Road Atlas

USA   CANADA   MEXICO

NORTH AMERICA

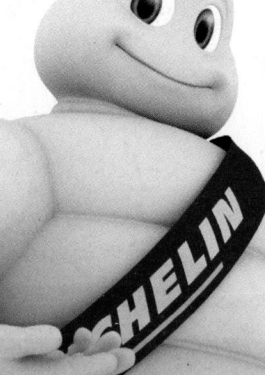

ROAD MAPS *are organized geographically.* United States, Canada, and Mexico road maps are organized in a grid layout, starting in the northwest of each country. To find your way, use either the **Key to Map Pages** inside the front cover, the **Listing of State and City Maps** on page 3, or the **index** in the back of the atlas.

COUNTRY COLORS
Colors represent countries throughout the atlas.
Red → Canada
Green → Mexico
Blue → United States
Purple → United States (Northeast Corridor)

MAP SCALES
Scale bars are shown at a constant length throughout the atlas for quick and easy scale comparison between regions.

DRIVING DISTANCES
Use this chart to check driving distances between major cities within each map. Refer to distance and driving time information at the back of the atlas for travel over greater distances.

LOCATOR MAPS
A quick glance at this miniature map lets you check which states and/or provinces are shown on each page.

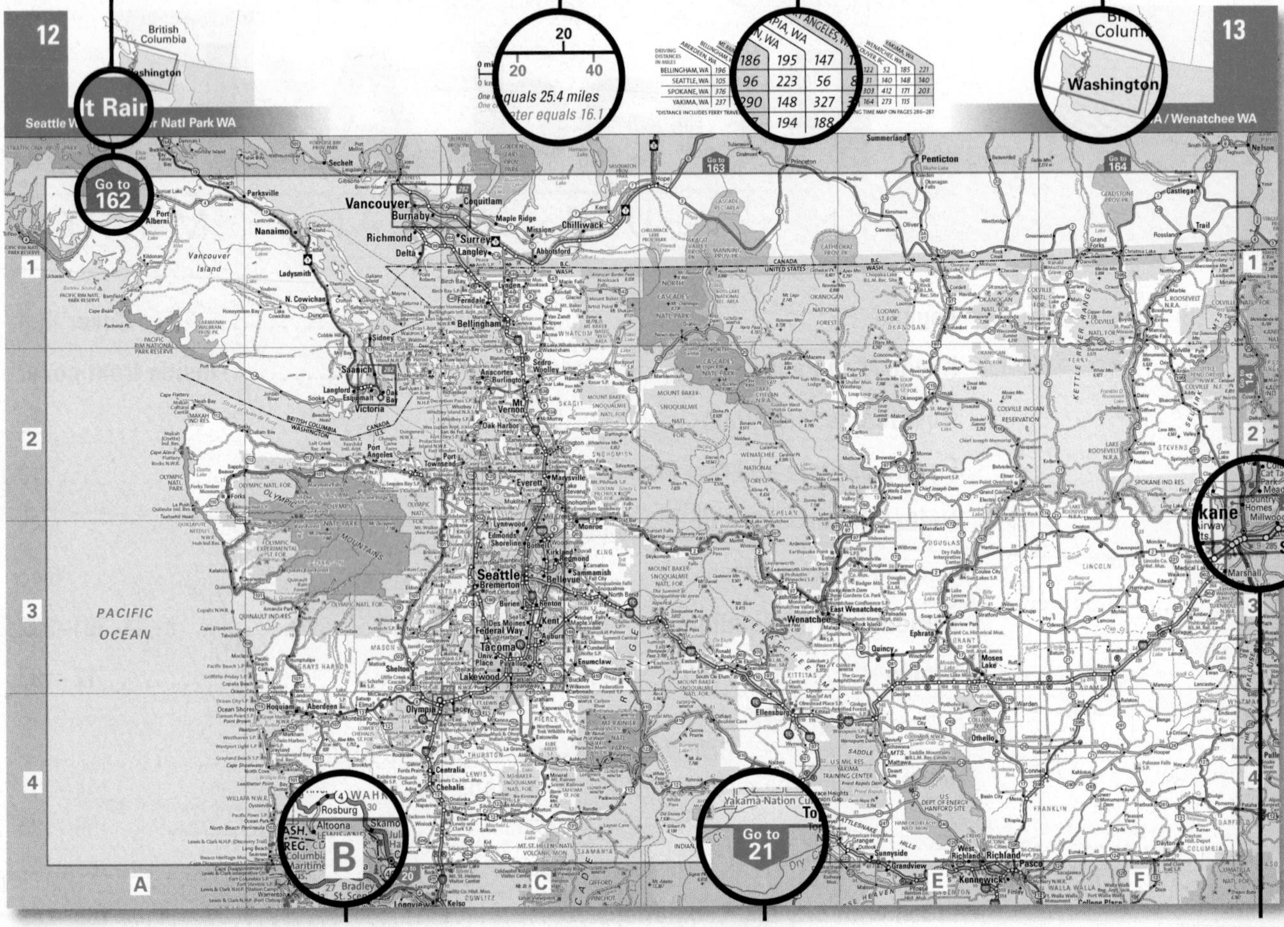

GRID REFERENCES
Use grid references to locate places listed in the index. For instance, Rosburg WA is listed in the index with "12" and "B4", indicating that the town may be found on page 12 in grid square B4.

"GO TO" POINTERS
Handy page tabs point the way to the next map, making navigation a breeze.

INSET MAP BOXES
These color-coded boxes outline areas that are featured in greater detail in the index section. The tab with "263" (above) indicates that a detailed map of Spokane may be found on page 263 (below).

HOW THE INDEX WORKS
Cities and towns are listed alphabetically, with separate indexes for the United States, Canada, and Mexico. Figures after entries indicate population, page number, and grid reference. Entries in bold color indicate cities with detailed inset maps. The U.S. index also includes counties and parishes, which are shown in bold black type.

INSET MAP INDEXES
Many inset maps have their own indexes. Metro area inset map indexes list cities and towns; downtown inset map indexes list points of interest.

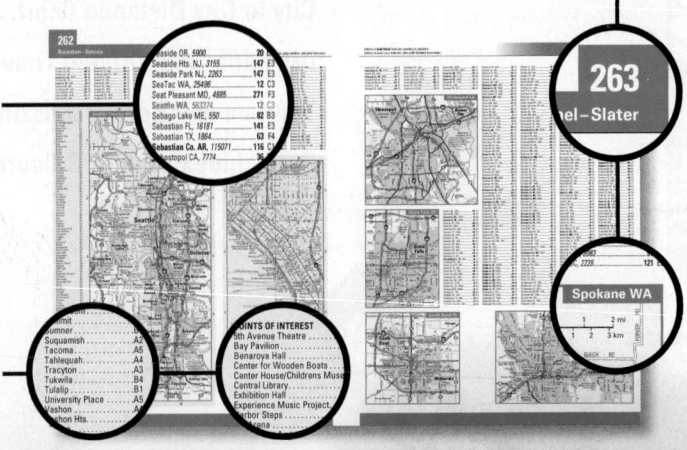

One inch equals 217 miles
One centimeter equals 138 kilometers

CANADA
ONTARIO
QUÉBEC
NEW BRUNSWICK
MINNESOTA
WISCONSIN
MICHIGAN
IOWA
ILLINOIS
INDIANA
OHIO
PA.
NEW YORK
VT.
N.H.
MAINE
MASS.
CT.
R.I.
N.J.
DEL.
MD.
WEST VIRGINIA
VIRGINIA
KENTUCKY
MISSOURI
TENNESSEE
NORTH CAROLINA
SOUTH CAROLINA
ARKANSAS
MISSISSIPPI
ALABAMA
GEORGIA
LOUISIANA
FLORIDA
BAHAMAS
CUBA
ATLANTIC OCEAN
GULF OF MEXICO
Lake Superior
Lake Michigan
Lake Huron
Lake Erie
Lake Ontario
APPALACHIAN MOUNTAINS
OZARK PLATEAU
Straits of Florida
Thunder Bay
Sault Ste. Marie
Sudbury
North Bay
Ottawa
Montréal
Québec
Toronto
Hamilton
London
Kitchener
Windsor
Duluth
Minneapolis
St. Paul
Milwaukee
Madison
Chicago
Detroit
Lansing
Grand Rapids
Toledo
Cleveland
Columbus
Cincinnati
Indianapolis
Louisville
Lexington
St. Louis
Kansas City
Des Moines
Pittsburgh
Buffalo
Rochester
Syracuse
Albany
Boston
Providence
Hartford
New Haven
New York
Newark
Philadelphia
Baltimore
Washington
Richmond
Norfolk
Virginia Beach
Charleston
Charlotte
Raleigh
Durham
Greensboro
Winston-Salem
Nashville
Knoxville
Memphis
Little Rock
Atlanta
Birmingham
Montgomery
Columbus
Macon
Savannah
Jacksonville
Orlando
Tampa
St. Petersburg
Miami
Fort Lauderdale
Key West
Jackson
Mobile
New Orleans
Baton Rouge
Lafayette
Shreveport
Houston
Galveston
Beaumont
Havana
Nassau

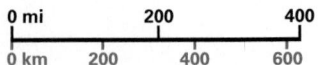

One inch equals 250 miles/Un pouce équivaut à 250 milles
One cm equals 159 km/Un cm équivaut à 159 km

NOTE: Legislated standard
time zone boundaries shown;
observed time may differ locally.

US National Parks

The seeds of America's national park system were planted in 1832 when the federal government created Hot Springs Reservation in central Arkansas to preserve the beneficial mineral springs found there. But not until 1872 did fierce lobbying by a dedicated group of citizens bring about the creation of Wyoming's Yellowstone National Park—America's first national park.

"FOR THE ENJOYMENT OF FUTURE GENERATIONS"

Preserving parklands east of the Mississippi River proved complicated by the early 20C, because so much territory was already developed or privately owned. In some cases, state parks were transferred to the care of the US government; in others, property was purchased outright with federal funds. American citizens mounted fundraising drives to buy and donate land for Great Smoky Mountains National Park, while industrialist John D. Rockefeller donated 11,000 acres of his personal property in Maine to help create Acadia National Park.

Established in 1916, the National Park Service's mandate is to conserve the scenery and the natural and historic objects therein "for the enjoyment of future generations." Today it oversees 59 national parks and more than 400 other monuments, historic sites, trails, seashores, military parks, recreation areas and byways. Great Smoky Mountains National Park is the most-visited park in the system, while the former Hot Springs

ℹ Info: ✆ 202-208-6843; www.nps.gov.

▶ Location: The Department of the Interior; National Park Service; 1849 C St. NW; Washington, DC 20240

Don't Miss: The America the Beautiful Annual Pass. Good for one year and includes admission to all national parks, sites and areas. Purchase at any park entrance; place order by calling ✆ 888-275-8747 x3; or purchase online at http://store.usgs.gov/pass.

Reservation is today Hot Springs National Park, the smallest, and only, urban park. Even the White House is a national park.

▶ ALASKA
Denali National Park★★★

George Parks Hwy. (Rte. 3), Denali Park; 125mi south of Fairbanks & 240mi north of Anchorage. ✆907-683-9532. www.nps.gov/dena. The main visitor center is located at Mile 1.5 on the park road.

At 9,375sq mi, Denali offers an incomparable cross section of the untamed Alaska Range, including the highest peak in North America, 20,310ft Mt. Denali, an Athabaskan word meaning "the high one" or "the great one." The park's geography varies from spruce forest to grassy tundra to austere granite pinnacles mantled in snow and ice. Glaciers have scoured cirques, and chiseled ridges and steep valleys, to create a remote Olympian landscape that often appears to float in a world of its own above the clouds.

Set aside as a refuge in 1917, the park harbors 37 mammal species and 157 bird species. Moose, wolves and grizzly bears roam. Caribou graze the tundra; Dall sheep dot the uplands.

Denali is the single largest exposed mountain in the world. Rising 18,000ft above the lowlands of Wonder Lake, it is 7,000ft higher than Everest from base to summit.

Early mornings and visits in March provide the best chance to view the often cloud-covered peak. Private vehicle travel in the park is restricted; shuttle-bus tours traverse forested taiga and open tundra, offering opportunities for wildlife sightings. Few trails cross this wilderness park.

▶ ARIZONA
Grand Canyon National Park★★★

△✕&🅿 ✆928-638-7888. www.nps.gov/grca.
If any single landscape feature symbolizes the United States in the minds of world travelers, it is Arizona's Grand Canyon. Most visitor activities in Grand Canyon National Park are focused along the **South Rim,** a 35mi strand of paved road that extends from the East Rim Entrance Station (29mi west of US-89 at Cameron) to Hermits Rest.

Between March and November, only free shuttle buses ply **West Rim Drive,** a 7mi road west from Grand Canyon Village. The drive passes **viewpoints★★★** at Maricopa Point, the John Wesley Powell Memorial, Hopi Point, Mohave Point and Pima Point before ending at **Hermits Rest★,** named for a 19C prospector, loner Louis Boucher.

East Rim Drive travels 24mi from Grand Canyon Village to the East Rim Entrance Station and passes numerous dizzying viewpoints. A small pueblo ruin marks the **Tusayan Ruin and Museum★,** 20mi east of the village. Displays trace the pre-13C culture of Ancestral Puebloans in the Grand Canyon region.

North Rim, Grand Canyon National Park, Arizona

© Leslie Forsberg/Michelin

SYMBOLS
△ campsites
✕ on-site eating facilities
& wheelchair accessible
🅿 on-site parking

MICHELIN STAR RATINGS
★ Highly recommended
★ Recommended
★ Interesting

The **Desert View Watchtower★**, 22mi from Grand Canyon Village, was modeled after an ancient Pueblo lookout. The three-story building is dominated by a circular 70ft tower that commands **views★★★** of the canyon and Colorado River far below. The Painted Desert appears on the far eastern horizon.

The drive from Grand Canyon Village (South Rim) to Grand Canyon Lodge on the **North Rim** (Rte. 64 east to Cameron, US-89 north to Marble Canyon, US-89A west to Jacob Lake, then Rte. 67 south; open 15 May–16 Oct, weather permitting; △✕&🄿) leads to a less developed part of the park. At 7,700-8,800ft above sea level, it is about 1,200ft higher than the South Rim, and several degrees cooler, with midsummer temperatures averaging in the high-70s (Fahrenheit).

The North Rim visitor center, adjacent to the Grand Canyon Lodge, offers a paved .5mi trail leading to Bright Angel Point, with glorious **views★★★** of the canyon. Also visible is the strenuous **North Kaibab Trail** (14.2mi), which descends 5,840ft to Phantom Ranch. Day hikers should not venture beyond Roaring Springs (4.7mi each way), water source for the entire park. Full- and half-day mule trips are available from the North Rim, but do not descend all the way to the river.

The **Cape Royal Road★** extends 23mi from the Grand Canyon Lodge southeast across the Walhalla Plateau to Vista Encantadora and Cape Royal, with a spur route to Point Imperial, the highest point on the canyon rim at 8,803ft.

◗ COLORADO
Mesa Verde National Park★★★

US-160, Mancos. △✕&🄿 ☏970-529-4465. www.nps.gov/meve.

The first US national park to preserve the works of man (as opposed to nature), Mesa Verde was created by Congress on September 29, 1906. Today this World Heritage Site attracts 500,000 annual visitors, mostly in summer, when they can walk through five major cliff dwellings and additional mesa-top structures displaying primitive construction methods used by Ancestral Puebloans between AD 750 and 1300. A newly constructed visitor center was opened in late 2012 at the park entrance.

The 21mi drive from the park entrance to the **Chapin Mesa Archeological Museum★** winds around the mesa, offering spectacular views of four states. Adjacent is **Spruce Tree House★★★**, a major cliff dwelling and the only one open year-round.

Nearby, the 6mi Mesa Top Loop Road is also open year-round. Overlooks provide views of **Square Tower House★★**, the **Twin Trees★** site and **Sun Temple★**. In warmer weather, guided tours are offered to spectacu-

lar sites built into overhanging cliffs at **Cliff Palace★★** and **Balcony House★★**.

◗ HAWAII
Hawai'i Volcanoes National Park★★★

Mamalahoa Hwy. (Rte. 11), Volcano, 28mi southwest of Hilo. ☏808-985-6000. www.nps.gov/havo.

This World Heritage Site is one of the few places to visit a live volcano. At the **Kilauea Visitor Center★★**, tourists may inspect exhibits and learn from rangers how to view the craters safely. Volcano House (☏808-441-7750; www.hawaiivolcanohouse.com), a recently reconstructed heritage hotel, sits on the brink of Kilauea Caldera, at 4,000ft elevation. Dangerous gases called "vog" (volcanic fog) rise from the caldera's deep **Halemaumau Crater★★**, which erupted most recently in 1982 and likely will again. On his 1866 tour of Hawaii, Mark Twain wrote that the lake of molten lava he found there "was like gazing at the sun at noon-day."

The **Crater Rim Drive★★** girdles the great pit and offers an opportunity to see (and smell) the fumes; dangerous sulfur dioxide levels have closed much of the drive. Along the drive, the **Thomas A. Jaggar Museum★** (3mi west of Volcano House) presents geological exhibits, and the 450ft-long **Thurston Lava Tube★** (2mi east of Volcano House) beckons visitors. Although the **Kilauea Volcano★★★** has been erupting since 1983, it is generally unseen. The 2,000°F molten magma moves through miles of lava tubes under the surface, and only where it breaks out near the island's southern shore is it sometimes visible. Active flow areas are closed to the public.

The 23mi **Chain of Craters Road★★**, extending off Crater Rim Drive 4mi southeast of Volcano House,

passes by old flows and reaches the shore near the place where a 2001 flow erased the end of the road.

Cliff Palace, Mesa Verde National Park, Colorado

© NPS Photo/Sandy Groves

DISCOVERING USA WEST NATIONAL PARKS

Nature and Safety in the Parks

In most parks, tampering with **plants or wildlife** is prohibited by law. When visiting any natural areas, remember that while the disturbance of a single person may be small, the cumulative impact of a large number of visitors may be disastrous. Avoid direct contact with any wildlife; an animal that does not shy away from humans may be sick. Some wildlife — bears in particular — may approach cars or campsites out of curiosity or if they smell food. Food storage guidelines: hang food 12ft off the ground and 10ft away from tree trunk; or store in a locking ice chest, car trunk or the lockers provided at some campgrounds. Improper storage of food is a violation of federal law and subject to a fine. If a bear approaches, try to frighten it by yelling and throwing rocks in its direction (not at the bear). Never approach a mother with cubs, as she will attack to protect her young.

When **hiking** in the backcountry, stay on marked trails; taking shortcuts is dangerous and causes erosion. It's best not to hike alone in the backcountry, but if you do, notify someone of your destination and planned return time. Since mountain roads tend to be narrow, steep and twisting, exercise caution when **driving.** Observe cautionary road signs and posted speed limits. Always check weather conditions before driving or hiking in mountainous areas. Flooding due to heavy rains can cause roads and bridges to become impassable and make camping and hiking in low terrain hazardous. Be prepared for snowstorms if you are camping or traveling in the mountains during winter months.

▶ MONTANA
Glacier National Park★★★

Going-to-the-Sun Road off US-2, 35mi east of Kalispell. △✕&🅿 ✆406-888-7800. www.nps.gov/glac.

Known to native Blackfeet as the "Land of Shining Mountains," Glacier Park was homesteaded in the late 19C. Pressure to establish the park began in 1891 with the arrival of the Great Northern Railway; the US Congress gave its nod in 1910. The railroad built numerous delightful Swiss-style chalets and hotels, several of which still operate.

Glacier's rugged mountainscape takes its name not from living glaciers, but from ancient rivers of ice that carved the peaks, finger lakes and U-shaped valleys. The remoteness of the park's 1,584sq mi makes it an ideal home for grizzly bears and mountain goats, bighorn sheep and bugling elk. The park's glaciers have been steadily disappearing, from 100 in 1910 to 25 in 2010 to, scientists estimate, zero by 2030.

The park's scenic highway, **Going-to-the-Sun Road★★★** (52mi from US-2 at West Glacier to US-89

Mt. Oberlin, Glacier National Park, Montana

at St. Mary. Closed mid Oct–late May due to snow.) is a National Historic Landmark and was deemed an engineering marvel when completed in 1932. The narrow, serpentine roadway climbs 3,500ft to the Continental Divide at Logan Pass, moving from forested valleys to alpine meadows to native grassland as it bisects the park west to east. Passenger vehicles (size restrictions prohibit large RVs) share the route with Glacier's trademark red "jammer" buses, which have carried sightseers for more than 60 years. At 6,646ft **Logan Pass★★★** (Mile 33), visitors enjoy broad alpine meadows of wildflowers and keep their eyes open for mountain goats on the 1.5mi walk to **Hidden Lake Overlook★★.**

From memorable views of and from craggy peaks to guided boat tours on pristine lakes, Glacier National Park abounds in beauty and adventures. Among the natural marvels, 8020ft **Triple Divide Peak** is the only place on the continent from which water flows to three oceans—Atlantic, Pacific and Arctic.

▶ NORTH DAKOTA
Theodore Roosevelt National Park★★

Off I-94 & US-85 between Medora & Watford City (3 units). △&🅿 ✆701-623-4730. www.nps.gov/thro.

The Little Missouri River links the 110sq mi park's South, Elkhorn Ranch and North Units, as does the 120mi Maah Daah Hey Trail. Erosion by wind, water and ice is the subtle artist, paring down softer rock, leaving behind the razor-sharp ridges and rugged buttes now called badlands. In the **North Unit★★** (US-85, 16mi south of Watford City), a 14mi scenic drive climbs to Oxbow Overlook, 500ft above the river. From here, the **Achenbach Trail** (16mi) approaches **Sperati Point★,** the narrowest gateway in the badlands. The **South Unit★★** (Rte. 10 Bypass off I-94, Medora, 16mi west of Belfield) is best seen on a paved 36mi scenic loop

drive. **Scoria Point Overlook** and **Boicourt Overlook** offer panoramas of yellow, gray and burnt-red buttes. **Wind Canyon Trail** (.2mi) negotiates the steep edge of a ridge. Wild horses grazing upland plateaus are a vision to behold, but prairie dogs are the darlings of the park. Behind the **South Unit Visitor Center** stands Roosevelt's Maltese Cross Cabin, restored and relocated here. At the site of **Elkhorn Ranch** (35mi north of Medora), foundation blocks are all that remain of Roosevelt's 1885 ranch.

▶ OREGON
Crater Lake National Park★★★

Rtes. 62 & 138 west of US-97, 145mi southeast of Eugene. ✆541-594-3000. www.nps.gov/crla.

The deepest lake in the US at 1,932ft rests in the crater of a collapsed volcano. Ringed by mountains blanketed with snow much of the year, this vivid sapphire lake, 6mi in diameter, attracts hikers, geologists and those compelled by the mysterious eye-like blue caldera. The cataclysmic eruption of Mt. Mazama 7,700 years ago hurled more than 18 cubic miles of pumice and ash into the air and surrounding landscape. The collapsed mountain created a bowl-shaped caldera that filled with snowmelt.

Most visitors take the awe-inspiring 33mi **Rim Drive★★,** which circles the lake and has spectacular **views.** Among the best are those from **Sinnott Memorial Overlook** (Rim Village, south side of lake) and **Cloudcap,** highest point on the Rim Drive (7,865ft). Better yet is the perspective from atop 8,929ft **Mount Scott★★,** requiring a strenuous 5mi round-trip hike to the park's highest summit. A 7mi spur road off Rim Drive leads to **The Pinnacles★,** 80ft tall hollow fossilized fumaroles.

There are ample other attractions here, including hikes through mid-elevation pine forests, and the famed

National Parks in British Columbia, Canada

PACIFIC RIM NATIONAL PARK RESERVE★★★ – *West side of Vancouver Island. Hwy. 1 north from Victoria to Parksville, Hwy. 4 west through Port Alberni to the park.* ⚠ *℘250-726-7721. www.pc.gc.ca. Open daily year-round; park facilities closed mid-Oct–mid-Mar.* Rocky headlands, sandy beaches, old-growth spruce forests and an inland sound with untouched islands are some of the varied elements that make up this natural preserve. Hugging the west coast of Vancouver Island, this Canadian National Park includes three distinct units: Long Beach, Broken Group Islands and West Coast Trail. The park's **visitor center** (open mid-Mar–mid-Oct daily 9am–6pm; ℘250-726-4212) is located just past the junction where Highway 4 turns north. Stretching from just north of Ucluelet in the south (where Hwy. 4 turns north) northward to within 4.8km/3mi of Tofino★, the **Long Beach★★** area is the only part of the park reachable by a road. The namesake beach has almost 32km/20mi of shoreline,

most of it open beach, with firm, gray sand for strolling, dozens of offshore sea stacks that send waves crashing upward, and open expanses where breaking waves draw hordes of surfers (Tofino is widely regarded as the surfing capital of Canada). About 29km/18mi north of the visitor center, the 300ft summit (highest on this stretch of coast) of **Radar Hill★★** affords a 360-degree **panorama★★** of the ocean and the island behind. The road ends in Tofino, 33.5km/21mi from the Ucluelet junction. **Broken Group Islands,** composed of more than 100 islands, is contained entirely within **Barkley Sound,** a small inland sound south of Ucluelet. It is one of the premier **saltwater kayaking** areas on earth.
West Coast Trail is a legendary 75km/47mi wilderness trail that traverses the coast between Bamfield and Port Renfrew. The arduous trek takes up to six days, the weather is notoriously temperamental, and reservations are necessary long in advance, as park

officials limit yearly use to about 8,000 hikers.

GULF ISLANDS NATIONAL PARK RESERVE★ – *Visitor center at 2220 Harbour Rd., Sidney; open year-round Mon–Fri 8am–4:30pm. Open daily year-round.* ⚠ *℘250-654-4000. www.pc.gc.ca.* Established in 2003, this Canadian reserve spreads across 15 of the Gulf Islands, encompassing 35sq km/13.5sq mi of numerous discrete pockets of island preserves inland and on the shore; and 26sq km/10sq mi of marine habitat. Many of these islands can be reached only by boat. One of the most interesting islands is **Russell Island,** a small islet near Salt Spring that was homesteaded by immigrant native Hawaiians around the turn of the 20C. Guided **kayak trips** to Russell Island are led by **Island Escapades** (℘250-537-2553; www.islandescapades.com).

For a complete listing of national parks in Canada, visit the Parks Canada website at www.pc.gc.ca.

---

boat tour to **Wizard Island★,** a small knob in the middle of the lake.

The historic (1915) **Crater Lake Lodge** offers cozy rooms and rockers on a wide veranda; the refurbished wood lodge is perched on the crater rim with excellent views (www.craterlakelodges.com).

◗ TEXAS
Big Bend National Park★★★

Rte. 118 south of Alpine or US-385 south of Marathon; Panther Junction is 320mi southeast of El Paso.
⚠✕⚙🅿 ℘432-477-2251. www.nps.gov/bibe.
Big Bend spans 1,252sq mi of spectacular canyons, lush bottomlands, sprawling desert and mountain woodlands on the north side of the Rio Grande. Ranging across more than 6,000ft of elevation, it boasts a wealth of animal and plant life. Big Bend has more

than 450 species of migratory and resident birds. Bats, rodents and other small mammals are nocturnal; javelina and deer are often seen; mountain lions, rarely. Reptiles thrive in the extreme climate. Torrential thunderstorms may follow droughts. Temperatures approach 120°F in summer but may drop below 10°F in winter. The area has a remarkable geological history, and a long and fascinating chronology of human habitation.

Park headquarters and the main visitor center are at **Panther Junction** (US-385 & Rio Grande Village Rd.) in the heart of Big Bend. Other visitor centers—at **Persimmon Gap** (US-385 at north entrance), **Chisos Basin** (Basin Rd.) and **Rio Grande Village** (Rio Grande Village Rd.)—also provide information on archaeology and ecotourism activities. Campgrounds and rustic lodges can be found at various locations.

Hikers can choose from 200mi of trails in the park, ranging from easy to strenuous. Naturalists guide walks year-round. Outfitters based outside the park offer Rio Grande float trips through rugged canyons.

◗ WASHINGTON
Olympic National Park★★★

Access via US-101 south and west of Port Angeles.
⚠✕⚙🅿 ℘360-565-3130. Visitor center, 3002 Mt. Angeles Rd., Port Angeles. www.nps.gov/olym.
Designated an International Biosphere Reserve and World Heritage Site, the 1,440sq-mi park has exceptional natural beauty and remarkable diversity within its three distinct wilderness ecosystems—glaciated mountain ranges, temperate rain forests and primitive coastal beaches. The park harbors more than 300 types of birds and 70 species of mammals, among them some 5,000 Roosevelt elk, the largest herd in the world. US Highway 101 runs around the perimeter of the national park on its east, north and west. Among its most accessible attractions is **Lake Crescent★★** (18mi west of Port Angeles), one of three large lakes in the park. Cupped within steep, forested hillsides, the deep glacial lake is popular with outdoor recreation lovers, who often base themselves at the rustic 1915 **Lake Crescent Lodge★** (416 Lake Crescent Rd.; t360-928-3211; www.nationalparkreservations.com). From here, a 1mi trail leads through old-growth forest to **Marymere Falls★,** a 90ft cascade. Nearby, Sol Duc Hot Springs offer mineral-rich bathing pools and rustic cabins for rent (www.olympicnationalparks.com).

Rio Grande, Big Bend National Park, Texas

© NPS Photo/Mark Schuler

Please turn to page 301 for more national parks.

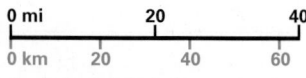

One inch equals 25.4 miles
One centimeter equals 16.1 kilometers

DRIVING DISTANCES IN MILES	ABERDEEN, WA	BELLINGHAM, WA	MT. RAINIER NP, WA	OKANOGAN, WA	OLYMPIA, WA	PORT ANGELES, WA	SEATTLE, WA	SPOKANE, WA	TACOMA, WA	VANCOUVER, BC	WENATCHEE, WA	YAKIMA, WA
BELLINGHAM, WA	196		186	195	147	127*	88	360	122	52	185	221
SEATTLE, WA	105	88	96	223	56	83*		278	31	140	148	140
SPOKANE, WA	376	360	290	148	327	362*	278		303	412	171	203
YAKIMA, WA	237	221	87	194	188	223*	140	203	164	273	115	

*DISTANCE INCLUDES FERRY TRAVEL

SEE ALSO DISTANCE AND DRIVING TIME MAP ON PAGES 286–287

Washington
B.C. Alta.
Montana
Idaho

0 mi   20   40
0 km   20   40   60
One inch equals 25.4 miles
One centimeter equals 16.1 kilometers

Spokane WA / Coeur d'Alene ID

DRIVING DISTANCES IN MILES	BONNERS FERRY, ID	BROWNING, MT	COEUR D'ALENE, ID	COLVILLE, WA	GREAT FALLS, MT	HELENA, MT	KALISPELL, MT	LEWISTON, ID	MISSOULA, MT	SHELBY, MT	SPOKANE, WA	WEST GLACIER, WA
GREAT FALLS, MT	369	124	364	471		85	222	420	199	82	398	192
LEWISTON, ID	196	413	118	176	420	334	315		221	448	103	348
MISSOULA, MT	244	201	167	274	199	114	116	221		227	201	136
SPOKANE, WA	110	336	34	73	398	313	238	103	201	426		271

SEE ALSO DISTANCE AND DRIVING TIME MAP ON PAGES 286–287

Alta.   Sask.

Montana   North Dakota

0 mi   20   40
0 km   20   40   60
One inch equals 25.4 miles
One centimeter equals 16.1 kilometers

DRIVING DISTANCES IN MILES	GLASGOW, MT	GLENDIVE, MT	GREAT FALLS, MT	HARLOWTON, MT	HAVRE, MT	LEWISTOWN, MT	MALTA, MT	MILES CITY, MT	ROUNDUP, MT	SHELBY, MT	WILLISTON, ND	WOLF POINT, MT
GLENDIVE, MT	147		351	309	306	242	217	74	219	408	106	98
GREAT FALLS, MT	277	351		133	118	109	207	329	183	82	422	326
HAVRE, MT	159	306	118	210		175	89	345	198	102	304	208
WILLISTON, ND	145	106	422	415	304	324	215	180	325	406		96

SEE ALSO DISTANCE AND DRIVING TIME MAP ON PAGES 286–287

Sask.
Manitoba
North Dakota
Minnesota
0 mi 20 40
0 km 20 40 60
One inch equals 25.4 miles
One centimeter equals 16.1 kilometers
Go to 166
Go to 17
Go to 26
CANADA
UNITED STATES
SASKATCHEWAN
NORTH DAKOTA
MANITOBA
NORTH DAKOTA
Halbrite
Midale
Benson
Lampman
Steelman
Macoun
Hitchcock
Estevan
Bienfait
Torquay
Roche Percee
Boundary Dam Res.
North Portal
Portal
Alameda
Frobisher
Oxbow
Glen Ewen
Carnduff
Alida
Storthoaks
Tilston
Carievale
Gainsborough
Pierson
Antler
Redvers
Bellegarde
Sinclair
Reston
Pipestone
Grande Clairière
Deleau
Hartney
Melita
Napinka
Lauder
Medora
Waskada
Deloraine
Goodlands
Carroll
Wawanesa
Nesbitt
Fairfax
Elgin
Minto
Regent
Dunrea
Boissevain
Whitewater
Ninga
Killarney
TURTLE MTN. PROV. PARK
Colgate
Goodwater
Tribune
Bromhead
Oungre
Colgan
Ambrose
Crosby
Fortuna
Noonan
Columbus
Larson
Lignite
Flaxton
Northgate
Bowbells
Sherwood
Antler
Westhope
Landa
Roth
Souris
Bottineau
Kelvin
St. John
Turtle Mtn. Chippewa Heritage Center
Belcourt
Dunseith
DIVIDE
BURKE
RENVILLE
BOTTINEAU
ROLETTE
WILLIAMS
MOUNTRAIL
WARD
MCHENRY
PIERCE
MCKENZIE
DUNN
MERCER
OLIVER
MCLEAN
SHERIDAN
WELLS
BILLINGS
STARK
MORTON
BURLEIGH
KIDDER
GRANT
HETTINGER
SLOPE
ADAMS
SIOUX
EMMONS
LOGAN
DES LACS N.W.R.
LOSTWOOD N.W.R.
UPPER SOURIS N.W.R.
J. CLARK SALYER N.W.R.
Kenmare
Mohall
Lansford
Tolley
Norma
Niobe
Coteau
Kenaston
Coulee
Donnybrook
Carpio
Grano
Glenburn
Wolseth
Deering
Minot A.F.B.
Newburg
Maxbass
Eckman
Russell
Gardena
Kramer
Omemee
Overly
Willow City
Upham
Bantry
Towner
Rugby
Denbigh
Geographic Center of North America
Grenora
Zahl
Alamo
Wildrose
Hamlet
McGregor
Appam
Battleview
Powers Lake
Lostwood
Bonetrail
Temple
Tioga
White Earth
Ray
Wheelock
Epping
Springbrook
Stanley
Ross
Palermo
Blaisdell
Tagus
Berthold
Burlington
Des Lacs
Minot
Surrey
Norwich
Granville
Berwick
Knox
Williston
Lewis and Clark S.P.
Lake Sakakawea
LITTLE MISSOURI NATL. GRASSLAND
Charlson
Keene
New Town
Three Affiliated Tribes Museum
FORT BERTHOLD IND. RES.
Plaza
Makoti
Parshall
Ryder
Douglas
Sawyer
Velva
Voltaire
Bergen
Balfour
Drake
Anamoose
Harvey
Alexander
Rawson
Arnegard
Watford City
THEODORE ROOSEVELT NATL. PARK (NORTH UNIT)
Mandaree
Roseglen
Raub
White Shield
Garrison
Max
Benedict
Ruso
Butte
Martin
Killdeer
Halliday
Dunn Center
Golden Valley
Zap
Beulah
Hazen
Stanton
Pick City
Riverdale
Coleharbor
Underwood
Turtle Lake
Mercer
McClusky
Denhoff
Goodrich
Hurdsfield
Falkirk
Washburn
Wilton
Regan
Wing
Tuttle
Robinson
Manning
Fairfield
Marshall
Hannover
Center
Price
Baldwin
Medora
Fryburg
Belfield
South Heart
Dickinson
Gladstone
Taylor
Richardton
Hebron
Glen Ullin
New Salem
Judson
Mandan
Bismarck
Menoken
McKenzie
Sterling
Driscoll
Steele
Dawson
Almont
Lincoln
Moffit
Lefor
New England
Mott
Regent
Elgin
Carson
Flasher
Breien
Solen
Fort Rice
Cannon Ball
Amidon
Rhame
Bowman
Scranton
Reeder
Gascoyne
Bentley
Leith
Heil
New Leipzig
Burt
Raleigh
Hazelton
Temvik
Linton
STANDING ROCK IND. RES.
Napoleon
Braddock
Kintyre
LONG LAKE N.W.R.
Huff Hills
THE HOGBACK
Lake Oahe
Lake Tschida
A
B
C
1
2
3
4

DRIVING DISTANCES IN MILES	BISMARCK, ND	BOTTINEAU, ND	DETROIT LAKES, MN	DICKINSON, ND	FARGO, ND	GRAND FORKS, ND	JAMESTOWN, ND	MINOT, ND	PEMBINA, ND	RUGBY, ND	THIEF RIVER FALLS, MN	WILLISTON, ND
BISMARCK, ND		189	244	97	199	274	105	116	347	153	319	229
FARGO, ND	199	271	45	291		79	97	268	152	221	113	424
GRAND FORKS, ND	274	198	125	367	79		173	212	77	148	61	340
MINOT, ND	116	76	313	178	268	212	171		238	64	276	128

SEE ALSO DISTANCE AND DRIVING TIME MAP ON PAGES 286–287

Washington

Oregon

0 mi   20   40
0 km   20   40   60
One inch equals 25.4 miles
One centimeter equals 16.1 kilometers

PACIFIC OCEAN

1
2
3
4

A   B   C

Go to 12

Go to 28

Major cities and places:

Astoria, Seaside, Cannon Beach, Manzanita, Nehalem, Wheeler, Rockaway Beach, Garibaldi, Bay City, Tillamook, Netarts, Oceanside, Sandlake, Pacific City, Cloverdale, Neskowin, Lincoln City, Gleneden Beach, Depoe Bay, Otter Rock, Newport, Toledo, Seal Rock, Waldport, Yachats, Florence, Dunes City, Gardiner, Reedsport, Winchester Bay, Lakeside, North Bend, Coos Bay, Charleston, Bandon

Longview, Kelso, St. Helens, Woodland, Battle Ground, Vancouver, Camas, Washougal, Portland, Gresham, Hillsboro, Forest Grove, Beaverton, Tigard, Lake Oswego, Damascus, Oregon City, Sandy, Wilsonville, Newberg, Dundee, Lafayette, McMinnville, Sheridan, Willamina, Dallas, Monmouth, Independence, Keizer, Salem, Four Corners, Stayton, Woodburn, Molalla, Mount Angel, Silverton, Corvallis, Philomath, Albany, Lebanon, Sweet Home, Junction City, Coburg, Eugene, Springfield, Creswell, Cottage Grove, Oakridge, Sutherlin, Oakland, Roseburg

Hood River, Cascade Locks, Mt. Hood, Detroit, Mt. Jefferson 10,497, Mt. Washington +7,794, Mt. Bachelor 9,065

WASHINGTON, COWLITZ, CLARK, SKAMANIA, CLATSOP, COLUMBIA, TILLAMOOK, YAMHILL, POLK, MARION, CLACKAMAS, LINCOLN, BENTON, LINN, LANE, DOUGLAS, COOS

PACIFIC, WAHKIAKUM, LEWIS

CASCADE RANGE, COAST RANGES, CALAPOOYA MTS., SIUSLAW NATIONAL FOREST, WILLAMETTE NATL. FOR., MT. HOOD NATL. FOR., GIFFORD PINCHOT NATL. FOR.

Highways: 5, 84, 101, 26, 30, 99W, 99E, 97, 20, 22, 34, 36, 38, 42, 58, 138, 126

DRIVING DISTANCES IN MILES

	ASTORIA, OR	BEND, OR	BURNS, OR	COOS BAY, OR	EUGENE, OR	KENNEWICK, WA	LA GRANDE, OR	NEWPORT, OR	PORTLAND, OR	SALEM, OR	THE DALLES, OR	WALLA WALLA, WA
BEND, OR	252		142	227	115	245	295	183	158	134	137	276
EUGENE, OR	216	115	257	105		328	377	101	112	65	198	359
KENNEWICK, WA	306	245	256	440	328		111	328	212	264	131	49
PORTLAND, OR	97	158	299	224	112	212	261	116		48	82	243

SEE ALSO DISTANCE AND DRIVING TIME MAP ON PAGES 286–287

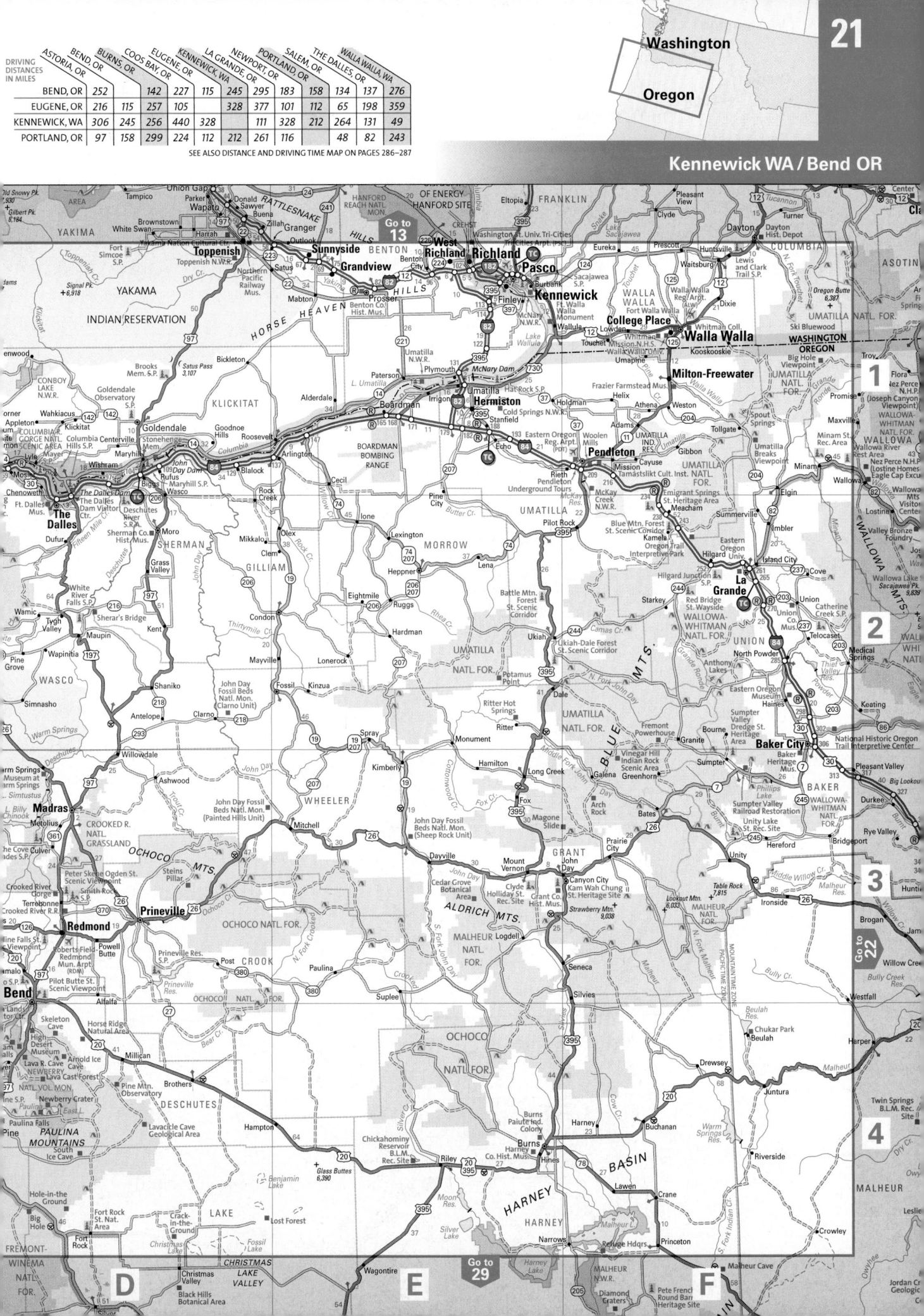

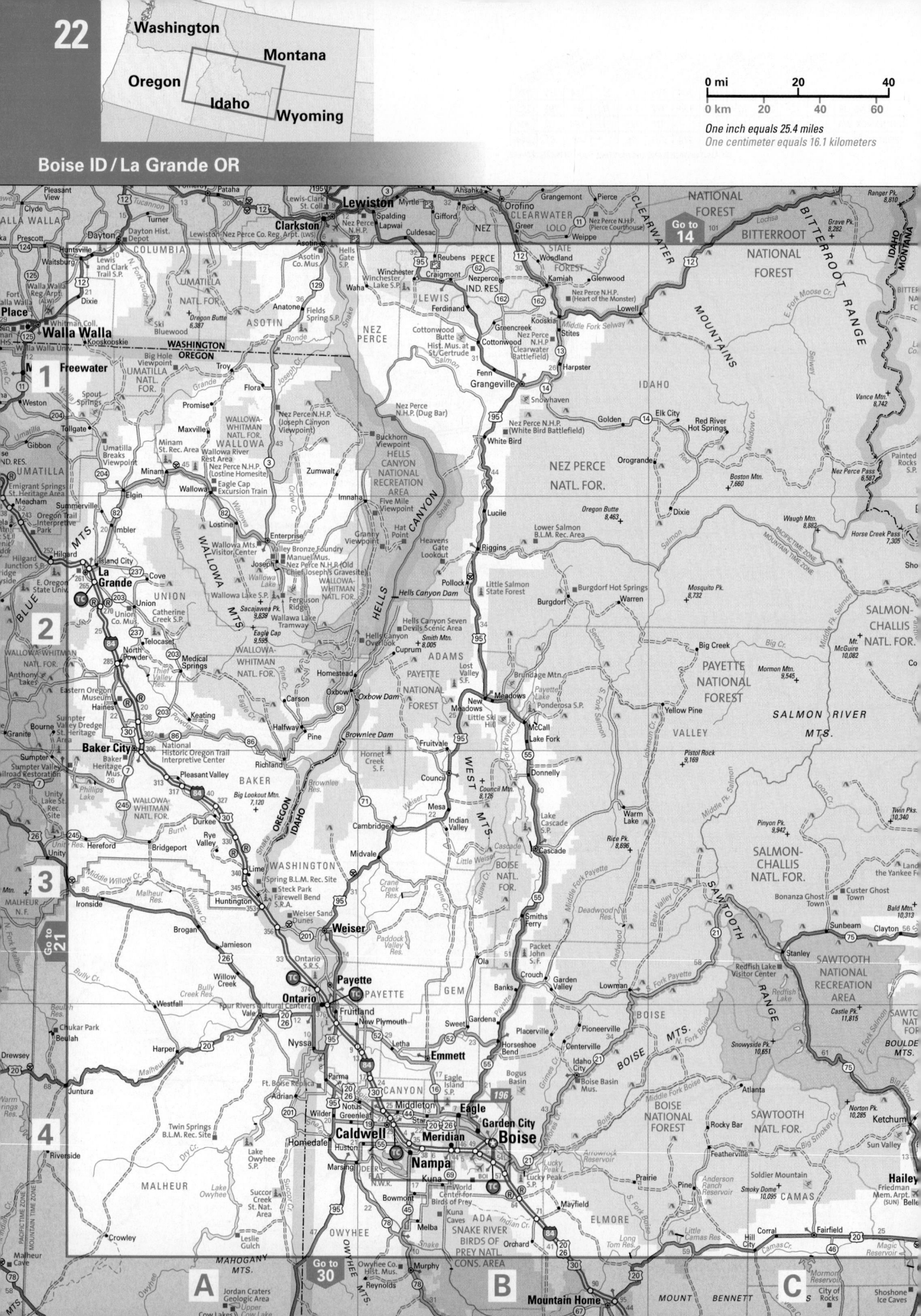

22

Washington
Montana
Oregon
Idaho
Wyoming

Boise ID / La Grande OR

0 mi   20   40
0 km   20   40   60
One inch equals 25.4 miles
One centimeter equals 16.1 kilometers

DRIVING DISTANCES IN MILES	BOISE, ID	BOZEMAN, MT	BUTTE, MT	GRANGEVILLE, ID	HAMILTON, MT	IDAHO FALLS, ID	JACKSON, WY	LA GRANDE, OR	ONTARIO, OR	SALMON, ID	SUN VALLEY, ID	W. YELLOWSTONE, MT
BOISE, ID		485	486	202	339	288	378	170	58	247	163	395
BUTTE, MT	486	81		290	103	203	275	566	541	150	312	162
IDAHO FALLS, ID	288	199	203	483	272		92	455	342	168	153	109
W. YELLOWSTONE, MT	395	90	162	451	264	109	128	562	449	244	252	

SEE ALSO DISTANCE AND DRIVING TIME MAP ON PAGES 286–287

Montana

North Dakota

Idaho

South Dakota

Wyoming

0 mi 20 40
0 km 20 40 60

One inch equals 25.4 miles
One centimeter equals 16.1 kilometers

Billings MT / Yellowstone Natl Park WY

DRIVING DISTANCES IN MILES

	BILLINGS, MT	BOZEMAN, MT	BUFFALO, WY	CODY, WY	GILLETTE, WY	JACKSON, WY	MILES CITY, MT	RAPID CITY, SD	SHERIDAN, WY	SPEARFISH, SD	W. YELLOWSTONE, MT	WORLAND, WY
BILLINGS, MT		141	165	111	233	287	144	379	131	333	232	161
BUFFALO, WY	165	306		180	70	342	237	216	34	170	396	91
SPEARFISH, SD	333	474	170	350	100	512	186	53	202		564	261
W. YELLOWSTONE, MT	232	90	396	147	464	128	376	610	363	564		236

SEE ALSO DISTANCE AND DRIVING TIME MAP ON PAGES 286–287

0 mi   20   40
0 km   20   40   60
One inch equals 25.4 miles
One centimeter equals 16.1 kilometers

DRIVING DISTANCES IN MILES	ABERDEEN, SD	BROOKINGS, SD	HOT SPRINGS, SD	HURON, SD	MITCHELL, SD	MOBRIDGE, SD	PIERRE, SD	RAPID CITY, SD	SIOUX FALLS, SD	WAHPETON, ND	WALL, SD	WATERTOWN, SD
ABERDEEN, SD		150	412	90	146	99	160	357	204	154	303	98
PIERRE, SD	160	188	247	115	155	107		193	226	301	138	189
RAPID CITY, SD	357	390	56	313	275	243	193		346	543	55	436
SIOUX FALLS, SD	204	57	401	127	73	303	226	346		210	292	103

SEE ALSO DISTANCE AND DRIVING TIME MAP ON PAGES 286–287

Oregon

California　Nevada

0 mi · 20 · 40
0 km · 20 · 40 · 60
One inch equals 25.4 miles
One centimeter equals 16.1 kilometers

PACIFIC OCEAN

COAST RANGE · KLAMATH MTS. · SISKIYOU MTS. · CASCADE RANGE

Coos Bay · North Bend · Charleston · Sumner · Bunker Hill · Coquille · Bandon · Norway · Myrtle Point · Riverton · Langlois · Denmark · Sixes · Port Orford · Ophir · Nesika Beach · Gold Beach · Wedderburn · Pistol River · Carpenterville · Brookings · Harbor · Smith River · Fort Dick · Crescent City · Gasquet

Sutherlin · Oakland · Wilbur · Roseburg · Winchester · Green · Winston · Dillard · Myrtle Creek · Tri-City · Days Creek · Riddle · Canyonville · Azalea · Glendale · Wolf Creek · Leland · Sunny Valley · Merlin · Grants Pass · Wilderville · Murphy · Selma · Kerby · Cave Junction · O'Brien · Takilma

Central Point · Medford · White City · Eagle Point · Gold Hill · Jacksonville · Phoenix · Talent · Ashland · Hilt · Siskiyou

Klamath Falls · Altamont · Keno · Midland · Merrill · Dorris · Macdoel

Yreka · Montague · Grenada · Gazelle · Weed · Mount Shasta · McCloud · Dunsmuir · Castella · Lamoine · Lakehead

Redwood Natl. Park · Klamath · Requa · Orick · Prairie Creek Redwoods · Trinidad · McKinleyville · Arcata · Eureka · Fortuna · Ferndale · Rio Dell · Scotia · Weott · Miranda · Phillipsville · Garberville · Redway

Willow Creek · Salyer · Hoopa · Weitchpec · Orleans · Somes Bar · Forks of Salmon · Cecilville · Etna · Fort Jones · Greenview · Callahan

KLAMATH NATL. FOR. · SISKIYOU NATL. FOR. · ROGUE RIVER–SISKIYOU NATL. FOR. · SHASTA-TRINITY NATL. FOR. · SIX RIVERS NATL. FOR. · TRINITY NATL. FOR. · WHISKEYTOWN-SHASTA-TRINITY NATL. REC. AREA

Weaverville · Junction City · Big Bar · Helena · Hayfork · Douglas City · Lewiston · Shasta Lake · Redding · Anderson · Cottonwood · Red Bluff

Crater Lake Natl. Park · Diamond Lake · Prospect · Fort Klamath · Chiloquin

Go to 20

Go to 36

A · B · C

1 · 2 · 3 · 4

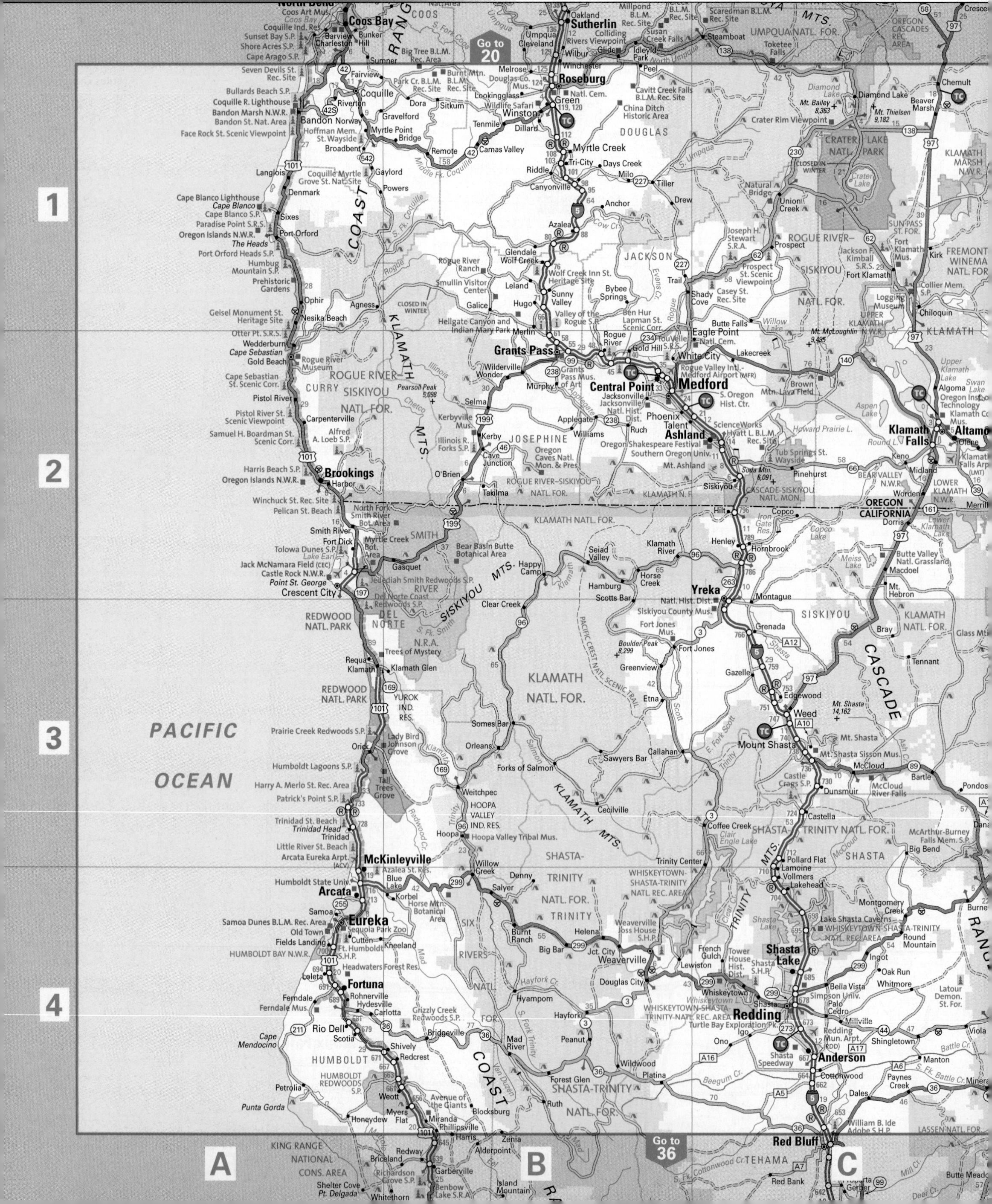

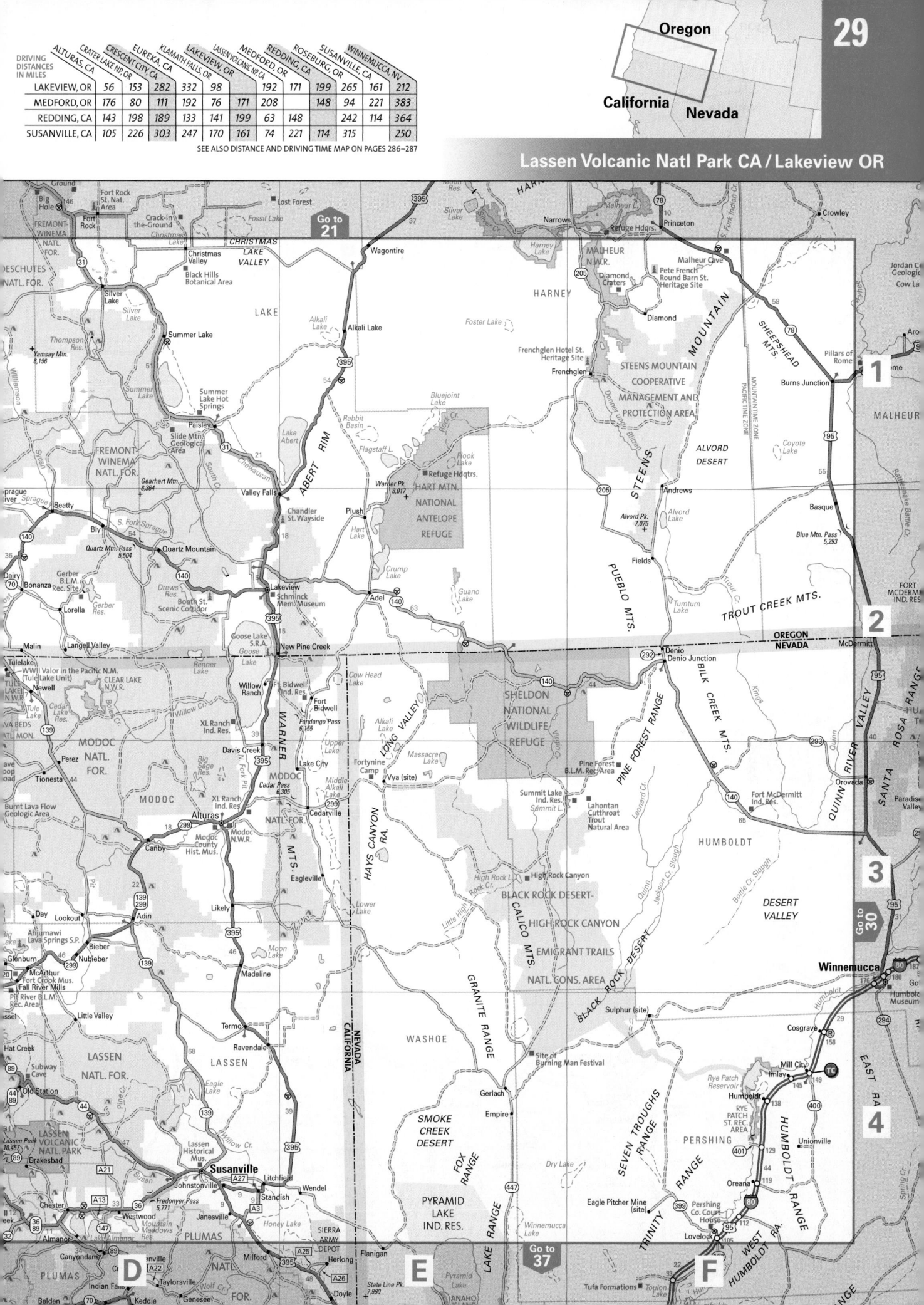

DRIVING
DISTANCES
IN MILES

	ALTURAS, CA	CRATER LAKE NP OR	CRESCENT CITY, CA	EUREKA, CA	KLAMATH FALLS, OR	LAKEVIEW, OR	LASSEN VOLCANIC NP CA	MEDFORD, OR	REDDING, CA	ROSEBURG, OR	SUSANVILLE, CA	WINNEMUCCA, NV
LAKEVIEW, OR	56	153	282	332	98		192	171	199	265	161	212
MEDFORD, OR	176	80	111	192	76	171	208		148	94	221	383
REDDING, CA	143	198	189	133	141	199	63	148		242	114	364
SUSANVILLE, CA	105	226	303	247	170	161	74	221	114	315		250

SEE ALSO DISTANCE AND DRIVING TIME MAP ON PAGES 286–287

0 mi   20   40

0 km   20   40   60

One inch equals 25.4 miles
One centimeter equals 16.1 kilometers

Oregon Idaho

Wyoming

Nevada Utah

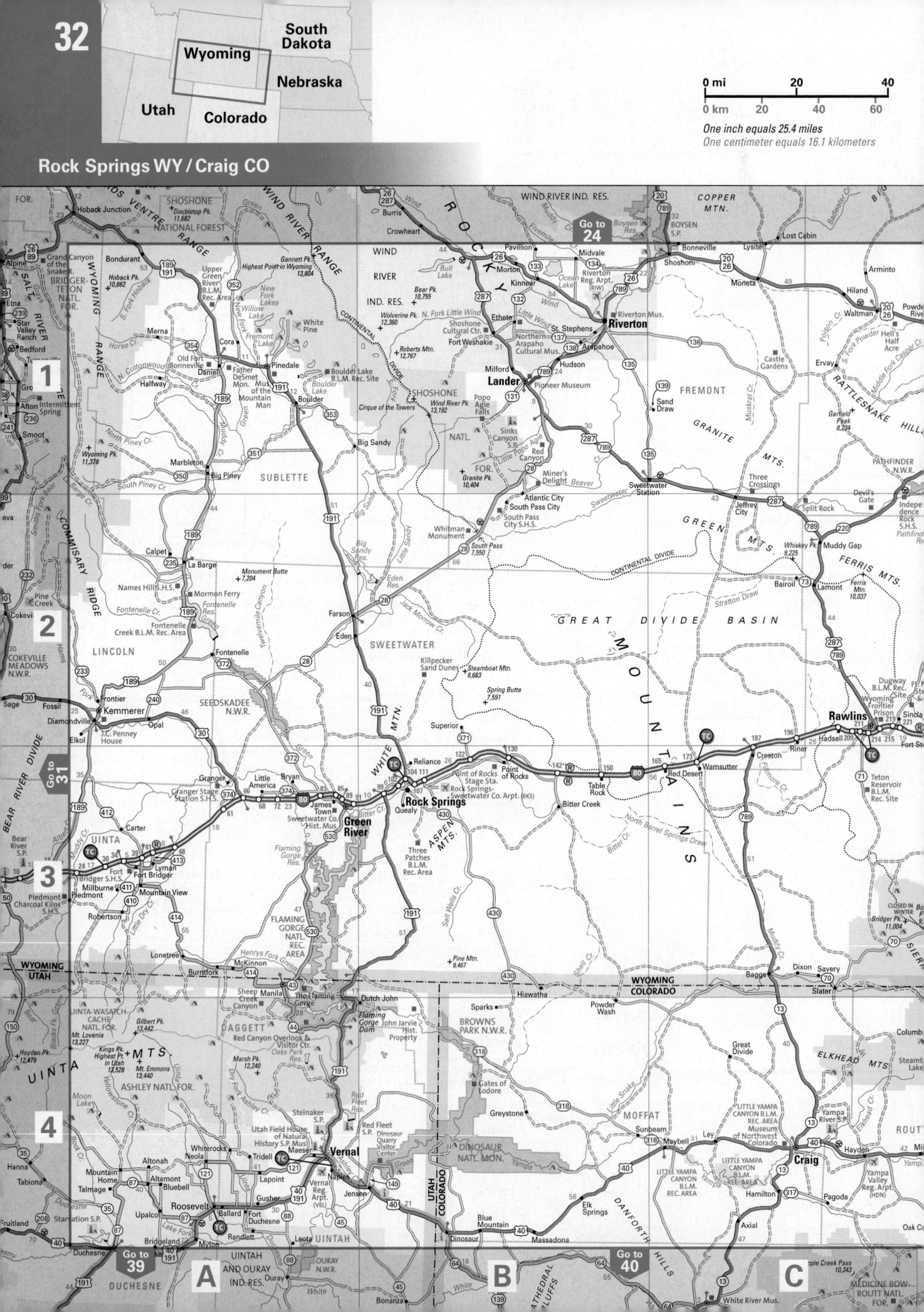

South Dakota
Wyoming
Nebraska
Utah
Colorado

0 mi   20   40
0 km   20   40   60
One inch equals 25.4 miles
One centimeter equals 16.1 kilometers

South Dakota
Wyoming
Nebraska
Utah
Colorado

DRIVING DISTANCES IN MILES	CASPER, WY	CHEYENNE, WY	CRAIG, CO	FORT COLLINS, CO	KEMMERER, WY	LANDER, WY	LARAMIE, WY	PINEDALE, WY	RAWLINS, WY	ROCK SPRINGS, WY	SCOTTSBLUFF, NE	VERNAL, UT
CASPER, WY		175	234	217	297	144	148	271	117	214	173	322
CHEYENNE, WY	175		221	44	342	276	52	355	151	260	111	367
CRAIG, CO	234	221		194	257	221	171	269	117	149	331	123
ROCK SPRINGS, WY	214	260	149	273	86	118	210	98	110		370	111

SEE ALSO DISTANCE AND DRIVING TIME MAP ON PAGES 286–287

South Dakota

Nebraska   Iowa

Colorado

0 mi   20   40
0 km   20   40   60
One inch equals 25.4 miles
One centimeter equals 16.1 kilometers

Go to 26

Go to 33

Go to 42

DRIVING DISTANCES IN MILES

	CHADRON, NE	GRAND ISLAND, NE	LINCOLN, NE	McCOOK, NE	NORFOLK, NE	NORTH PLATTE, NE	OGALLALA, NE	OMAHA, NE	SCOTTSBLUFF, NE	SIOUX CITY, IA	STERLING, CO	YANKTON, SD
GRAND ISLAND, NE	373		95	147	105	143	196	150	318	180	281	167
LINCOLN, NE	453	95		226	119	223	275	58	397	153	361	218
NORTH PLATTE, NE	230	143	223		67	248	53	278	175	373	138	310
OMAHA, NE	508	150	58	281	115	278	330		452	99	416	163

SEE ALSO DISTANCE AND DRIVING TIME MAP ON PAGES 286–287

California Nevada

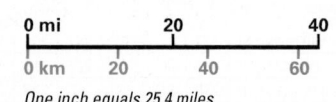

0 mi 20 40
0 km 20 40 60
One inch equals 25.4 miles
One centimeter equals 16.1 kilometers

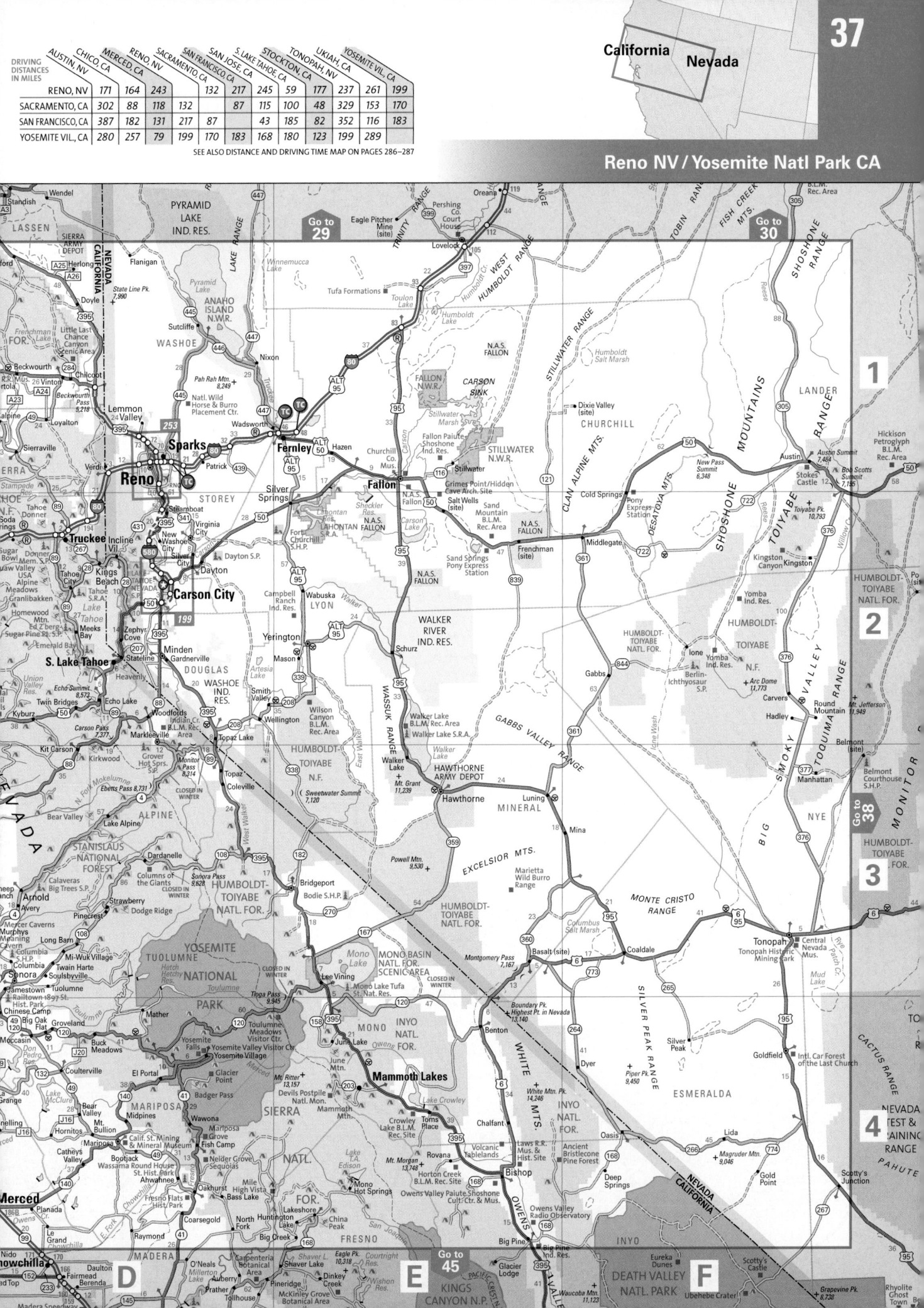

DRIVING DISTANCES IN MILES	AUSTIN, NV	CHICO, CA	MERCED, CA	RENO, NV	SACRAMENTO, CA	SAN FRANCISCO, CA	SAN JOSE, CA	S. LAKE TAHOE, CA	STOCKTON, CA	TONOPAH, NV	UKIAH, CA	YOSEMITE VIL., CA
RENO, NV	171	164	243		132	217	245	59	177	237	261	199
SACRAMENTO, CA	302	88	118	132		87	115	100	48	329	153	170
SAN FRANCISCO, CA	387	182	131	217	87		43	185	82	352	116	183
YOSEMITE VIL., CA	280	257	79	199	170	183	168	180	123	199	289	

SEE ALSO DISTANCE AND DRIVING TIME MAP ON PAGES 286–287

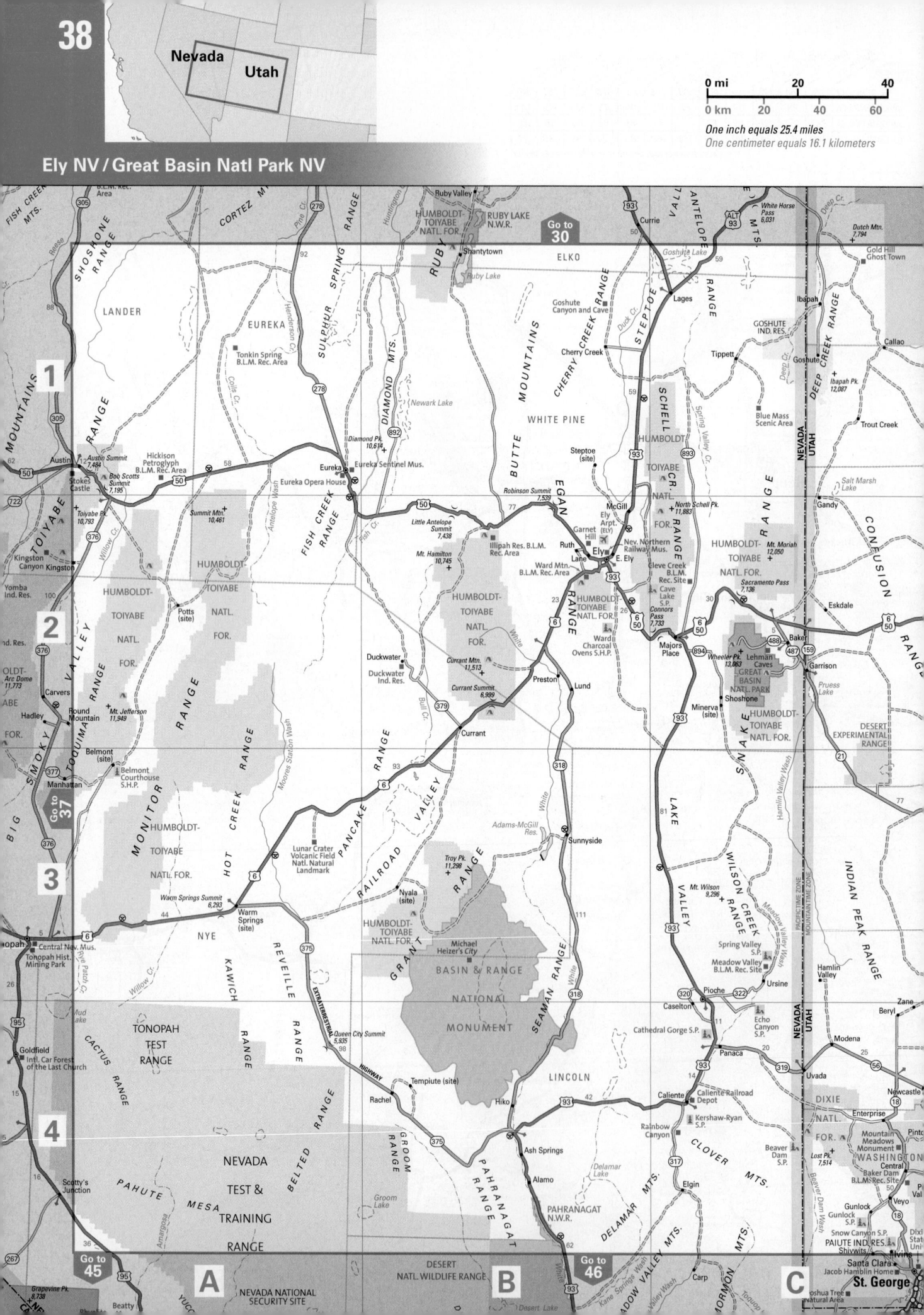

Nevada

Utah

0 mi   20   40
0 km   20   40   60
One inch equals 25.4 miles
One centimeter equals 16.1 kilometers

Go to 30

Go to 37

Go to 45

Go to 46

A   B   C

1   2   3   4

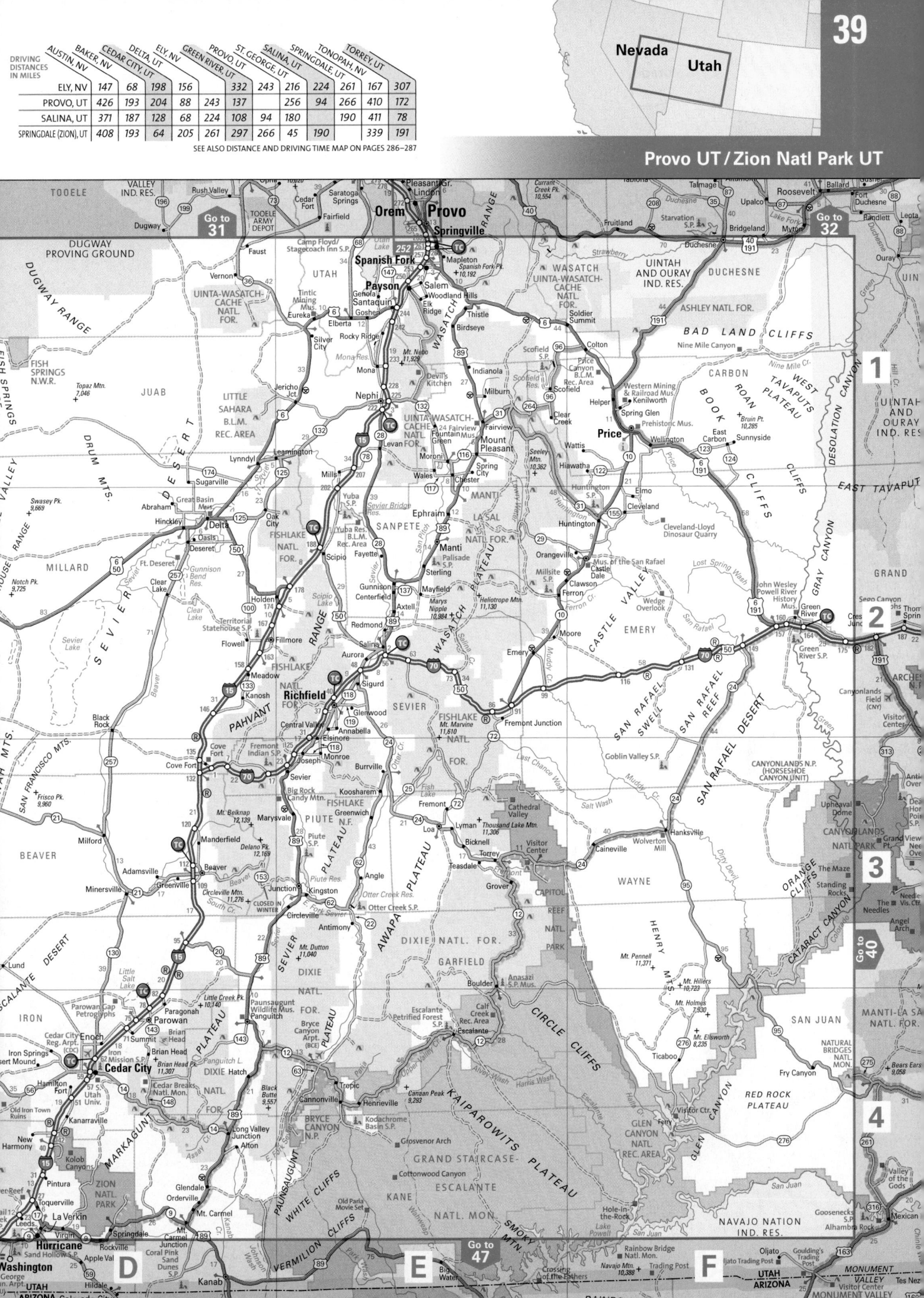

DRIVING DISTANCES IN MILES

	AUSTIN, NV	BAKER, NV	CEDAR CITY, UT	DELTA, UT	ELY, NV	GREEN RIVER, UT	PROVO, UT	ST. GEORGE, UT	SALINA, UT	SPRINGDALE, UT	TONOPAH, NV	TORREY, UT
ELY, NV	147	68	198	156		332	243	216	224	261	167	307
PROVO, UT	426	193	204	88	243	137		256	94	266	410	172
SALINA, UT	371	187	128	68	224	108	94	180		190	411	78
SPRINGDALE (ZION), UT	408	193	64	205	261	297	266	45	190		339	191

SEE ALSO DISTANCE AND DRIVING TIME MAP ON PAGES 286–287

Utah | Colorado

0 mi   20   40
0 km   20   40   60
One inch equals 25.4 miles
One centimeter equals 16.1 kilometers

Go to 32
Go to 39
Go to 48

DRIVING DISTANCES IN MILES	ALAMOSA, CO	ASPEN, CO	COLORADO SPRS, CO	CORTEZ, CO	DENVER, CO	DURANGO, CO	GRAND JUNCTION, CO	GREEN RIVER, UT	MOAB, UT	MONTROSE, CO	PUEBLO, CO	TRINIDAD, CO
COLORADO SPRS., CO	162	157		359	70	314	318	404	418	236	43	127
DENVER, CO	230	164	70	452		337	250	350	337	277	111	196
DURANGO, CO	152	244	314	45	337		169	214	160	107	271	260
GRAND JUNCTION, CO	261	135	318	203	250	169		102	88	62	360	444

SEE ALSO DISTANCE AND DRIVING TIME MAP ON PAGES 286–287

42
Nebraska
Colorado
Kansas
Garden City KS / Dodge City KS
0 mi 20 40
0 km 20 40 60
One inch equals 25.4 miles
One centimeter equals 16.1 kilometers
Go to 34
Go to 41
Go to 50
COLORADO NEBRASKA
NEBRASKA KANSAS
COLORADO KANSAS
COLORADO OKLAHOMA
WASHINGTON
YUMA
DUNDY
HITCHCOCK
RED WILLOW
FURNAS
GOSPER
CHEYENNE
RAWLINS
DECATUR
NORTON
KIT CARSON
SHERMAN
THOMAS
SHERIDAN
GRAHAM
WALLACE
LOGAN
GOVE
TREGO
WICHITA
SCOTT
LANE
NESS
KIOWA
GREELEY
HAMILTON
KEARNY
FINNEY
HODGEMAN
PROWERS
BENT
GRAY
FORD
HASKELL
GRANT
STANTON
MEADE
CLARK
BACA
MORTON
STEVENS
SEWARD
McCook
Colby
Goodland
Burlington
Lamar
Garden City
Dodge City
Ulysses
Liberal
Scott City
Oakley
Oberlin
Norton
WaKeeney
Atwood
Hugoton
Syracuse
Sharon Springs
Tribune
Leoti
Lakin
Meade
Cimarron
Ness City
Dighton
Jetmore
Springfield
Eads
Las Animas
Cheyenne Wells
Kit Carson
Wray
Yuma
Akron
Trenton
St. Francis
Hoxie
Hill City
Johnson City
Elkhart
Ashland
COMANCHE NATL. GRASSLAND
CIMARRON NATL. GRASSLAND
SAND CREEK MASSACRE NATL. HIST. SITE
Mt. Sunflower Highest Pt in Kansas 4,039
Monument Rocks Natl. Landmark
A
B
C
1
2
3
4

DRIVING DISTANCES IN MILES	BURLINGTON, CO	DODGE CITY, KS	EMPORIA, KS	GARDEN CITY, KS	HAYS, KS	LAMAR, CO	MANHATTAN, KS	MCCOOK, NE	OAKLEY, KS	SALINA, KS	TOPEKA, KS	WICHITA, KS
GARDEN CITY, KS	167	52	290		139	98	272	167	79	204	311	205
OAKLEY, KS	88	136	293	79	87	156	247	88		179	286	268
SALINA, KS	266	164	118	204	93	335	72	240	179		111	92
WICHITA, KS	354	153	85	205	181	303	131	329	268	92	137	

SEE ALSO DISTANCE AND DRIVING TIME MAP ON PAGES 286–287

Nebraska

Colorado

Kansas

Nevada

California

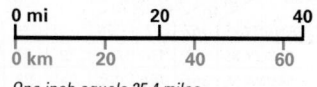

One inch equals 25.4 miles
One centimeter equals 16.1 kilometers

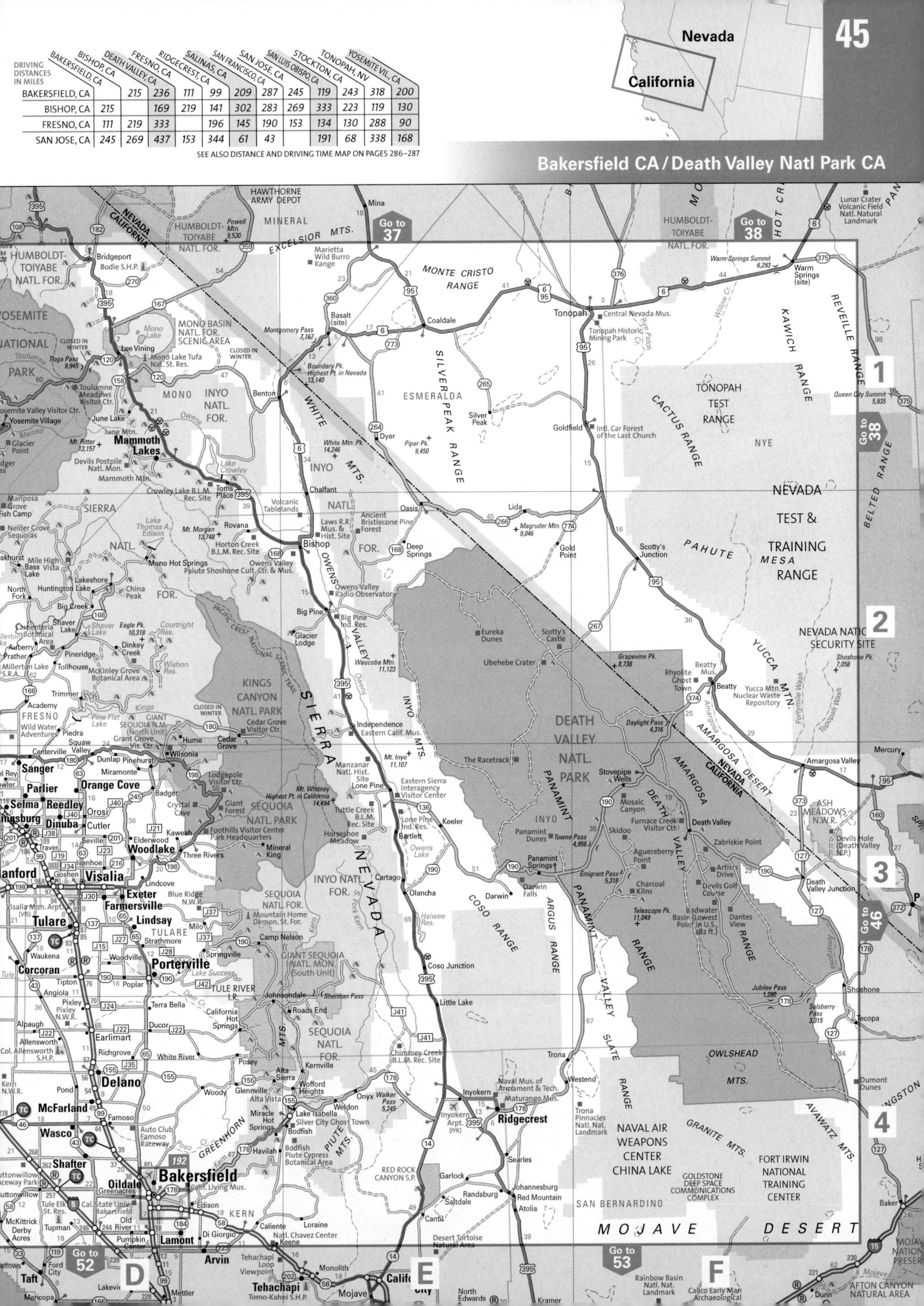

DRIVING DISTANCES IN MILES	BISHOP, CA	DEATH VALLEY, CA	FRESNO, CA	RIDGECREST, CA	SALINAS, CA	SAN FRANCISCO, CA	SAN JOSE, CA	SAN LUIS OBISPO, CA	STOCKTON, CA	TONOPAH, NV	YOSEMITE VIL., CA
BAKERSFIELD, CA	215	236	111	99	209	287	245	119	243	318	200
BISHOP, CA	215	169	219	141	302	283	269	333	223	119	130
FRESNO, CA	111	219	333	196	145	190	153	134	130	288	90
SAN JOSE, CA	245	269	437	153	344	61	43	191	68	338	168

SEE ALSO DISTANCE AND DRIVING TIME MAP ON PAGES 286–287

Nevada   Utah

California

Arizona

0 mi   20   40
0 km   20   40   60
One inch equals 25.4 miles
One centimeter equals 16.1 kilometers

MESA

NEVADA
TEST &
TRAINING
RANGE

NEVADA NATIONAL
SECURITY SITE

Shoshone Pk.
7,058

NYE

Amargosa Valley   Mercury
Ash Meadows N.W.R.
Death Valley Junction
Devils Hole (Death Valley N.P.)

Pahrump

SPRING MOUNTAINS N.R.A.

Indian Springs
Creech A.F.B.

Charleston Pk.
11,918

Las Vegas Ski and Snowboard

Las Vegas

Red Rock Canyon N.C.A.

Spring Mtn. Ranch S.P.
Blue Diamond

Sloan

Shoshone
Tecopa

Goodsprings
Sandy Valley   Jean

Primm
Buffalo Bill's
Clark Mtn. 7,929
Mountain Pass
Mountain Pass 4,730

Halloran Springs
Baker

Silver Lake
Cima Dome
Cinder Cones   Cima
Ivanpah

MOJAVE NATIONAL PRESERVE

DEVILS PLAYGROUND

Kelso
Providence Mountains St. Rec. Area
Kelso Dunes
Mitchell Caverns

SAN BERNARDINO

BRISTOL MTS.

Ludlow
Bagdad
Amboy Crater Natl. Nat. Landmark
Amboy   Cadiz

MARINE CORPS AIR GROUND COMBAT CENTER
TWENTYNINE PALMS

Twentynine Palms
Yucca Valley
Joshua Tree Natl. Park

DESERT

SPOTTED RANGE

SHEEP RANGE

NATL. WILDLIFE RANGE

Hayford Pk. 9,912

CLARK

TULE SPRINGS FOSSIL BEDS NATL. MON.

Floyd Lamb Park

North Las Vegas

Henderson

Boulder City

SLOAN CANYON N.C.A.

MC CULLOUGH RANGE

Searchlight
Nipton
Nelson

NEW YORK MTS.

LANFAIR VALLEY

Goffs

Fenner   Essex

PIUTE MTS.
Danby
OLD WOMAN MTS.

SHEEP HOLE MTS.

PAHRANAGAT N.W.R.

LINCOLN

Carp

MEADOW VALLEY MTS.

Mormon Pk. 7,411

Moapa
Glendale
Logandale
Overton

MOAPA RIVER IND. RES.

VALLEY OF FIRE S.P.
Lost City Mus.

Hoover Dam

LAKE MEAD NATL. REC. AREA

Fortification Hill 3,718

Temple Bar

Meadview

Willow Beach

ELDORADO MTS.

ARIZONA
NEVADA

BLACK MTS.

Mt. Perkins 5,456

Cottonwood Cove
Lake Mohave

Dolan Springs

WHITE HILLS

Joshua Tree Forest

Garnet Mtn. 8,440
Red Lake

Davis Dam
Colorado River Museum

Laughlin

Bullhead City

Mohave Valley
FORT MOJAVE IND. RES.

Needles

HAVASU N.W.R.
Topock
Moabi Reg. Park

CHEMEHUEVI VALLEY

Havasu Lake

Lake Havasu City
London Bridge
Lake Havasu S.P.

CHEMEHUEVI IND. RES.

WHIPPLE MTS.

Vidal Jct.
Big River
Vidal
Parker

NEVADA
UTAH

Go to 38

WASHINGTON
ZION NATL. PARK

Gunlock
Veyo
Silver Reef
Toquerville
La Verkin
Snow Canyon S.P.
Dixie State Univ.
Santa Clara
Ivins
St. George
Hurricane
Rockville
Springdale
Washington
St. George Mun. Arpt. (SGU)
UTAH
ARIZONA
Colorado City
Hildale

Beaver Dam
Littlefield
Virgin River Canyon B.L.M. Rec. Area

Mesquite
Bunkerville

Mt. Bangs 8,012

VIRGIN MTS.

SHIVWITS

Poverty Mtn. 6,791
Mt. Trumbull 8,028

GRAND WASH CLIFFS

GRAND CANYON-PARASHANT NATL. MONUMENT

UINKARET PLATEAU

Ranger Station

LAKE MEAD NATL. REC. AREA

Toroweap Overlook

GRAND CANYON WEST PLATEAU

Grand Canyon West & Skywalk
Grand Canyon West Arpt. (GCW)

GRAND CANYON NATL. PARK

Natural Bridge

HUALAPAI IND. RES.

MOHAVE

Truxton Wash

Windy Point B.L.M. Rec. Site
Chloride

Peach Springs
Nelson
Yampai
Truxton

Grand Canyon Caverns

AUBREY CLIFFS

CERBAT MTS.

Mt. Tipton 7,148

Hackberry
Valentine

SACRAMENTO MTS.

Kingman
Kingman Arpt. (IGM)
McConnico

HUALAPAI VALLEY

Hualapai Mtn. Park
Hualapai Pk. 8,417
Wild Cow Springs B.L.M. Rec. Site

Yucca

Golden Shores

Oatman

Mohave Mus. of History & Arts and Historic Rt. 66 Mus.

BLACK MESA

DUTCH FLAT

MC CRACKEN MTS.

AQUARIUS MOUNTAINS

Mohon Pk. 7,499
Mt. Hope 7,263
Snow Mtn. 5,879
Cross Mtn. 6,463
Hyde Creek Mtn. 7,272

Wikieup
Aubrey Pk. 5,078

Burro Creek B.L.M. Rec. Site
Bagdad

JUNIPER MTS.

PRESCOTT NATL. FOR.

Seligman

Cypress Mtn. 6,251

POACHIE RANGE

Hillside
Date

JOSHUA FOREST PARKWAY

Kirkland

Parker Dam
Bill Williams River
Buckskin Mountain S.P.
B.L.M. Rec. Area
Alamo Dam
Alamo Lake S.P.

Swansea Ghost Town
Tres Alamos 4,293

Congress

Colorado River Indian Tribes Mus.
Poston

CACTUS PLAIN

LA PAZ

Go to 54

Go to 45

Go to 53

BULLION

INYO

KINGSTON RANGE

SHADOW VALLEY

Dumont Dunes

Mesquite Lake

Roach Lake

Ivanpah Lake

AVAWATZ MTS.

CADY MTS.

Pisgah Crater

Afton Canyon Natural Area

Soda Lake

DRIVING DISTANCES IN MILES

	CHINLE, AZ	FLAGSTAFF, AZ	GRAND CANYON, AZ	HOLBROOK, AZ	KAYENTA, AZ	KINGMAN, AZ	LAKE HAVASU CITY, AZ	LAS VEGAS, NV	LAUGHLIN, NV	PAGE, AZ	PRESCOTT, AZ	ST. GEORGE, UT
FLAGSTAFF, AZ	216		89	93	152	148	209	249	182	135	89	271
GRAND CANYON, AZ	232	89		182	153	175	236	276	209	136	131	272
LAS VEGAS, NV	465	249	276	341	374	103	154		94	277	251	118
ST. GEORGE, UT	358	271	272	353	255	221	272	118	212	159	369	

SEE ALSO DISTANCE AND DRIVING TIME MAP ON PAGES 286–287

Utah Colorado
Arizona **New Mexico** Okla.
Texas

0 mi   20   40
0 km   20   40   60
One inch equals 25.4 miles
One centimeter equals 16.1 kilometers

San Juan
Montezuma Creek
Bluff
Aneth
Red Mesa
Mexican Water
Sweetwater
Teec Nos Pos
Beklabito
Four Corners Mon. & Navajo Tribal Park
UTAH / ARIZONA
COLORADO / NEW MEXICO
Shiprock
Waterflow Fruitland
Kirtland **Farmington**
Bloomfield
Aztec
Flora Vista
Blanco
Durango & Silverton Narrow Gauge Railroad
Durango
Fort Lewis Coll.
Grandview
Hesperus
Bayfield
Chimney Rock
Pagosa Springs
Summit Peak 13,300
ARCHULETA
CONEJOS
MESA VERDE NATL. PARK
LA PLATA
SOUTHERN UTE IND. RES.
Ignacio
Tiffany
Allison
Arboles
Chromo
Chama
UTE MOUNTAIN IND. RES.
Towaoc
Cortez Mun. Arpt. (CEZ)
Yucca House Natl. Mon.
MONTEZUMA
CHINLE ALLEY
NAVAJO NATION INDIAN RES.
CARRIZO MTS.
Rock Point
Round Rock
Cove
Red Rock
Lukachukai
Tsaile
Many Farms
CHUSKA MTS.
Chinle
CANYON DE CHELLY NATL. MON.
Spider Rock Overlook
Antelope House Ruins
Mummy Cave Ruin
White House Ruin
Nazlini
Sawmill
Navajo
Fort Defiance
St. Michaels
Window Rock
Hubbell Trading Post N.H.S.
Ganado
DEFIANCE PLATEAU
Pine Springs
Houck
Lupton
Manuelito
Gallup
Gallup Mun. Arpt. (GUP)
Gallup Cultural Ctr.
McGaffey
Fort Wingate
Continental Divide
Thoreau
Prewitt
Bluewater Lake S.P.
Milan
Grants
ZUNI MTS.
CIBOLA NATL. FOR.
Ramah
El Morro Natl. Mon.
ZUNI IND. RES.
Zuni Pueblo
A:shiwi A:wan Mus. & Heritage Ctr.
Black Rock
Pescado
Pine Hill
EL MALPAIS NATL. MON.
Bandera Crater & Ice Caves
La Ventana Natural Arch
NAVAJO (RAMAH) IND. RES.
Fence Lake
NORTH PLAINS
EL MALPAIS NATL. CONS. AREA
Cebolleta Pk. 8,762
St. Johns
Salado
Lyman Lake S.P.
White Mtn. Arch. Ctr. and Raven Site Ruins
Casa Malpais Arch. Park
Springerville
Eagar
Quemado
Omega
Red Hill
Pie Town
Datil
DATIL MTS.
National Radio Astronomy Observatory Very Large Array
Magdalena
Kelly Ghost Town
N. Mex. Inst. of Mining & Tech.
Socorro
San Acacia
Luis Lopez
San Antonio
SEVILLETA N.W.R.
La Joya
Bernardo
Belen
Jarales
Bosque
Los Lunas
Peralta
Valencia
Los Chavez
Tome
VALENCIA
ISLETA PUEBLO
San Agustin Mission
Bosque Farms
Albuquerque
Los Ranchos de Albuquerque
Petroglyph Natl. Mon.
Paradise Hills
Rio Rancho
Corrales
Alameda
KIRTLAND A.F.B.
Cedar Crest
Tijeras
Edgewood
SANDIA MTS.
Sandia Park
Cedar Grove
Wildlife West Nature Park
BERNALILLO
Bernalillo
Placitas
Algodones
ZIA PUEBLO
SANTA ANA PUEBLO
SAN FELIPE PUEBLO
SANTO DOMINGO PUEBLO
San Ysidro
Zia Pueblo
Jemez Pueblo
Jemez Springs
JEMEZ MTS.
Cañon
Ponderosa
Cochiti Pueblo
Pena Blanca
La Cienega
Madrid
Cerrillos
Golden
SANDOVAL
CIBOLA
Seboyeta
Paguate
Laguna
Mesita
Paraje
LAGUNA PUEBLO
Mesa
Acoma Pueblo
San Esteban del Rey Mission
Enchanted Mesa
ACOMA PUEBLO
McCartys
Acomita Lake
Casa Blanca
San Fidel
Cubero
Correo
ISLETA PUEBLO
Laguna Pueblo
Rio Puerco
Mt. Taylor 11,301
New Mex. Mining Museum
SAN MATEO MTS.
San Mateo
Marquez
Cabezon Peak
IGNACIO CHAVEZ SPECIAL MANAGEMENT AREA
Star Lake
White Horse
Seven Lakes
CHACO MESA
Torreon
Hospah
Crownpoint
Ambrosia Lake
Smith Lake
MCKINLEY
Twin Lakes
Mentmore
Gamerco
Allison
Coolidge
Iyanbito
Mariano Lake
Pinedale
Rehoboth
Red Rock State Park
Yah-ta-hey
Church Rock
CIBOLA NATL. FOR.
ZUNI IND. RES.
Vander Wagen
Upper Nutria
Ojo Caliente
Zuni Pueblo
CHACO CULTURE N.H.P.
Pueblo Bonito Ruins
ONLY PUBLIC ACCESS TO PARK
Lake Valley
White Rock
Pueblo Pintado
NAVAJO NATION INDIAN RES.
Standing Rock
Coyote Canyon
Sheep Springs
Newcomb
Toadlena
Burnham
SAN JUAN BASIN
Bisti Wilderness Area
De-Na-Zin Wilderness Area
Nageezi
Counselor
Cuba
La Jara
Regina
Gallina
Coyote
Youngsville
Abiquiu
Medanales
Chili
Hernandez
Espanol
Puye Cliff Dwellings
SANTA CLARA PUEBLO
SAN ILDEFONSO
Los Alamos
White Rock
VALLES CALDERA
Bandelier Natl. Mon.
JEMEZ NATL. REC. AREA
Fenton Lake S.P.
Ghost Ranch Living Mus.
Echo Amphitheater
El Rito
Abiquiu Lake
SANTA FE NATL. FOR.
RIO ARRIBA
Gobernador
Blanco Trading Post
Angel Peak B.L.M. Rec. Area
JICARILLA APACHE IND. RES.
Gavilan
Lindrith
Llaves
Canjilon
Vallecitos
Cebolla
El Vado
El Vado Lake S.P.
Tierra Amarilla
Los Ojos
Heron Lake S.P.
BRAZOS CLIFFS
CARSON NATL. FOR.
Rutheron
Ensenada
Las Nutrias
Canon Plaza
Las Nutrias
CARSON
Dulce
Monero
Lumberton
Navajo Lake S.P.
Navajo Dam
Simon Canyon B.L.M. Rec. Area
Aztec Ruins N.M.
Cedar Hill
Negro Canyon B.L.M. Rec. Area
La Plata
NAVAJO NATION INDIAN RES.
Salmon Ruins & Heritage Park
Dunes B.L.M. OHV Rec. Area
Turley
Archuleta
Aztec Museum
Four Corners Reg. Arpt. (FMN)
Pagosa Junction
Cumbres and Toltec Scenic R.R.
La Manga Pass 10,230
Cumbres Pass 10,022
Fox Creek
San Miguel
CONTINENTAL DIVIDE
CATRON
GALLINAS MTS.
Datil Well B.L.M. Rec. Area
DATIL MTS.
MANGAS MTS.
Alegres Mtn. 10,244
SOCORRO
Ladron Pk. 9,176
San Lorenzo Canyon B.L.M. Rec. Area
Polvadera
Lemitar
Escondida
Abeytas
Veguita
Sabinal
Las Nutrias
Jarales
San Agustin Plains

Go to 40
Go to 47
Go to 56

1 2 3 4
A B C

Utah Colorado

Arizona New Mexico Okla.

Texas

0 mi   20   40

0 km   20   40   60

One inch equals 25.4 miles
One centimeter equals 16.1 kilometers

DRIVING DISTANCES IN MILES	AMARILLO, TX	ARDMORE, OK	BARTLESVILLE, OK	CHILDRESS, TX	CLINTON, OK	ENID, OK	LAWTON, OK	LIBERAL, KS	OKLAHOMA CITY, OK	STILLWATER, OK	TULSA, OK	WOODWARD, OK
AMARILLO, TX		361	419	118	177	298	240	165	262	329	371	177
LAWTON, OK	240	103	243	124	98	142		287	85	152	194	175
OKLAHOMA CITY, OK	262	99	157	225	85	84	85	259		67	109	143
TULSA, OK	371	206	48	334	194	117	194	321	109	71		205

SEE ALSO DISTANCE AND DRIVING TIME MAP ON PAGES 286–287

Colorado   Kansas

Oklahoma

Texas

Nev.

California Arizona

Mexico

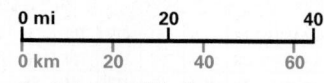

0 mi   20   40
0 km   20   40   60

One inch equals 25.4 miles
One centimeter equals 16.1 kilometers

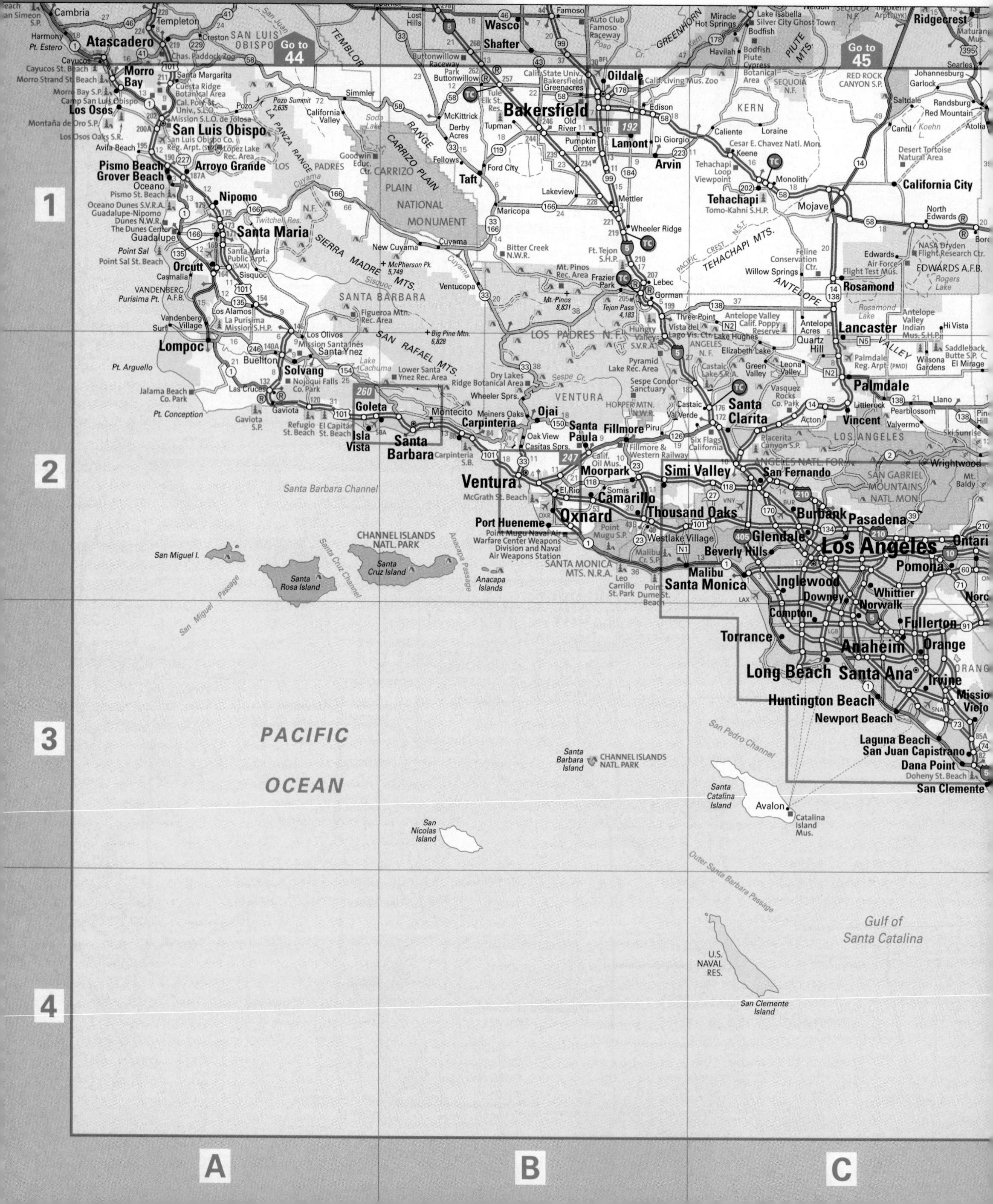

1

2

3

4

A   **B**   **C**

San Simeon
San Simeon S.P.
Harmony
Cambria
Pt. Estero
Cayucos
Cayucos St. Beach
Morro Bay S.P.
Morro Strand St. Beach
Camp San Luis Obispo
Montaña de Oro S.P.
Los Osos Oaks S.R.
Avila Beach
Atascadero
Templeton
Creston
Morro Bay
Los Osos
San Luis Obispo
Santa Margarita
Cuesta Ridge Botanical Area
Cal. Poly. St. Univ., S.L.O.
Mission S.L.O. de Tolosa
San Luis Obispo Co. Rg. Arpt. (SBP)
Lopez Lake Rec. Area
Pozo
Pismo Beach
Grover Beach
Oceano
Pismo St. Beach
Oceano Dunes S.V.R.A.
Guadalupe-Nipomo Dunes N.W.R.
The Dunes Center
Guadalupe
Casmalia
Nipomo
Arroyo Grande
Point Sal
Point Sal St. Beach
Santa Maria
Santa Maria Public Arpt. (SMX)
Orcutt
Sisquoc
VANDENBERG A.F.B.
Purisima Pt.
Vandenberg Village
Surf
La Purisima Mission S.H.P.
Los Alamos
Los Olivos
Mission Santa Inés
Lompoc
Santa Ynez
Solvang
Buellton
Pt. Arguello
Jalama Beach Co. Park
Las Cruces
Nojoqui Falls Co. Park
Gaviota
Gaviota S.P.
Pt. Conception
Refugio St. Beach
El Capitán St. Beach
Goleta
Isla Vista
Santa Barbara
Montecito
Carpinteria

TEMBLOR
RANGE
Lost Hills
Wasco
Shafter
Buttonwillow Raceway Park
Buttonwillow
McKittrick
Derby Acres
Fellows
Taft
Ford City
Maricopa
CARRIZO PLAIN
CARRIZO PLAIN NATIONAL MONUMENT
LA PANZA RANGE
Pozo Summit 2,635
California Valley
Soda Lake
Twitchell Res.
Simmler
SIERRA MADRE MTS.
New Cuyama
Cuyama
McPherson Pk. 5,749
Figueroa Mtn. Rec. Area
Big Pine Mtn. 6,828
SANTA BARBARA
SAN RAFAEL MTS.
Lake Cachuma
Lower Santa Ynez Rec. Area
Ventucopa
Bitter Creek N.W.R.
Lakeview
Wheeler Sprs.
Dry Lakes Ridge Botanical Area
Meiners Oaks
Oak View
Casitas Sprs.
Ojai
Santa Paula
Fillmore
LOS PADRES N.F.
Pyramid Lake Rec. Area
Sespe Condor Sanctuary

Famoso
Auto Club Famoso Raceway
Oildale
Bakersfield
Calif. State Univ. Bakersfield
Greenacres
Old River
Pumpkin Center
Lamont
Di Giorgio
Arvin
Edison
Mettler
Wheeler Ridge
Ft. Tejon S.H.P.
Tejon Pass 4,183
Lebec
Gorman
Frazier Park
Mt. Pinos 8,831
Three Points
Hungry Valley S.V.R.A.
Castaic
Val Verde
Piru
Fillmore & Western Railway
Six Flags California
Castaic Lake S.R.A.
Santa Clarita
Placerita Canyon S.P.
San Fernando

GREENHORN
PIUTE MTS.
Miracle Hot Springs
Bodfish
Lake Isabella
Silver City Ghost Town
Havilah
Bodfish Piute Cypress Botanical Area
SEQUOIA N.F.
Cesar E. Chavez Natl. Mon.
Caliente
Loraine
Keene
Tehachapi
Tomo-Kahni S.H.P.
Monolith
Tehachapi Loop Viewpoint
TEHACHAPI MTS.
PACIFIC CREST N.S.T.
Willow Springs
Feline Conservation Ctr.
ANTELOPE VALLEY
Antelope Valley Calif. Poppy Reserve
Antelope Acres
Lancaster
Elizabeth Lake
Green Valley
Leona Valley
Quartz Hill
Palmdale
Palmdale Reg. Arpt. (PMD)
Littlerock
Pearblossom
Vasquez Rocks Co. Park
Acton
Vincent
Valyermo
LOS ANGELES
Wasco

Ridgecrest
Matura Mus.
Go to 45
Johannesburg
Garlock
Randsburg
Red Mountain
Saltdale
Koehn
Atolia
Cantil
RED ROCK CANYON S.P.
California City
Mojave
North Edwards
EDWARDS A.F.B.
Rogers Lake
NASA Dryden Flight Research Ctr.
Air Force Flight Test Mus.
Edwards
Rosamond
Rosamond Lake
Hi Vista
Saddleback Butte S.P.
El Mirage
Wilsona Gardens
Llano
Wrightwood
SAN GABRIEL MOUNTAINS NATL. MON.
Mt. Baldy
Ski Sunrise

Go to 44
KERN
SEQUOIA N.F.
Califi Living Mus. Zoo

Carpinteria
Ventura
McGrath St. Beach
Moorpark
Camarillo
Oxnard
Port Hueneme
Point Mugu Naval Air Warfare Center Weapons Division and Naval Air Weapons Station
Point Mugu S.P.
Simi Valley
Thousand Oaks
Westlake Village
SANTA MONICA MTS. N.R.A.
Leo Carrillo St. Park
Point Dume St. Beach
Malibu
Santa Monica
San Fernando
Burbank
Glendale
Beverly Hills
LAX
Inglewood
Pasadena
Los Angeles
Downey
Compton
Whittier
Norwalk
Torrance
Pomona
Ontari
Norc
Fullerton
Anaheim
Orange
Long Beach
Santa Ana
Irvine
Missio Viejo
Huntington Beach
Newport Beach
Laguna Beach
San Juan Capistrano
Dana Point
Doheny St. Beach
San Clemente
ORANG

Santa Barbara Channel
CHANNEL ISLANDS NATL. PARK
San Miguel I.
Santa Rosa Island
Santa Cruz Island
San Miguel Passage
Santa Cruz Channel
Anacapa Passage
Anacapa Islands

PACIFIC

OCEAN

San Nicolas Island

Santa Barbara Island
CHANNEL ISLANDS NATL. PARK

San Pedro Channel
Santa Catalina Island
Avalon
Catalina Island Mus.

Outer Santa Barbara Passage

Gulf of Santa Catalina

U.S. NAVAL RES.
San Clemente Island

DRIVING DISTANCES IN MILES

	BAKERSFIELD, CA	BARSTOW, CA	BLYTHE, CA	EL CENTRO, CA	LOS ANGELES, CA	NEEDLES, CA	PALM SPRINGS, CA	SAN BERNARDINO, CA	SAN DIEGO, CA	SAN LUIS OBISPO, CA	SANTA BARBARA, CA	YUMA, AZ
LOS ANGELES, CA	111	118	230	234		263	110	62	124	190	97	294
SAN DIEGO, CA	234	181	211	117	124	326	143	111		314	221	177
SANTA BARBARA, CA	150	213	325	330	97	358	205	157	221	93		391
YUMA, AZ	403	294	103	65	294	187	171	225	177	483	391	

SEE ALSO DISTANCE AND DRIVING TIME MAP ON PAGES 286–287

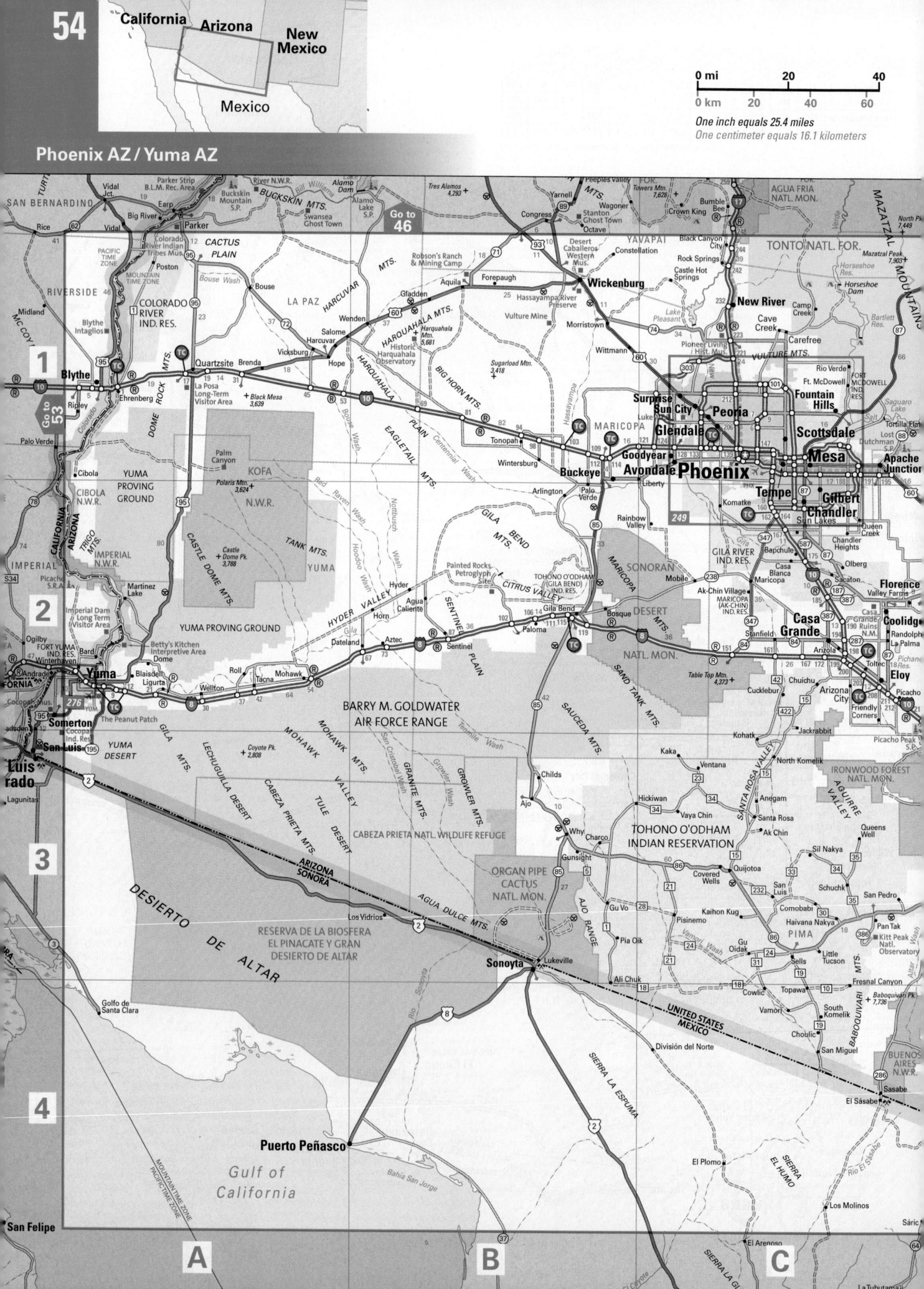

California Arizona New Mexico
Mexico

0 mi   20   40
0 km   20   40   60
One inch equals 25.4 miles
One centimeter equals 16.1 kilometers

DRIVING DISTANCES IN MILES	BLYTHE, CA	CASA GRANDE, AZ	DOUGLAS, AZ	EAGAR, AZ	GLOBE, AZ	LORDSBURG, NM	NOGALES, AZ	PHOENIX, AZ	SAFFORD, AZ	SILVER CITY, NM	TUCSON, AZ	YUMA, AZ
LORDSBURG, NM	417	228	101	184	155		185	278	77	45	161	401
PHOENIX, AZ	140	50	237	227	92	278	181		169	322	118	183
TUCSON, AZ	258	68	120	242	106	161	65	118	128	205		241
YUMA, AZ	103	179	360	401	265	401	304	183	368	446	241	

SEE ALSO DISTANCE AND DRIVING TIME MAP ON PAGES 286–287

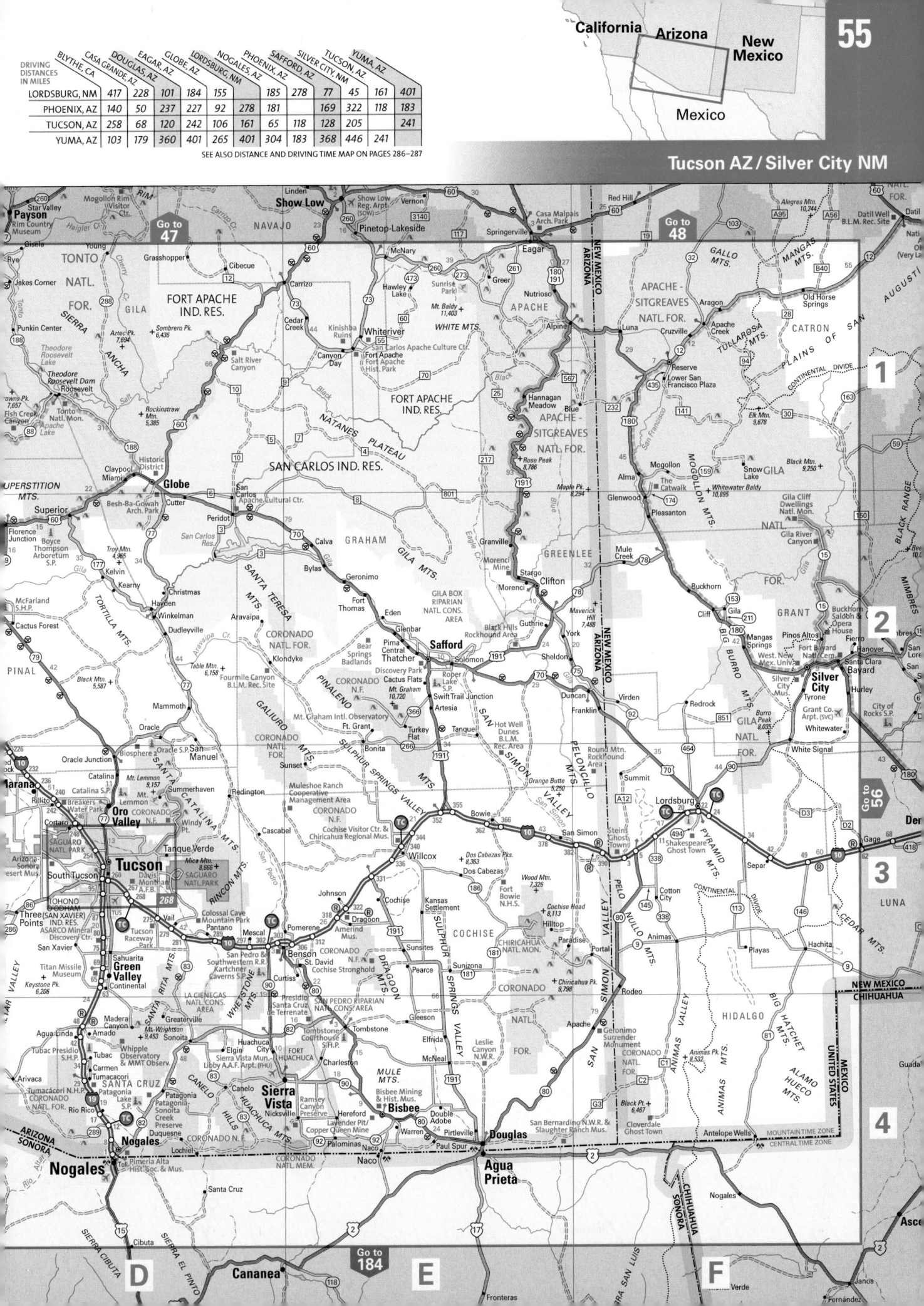

Go to 47

Go to 48

Go to 56

Go to 184

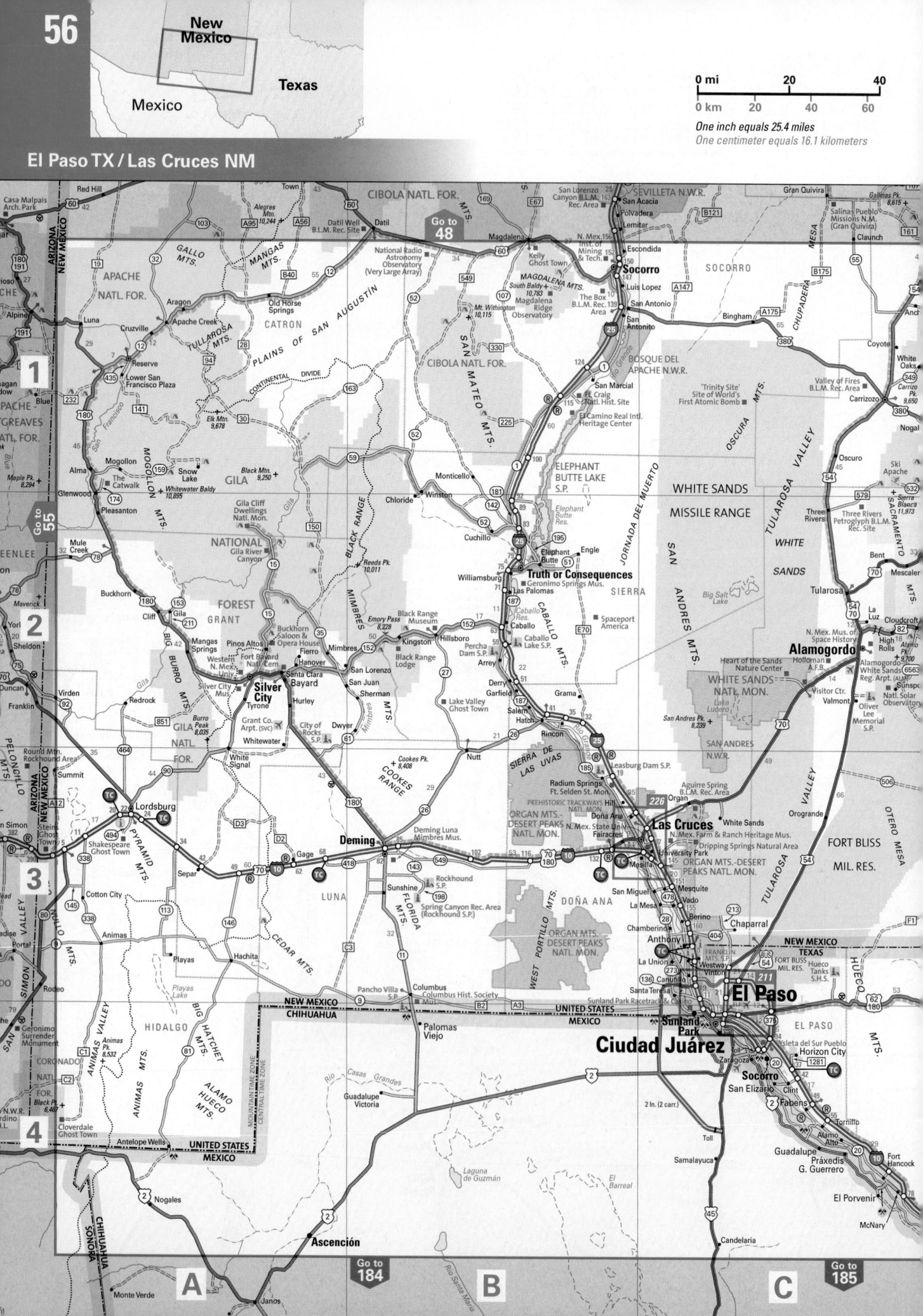

New Mexico

Texas

Mexico

0 mi   20   40
0 km   20   40   60
One inch equals 25.4 miles
One centimeter equals 16.1 kilometers

DRIVING DISTANCES IN MILES

	ALAMOGORDO, NM	CARLSBAD, NM	EL PASO, TX	HOBBS, NM	LAS CRUCES, NM	LORDSBURG, NM	ODESSA, TX	PECOS, TX	PORTALES, NM	ROSWELL, NM	SILVER CITY, NM	SOCORRO, NM
CARLSBAD, NM	144		162	70	203	321	137	87	168	76	311	241
EL PASO, TX	86	162		232	42	160	285	209	295	203	150	190
LAS CRUCES, NM	65	203	42	250		122	325	250	274	182	111	146
ROSWELL, NM	117	76	203	117	182	304	201	163	92		293	164

SEE ALSO DISTANCE AND DRIVING TIME MAP ON PAGES 286–287

New Mexico
Texas
Mexico
Roswell
Carlsbad
Artesia
Hobbs
Lovington
Portales
Pecos
Kermit
Monahans
Andrews
Seminole
Levelland
Littlefield
West Odessa
Go to 49
Go to 58
Go to 62
CARLSBAD CAVERNS NATL PARK
GUADALUPE MOUNTAINS NATL. PARK
LLANO ESTACADO
NEW MEXICO
TEXAS

0 mi   20   40
0 km   20   40   60
One inch equals 25.4 miles
One centimeter equals 16.1 kilometers

Oklahoma

Texas

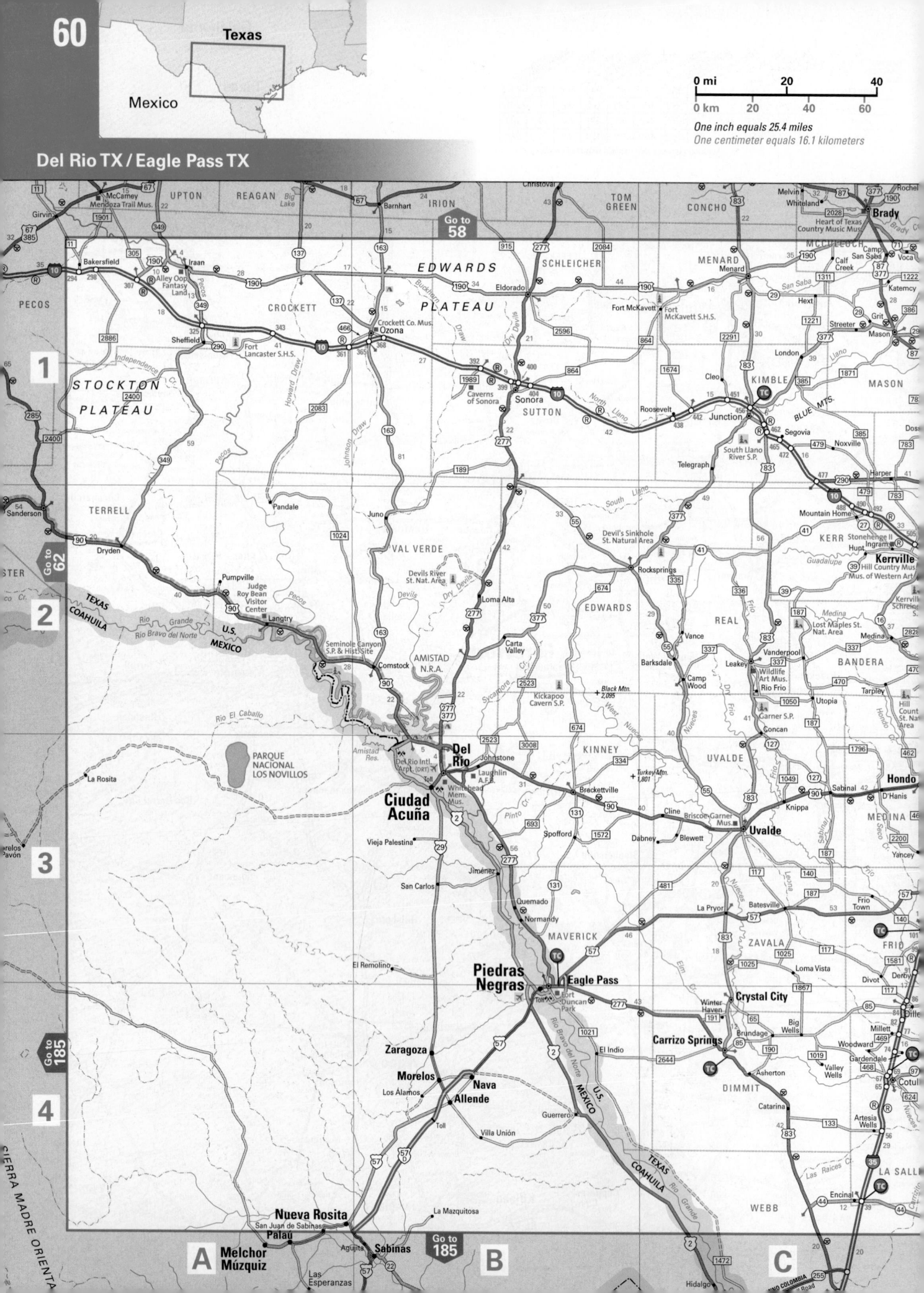
Texas
Mexico
0 mi 20 40
0 km 20 40 60
One inch equals 25.4 miles
One centimeter equals 16.1 kilometers
Go to 58
Go to 62
Go to 185
Go to 185
1
2
3
4
A
B
C
UPTON
REAGAN
IRION
TOM GREEN
CONCHO
PECOS
CROCKETT
EDWARDS PLATEAU
SCHLEICHER
MENARD
MCCULLOCH
STOCKTON PLATEAU
SUTTON
KIMBLE
MASON
TERRELL
VAL VERDE
EDWARDS
REAL
KERR
BANDERA
KINNEY
UVALDE
MEDINA
MAVERICK
ZAVALA
FRIO
DIMMIT
WEBB
LA SALLE
TEXAS
COAHUILA
U.S.
MEXICO
Rio Grande
Rio Bravo del Norte
BLUE MTS.
PARQUE NACIONAL LOS NOVILLOS
SIERRA MADRE ORIENTAL
Del Rio
Ciudad Acuña
Piedras Negras
Eagle Pass
Uvalde
Crystal City
Carrizo Springs
Hondo
Kerrville
Brady
Junction
Sonora
Ozona
Nueva Rosita
Melchor Múzquiz
Sabinas
Zaragoza
Morelos
Nava
Allende
McCamey
Mendoza Trail Mus.
Barnhart
Girvin
Bakersfield
Iraan
Alley Oop Fantasy Land
Sheffield
Fort Lancaster S.H.S.
Crockett Co. Mus.
Eldorado
Fort McKavett
Fort McKavett S.H.S.
Menard
Caverns of Sonora
Roosevelt
Telegraph
South Llano River S.P.
Segovia
Noxville
Harper
Mountain Home
Hunt
Ingram
Hill Country Mus.
Mus. of Western Art
Sanderson
Dryden
Pandale
Juno
Devils River St. Nat. Area
Devil's Sinkhole St. Natural Area
Rocksprings
Pumpville
Judge Roy Bean Visitor Center
Langtry
Seminole Canyon S.P. & Hist. Site
Comstock
Amistad N.R.A.
Loma Alta
Carta Valley
Kickapoo Cavern S.P.
Black Mtn. 2,095
Turkey Mtn. 1,801
Vance
Barksdale
Camp Wood
Leakey
Vanderpool
Lost Maples St. Nat. Area
Medina
Wildlife Art Mus.
Rio Frio
Garner S.P.
Concan
Utopia
Tarpley
Johnstone
Laughlin A.F.B.
Del Rio Intl. Arpt. (DRT)
Whitehead Mem. Mus.
Brackettville
Cline
Briscoe Garner Mus.
Spofford
Dabney
Blewett
Knippa
Sabinal
D'Hanis
Yancey
La Rosita
Vieja Palestina
Jiménez
San Carlos
Quemado
Normandy
La Pryor
Batesville
Frio Town
El Remolino
Fort Duncan Park
Winter Haven
Brundage
Big Wells
Loma Vista
Divot
El Indio
Asherton
Valley Wells
Catarina
Artesia Wells
Encinal
Los Álamos
Guerrero
Villa Unión
La Mazquitosa
San Juan de Sabinas
Palaú
Agujita
Las Esperanzas
Hidalgo
Melvin
Whiteland
Heart of Texas Country Music Mus.
Calf Creek
San Saba
Voca
Katemcy
Hext
Streeter
Grit
Mason
London
Cleo
Stonehenge II
Dilley
Millett
Woodward
Gardendale
Cotulla
Derby
Pearsall

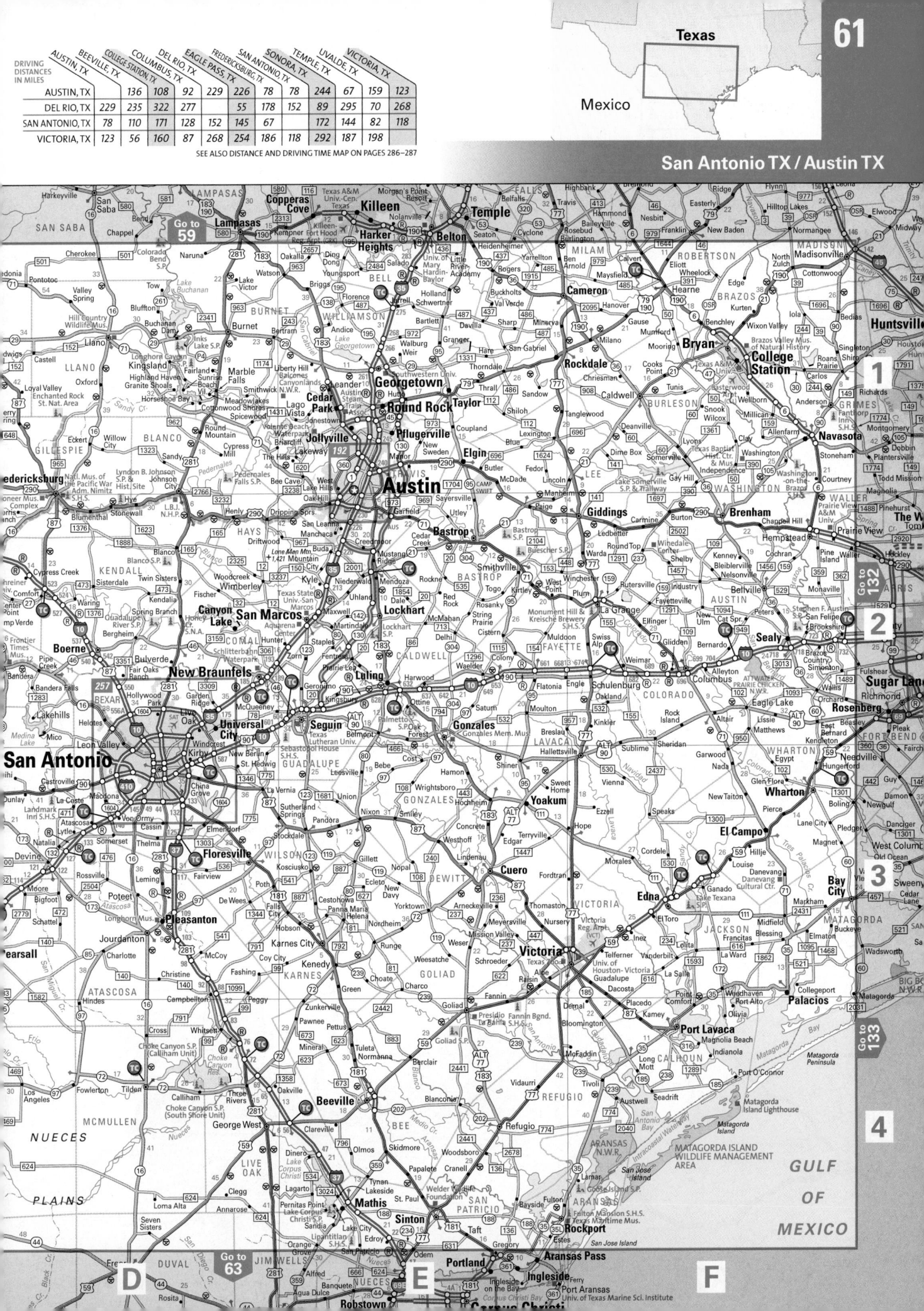

DRIVING DISTANCES IN MILES	AUSTIN, TX	BEEVILLE, TX	COLLEGE STATION, TX	COLUMBUS, TX	DEL RIO, TX	EAGLE PASS, TX	FREDERICKSBURG, TX	SAN ANTONIO, TX	SONORA, TX	TEMPLE, TX	UVALDE, TX	VICTORIA, TX
AUSTIN, TX		136	108	92	229	226	78	78	244	67	159	123
DEL RIO, TX	229	235	322	277		55	178	152	89	295	70	268
SAN ANTONIO, TX	78	110	171	128	152	145	67		172	144	82	118
VICTORIA, TX	123	56	160	87	268	254	186	118	292	187	198	

SEE ALSO DISTANCE AND DRIVING TIME MAP ON PAGES 286–287

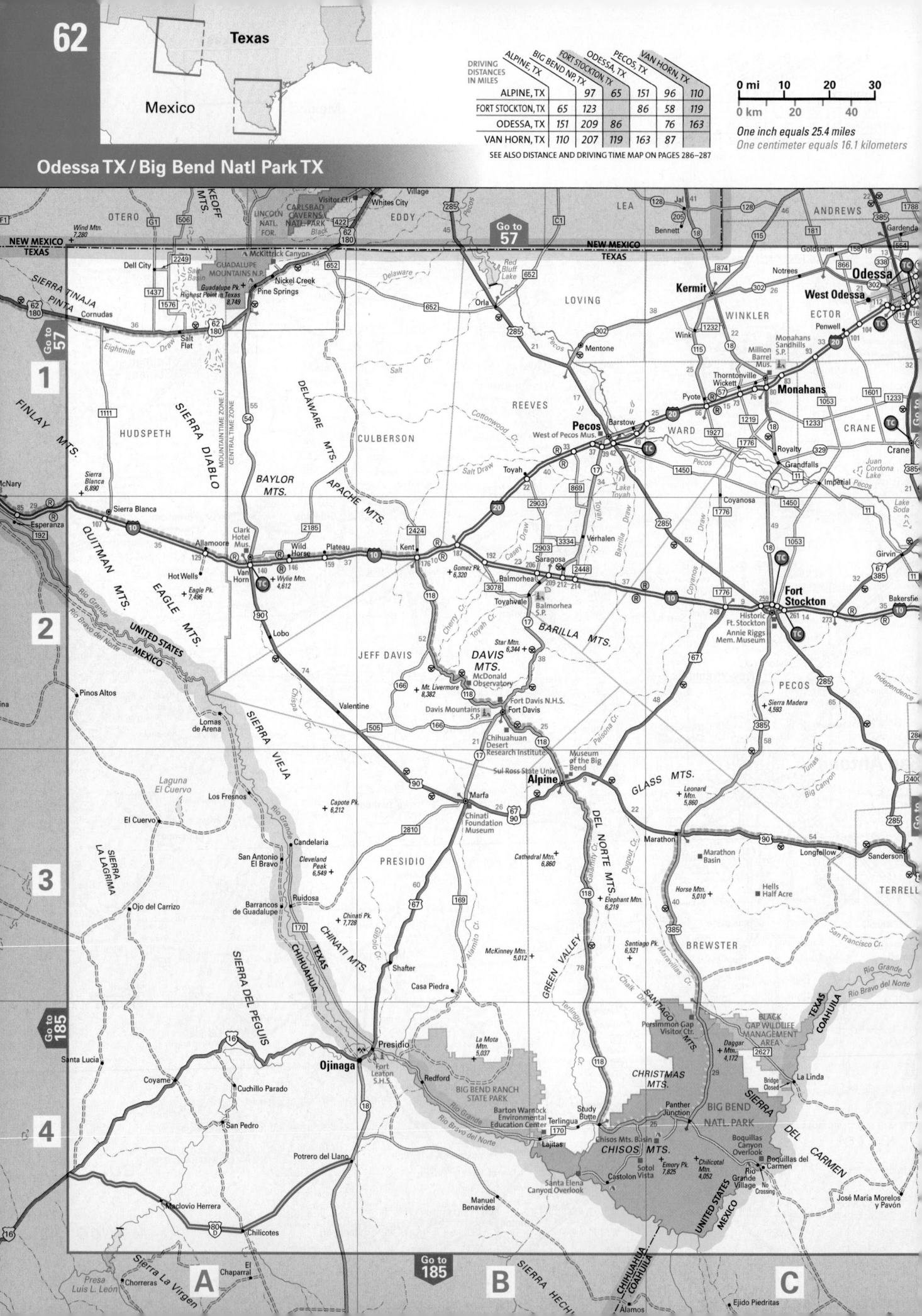

DRIVING DISTANCES IN MILES	ALPINE, TX	FORT STOCKTON, TX	BIG BEND NP, TX	ODESSA, TX	PECOS, TX	VAN HORN, TX
ALPINE, TX		97	65	151	96	110
FORT STOCKTON, TX	65		123	86	58	119
ODESSA, TX	151	209	86		76	163
VAN HORN, TX	110	207	119	163	87	

SEE ALSO DISTANCE AND DRIVING TIME MAP ON PAGES 286–287

0 mi 10 20 30
0 km 20 40

One inch equals 25.4 miles
One centimeter equals 16.1 kilometers

DRIVING DISTANCES IN MILES	BEEVILLE, TX	BROWNSVILLE, TX	CARRIZO SPRS., TX	CORPUS CHRISTI, TX	HARLINGEN, TX	KINGSVILLE, TX	LAREDO, TX	McALLEN, TX	VICTORIA, TX
BROWNSVILLE, TX	192		282	157	27	119	202	61	226
CORPUS CHRISTI, TX	59	157	199		131	38	141	152	94
LAREDO, TX	130	202	79	141	176	124		144	186
McALLEN, TX	168	61	223	152	35	114	144		221

SEE ALSO DISTANCE AND DRIVING TIME MAP ON PAGES 286–287

Manitoba

Ontario

Minnesota

Michigan

Wisconsin

0 mi   20   40

0 km   20   40   60

One inch equals 25.4 miles
One centimeter equals 16.1 kilometers

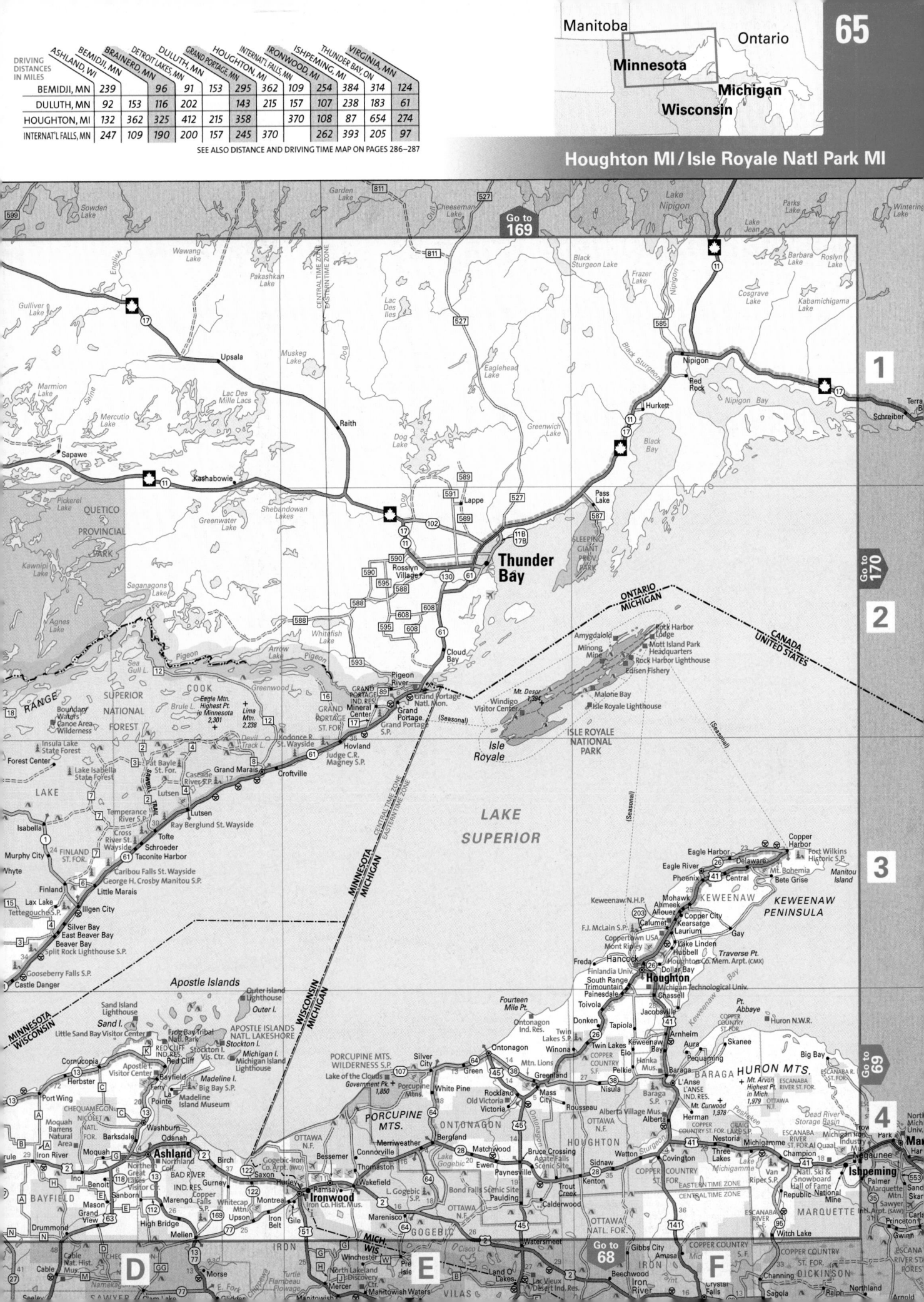

DRIVING DISTANCES IN MILES	ASHLAND, WI	BEMIDJI, MN	BRAINERD, MN	DETROIT LAKES, MN	DULUTH, MN	GRAND PORTAGE, MN	HOUGHTON, MI	INTERNAT'L FALLS, MN	IRONWOOD, MI	ISHPEMING, MI	THUNDER BAY, ON	VIRGINIA, MN
BEMIDJI, MN	239		96	91	153	295	362	109	254	384	314	124
DULUTH, MN	92	153	116	202		143	215	157	107	238	183	61
HOUGHTON, MI	132	362	325	412	215	358		370	108	87	654	274
INTERNAT'L FALLS, MN	247	109	190	200	157	245	370		262	393	205	97

SEE ALSO DISTANCE AND DRIVING TIME MAP ON PAGES 286–287

Manitoba   Ontario

Minnesota

Michigan

Wisconsin

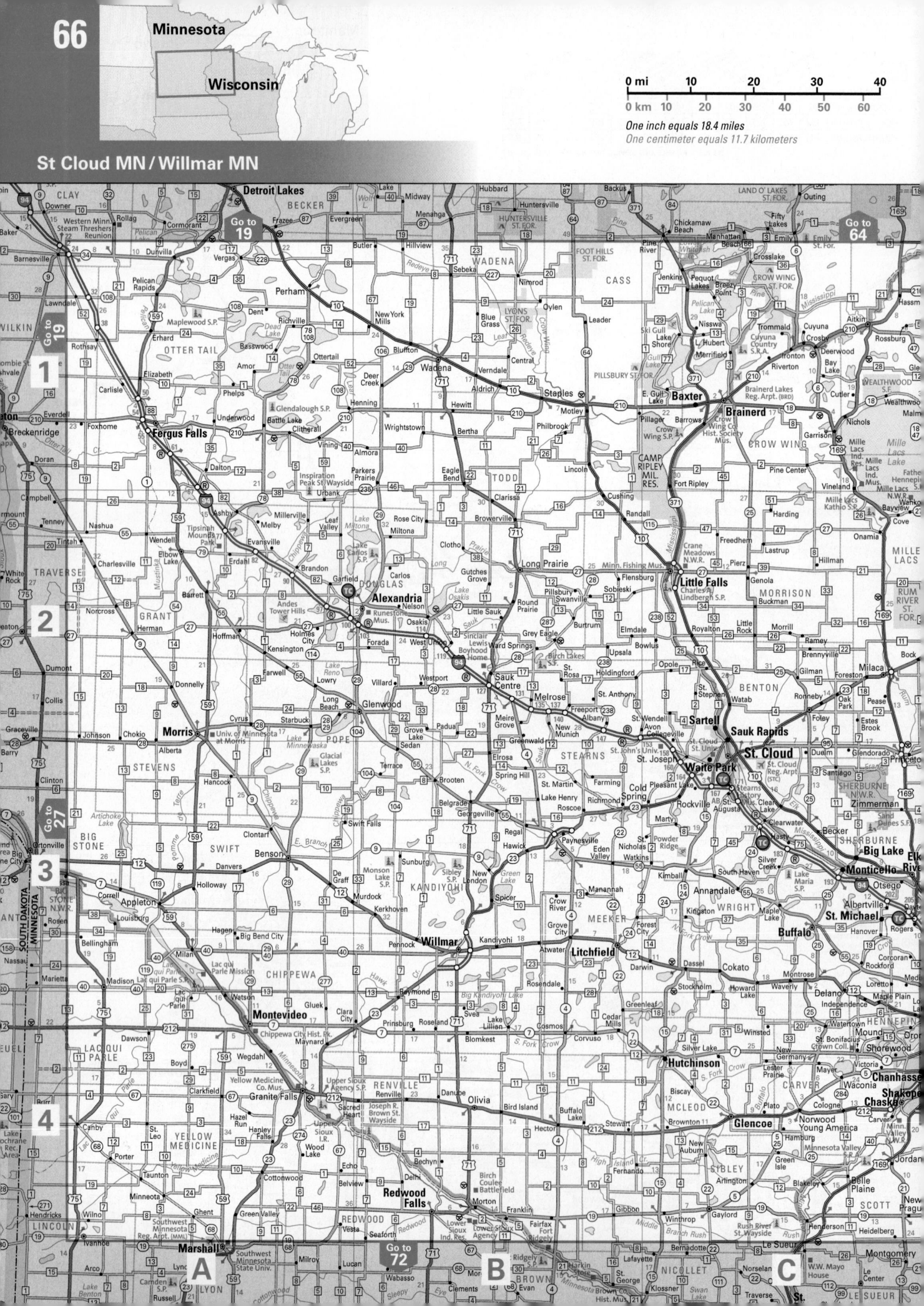

0 mi   10   20   30   40
0 km 10 20 30 40 50 60
One inch equals 18.4 miles
One centimeter equals 11.7 kilometers

DRIVING DISTANCES IN MILES	ASHLAND, WI	BRAINERD, MN	DULUTH, MN	EAU CLAIRE, WI	FERGUS FALLS, MN	MARSHALL, MN	MINNEAPOLIS, MN	MORRIS, MN	RICE LAKE, MN	ST. CLOUD, MN	ST. PAUL, MN	WILLMAR, MN
EAU CLAIRE, WI	167	220	155		267	236	93	247	57	156	83	193
MINNEAPOLIS, MN	196	129	158	93	176	148		156	103	64	10	92
ST. CLOUD, MN	205	62	149	156	117	131	64	98	155		73	63
WILLMAR, MN	263	112	206	193	113	68	92	57	196	63	102	

SEE ALSO DISTANCE AND DRIVING TIME MAP ON PAGES 286–287

Wisconsin
Michigan
0 mi 10 20 30 40
0 km 10 20 30 40 50 60
One inch equals 18.4 miles
One centimeter equals 11.7 kilometers
LAKE SUPERIOR
Go to 65
Go to 67
Go to 74
Ashland
Ironwood
Bessemer
Wakefield
Hurley
Mellen
Park Falls
Phillips
Medford
Rhinelander
Tomahawk
Merrill
Wausau
Weston
Antigo
Marshfield
Stevens Point
Wisconsin Rapids
Plover
Shawano
Waupaca
New London
Clintonville
Iron River
Iron Mountain
Kingsford
Crystal Falls
Eagle River
Minocqua
Woodruff
Green Bay
Ashwaubenon
De Pere
Howard
Neillsville
Oconto Falls
ONTONAGON
HOUGHTON
BARAGA
GOGEBIC
IRON
VILAS
ONEIDA
FOREST
FLORENCE
MARINETTE
LANGLADE
LINCOLN
PRICE
TAYLOR
CLARK
MARATHON
SHAWANO
OCONTO
WOOD
PORTAGE
WAUPACA
JACKSON
RUSK
SAWYER
ASHLAND
MENOMINEE
MICHIGAN
WISCONSIN
PORCUPINE MTS.
OTTAWA N.F.
OTTAWA NATL. FOR.
CHEQUAMEGON-NICOLET NATL. FOR.
COPPER COUNTRY ST. FOR.
NORTHERN HIGHLAND AMERICAN LEGION ST. FOR.
MENOMINEE IND. RES.
LAC DU FLAMBEAU IND. RES.
Timms Hill Highest Pt. in Wisconsin 1,951
1
2
3
4
A
B
C

DRIVING DISTANCES IN MILES	ESCANABA, MI	GREEN BAY, WI	IRON MOUNTAIN, MI	IRONWOOD, MI	L'ANSE, MI	MARINETTE, WI	MARQUETTE, MI	MANISTIQUE, MI	RHINELANDER, WI	STEVENS POINT, WI	TRAVERSE CITY, MI	WAUSAU, WI
ESCANABA, MI		111	52	178	134	54	57	65	132	185	252	171
GREEN BAY, WI	111		96	202	178	165	54	175	124	87	363	93
MARQUETTE, MI	65	175	79	145	70	86	122		147	238	269	204
WAUSAU, WI	171	93	133	121	176	225	112	204	58	35	423	

SEE ALSO DISTANCE AND DRIVING TIME MAP ON PAGES 286–287

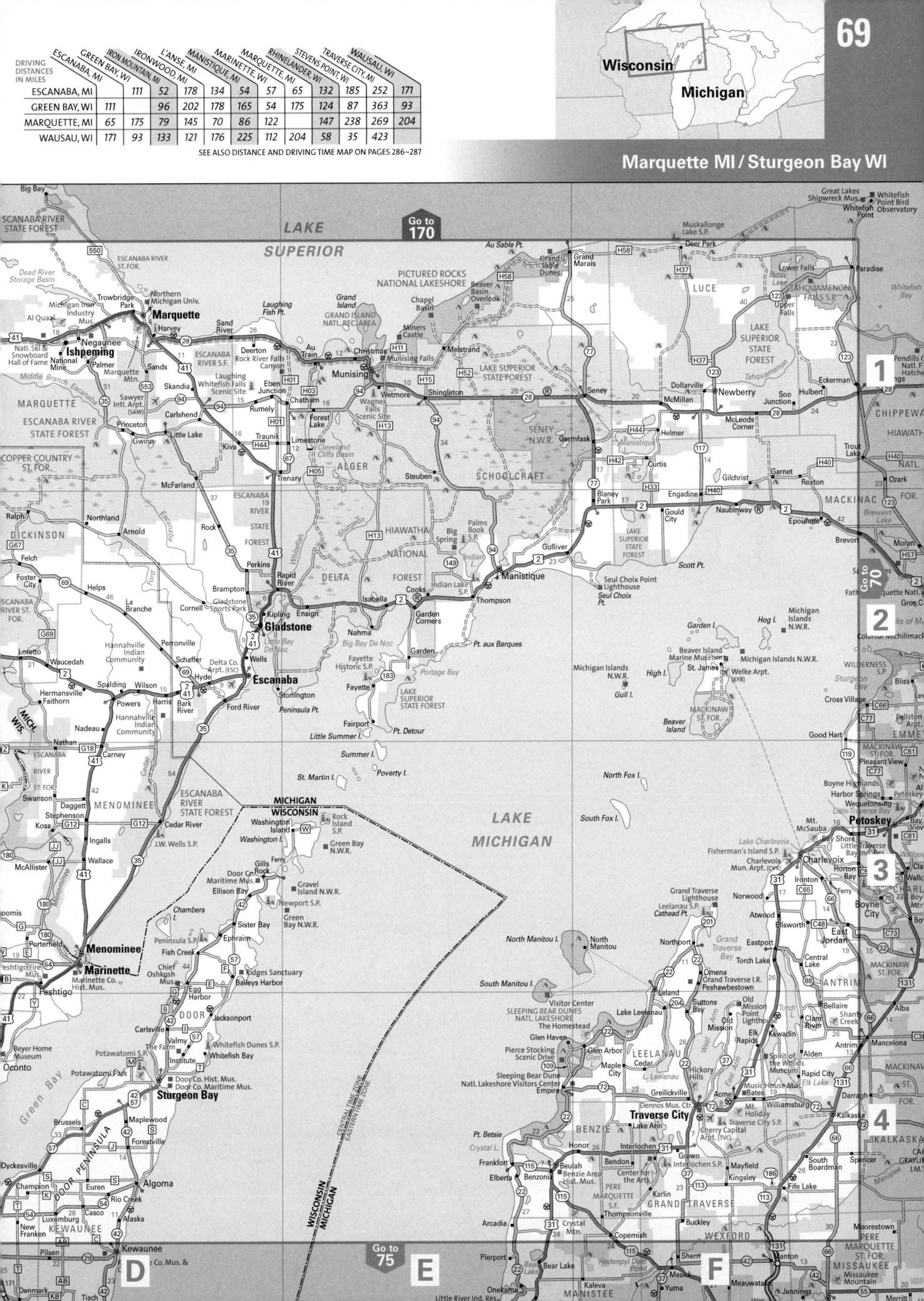

Ontario

Michigan

0 mi 10 20 30 40
0 km 10 20 30 40 50 60
One inch equals 18.4 miles
One centimeter equals 11.7 kilometers

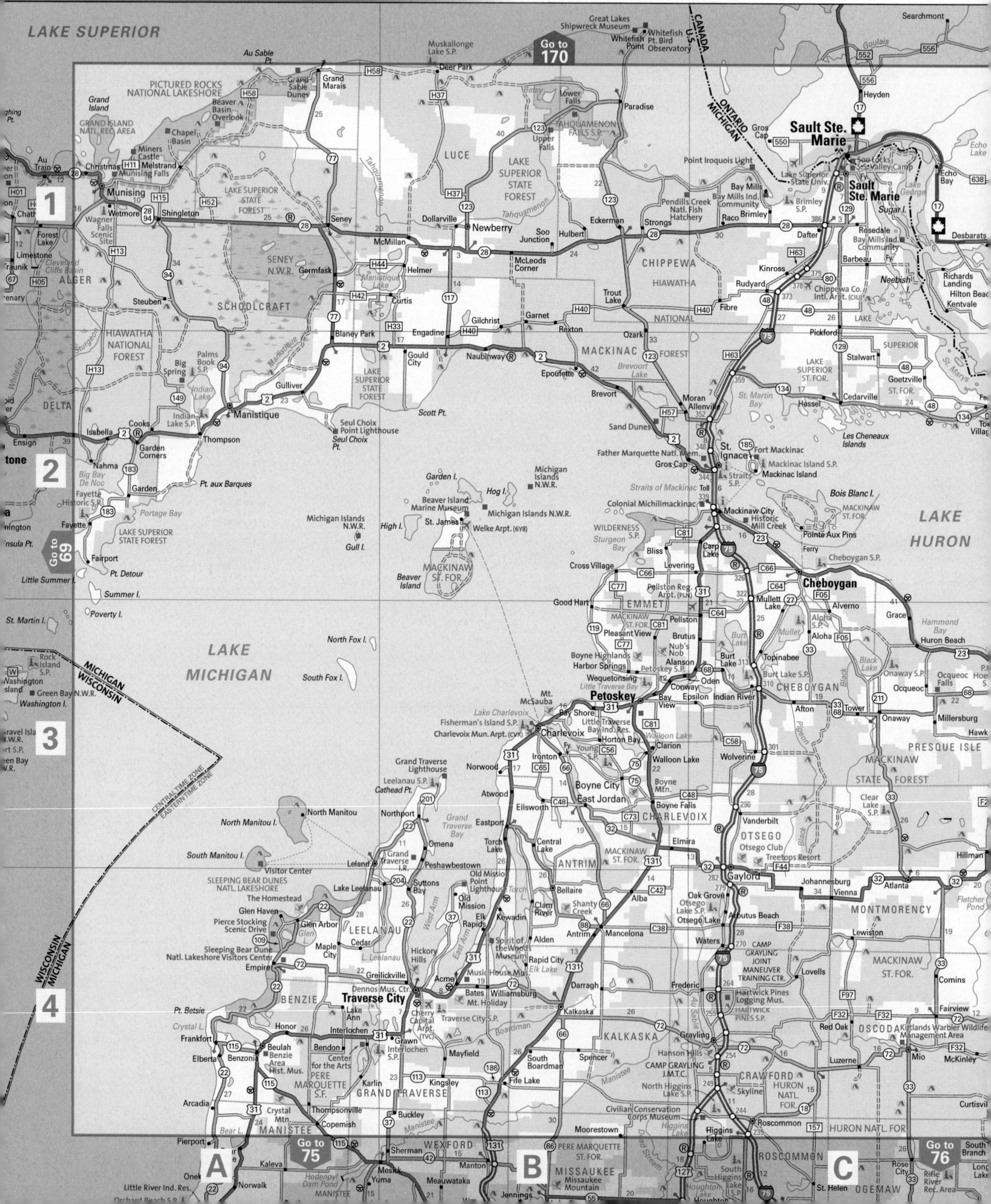

LAKE SUPERIOR

Go to 170

CANADA
ONTARIO
MICHIGAN

Searchmont

552 556
556
Heyden
550 17
Gros Cap
Sault Ste. Marie
Soo Locks
Valley Camp
80 386 3 **Sault Ste. Marie**
Sugar I.
Echo Bay
Echo Lake
638

Great Lakes Shipwreck Museum
Whitefish Pt. Bird Observatory
Whitefish Point
Point Iroquois Light
Paradise

123
TAHQUAMENON FALLS S.P.
Upper Falls
Lower Falls

PICTURED ROCKS NATIONAL LAKESHORE
Au Sable Pt.
Grand Sable Dunes
Grand Marais
Deer Park
Muskallonge Lake S.P.
H58
Betsy
25

GRAND ISLAND NATL. REC AREA
Grand Island
Beaver Basin Overlook
H58
Chapel Basin
Miners Castle
Melstrand
Munising Falls

Lake Superior State Univ.
Bay Mills Community
Brimley
Bay Mills Ind. Community
Dafter
Rosedale
Bay Mills Ind. Community
129
Barbeau
Fy.
Neebish
Richards Landing
Hilton Beach
Kentvale

Pendills Creek Natl. Fish Hatchery
Strongs
Eckerman
Raco
28
30
H63
Kinross
379 80
Rudyard
378 373
27
Chippewa Co. Intl. Arpt. (CIU)
48
Fibre
26

H01
Christmas
Munising
Au Train
28
Wetmore
Shingleton
H15
H52
LAKE SUPERIOR STATE FOREST
77
Seney
28
McMillan
Newberry
123
Dollarville
Soo Junction
McLeods Corner
Hulbert
24
CHIPPEWA
HIAWATHA
NATIONAL
H40
H63
Stalwart
48
LAKE SUPERIOR ST. FOR.
129
Goetzville
St. Marys
Cedarville
48
Tor Villa

Chat
1
H11
Forest Lake
Limestone
H13
12
ALGER
67
H05
raunik
Cleveland Cliffs Basin
Sturgeon
34
Steuben
94
Germfask
SENEY N.W.R.
Helmer
H44
H42
Curtis
117
Manistique Lake
Gilchrist
Garnet
Rexton
MACKINAC
Trout Lake
Ozark
33
FOREST
H57
Moran
352
Allenville
St. Martin Bay
134
Hessel
Les Cheneaux Islands
LAKE HURON
24

1
H13
Big Spring
Palms Book S.P.
94
Manistique
Gulliver
149
Indian Lake S.P.
23
2
Scott Pt.
Blaney Park
H33
17
Gould City
Naubinway
2
Epoufette
42
Brevort
Brevoort Lake
123
St. Ignace
Mackinac Island S.P.
Bois Blanc I.
MACKINAW ST. FOR.
Pointe Aux Pins

DELTA
Cooks
Isabella
2
Thompson
Garden Corners
Nahma
183
Garden
Indian Lake S.P.
Pt. aux Barques
Seul Choix Point Lighthouse
Seul Choix Pt.
Sand Dunes
Father Marquette Natl. Mem.
Gros Cap
348
344
339
Straits of Mackinac
Straits S.P.
185
Fort Mackinac
Mackinac Island
Colonial Michilimackinac
Mackinac Island
336
Carp Lake
75
23
Cheboygan S.P.

2
stone
Go to 69

Big Bay De Noc
Fayette Historic S.P.
183
Fayette
Portage Bay
LAKE SUPERIOR STATE FOREST
Fairport
Pt. Detour
Garden I.
Hog I.
Michigan Islands N.W.R.
Beaver Island Marine Museum
St. James
High I.
Michigan Islands N.W.R.
Welke Arpt. (6Y8)
Gull I.
MACKINAW ST. FOR.
Beaver Island
WILDERNESS S.P.
Sturgeon Bay
Bliss
Colonial Michilimackinac Historic Mill Creek
Mackinaw City
C81
Levering
C66
Carp Lake
Cheboygan S.P.
Ferry
Cheboygan
F05
Alverno
Grace
Hammond Bay
Huron Beach

Little Summer I.
St. Martin I.
Poverty I.
Summer I.
North Fox I.
Cross Village
Good Hart
EMMET
119
MACKINAW ST. FOR.
Pleasant View
Pellston
C81
Brutus
C64
25
Mullett Lake
27
Mullett Lake
S.P.
Aloha
F05
Aloha
Black Lake
41
Onaway S.P.
Ocqueoc Falls
Ocqueoc
22
68

3
W
Washington I.
Rock Island S.P.
Green Bay N.W.R.
Washington I.
LAKE MICHIGAN
South Fox I.
North Manitou I.
Boyne Highlands
Nub's Nob
Harbor Springs
Petoskey S.P.
Wequetonsing
C81
Mt. McSauba
Bay Shore
Charlevoix Mun. Arpt. (CVX)
Fisherman's Island S.P.
Little Traverse Bay
Pellston Reg. Arpt. (PLN)
322
C64
119
Brutus
68
Burt Lake S.P.
Burt Lake
Oden
Conway
Epsilon
Indian River
Afton
Tower
33
CHEBOYGAN
33
68
Onaway
211
Millersburg
PRESQUE ISLE
Hawk

Gravel Isl. N.W.R.
Spider Isl. N.W.R.
Green Bay N.W.R.
Petoskey
31
Walloon Lake
C58
Wolverine
301
75
Clear Lake S.P.
33
MACKINAW STATE FOREST

MICHIGAN
WISCONSIN
Grand Traverse Lighthouse
Leelanau S.P.
Cathead Pt.
North Manitou I.
North Manitou
Northport
201
Grand Traverse I.R.
11
Omena
Peshawbestown
Suttons Bay
204
Old Mission Point Lighthouse
Charlevoix
Ironton
Norwood
C65
Boyne City
East Jordan
C48
Atwood
Ellsworth
Eastport
Central Lake
19
32
CHARLEVOIX
Elmira
Boyne Falls
Boyne Mtn.
Vanderbilt
290
28
OTSEGO
Otsego Club
Treetops Resort
F44
Hillman
19

Horton Bay
Clarion
Walloon Lake
75
Fy. Young
C56
31
17
66
131
CENTRAL TIME ZONE
EASTERN TIME ZONE

3
Leland
Grand Traverse I.R.
South Manitou I.
Visitor Center
SLEEPING BEAR DUNES NATL. LAKESHORE
The Homestead
Natl. Lakeshore Visitors Center
Lake Leelanau
Cedar
LEELANAU
Suttons Bay
Old Mission Point Lighthouse
Torch
West Arm
East Arm
37
Elk Rapids
Kewadin
Torch Lake
Clam River
Bellaire
Shanty Creek
Alba
66
C42
ANTRIM
Mancelona
C38
Gaylord
279
Oak Grove
Otsego Lake S.P.
Otsego Lake
270
Arbutus Beach
F38
Johannesburg
34
Vienna
32
Atlanta
32
MONTMORENCY
Lewiston
19

Glen Haven
Pierce Stocking Scenic Drive
Sleeping Bear Dune
108
Glen Arbor
Maple City
Empire
72
L. Leelanau
BENZIE
Greilickville
Pt. Betsie
Traverse City
Lake Ann
22
Cherry Capital Arpt. (TVC)
Traverse City S.P.
Acme
Williamsburg
Kalkaska
Grand Traverse Lighthouse
Music House Mus.
Spirit of the Woods Museum
Rapid City
Alden
131
Waters
270
CAMP GRAYLING JOINT MANEUVER TRAINING CTR.
Lovells
Comins
MACKINAW ST. FOR.
33

4
Frankfort
Crystal L.
Elberta
Benzonia
Honor
31
Beulah
Benzie Area Hist. Mus.
115
22
115
Interlochen
Bendon
Center for the Arts
Karlin
PERE MARQUETTE S.F.
Interlochen S.P.
Grawn
Mayfield
186
113
Kingsley
Fife Lake
South Boardman
66
KALKASKA
Grayling
Hanson Hills
Hartwick Pines Logging Mus.
Hartwick Pines S.P.
Frederic
264
CAMP GRAYLING J.M.T.C.
North Higgins Lake S.P.
75
254
F97
Red Oak
F32
F32
OSCODA
Luzerne
Mio
McKinley
F32
Fairview
Kirtlands Warbler Wildlife Management Area

Elberta
22
115
Arcadia
27
31
Crystal Mtn.
Thompsonville
Copemish
37
Manistee
MANISTEE
Buckley
113
WEXFORD
GRAND TRAVERSE
Boardman
Spencer
72
South Higgins Lake S.P.
244
Skyline
Civilian Conservation Corps Museum
Higgins Lake
157
HURON NATL. FOR.
Moorestown
Roscommon
CRAWFORD
HURON NATL. FOR.
33
Curtisville

A
Pierport
Onek
31
Kaleva
Mesick
Hodenpyl Dam Pond
Little River Ind. Res.
Norwalk
Yuma
Meauwataka
Go to 75
B
Sherman
Manton
15
131
66
Jennings
MISSAUKEE
Missaukee Mountain
Dar Stream
Manistee
Fletcher
55
C
Houghton Lake
127
St. Helen
South Higgins Lake S.P.
112
Higgins Lake
239
Roscommon
Rose City
33
Lone
Long Lake
OGEMAW
Rifle River Rec. Area
Go to 76
South Branch

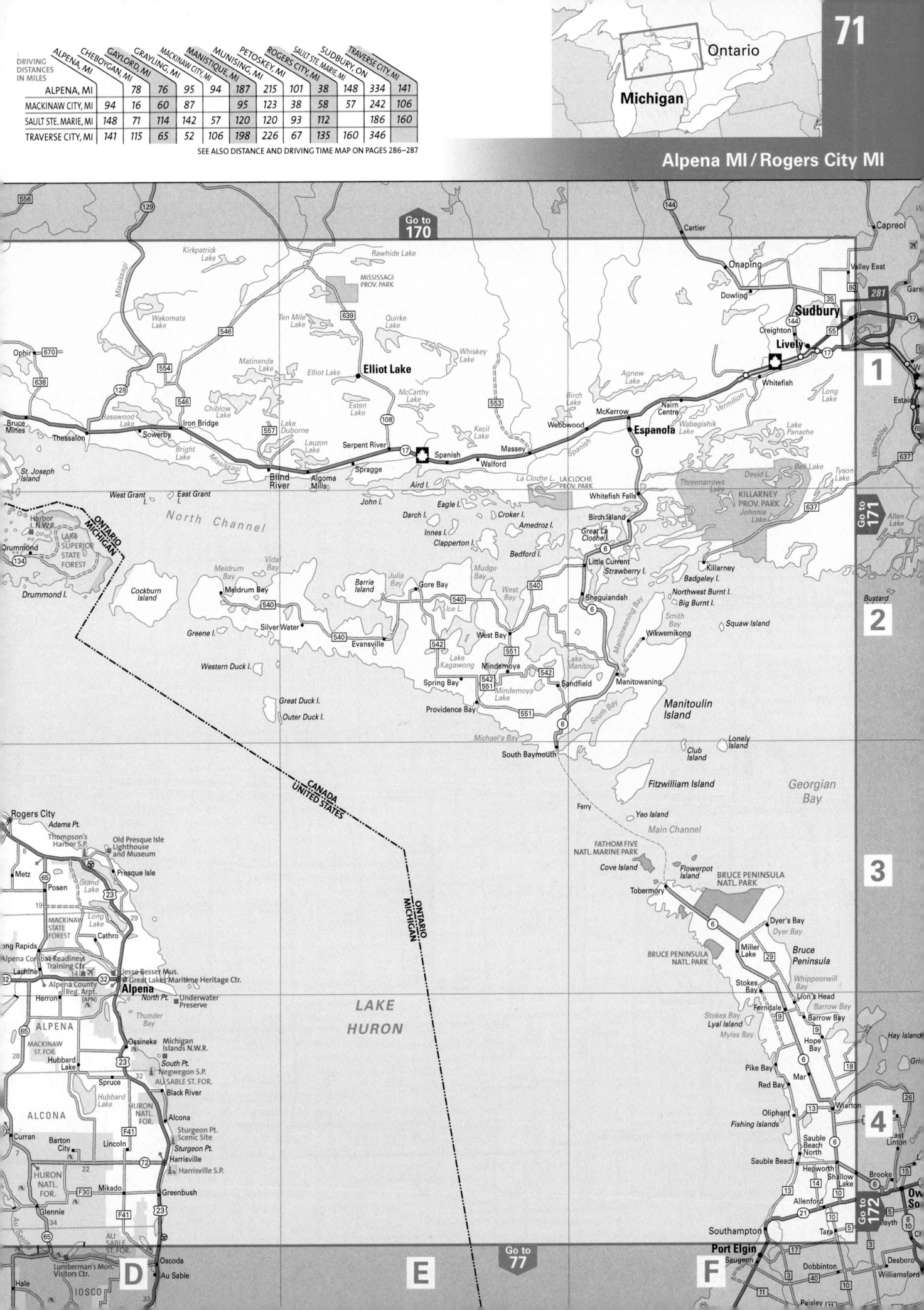

DRIVING DISTANCES IN MILES	ALPENA, MI	CHEBOYGAN, MI	GAYLORD, MI	GRAYLING, MI	MACKINAW CITY, MI	MANISTIQUE, MI	MUNISING, MI	PETOSKEY, MI	ROGERS CITY, MI	SAULT STE. MARIE, MI	SUDBURY, ON	TRAVERSE CITY, MI
ALPENA, MI		78	76	95	94	187	215	101	38	148	334	141
MACKINAW CITY, MI	94	16	60	87		95	123	38	58	57	242	106
SAULT STE. MARIE, MI	148	71	114	142	57	120	120	93	112		186	160
TRAVERSE CITY, MI	141	115	65	52	106	198	226	67	135	160	346	

SEE ALSO DISTANCE AND DRIVING TIME MAP ON PAGES 286–287

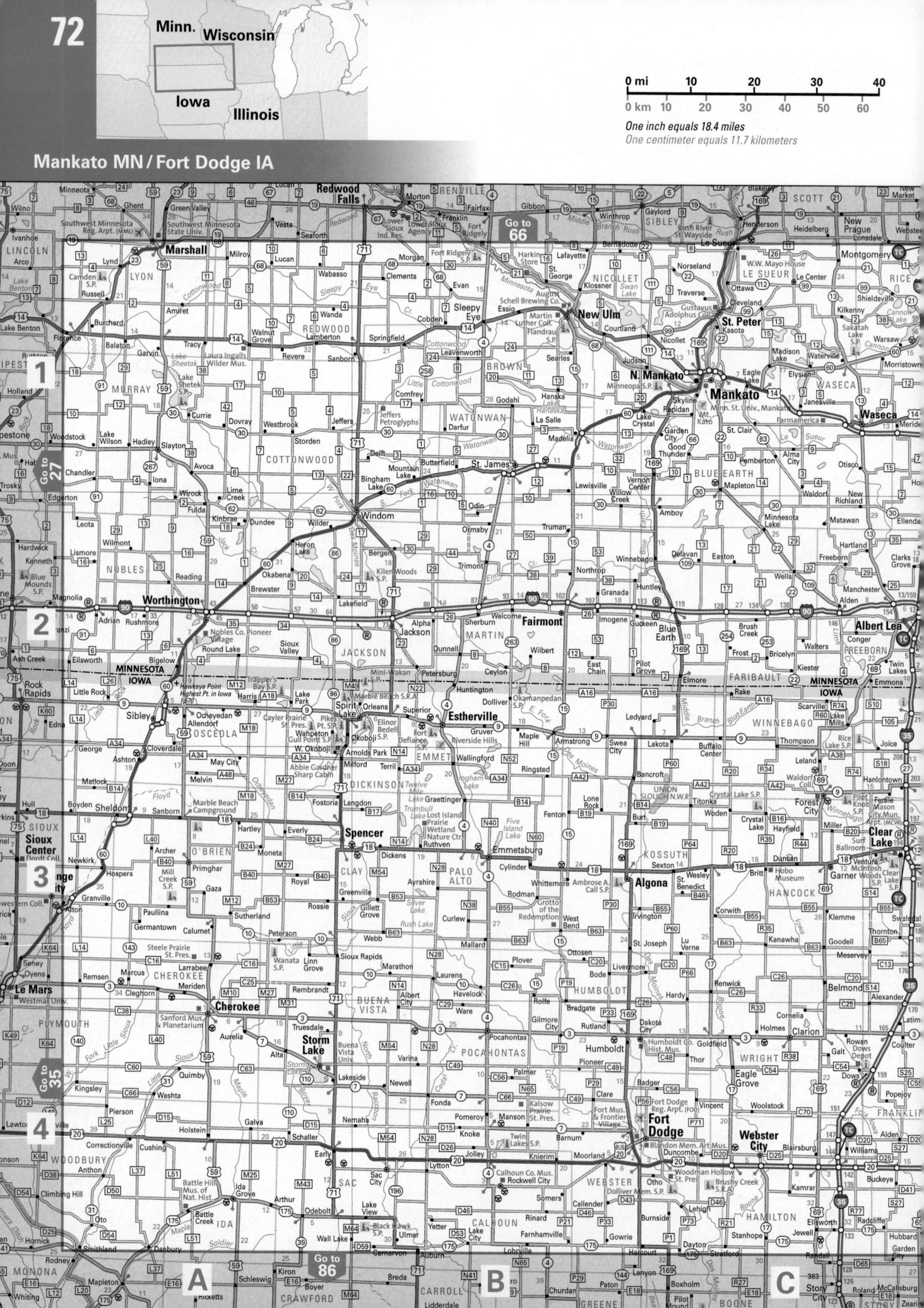
Minn.
Wisconsin
Iowa
Illinois
Mankato MN / Fort Dodge IA
0 mi 10 20 30 40
0 km 10 20 30 40 50 60
One inch equals 18.4 miles
One centimeter equals 11.7 kilometers
Go to 66
Go to 27
Go to 35
Go to 86
MINNESOTA
IOWA
Marshall
Redwood Falls
New Ulm
St. Peter
N. Mankato
Mankato
Waseca
Worthington
Fairmont
Albert Lea
Jackson
Windom
St. James
Estherville
Spencer
Algona
Clear Lake
Storm Lake
Cherokee
Le Mars
Fort Dodge
Webster City
Sheldon
Sioux Center
1
2
3
4
A
B
C

DRIVING DISTANCES IN MILES	ALBERT LEA, MN	DECORAH, IA	DUBUQUE, IA	FORT DODGE, IA	LA CROSSE, WI	MANKATO, MN	MASON CITY, IA	ROCHESTER, MN	SPENCER, IA	WATERLOO, IA	WINONA, MN	WORTHINGTON, MN
FORT DODGE, IA	124	186	200		245	138	97	183	95	108	225	148
MANKATO, MN	56	151	253	138	149		100	80	123	186	186	108
ROCHESTER, MN	62	68	170	183	71	80	103		189	116	51	174
WATERLOO, IA	130	79	93	108	138	186	79	116	189		144	244

SEE ALSO DISTANCE AND DRIVING TIME MAP ON PAGES 286–287

Wisconsin
Michigan
Iowa
Illinois

0 mi 10 20 30 40
0 km 10 20 30 40 50 60
One inch equals 18.4 miles
One centimeter equals 11.7 kilometers

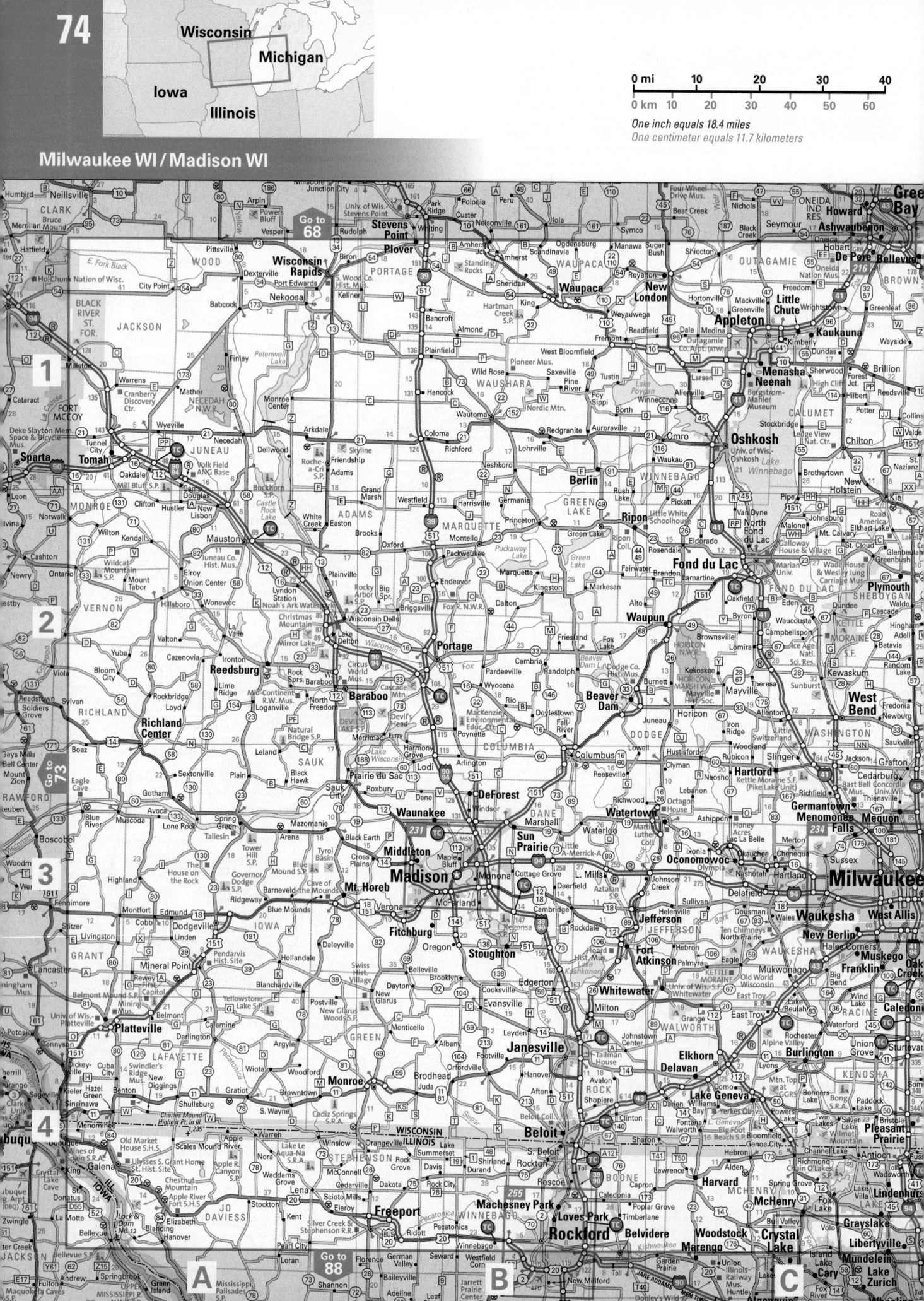

DRIVING
DISTANCES
IN MILES

	CADILLAC, MI	DUBUQUE, IA	GRAND RAPIDS, MI	GREEN BAY, WI	KALAMAZOO, MI	MADISON, WI	MILWAUKEE, WI	MUSKEGON, MI	OSHKOSH, WI	ROCKFORD, IL	SHEBOYGAN, WI	TOMAH, WI
GRAND RAPIDS, MI	99	364		393	53	335	277	40	363	271	332	424
GREEN BAY, WI	492	229	393		362	135	115	400	50	211	61	162
MADISON, WI	434	93	335	135	304		78	341	86	78	132	98
MILWAUKEE, WI	377	167	277	115	247	78		285	87	95	54	168

SEE ALSO DISTANCE AND DRIVING TIME MAP ON PAGES 286–287

Ontario

Michigan

Detroit MI / Lansing MI

0 mi 10 20 30 40

0 km 10 20 30 40 50 60

One inch equals 18.4 miles

One centimeter equals 11.7 kilometers

LAKE HURON

Saginaw Bay

Lake St. Clair

Go to 70

Go to 75

Go to 90

Detroit

Windsor

Lansing

E. Lansing

Flint

Saginaw

Bay City

Midland

Mt. Pleasant

Ann Arbor

Jackson

Battle Creek

Pontiac

Sterling Hts.

Rochester Hills

Warren

Livonia

Dearborn

Westland

Southfield

Port Huron

Marysville

Cadillac

Alma

Owosso

Lapeer

Howell

Brighton

DRIVING DISTANCES IN MILES

	ANN ARBOR, MI	BAD AXE, MI	BATTLE CREEK, MI	CADILLAC, MI	DETROIT, MI	FLINT, MI	HAMILTON, ON	LANSING, MI	LONDON, ON	MT. PLEASANT, MI	PORT HURON, MI	SAGINAW, MI
DETROIT, MI	42	107	116	209		62	203	86	128	149	58	97
LANSING, MI	63	140	56	131	86	53	270		191	67	117	86
PORT HURON, MI	101	81	175	211	58	64	154	117	75	155		100
SAGINAW, MI	87	64	142	116	97	36	253	86	174	60	100	

SEE ALSO DISTANCE AND DRIVING TIME MAP ON PAGES 286–287

Ontario
New York
0 mi 10 20 30 40
0 km 10 20 30 40 50 60
One inch equals 18.4 miles
One centimeter equals 11.7 kilometers
Go to 173
Go to 77
Go to 92
LAKE ONTARIO
LAKE ERIE
ONTARIO
NEW YORK
CANADA
UNITED STATES
PENNSYLVANIA
NEW YORK
1
2
3
4
A
B
C
Barrie
Lindsay
Peterborough
Belleville
Trenton
Oshawa
Bowmanville
Cobourg
Port Hope
Markham
Richmond Hill
Pickering
Ajax
Brampton
Toronto
Mississauga
Milton
Oakville
Burlington
Hamilton
St. Catharines
Niagara Falls
Welland
Dunnville
Port Colborne
Newmarket
Aurora
Bolton
Alliston
Bradford
Uxbridge
Port Perry
Keswick
Sutton
Angus
Wasaga Beach
Lockport
Medina
Albion
Brockport
Rochester
Irondequoit
Greece
Gates
Brighton
Fairport
Batavia
Le Roy
Buffalo
Cheektowaga
Lancaster
Tonawanda
N. Tonawanda
Kenmore
West Seneca
Lackawanna
Hamburg
Dunkirk
Fredonia
Geneseo
Dansville
Hornell
Bath
Canandaigua
Newark
Penn Yan
Salamanca
Westfield
Lake Simcoe
Rice Lake
Wyoming
Livingston
Genesee
Orleans
Niagara
Monroe
Ontario
Yates
Steuben
Allegany
Cattaraugus
Chautauqua
Erie

DRIVING DISTANCES IN MILES	BATH, NY	BUFFALO, NY	ITHACA, NY	NIAGARA FALLS, NY	ONEONTA, NY	OSWEGO, NY	ROCHESTER, NY	SYRACUSE, NY	TORONTO, ON	TUPPER LAKE, NY	UTICA, NY	WATERTOWN, NY
BUFFALO, NY	113		153	20	263	158	74	152	106	321	199	210
ROCHESTER, NY	78	74	89	88	200	73		88	181	257	135	146
SYRACUSE, NY	105	152	59	166	118	38	88		260	176	53	65
UTICA, NY	152	199	108	213	65	81	135	53	307	131		86

SEE ALSO DISTANCE AND DRIVING TIME MAP ON PAGES 286–287

Ontario

New York

Québec
Maine
Ontario
Vt.
N.H.
New York
0 mi 10 20 30 40
0 km 10 20 30 40 50 60
One inch equals 18.4 miles
One centimeter equals 11.7 kilometers
Go to 174
Go to 79
Go to 79
1
2
3
4
A
B
C
Ottawa
Carleton Place
Smiths Falls
Perth
Kemptville
Cornwall
Salaberry-de-Valleyfield
Massena
Malone
Brockville
Ogdensburg
Potsdam
Canton
Gananoque
Kingston
THOUSAND ISLANDS
Watertown
Saranac Lake
Lake Placid
Tupper Lake
ADIRONDACK PARK
ADIRONDACK MOUNTAINS
ST. LAWRENCE
FRANKLIN
JEFFERSON
LEWIS
HAMILTON
HERKIMER
OSWEGO
ONEIDA
WARREN
SARATOGA
FULTON
ONONDAGA
ESSEX
LAKE ONTARIO
Oswego
Fulton
Syracuse
Rome
Oneida
Utica
Herkimer
Little Falls
Gloversville
Johnstown
Amsterdam
Saratoga Springs
QUÉBEC
NEW YORK
CANADA
U.S.
ONTARIO
NEW YORK
Mt. Marcy Highest Pt. in New York 5,344
Whiteface Mtn. 4,867
Santanoni Peak 4,607
FORT DRUM MIL. RES.

Go to 175
Go to 84
Go to 82
Go to 82
Go to 94
Go to 95

DRIVING DISTANCES IN MILES	BURLINGTON, VT	CONCORD, NH	LAKE PLACID, NY	OGDENSBURG, NY	PLATTSBURGH, NY	RUTLAND, VT	ST. JOHNSBURY, VT	SARATOGA SPRS., NY	SYRACUSE, NY	UTICA, NY	WATERTOWN, NY	WHITE RIVER JCT., VT
BURLINGTON, VT		150	68	208	51	69	76	115	230	183	195	91
CONCORD, NH	150		215	357	198	104	104	173	280	228	312	59
LAKE PLACID, NY	68	215		96	49	133	141	106	192	148	126	156
WATERTOWN, NY	195	312	126	68	167	244	319	179	65	86		289

SEE ALSO DISTANCE AND DRIVING TIME MAP ON PAGES 286–287

Québec
N.B.
Maine
Nova Scotia
Vt.
N.H.
0 mi 10 20 30 40
0 km 10 20 30 40 50 60
One inch equals 18.4 miles
One centimeter equals 11.7 kilometers
Go to 84
Go to 81
Go to 95
Gulf of Maine
Portland
S. Portland
Augusta
Lewiston
Auburn
Waterville
Winslow
Skowhegan
Brunswick
Bath
Gardiner
Rockland
Biddeford
Saco
Sanford
Rochester
Somersworth
Dover
Portsmouth
Manchester
Concord
Laconia
Franklin
Berlin
Westbrook
Farmington
Rumford
Exeter
Hampton
Belfast
Camden
ESSEX
COOS
OXFORD
FRANKLIN
SOMERSET
KENNEBEC
ANDROSCOGGIN
CUMBERLAND
SAGADAHOC
LINCOLN
KNOX
WALDO
YORK
CARROLL
GRAFTON
BELKNAP
STRAFFORD
ROCKINGHAM
MERRIMACK
HILLSBOROUGH
WHITE MTS.
WHITE MTN. NATL. FOR.
1
2
3
4
A
B
C

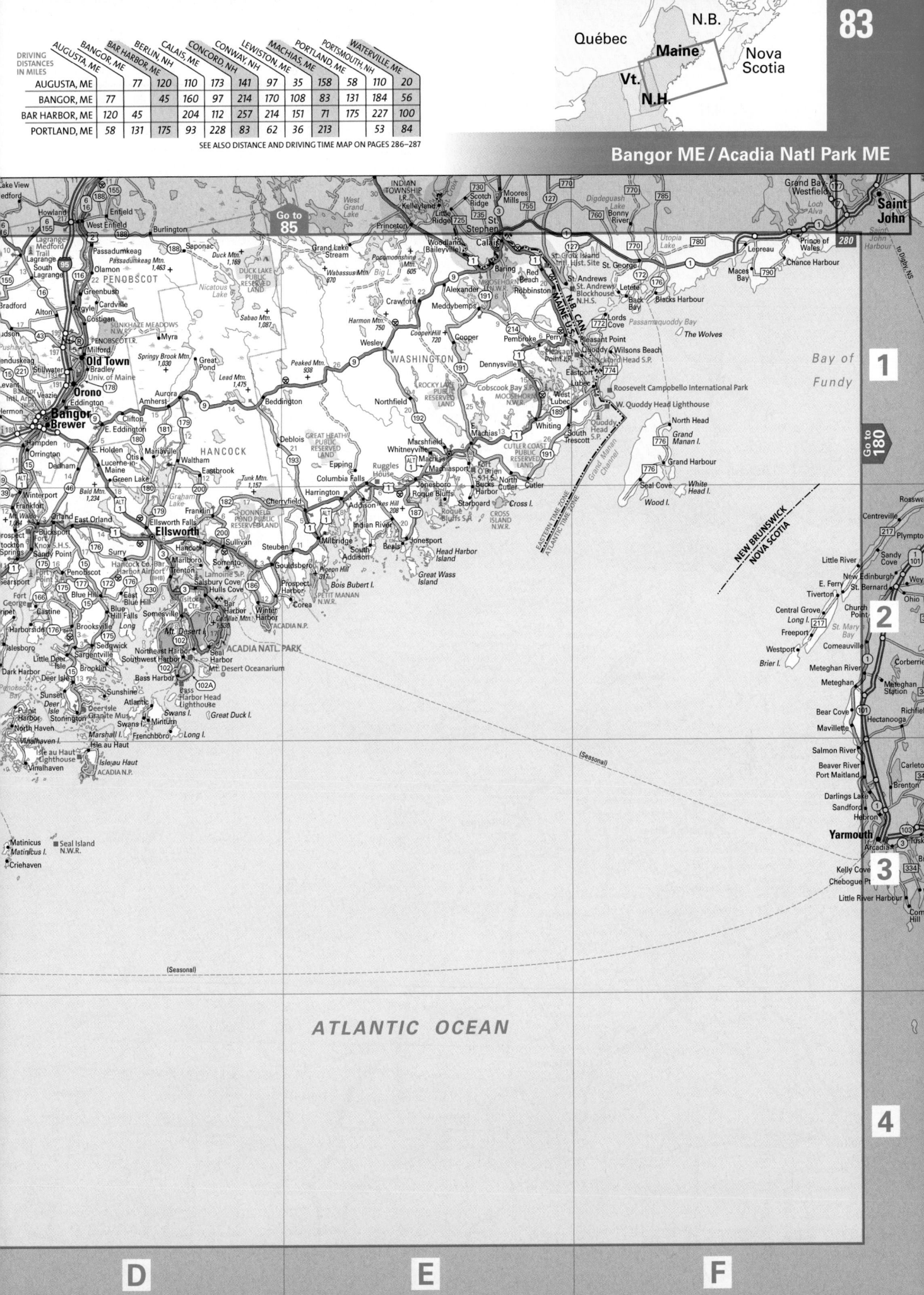

DRIVING DISTANCES IN MILES	AUGUSTA, ME	BANGOR, ME	BAR HARBOR, ME	BERLIN, NH	CALAIS, ME	CONCORD, NH	CONWAY, NH	LEWISTON, ME	MACHIAS, ME	PORTLAND, ME	PORTSMOUTH, NH	WATERVILLE, ME
AUGUSTA, ME		77	120	110	173	141	97	35	158	58	110	20
BANGOR, ME	77		45	160	97	214	170	108	83	131	184	56
BAR HARBOR, ME	120	45		204	112	257	214	151	71	175	227	100
PORTLAND, ME	58	131	175	93	228	83	62	36	213		53	84

SEE ALSO DISTANCE AND DRIVING TIME MAP ON PAGES 286–287

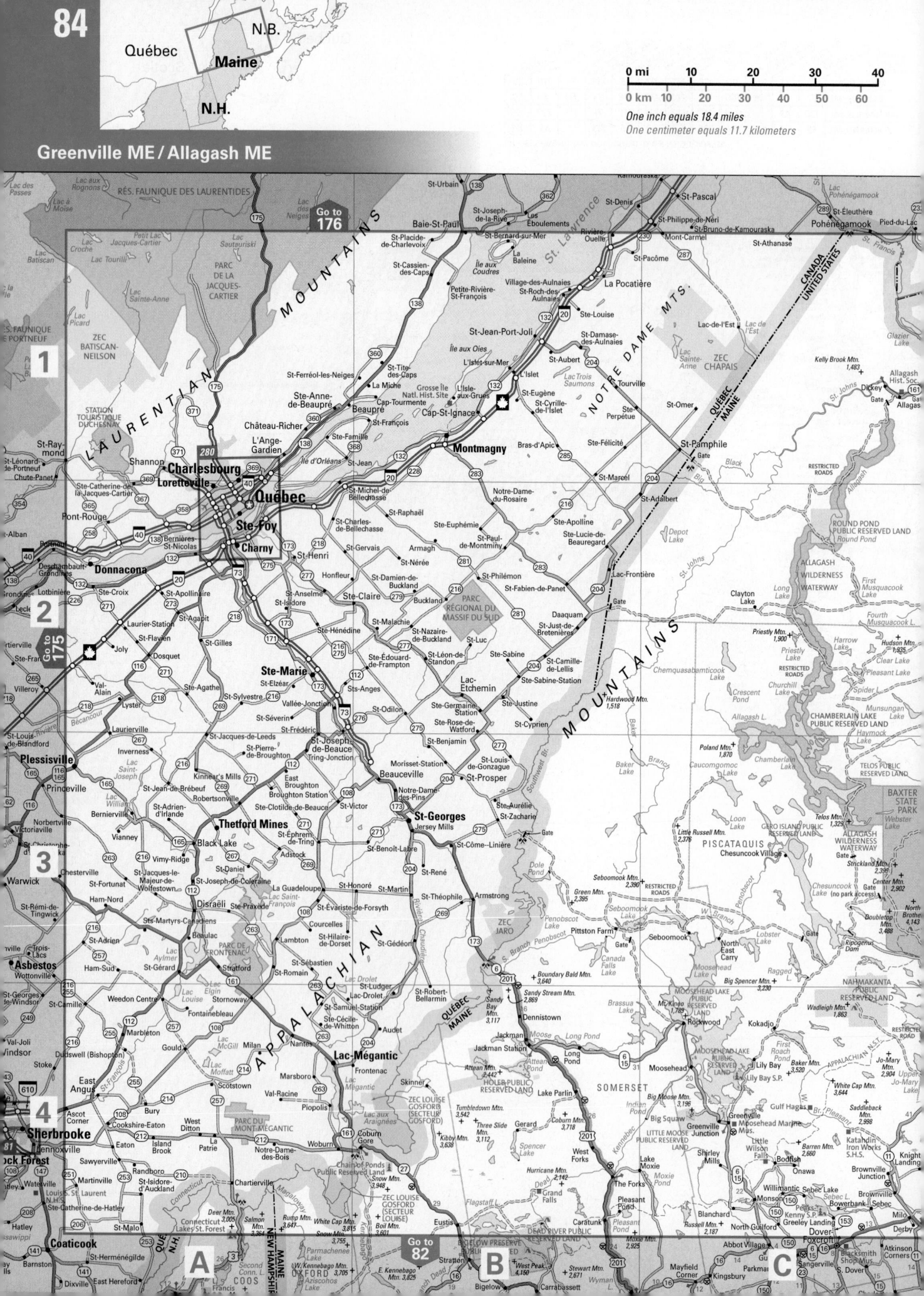

N.B.
Québec
Maine
N.H.

0 mi 10 20 30 40
0 km 10 20 30 40 50 60
One inch equals 18.4 miles
One centimeter equals 11.7 kilometers

Go to 178

Go to 179

Go to 180

Go to 83

DRIVING DISTANCES IN MILES	BANGOR, ME	CALAIS, ME	CARIBOU, ME	FREDERICTON, NB	GREENVILLE, ME	HOULTON, ME	JACKMAN, ME	LINCOLN, ME	MADAWASKA, ME	MILLINOCKET, ME	PRESQUE ISLE, ME	QUÉBEC, QC
HOULTON, ME	122	91	55	73	155		204	83	102	73	42	286
LINCOLN, ME	51	77	135	114	83	83	132		174	35	122	231
MADAWASKA, ME	214	207	50	167	212	102	269	174		164	62	182
PRESQUE ISLE, ME	162	133	13	113	166	42	215	122	62	113		246

SEE ALSO DISTANCE AND DRIVING TIME MAP ON PAGES 286–287

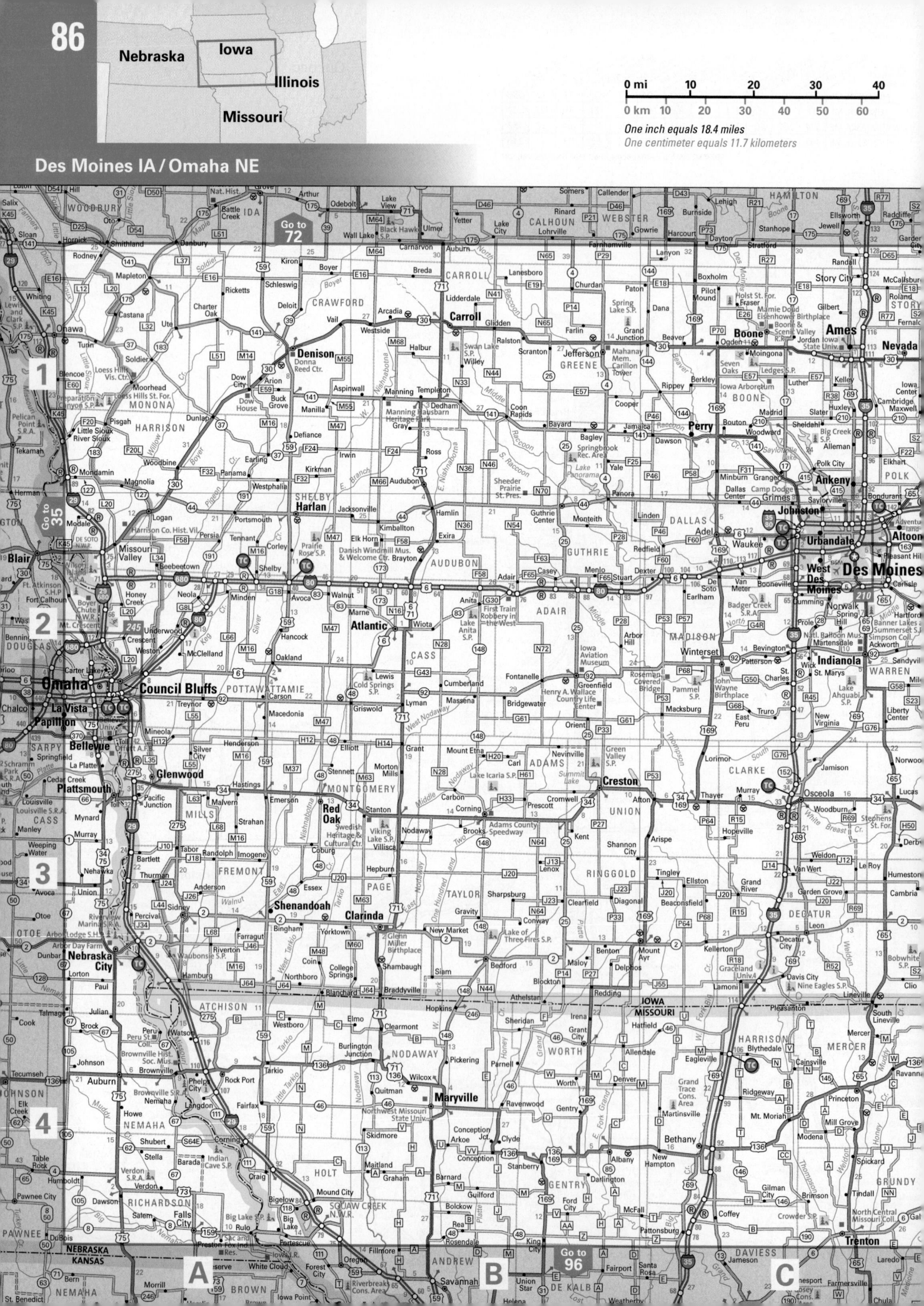

0 mi   10   20   30   40
0 km 10   20   30   40   50   60
One inch equals 18.4 miles
One centimeter equals 11.7 kilometers

DRIVING DISTANCES IN MILES	AMES, IA	BURLINGTON, IA	CARROLL, IA	CEDAR RAPIDS, IA	CRESTON, IA	DAVENPORT, IA	DES MOINES, IA	IOWA CITY, IA	KIRKSVILLE, MO	MARYVILLE, MO	OMAHA, NE	OTTUMWA, IA
CEDAR RAPIDS, IA	108	106	173		211	87	129	28	170	276	266	111
DES MOINES, IA	34	157	90	129	81	171		113	145	146	136	86
IOWA CITY, IA	136	82	195	28	195	59	113		143	260	250	83
OMAHA, NE	171	328	97	266	98	308	136	250	275	112		221

SEE ALSO DISTANCE AND DRIVING TIME MAP ON PAGES 286–287

Michigan
Iowa
Illinois
Indiana
0 mi 10 20 30 40
0 km 10 20 30 40 50 60
One inch equals 18.4 miles
One centimeter equals 11.7 kilometers
Go to 74
Go to 87
Go to 98
Rockford
Freeport
Machesney Park
Loves Park
Belvidere
McHenry
Crystal Lake
Carpentersville
Elgin
St. Charles
DeKalb
Rochelle
Sycamore
Geneva
Batavia
Aurora
Naperville
Oswego
Plainfield
Sandwich
Dixon
Sterling
Rock Falls
Clinton
De Witt
Maquoketa
Davenport
Bettendorf
Rock Island
Moline
E. Moline
Geneseo
Kewanee
Princeton
Mendota
Peru
LaSalle
Ottawa
Morris
Spring Valley
Streator
Galesburg
Monmouth
Macomb
Canton
Peoria
E. Peoria
Washington
Pekin
Morton
Chillicothe
Bloomington
Normal
Pontiac
Lincoln
Clinton
Champaign
Urbana
Beardstown
Rushville
Havana
Monticello
Rantoul
Dwight
Wilmington
Braidwood
JO DAVIESS
STEPHENSON
WINNEBAGO
BOONE
CARROLL
OGLE
DE KALB
KANE
KENDALL
LEE
WHITESIDE
HENRY
BUREAU
LA SALLE
GRUNDY
ROCK ISLAND
MERCER
KNOX
STARK
PUTNAM
MARSHALL
WARREN
PEORIA
WOODFORD
LIVINGSTON
FULTON
TAZEWELL
MCLEAN
MCDONOUGH
SCHUYLER
MASON
MENARD
LOGAN
DE WITT
MACON
BROWN
CASS
JACKSON
CLINTON
SCOTT
MUSCATINE
JONES
A
B
C
1
2
3
4

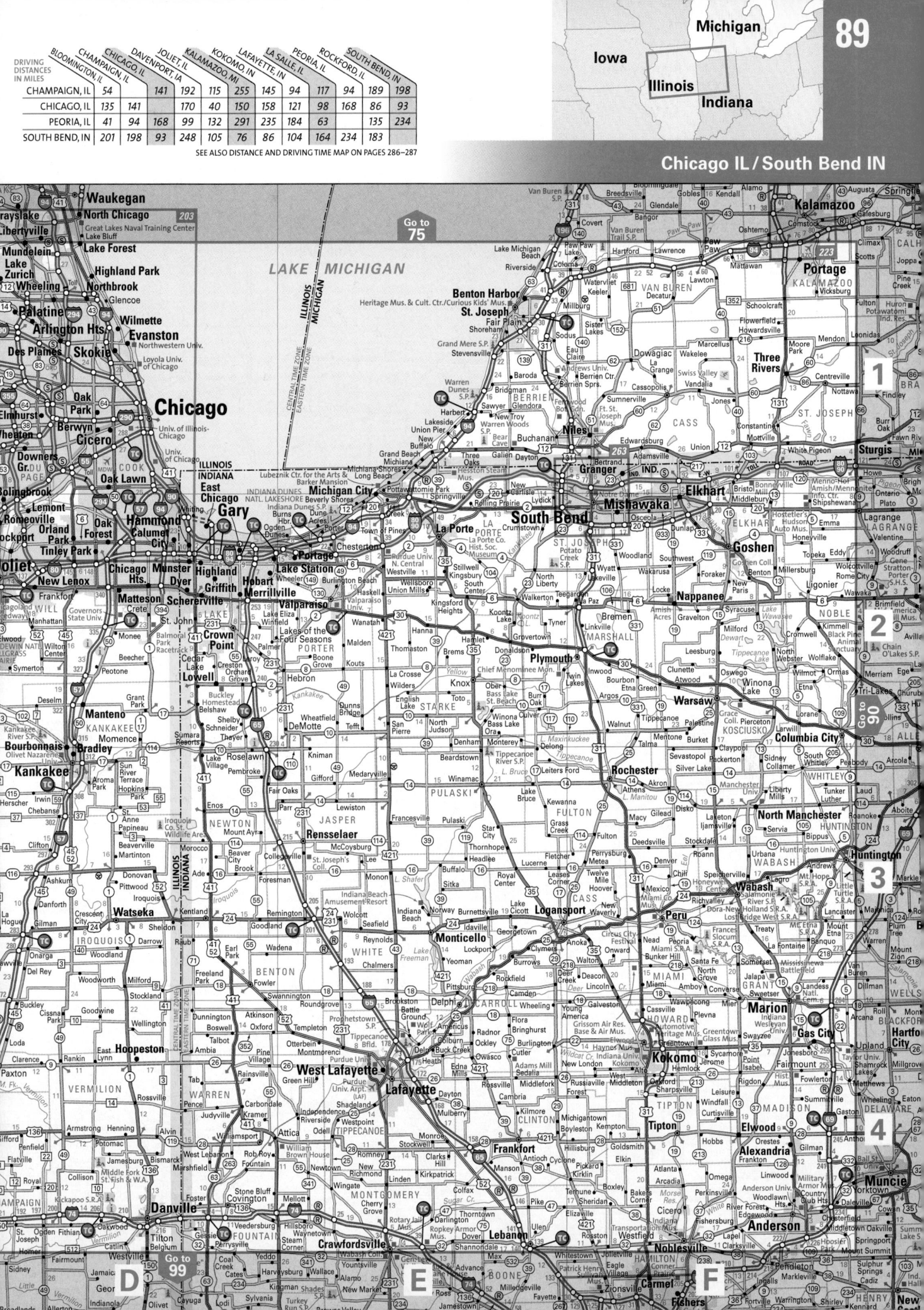

DRIVING DISTANCES IN MILES	BLOOMINGTON, IL	CHAMPAIGN, IL	CHICAGO, IL	DAVENPORT, IA	JOLIET, IL	KALAMAZOO, MI	KOKOMO, IN	LAFAYETTE, IN	LA SALLE, IL	PEORIA, IL	ROCKFORD, IL	SOUTH BEND, IN
CHAMPAIGN, IL	54		141	192	115	255	145	94	117	94	189	198
CHICAGO, IL	135	141		170	40	150	158	121	98	168	86	93
PEORIA, IL	41	94	168	99	132	291	235	184	63		135	234
SOUTH BEND, IN	201	198	93	248	105	76	86	104	164	234	183	

SEE ALSO DISTANCE AND DRIVING TIME MAP ON PAGES 286–287

0 mi   10   20   30   40
0 km 10   20   30   40   50   60
One inch equals 18.4 miles
One centimeter equals 11.7 kilometers

DRIVING DISTANCES IN MILES	AKRON, OH	CLEVELAND, OH	COLUMBUS, OH	DETROIT, MI	ERIE, PA	FORT WAYNE, IN	LIMA, OH	MANSFIELD, OH	MUNCIE, IN	TOLEDO, OH	WHEELING, WV	YOUNGSTOWN, OH
CLEVELAND, OH	38		144	171	106	214	163	81	287	119	16	275
FORT WAYNE, IN	237	214	186	170	322		66	151	75	109	290	274
MANSFIELD, OH	66	81	67	156	179	151	93		209	105	141	112
TOLEDO, OH	142	119	148	60	227	109	83	105	180		261	179

SEE ALSO DISTANCE AND DRIVING TIME MAP ON PAGES 286–287

New York
Pennsylvania
New Jersey
0 mi 10 20 30 40
0 km 10 20 30 40 50 60
One inch equals 18.4 miles
One centimeter equals 11.7 kilometers
LAKE ERIE
Go to 77
Go to 78
Go to 91
Go to 102
Erie
Jamestown
Salamanca
Olean
Wellsville
Meadville
Titusville
Warren
Bradford
Oil City
Franklin
Sugarcreek
St. Marys
Clarion
DuBois
Clearfield
Grove City
New Castle
Butler
Punxsutawney
Indiana
Altoona
State College
Bellefonte
Huntingdon
Pittsburgh
McCandless
Monroeville
Murrysville
Greensburg
Latrobe
Johnstown
Washington
Somerset
Connellsville
Chambersburg
ALLEGHENY NATIONAL FOREST
ALLEGHENY PLATEAU
NEW YORK
PENNSYLVANIA
1
2
3
4
A
B
C

DRIVING DISTANCES IN MILES

	ALLENTOWN, PA	ALTOONA, PA	BINGHAMTON, NY	ELMIRA, NY	ERIE, PA	HARRISBURG, PA	JOHNSTOWN, PA	PITTSBURGH, PA	READING, PA	SCRANTON, PA	STATE COLLEGE, PA	WILLIAMSPORT, PA
ALLENTOWN, PA		218	132	188	361	82	217	284	37	76	165	116
HARRISBURG, PA	82	140	181	157	298		138	205	65	119	88	83
PITTSBURGH, PA	284	99	363	284	126	205	73		262	301	139	215
SCRANTON, PA	76	185	61	117	317	119	233	301	103		149	83

SEE ALSO DISTANCE AND DRIVING TIME MAP ON PAGES 286–287

Vt.
N.H.
Massachusetts
New York
Rhode Island
Connecticut
Pa.
N.J.
0 mi 10 20 30 40
0 km 10 20 30 40 50 60
One inch equals 18.4 miles
One centimeter equals 11.7 kilometers
Hartford CT / Albany NY
Go to 80
Go to 81
Go to 79
Go to 150
Go to 93
Go to 148
Go to 105
1
2
3
4
A
B
C

DRIVING DISTANCES IN MILES	ALBANY, NY	BOSTON, MA	HARTFORD, CT	MANCHESTER, NH	NEWBURGH, NY	NEW HAVEN, CT	NEW YORK, NY	ONEONTA, NY	PROVIDENCE, RI	PROVINCETOWN, MA	SPRINGFIELD, MA	WORCESTER, MA
ALBANY, NY		172	111	145	89	150	151	81	170	271	86	133
BOSTON, MA	172		102	54	201	139	215	251	52	117	95	46
HARTFORD, CT	111	102		131	99	39	115	190	73	200	25	62
NEW YORK, NY	151	215	115	245	56	78		193	177	292	141	176

SEE ALSO DISTANCE AND DRIVING TIME MAP ON PAGES 286–287

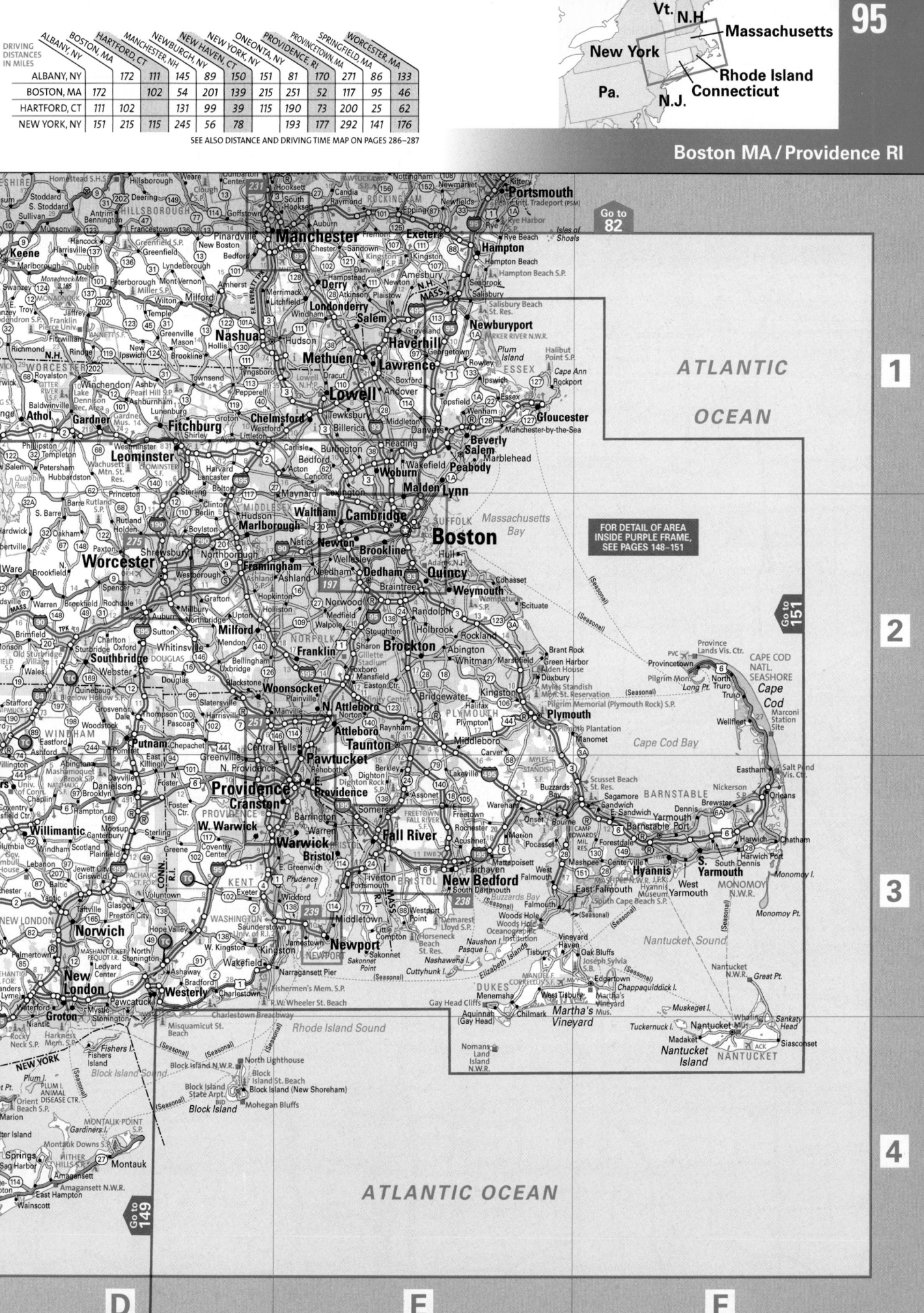

0 mi   10   20   30   40

0 km 10 20 30 40 50 60

One inch equals 18.4 miles
One centimeter equals 11.7 kilometers

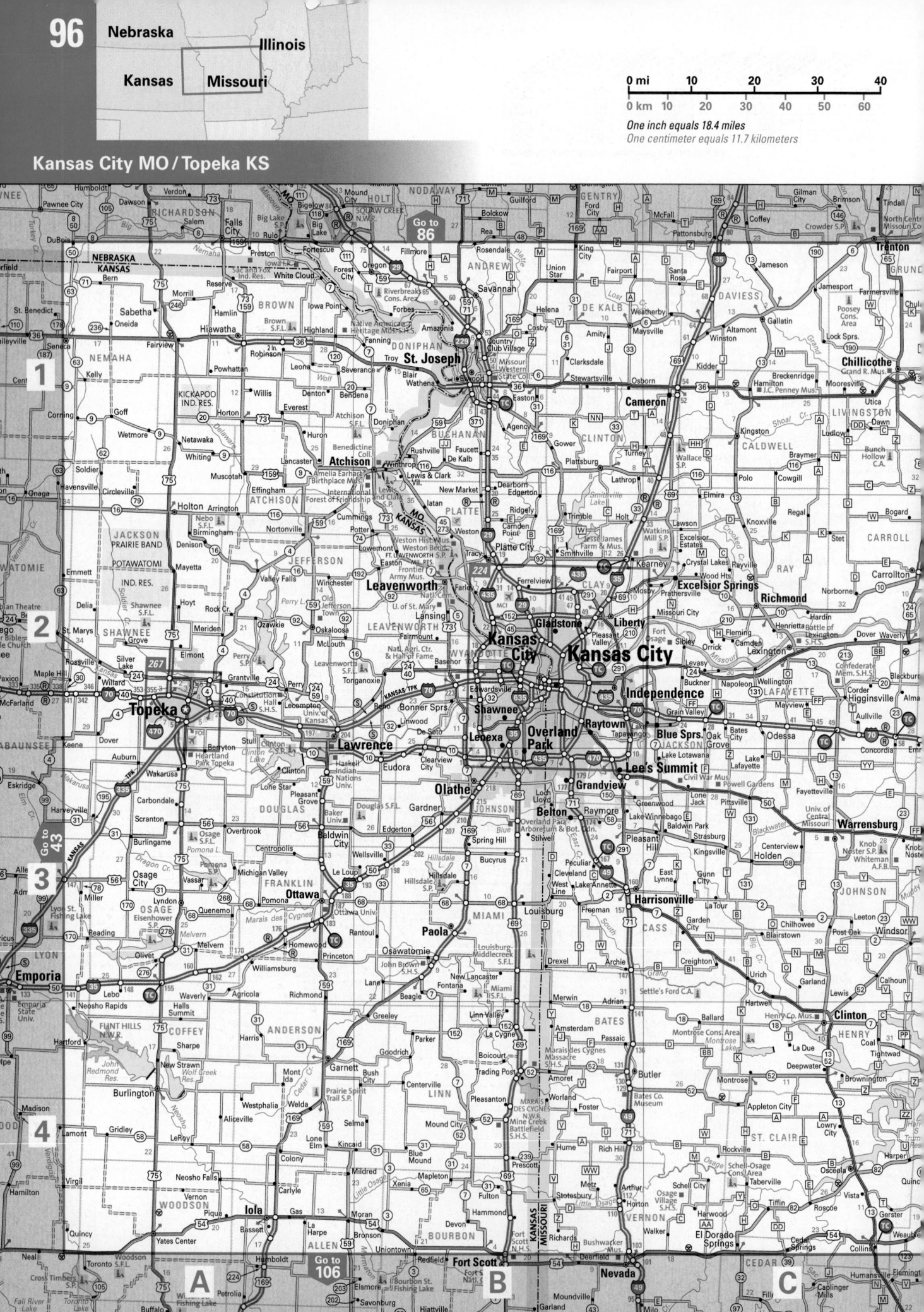

Nebraska

Illinois

Kansas   Missouri

DRIVING DISTANCES IN MILES

	COLUMBIA, MO	IOLA, KS	JEFFERSON CITY, MO	KANSAS CITY, MO	LAWRENCE, KS	MACON, MO	OSAGE BEACH, MO	QUINCY, IL	ROLLA, MO	ST. JOSEPH, MO	SEDALIA, MO	TOPEKA, KS
JEFFERSON CITY, MO	32	263		161	198	88	44	131	65	217	64	225
KANSAS CITY, MO	129	106	161		37	148	173	251	226	56	97	63
ST. JOSEPH, MO	185	154	217	56	76	131	229	210	282		153	71
TOPEKA, KS	193	100	225	63	26	209	236	314	289	71	161	

SEE ALSO DISTANCE AND DRIVING TIME MAP ON PAGES 286–287

One inch equals 18.4 miles
One centimeter equals 11.7 kilometers

DRIVING DISTANCES IN MILES	BLOOMINGTON, IN	CHAMPAIGN, IL	DECATUR, IL	EFFINGHAM, IL	EVANSVILLE, IN	INDIANAPOLIS, IN	LOUISVILLE, KY	MT. VERNON, IL	ST. LOUIS, MO	SPRINGFIELD, IL	TERRE HAUTE, IN	VINCENNES, IN
EVANSVILLE, IN	117	192	184	117		166	114	90	170	247	107	51
INDIANAPOLIS, IN	47	123	177	137	166		112	205	239	212	77	123
ST. LOUIS, MO	223	179	116	103	170	239	264	81		97	169	185
SPRINGFIELD, IL	209	87	40	89	247	212	326	158	97		155	169

SEE ALSO DISTANCE AND DRIVING TIME MAP ON PAGES 286–287

Ohio
Indiana
W.Va.
Kentucky
Cincinnati OH / Louisville KY
0 mi 10 20 30 40
0 km 10 20 30 40 50 60
One inch equals 18.4 miles
One centimeter equals 11.7 kilometers
Go to 90
Go to 99
Go to 110
1
2
3
4
A
B
C
Cincinnati
Louisville
Dayton
Lexington
Frankfort
Covington
Newport
Hamilton
Middletown
Springfield
Richmond
Anderson
Columbus
Madison
Maysville
Georgetown
Winchester
Nicholasville
Versailles
Shelbyville
Mt. Sterling
Morehead
Paris
Cynthiana
Lebanon
Xenia
Wilmington
Hillsboro
Greenfield
Shelbyville
Greensburg
Batesville
Rushville
Connersville
New Castle
Seymour
North Vernon
Scottsburg
Jeffersonville
Clarksville
New Albany
Radcliff
Bardstown
Harrodsburg
Eaton
Oxford
Fairfield
Mason
Kettering
Beavercreek
Troy
Piqua
Urbana
Greenville
Winchester
Florence
Erlanger
Independence
Williamstown
Carrollton
La Grange
Lawrenceburg
Mt. Washington
Shepherdsville

DRIVING
DISTANCES
IN MILES

	CHARLESTON, WV	CHILLICOTHE, OH	CINCINNATI, OH	COLUMBUS, OH	DAYTON, OH	HUNTINGTON, WV	LEXINGTON, KY	LOUISVILLE, KY	MAYSVILLE, KY	PARKERSBURG, WV	WHEELING, OH	ZANESVILLE, OH
CHARLESTON, WV		121	202	168	198	52	176	251	155	73	176	155
CINCINNATI, OH	202	108		109	52	150	85	100	63	191	235	164
COLUMBUS, OH	168	47	109		70	135	193	207	114	108	130	58
LEXINGTON, KY	176	191	85	193	135	126		80	67	249	319	247

SEE ALSO DISTANCE AND DRIVING TIME MAP ON PAGES 286–287

Pennsylvania
Ohio
W.Va. Md. —Delaware
Virginia

0 mi 10 20 30 40
0 km 10 20 30 40 50 60
One inch equals 18.4 miles
One centimeter equals 11.7 kilometers

Charlottesville VA / Morgantown WV

DRIVING DISTANCES IN MILES	CHARLOTTESVILLE, VA	CUMBERLAND, MD	ELKINS, WV	FREDERICKSBURG, VA	FRONT ROYAL, VA	GETTYSBURG, PA	HAGERSTOWN, MD	MORGANTOWN, WV	SALISBURY, MD	WASHINGTON, DC	WHEELING, WV
BALTIMORE, MD	161	140	229	98	110	62	76	211	106	38	290
CHARLOTTESVILLE, VA		161	163	142	70	74	190	141	204	235	118	279
MORGANTOWN, WV	211	204	71	62	252	161	181	138		317	205	76
WASHINGTON, DC	38	118	134	192	54	73	80	70	205	115		284

SEE ALSO DISTANCE AND DRIVING TIME MAP ON PAGES 286–287

N.Y.
Pennsylvania
New Jersey
Md.
Delaware
Virginia
0 mi 10 20 30 40
0 km 10 20 30 40 50 60
One inch equals 18.4 miles
One centimeter equals 11.7 kilometers
Go to 93
Go to 144
Go to 103
Go to 146
Go to 145
Go to 114
Bloomsburg
Berwick
Hazleton
E. Stroudsburg
Stroudsburg
Lewisburg
Milton
Sunbury
Shamokin
Selinsgrove
Mount Carmel
Shenandoah
Lehighton
Tamaqua
Pottsville
Schuylkill Haven
Northampton
Easton
Phillipsburg
Whitehall
Bethlehem
Allentown
Emmaus
Quakertown
Hamburg
Kutztown
Bangor
Washington
Harrisburg
Carlisle
Hershey
Lebanon
Reading
Wyomissing
Doylestown
Trenton
Levittown
Elizabethtown
Lititz
Ephrata
Pottstown
Lansdale
Norristown
Phoenixville
Lancaster
Millersville
Columbia
York
Philadelphia
Camden
West Chester
Coatesville
Gettysburg
Hanover
Taneytown
Thurmont
Westminster
Chester
Wilmington
Newark
Elkton
Glassboro
Vineland
Millville
Bridgeton
Havre de Grace
Aberdeen
Cockeysville
Reisterstown
Owings Mills
Towson
Perry Hall
Edgewood
Baltimore
Middle River
Essex
Dundalk
Frederick
Mount Airy
Catonsville
Ellicott City
Columbia
Elkridge
Glen Burnie
Severna Park
Annapolis
Germantown
Gaithersburg
Rockville
Bethesda
Silver Spr.
Greenbelt
Bowie
Laurel
Odenton
Crofton
Arnold
Reston
McLean
Washington
Arlington
Alexandria
Fairfax
Springfield
Franconia
Oxon Hill
Clinton
Waldorf
Woodbridge
Dale City
Lake Ridge
Smyrna
Dover
Milford
Easton
Denton
Seaford
Georgetown
Lewes
Cape May Court House
Wildwood
Hammonton
Lindenwold
Salem
A
B
C
1
2
3
4

DRIVING DISTANCES IN MILES

	ALLENTOWN, PA	ATLANTIC CITY, NJ	BALTIMORE, MD	DOVER, DE	HARRISBURG, PA	LANCASTER, PA	NEWARK, NJ	NEW YORK, NY	PHILADELPHIA, PA	TRENTON, NJ	WASHINGTON, DC	WILMINGTON, DE
HARRISBURG, PA	82	171	83	126		44	154	165	109	135	123	102
NEW YORK, NY	84	125	192	160	165	165	11		91	55	228	120
PHILADELPHIA, PA	63	62	104	74	109	79	80	91		34	140	30
WASHINGTON, DC	188	186	38	94	123	123	218	228	140	179		110

SEE ALSO DISTANCE AND DRIVING TIME MAP ON PAGES 286–287

N.Y.
Pennsylvania
New Jersey
Md.
Delaware
Virginia

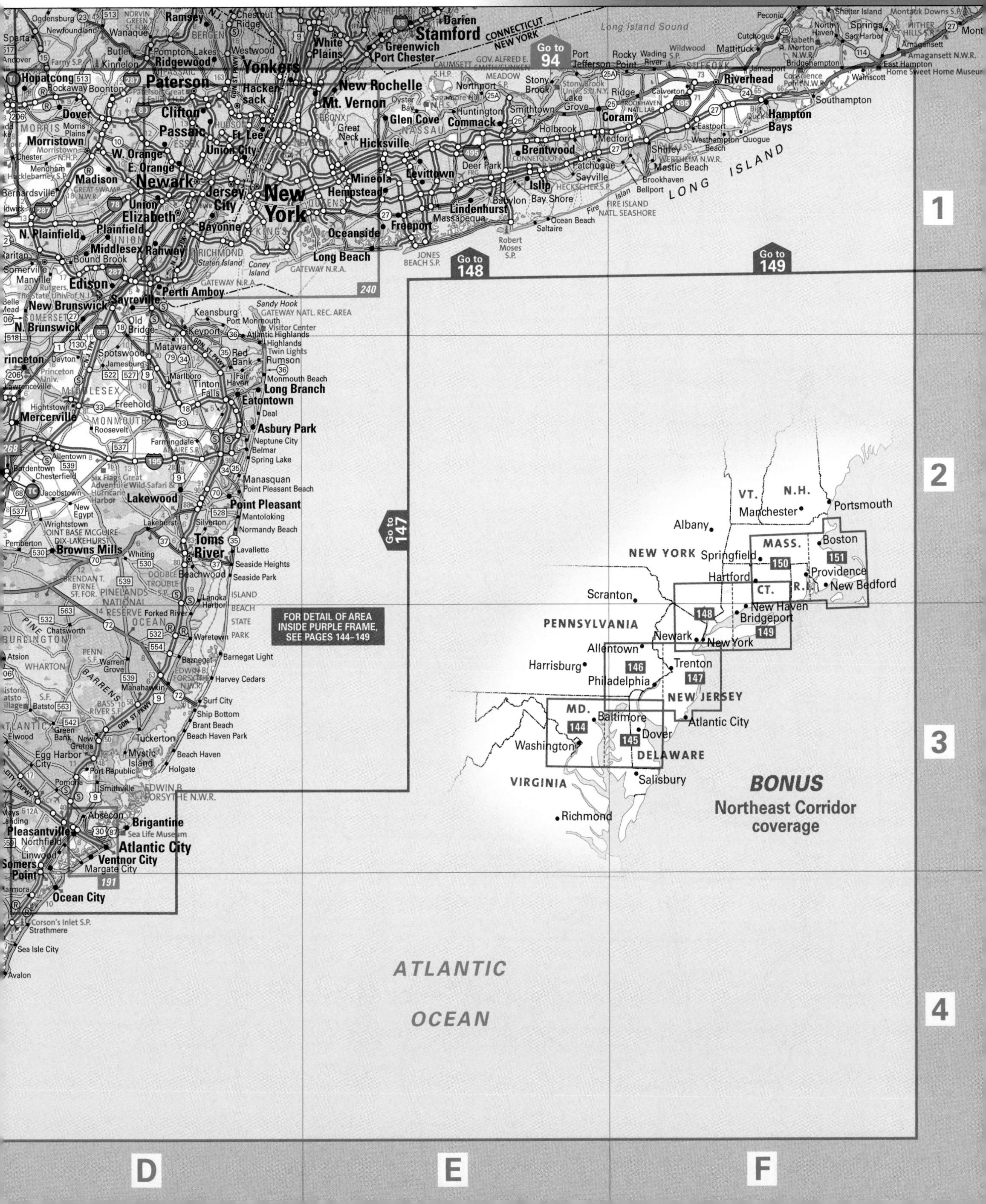

Go to 94

Go to 148

Go to 149

Go to 147

FOR DETAIL OF AREA INSIDE PURPLE FRAME, SEE PAGES 144–149

VT. N.H.
Manchester Portsmouth
Albany
NEW YORK Springfield MASS. Boston
Hartford 150 151
Scranton CT. Providence New Bedford
R.I.
148 New Haven
PENNSYLVANIA Bridgeport
Newark 149
Allentown New York
Harrisburg 146 Trenton
Philadelphia 147
NEW JERSEY
MD. Atlantic City
144 Baltimore
Washington 145 Dover

DELAWARE
VIRGINIA Salisbury

Richmond

BONUS
Northeast Corridor coverage

ATLANTIC

OCEAN

1
2
3
4

D
E
F

Tulsa OK / Fayetteville AR

Kansas
Missouri
Oklahoma
Arkansas
0 mi 10 20 30 40
0 km 10 20 30 40 50 60
One inch equals 18.4 miles
One centimeter equals 11.7 kilometers
Go to 96
Go to 43
Go to 51
Go to 116
1
2
3
4
A
B
C
KANSAS
OKLAHOMA
MISSOURI
ARKANSAS
Iola
Fort Scott
Nevada
Chanute
Pittsburg
Parsons
Independence
Coffeyville
Joplin
Webb City
Carthage
Lamar
Bartlesville
Miami
Neosho
Monett
Aurora
Vinita
Grove
Bella Vista
Bentonville
Rogers
Springdale
Fayetteville
Siloam Sprs.
Pryor
Claremore
Owasso
Tulsa
Sand Sprs.
Jenks
Broken Arrow
Sapulpa
Bixby
Wagoner
Tahlequah
Muskogee
Okmulgee
Stilwell
Cassville
Berryville
WOODSON
ALLEN
BOURBON
VERNON
ST. CLAIR
CEDAR
WILSON
NEOSHO
CRAWFORD
DADE
BARTON
ELK
MONTGOMERY
LABETTE
CHEROKEE
JASPER
LAWRENCE
CHAUTAUQUA
WASHINGTON
NOWATA
CRAIG
OTTAWA
NEWTON
BARRY
MCDONALD
OSAGE
ROGERS
MAYES
DELAWARE
BENTON
TULSA
WAGONER
CHEROKEE
ADAIR
WASHINGTON
MADISON
OKMULGEE
MUSKOGEE
SEQUOYAH
CRAWFORD
FRANKLIN
BOSTON MTS.
OZARK-ST. FRANCIS NATL. FOR.
MARK TWAIN N.F.

DRIVING DISTANCES IN MILES

	BARTLESVILLE, OK	BRANSON, MO	FAYETTEVILLE, AR	INDEPENDENCE, KS	JOPLIN, MO	MOUNTAIN HOME, AR	MUSKOGEE, OK	NEWPORT, AR	ROLLA, MO	SPRINGFIELD, MO	TULSA, OK	WEST PLAINS, MO
BRANSON, MO	213		95	188	111	84	181	178	147	41	225	109
FAYETTEVILLE, AR	154	95		165	88	127	86	241	227	121	113	182
SPRINGFIELD, MO	177	41	121	153	70	112	193	219	110		189	109
TULSA, OK	48	225	113	86	116	237	52	344	295	189		293

SEE ALSO DISTANCE AND DRIVING TIME MAP ON PAGES 286–287

108

Illinois Ind.
Missouri
Kentucky
Tennessee
Arkansas

Jonesboro AR / Cape Girardeau MO

Illinois Ind.
Missouri
Kentucky
Arkansas Tennessee

DRIVING DISTANCES IN MILES	BOWLING GREEN, KY	CAPE GIRARDEAU, MO	CARBONDALE, IL	CLARKSVILLE, TN	DYERSBURG, TN	HOPKINSVILLE, KY	JACKSON, TN	JONESBORO, AR	NASHVILLE, TN	OWENSBORO, KY	PADUCAH, KY	POPLAR BLUFF, MO
BOWLING GREEN, KY		199	206	63	217	63	196	349	68	67	135	239
CAPE GIRARDEAU, MO	199		46	155	112	136	161	155	197	168	67	75
JONESBORO, AR	349	155	199	268	101	249	160		285	304	178	81
NASHVILLE, TN	68	197	204	46	178	68	132	285		141	133	237

SEE ALSO DISTANCE AND DRIVING TIME MAP ON PAGES 286–287

Knoxville TN / Richmond KY

One inch equals 18.4 miles
One centimeter equals 11.7 kilometers

DRIVING DISTANCES IN MILES	ASHEVILLE, NC	BECKLEY, WV	BRISTOL, TN/VA	COOKEVILLE, TN	GATLINBURG, TN	HICKORY, NC	JOHNSON CITY, TN	KNOXVILLE, TN	LONDON, KY	MAMMOTH CAVE NP., KY	PIKEVILLE, KY	RICHMOND, VA
BRISTOL, TN/VA	83	140		224	118	98		98	24	117	213	348	116	265
HICKORY, NC	78	196	98	291	147		98	185	280	415	214	332
KNOXVILLE, TN	109	256	117	107	40	185	107		100	234	202	151
LONDON, KY	205	287	213	129	136	280	203	100		136	121	53

SEE ALSO DISTANCE AND DRIVING TIME MAP ON PAGES 286–287

0 mi   10   20   30   40

0 km   10   20   30   40   50   60

One inch equals 18.4 miles
One centimeter equals 11.7 kilometers

DRIVING DISTANCES IN MILES	DANVILLE, VA	GREENSBORO, NC	LYNCHBURG, VA	NORFOLK, VA	RALEIGH, NC	RICHMOND, VA	ROANOKE, VA	ROANOKE RAPIDS, NC	ROCKY MOUNT, NC	WILLIAMSBURG, VA	WINSTON-SALEM, NC	WYTHEVILLE, VA
GREENSBORO, NC	46		106	230	69	200	101	132	124	237	30	120
RALEIGH, NC	89	69	140	179		157	156	84	54	204	96	186
RICHMOND, VA	160	200	114	91	157		192	91	127	49	228	256
ROANOKE, VA	83	101	55	285	156	192		190	211	243	107	78

SEE ALSO DISTANCE AND DRIVING TIME MAP ON PAGES 286–287

Go to 103
Go to 114
Go to 115
Go to 123

Md — Delaware
Virginia
North Carolina

0 mi   10   20   30   40
0 km 10 20 30 40 50 60
One inch equals 18.4 miles
One centimeter equals 11.7 kilometers

DRIVING DISTANCES IN MILES	ELIZABETH CITY, NC	GREENVILLE, NC	MOREHEAD CITY, NC	NAGS HEAD, NC	NEW BERN, NC	NORFOLK, VA	OCEAN CITY, MD	RICHMOND, VA	SALISBURY, MD	VIRGINIA BEACH, VA	WASHINGTON, DC	WILLIAMSBURG, VA
MOREHEAD CITY, NC	150	82		184	35	185	326	241	321	206	352	221
NAGS HEAD, NC	59	135	184		149	82	214	179	209	94	284	131
NORFOLK, VA	50	130	185	82	151		138	91	133	18	196	43
WASHINGTON, DC	243	270	352	284	317	196	139	108	115	212		153

SEE ALSO DISTANCE AND DRIVING TIME MAP ON PAGES 286–287

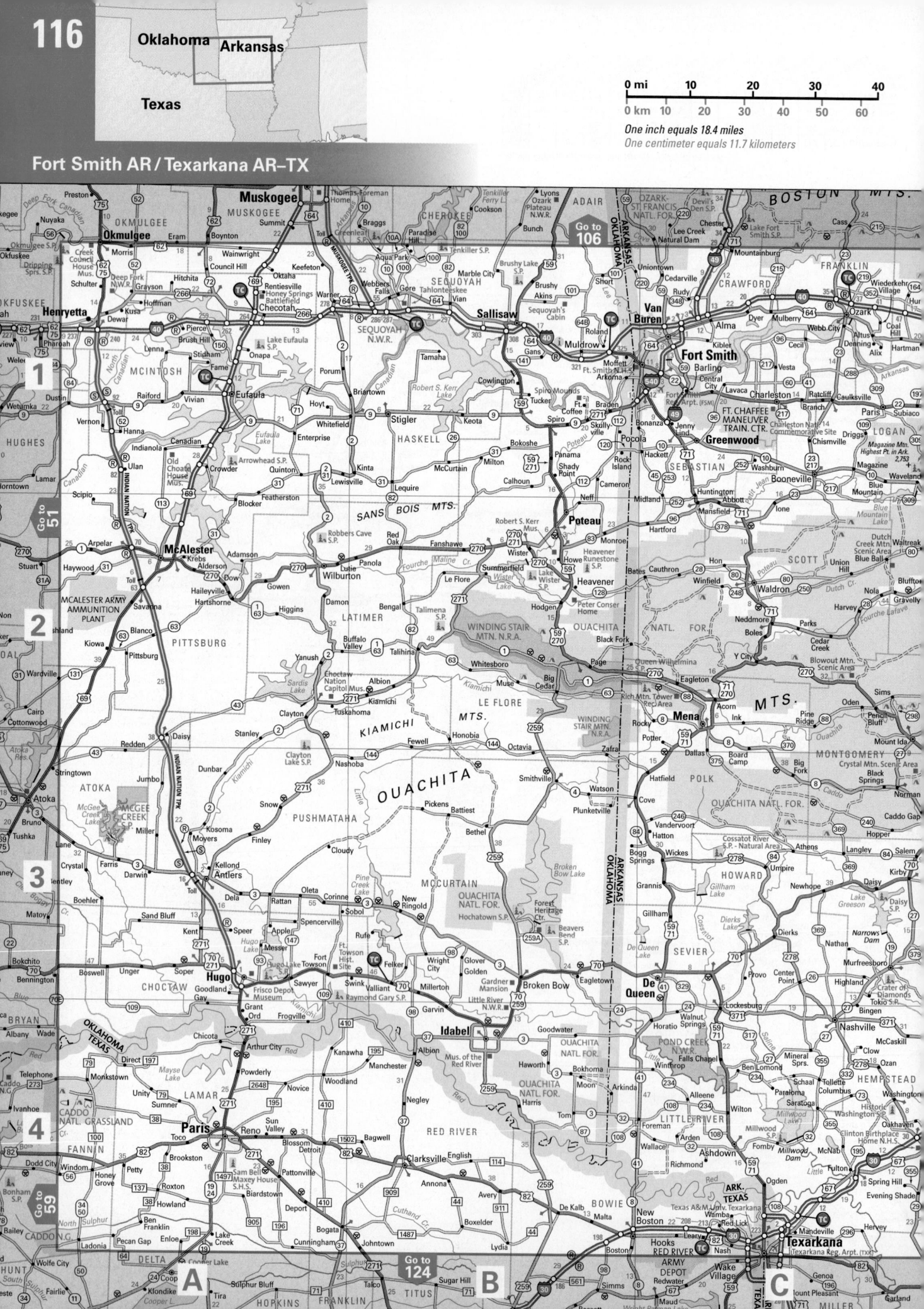

Oklahoma Arkansas

Texas

0 mi   10   20   30   40
0 km 10 20 30 40 50 60
One inch equals 18.4 miles
One centimeter equals 11.7 kilometers

Oklahoma Arkansas

Texas

DRIVING DISTANCES IN MILES	ARKADELPHIA, AR	FORT SMITH, AR	HENRYETTA, OK	HOT SPRINGS, AR	LITTLE ROCK, AR	MCALESTER, OK	MENA, AR	NEWPORT, AR	PARIS, TX	PINE BLUFF, AR	RUSSELLVILLE, AR	TEXARKANA, AR/TX
FORT SMITH, AR	152		100	126	165	114	81	220	214	210	87	180
HOT SPRINGS, AR	37	126	224			65	193	75	154	207	76	67	117
LITTLE ROCK, AR	72	165	263	65			278	141	89	242	45	81	153
TEXARKANA, AR/TX	83	180	227	117	153		188	99	241	92	163	180	

SEE ALSO DISTANCE AND DRIVING TIME MAP ON PAGES 286–287

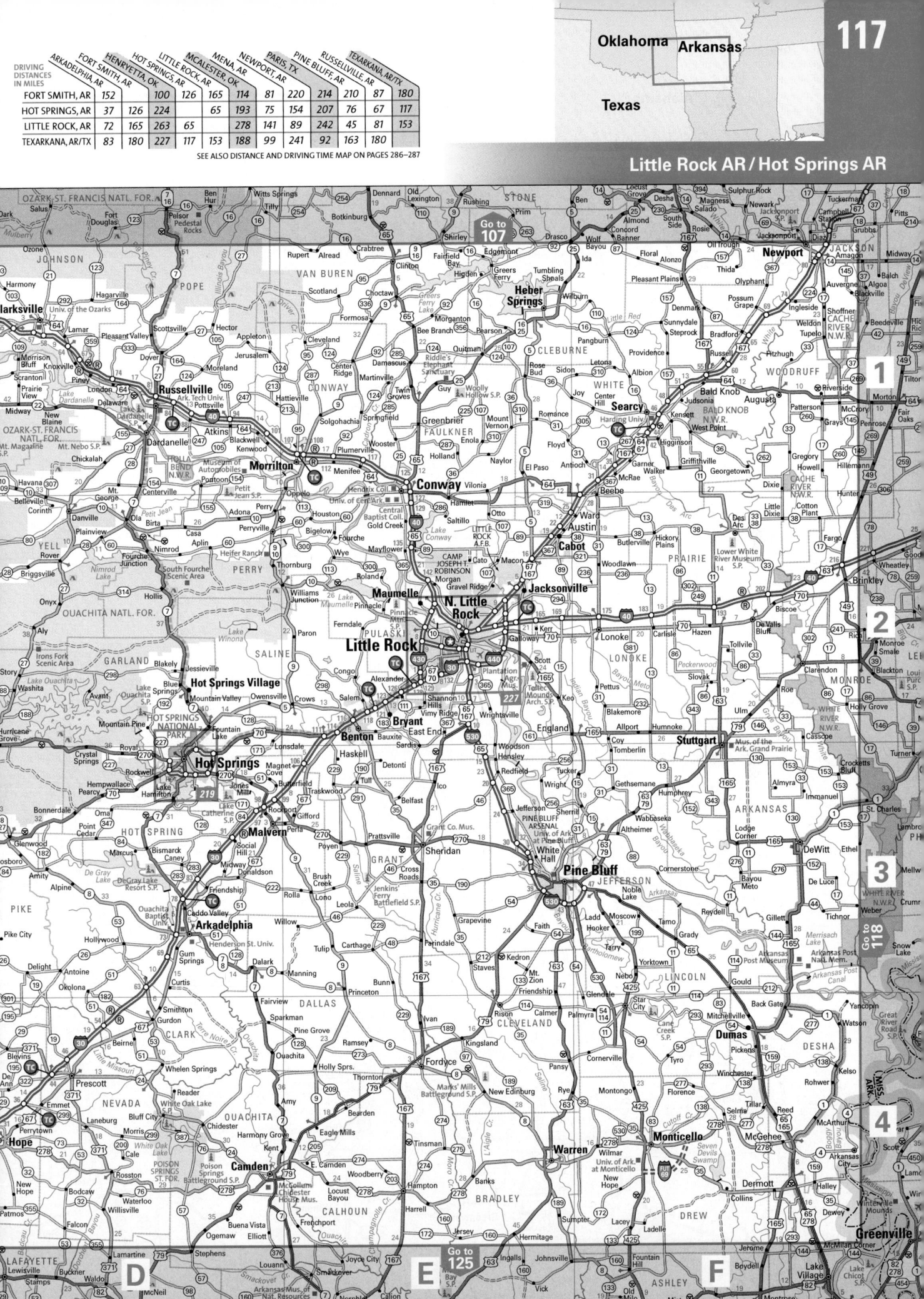

0 mi   10   20   30   40
0 km 10 20 30 40 50 60
One inch equals 18.4 miles
One centimeter equals 11.7 kilometers

DRIVING DISTANCES IN MILES	CLARKSDALE, MS	COLUMBIA, TN	COLUMBUS, MS	DECATUR, AL	FLORENCE, AL	GREENVILLE, MS	HUNTSVILLE, AL	JACKSON, TN	MEMPHIS, TN	OXFORD, MS	TUPELO, MS
BIRMINGHAM, AL	248	161	122	83	121	286	101	223	241	185	136
HUNTSVILLE, AL	101	260	79	163	25	65	318		205	216	196	148
MEMPHIS, TN	241	76	210	175	191	156	148	216		85	109
TUPELO, MS	136	113	159	66	123	92	172	148	107	109	50

SEE ALSO DISTANCE AND DRIVING TIME MAP ON PAGES 286–287

One inch equals 18.4 miles
One centimeter equals 11.7 kilometers

Go to 111

Go to 122

Go to 129

Go to 130

DRIVING DISTANCES IN MILES	ANNISTON, AL	ASHEVILLE, NC	ATHENS, GA	ATLANTA, GA	AUGUSTA, GA	CHATTANOOGA, TN	GADSDEN, AL	GATLINBURG, TN	GREENVILLE, SC	HUNTSVILLE, AL	MANCHESTER, TN	SPARTANBURG, SC
ATLANTA, GA	91	207	70		149	113	117	187	146	191	180	173
AUGUSTA, GA	240	179	97	149		266	266	240	110	334	333	118
CHATTANOOGA, TN	120	225	170	113	266		94	156	245	109	69	272
GREENVILLE, SC	238	64	104	146	110	245	264	125		313	311	30

SEE ALSO DISTANCE AND DRIVING TIME MAP ON PAGES 286-287

North Carolina
South Carolina

0 mi 10 20 30 40
0 km 10 20 30 40 50 60
One inch equals 18.4 miles
One centimeter equals 11.7 kilometers

Charlotte NC / Columbia SC

Go to 111
Go to 112
Go to 121
Go to 131
Go to 130

1 **2** **3** **4**

A **B** **C**

Hickory · Conover · Newton · Salisbury · Asheboro · Siler City · Mooresville · Davidson · Cornelius · Kannapolis · Concord · Huntersville · Lincolnton · Shelby · Gastonia · Albemarle · Charlotte · Mint Hill · Matthews · Pinehurst · Southern Pines · Aberdeen · Gaffney · York · Indian Trail · Monroe · Rock Hill · Wadesboro · Rockingham · Hamlet · Laurinburg · Chester · Lancaster · Cheraw · Bennettsville · Dillon · Union · Newberry · Winnsboro · Camden · Hartsville · Darlington · Florence · Marion · Lexington · Irmo · Columbia · Cayce · Sumter · Lake City · Batesburg-Leesville · Aiken · Orangeburg · Manning · Kingstree · Georgetown

U.S. DEPT. OF ENERGY SAVANNAH RIVER SITE

CONGAREE NATL. PARK

FRANCIS MARION NATL. FOR.

North
Carolina
South
Carolina

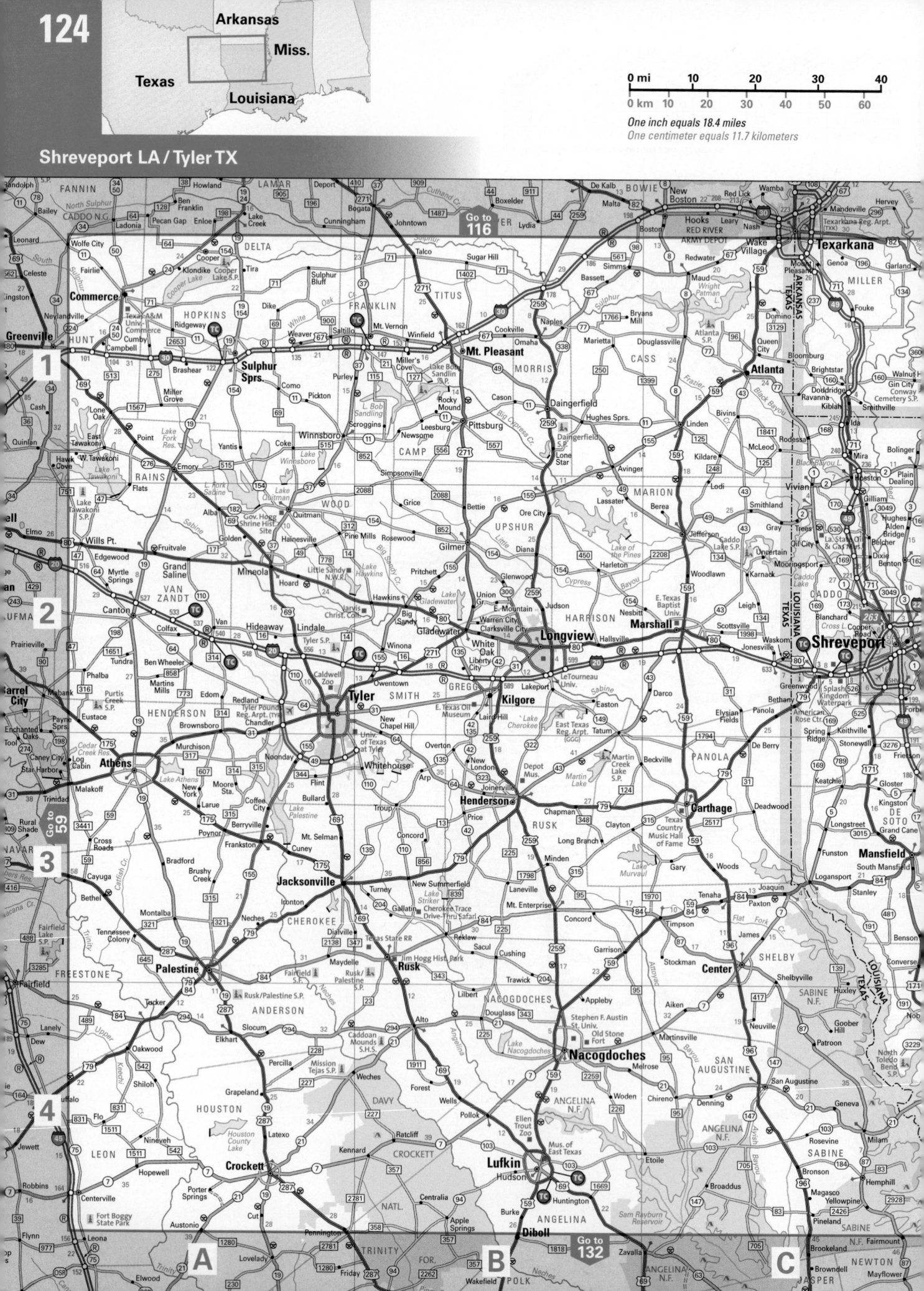

Arkansas

Miss.

Texas

Louisiana

0 mi 10 20 30 40
0 km 10 20 30 40 50 60
One inch equals 18.4 miles
One centimeter equals 11.7 kilometers

DRIVING DISTANCES IN MILES

	EL DORADO, AR	GREENVILLE, TX	LONGVIEW, TX	LUFKIN, TX	MONROE, LA	NACOGDOCHES, LA	NATCHEZ, MS	NATCHITOCHES, LA	SHREVEPORT, LA	TEXARKANA, AR/TX	TYLER, TX
ALEXANDRIA, LA	147	276	179	160	96	167	76	55	121	190	213
MONROE, LA	96	86	267	170	223	203	95	100	103	172	204
SHREVEPORT, LA	121	96	165	68	121	103	101	198	73	69	102
TYLER, TX	213	196	77	42	82	204	76	288	164	102	118

SEE ALSO DISTANCE AND DRIVING TIME MAP ON PAGES 286–287

Arkansas

Miss. Alabama

Louisiana

0 mi   10   20   30   40

0 km   10   20   30   40   50   60

One inch equals 18.4 miles
One centimeter equals 11.7 kilometers

Arkansas
Miss. Alabama
Louisiana

DRIVING DISTANCES IN MILES

	BIRMINGHAM, AL	EVERGREEN, AL	GREENVILLE, MS	HATTIESBURG, MS	JACKSON, MS	MCCOMB, MS	MERIDIAN, MS	NATCHEZ, MS	SELMA, AL	TUSCALOOSA, AL	VICKSBURG, MS	WINONA, MS
HATTIESBURG, MS	239	184	215		90	75	89	142	193	183	132	180
JACKSON, MS	241	243	125	90		76	91	102	195	185	42	94
MERIDIAN, MS	149	152	216	89	91	167		194	104	94	133	113
TUSCALOOSA, AL	61	211	225	183	185	261	94	287	82		227	144

SEE ALSO DISTANCE AND DRIVING TIME MAP ON PAGES 286–287

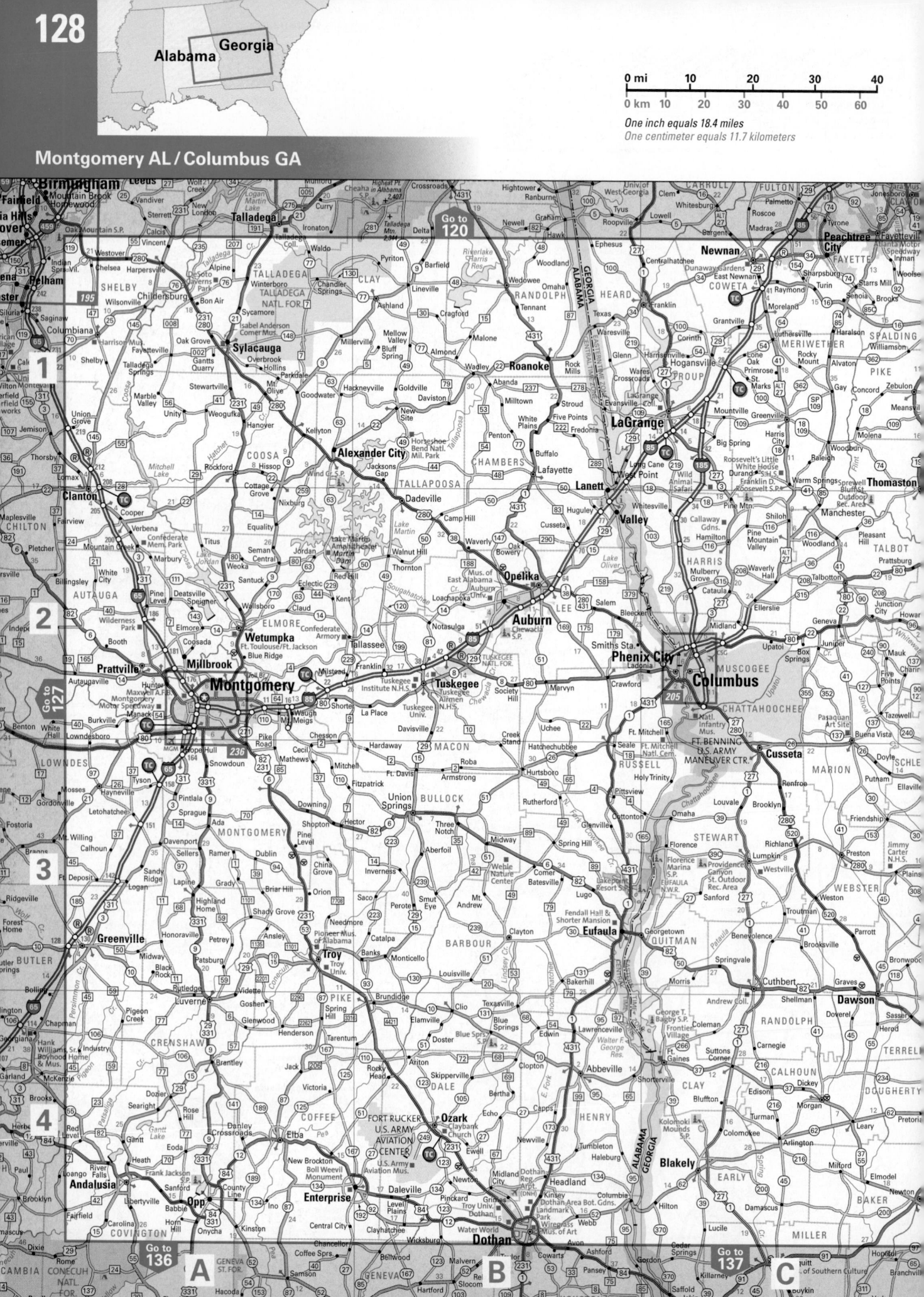

Alabama Georgia

0 mi   10   20   30   40
0 km   10   20   30   40   50   60
One inch equals 18.4 miles
One centimeter equals 11.7 kilometers

DRIVING DISTANCES IN MILES	ALBANY, GA	ATLANTA, GA	AUBURN, AL	AUGUSTA, GA	BIRMINGHAM, AL	COLUMBUS, GA	DOTHAN, AL	LA GRANGE, GA	MACON, GA	MONTGOMERY, AL	TIFTON, GA	WAYCROSS, GA
ALBANY, GA		180	121	226	253	86	83	129	102	165	43	116
COLUMBUS, GA	86	106	34	249	167		97	46	95	79	135	208
MACON, GA	102	84	151	123	234	95	186	114		203	102	159
MONTGOMERY, AL	165	158	54	301	88	79	103	95	203		214	287

SEE ALSO DISTANCE AND DRIVING TIME MAP ON PAGES 286–287

South Carolina

Georgia

0 mi 10 20 30 40
0 km 10 20 30 40 50 60
One inch equals 18.4 miles
One centimeter equals 11.7 kilometers

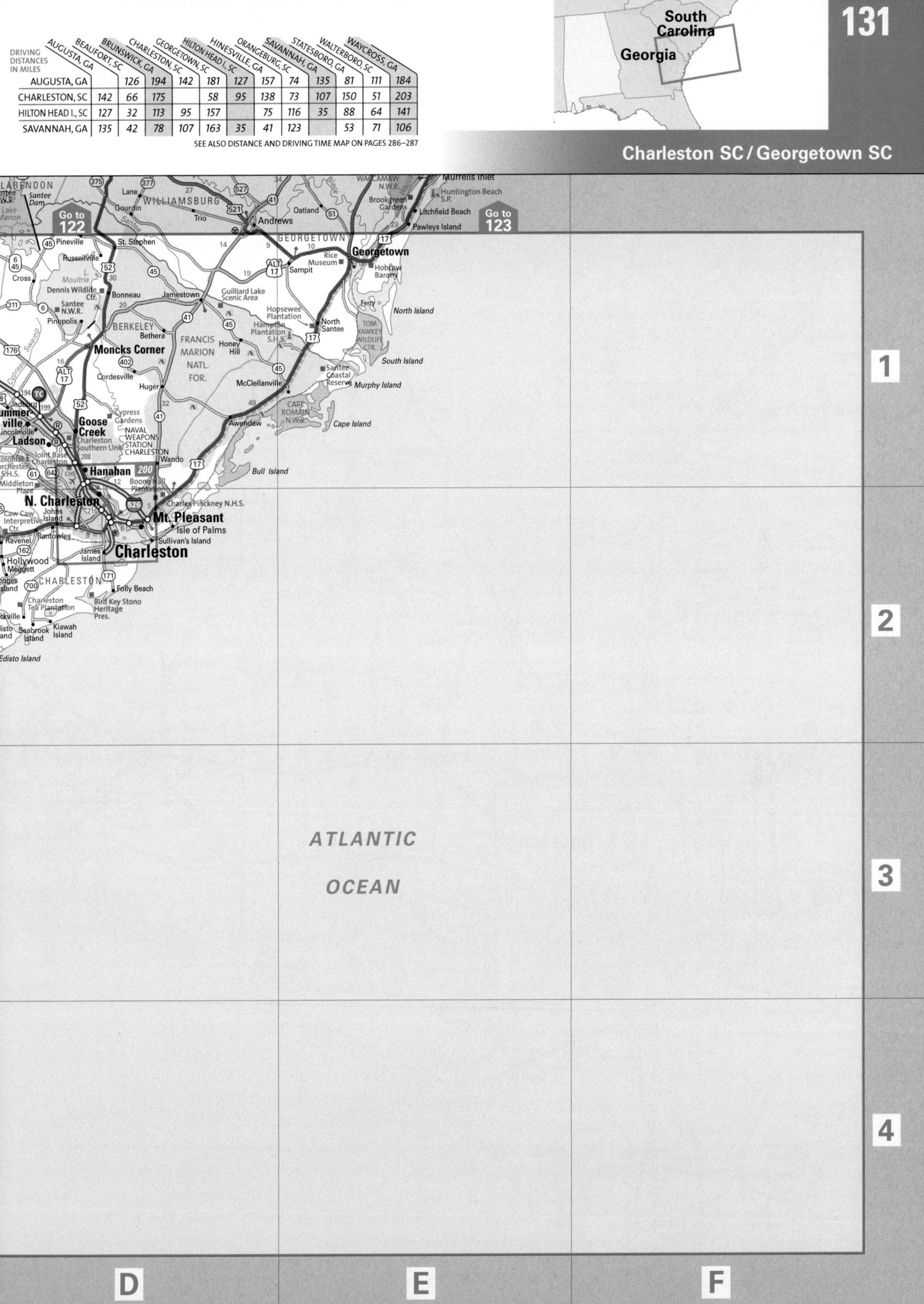

South Carolina

Georgia

DRIVING DISTANCES IN MILES	AUGUSTA, GA	BEAUFORT, SC	BRUNSWICK, GA	CHARLESTON, SC	GEORGETOWN, SC	HILTON HEAD I., SC	HINESVILLE, GA	ORANGEBURG, SC	SAVANNAH, GA	STATESBORO, GA	WALTERBORO, SC	WAYCROSS, GA
AUGUSTA, GA		126	194	142	181	127	157	74	135	81	111	184
CHARLESTON, SC	142	66	175		58	95	138	73	107	150	51	203
HILTON HEAD I., SC	127	32	113	95	157		75	116	35	88	64	141
SAVANNAH, GA	135	42	78	107	163	35	41	123		53	71	106

SEE ALSO DISTANCE AND DRIVING TIME MAP ON PAGES 286–287

Miss.

Texas

Louisiana

0 mi   10   20   30   40

0 km   10   20   30   40   50   60

One inch equals 18.4 miles
One centimeter equals 11.7 kilometers

Miss.

Texas

Louisiana

DRIVING DISTANCES IN MILES

	ALEXANDRIA, LA	BEAUMONT, TX	DE RIDDER, LA	FREEPORT, TX	GALVESTON, TX	HOUSTON, TX	HUNTSVILLE, TX	LAFAYETTE, LA	LAKE CHARLES, LA	LUFKIN, TX	OPELOUSAS, LA	PORT ARTHUR, TX
BEAUMONT, TX	157		82	143	75	84	84	157	133	57	112	144	18
HOUSTON, TX	241	84	166	61	53		75	217	141	121	228	93
LAFAYETTE, LA	87	133	119	276	208	217	290		76	216	27	130
LAKE CHARLES, LA	100	57	49	200	132	141	214	76		140	87	54

SEE ALSO DISTANCE AND DRIVING TIME MAP ON PAGES 286–287

Miss. Alabama

Louisiana Florida

0 mi 10 20 30 40
0 km 10 20 30 40 50 60
One inch equals 18.4 miles
One centimeter equals 11.7 kilometers

DRIVING DISTANCES IN MILES	BATON ROUGE, LA	BILOXI, MS	GULFPORT, MS	GULF SHORES, AL	HAMMOND, LA	HATTIESBURG, MS	HOUMA, LA	McCOMB, MS	MOBILE, AL	NEW ORLEANS, LA	PASCAGOULA, MS	PENSACOLA, FL
BATON ROUGE, LA		151	140	254	51	174	101	102	205	91	170	264
BILOXI, MS	151		12	110	106	82	148	161	61	93	20	120
MOBILE, AL	205	61	75	48	159	97	201	215		146	41	58
NEW ORLEANS, LA	91	93	81	195	57	115	57	111	146		112	205

SEE ALSO DISTANCE AND DRIVING TIME MAP ON PAGES 286–287

Alabama Georgia

Florida

0 mi   10   20   30   40
0 km 10   20   30   40   50   60
One inch equals 18.4 miles
One centimeter equals 11.7 kilometers

GULF OF MEXICO

A   B   C

1   2   3   4

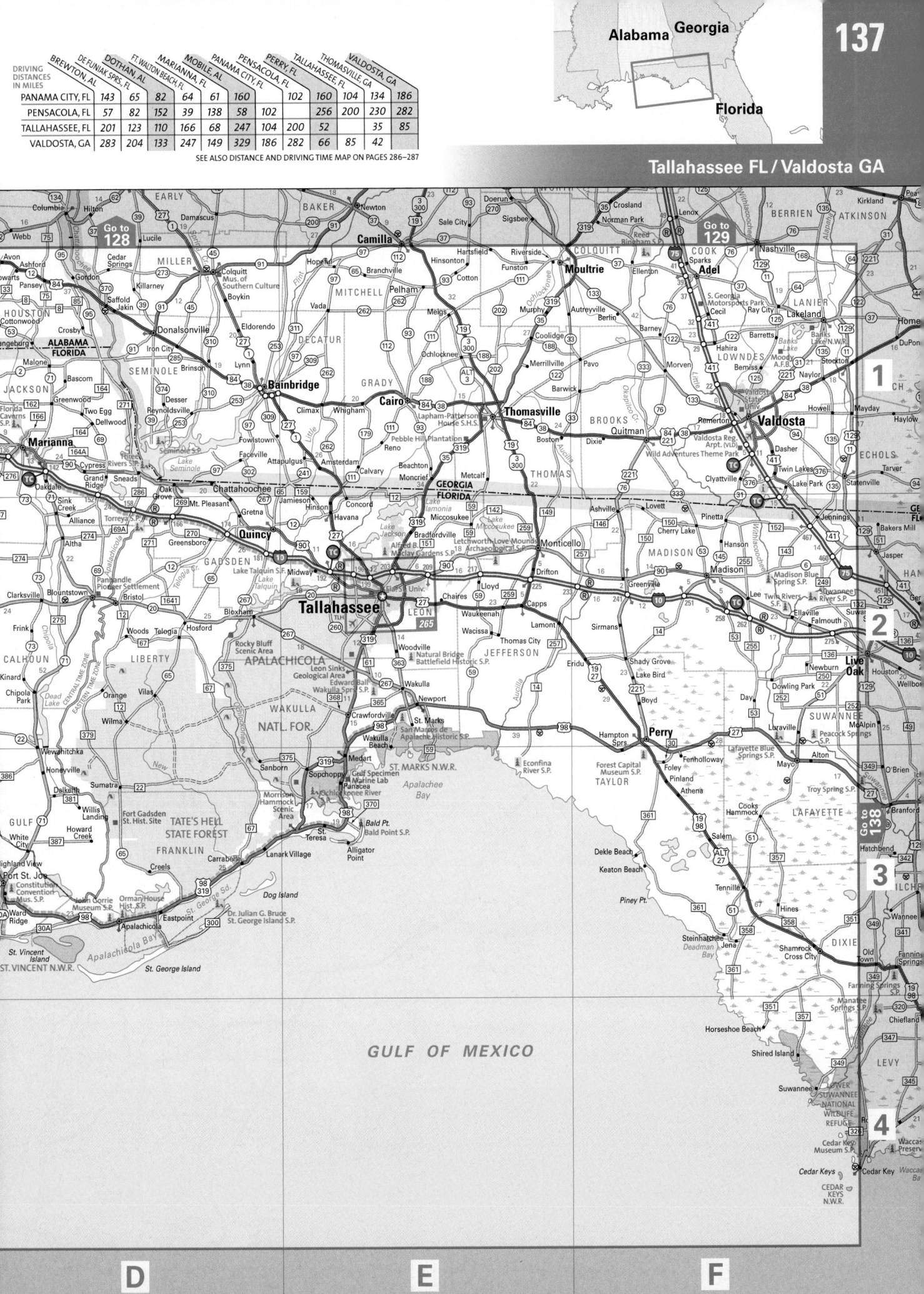

Alabama Georgia

Florida

DRIVING DISTANCES IN MILES

	BREWTON, AL	DE FUNIAK SPRS., AL	DOTHAN, AL	FT. WALTON BEACH, FL	MARIANNA, FL	MOBILE, AL	PANAMA CITY, FL	PENSACOLA, FL	PERRY, FL	TALLAHASSEE, FL	THOMASVILLE, GA	VALDOSTA, GA
PANAMA CITY, FL	143	65	82	64	61	160		102	160	104	134	186
PENSACOLA, FL	57	82	152	39	138	58	102		256	200	230	282
TALLAHASSEE, FL	201	123	110	166	68	247	104	200	52		35	85
VALDOSTA, GA	283	204	133	247	149	329	186	282	66	85	42	

SEE ALSO DISTANCE AND DRIVING TIME MAP ON PAGES 286–287

Georgia
Florida
0 mi 10 20 30 40
0 km 10 20 30 40 50 60
One inch equals 18.4 miles
One centimeter equals 11.7 kilometers
Go to 129
Go to 137
Go to 140
1
2
3
4
A
B
C
GULF
OF
MEXICO
GEORGIA
FLORIDA
Apalachee Bay
Camilla
Moultrie
Adel
Nashville
Waycross
Blackshear
Homerville
Valdosta
Thomasville
Cairo
Bainbridge
Quitman
Tallahassee
Monticello
Madison
Jasper
Live Oak
Lake City
Perry
Mayo
Branford
High Sprs.
Alachua
Gainesville
Starke
Waldo
Newberry
Trenton
Chiefland
Bronson
Williston
Ocala
Cedar Key
Crystal River
Hernando
Cross City
Steinhatchee
Crawfordville
Sopchoppy
Lake Butler
Macclenny
Olustee
Fargo
Okefenokee
Suwannee Canal Rec. Area
N.W.R.
Osceola N.F.
Lower Suwannee National Wildlife Refuge
Cedar Keys N.W.R.
St. Marks N.W.R.
Mitchell
Grady
Decatur
Thomas
Brooks
Lowndes
Lanier
Clinch
Ware
Charlton
Echols
Colquitt
Cook
Berrien
Atkinson
Gadsden
Leon
Jefferson
Madison
Hamilton
Columbia
Baker
Union
Bradford
Suwannee
Lafayette
Taylor
Dixie
Gilchrist
Alachua
Levy
Marion
Sumter

DRIVING DISTANCES IN MILES	BRUNSWICK, GA	DAYTONA BEACH, FL	GAINESVILLE, FL	JACKSONVILLE, FL	LAKE CITY, FL	OCALA, FL	PERRY, FL	ST. AUGUSTINE, FL	STARKE, FL	TALLAHASSEE, FL	VALDOSTA, GA	WAYCROSS, GA
DAYTONA BEACH, FL	160		99	91	154	77	225	53	92	258	209	173
JACKSONVILLE, FL	69	91	70		62	101	133	41	45	166	117	78
OCALA, FL	171	77	40	101	80		120	81	57	186	137	170
TALLAHASSEE, FL	235	258	152	166	109	186	52	207	145		85	146

SEE ALSO DISTANCE AND DRIVING TIME MAP ON PAGES 286–287

0 mi   10   20   30   40
0 km 10   20   30   40   50   60
One inch equals 18.4 miles
One centimeter equals 11.7 kilometers

GULF

OF

MEXICO

1

2

3

4

A   **B**   **C**

Go to 138

Go to 142

Yankeetown   Inglis
Crystal River Pres. S.P. & Archaeological S.P.
Crystal River N.W.R.
Crystal River
Homosassa Sprs.
Homosassa Springs Wildlife S.P.
Homosassa
Yulee Sugar Mill Ruins Historic S.P.
Homosassa Bay
Chassahowitzka
CHASSAHOWITZKA N.W.R.
HERNANDO
Bayport
Weeki Wachee Gardens
Weeki Wachee Springs S.P. and Buccaneer Bay
Hernando Beach
Weeki Wachee
Spring Hill
Aripeka
Hudson
Bayonet Point
Werner-Boyce Salt Springs S.P.
Jasmine Estates
Port Richey
New Port Richey
Anclote Key Preserve S.P.
Elfers
Holiday
Tarpon Sprs.
Palm Harbor
Honeymoon Island S.P.
Caladesi Island S.P.
Oldsmar
Dunedin
Clearwater
Safety Harbor
Bellair
Belleair Beach
Largo
Indian Rocks Beach
Seminole
Pinellas Park
Redington Beach
Madeira Beach
Treasure Island
South Pasadena
Gulfport
St. Pete Beach
St. Petersburg
Ruskin
Fort De Soto
Egmont Key S.P.
Palmetto
Anna Maria
Bradenton
Holmes Beach
Cortez
Bradenton Beach
Longboat Key
Whitfield
Sarasota
Ringling Mus. of Art
Siesta Key
Coral Cove
Vamo
Osprey
Oscar Scherer S.P.
Laurel
Nokomis
Venice
South Venice
Venice Gardens
North Port
Englewood
Englewood Beach
Grove City
Don Pedro Island S.P.
Placida
Gasparilla Island
Gasparilla Island S.P.
Boca Grande
Old Port Boca Grande Lighthouse
Cayo Costa S.P.
Pine Island N.W.R.
Bokeelia
Pinelang
Matlacha
Ft. Myers
Fort Myers
Punta Gorda
Port Charlotte
Charlotte Harbor
Cleveland
Solana
Harbour Heights
Murdock
Charlotte Harbor Pres. S.P.
Charlotte Harbor
Pirate Harbor
Babcock Wilderness Adventures
CHARLOTTE
DE SOTO
Arcadia
Nocatee
Ft. Ogden
Hull
Brownsville
Sandy
Old Myakka
Myakka City
MYAKKA RIVER S.P.
Pine Level
Solomon's Castle
Limestone
Gardner
Zolfo Sprs.
Wauchula
Ona
Griffins Corner
Bowling Green
Ft. Green
Duette
Paynes Creek Historic S.P.
HARDEE
Ft. Meade
POLK
Bowling Green
Homeland
Pembroke
Bartow
Alturas
Mulberry
Nichols
Highland City
Medulla
Plant City
Lakeland
Winter Haven
Auburndale
Polk City
Fantasy of Flight
Lake Alfred
Eagle Lake
Legoland Florida
Kathleen
Providence
Crystal Sprs.
Thonotosassa
Temple Terrace
Tampa
Brandon
Riverview
Gibsonton
Sun City Center
Wimauma
Balm
Picnic
Alafia River S.P.
Brewster
Baird
Little Manatee River St. Rec. Area
Parrish
Memphis
Lake Manatee S.P.
Verna
Oneco
Bee Ridge
Bradley Jct.
Pinecrest
Boyette
HILLSBOROUGH
MANATEE
SARASOTA
Plant City
Dover
Lutz
Land O' Lakes
Wesley Chapel
Zephyrhills
Crystal Sprs.
Denham
Betmar Acres
Lumberton
Dade City
Pasco
San Antonio
St. Leo Univ.
St. Leo
PASCO
Gower's Corner
San Antonio
Colt Creek S.P.
Berry
Eva
Withlacoochee
Blanton
Lacoochee
Trilby
Ridge Manor
Masaryktown
Spring Lake
Brooksville
Bushnell
Nobleton
Istachatta
Floral City
Inverness
Hernando
Beverly Hills
Holder
Dunnellon
Citrus Sprs.
CITRUS
WITHLACOOCHEE ST. FOR.
Lecanto
Floral City
Lake Panasoffkee
Sumterville
Coleman
SUMTER
Wildwood
Leesburg
Lady Lake
Tavares
Eustis
Clermont
Minneola
Groveland
Mascotte
Center Hill
Webster
Bushnell
Dade Battlefield Historic S.P.
Fla. Natl. Cem.
Howey-in-the-Hills
Yalaha
Astatula
Montverde
MARION
Ocklawaha
Belleview
Summerfield
Weirsdale
The Villages
Oxford
Lake Griffin S.P.
Fruitland Pk.
Eastlake Weir
Pedro
Candler
Ross Prairie State Forest
Marion Oaks
Springs S.P.
Florida Horse Park
FOREST
LEE

266

214

DRIVING DISTANCES IN MILES	FORT MYERS, FL	FORT PIERCE, FL	LAKELAND, FL	MELBOURNE, FL	OKEECHOBEE, FL	ORLANDO, FL	PUNTA GORDA, FL	ST. PETERSBURG, FL	SARASOTA, FL	TAMPA, FL	TITUSVILLE, FL	W. PALM BEACH, FL
FORT PIERCE, FL	126		122	57	36	120	127	197	150	172	95	57
ORLANDO, FL	155	120	56	72	108		131	107	130	82	40	169
SARASOTA, FL	74	150	85	190	114	130	50	35		60	170	184
TAMPA, FL	123	172	37	142	162	82	99	25	60		121	223

SEE ALSO DISTANCE AND DRIVING TIME MAP ON PAGES 286–287

0 mi | 10 | 20 | 30 | 40
0 km | 10 | 20 | 30 | 40 | 50 | 60
One inch equals 18.4 miles
One centimeter equals 11.7 kilometers

1

2

3

4

A **B** **C**

GULF

OF

MEXICO

Go to 140

Don Pedro Island S.P.
Gasparilla Island
Placida
Toll
771
775
Island Bay
Charlotte Harbor Pres. S.P.
Pirate Harbor
31
765
R
41
23
158
Babcock Wilderness Adventures
75
31

Gasparilla Island S.P.
Boca Grande
Old Port Boca Grande Lighthouse
Cayo Costa S.P.
Pine Island N.W.R.
Bokeelia
Pineland
Matlacha
N. Ft. Myers
Tice
765
78
143
Ft. Myers Shores
141
75

Captiva I.
Captiva
St. James City
Sanibel
Sanibel I.
767
767
Punta Rassa
Iona
Toll
869
San Carlos Park
Estero
Ft. Myers Beach
Lovers Key S.P.
865
41
Fort Myers
Cape Coral
Ft. Myers Villas
884
135
136
128
123
39
36
RSW
LEE
82
131
Everglade Wonder Gardens

214
Bonita Springs
116
865
75
84
111

Delnor-Wiggins Pass S.P.
Naples Park
Golden Gate
North Naples
Artis-Naples Philharmonic
Naples Zoo at Caribbean Gardens
Naples Municipal Arpt. (APF)
Naples
Naples Botanical Garden
E. Naples
Naples Manor
31
107
7
84
8
95
95

Marco Island
Marco Island
Marco I. Trolley Tours
Cape Romano

DRY TORTUGAS
NATL. PARK
Fort Jefferson

KEY WEST
N.W.R.
Marquesas Keys
Stock Island
Key West
EYW
Naval Air Station Key West
224
1

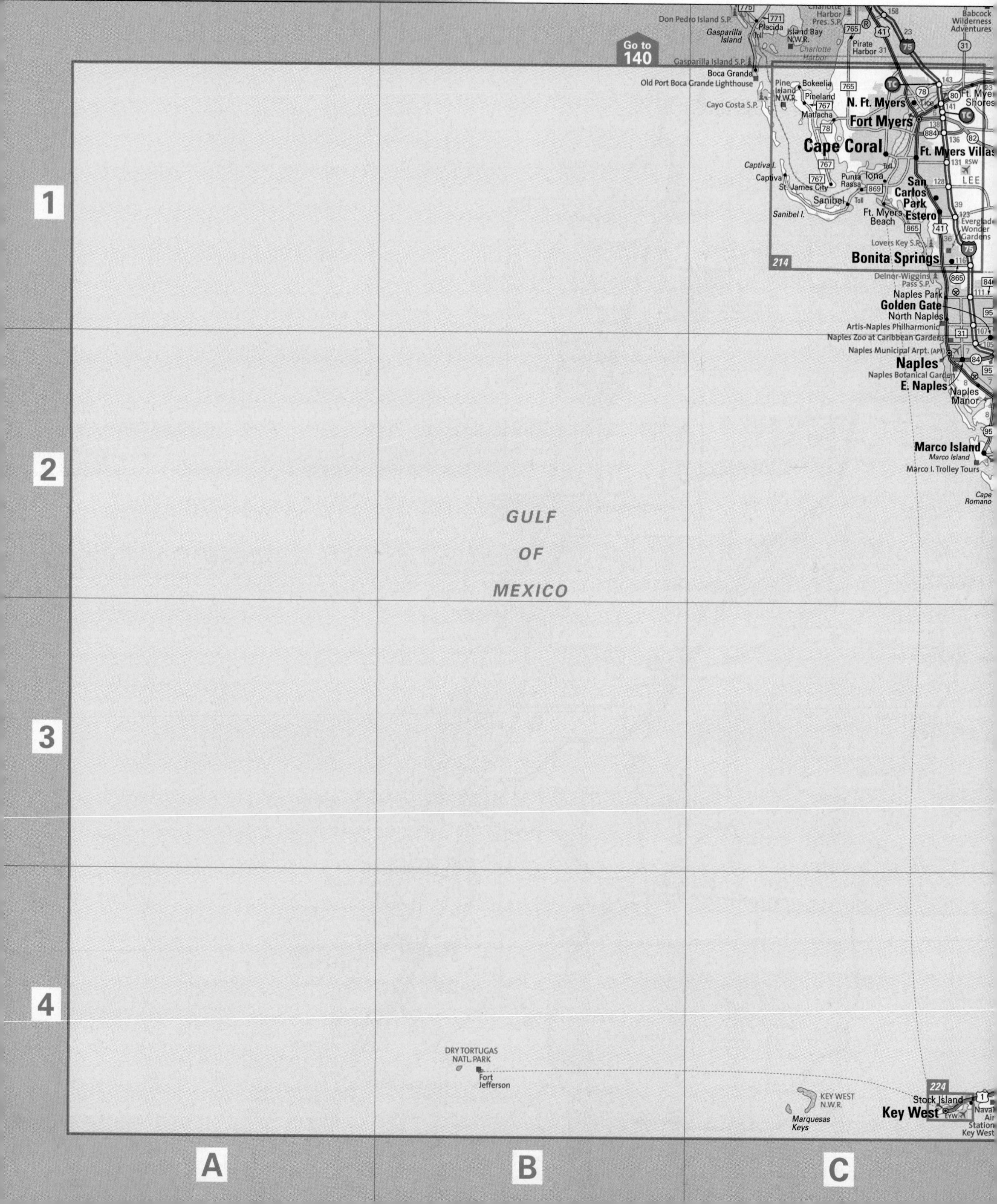

DRIVING DISTANCES IN MILES

	BELLE GLADE, FL	BOCA RATON, FL	FLAMINGO, FL	FORT LAUDERDALE, FL	FORT MYERS, FL	HOMESTEAD, FL	KEY LARGO, FL	KEY WEST, FL	MARATHON, FL	MIAMI, FL	NAPLES, FL	W. PALM BEACH, FL
FORT MYERS, FL	84	155	227	139		174	195	308	260	155	36	125
KEY WEST, FL	235	211	181	190	308	133	113		48	168	273	234
MIAMI, FL	83	44	87	23	155	34	55	168	120		121	67
W. PALM BEACH, FL	41	28	153	48	125	100	121	234	186	67	144	

SEE ALSO DISTANCE AND DRIVING TIME MAP ON PAGES 286–287

BONUS MAPS!

0 mi 5 10 15 20
0 km 5 10 15 20 25 30
One inch equals 9.85 miles
One centimeter equals 6.25 kilometers

Pa. New Jersey
W.Va. Md. Delaware
Virginia

DRIVING DISTANCES IN MILES	ANNAPOLIS, MD	BALTIMORE, MD	CAMBRIDGE, MD	DOVER, DE	ELKTON, MD	FREDERICK, MD	HAGERSTOWN, MD	LEESBURG, VA	MANASSAS, VA	REHOBOTH BEACH, DE	VINELAND, NJ	WASHINGTON, DC
BALTIMORE, MD	25		78	98	58	51	76	71	67	111	109	38
DOVER, DE	62	98	64		40	135	160	135	131	43	77	94
FREDERICK, MD	73	51	128	135	106		28	25	61	161	158	44
WASHINGTON, DC	31	38	87	94	94	44	70	38	31	120	145	

SEE ALSO DISTANCE AND DRIVING TIME MAP ON PAGES 286–287

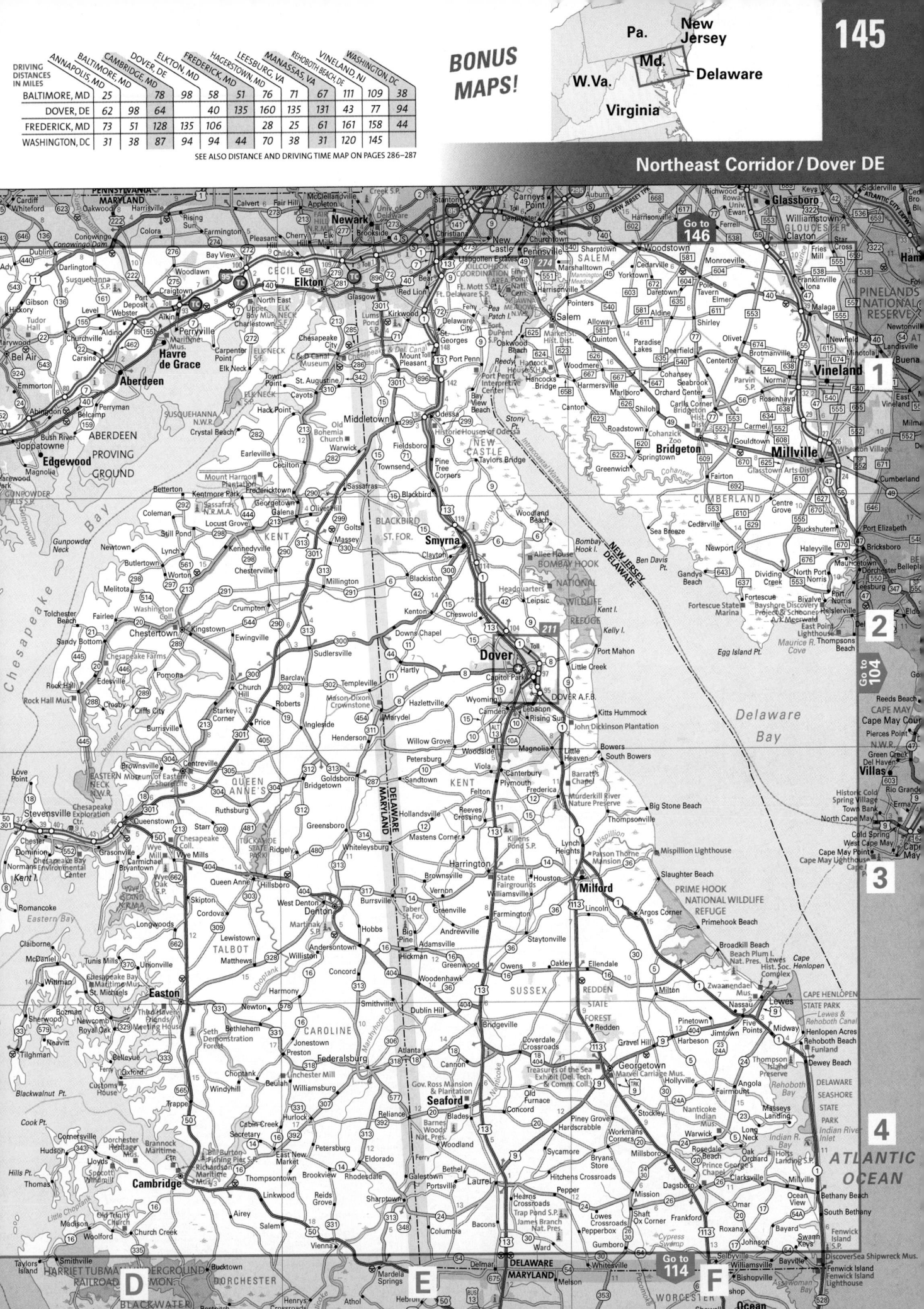

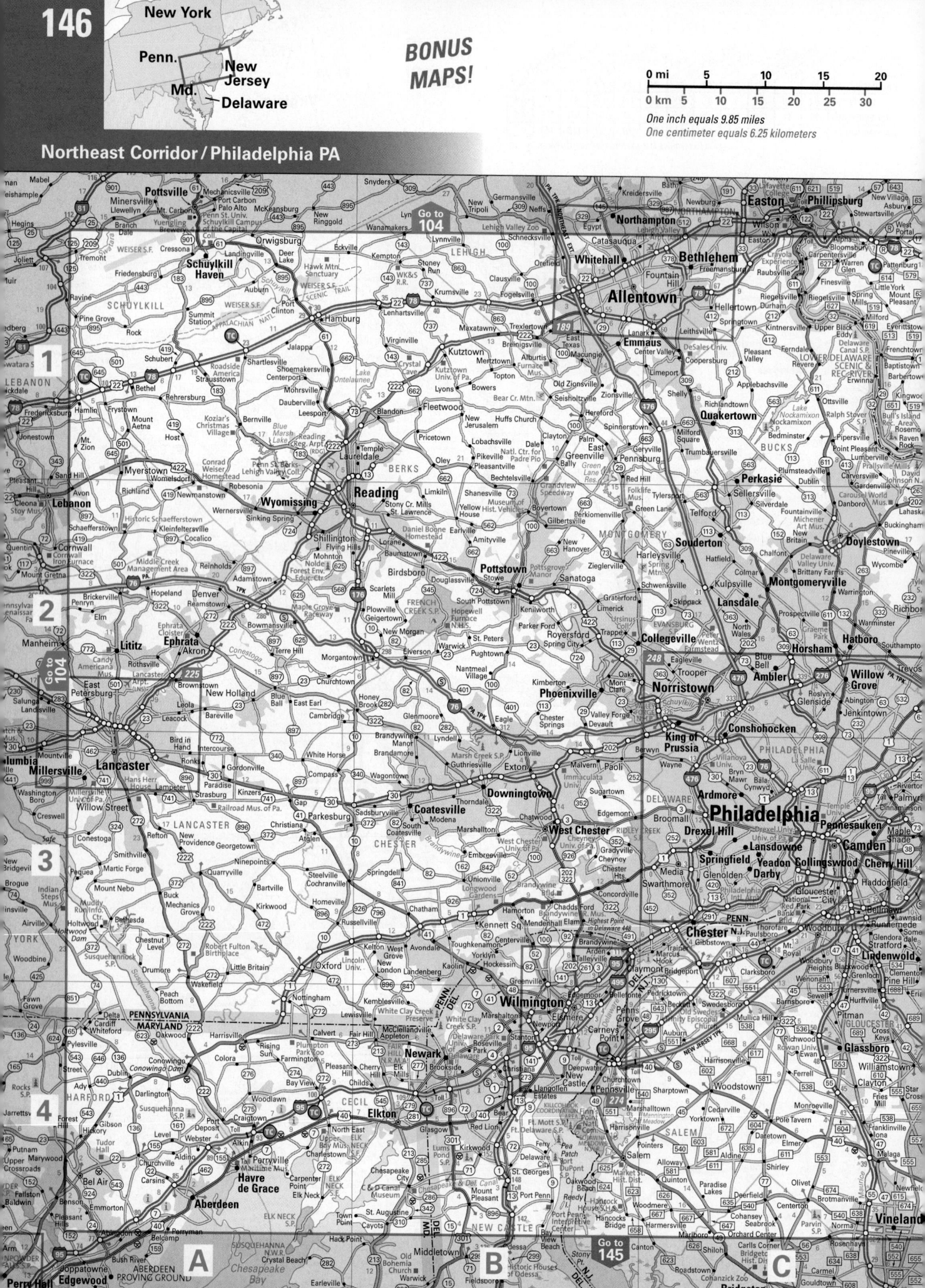

New York
Penn.
New Jersey
Md.
Delaware
BONUS MAPS!
Northeast Corridor / Philadelphia PA
0 mi 5 10 15 20
0 km 5 10 15 20 25 30
One inch equals 9.85 miles
One centimeter equals 6.25 kilometers
Go to 104
Go to 145

BONUS MAPS!

DRIVING DISTANCES IN MILES	ALLENTOWN, PA	ATLANTIC CITY, NJ	ELKTON, MD	LANCASTER, PA	LONG BRANCH, NJ	NEW BRUNSWICK, NJ	NEW YORK, NY	PHILADELPHIA, PA	READING, PA	TOMS RIVER, NJ	TRENTON, NJ	WILMINGTON, DE
NEW YORK, NY	84	125	137	165	55	34		91	118	75	55	120
PHILADELPHIA, PA	63	62	50	79	77	55	91		63	58	34	30
TRENTON, NJ	66	77	88	105	53	22	55	34	89	48		68
WILMINGTON, DE	77	86	20	53	106	90	120	30	56	85	68	

SEE ALSO DISTANCE AND DRIVING TIME MAP ON PAGES 286–287

New York
Penn.
New Jersey
Md.
Delaware
Go to 148
New York
Elizabeth
LONG ISLAND
Edison
New Brunswick
Perth Amboy
Trenton
Princeton
Long Branch
Asbury Park
Lakewood
Toms River
Point Pleasant
JOINT BASE MCGUIRE-DIX-LAKEHURST
PINELANDS NATIONAL RESERVE
ATLANTIC OCEAN
Atlantic City
Ocean City
Hammonton
FOR CONTINUATION SEE INSET AT RIGHT
Go to 105
1
2
3
4
D
E
F

New York
Rhode Island
Pa.
Conn.
New Jersey

BONUS MAPS!

0 mi 5 10 15 20
0 km 5 10 15 20 25 30
One inch equals 9.85 miles
One centimeter equals 6.25 kilometers

BONUS MAPS!

New York
Pa.
New Jersey
Rhode Island
Conn.

SEE ALSO DISTANCE AND DRIVING TIME MAP ON PAGES 286–287

DRIVING DISTANCES IN MILES	BRIDGEPORT, CT	DANBURY, CT	HARTFORD, CT	NEWARK, NJ	NEWBURGH, NY	NEW HAVEN, CT	NEW LONDON, CT	NEW YORK, NY	PATERSON, NJ	RIVERHEAD, NY	STAMFORD, CT	WATERBURY, CT
BRIDGEPORT, CT		31	56	69	73	19	64	60	77	115	21	33
NEWARK, NJ	69	79	125		66	88	134	11	18	88	48	108
NEW HAVEN, CT	19	35	39	88	78		46	78	89	133	40	30
NEW YORK, NY	60	69	115	11	56	78	124		16	78	38	99

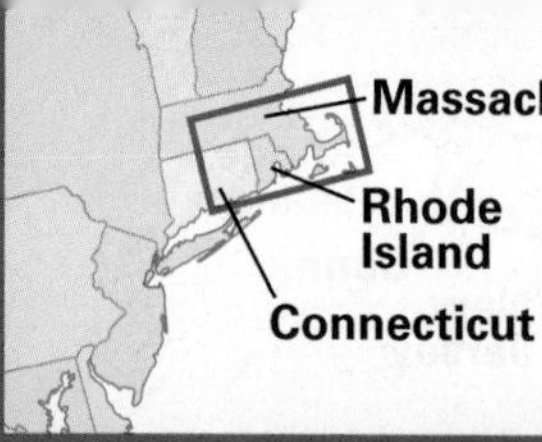

Massachusetts
Rhode Island
Connecticut

BONUS MAPS!

0 mi   5   10   15   20
0 km 5 10 15 20 25 30
One inch equals 9.85 miles
One centimeter equals 6.25 kilometers

Northeast Corridor / Hartford CT

Go to 94
Go to 95
Go to 94
Go to 149

BONUS MAPS!

Massachusetts
Rhode Island
Connecticut

DRIVING DISTANCES IN MILES	BOSTON, MA	GLOUCESTER, MA	HARTFORD, CT	HYANNIS, MA	NEW BEDFORD, MA	NEW LONDON, CT	NEWPORT, RI	PLYMOUTH, MA	PROVIDENCE, RI	SPRINGFIELD, MA	WORCESTER, MA
BOSTON, MA		35	102	72	60	109	73	41	52	117	95	46
HARTFORD, CT	102	136		155	104	46	85	127	73	200	25	62
PROVIDENCE, RI	52	92	73	71	33	58	33	41		117	75	43
SPRINGFIELD, MA	95	129	25	148	127	71	111	120	75	193		55

SEE ALSO DISTANCE AND DRIVING TIME MAP ON PAGES 286–287

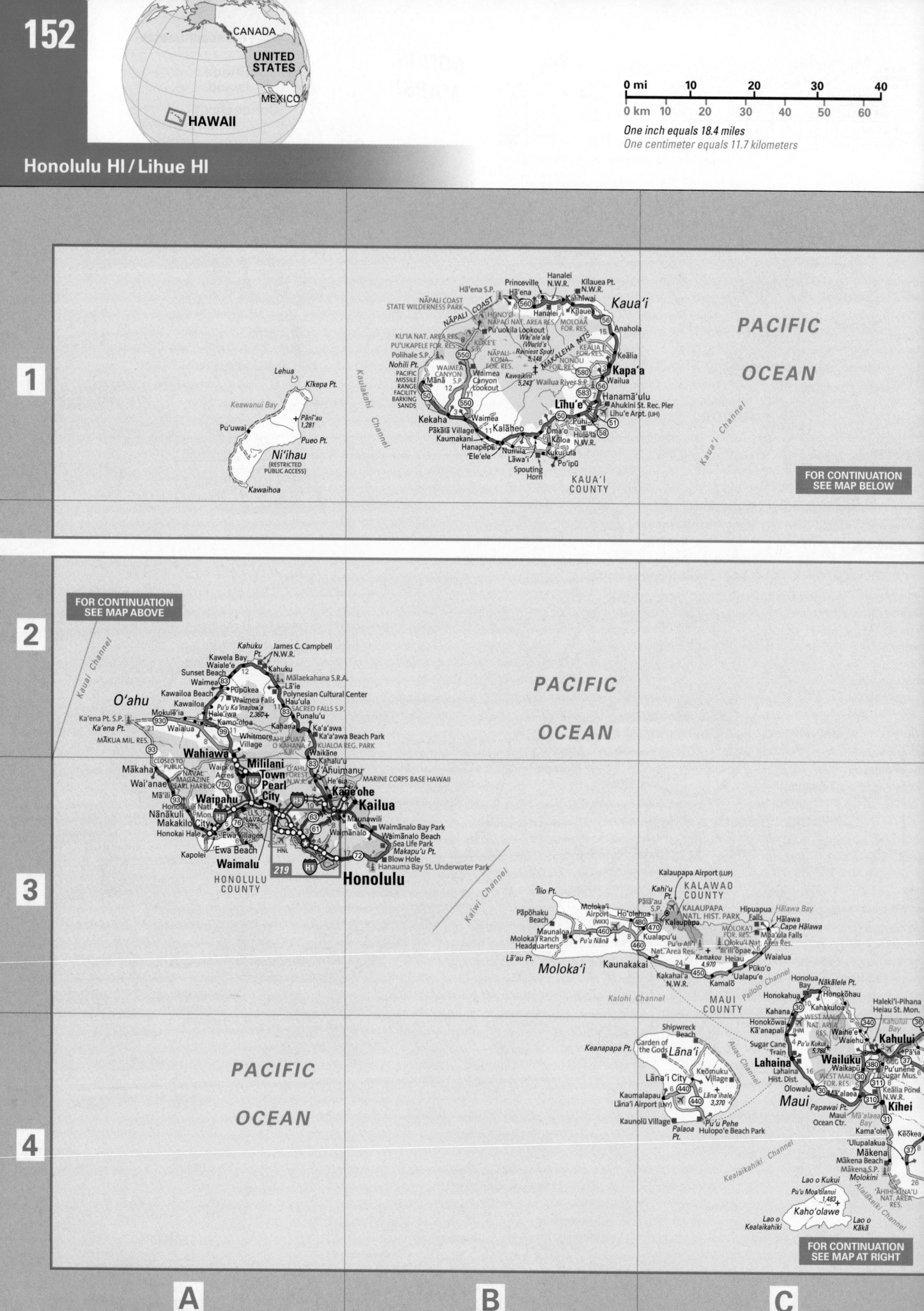

CANADA
UNITED STATES
MEXICO
HAWAII

0 mi   10   20   30   40
0 km 10   20   30   40   50   60
One inch equals 18.4 miles
One centimeter equals 11.7 kilometers

1

Lehua

Kīkepa Pt.

Keawanui Bay

Puʻuwai
+ Pānīʻau
1,281
Pueo Pt.

Niʻihau
(RESTRICTED PUBLIC ACCESS)

Kawaihoa

Kaulakahi Channel

NĀPALI COAST
STATE WILDERNESS PARK

NĀPALI NAT. AREA RES.
KUʻIA NAT. AREA RES.
PUʻUKAPELE FOR. RES.
Polihale S.P.
Nohili Pt.
PACIFIC MISSILE RANGE FACILITY BARKING SANDS

HONOʻO
Puʻuokila Lookout
KOKEʻE
Waiʻaleʻale (World's Rainiest Spot) 5,148
Kawaikini 5,243
WAIMEA CANYON S.P.
Waimea Canyon Lookout
Mānā
Kekaha
Pākālā Village
Kaumakani
Hanapēpē
ʻEleʻele
Numila
Lāwaʻi
Spouting Horn
Waimea
Kalāheo
Ōmaʻo
Kōloa
Poʻipū
Kukuiʻula

Hāʻena S.P.
Hāʻena
Princeville
Hanalei N.W.R.
Hanalei
Kīlauea Pt. N.W.R.
Kīlauea
Kalihiwai
Kīlauei

Kauaʻi

MOLOAʻA FOR. RES.
Anahola
Keālia
NONOU FOR. RES.
MAKALEHA MTS.
KEALIA FOR. RES.
Wailua River S.P.
Wailua
Kapaʻa
Hanamāʻulu
Ahukini St. Rec. Pier
Līhuʻe
Līhuʻe Arpt. (LIH)
Puhi
HULĒʻIA N.W.R.

PACIFIC OCEAN

Kauaʻi Channel

KAUAʻI COUNTY

FOR CONTINUATION
SEE MAP BELOW

2

FOR CONTINUATION
SEE MAP ABOVE

Kauai Channel

Oʻahu

Kaʻena Pt. S.P.
Kaʻena Pt.
MĀKUA MIL. RES.
Mokulēʻia
Waialua

Mākaha
Waiʻanae
Māʻili
Nānākuli
Makakilo City
Honokai Hale
Kapolei

Kahuku Pt.
Kawela Bay
Waialeʻe
Sunset Beach
Waimea
Kawailoa Beach
Kawailoa
Haleʻiwa
Kamoʻoloa
Whitmore Village
Wahiawā
Mililani Town
Waipiʻo Acres
NAVAL MAGAZINE PEARL HARBOR
Pearl City
Waipahu
Honolulu Intl.
Mon.
NAVAL RES.
Ewa Villages
Ewa Beach
Waimalu
HONOLULU COUNTY

James C. Campbell N.W.R.
Kahuku
Mālaekahana S.R.A.
Lāʻie
Polynesian Cultural Center
Pūpūkea
Hauʻula
Puʻu Kaʻinapuaʻa 2,360
SACRED FALLS S.P.
Punaluʻu
Kahana
AHUPUAʻA O KAHANA S.P.
Kaʻaʻawa
Kaʻaʻawa Beach Park
Waikāne
KUALOA REG. PARK
Kahaluʻu
Kāneʻohe
ʻAhuimanu
Heʻeia
MARINE CORPS BASE HAWAII
Kailua
Maunawili
Waimānalo
Waimānalo Bay Park
Waimānalo Beach
Sea Life Park
Makapuʻu Pt.
Blow Hole
Hanauma Bay St. Underwater Park

Honolulu

PACIFIC OCEAN

3

Kaiwi Channel

ʻĪlio Pt.
Pāpōhaku Beach
Maunaloa
Molokaʻi Ranch Headquarters
Lāʻau Pt.

Kalaupapa Airport (LUP)
Kahiʻu Pt.
Hoʻolehua
PSIʻaʻu S.P.
KALAUPAPA NATL. HIST. PARK
Kalaupapa
Kualapuʻu
Puʻu Nānā
Kaunakakai
Kakahaiʻa N.W.R.
Kamalō

KALAWAO COUNTY
Hīpuapua Falls
Hālawa Bay
Moaʻula Falls
Hālawa
Cape Hālawa
ʻĪliʻiliʻōpae
ʻUalu Nat. Area Res.
Puʻu Aliʻi Nat. Area Res.
Kamakou Heiau 4,970
Waialua
Pūkoʻo
ʻUalapuʻe

Molokaʻi

Kalohi Channel

MAUI COUNTY

PACIFIC OCEAN

Shipwreck Beach
Keanapapa Pt.
Garden of the Gods
Lānaʻi
Keōmuku Village
Keōmuku
Kaumalapau
Lānaʻi City
Lānaʻi Airport (LNY)
Kaunolū Village
Palaoa Pt.
Puʻu Pehe
Hulopoʻe Beach Park
Lānaʻihale 3,370

Auau Channel

Honokōwai
Kāʻanapali
Sugar Cane Train
Lahaina
Lahaina Hist. Dist.
Olowalu
Māʻalaea
Papawai Pt.
Maui Ocean Ctr.

Honolua Bay
Nākālele Pt.
Honokōhau
Honokahua
Kahana
Honokōhau
WEST MAUI NAT. AREA RES.
Puʻu Kukui 5,788
WEST MAUI FOR. RES.
Waiheʻe
Waiheʻe
Wailuku
Waikapū
Kahului
Pāʻia
OGG
Puʻunēnē
Puʻunēnē Sugar Mus.
Keālia Pond N.W.R.
Kihei
Kamaʻole
Haleki'i-Pihana Heiau St. Mon.
Kahului Bay

Maui

Māʻalaea Bay

4

PACIFIC OCEAN

Kealaikahiki Channel

Alalākeiki Channel

Lao o Kukui
Puʻu Moaʻulanui 1,483
Lao o Kealaikahiki
Lao o Kākā
Kahoʻolawe
Molokini
ʻAHIHI-KINAʻU NAT. AREA RES.
Keōkea
Mākena
Mākena Beach
Mākena S.P.
ʻUlupalakua

FOR CONTINUATION
SEE MAP AT RIGHT

A   B   C

DRIVING DISTANCES IN MILES	HĀNA	HILO	HONOLULU	HO'OLEHUA	KAHULUI	KAILUA	KAILUA-KONA	LAHAINA	LANAI CITY	LIHUE	WAHIAWĀ	WAIMEA
HILO	149*		217*	169*	121*	235*	88	142*	155*	319*	234*	54
HONOLULU	129*	217*		54*	101*	14	185*	92*	74*	102*	23	172*
KAHULUI	42	121*	101*	76*		119*	109*	23	57*	202*	118*	79*
LIHUE	230*	319*	102*	156*	202*	120*	285*	225*	176*		119*	174*

*DISTANCE INCLUDES AIR TRAVEL

SEE ALSO DISTANCE AND DRIVING TIME MAP ON PAGES 286–287

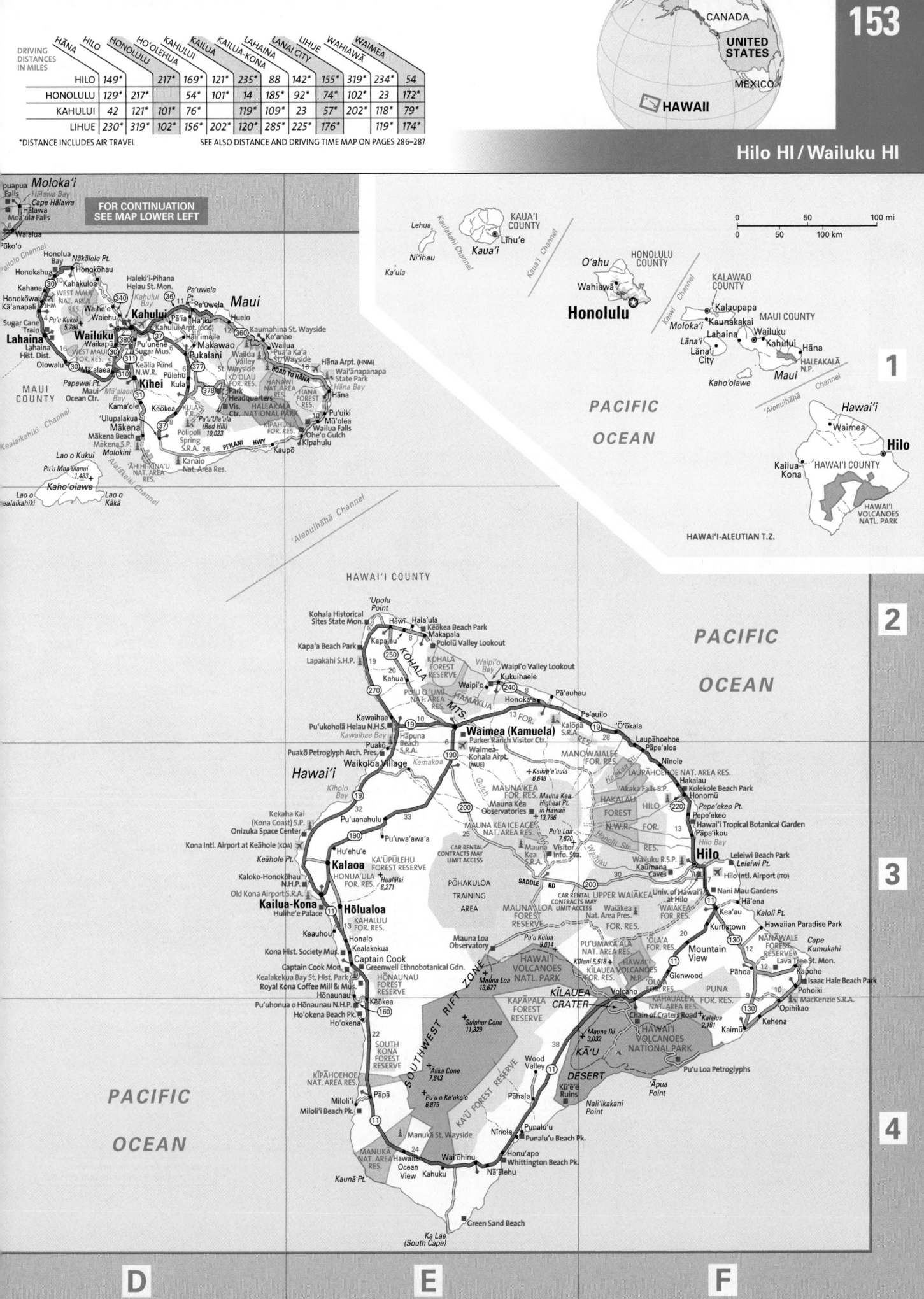

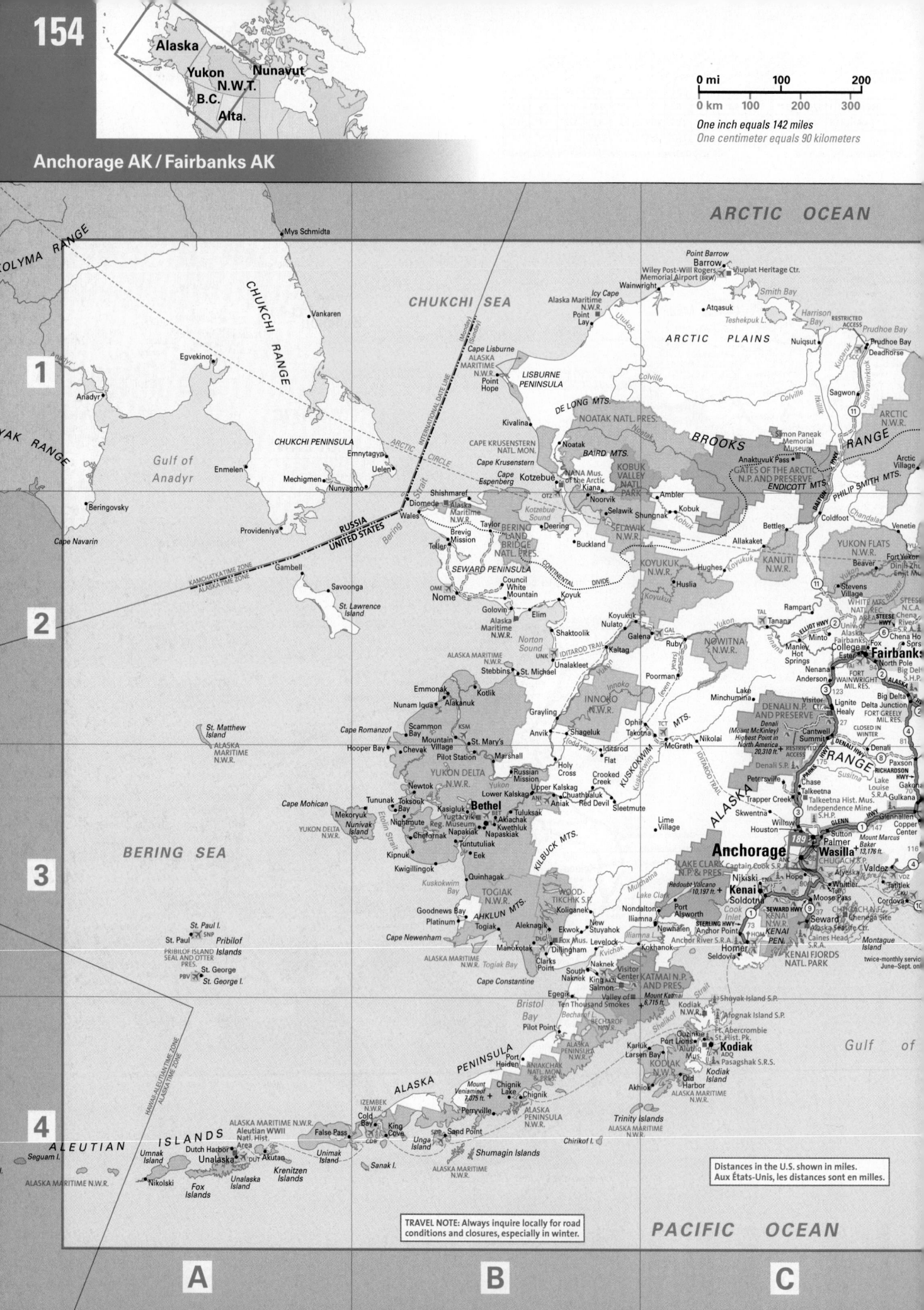

Alaska

Yukon   Nunavut
N.W.T.
B.C.
Alta.

0 mi   100   200
0 km   100   200   300
One inch equals 142 miles
One centimeter equals 90 kilometers

ARCTIC OCEAN

KOLYMA RANGE

CHUKCHI SEA

Point Barrow
Barrow
Wiley Post-Will Rogers   Iñupiat Heritage Ctr.
Memorial Airport (BRW)

Icy Cape   Alaska Maritime   Atqasuk   Teshekpuk L.   Harrison   RESTRICTED
Wainwright   N.W.R.   Smith Bay   Bay   ACCESS
Point   Prudhoe Bay
Lay   Nuiqsut   Deadhorse

Mys Schmidta   ARCTIC PLAINS   Sagwon

CHUKCHI RANGE   Vankaren   Colville

Cape Lisburne   Colville
Egvekinot   ALASKA   LISBURNE   DE LONG MTS.   BROOKS   11
Emnytagyn   MARITIME   PENINSULA   NOATAK NATL. PRES.   RANGE   Arctic
N.W.R.   Simon Paneak   Village
Anadyr   Point   Noatak   BAIRD MTS.   Memorial Museum   ARCTIC
Hope   Anaktuvuk Pass   N.W.R.

YAK RANGE   Kivalina   NANA Mus.   KOBUK   GATES OF THE ARCTIC   PHILIP SMITH MTS.
of the Arctic   VALLEY   N.P. AND PRESERVE
CHUKCHI PENINSULA   Cape Krusenstern   Kiana   NATL   ENDICOTT MTS.
Uelen   CAPE KRUSENSTERN   Kotzebue   PARK   Bettles
NATL. MON.   Noorvik   Ambler   Coldfoot   Venetie
Gulf of   Mechigmen   Cape   Selawik   Shungnak   Kobuk   Chandalar
Anadyr   Enmelen   Espenberg   OTZ   SELAWIK   Allakaket   YUKON FLATS
Emmelen   Kotzebue   N.W.R.   KANUTI   N.W.R.
Beringovsky   Shishmaref   Sound   Deering   KOYUKUK   Hughes   N.W.R.   Fort Yukon
Nunyamo   Diomede   Wales   Buckland   N.W.R.   Beaver   Dinjii Zhu
Cape Navarin   Alaska   Taylor   BERING   Huslia   Enit NCA
Maritime   Brevig   LAND   Koyuk   Stevens
RUSSIA   N.W.R.   Mission   BRIDGE   CONTINENTAL   Village   11
Providentiya   UNITED STATES   Teller   NATL. PRES.   Koyukuk   Rampart   WHITE
Nulato   MTS   NCA
KAMCHATKA TIME ZONE   SEWARD PENINSULA   DIVIDE   Galena   Tanana   STEESE
ALASKA TIME ZONE   OME   Council   NOWITNA   Minto   NATL. REC. Chena Ho
Gambell   White   N.W.R.   Manley   ELLIOT HWY   Spr
Savoonga   Nome   Mountain   Koyuk   Ruby   Hot   2   Alaska-   Chena Ho
St. Lawrence   Golovin   Springs   ELY   Fairbanks   Spr
Island   Elim   IDITAROD TRAIL   Poorman   Lake   Ester   College   Fox   Fairbanks
Shaktoolik   Minchumina   Nenana   North Pole   Big Del
St. Matthew   UNK   Anderson   FORT   2   ALASKA HWY
Island   Kaltag   WAINWRIGHT   Big Delta
Emmonak   Norton   Stebbins   123   MIL. RES.   Delta Junction
ALASKA   Nunam Iqua   Kotlik   Sound   Ophir   DENALI N.P.   Lignite   FORT GREELY
MARITIME   Alakanuk   St. Michael   Grayling   AND PRESERVE   Healy   MIL. RES.
N.W.R.   Scammon   KSM   Anvik   Shageluk   Takotna   Denali   Cantwell   Denali
Cape Romanzof   Bay   Mountain   Nikolai   (Mount McKinley)   Summit   4
Hooper Bay   Chevak   Village   St. Mary's   McGrath   Highest Point in   CLOSED IN
Pilot Station   IDITAROD TRAIL   North America   RESTRICTED   8   Paxson
Marshall   Iditarod   20,310 ft.   ACCESS   RANGE   RICHARDSON
YUKON DELTA   Holy   Flat   Denali S.P.   ALASKA   Gakona   HWY
N.W.R.   Russian   Cross   Crooked   KUSKOKWIM   Petersville   Gulkana
Mission   Creek   MTS.   Chase   Lake   Copper
Newtok   Upper Kalskag   Nikolai   Talkeetna   Louise   Center
Cape Mohican   Tununak   Lower Kalskag   ANI   Red Devil   Talkeetna Hist. Mus.   S.R.A.   147
Mekoryuk   Toksook   Chuathbaluk   Sleetmute   Independence Mine   GLENN
Nunivak   Bay   Kasigluk   BET   Aniak   S.H.P.   HWY   116
Island   Nightmute   Yugtarvik   Akiachak   Skwentna   Sutton   Mount Marcus
Bethel   Kwethluk   Lime   Willow   189   Palmer   Baker
YUKON DELTA   Chefornak   Reg. Museum   Napakiak   Tuluksak   Village   Houston   Wasilla   13,176 ft.
N.W.R.   Napaskiak   Anchorage   CHUGACH
Tuntutuliak   Eek   KILBUCK MTS.   LAKE CLARK   Palmer   MTS.
BERING SEA   Kipnuk   Redoubt Volcano   N.P. & PRES.   Niklski   Hope   Valdez
Kwigillingok   10,197 ft.   Captain Cook S.R.A.   Whittier   Tatitlek   VDZ
Quinhagak   Kenai   Moose Pass   CHUGACH N.F.   Cordova
St. Paul I.   WOOD-   Soldotna   37   CKU
St. Paul   SNP   TIKCHIK S.P.   Nondalton   Port   Seward   Alaska Sealife Ctr.
Pribilof   Goodnews Bay   Iliamna   Alsworth   STERLING HWY   SEWARD HWY   9
PRIBILOF ISLAND   Islands   Platinum   AHKLUN MTS.   New   Anchor Point   73   KENAI   Seward
SEAL AND OTTER   Togiak   Aleknagik   Stuyahok   Iliamna L.   KENAI   PEN.   KENAI FJORDS
PRES.   PBV   St. George   Manokotak   Ekwok   Kvichak   Homer   N.W.R.   Caines Head   NATL. PARK
St. George I.   TOGIAK   Dillingham   Newhalen   Anchor River   S.R.A.
N.W.R.   Clarks   Kohkanok   Seldovia   Montague
Point   South   Island
Cape Newenham   Naknek   twice-monthly service
Cape Constantine   Egegik   King   Visitor   June–Sept. only
Salmon   Center   KATMAI N.P.
Bristol   Ten Thousand   Valley of   AND PRES.   Shuyak Island S.P.
Bay   Smokes   Mount Katmai   Kodiak
Pilot Point   Becharof   6,715 ft.   N.W.R.   Afognak Island S.P.
BECHAROF   Ouzinkie   Ft. Abercrombie
Port   N.W.R.   Port Lions   St. Hist. Pk.
Heiden   ALASKA   Alutiiq   Kodiak
PENINSULA   Karluk   Mus.   ADQ
ALASKA   NATL. MON.   Larsen Bay   Pasagshak S.R.S.
Mount   & PRES.   KODIAK   Kodiak
Veniaminof   Chignik   Akhiok   Old   Island
IZEMBEK   7,075 ft.   Lake   Harbor   ALASKA MARITIME
N.W.R.   Chignik   N.W.R.
Cold   Perryville
Bay   King   ALASKA   Gulf of
Cove   PENINSULA
False Pass   Sand Point   N.W.R.   Trinity Islands
CDB   Unga   Chirikof I.   ALASKA MARITIME
Island   N.W.R.
ALEUTIAN   ISLANDS   Shumagin Islands   Distances in the U.S. shown in miles.
Seguam I.   Umnak   Dutch Harbor   Unimak Island   Sanak I.   Aux États-Unis, les distances sont en milles.
Island   Akutan
Nikolski   Unalaska   DUT   Krenitzen
Fox   Unalaska   Islands
Islands   Island
ALASKA MARITIME N.W.R.   TRAVEL NOTE: Always inquire locally for road   PACIFIC OCEAN
conditions and closures, especially in winter.

A   B   C

DRIVING DISTANCES IN MILES	ANCHORAGE, AK	DAWSON CREEK, BC	DENALI NP, AK	FAIRBANKS, AK	HOMER, AK	JUNEAU, AK	PRINCE GEORGE, BC	PRINCE RUPERT, BC	SKAGWAY, AK	TOK, AK	WHITEHORSE, YT	YELLOWKNIFE, NT
ANCHORAGE, AK		1516	275	378	225	841*	1679	1514	807	323	697	1844
DAWSON CREEK, BC	1516		1503	1400	1740	963*	224	625	862	1193	819	741
FAIRBANKS, AK	378	1400	103		603	726*	1564	1398	691	207	581	1729
WHITEHORSE, YT	697	819	684	581	921	211*	982	817	110	374		1147

*DISTANCE INCLUDES FERRY TRAVEL

SEE ALSO DISTANCE AND DRIVING TIME MAP ON PAGES 286–287

Distances in Canada shown in kilometers.
Au Canada, les distances sont en kilomètres.

The Alaska Marine Highway—with ferry service to
30 communities in Alaska, plus Bellingham WA and
Prince Rupert BC—is an All-American Road

Alaska

British Columbia Alberta

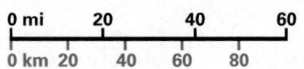

One inch equals 40.3 miles/Un pouce équivaut à 40.3 milles
One centimeter equals 25.4 km/Un cm équivaut à 25.4 km

Distances in Canada shown in kilometers.
Au Canada, les distances sont en kilomètres.

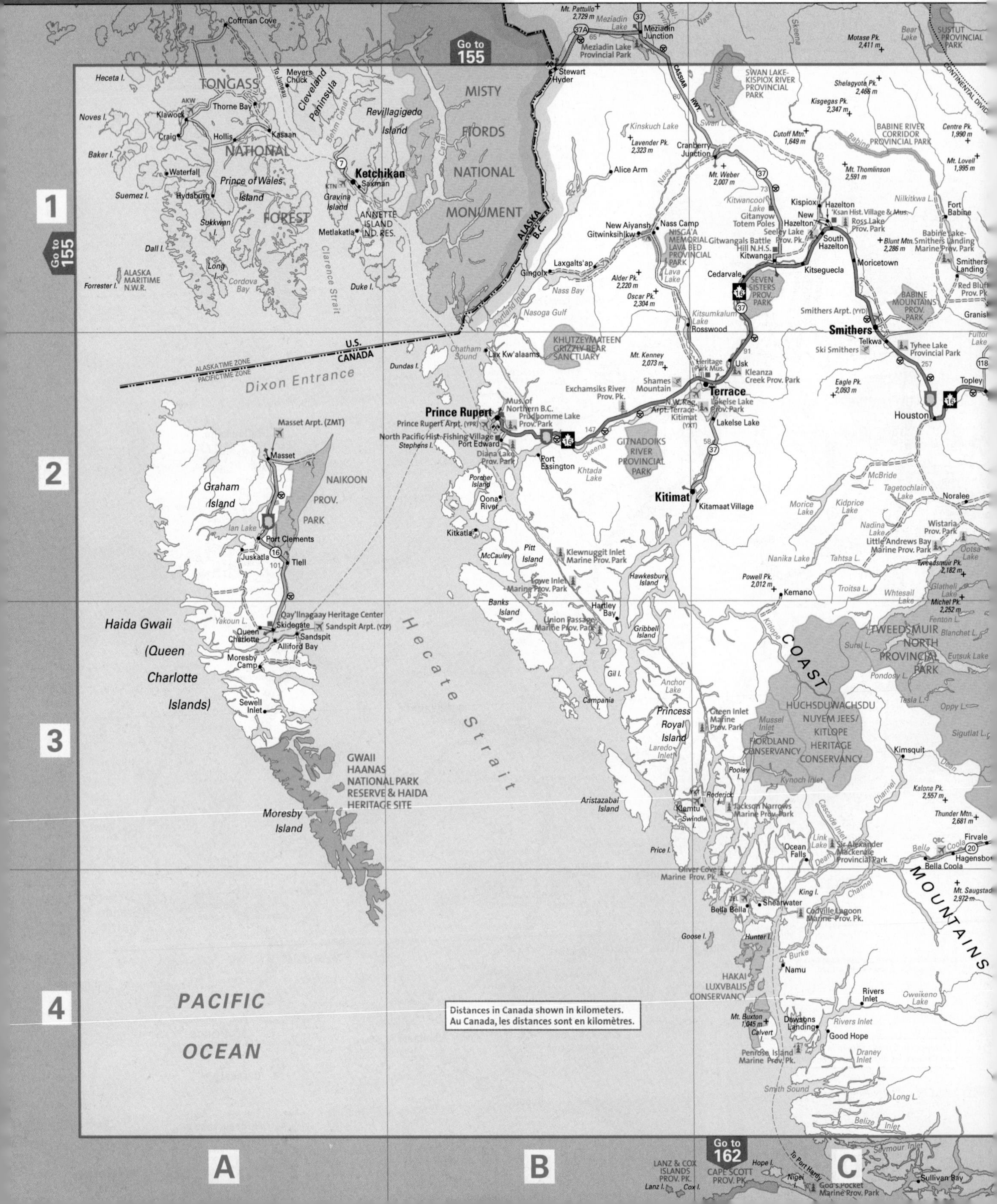

DRIVING DISTANCES IN KM / DISTANCES ROUTIÈRES EN KM

	DAWSON CREEK, BC	GRANDE PRAIRIE, AB	KAMLOOPS, BC	KITIMAT, BC	100 MILE HOUSE, BC	PRINCE GEORGE, BC	PRINCE RUPERT, BC	SMITHERS, BC	STEWART, BC	TERRACE, BC	VALEMOUNT, BC	WILLIAMS LAKE, BC
DAWSON CREEK, BC		124	931	1041	734	406	1130	777	1109	983	642	644
PRINCE GEORGE, BC	406	530	525	635	328		724	371	703	577	295	238
PRINCE RUPERT, BC	1130	1254	1249	205	1052	724		353	463	147	1019	962
WILLIAMS LAKE, BC	644	768	287	873	90	238	962	609	941	815	332	

SEE ALSO DISTANCE AND DRIVING TIME MAP ON PAGES 286–287 / VOIR AUSSI CARTE DES DISTANCES ET DES TEMPS DE PARCOURS PAGES 286–287

British Columbia — Alaska — Alberta

British Columbia · Alberta · Sask.

Go to 155
Go to 155
Go to 157
Go to 164

0 mi 20 40 60
0 km 20 40 60 80
One inch equals 40.3 miles/Un pouce équivaut à 40.3 milles
One centimeter equals 25.4 km/Un cm équivaut à 25.4 km

DRIVING DISTANCES IN KM / DISTANCES ROUTIÈRES EN KM	DAWSON CREEK, BC	EDMONTON, AB	FORT McMURRAY, AB	GRANDE PRAIRIE, AB	JASPER, AB	LLOYDMINSTER, AB/SK	MEADOW LAKE, SK	N. BATTLEFORD, SK	PEACE RIVER, AB	SLAVE LAKE, AB	VALEMOUNT, BC	WHITECOURT, AB
EDMONTON, AB	597		439	462	367	238	415	375	484	251	488	177
GRANDE PRAIRIE, AB	124	462	756		397	700	824	837	197	318	518	279
JASPER, AB	521	367	796	397		605	782	742	578	464	121	271
N. BATTLEFORD, SK	972	375	814	837	742	137	158		866	633	863	559

0 mi   20   40   60

0 km 20   40   60   80

One inch equals 40.3 miles/Un pouce équivaut à 40.3 milles
One centimeter equals 25.4 km/Un cm équivaut à 25.4 km

Alberta Sask. Manitoba Ontario

SEE ALSO DISTANCE AND DRIVING TIME MAP ON PAGES 286–287 / VOIR AUSSI CARTE DES DISTANCES ET DES TEMPS DE PARCOURS PAGES 286–287

DRIVING DISTANCES IN KM / DISTANCES ROUTIÈRES EN KM

	FLIN FLON, MB	GILLAM, MB	GRAND RAPIDS, MB	LA LOCHE, SK	LA RONGE, SK	LYNN LAKE, MB	MEADOW LAKE, SK	NIPAWIN, SK	N. BATTLEFORD, SK	PRINCE ALBERT, SK	THE PAS, MB	THOMPSON, MB
FLIN FLON, MB		676	402	889	613	703	633	388	571	375	141	380
MEADOW LAKE, SK	633	1309	867	305	496	1336		399	158	258	569	1013
PRINCE ALBERT, SK	375	1051	609	514	238	1078	258	141	196		311	781
THOMPSON, MB	380	296	328	1269	697	323	1013	640	977	781	470	

Distances in Canada shown in kilometers.
Au Canada, les distances sont en kilomètres.

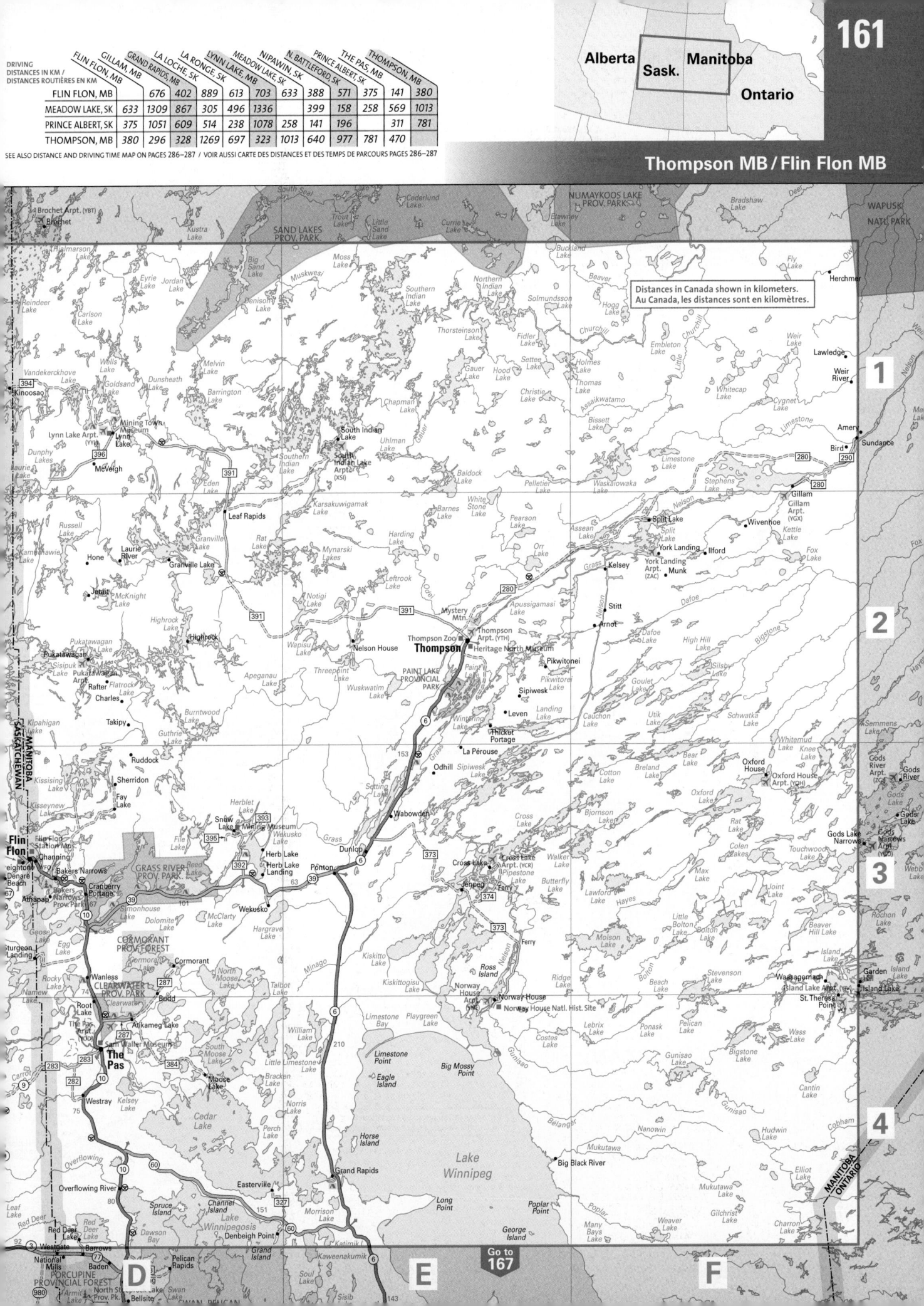

British Columbia

Washington

0 mi   20   40
0 km   20   40   60
One inch equals 25.4 miles/Un pouce équivaut à 25.4 milles
One cm equals 16.1 km/Un cm équivaut à 16.1 km

Go to 156

Long Lake
Belize Inlet
Seymour Inlet
MacKenzie Sound
Kingcome Inlet
Thompson Sound
Knight Inlet
Loughborough Inlet
Phillips Arm
Bute Inlet
Toba Inlet

HOMATHKO RIVER - TATLAYOKO PROTECTED AREA
Mt. Tatlow 3,066 m
Mt. Queen Bess 3,298 m
Chilko Lake
Yohetta Lake
TS'IL-OS PROV. PARK
Good Hope Mtn. 3,240 m
Mt. Grenville 3,109 m
Bishop
Monmouth Mtn. 3,194 m
Mt. Raleigh 3,078 m
BISHOP RIVER PROV. PARK
Toba L. 2,896 m
Mt. Gilbert 3,109 m
Costello Peak 1,713 m
Mt. Rodell 2,187 m
Mt. Everard 2,182 m
Mt. Cridge 1,795 m
Mt. Kennedy 2,028 m
Mt. Smith 2,299 m
Superb Mtn. 2,469 m
Granite Pk. 2,048 m
UPPER LILLOOET PROV. PARK
COAST MOUNTAINS
Homathko
Southgate
Homathko River
CLENDINNING PROV. PK.

Hope I.
Nigei I.
William Lake
CAPE SCOTT PROV. PARK
God's Pocket Marine Prov. Pk.
Sullivan Bay
Broughton I.
Simoom Sound
Gilford I.
Tribune Ch.
Turnour I.
Minstrel Island
Port Neville
Phillips Arm

Holberg
Port Hardy
Bear Cove
Holberg Inlet
Coal Harbour
19
Sointula
Malcolm I.
Alert Bay
U'Mista Cult. Ctr.
Kokish
Telegraph Cove
Beaver Cove
Cracroft Is.
Call Inlet
Blind Channel
Big Bay
Stuart Island
Walsh Cove Prov. Park

Winter Harbour
Quatsino Prov. Park
Quatsino
Marble River Prov. Park
30
Port McNeill
36
Neroutsos Inlet
Nimpkish Lake
68
Hardwicke I.
W. Thurlow I.
Sayward
Sonora I.
Surge Narrows Prov. Park
Refuge Cove
Princess Louisa Marine Prov. Pk.
DESOLATION SOUND MARINE PROV. PARK

Port Alice
Victoria Lake
Nimpkish Lake Prov. Park
Woss
19
Mt. Cain
62
64
Thurston Bay Marine Prov. Pk.
Rock Bay
Granite Bay
Ha'thayim Marine Prov. Pk.
Whaletown
Mansons Landing
Okeover Arm Prov. Park
Lund
Jervis Inlet

Brooks Bay
BROOKS PENINSULA PROV. PARK
Big Bunsby Marine Prov. Pk.
Checleset Bay
Kyuquot
TAHSISH-KWOIS PROV. PARK
Tahsish Inlet
Woss Lake
Woss Lake Prov. Park
SCHOEN LAKE PROV. PARK
Victoria Pk. 2,163 m
Morton Lake Prov. Park
Main Lake Prov. Park
Quadra I.
Heriot Bay
Quathiaski Cove
Mansons Landing
Smelt Bay Prov. Park
Inland Lake Prov. Park
Harmony Islands Marine Prov. Pk.

Kyuquot Sound
Rugged Point Marine Prov. Pk.
Zeballos
Vernon Lake
Elk Falls Prov. Park
Campbell River
Campbell River Arpt. (YBL)
19A
Kwagiulth Mus.
Lund
Skookumchuc Narrows Prov. Park

Catala Island Marine Prov. Park
Esperanza Inlet
Tahsis
Nuchatlitz Prov. Park
Nootka Island
Upper Campbell Lake
28
Gold River
Butte Lake
Mt. Washington
Miracle Beach
Miracle Bch. Prov. Park
Black Creek
Powell River
Powell River Arpt. (YPW)
Westview
Saltery Bay
Texada I.
Earls Cove
Nelson I.
Garden Bay
Sechelt Inlet

STRATHCONA
89
46
Merville
Little River
Lazo
Comox Valley Arpt. (YQQ)
Gillies Bay
Van Anda
Blubber Bay
Texada I.
Kleindale
81
Porpoise Bay Prov. Park

Tlupana Inlet
Bligh Island Marine Prov. Pk.
Muchalat Inlet
PROV. PARK
Courtenay
Comox
Royston
Cumberland
Comox L.
19A
Union Bay
Denman I.
Sandy I. Marine Prov. Pk.
Fillongley Prov. Park
Hornby I.
False Bay
Jedediah Island Marine Prov. Pk.
Halfmoon Bay
Simson Prov. Park
Sechelt

Yuquot
Nootka Sound
Hesquiat Lake Prov. Park
Boat Basin
Sulphur Passage Prov. Park
Buckley Bay
Fanny Bay
Rosewall Creek Prov. Pk.
Bowser
Lasqueti I.
Squitty Bay Prov. Park
Sargeant Bay Prov. Park
Robert Creek Prov. Pk.

HESQUIAT PEN. PROV. PARK
Maquinna Marine Prov. Park
Stewardson Inlet
Herbert Inlet
Flores I.
Bedwell Sound
Great Central L.
Stamp River Prov. Park
92
Horne Lake Caves Prov. Park
Qualicum Beach
French Creek
XOU
Rathtrevor Beach Prov. Park
Gabriola Island

Flores Island Prov. Park
Ahousat
Gibson Marine Prov. Pk.
Epper Passage Prov. Park
Clayoquot Plateau Prov. Park
Taylor Arm Prov. Park
MacMillan Prov. Park
4
Coombs
Errington
Little Qualicum Falls Prov. Park
Englishman River Falls Prov. Park
Parksville
35
Nanoose Bay
19A
Lantzville
Nanaimo

Vargas Island Prov. Park
Whale Centre Museum
Clayoquot Sound
Dawley Passage Prov. Park
Clayoquot Arm Prov. Park
Tofino
Tofino Arpt. (YAZ)
34
Sproat Lake Prov. Park
Sproat L.
Port Alberni
Alberni Valley Museum
47
Cedar

PACIFIC RIM NATIONAL PARK RESERVE (Long Beach Unit)
4
Kennedy L.
Alberni Inlet
Nahmint
Kildonan
Green Cove
RESTRICTED ROAD
Cassidy
Ladysmith

Ucluelet
Barkley Sound
Sarita
Cowichan Lake
Youbou
Thetis
Chemainus
N. Cowichan

PACIFIC RIM NATIONAL PARK RESERVE (Broken Group Islands Unit)
Bamfield
Hitchie Creek Prov. Park
Gordon Bay Prov. Park
Honeymoon Bay
Mesachie L.
Cowichan
30
Quw'utsun' Cult. Ctr.
18
Duncan
Cowichan River Prov. Pk.

PACIFIC OCEAN

Distances in Canada shown in kilometers.
Au Canada, les distances sont en kilomètres.

Nitinat Lake
CARMANAH WALBRAN PROV. PARK
Clo-oose
RESTRICTED ROAD
PACIFIC RIM NATIONAL PARK RESERVE (West Coast Trail Unit)
Port Renfrew
14
102
Juan de Fuca Prov. Pk.
River Jordan
Milnes Landing
Sooke

B.C. WASH.
Cape Flattery
Neah Bay
112
MAKAH IND. RES.
Clallam Bay
Strait of Juan de Fuca
Juan de Fuca Prov. Pk.
French Beach Prov. Pk.
Beechey Head

Cape Alava
Flattery Rocks N.W.R.
113
Sappho
101
Joyce

Go to 12

Ozette Lake
OLYMPIC NATL. PARK
OLYMPIC NATL. FOR.
Sol Duc
Forks
OLY...
L. Crescent

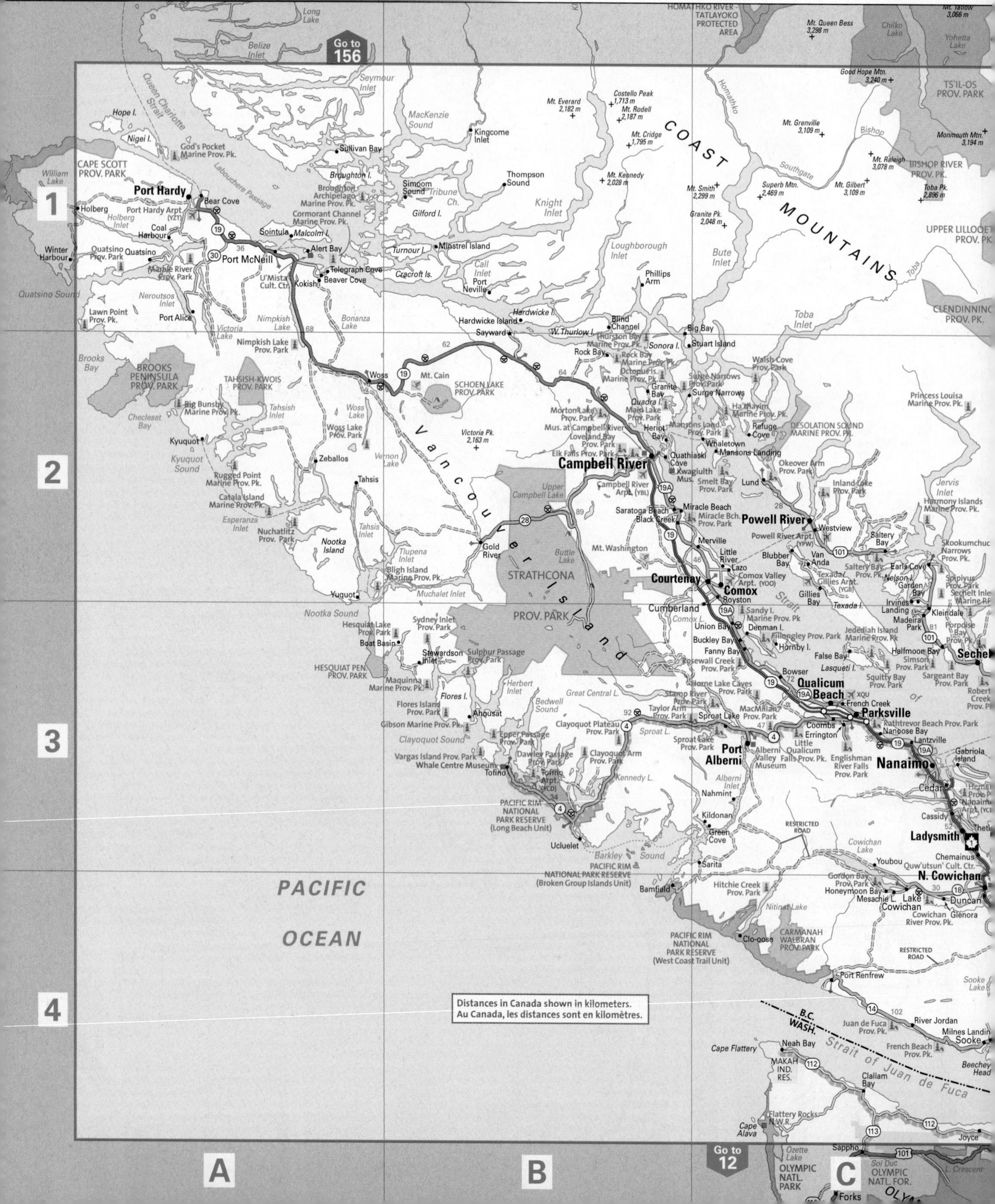

DRIVING DISTANCES IN KM /
DISTANCES ROUTIÈRES EN KM

	CAMPBELL RIVER, BC	KAMLOOPS, BC	KELOWNA, BC	MERRITT, BC	NANAIMO, BC	OSOYOOS, BC	PORT ALBERNI, BC	PORT HARDY, BC	SALMON ARM, BC	VANCOUVER, BC	VICTORIA, BC	WHISTLER, BC
KAMLOOPS, BC	512		163	163	87	363	231	441	750	108	355	393	475
NANAIMO, BC	153	363	403	279		404	82	391	471	23	113	104
VANCOUVER, BC	172	355	395	271	23	396	101	410	463		69	123
VICTORIA, BC	266	393	433	309	113	434	195	504	501	69		192

SEE ALSO DISTANCE AND DRIVING TIME MAP ON PAGES 286–287 / VOIR AUSSI CARTE DES DISTANCES ET DES TEMPS DE PARCOURS PAGES 286–287

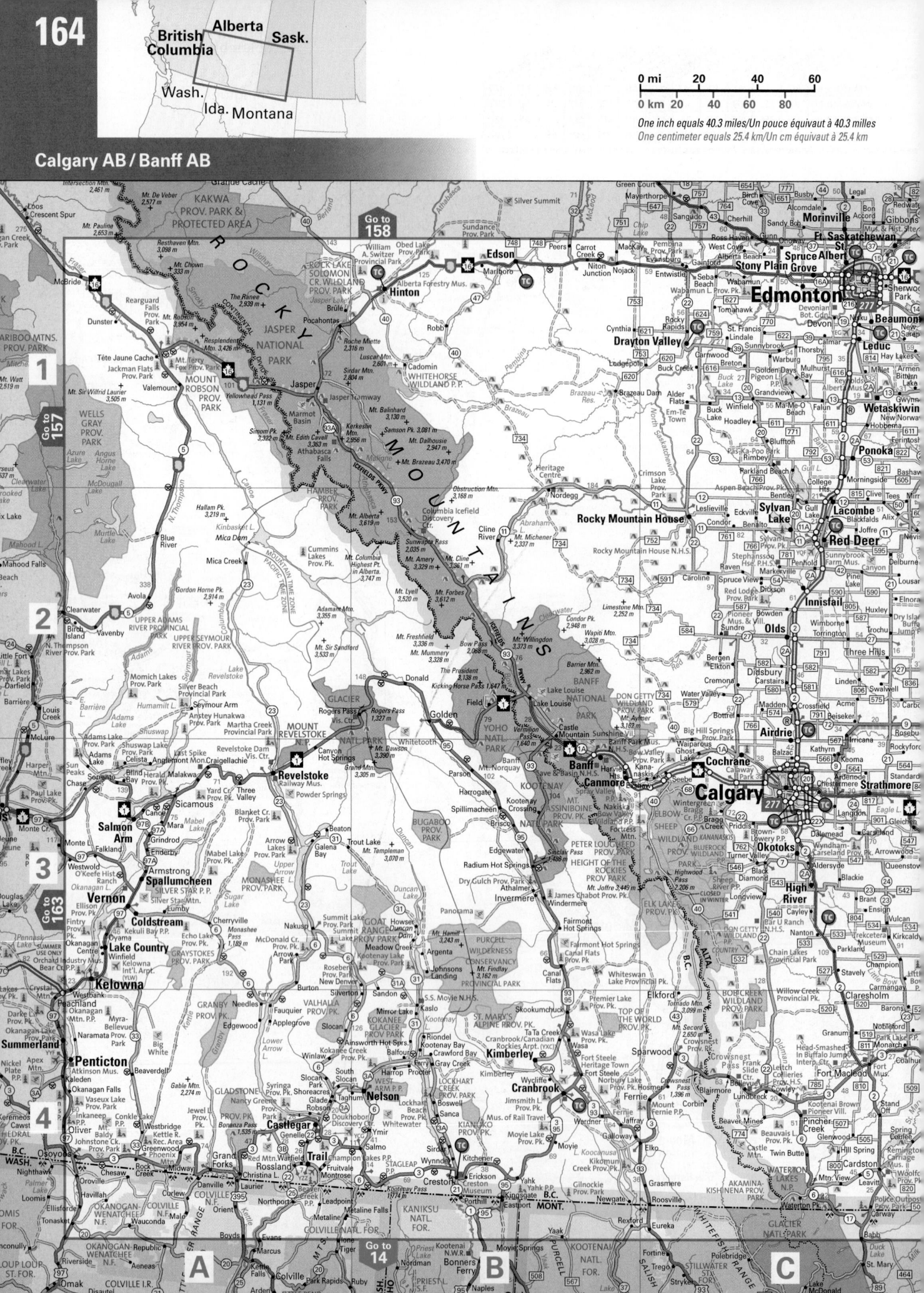
British Columbia
Alberta
Sask.
Wash.
Ida.
Montana
0 mi 20 40 60
0 km 20 40 60 80
One inch equals 40.3 miles/Un pouce équivaut à 40.3 milles
One centimeter equals 25.4 km/Un cm équivaut à 25.4 km
Go to 158
Go to 157
Go to 163
Go to 14
ROCKY MOUNTAINS
Edmonton
Calgary
Red Deer
Jasper
Banff
Lake Louise
Canmore
Cochrane
Airdrie
Okotoks
High River
Kelowna
Penticton
Vernon
Revelstoke
Nelson
Cranbrook
Kimberley
Golden
Hinton
Edson
JASPER NATIONAL PARK
BANFF NATIONAL PARK
YOHO NATL. PARK
KOOTENAY NATL. PARK
GLACIER NATL. PARK
WATERTON LAKES N.P.
1
2
3
4
A
B
C

DRIVING
DISTANCES IN KM /
DISTANCES ROUTIÈRES EN KM

	BANFF, AB	CALGARY, AB	CRANBROOK, BC	EDMONTON, AB	JASPER, AB	KELOWNA, BC	LETHBRIDGE, AB	LLOYDMINSTER AB/SK	MEDICINE HAT, AB	RED DEER, AB	SASKATOON, SK	SWIFT CURRENT, SK
CALGARY, AB	128		383	296	396	638	216	534	285	145	620	503
EDMONTON, AB	412	296	679		367	934	512	238	579	150	513	676
LETHBRIDGE, AB	344	216	306	512	612	809		605	164	360	650	382
SASKATOON, SK	748	620	969	513	880	1255	650	275	486	639		267

SEE ALSO DISTANCE AND DRIVING TIME MAP ON PAGES 286–287 / VOIR AUSSI CARTE DES DISTANCES ET DES TEMPS DE PARCOURS PAGES 286–287

Distances in Canada shown in kilometers.
Au Canada, les distances sont en kilomètres.

Sask.
Manitoba
Ontario
Montana
N.D.
Minn.
0 mi 20 40 60
0 km 20 40 60 80
One inch equals 40.3 miles/Un pouce équivaut à 40.3 milles
One centimeter equals 25.4 km/Un cm équivaut à 25.4 km
Go to 160
Go to 165
Go to 17
Go to 18
A
B
C
1
2
3
4
PRINCE ALBERT NATL. PARK
North Battleford
Battleford
Prince Albert
Melfort
Tisdale
Nipawin
Saskatoon
Humboldt
Yorkton
Melville
Moose Jaw
Regina
Swift Current
Weyburn
Estevan
The Pas
Swan River
GRASSLANDS NATL. PARK
SASKATCHEWAN
MONTANA
SASKATCHEWAN MANITOBA
SASK. N. DAK.
CANADA
U.S.
CENTRAL T.Z.
MOUNTAIN T.Z.
FORT PECK IND. RES.
MOOSE MTN. PROV. PARK
DUCK MTN. PROV. PARK
GREENWATER L. PROV. PARK
GOOD SPIRIT PROV. PARK
DOUGLAS PROV. PARK
DANIELSON PROV. PARK
SASKATCHEWAN LANDING PROV. PARK
BUFFALO POUND PROV. PARK
WILDCAT HILL PROV. PARK
PASQUIA HILLS
PORCUPINE HILLS

DRIVING DISTANCES IN KM / DISTANCES ROUTIÈRES EN KM

	BRANDON, MB	DAUPHIN, MB	GRAND RAPIDS, MB	MOOSE JAW, SK	PORTAGE LA PRAIRIE, MB	PRINCE ALBERT, SK	REGINA, SK	SASKATOON, SK	SWIFT CURRENT, SK	THE PAS, MB	WINNIPEG, MB	YORKTON, SK
BRANDON, MB		166	525	448	134	745	377	639	618	570	216	270
REGINA, SK	377	366	787	68	511	368		261	241	557	593	195
SASKATOON, SK	639	502	689	224	691	141	261		267	578	773	331
WINNIPEG, MB	216	322	430	664	82	819	593	773	834	611		442

SEE ALSO DISTANCE AND DRIVING TIME MAP ON PAGES 286–287 / VOIR AUSSI CARTE DES DISTANCES ET DES TEMPS DE PARCOURS PAGES 286–287

Sask. Manitoba
Ontario
Montana   N.D.   Minn.

Distances in Canada shown in kilometers.
Au Canada, les distances sont en kilomètres.

Go to 161

Go to 168

Go to 19

Manitoba

Ontario

N.D. Minn.

Mich.

0 mi   20   40   60

0 km 20   40   60   80

One inch equals 40.3 miles/Un pouce équivaut à 40.3 milles
One centimeter equals 25.4 km/Un cm équivaut à 25.4 km

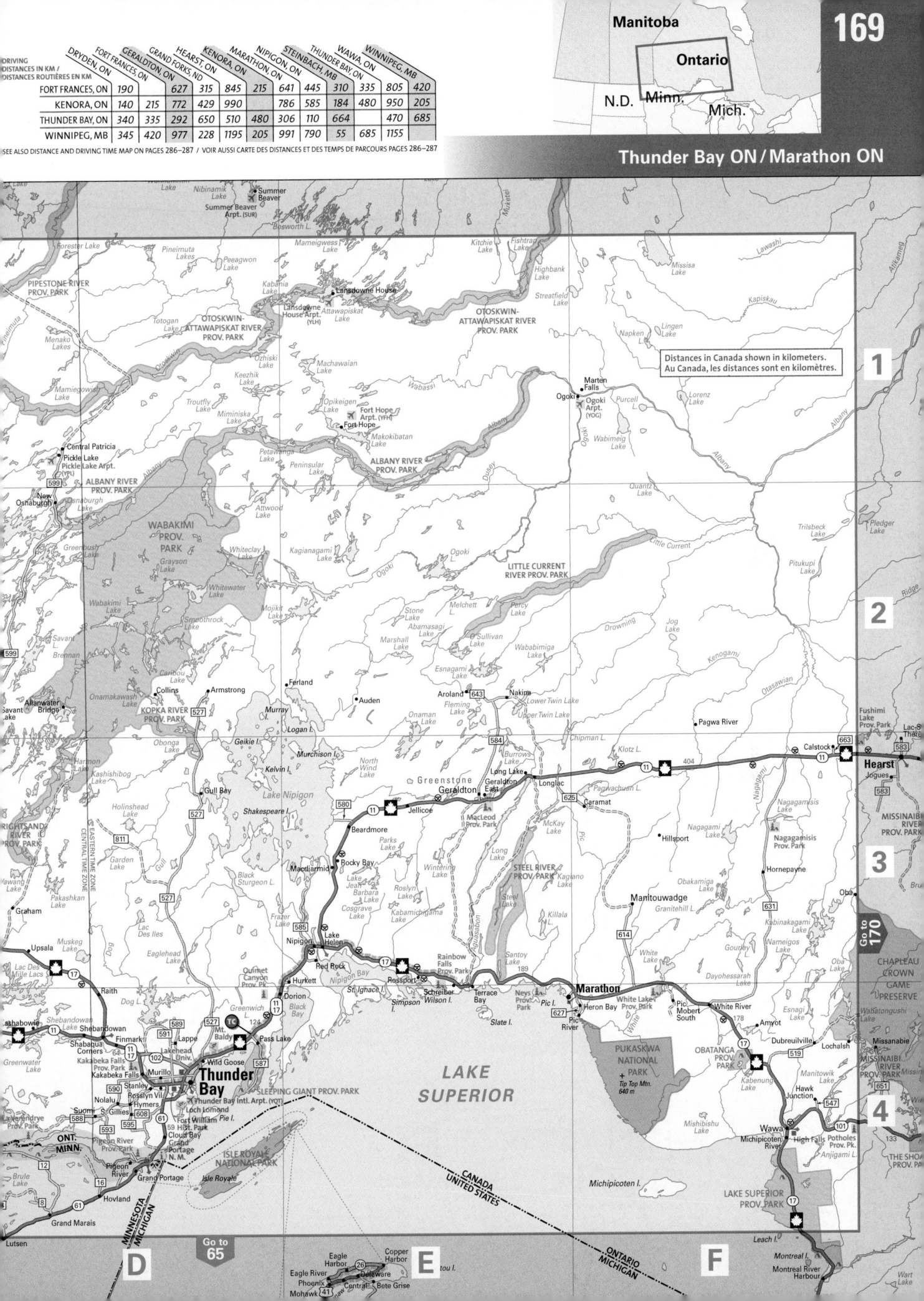

Manitoba

Ontario

N.D. Minn. Mich.

DRIVING
DISTANCES IN KM /
DISTANCES ROUTIÈRES EN KM

	DRYDEN, ON	FORT FRANCES, ON	GERALDTON, ON	GRAND FORKS, ND	HEARST, ON	KENORA, ON	MARATHON, ON	NIPIGON, ON	STEINBACH, MB	THUNDER BAY, ON	WAWA, ON	WINNIPEG, MB
FORT FRANCES, ON	190		627	315	845	215	641	445	310	335	805	420
KENORA, ON	140	215	772	429	990		786	585	184	480	950	205
THUNDER BAY, ON	340	335	292	650	510	480	306	110	664		470	685
WINNIPEG, MB	345	420	977	228	1195	205	991	790	55	685	1155	

SEE ALSO DISTANCE AND DRIVING TIME MAP ON PAGES 286–287 / VOIR AUSSI CARTE DES DISTANCES ET DES TEMPS DE PARCOURS PAGES 286–287

Distances in Canada shown in kilometers.
Au Canada, les distances sont en kilomètres.

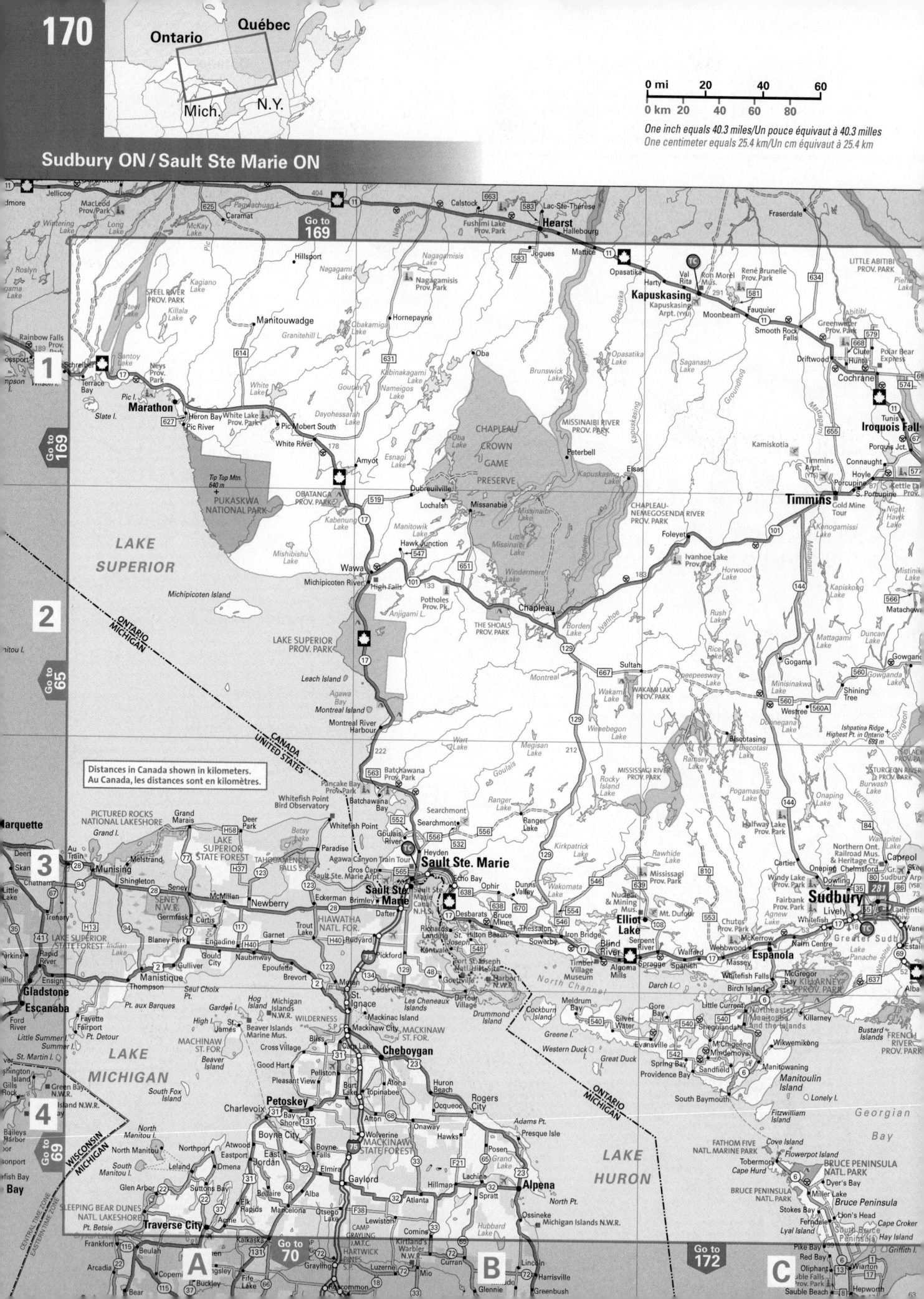

Ontario   Québec

Mich.   N.Y.

0 mi   20   40   60
0 km 20   40   60   80

One inch equals 40.3 miles/Un pouce équivaut à 40.3 milles
One centimetre equals 25.4 km/Un cm équivaut à 25.4 km

Distances in Canada shown in kilometers.
Au Canada, les distances sont en kilomètres.

LAKE SUPERIOR

LAKE MICHIGAN

LAKE HURON

Georgian Bay

DRIVING DISTANCES IN KM / DISTANCES ROUTIÈRES EN KM

	HEARST, ON	HUNTSVILLE, ON	KIRKLAND LAKE, ON	MONT-LAURIER, QC	NORTH BAY, ON	ORILLIA, ON	OTTAWA, ON	ROUYN-NORANDA, QC	SAULT STE. MARIE, ON	SUDBURY, ON	TIMMINS, ON	WAWA, ON
KIRKLAND LAKE, ON	370	370		505	250	578	610	154	580	315	140	475
OTTAWA, ON	955	350	610	209	364	415		456	787	488	730	1015
SAULT STE. MARIE, ON	545	560	580	1004	430	562	787	734		305	440	225
SUDBURY, ON	550	250	315	699	124	263	488	469	305		290	530

SEE ALSO DISTANCE AND DRIVING TIME MAP ON PAGES 286–287 / VOIR AUSSI CARTE DES DISTANCES ET DES TEMPS DE PARCOURS PAGES 286–287

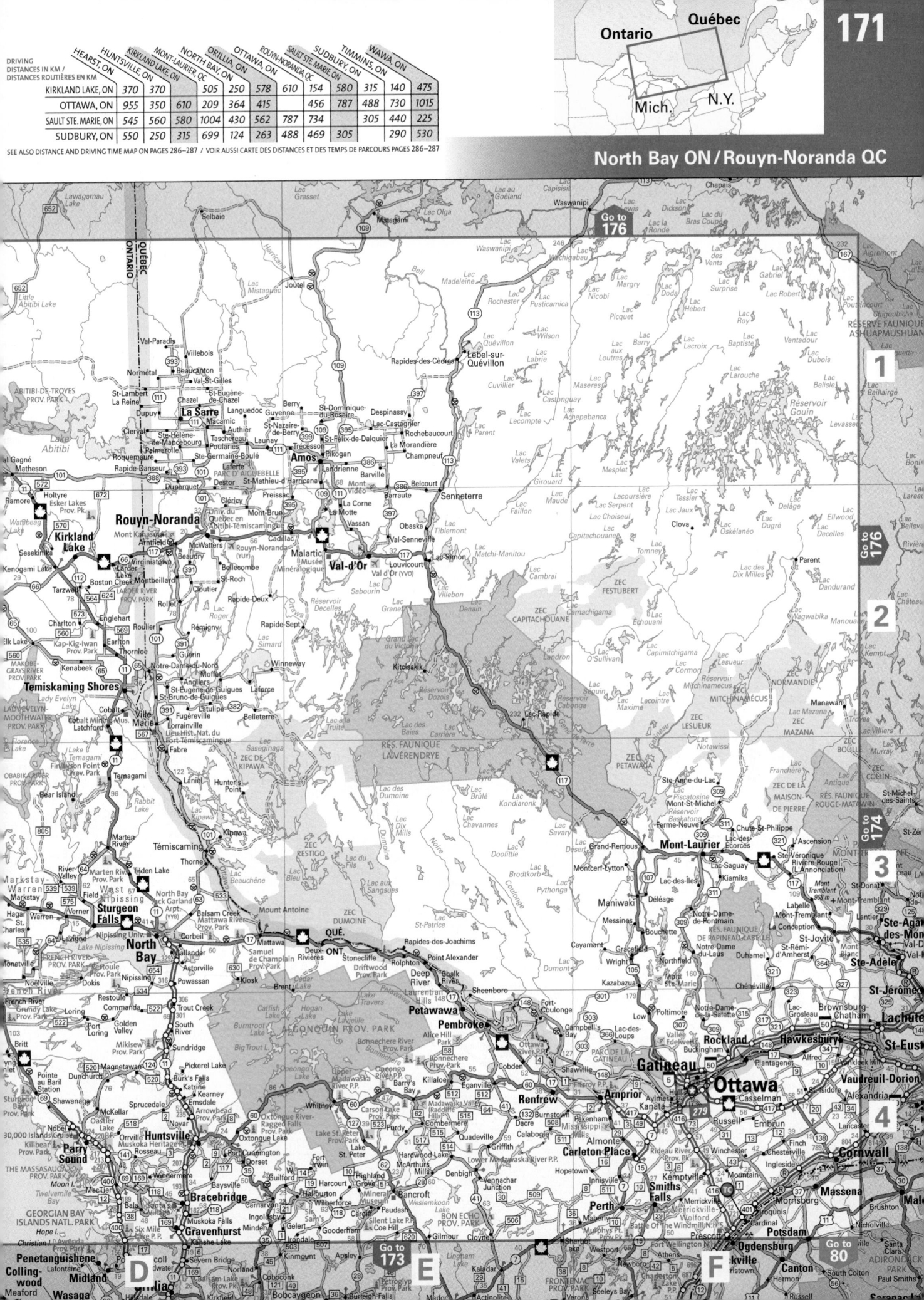

Ontario
Mich.
N.Y.
Pa.
Ohio

0 mi 20 40
0 km 20 40 60
One inch equals 25.4 miles/Un pouce équivaut à 25.4 milles
One cm equals 16.1 km/Un cm équivaut à 16.1 km

Distances in Canada shown in kilometers.
Au Canada, les distances sont en kilomètres.

Go to 170

LAKE HURON

Georgian Bay
GEORGIAN BAY ISLANDS NATL. PARK
Giants Tomb Island

Bruce Peninsula
South Bruce Peninsula
Owen Sound
Port Elgin
Kincardine
Walkerton
Hanover
Durham
Shelburne
Orangeville
Collingwood
Wasaga Beach
Midland
Penetanguishene

Goderich
Listowel
Elmira
Fergus
Guelph
Acton
Georgetown
Milton

Clinton
Seaforth
Stratford
Waterloo
Kitchener
Cambridge
Hamilton
Paris
Brantford
Caledonia

Exeter
St. Marys
New Hamburg
Woodstock
Ingersoll
London
St. Thomas
Aylmer
Tillsonburg
Simcoe
Port Dover

Sarnia
Strathroy
Petrolia
Port Huron
Marysville

Chatham
Ridgetown
Blenheim
Leamington
Kingsville
Essex
Amherstburg
Harrow

Windsor
Detroit
Dearborn
Warren
Sterling Hts.
Pontiac
Livonia
Taylor
LaSalle
Wallaceburg

LAKE ST. CLAIR
LAKE ERIE
POINT PELEE NATL. PARK
RONDEAU PROV. PARK
LONG POINT

Lapeer
Monroe
Toledo

CANADA / UNITED STATES
ONTARIO / MICHIGAN
MICHIGAN / OHIO
ONTARIO / OHIO

Erie
Ashtabula
Conneaut
Geneva
Edinboro
Painesville

Go to 76
Go to 90
Go to 91

Ontario
Mich.   N.Y.
Ohio   Pa.

Québec
Ontario
Me.
N.H.
N.Y.
Vermont
0 mi 20 40
0 km 20 40 60
One inch equals 25.4 miles/Un pouce équivaut à 25.4 milles
One cm equals 16.1 km/Un cm équivaut à 16.1 km
Ottawa ON / Montréal QC
Go to 171
Go to 176
Go to 173
Go to 80
Distances in Canada shown in kilometers.
Au Canada, les distances sont en kilomètres.
1
2
3
4
A
B
C
ZEC MITCHINAMÉCUS
ZEC NORMANDIE
ZEC LESUEUR
ZEC PETAWAGA
ZEC MAZANA
ZEC BOULLÉ
ZEC DU GROS-BROCHET
ZEC CHAPEAU-DE-PAIL
ZEC DE LA MAISON-DE PIERRE
RÉS. FAUNIQUE ROUGE-MATAWIN
RÉSERVE FAUNIQUE MASTIGOUCHE
PARC DU MONT-TREMBLANT
RÉS. FAUNIQUE DE PAPINEAU-LABELLE
ADIRONDACK PARK
Mont-Laurier
Maniwaki
Gatineau
Ottawa
Rockland
Hawkesbury
Lachute
St-Jérôme
Ste-Adèle
Ste-Agathe-des-Monts
Joliette
Laval
Montréal
Terrebonne
Repentigny
Blainville
St-Eustache
Vaudreuil-Dorion
Châteauguay
Salaberry-de-Valleyfield
Cornwall
Massena
Malone
Plattsburgh
Potsdam
Canton
Ogdensburg
Brockville
Gananoque
Kingston
Napanee
Belleville
Smiths Falls
Perth
Carleton Place
Arnprior
Renfrew
Pembroke
Petawawa
Saranac Lake

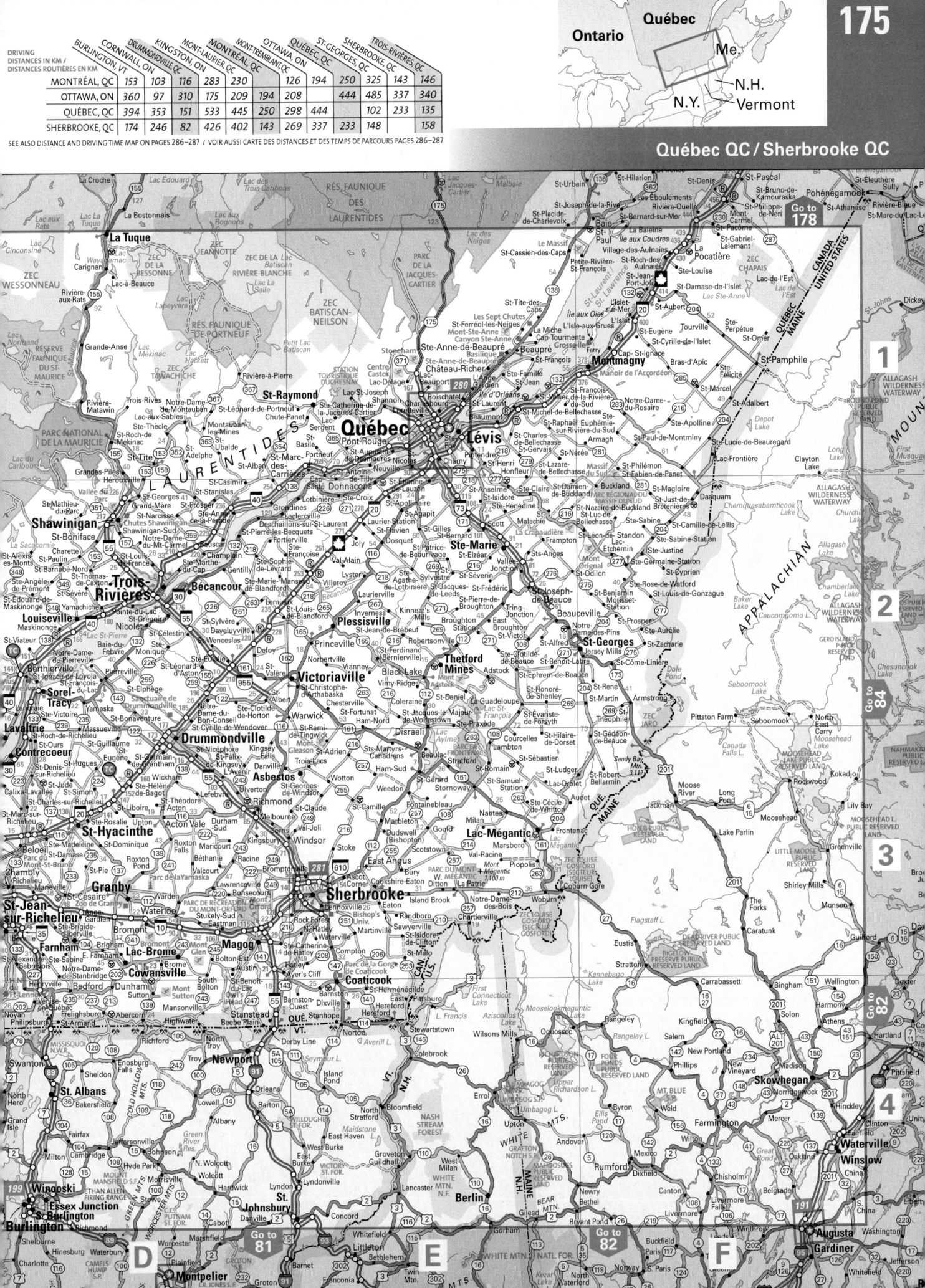

Ontario · Québec · Me. · N.H. · N.Y. · Vermont

DRIVING
DISTANCES IN KM /
DISTANCES ROUTIÈRES EN KM

	BURLINGTON, VT	CORNWALL, ON	DRUMMONDVILLE, QC	KINGSTON, ON	MONT-LAURIER, QC	MONTRÉAL, QC	MONT-TREMBLANT, QC	OTTAWA, ON	QUÉBEC, QC	ST-GEORGES, QC	SHERBROOKE, QC	TROIS-RIVIÈRES, QC
MONTRÉAL, QC	153	103	116	283	230		126	194	250	325	143	146
OTTAWA, ON	360	97	310	175	209	194	208		444	485	337	340
QUÉBEC, QC	394	353	151	533	445	250	298	444			102	233	135
SHERBROOKE, QC	174	246	82	426	402	143	269	337	233	148		158

SEE ALSO DISTANCE AND DRIVING TIME MAP ON PAGES 286–287 / VOIR AUSSI CARTE DES DISTANCES ET DES TEMPS DE PARCOURS PAGES 286–287

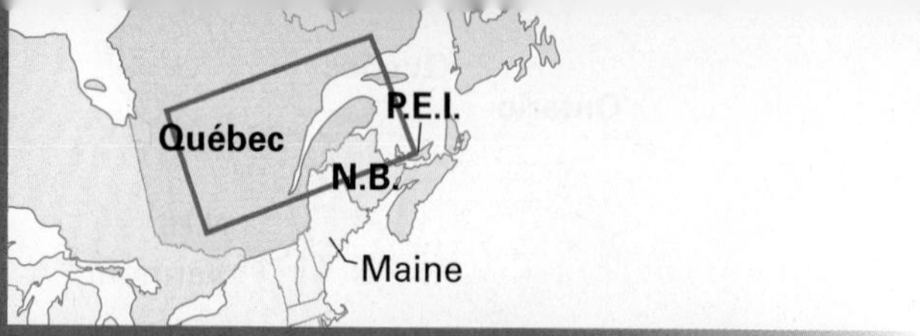

Québec
P.E.I.
N.B.
Maine

0 mi 20 40 60
0 km 20 40 60 80
One inch equals 40.3 miles/Un pouce équivaut à 40.3 milles
One centimeter equals 25.4 km/Un cm équivaut à 25.4 km

Distances in Canada shown in kilometers.
Au Canada, les distances sont en kilomètres.

DRIVING DISTANCES IN KM / DISTANCES ROUTIÈRES EN KM

	BAIE-COMEAU, QC	CAMPBELLTON, NB	CHIBOUGAMAU, QC	CHICOUTIMI, QC	EDMUNDSTON, NB	GASPÉ, QC	HAVRE-ST-PIERRE, QC	MATANE, QC	MIRAMICHI, QC	QUÉBEC, QC	RIMOUSKI, QC	SEPT-ÎLES, QC
CHICOUTIMI, QC	435	444	359		269	771	884	348	622	211	253	667
EDMUNDSTON, NB	368	188	628	269		534	817	249	268	317	180	600
GASPÉ, QC	287	340	1130	771	534		743	294	518	706	389	526
QUÉBEC, QC	408	508	570	211	317	706	857	412	582		507	640

SEE ALSO DISTANCE AND DRIVING TIME MAP ON PAGES 286–287 / VOIR AUSSI CARTE DES DISTANCES ET DES TEMPS DE PARCOURS PAGES 286–287

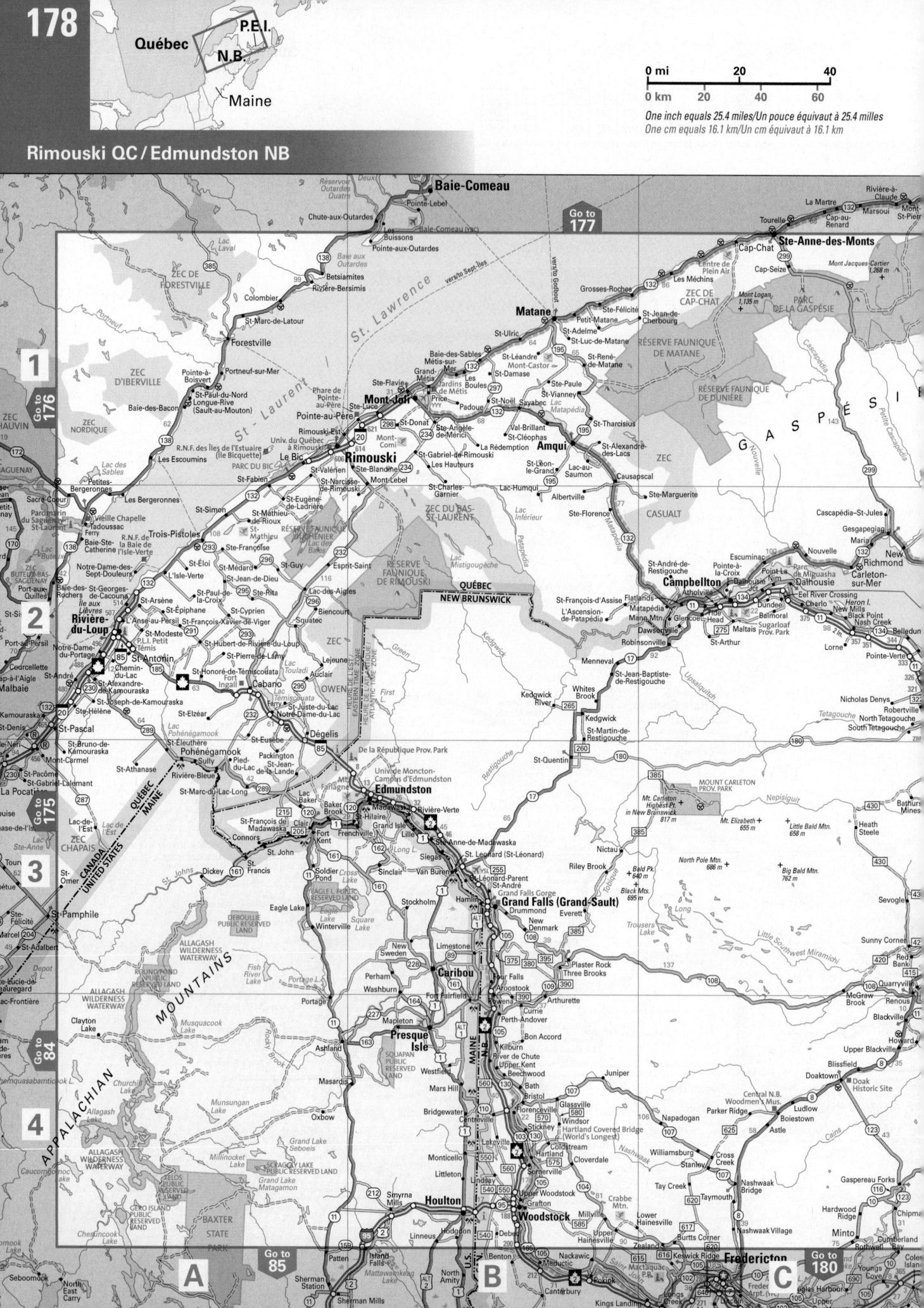

One inch equals 25.4 miles/Un pouce équivaut à 25.4 milles
One cm equals 16.1 km/Un cm équivaut à 16.1 km

0 mi 20 40
0 km 20 40 60

Go to 177

Go to 176

Go to 175

Go to 84

Go to 85

Go to 180

DRIVING DISTANCES IN KM / DISTANCES ROUTIÈRES EN KM

	BATHURST, NB	BORDEN-CARLETON, PE	CAMPBELLTON, NB	CHARLOTTETOWN, PE	EDMUNDSTON, NB	FREDERICTON, NB	GASPÉ, QC	GRAND FALLS, NB	MATANE, QC	MIRAMICHI, NB	MONCTON, NB	RIMOUSKI, QC
CHARLOTTETOWN, PE	338	56	438		629	362	791	581	562	273	164	596
EDMUNDSTON, NB	189	428	188	638		279	534	57	249	268	447	180
MATANE, QC	262	506	168	562	249	553	294	331		346	487	95
MONCTON, NB	206	108	306	164	447	170	659	390	487	141		502

SEE ALSO DISTANCE AND DRIVING TIME MAP ON PAGES 286–287 / VOIR AUSSI CARTE DES DISTANCES ET DES TEMPS DE PARCOURS PAGES 286–287

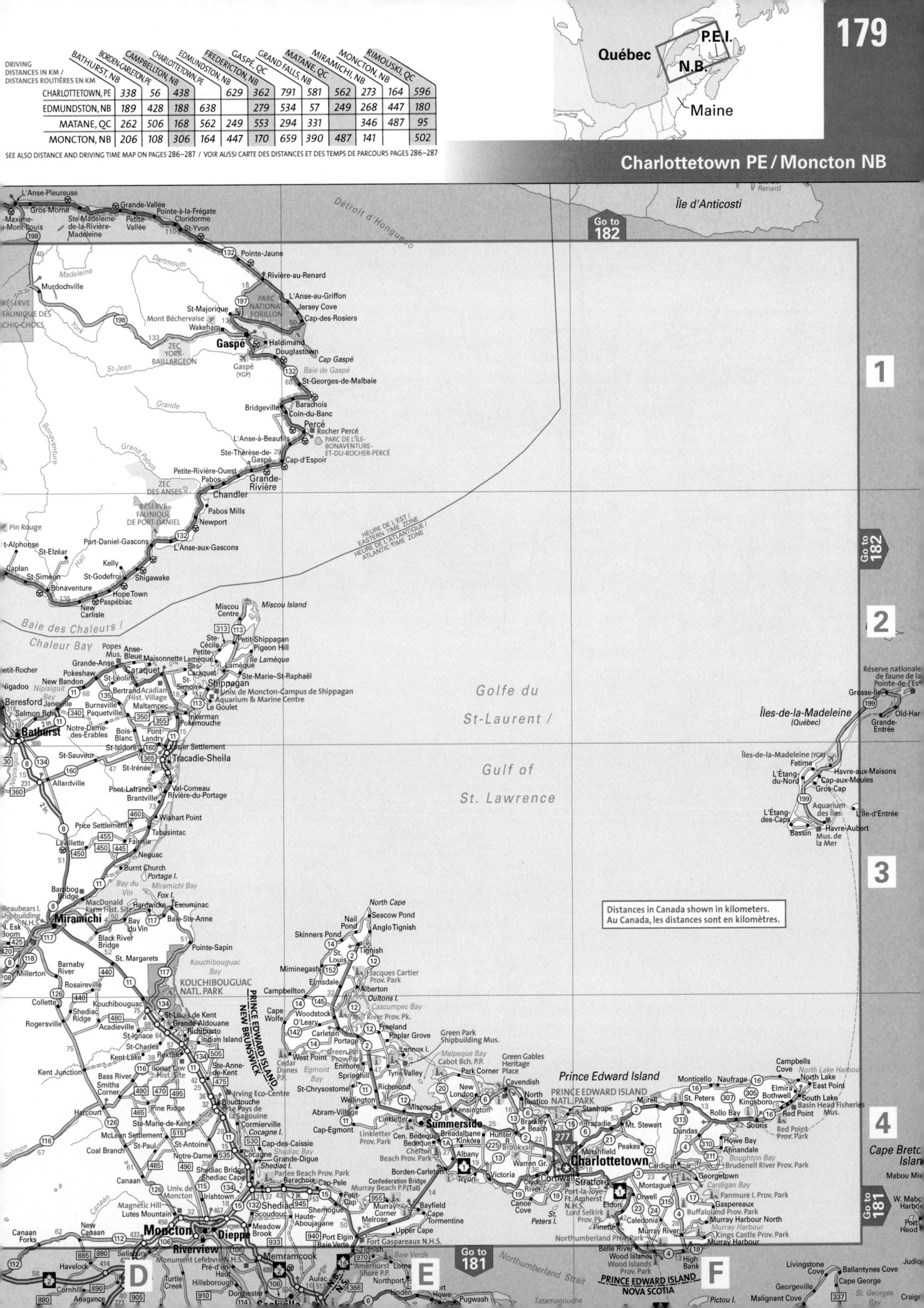

P.E.I.

N.B.

Nova Scotia

Maine

0 mi	20	40
0 km	20	40	60

One inch equals 25.4 miles/Un pouce équivaut à 25.4 milles
One cm equals 16.1 km/Un cm équivaut à 16.1 km

Go to 178

Go to 179

Go to 85

Go to 83

New Brunswick / Nova Scotia

PRINCE EDWARD ISLAND / NEW BRUNSWICK

Gulf of Maine

Bay of Fundy

Major places: Houlton, Woodstock, Fredericton, Oromocto, Saint John, Quispamsis, Grand Bay-Westfield, St. Stephen, Calais, St. Andrews, Moncton, Riverview, Dieppe, Sackville, Amherst, Kentville, Wolfville, Windsor, Kingston, Bridgewater, Lunenburg, Liverpool, Yarmouth, Digby

to Bar Harbor, Maine

to Portland, Maine

EASTERN TIME ZONE / ATLANTIC TIME ZONE

KEJIMKUJIK NATL. PARK

FUNDY N.P.

1 2 3 4

A B C

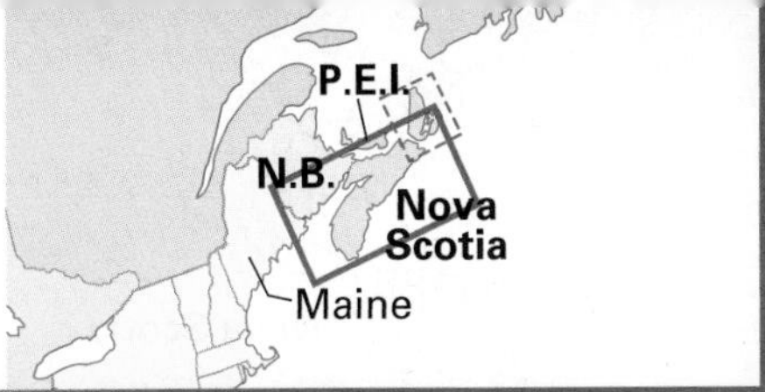

DRIVING DISTANCES IN KM / DISTANCES ROUTIÈRES EN KM	CHÉTICAMP, NS	CHARLOTTETOWN, PE	DIGBY, NS	FREDERICTON, NB	HALIFAX, NS	MONCTON, NB	PORT HAWKESBURY, NS	SAINT JOHN, NB	ST. STEPHEN, NB	SYDNEY, NS	TRURO, NS	YARMOUTH, NS
HALIFAX, NS	322	425	235	462		260	265	410	515	415	89	339
MONCTON, NB	164	481	231	170	260		374	150	278	497	182	599
SAINT JOHN, NB	350	640	72	114	410	150	497		119	647	321	176
SYDNEY, NS	374	173	623	689	415	497	123	647	766		326	727

SEE ALSO DISTANCE AND DRIVING TIME MAP ON PAGES 286–287 / VOIR AUSSI CARTE DES DISTANCES ET DES TEMPS DE PARCOURS PAGES 286–287

P.E.I.
N.B.
Nova Scotia
Maine

Cape Breton Island

FOR CONTINUATION SEE INSET LOWER RIGHT

Go to 182

PRINCE EDWARD ISLAND
NOVA SCOTIA

ATLANTIC OCEAN

Cape Breton Island

Distances in Canada shown in kilometers.
Au Canada, les distances sont en kilomètres.

1
2
3
4
D
E
F

Nfld. & Lab.

P.E.I.

Québec   Nova Scotia

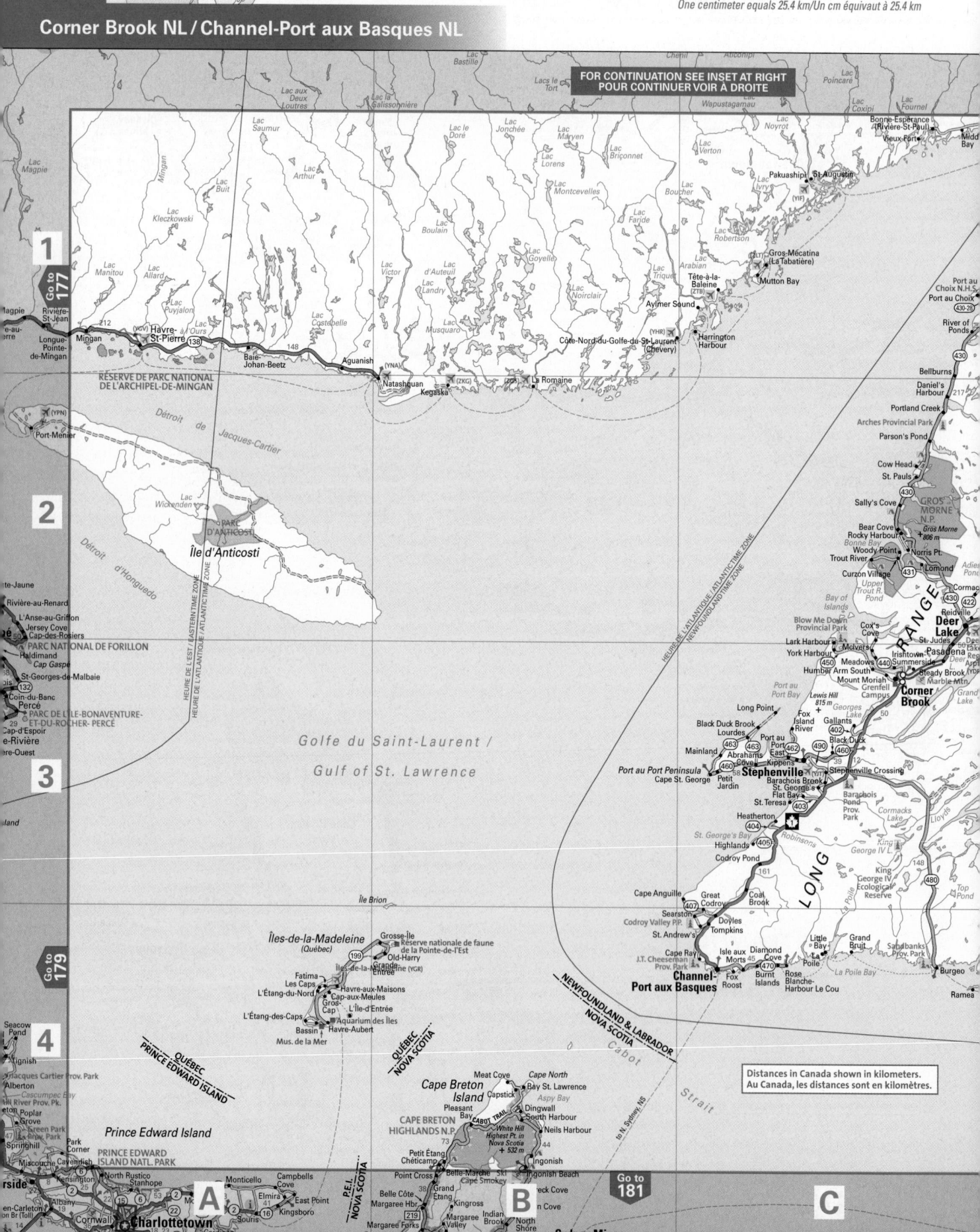

FOR CONTINUATION SEE INSET AT RIGHT
POUR CONTINUER VOIR À DROITE

Distances in Canada shown in kilometers.
Au Canada, les distances sont en kilomètres.

DRIVING DISTANCES IN KM / DISTANCES ROUTIÈRES EN KM	ARGENTIA, NL	BISHOP'S FALLS, NL	BONAVISTA, NL	CHAN.-PT. AUX BASQUES, NL	CORNER BROOK, NL	DEER LAKE, NL	GANDER, NL	GRAND FALLS-WINDSOR, NL	MARYSTOWN, NL	ST. ANTHONY, NL	ST. JOHN'S, NL	STEPHENVILLE, NL
BISHOP'S FALLS, NL	363		307	482	280	225	72	18	384	628	393	339
CHAN.-PT. AUX BASQUES, NL	845	482	789		202	257	554	464	866	660	875	151
CORNER BROOK, NL	643	280	587	202		55	352	262	664	458	673	59
ST. JOHN'S, NL	134	393	296	875	673	618	321	411	293	1021		732

SEE ALSO DISTANCE AND DRIVING TIME MAP ON PAGES 286–287 / VOIR AUSSI CARTE DES DISTANCES ET DES TEMPS DE PARCOURS PAGES 286–287

NOTE: Legislated standard time zone boundaries are shown; however, Labrador — except for the coastal area from L'Anse-au-Clair to Cartwright — operates on Atlantic Standard Time.

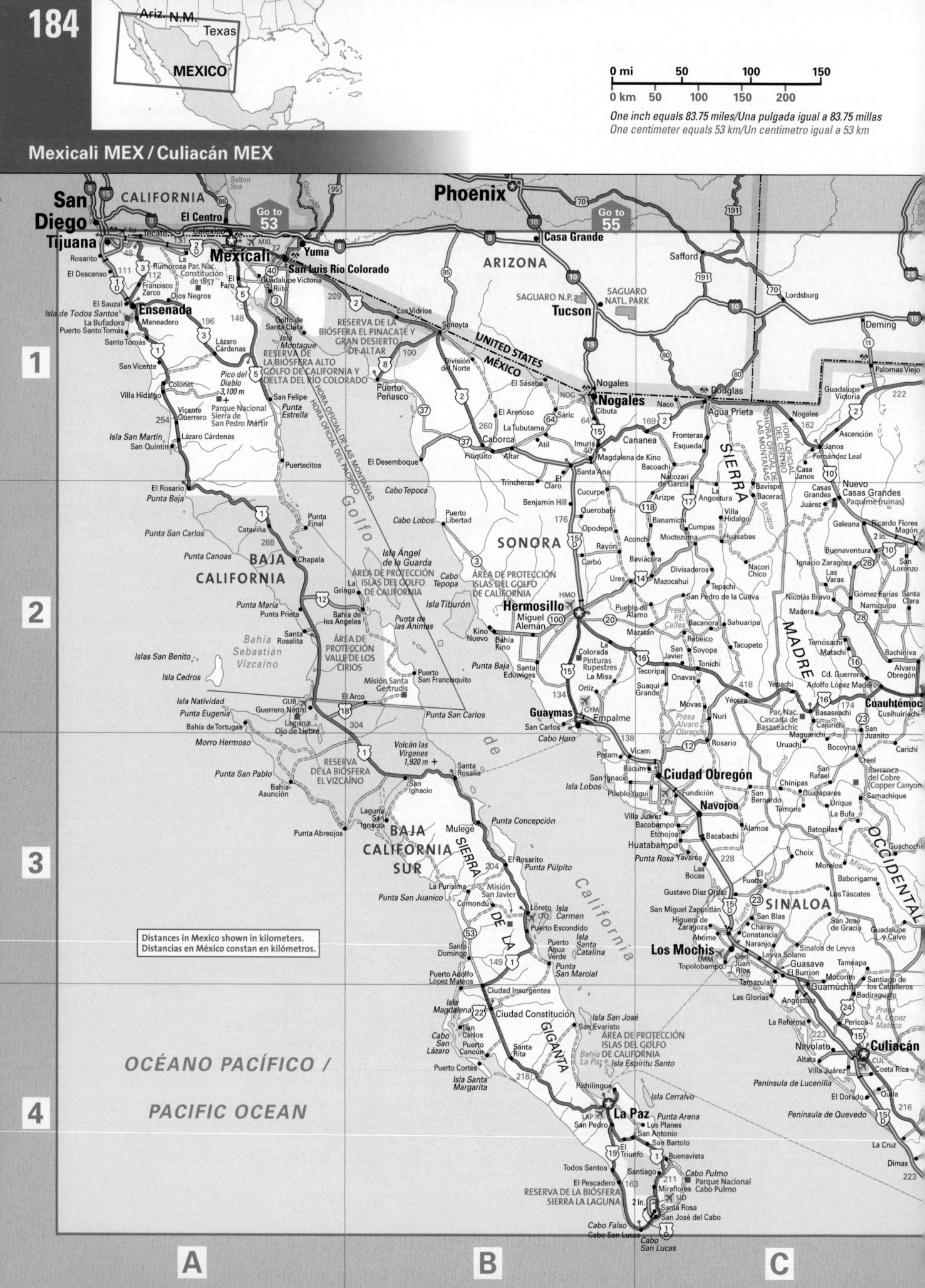
Ariz.
N.M.
Texas
MEXICO
0 mi 50 100 150
0 km 50 100 150 200
One inch equals 83.75 miles/Una pulgada igual a 83.75 millas
One centimeter equals 53 km/Un centímetro igual a 53 km
Go to 53
Go to 55
CALIFORNIA
ARIZONA
SONORA
BAJA CALIFORNIA
BAJA CALIFORNIA SUR
SINALOA
SIERRA MADRE OCCIDENTAL
SIERRA DE LA GIGANTA
UNITED STATES
MÉXICO
Golfo de California
OCÉANO PACÍFICO /
PACIFIC OCEAN
San Diego
Tijuana
Mexicali
El Centro
Calexico
Yuma
San Luis Río Colorado
Phoenix
Casa Grande
Tucson
Safford
Lordsburg
Deming
Nogales
Douglas
Agua Prieta
Ensenada
Rosarito
El Descanso
Tecate
San Felipe
Puerto Peñasco
Caborca
Hermosillo
Guaymas
Empalme
Ciudad Obregón
Navojoa
Los Mochis
Topolobampo
Guasave
Guamúchil
Culiacán
Cuauhtémoc
Nuevo Casas Grandes
Santa Rosalía
Mulegé
Loreto
Ciudad Constitución
La Paz
Todos Santos
San José del Cabo
Cabo San Lucas
Cananea
Magdalena de Kino
Santa Ana
Sonoyta
SAGUARO N.P.
SAGUARO NATL. PARK
RESERVA DE LA BIÓSFERA EL PINACATE Y GRAN DESIERTO DE ALTAR
RESERVA DE LA BIÓSFERA ALTO GOLFO DE CALIFORNIA Y DELTA DEL RÍO COLORADO
RESERVA DE LA BIÓSFERA EL VIZCAÍNO
RESERVA DE LA BIÓSFERA SIERRA LA LAGUNA
ÁREA DE PROTECCIÓN ISLAS DEL GOLFO DE CALIFORNIA
ÁREA DE PROTECCIÓN VALLE DE LOS CIRIOS
Parque Nacional Sierra de San Pedro Mártir
Parque Nacional Cabo Pulmo
Parque Nacional Cascada de Basaseachic
Isla Ángel de la Guarda
Isla Tiburón
Isla Cedros
Bahía Sebastián Vizcaíno
HORA OFICIAL DE LAS MONTAÑAS
HORA OFICIAL DEL PACÍFICO
HORA OFICIAL DEL CENTRO
Distances in Mexico shown in kilometers.
Distancias en México constan en kilómetros.
1
2
3
4
A
B
C

DRIVING DISTANCES IN KM / DISTANCIAS DE MANEJO EN KM

	CHIHUAHUA	CIUDAD JUÁREZ	CIUDAD VICTORIA	CULIACÁN	DURANGO	HERMOSILLO	MAZATLÁN	MÉXICO	MONTERREY	SAN LUIS POTOSÍ	TIJUANA	TORREÓN
CHIHUAHUA		385	1086	919	686	579	1209	1538	808	1155	1456	449
HERMOSILLO	579	795	1666	706	941		729	1810	1387	1416	884	1028
MONTERREY	808	1236	288	924	689	1387	901	892		509	2362	359
TORREÓN	449	834	637	914	266	1028	892	1089	359	706	1905	

SEE ALSO DISTANCE AND DRIVING TIME MAP ON PAGES 286–287 / CONSULTE, PARA DISTANCIAS Y TIEMPO DE MANEJO, EN LAS PÁGINAS 286–287

MEXICO

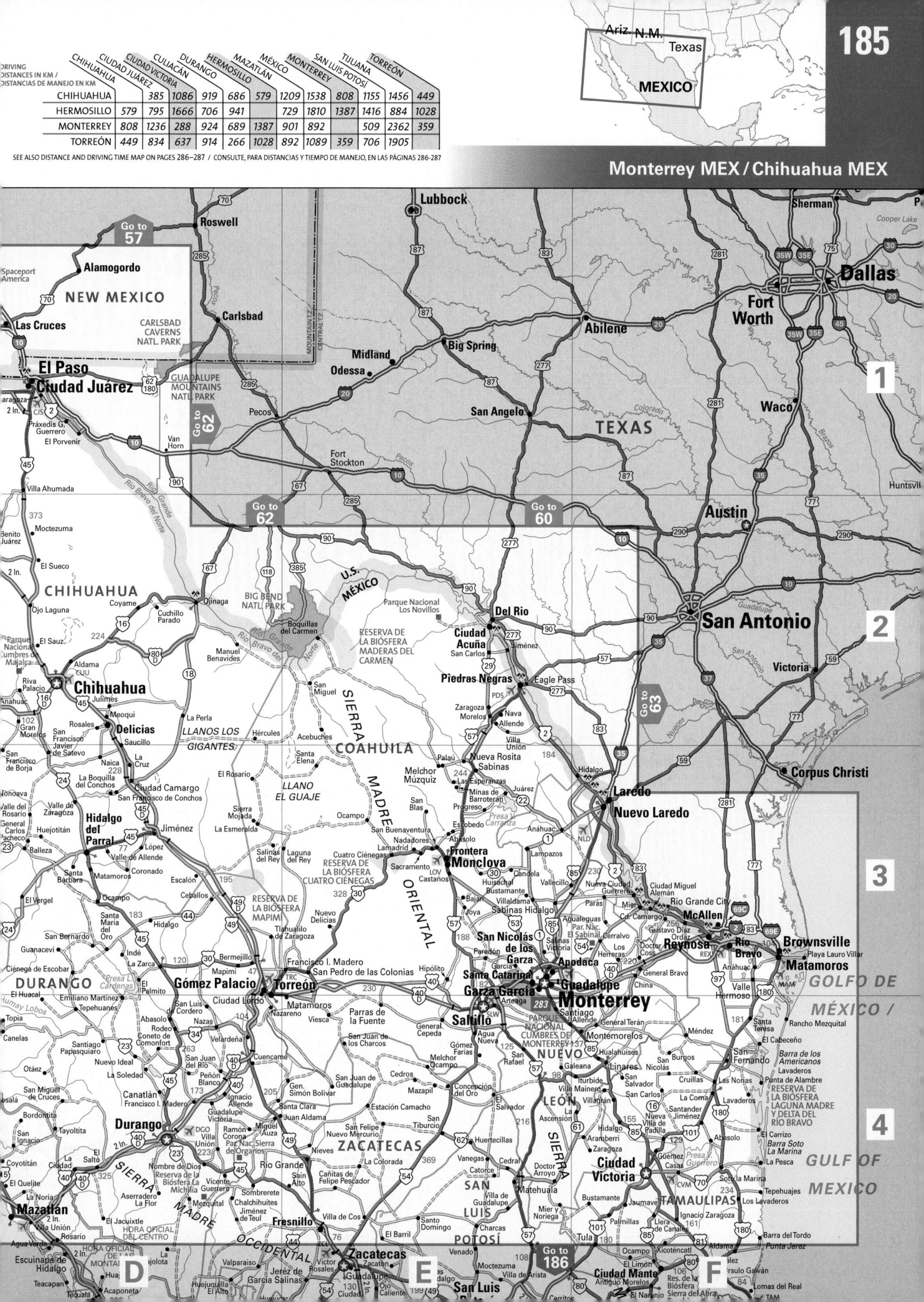

Puerto
Rico

0 mi   50   100   150
0 km   50   100   150   200

One inch equals 83.75 miles/Una pulgada igual a 83.75 millas
One centimeter equals 53 km/Un centímetro igual a 53 km

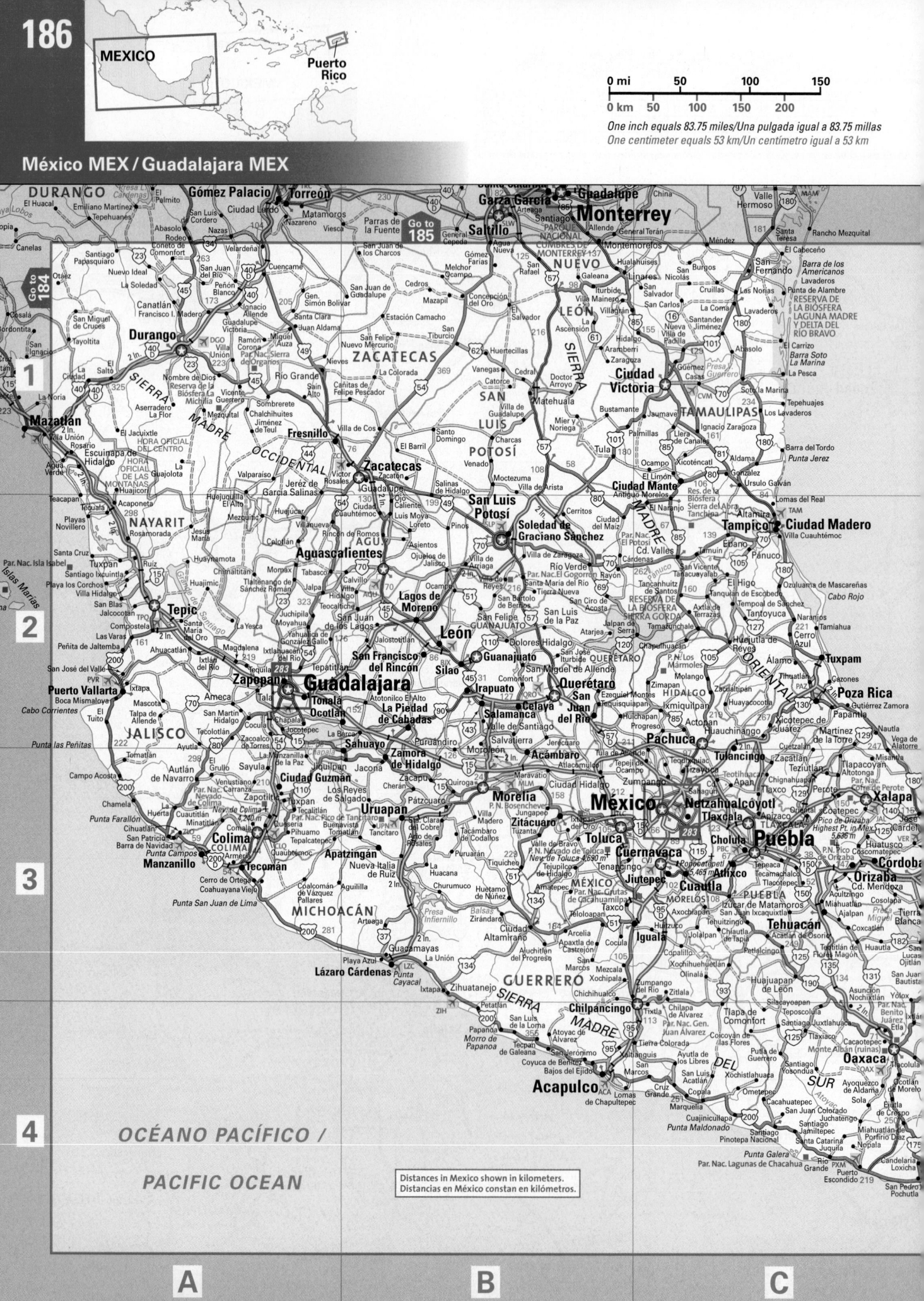

Distances in Mexico shown in kilometers.
Distancias en México constan en kilómetros.

OCÉANO PACÍFICO /

PACIFIC OCEAN

A   B   C

MEXICO

Puerto Rico

DRIVING DISTANCES IN KM / DISTANCIAS DE MANEJO EN KM

	ACAPULCO	CANCÚN	CIUDAD VICTORIA	DURANGO	GUADALAJARA	MAZATLÁN	MÉRIDA	MÉXICO	PUEBLA	SAN LUIS POTOSÍ	TUXTLA GUTIÉRREZ	VERACRUZ
GUADALAJARA	897	2275	774	599		523	1904	578	691	336	1510	943
MÉRIDA	1777	321	1725	2182	1904	2408		1326	1282	1707	786	995
MÉXICO	422	1736	682	856	578	1081	1326		133	381	932	365
SAN LUIS POTOSÍ	834	2161	438	475	336	687	1707	381	496		1313	747

SEE ALSO DISTANCE AND DRIVING TIME MAP ON PAGES 286–287 / CONSULTE, PARA DISTANCIAS Y TIEMPO DE MANEJO, EN LAS PÁGINAS 286–287

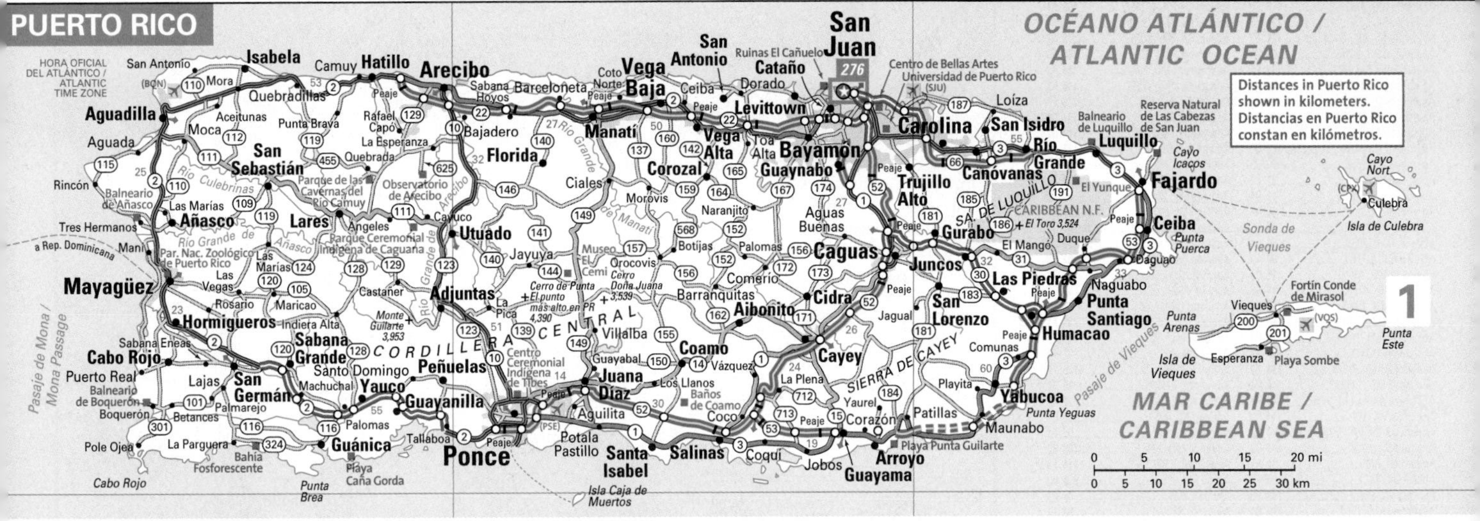

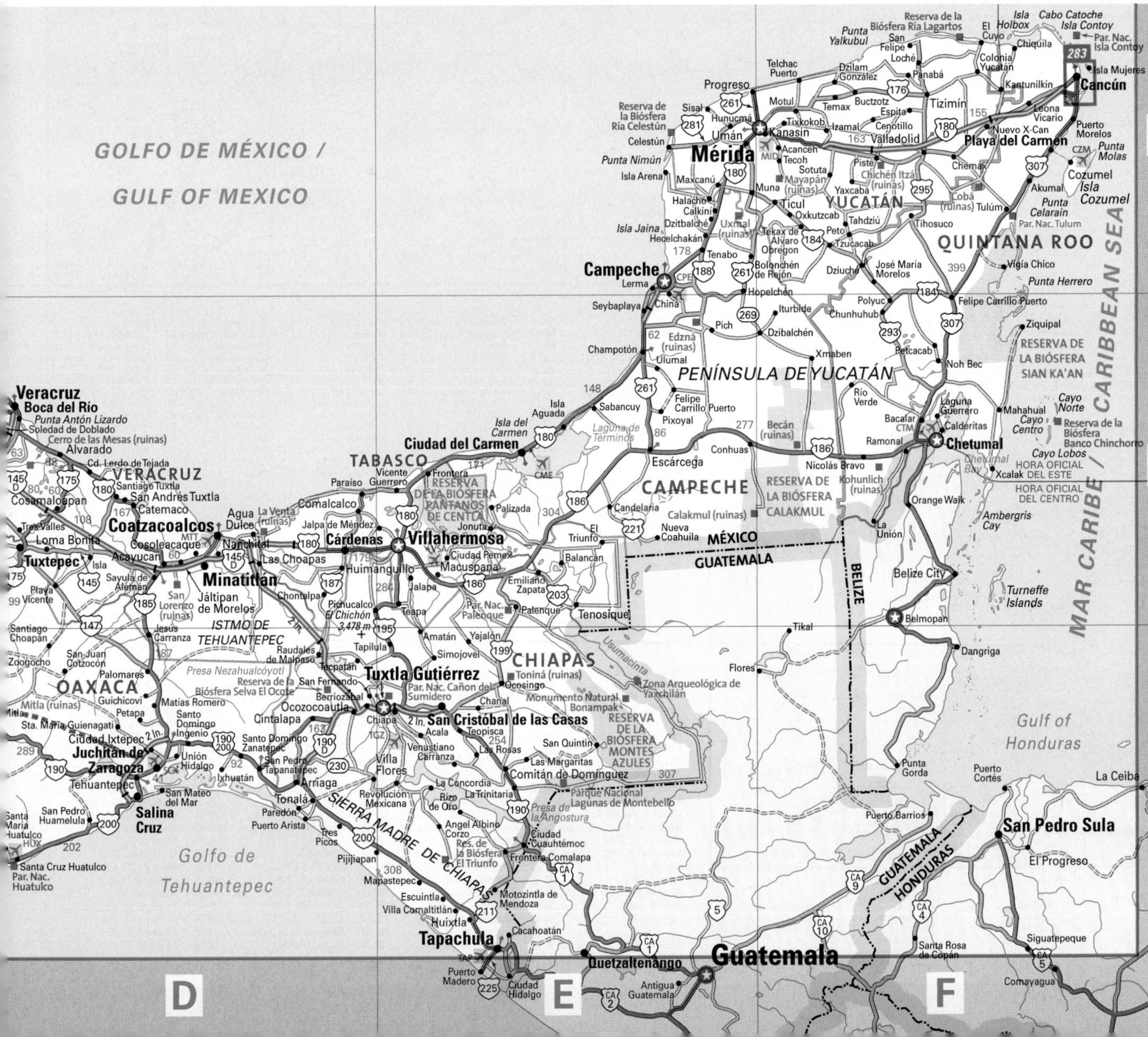

PUERTO RICO

OCÉANO ATLÁNTICO / ATLANTIC OCEAN

HORA OFICIAL DEL ATLÁNTICO / ATLANTIC TIME ZONE

Distances in Puerto Rico shown in kilometers.
Distancias en Puerto Rico constan en kilómetros.

MAR CARIBE / CARIBBEAN SEA

| 0 | 5 | 10 | 15 | 20 mi |
| 0 | 5 | 10 | 15 | 20 | 25 | 30 km |

GOLFO DE MÉXICO / GULF OF MEXICO

PENÍNSULA DE YUCATÁN

YUCATÁN

QUINTANA ROO

CAMPECHE

TABASCO

VERACRUZ

OAXACA

ISTMO DE TEHUANTEPEC

CHIAPAS

SIERRA MADRE DE CHIAPAS

Golfo de Tehuantepec

MAR CARIBE / CARIBBEAN SEA

RESERVA DE LA BIÓSFERA SIAN KA'AN

RESERVA DE LA BIÓSFERA CALAKMUL

MÉXICO
GUATEMALA

BELIZE

Gulf of Honduras

GUATEMALA
HONDURAS

Guatemala

Figures after entries indicate population, page number, and grid reference.

UNITED STATES

A

Abbeville AL, 2688 128 B4
Abbeville GA, 2908 129 E3
Abbeville LA, 12257 133 F3
Abbeville MS, 419 118 C3
Abbeville SC, 5237 121 E3
Abbeville Co. SC, 25417 121 E3
Abbotsford WI, 2310 68 A4
Abbottstown PA, 1011 103 E1
Abercrombie ND, 263 19 F4
Aberdeen ID, 1994 31 E1
Aberdeen MD, 14959 145 D1
Aberdeen MS, 5612 119 D4
Aberdeen NC, 6350 122 C1
Aberdeen OH, 1638 100 C3
Aberdeen SD, 26091 27 E2
Aberdeen WA, 16896 12 B4
Abernathy TX, 2805 58 A1
Abilene KS, 6844 43 E2
Abilene TX, 117063 58 C3
Abingdon IL, 3319 88 A3
Abingdon MD, 950 145 D1
Abingdon VA, 8191 111 E3
Abington MA, 15985 151 D2
Abita Sprs. LA, 2365 134 B2
Absarokee MT, 1150 24 B2
Absecon NJ, 8411 147 F4
Acadia Par. LA, 61773 133 E2
Accokeek MD, 10573 144 B4
Accokeek Acres MD, 1500 144 B4
Accomac VA, 519 114 C3
Accomack Co. VA, 33164 114 C3
Accord MA, 2300 151 D2
Accord NY, 562 94 A3
Achille OK, 492 59 F1
Achilles VA, 650 113 F2
Ackerman MS, 1510 126 C1
Ackley IA, 1589 73 D4
Acme MI, 650 69 F4
Acomita Lake NM, 416 48 B3
Acton CA, 7596 52 C2
Acton MA, 21924 150 C1
Acushnet MA, 3073 151 D3
Acworth GA, 20425 120 C3
Ada MN, 1707 19 F3
Ada OH, 5952 90 B3
Ada OK, 16810 51 F4
Ada Co. ID, 392365 22 B4
Adair IA, 781 86 B2
Adair OK, 790 106 A3
Adair Co. IA, 7682 86 B2
Adair Co. KY, 18656 110 B2
Adair Co. MO, 25607 87 D4
Adair Co. OK, 22683 106 B4
Adairsville GA, 4648 120 B3
Adair Vil. OR, 840 20 B3
Adairville KY, 852 109 F3
Adams MA, 5515 94 C1
Adams MN, 787 73 D2
Adams NE, 573 35 F4
Adams NY, 1775 79 E2
Adams OR, 350 21 F1
Adams TN, 633 109 E3
Adams WI, 1967 74 A1
Adams Ctr. NY, 1568 79 E2
Adams Co. CO, 441603 41 F1
Adams Co. ID, 3976 22 B2
Adams Co. IL, 67103 87 F4
Adams Co. IN, 34387 90 A3
Adams Co. IA, 4029 86 B3
Adams Co. MS, 32297 126 A4
Adams Co. NE, 31364 35 D4
Adams Co. ND, 2343 26 A1
Adams Co. OH, 28550 100 C3
Adams Co. PA, 101407 103 E1
Adams Co. WA, 18728 13 F4
Adams Co. WI, 20875 74 A2
Adamston NJ, 4900 147 E3
Adamstown MD, 2372 144 A2
Adamstown PA, 1789 146 A2
Adamsville AL, 4522 119 F4
Adamsville RI, 550 151 D4
Adamsville TN, 2207 119 D1
Addis LA, 3593 134 A2
Addison AL, 758 119 E3
Addison IL, 36942 203 C4
Addison ME, 300 83 E2
Addison MI, 605 90 B1
Addison NY, 1763 93 D1
Addison TX, 13056 207 D1
Addison Co. VT, 36821 81 D3
Adel GA, 5334 137 F1
Adel IA, 3682 86 C2
Adelanto CA, 31765 53 D2
Adelphi MD, 15086 270 E1
Adelphia NJ, 700 147 E2
Adena OH, 759 91 F4
Adrian GA, 664 129 F2
Adrian MI, 21133 90 B1
Adrian MN, 1209 72 A2
Adrian MO, 1677 96 B4
Advance IN, 477 99 E1
Advance MO, 1347 108 B2
Adwolf VA, 1530 111 F2
Affton MO, 20307 256 B3
Afton IA, 845 86 C3
Afton NY, 822 93 F1
Afton OK, 1049 106 B3
Afton WY, 1911 31 F1
Agawam MA, 28438 150 A2
Agency IA, 638 87 E3
Agency MO, 684 96 B1
Agoura Hills CA, 20330 228 A2
Agua Dulce TX, 3014 63 E2
Agua Fria NM, 2800 49 D2
Aguilar CO, 538 41 E4
Ahoskie NC, 5039 113 F3
Ahsahka ID, 600 14 B4
Ahuimanu HI, 8810 152 A3
Aiken SC, 29524 121 F4
Aiken Co. SC, 160099 122 A4
Ainsworth IA, 567 87 F2
Ainsworth NE, 1728 34 C1
Airmont NY, 8628 148 B3
Airport Drive MO, 698 106 B2
Airway Hts. WA, 6114 13 F3
Aitkin MN, 2165 64 B4
Aitkin Co. MN, 16202 64 B4
Ajo AZ, 3304 54 B3
Ak-Chin Vil. AZ, 862 54 C2
Akiachak AK, 627 154 B3
Akins OK, 493 116 B1
Akron AL, 356 127 E1
Akron CO, 1702 41 F1
Akron IN, 1167 89 F3
Akron IA, 1486 35 F1
Akron MI, 402 76 B2
Akron NY, 2868 78 B3

Albany D3
Alplaus C1
Best E3
Bethlehem Ctr. D3
Boght Corners E1
Calico Colony D1
Clifton Gardens D1
Clifton Park D1
Clifton Park Ctr. D1
Clinton Park E3
Cohoes E2
Colonie D2
Crescent E1
Defreestville E3
Delmar D3
Dunnsville C2
Dunsbach Ferry E1
E. Greenbush E3
Elsmere D3
Ft. Hunter C2
Glenmont D3
Glenridge C1
Grant Hollow E1
Green Island E2
Grooms Corners D1
Guilderland C2
Guilderland Ctr. C2
Halfmoon E1
Hartmans Corners C2
Hawthorne Hill D1
Latham E2
Loudonville E2
Luther E3
Maple Wood E2
Maywood D2
McCormack Corners C2
McKownville D3
Meadowdale C3
Menands E3
Mohawk View D2
New Salem C3
New Scotland C3
Newtonville E2
Niskayuna D2
Normanville D3
N. Bethlehem D3
Rensselaer E3
Rexford D1
Roessleville D2
Rotterdam C1
Schenectady C1
Scotia C1
Sherwood Park E3
Slingerlands D3
Snyders Corners E3
Speigletown E1
Sycaway E2
Troy E2
Unionville D3
Verdoy D2
Vischer Ferry D1
Voorheesville C3
Waterford E1
Watervliet E2
W. Hill C1
Westmere D2
Wynantskill E2

Akron OH, 199110 91 E3
Akron PA, 3876 146 A2
Akutan AK, 1027 154 A4
Alabaster AL, 30352 127 F1
Alachua FL, 9059 138 C3
Alachua Co. FL, 247336 138 C3
Alakanuk AK, 677 154 B2
Alamance Co. NC, 151131 112 C4
Alameda CA, 73812 259 C3
Alameda NM, 4200 48 C3
Alameda Co. CA, 1510271 36 B4
Alamo CA, 14570 259 D2
Alamo GA, 2797 129 E3
Alamo NM, 1085 48 B4
Alamo TN, 2461 108 C4
Alamo TX, 18353 63 E4
Alamogordo NM, 30403 56 C2
Alamo Hts. TX, 7031 257 E2
Alamosa CO, 8780 41 D4
Alamosa Co. CO, 15445 41 D4
Alanson MI, 738 70 C3
Alapaha GA, 668 129 E4
Alba MO, 555 106 B2
Albany CA, 18539 259 C2
Albany GA, 77434 129 D4
Albany IL, 891 88 A1
Albany IN, 2165 90 A4
Albany KY, 2033 110 B3
Albany LA, 1088 134 B2
Albany MN, 2561 66 B2
Albany MO, 1730 86 B4
Albany NY, 97856 94 B1
Albany OH, 828 101 E2
Albany OR, 50158 20 B3
Albany TX, 2034 58 C2
Albany WI, 1018 74 B4
Albany Co. NY, 304204 94 B1
Albany Co. WY, 36299 33 E2
Albemarle NC, 15903 122 B1
Albemarle Co. VA, 98970 102 C4
Albers IL, 1190 98 B3
Albert City IA, 699 72 B4
Albert Lea MN, 18016 72 C2
Alberton MT, 420 15 D4
Albertville AL, 21160 120 A3
Albertville MN, 7044 66 C3
Albia IA, 3766 87 D3
Albin VA, 700 102 C2
Albion ID, 267 31 D2
Albion IL, 1988 99 D4
Albion IN, 2349 90 A2
Albion IA, 505 87 D1
Albion MI, 8616 76 A4
Albion NE, 1650 35 E3
Albion NY, 6056 78 B3
Albion PA, 1516 91 F1
Albion WA, 579 14 A4
Albuquerque NM, 545852 48 C3
Alburg VT, 497 81 D1
Alburnett IA, 673 87 E1
Alburtis PA, 2361 146 B1
Alcalde NM, 285 49 D2
Alcester SD, 807 35 F1
Alcoa TN, 8449 110 C4
Alcona Co. MI, 10942 71 D4
Alcorn MS, 1017 126 A3
Alcorn Co. MS, 37057 119 D2
Alda NE, 642 35 D4
Aldan PA, 4152 248 B4
Alden IA, 787 72 C4
Alden MN, 661 72 C2
Alden NY, 2605 78 B3
Alderson WV, 1184 112 A1
Alderwood Manor WA, 8442 262 B2
Aldine TX, 15869 220 C1
Aledo IL, 3640 87 F2
Aledo TX, 2716 59 E2
Alex OK, 550 51 E3
Alexander AR, 2901 117 E2
Alexander ND, 223 17 F2
Alexander City AL, 14875 128 A1
Alexander Co. IL, 8238 108 C2
Alexander Co. NC, 37198 112 A4
Alexandria AL, 3917 120 A4
Alexandria IN, 5145 89 F4
Alexandria KY, 8477 100 B3
Alexandria LA, 47723 125 E4
Alexandria MN, 11070 66 B2
Alexandria SD, 615 27 E4
Alexandria TN, 966 110 A4
Alexandria VA, 139966 144 B3
Alexandria Bay NY, 1078 79 E1
Alexis IL, 831 88 A3
Alfalfa Co. OK, 5642 51 D1
Alford FL, 489 136 C1
Alfred ME, 2497 82 B4
Alfred NY, 4174 92 C1
Alger OH, 860 90 B3
Alger Co. MI, 9601 69 E1
Algoa TX, 900 132 B4
Algodones NM, 814 48 C3
Algoma MS, 590 118 C3
Algoma WI, 3167 69 D4
Algona IA, 5560 72 B3
Algona WA, 3014 262 B5
Algonac MI, 4110 76 C4
Algonquin IL, 30046 88 C1
Algood TN, 3495 110 A3
Alhambra CA, 83089 228 D2
Alhambra IL, 681 98 B3
Alice TX, 19104 63 E2
Aliceville AL, 2486 127 E1
Ali Chuk AZ, 161 54 B3
Aliquippa PA, 9438 91 F3
Aliso Viejo CA, 47823 229 G6
Allamakee Co. IA, 14330 73 F3
Allamuchy NJ, 78 94 A4
Allardt TN, 634 110 B3
Allegan MI, 4998 75 F4
Allegan Co. MI, 111408 75 F4
Allegany NY, 1816 92 C1
Allegany Co. MD, 75087 102 C1
Allegany Co. NY, 48946 78 C4
Alleghany Co. NC, 11155 111 F3
Alleghany Co. VA, 16250 102 A4
Allegheny Co. PA, 1223348 92 A4
Allen NE, 377 35 F2
Allen OK, 932 51 F3
Allen SD, 420 26 B4
Allen TX, 84246 59 F2
Allen Co. IN, 355329 90 A3
Allen Co. KS, 13371 96 A4
Allen Co. KY, 19956 109 F2
Allen Co. OH, 106331 90 B3
Allendale MI, 17579 75 F3
Allendale NJ, 6505 148 B3
Allendale SC, 3482 130 B1
Allendale Co. SC, 10419 130 B1
Allenhurst GA, 695 130 B3
Allenhurst NJ, 496 147 F2
Allen Par. LA, 25764 133 E1
Allen Park MI, 28210 210 B4
Allenspark CO, 528 41 D1
Allenton RI, 1400 150 C4
Allenton WI, 823 74 C2
Allentown NJ, 1828 147 D2
Allentown PA, 118032 146 B1
Allenwood NJ, 925 147 E2
Allerton IA, 501 87 D3

Akron OH

Akron A1
Barberton A2
Copley A1
Cuyahoga Falls B1
Fairlawn A1
Ghent A1
Lakemore B2
Mogadore B2
Montrose A1
Munroe Falls B1
Norton A2
Portage Lakes A2
Silver Lake B1
Stow B1
Tallmadge B1

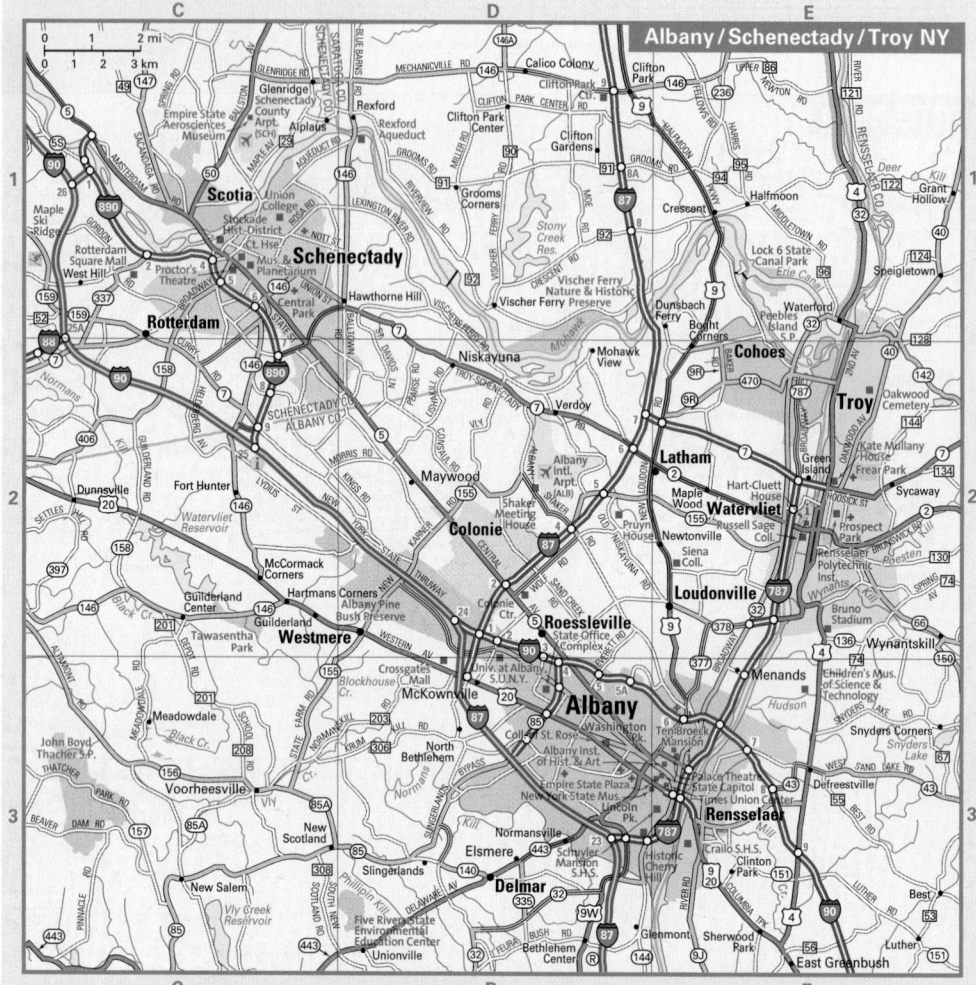

Entries in **bold black** indicate counties or parishes.
Entries in **bold color** indicate cities with detailed inset maps.

Albuquerque NM

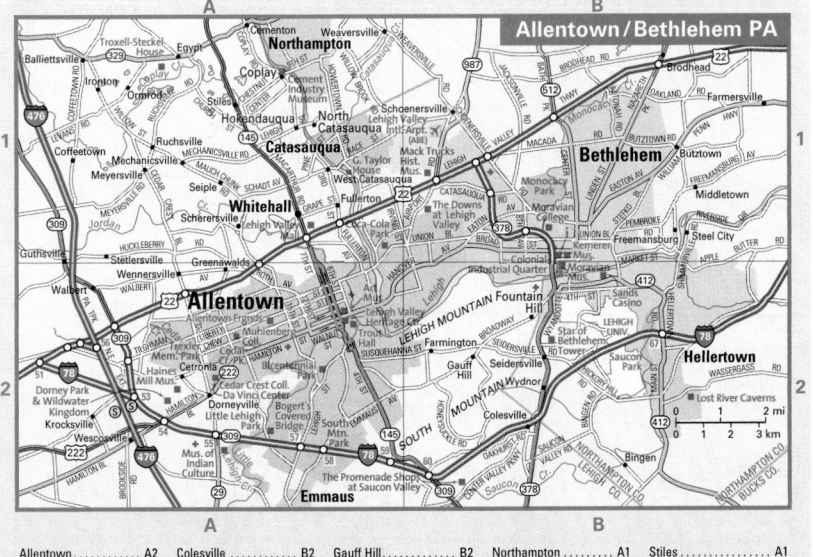

Amarillo TX

Anchorage AK

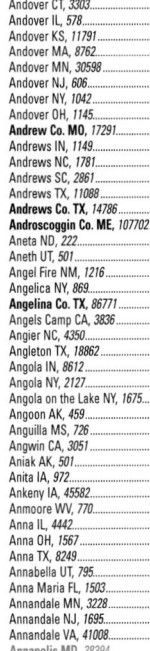

Allentown / Bethlehem PA

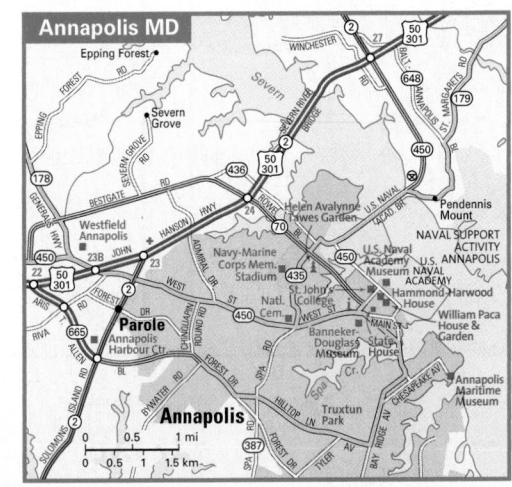

Annapolis MD

190

Anoka County–Arcade

Figures after entries indicate population, page number, and grid reference.

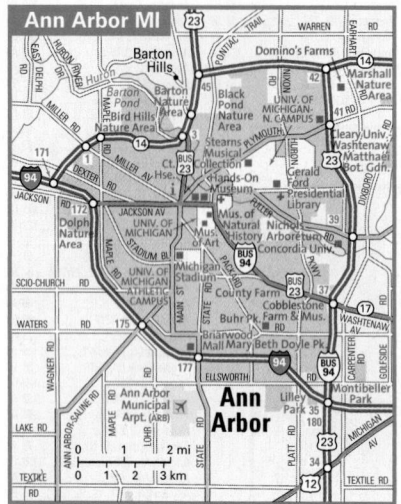

Ann Arbor MI

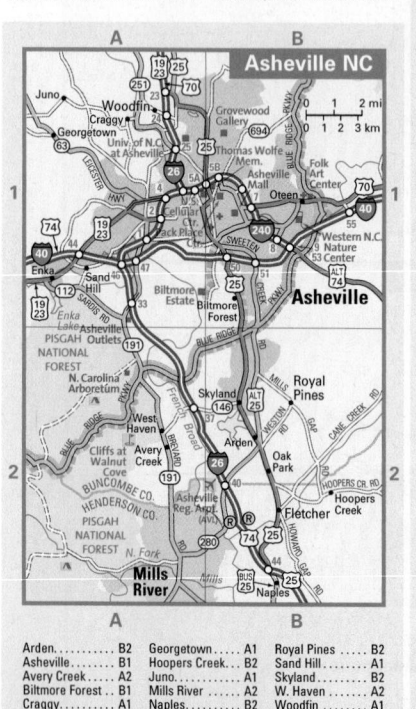

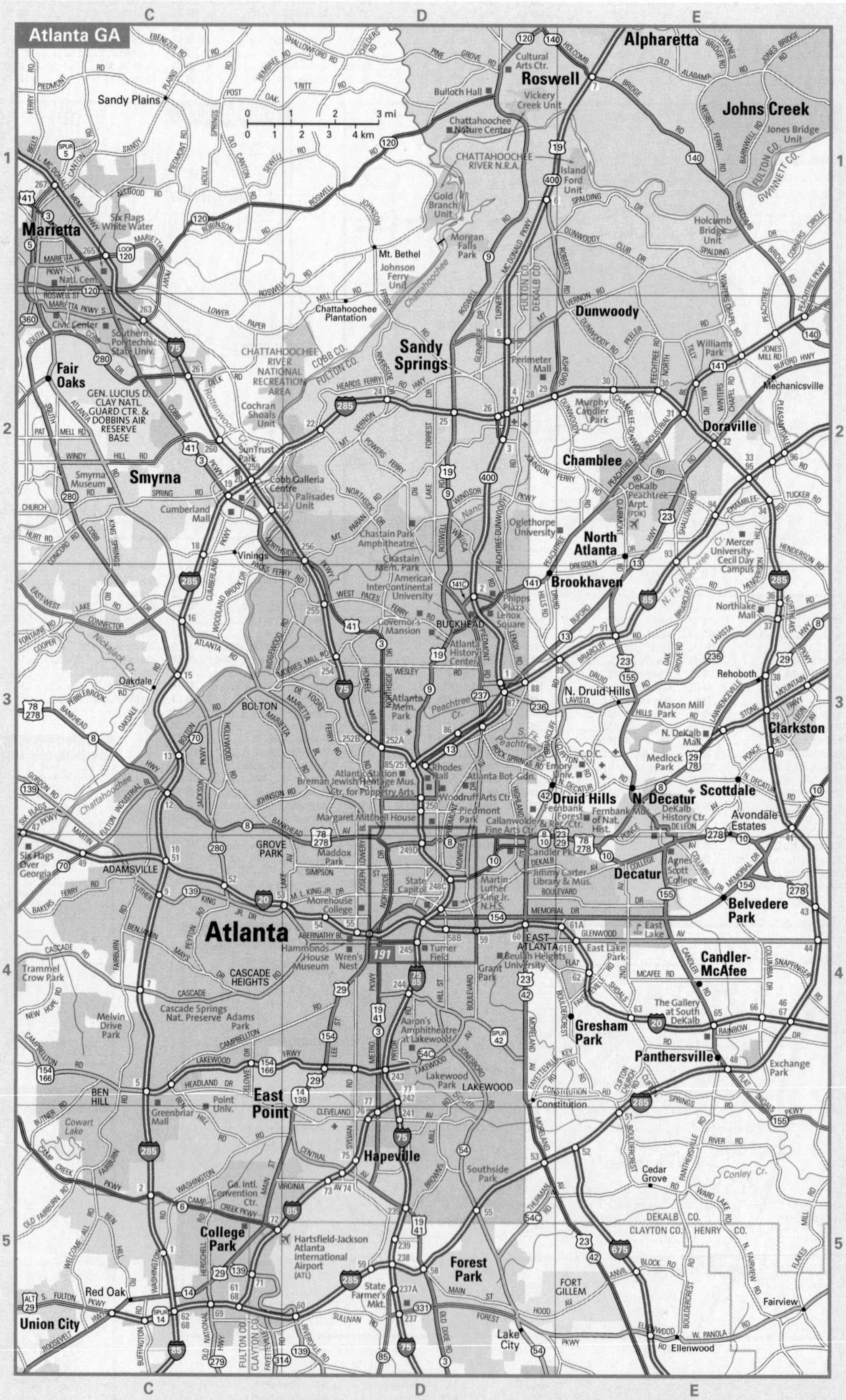

Asheville NC

Atlanta GA

Entries in **bold black** indicate counties or parishes.
Entries in **bold color** indicate cities with detailed inset maps.

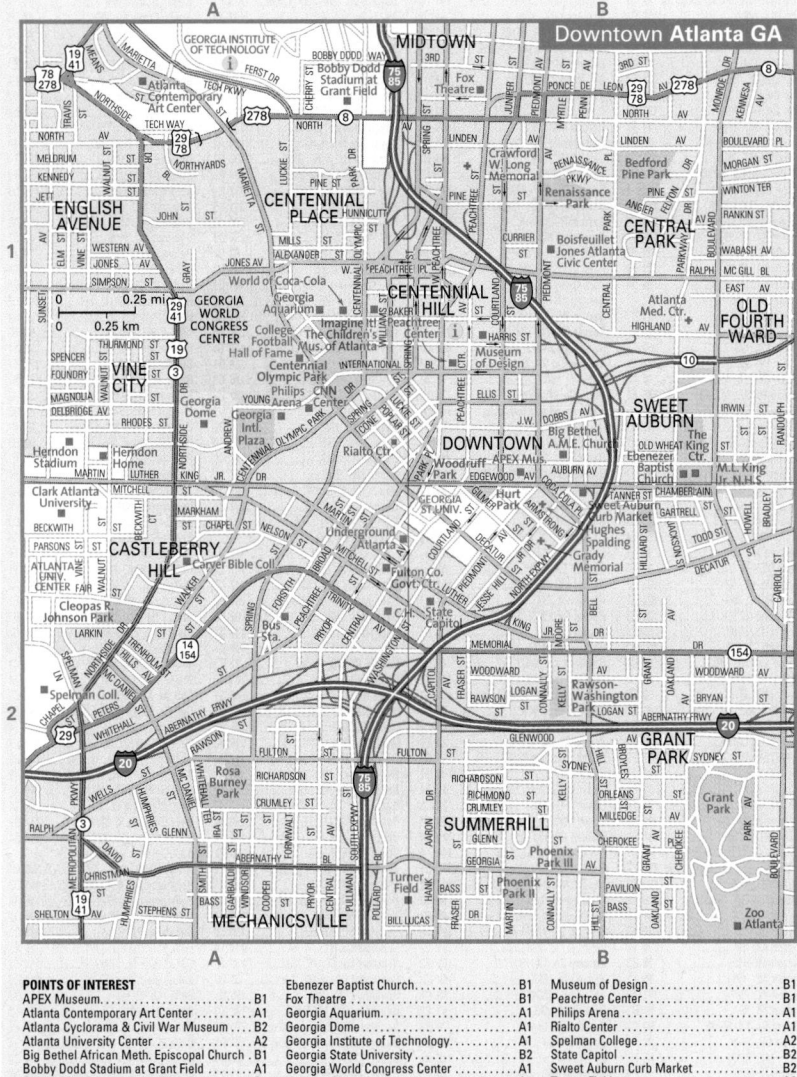

Downtown Atlanta GA

POINTS OF INTEREST

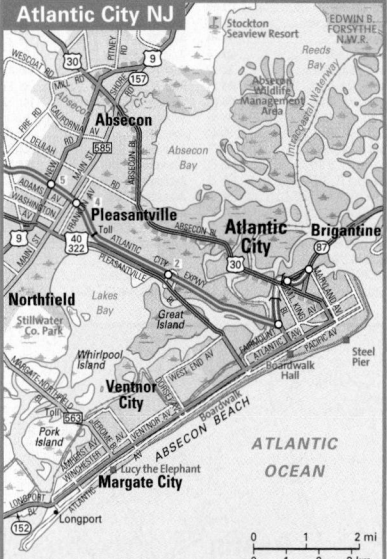

Atlantic City NJ

Augusta GA

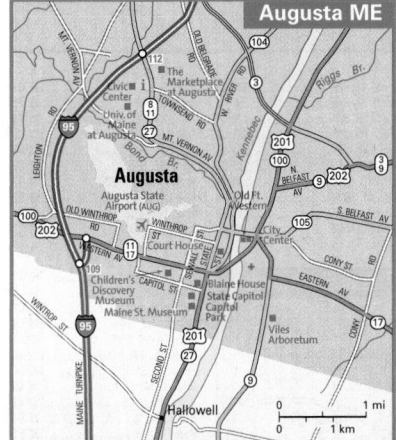

Augusta ME

192
Aulander–Belmont

Figures after entries indicate population, page number, and grid reference.

Aulander NC, *895* 113 E3
Ault CO, *1519* 33 E4
Aumsville OR, *3584* 20 B2
Aurelia IA, *1036* 72 A4
Aurora CO, *325078* 41 E1
Aurora IL, *197899* 88 C1
Aurora IN, *3750* 100 B2
Aurora MN, *1682* 64 C3
Aurora MO, *7508* 106 C2
Aurora NE, *4479* 35 E4
Aurora NY, *724* 79 D4
Aurora NC, *520* 115 D3
Aurora OH, *15548* 91 E2
Aurora OR, *918* 20 C2
Aurora SD, *532* 27 F3
Aurora TX, *1220* 59 E2
Aurora UT, *1016* 39 E2
Aurora Co. SD, *2710* 27 D4
Au Sable MI, *1404* 76 C1
Autaugaville AL, *870* 127 F2
Auxvasse MO, *983* 97 E2
Ava IL, *654* 98 B4
Ava MO, *2993* 107 E2
Avalon CA, *3728* 52 C3
Avalon NJ, *1334* 105 D4
Avalon PA, *4705* 250 A1
Avawam KY, *450* 111 D2
Avella PA, *804* 91 F4
Avenal CA, *15505* 44 C3
Avenel NJ, *17011* 147 E1
Aventura FL, *35762* 143 F2
Averill Park NY, *1693* 94 B1
Avery CA, *646* 37 D3
Avery Co. NC, *17797* 111 F4
Avery Creek NC, *1950* 121 E1
Avilla IN, *2401* 90 A2
Avis PA, *1484* 93 D2
Aviston IL, *1945* 98 B3
Avon MN, *1396* 66 C2
Avon NY, *3394* 78 C3
Avon NC, *776* 115 F3
Avon OH, *21193* 91 D2
Avon PA, *1667* 146 A2
Avon SD, *590* 35 E1
Avon-by-the-Sea NJ, *1901* 147 F2
Avondale AZ, *76238* 54 C1
Avondale CO, *674* 41 E3
Avondale LA, *4954* 134 B3
Avondale MO, *440* 224 C2
Avondale PA, *1265* 146 B3
Avondale RI, *425* 149 F2
Avondale Estates GA, *2960* 190 E3
Avonia PA, *1205* 91 F1
Avon Lake OH, *22581* 91 D2
Avonmore PA, *1011* 92 A4
Avon Park FL, *8836* 141 D3
Avoyelles Par. LA, *42073* 125 F4

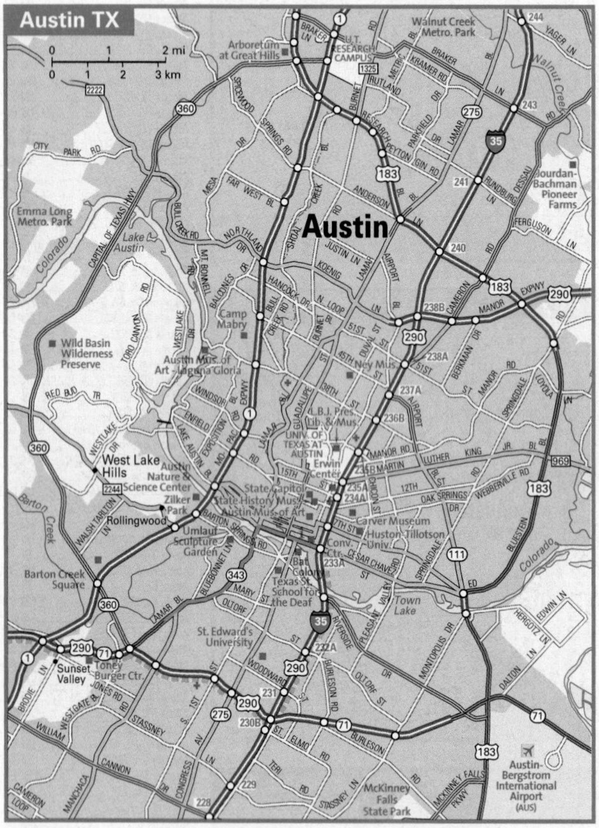
Austin TX
0 1 2 mi
0 1 2 3 km
Austin
Arboretum at Great Hills
U.T. Research Campus
Walnut Creek Metro. Park
Jourdan-Bachman Pioneer Farms
Emma Long Metro. Park
Lake Austin
Camp Mabry
Wild Basin Wilderness Preserve
Austin Mus. of Art - Laguna Gloria
West Lake Hills
Austin Nature & Science Center
Zilker Park
Rollingwood
Umlauf Sculpture Garden
State Capitol
State History Mus.
Austin Mus. of Art
Carver Museum
Huston-Tillotson Univ.
Barton Creek Square
St. Edward's University
Texas School for the Deaf
Town Lake
Sunset Valley
Toney Burger Ctr.
McKinney Falls State Park
Austin-Bergstrom International Airport (AUS)
Colorado

Au Sable Forks NY, *559* 81 D2
Austin AR, *2038* 117 E2
Austin IN, *4295* 99 F3
Austin MN, *24718* 73 D2
Austin NV, *192* 37 F1
Austin PA, *562* 92 C2
Austin TX, *790390* 61 E1
Austin Co. TX, *28417* 61 F2
Austintown OH, *29677* 91 F3
Autauga Co. AL, *54571* 127 F2
Avoca AR, *488* 106 C3
Avoca IA, *1506* 86 A2
Avoca NY, *946* 78 C4
Avoca PA, *2661* 261 C2
Avoca WI, *637* 74 A3
Avon AL, *543* 137 D1
Avon CO, *6447* 40 C1
Avon CT, *18098* 94 C3
Avon IL, *799* 88 A3
Avon IN, *12446* 99 F1
Awendaw SC, *1294* 131 D1
Axtell KS, *406* 43 F1
Axtell NE, *726* 35 D4
Ayden NC, *4932* 115 D3
Ayer MA, *2868* 95 D1
Aynor SC, *560* 122 C3
Azalea Park FL, *12556* 246 D2
Azle TX, *10947* 59 E2
Aztec NM, *6763* 48 B1
Azusa CA, *46361* 228 E2

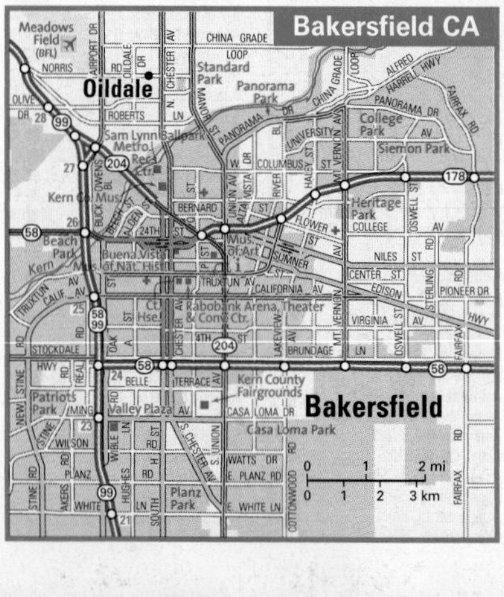
Bakersfield CA
Meadows Field (BFL)
Oildale
Standard Park
Panorama Park
Sam Lynn Ballpark
College Park
Kern Co. Mus.
Beach Park
Buena Vista Mus. of Nat. Hist.
Mus. of Art
Heritage Park
Rabobank Arena, Theater & Conv. Ctr.
Patriots Park
Valley Plaza
Kern County Fairgrounds
Bakersfield
Casa Loma Park
Planz Park
0 1 2 mi
0 1 2 3 km

B

Babbie AL, *603* 128 A4
Babbitt MN, *1475* 64 C3
Babson Park FL, *1356* 141 D3
Babylon NY, *12166* 148 C4
Baca Co. CO, *3788* 42 A4
Bacon Co. GA, *11096* 129 F4
Baconton GA, *915* 129 D4
Bad Axe MI, *3129* 76 C2
Baden PA, *4135* 92 A3
Badger IA, *561* 72 C4
Badin NC, *1974* 122 B1
Bagdad AZ, *1876* 46 C4
Bagdad FL, *3761* 135 F2
Baggs WY, *440* 32 C3
Bagley MN, *1392* 64 A3
Bahama NC, *550* 112 C4
Bailey NC, *569* 113 D4
Bailey Co. TX, *7165* 49 F4
Bailey Island ME, *400* 82 B3
Bailey's Crossroads VA, *23643* 270 B4
Bailey's Prairie TX, *727* 132 A4
Baileyton AL, *610* 119 F3
Baileyton TN, *431* 111 D3
Bainbridge GA, *12697* 137 D1
Bainbridge IN, *746* 99 E1
Bainbridge NY, *1355* 79 E4
Bainbridge OH, *3267* 101 D2
Bainbridge Island WA, *23025* 12 C3
Baird TX, *1496* 58 C3
Baiting Hollow NY, *1642* 149 E3
Baker LA, *13895* 134 A2
Baker MT, *1741* 17 F4
Baker City OR, *9828* 21 F2
Baker Co. FL, *27115* 138 C2
Baker Co. GA, *3451* 128 C4
Baker Co. OR, *16134* 21 F3
Bakersfield CA, *347483* 45 D4
Bakersville NC, *464* 111 E4
Bala-Cynwyd PA, *10300* 146 C3
Balaton MN, *643* 72 A1
Balch Sprs. TX, *23728* 207 E3
Balcones Hts. TX, *2941* 257 E2
Bald Knob AR, *2897* 117 F1
Baldwin FL, *1425* 139 D2
Baldwin GA, *3279* 121 D3
Baldwin IL, *373* 98 B4
Baldwin LA, *2436* 133 F3
Baldwin MD, *850* 144 C1
Baldwin MI, *1208* 75 F2
Baldwin PA, *19767* 250 C3
Baldwin WI, *3957* 67 E4
Baldwin City KS, *4515* 96 A3
Baldwin Co. AL, *182265* 135 E1
Baldwin Co. GA, *45720* 129 E1
Baldwin Harbor NY, *8102* 147 F1
Baldwin Park CA, *75390* 228 E2
Baldwinsville NY, *7378* 79 D3
Baldwinville MA, *2028* 95 D1
Baldwyn MS, *3297* 119 D3
Balfour NC, *1187* 121 E1
Bal Harbour FL, *2513* 233 B3
Ball LA, *4000* 125 E4
Ballantine MT, *320* 24 C1
Ballard UT, *801* 32 A4
Ballard Co. KY, *8249* 108 C2
Ballentine SC, *850* 122 A3
Ball Ground GA, *1433* 120 C3
Ballinger TX, *3767* 58 C4
Ballouville CT, *950* 150 B3
Ballston Spa NY, *5409* 80 C4
Ballville OH, *2976* 90 C2
Ballwin MO, *30404* 98 A3
Bally PA, *1090* 146 B1
Balmorhea TX, *479* 62 B2
Balmville NY, *3178* 148 B1
Balsam Lake WI, *1009* 67 E3
Baltic CT, *1250* 149 F1
Baltic OH, *795* 91 E4
Baltic SD, *1089* 27 F4
Baltimore MD, *620961* 144 C2
Baltimore OH, *2966* 101 D1
Baltimore Co. MD, *805029* 144 C1
Baltimore Highlands MD, *7019* 193 C4
Bamberg SC, *3607* 130 C1
Bamberg Co. SC, *15987* 130 B1
Bancroft ID, *377* 31 E1
Bancroft IA, *732* 72 B3
Bancroft KY, *494* 230 F1
Bancroft MI, *545* 76 B3
Bancroft NE, *495* 35 F2
Bancroft WV, *587* 101 E3
Bandera TX, *857* 61 D2
Bandera Co. TX, *20485* 60 C2
Bandon OR, *3066* 28 A1
Bangor ME, *33039* 83 D1
Bangor MI, *1885* 75 E4
Bangor PA, *5273* 93 F3
Bangor WI, *1459* 73 F2
Bangs TX, *1603* 59 D4
Banks OR, *1777* 20 B1
Banks Co. GA, *18395* 121 D3
Banner Co. NE, *690* 33 F3
Banner Elk NC, *1028* 111 F4
Banner Hill TN, *1497* 111 E4
Bannertown NC, *950* 112 A3
Banning CA, *29603* 53 D2
Bannockburn IL, *1583* 203 C2
Bannock Co. ID, *82839* 31 E1
Banquete TX, *726* 63 F2
Bantam CT, *759* 94 C3
Baraboo WI, *12048* 74 A2
Baraga MI, *2053* 65 F4
Baraga Co. MI, *8860* 65 F4
Barataria LA, *1109* 134 B3
Barber Co. KS, *4861* 43 D4
Barberton OH, *26550* 91 E3
Barbour Co. AL, *27457* 128 B3
Barbour Co. WV, *16589* 102 A2
Barbourmeade KY, *1218* 230 F1
Barboursville WV, *3964* 101 E4
Barbourville KY, *3165* 110 C2
Bardstown KY, *11700* 110 A1
Bardwell KY, *723* 108 C2
Bardwell TX, *649* 59 F3
Bareville PA, *6625* 146 A2
Bargersville IN, *4013* 99 F1
Bar Harbor ME, *2552* 83 D2
Barker NY, *533* 78 B3
Barling AR, *4649* 116 C1
Barlow KY, *675* 108 C2
Bar Mills ME, *800* 82 B3
Barnegat NJ, *2817* 147 E4
Barnegat Light NJ, *574* 147 E4
Barnegat Pines NJ, *1300* 147 E3
Barnes Co. ND, *11066* 19 D4
Barnesville GA, *6755* 129 D1
Barnesville MN, *2563* 19 F4
Barnesville OH, *4193* 101 F1
Barneveld WI, *1231* 74 A3
Barnhart MO, *5682* 98 A4
Barnsboro NJ, *2500* 146 C4
Barnsdall OK, *1243* 51 F1
Barnstable MA, *45193* 151 F3
Barnstable Co. MA, *215888* 151 E4
Barnum MN, *613* 64 C4
Bar Nunn WY, *2213* 33 D1
Barnwell SC, *4750* 130 B1
Barnwell Co. SC, *22621* 130 B1
Baroda MI, *873* 89 E1
Barrackville WV, *1302* 102 A1
Barre MA, *1009* 150 B1
Barre VT, *9052* 81 E2
Barren Co. KY, *42173* 110 A2
Barre Plains MA, *1200* 150 B1
Barrett TX, *3199* 132 B3
Barrington IL, *10327* 203 B2
Barrington NH, *8576* 81 F4
Barrington NJ, *6983* 248 D4
Barrington RI, *16310* 151 D3
Barrington Hills IL, *4209* 203 A2
Barron WI, *3423* 67 E3
Barron Co. WI, *45870* 67 E3
Barrow AK, *4212* 154 C1
Barrow Co. GA, *69367* 121 D3
Barry IL, *1318* 97 F1
Barry Co. MI, *59173* 75 F4
Barry Co. MO, *35597* 106 C2
Barstow CA, *22639* 53 D1
Barstow MD, *750* 144 C4
Bartelso IL, *595* 98 B3
Bartholomew Co. IN, *76794* 99 F2
Bartlesville OK, *35750* 51 F1
Bartlett IL, *41208* 203 A3
Bartlett NE, *117* 35 D2
Bartlett NH, *373* 81 F2
Bartlett TN, *54613* 118 B1
Bartlett TX, *1623* 61 E1
Barton MD, *457* 102 C1
Barton VT, *737* 81 E1
Barton Co. KS, *27674* 43 D3
Barton Co. MO, *12402* 106 B1
Bartonsville MD, *1451* 144 A1
Bartonville IL, *6471* 88 B3
Bartow FL, *17298* 140 C2
Bartow Co. GA, *100157* 120 B3
Barview OR, *1844* 20 A4
Basalt CO, *3857* 40 C2
Basalt ID, *394* 23 E4
Basehor KS, *4613* 96 B2
Basile LA, *1821* 133 E2
Basin MT, *212* 15 E4
Basin WY, *1285* 24 C3
Basin City WA, *1092* 13 E4
Baskett KY, *550* 99 E4
Basking Ridge NJ, *3600* 148 A4
Bassett NE, *619* 35 D1
Bassett VA, *1100* 112 B2
Bass Harbor ME, *600* 83 D2
Bass Lake IN, *1195* 89 E2
Bastrop LA, *11365* 125 F2
Bastrop TX, *7218* 61 E2
Bastrop Co. TX, *74171* 61 E2
Basye VA, *1253* 102 C3
Batavia IL, *26045* 88 C1
Batavia IA, *499* 87 E3
Batavia NY, *15465* 78 B3
Batavia OH, *1509* 100 B2
Batesburg-Leesville SC, *5362* 122 A4
Bates Co. MO, *17049* 96 B4
Batesville AR, *10248* 107 F4
Batesville IN, *6520* 100 A2
Batesville MS, *7463* 118 B3
Batesville TX, *1068* 60 C3
Bath ME, *8514* 82 C3
Bath MI, *2083* 76 A3
Bath NY, *5786* 78 C4
Bath PA, *2693* 93 F3
Bath Co. KY, *11591* 100 C4
Bath Co. VA, *4731* 102 B4
Baton Rouge LA, *229493* 134 A2
Battle Creek IA, *713* 72 A4
Battle Creek MI, *52347* 75 F4
Battle Creek NE, *1207* 35 E2
Battlefield MO, *5590* 107 D2
Battle Ground IN, *1334* 89 E4
Battle Ground WA, *17571* 20 C1
Battle Lake MN, *875* 19 F4
Battlement Mesa CO, *4471* 40 B2
Battle Mtn. NV, *3635* 30 A4
Baudette MN, *1106* 64 A1
Baumstown PA, *422* 146 B2
Bauxite AR, *487* 117 E2
Bawcomville LA, *3588* 125 E2
Baxley GA, *4400* 129 F3
Baxter IA, *1101* 87 D1
Baxter MN, *7610* 64 A4
Baxter TN, *1365* 110 A4
Baxter Co. AR, *41513* 107 E4
Baxter Estates NY, *999* 241 G2
Baxter Sprs. KS, *4238* 106 B2
Bay AR, *1801* 108 A4
Bayard IA, *471* 86 B1
Bayard NE, *1209* 33 F2
Bayard NM, *2328* 55 F2
Bayboro NC, *1263* 115 D3
Bay City MI, *34932* 76 B2
Bay City OR, *1286* 20 B2
Bay City TX, *17614* 61 F3
Bay Co. FL, *168852* 136 C2
Bay Co. MI, *107771* 76 B2
Bayfield CO, *2333* 40 C4
Bayfield WI, *487* 65 D4
Bayfield Co. WI, *15014* 65 D4
Bay Harbor Islands FL, *5628* 233 C4
Bay Head NJ, *968* 147 E3
Bay Hill FL, *4884* 246 B3
Baylor Co. TX, *3726* 59 D1
Bay Minette AL, *8044* 135 E1
Bayonet Pt. FL, *23467* 140 B2
Bayonne NJ, *63024* 148 B4
Bayou Cane LA, *19355* 134 A3
Bayou George FL, *800* 136 C2
Bayou Goula LA, *612* 134 A2
Bayou La Batre AL, *2558* 135 E2
Bayou Vista LA, *4652* 134 A3
Bayou Vista TX, *1537* 132 B4
Bay Park NY, *2212* 241 G5
Bay Pines FL, *2931* 266 A3
Bay Pt. CA, *21349* 259 D1
Bayport MN, *3471* 67 D4
Bayport NY, *8896* 149 D4
Bay Ridge MD, *2300* 144 C3
Bay St. Louis MS, *9260* 134 C2
Bay Shore NY, *26337* 149 D4
Bayshore Gardens FL, *16323* 266 B5
Bay Side NJ, *1800* 147 E4
Bayside WI, *4389* 234 D1
Bay Sprs. MS, *1786* 126 C3
Baytown TX, *71802* 132 B3
Bay View OH, *632* 91 D2
Bay Vil. OH, *15651* 204 D2
Bayville NJ, *4700* 147 E3
Bayville NY, *6669* 148 C3
Beach ND, *1019* 17 F4
Beach City OH, *1033* 91 E3
Beach City TX, *2198* 132 B3
Beach Haven NJ, *1170* 147 E4
Beach Haven Gardens NJ, *1200* 147 E4
Beach Haven Terrace NJ, *1100* 147 E4
Beachwood NJ, *11045* 147 E3
Beachwood OH, *11953* 204 G2
Beacon IA, *494* 87 D2
Beacon NY, *15541* 148 B1
Beacon Falls CT, *5596* 149 D1
Beadle Co. SD, *17398* 27 D3
Bealeton VA, *4435* 103 D3
Beals ME, *618* 83 E2
Bean Sta. TN, *2826* 111 D3
Bear DE, *19371* 145 E1
Bear Creek AL, *1070* 119 E3
Bearden AR, *966* 117 E4
Beardstown IL, *6123* 98 A1
Bear Lake Co. ID, *5986* 31 F2
Bear River City UT, *853* 31 E3
Beasley TX, *641* 132 A4
Beatrice AL, *301* 127 F4
Beatrice NE, *12459* 35 F4
Beatty NV, *1010* 45 F2
Beattyville KY, *1307* 110 C1
Beatyestown NJ, *3223* 94 A4
Beaufort NC, *4039* 115 E4
Beaufort SC, *12361* 130 C2
Beaufort Co. NC, *47759* 113 F4
Beaufort Co. SC, *162233* 130 C3
Beaumont CA, *36877* 53 D2
Beaumont MS, *951* 135 D1
Beaumont TX, *118296* 132 C3
Beaumont Place TX, *4500* 220 D2
Beauregard Par. LA, *35654* 133 D2
Beaver OK, *1515* 50 C1
Beaver PA, *4531* 91 F3
Beaver UT, *3112* 39 D3
Beaver WV, *1308* 111 F1
Beaver City NE, *609* 42 C1
Beaver Co. OK, *5636* 50 C1
Beaver Co. PA, *170539* 91 F3
Beaver Co. UT, *6629* 39 D3
Beavercreek OH, *45193* 100 C1
Beaver Crossing NE, *403* 35 E4
Beaverdale PA, *1035* 92 B4
Beaver Dam KY, *3409* 109 E1
Beaver Dam WI, *16214* 74 B2
Beaver Falls PA, *8987* 91 F3
Beaverhead Co. MT, *9246* 23 D2
Beaver Meadows PA, *869* 93 E3
Beaver Sprs. PA, *674* 93 D3
Beaverton MI, *1071* 76 A2
Beaverton OR, *89803* 20 C2
Beavertown PA, *965* 93 D3
Bechtelsville PA, *942* 146 B1
Beckemeyer IL, *1040* 98 B3
Becker MN, *4538* 66 C3
Becker Co. MN, *32504* 19 F3
Beckett NJ, *4847* 146 C4
Beckham Co. OK, *22119* 50 C3
Beckley WV, *17614* 111 F1
Beckville TX, *847* 124 C3
Bedford IN, *13413* 99 F3
Bedford IA, *1440* 86 B3
Bedford KY, *599* 100 A3
Bedford MA, *13320* 151 D1
Bedford NH, *21203* 95 D1
Bedford NY, *1834* 148 C2
Bedford OH, *13074* 204 G3
Bedford PA, *2841* 102 C1
Bedford TX, *46979* 207 B2
Bedford VA, *6222* 112 B1
Bedford Co. PA, *49762* 92 C4
Bedford Co. TN, *45058* 120 A1
Bedford Co. VA, *68676* 112 B1
Bedford Hts. OH, *10751* 204 G3
Bedford Hills NY, *3001* 148 C2
Bedford Park IL, *580* 203 D5
Beebe AR, *7315* 117 F2
Bee Cave TX, *3925* 61 E1
Beech Bottom WV, *523* 91 F4
Beech Creek PA, *701* 93 D3
Beecher IL, *4359* 89 D2
Beech Grove IN, *14192* 99 F1
Beechwood Vil. KY, *1324* 230 E1
Bee Co. TX, *31861* 61 E4
Beemer NE, *678* 35 F2
Bee Ridge FL, *9598* 140 B4
Beersheba Sprs. TN, *477* 120 A1
Beesleys Pt. NJ, *1400* 147 F4
Beeville TX, *12863* 61 E4
Beggs OK, *1321* 51 F2
Bel Air MD, *1258* 145 D1
Belcamp MD, *1900* 145 D1
Belchertown MA, *2899* 150 A1
Belcourt ND, *2078* 18 C1
Belding MI, *5757* 75 F3
Belen NM, *7269* 48 C4
Belfair WA, *3931* 12 C3
Belfast ME, *6668* 82 C2
Belfast NY, *837* 78 B4
Belfast PA, *1257* 93 F3
Belfield ND, *800* 18 A4
Belford NJ, *1768* 147 E1
Belfry MT, *218* 24 B2
Belgium WI, *2245* 75 D2
Belgrade MN, *740* 66 B3
Belgrade MT, *7389* 23 F1
Belgrade Lakes ME, *350* 82 B2
Belhaven NC, *1688* 115 E3
Belinda City TN, *2100* 109 F4
Belington WV, *1921* 102 A2
Belknap Co. NH, *60088* 81 F4
Bell CA, *35477* 228 D3
Bellair FL, *16539* 222 C4
Bellaire MI, *1086* 69 F4
Bellaire OH, *4278* 101 F1
Bellaire TX, *16855* 132 A3
Bellamy AL, *543* 127 E2
Bella Villa MO, *729* 256 B3
Bella Vista AR, *26461* 106 C3
Bella Vista CA, *2781* 28 C4
Bellbrook OH, *6943* 100 C1
Bell Buckle TN, *500* 119 F1
Bell Co. KY, *28691* 110 C3
Bell Co. TX, *310235* 61 E1
Belle MO, *1545* 97 F4
Belle WV, *1260* 101 F4
Belleair FL, *3869* 140 B2
Belleair Beach FL, *1560* 140 B2
Belleair Bluffs FL, *2031* 266 A2
Belle Ctr. OH, *813* 90 C4
Belle Chasse LA, *12679* 134 B3
Bellefontaine OH, *13370* 90 B4
Bellefontaine Neighbors MO, *10860* 256 C1
Bellefonte AR, *454* 107 D3
Bellefonte DE, *1193* 146 B4
Bellefonte KY, *888* 101 D3
Bellefonte PA, *6187* 92 C3
Belle Fourche SD, *5594* 25 F3
Belle Glade FL, *17467* 143 E1
Belle Haven VA, *532* 114 B3
Belle Isle FL, *5988* 141 D1
Bellemeade KY, *865* 230 F2
Belle Plaine IA, *2534* 87 E1
Belle Plaine KS, *1681* 43 E4
Belle Plaine MN, *6661* 66 C4
Belle Rose LA, *1902* 134 A3
Bellerose NY, *1193* 241 G3
Bellerose Terrace NY, *2198* 241 G3
Belle Terre NY, *792* 149 D3
Belle Vernon PA, *1093* 92 A4
Belleview FL, *4492* 139 D4
Belleville IL, *44478* 98 B3
Belleville KS, *1991* 43 E1
Belleville MI, *3991* 90 C1
Belleville NJ, *35926* 148 B4
Belleville PA, *1827* 92 C4
Belleville WI, *2385* 74 B3
Bellevue ID, *2287* 22 C4
Bellevue IL, *1978* 88 B3
Bellevue IA, *2191* 74 A4
Bellevue KY, *5955* 204 B3
Bellevue MI, *1282* 76 A4
Bellevue NE, *50137* 86 A2
Bellevue OH, *8202* 204 B3
Bellevue PA, *8370* 92 A4
Bellevue WA, *122363* 12 C3
Bellevue WI, *14570* 74 C1
Bellflower CA, *76616* 228 D3
Bell Gardens CA, *42072* 228 D3
Bellingham MA, *4854* 150 C2
Bellingham WA, *80885* 12 C1
Bellmawr NJ, *11583* 146 C3
Bellmead TX, *9901* 59 E4
Bellows Falls VT, *3148* 81 E4
Bellport NY, *2084* 149 D4
Bells TN, *2437* 108 C4
Bells TX, *1392* 59 F1
Bellview FL, *23355* 247 A1
Bellville OH, *1918* 91 D3
Bellville TX, *4097* 61 F2
Bellwood IL, *19071* 203 C4
Bellwood NE, *435* 35 E3
Bellwood PA, *1828* 92 C4
Bellwood VA, *6352* 254 B3
Belmar NJ, *5794* 147 F2
Belmond IA, *2376* 72 C3
Belmont CA, *25835* 259 B5
Belmont MA, *24729* 151 D1
Belmont MS, *2021* 119 D3
Belmont NH, *1301* 81 F4

Entries in **bold black** indicate counties or parishes.
Entries in **bold color** indicate cities with detailed inset maps.

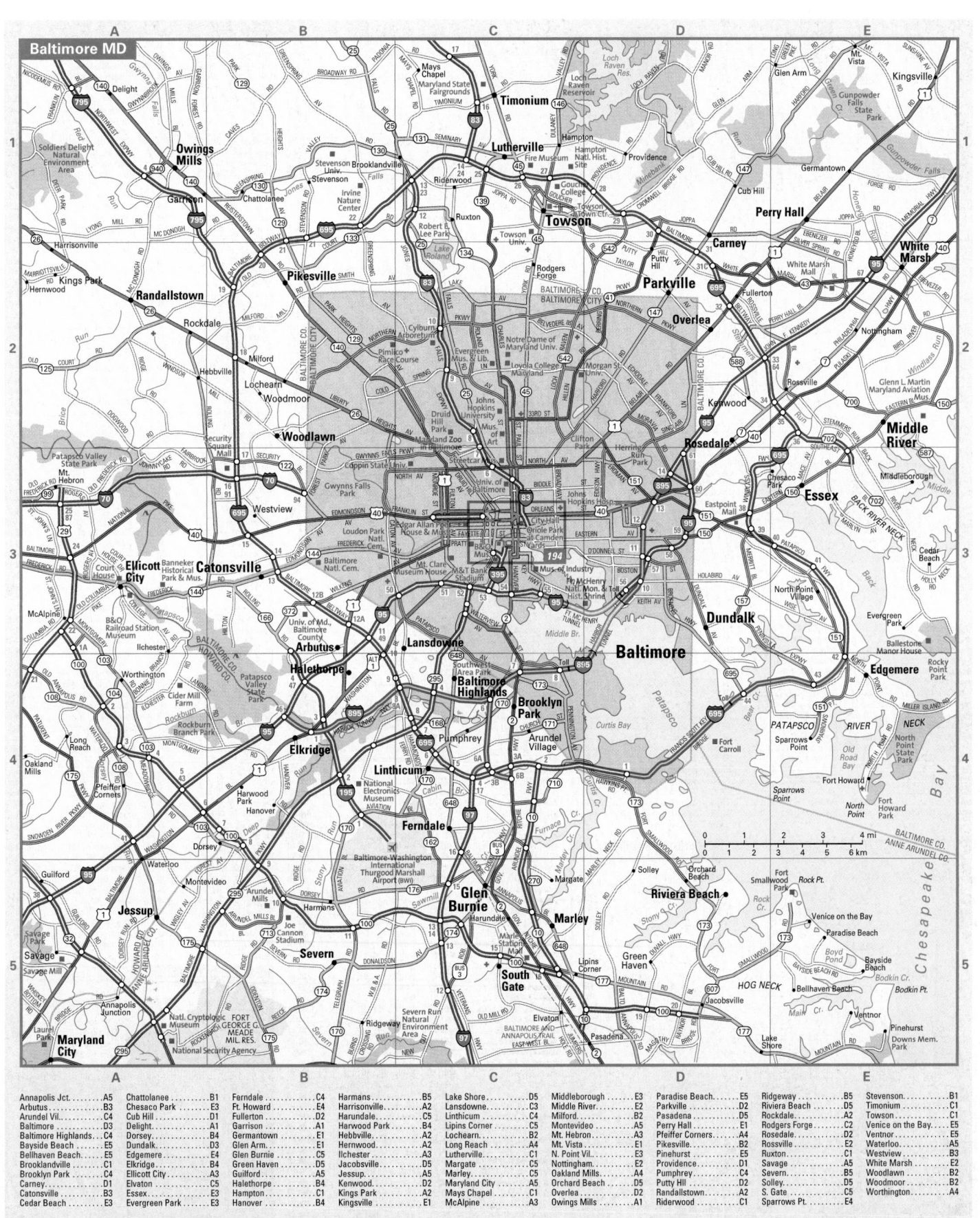

Baltimore MD

Figures after entries indicate population, page number, and grid reference.

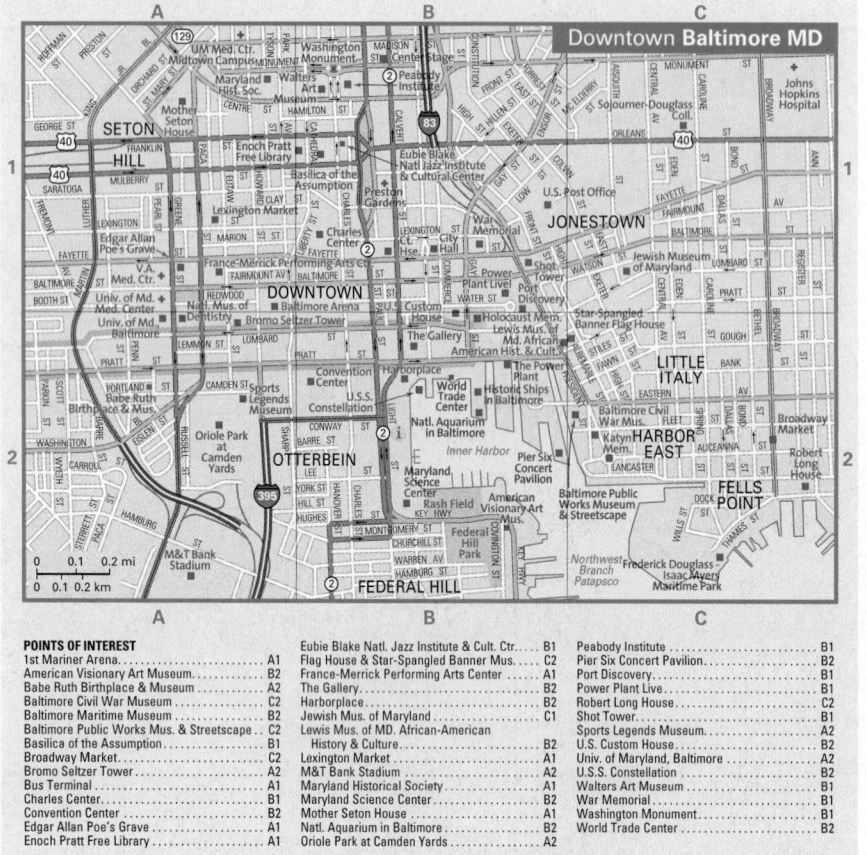

POINTS OF INTEREST

1st Mariner Arena A1
American Visionary Art Museum B2
Babe Ruth Birthplace & Museum A2
Baltimore Civil War Museum C2
Baltimore Maritime Museum B2
Baltimore Public Works Mus. & Streetscape .. C2
Basilica of the Assumption B1
Broadway Market C2
Bromo Seltzer Tower A2
Bus Terminal A1
Charles Center B1
Convention Center B2
Edgar Allan Poe's Grave A1
Enoch Pratt Free Library A1
Eubie Blake Natl. Jazz Institute & Cult. Ctr. B1
Flag House & Star-Spangled Banner Mus. C2
France-Merrick Performing Arts Center A1
The Gallery B2
Harborplace B2
Jewish Mus. of Maryland C1
Lewis Mus. of MD. African-American History & Culture B2
Lexington Market A1
M&T Bank Stadium A2
Maryland Historical Society A1
Maryland Science Center B2
Mother Seton House A1
Natl. Aquarium in Baltimore B2
Oriole Park at Camden Yards A2
Peabody Institute B1
Pier Six Concert Pavilion B2
Port Discovery B1
Power Plant Live B1
Robert Long House C2
Shot Tower B1
Sports Legends Museum A2
U.S. Custom House B2
Univ. of Maryland, Baltimore A2
U.S.S. Constellation B2
Walters Art Museum B1
War Memorial B1
Washington Monument B1
World Trade Center B2

Belmont NY, *969* **92** C1
Belmont NC, *10076* **122** A1
Belmont WV, *903* **101** F2
Belmont WI, *986* **74** A4
Belmont Corner ME, *375* **82** C2
Belmont Co. OH, *70400* **101** F1
Bel-Nor MO, *1499* **256** B2
Beloit KS, *3835* **43** E1
Beloit OH, *978* **91** F3
Beloit WI, *36966* **74** B4
Belpre OH, *6441* **101** E2
Bel-Ridge MO, *2737* **256** B2
Belt MT, *597* **15** F3
Belton KY, *500* **109** E2
Belton MO, *23116* **96** B3
Belton SC, *4134* **121** E3
Belton TX, *18216* **59** E4
Beltrami Co. MN, *44442* **64** A2
Beltsville MD, *16772* **144** B3
Belvedere CA, *2068* **259** B2
Belvedere SC, *5792* **121** F4
Belvedere Park GA, *15152* **190** E4
Belvidere IL, *25585* **74** B4
Belvidere NJ, *2681* **93** F3
Belwood NC, *950* **121** F1
Belzoni MS, *2235* **126** B1
Bement IL, *1730* **98** C1
Bemidji MN, *13431* **64** A3
Bemiss GA, *1500* **137** F1
Benavides TX, *1362* **63** E2
Ben Avon PA, *1781* **250** A1
Benbrook TX, *21234* **207** A3
Bend OR, *76639* **21** D3
Bendersville PA, *641* **103** E1
Benewah Co. ID, *9285* **14** B3
Benham KY, *500* **111** D2
Ben Hill Co. GA, *17634* **129** E3
Benicia CA, *26997* **36** B3
Benjamin TX, *258* **58** C1
Benkelman NE, *953* **42** B1
Benld IL, *1556* **98** B2
Ben Lomond CA, *6234* **44** A2
Bennet NE, *719* **35** F4
Bennett CO, *2308* **41** E1
Bennett Co. SD, *3431* **26** B4
Bennettsville SC, *9069* **122** C2
Bennington KS, *672* **43** E2
Bennington NE, *1458* **35** F3
Bennington NH, *381* **81** E4
Bennington VT, *9074* **94** C1
Bennington Co. VT, *37125* **81** D4
Benoit MS, *477* **118** A4
Bensenville IL, *18352* **203** C4
Bensley VA, *5819* **113** E1
Benson AZ, *5105* **55** D3
Benson MD, *950* **144** C1
Benson MN, *3240* **66** A3
Benson NC, *3311* **123** D1
Benson Co. ND, *6660* **19** D2
Bent Co. CO, *6499* **41** F3
Bent Creek NC, *1287* **121** E1
Bentleyville OH, *864* **204** G3
Bentleyville PA, *2581* **92** A4
Benton AR, *30681* **117** E2
Benton IL, *7087* **98** C4
Benton KS, *880* **43** F4
Benton KY, *4349* **109** D2
Benton LA, *1948* **124** C2
Benton ME, *2557* **82** C2
Benton MO, *863* **108** B2
Benton PA, *824* **93** E2
Benton TN, *1385* **120** C1
Benton WI, *973* **74** A4
Benton City WA, *3038* **21** E1
Benton Co. AR, *221339* **106** B3
Benton Co. IN, *8854* **89** D3
Benton Co. IA, *26076* **87** E1
Benton Co. MN, *38451* **66** C2
Benton Co. MS, *8729* **118** C2
Benton Co. MO, *19056* **97** D4
Benton Co. OR, *85579* **20** B3
Benton Co. TN, *16489* **109** D4
Benton Co. WA, *175177* **21** E1
Benton Harbor MI, *10038* **89** E1
Bentonia MS, *440* **126** B2
Bentonville AR, *35301* **106** C3
Benzie Co. MI, *17525* **69** F4
Benzonia MI, *497* **69** E4
Berea KY, *13561* **110** C1
Berea OH, *19093* **91** E2
Berea SC, *14295* **217** A2
Beresford SD, *2005* **35** F1
Bergen NY, *1176* **78** B3
Bergen Co. NJ, *905116* **148** B3
Bergenfield NJ, *26764* **148** B3
Bergholz OH, *664* **91** F4
Bergman AR, *439* **107** D3
Berino NM, *1441* **56** C3
Berkeley CA, *112580* **36** B4
Berkeley IL, *5209* **203** C4
Berkeley MO, *8978* **256** B1
Berkeley RI, *2800* **150** C3
Berkeley Co. SC, *177843* **131** D1
Berkeley Co. WV, *104169* **103** D2
Berkeley Hts. NJ, *13183* **148** A4
Berkeley Sprs. WV, *624* **102** C1
Berkley MA, *5749* **151** D3
Berkley MI, *14970* **210** B2
Berks Co. PA, *411442* **146** B1
Berkshire CT, *950* **149** D2
Berkshire Co. MA, *131219* **94** C2
Berlin CT, *19590* **149** E1
Berlin GA, *551* **137** F1
Berlin MD, *4485* **114** C2
Berlin MA, *2866* **150** C1
Berlin NH, *10051* **81** F2
Berlin NJ, *7588* **147** D3
Berlin OH, *898* **91** E4
Berlin PA, *2104* **102** C1
Berlin WI, *5524* **74** B1
Berlin Hts. OH, *714* **91** D2
Bermuda Run NC, *1725* **112** A4
Bernalillo NM, *8320* **48** C3
Bernalillo Co. NM, *662564* **48** C3
Bernardston MA, *2155* **94** C1
Bernardsville NJ, *7707* **148** A4
Berne IN, *3999* **90** A3
Bernice LA, *1689* **125** E2
Bernice OK, *562* **106** B3
Bernie MO, *1958* **108** B3
Bernstadt KY, *475* **110** C2
Bernville PA, *955* **146** A1
Berrien Co. GA, *19286* **129** E4
Berrien Co. MI, *156813* **89** E1
Berrien Sprs. MI, *1800* **89** E1
Berry AL, *1148* **119** E4
Berryville AR, *5356* **106** C3
Berryville TX, *975* **124** A3
Berryville VA, *4185* **103** D2
Berthold ND, *454* **18** B2
Berthoud CO, *5105* **33** E4
Bertie Co. NC, *21282* **113** F4
Bertram IA, *294* **87** F1
Bertram TX, *1353* **61** D1
Bertrand MI, *1700* **89** F1
Bertrand MO, *821* **108** B2
Bertrand NE, *750* **35** D4
Berwick LA, *4946* **134** A3
Berwick ME, *2187* **82** A4
Berwick PA, *10477* **93** E3
Berwyn IL, *56657* **89** D1
Berwyn PA, *3631* **146** B3
Berwyn Hts. MD, *3123* **270** E2
Bessemer AL, *27456* **127** F1
Bessemer MI, *1905* **65** E4
Bessemer PA, *1111* **91** F3
Bessemer City NC, *5340* **122** A1
Bethalto IL, *9521* **98** B3
Bethany CT, *5473* **149** D1
Bethany IL, *1352* **98** C1
Bethany MO, *3292* **86** C4
Bethany OK, *19051* **51** E3
Bethany WV, *1036* **91** F4
Bethany Beach DE, *1060* **145** F4
Bethel AK, *6080* **154** B3
Bethel CT, *9549* **148** C2
Bethel DE, *171* **145** E4
Bethel ME, *2411* **82** B2
Bethel NC, *1577* **113** E4
Bethel OH, *2711* **100** C2
Bethel VT, *569* **81** E3
Bethel VA, *500* **103** D3
Bethel Acres OK, *2895* **51** F3
Bethel Hts. AR, *2372* **106** C3
Bethel Park PA, *32313* **92** A4
Bethel Sprs. TN, *718* **119** D1
Bethesda MD, *60858* **144** B3
Bethesda OH, *1256* **101** F1
Bethlehem CT, *3596* **149** D1
Bethlehem GA, *601* **121** D4
Bethlehem MD, *600* **145** D4
Bethlehem NH, *972* **81** F2
Bethlehem NC, *4214* **111** F4
Bethlehem PA, *74982* **146** C1
Bethlehem Ctr. NY, *2500* **188** D3
Bethpage NY, *16429* **148** C4
Betmar Acres FL, *4000* **140** C2
Bettendorf IA, *33217* **88** A2
Bettsville OH, *661* **90** C2
Beulah CO, *1164* **41** E3
Beulah MI, *342* **69** E4
Beulah MS, *348* **118** A4
Beulah ND, *3121* **18** B3
Beulaville NC, *1296* **123** E2
Beverly MA, *39502* **151** F1
Beverly NJ, *2577* **147** D3
Beverly OH, *1313* **101** E1
Beverly WV, *702* **102** B3
Beverly Beach FL, *338* **139** E4
Beverly Beach MD, *1600* **144** C3
Beverly Hills CA, *34109* **52** C2
Beverly Hills FL, *8445* **140** B1
Beverly Hills MI, *10267* **210** B2
Beverly Hills MO, *574* **256** B2
Beverly Shores IN, *613* **89** E2
Bevier MO, *718* **97** E1
Bevil Oaks TX, *1274* **132** C2
Bevis OH, *5700* **204** A1
Bexar Co. TX, *1714773* **61** D2
Bexley OH, *13057* **206** C2
Bibb Co. AL, *22915* **127** F1
Bibb Co. GA, *155547* **129** D2
Bicknell IN, *2915* **99** E3
Bicknell UT, *327* **39** E3
Biddeford ME, *21277* **82** B4
Bienville Par. LA, *14353* **125** D2
Big Bear City CA, *12304* **53** D2
Big Bear Lake CA, *5019* **53** D2
Big Beaver PA, *1970* **91** F3
Big Bend WI, *1290* **74** C3
Big Chimney WV, *627* **101** F3
Big Coppitt Key FL, *2458* **143** D4
Big Delta AK, *591* **154** C2
Big Flats NY, *5277* **93** D1
Bigfork MT, *4270* **15** D2
Biggs CA, *1707* **36** B2
Big Horn Co. MT, *12865* **24** C2
Big Horn Co. WY, *11668* **24** C3
Big Lake MN, *443* **66** C3
Big Lake TX, *2936* **58** A4
Big Lake WA, *1835* **12** C2
Biglerville PA, *1200* **103** E1
Big Oak Flat CA, *3388* **37** D4
Big Pine CA, *1756* **37** E4
Big Pine Key FL, *4252* **143** D4
Big Piney WY, *552* **32** A1
Big Rapids MI, *10601* **75** F2
Big River CA, *1327* **46** B4
Big Run PA, *624* **92** B3
Big Sandy MT, *598* **16** B2
Big Sandy TN, *557* **109** D3
Big Sandy TX, *1343* **124** B2
Big Sky MT, *2308* **23** F2
Big Spr. TX, *27282* **58** A3
Big Sprs. NE, *400* **34** B3
Big Stone City SD, *467* **27** F2
Big Stone Co. MN, *5269* **27** F2
Big Stone Gap VA, *5614* **111** E2
Big Timber MT, *1641* **24** A1
Big Water UT, *475* **47** D1
Big Wells TX, *697* **60** C4
Billerica MA, *40243* **95** E1
Billings MO, *1035* **106** C2
Billings MT, *104170* **24** C1
Billings NY, *800* **148** B1
Billings OK, *509* **51** E1
Billings Co. ND, *783* **18** A3
Billington Hts. NY, *1685* **78** B4
Biloxi MS, *44054* **135** D2
Biltmore Forest NC, *1343* **121** E1
Bingen PA, *1300* **189** B2
Binger OK, *672* **51** D3
Bingham ME, *758* **82** B1
Bingham Co. ID, *45607* **23** E4
Bingham Farms MI, *1111* **210** B2
Binghamton NY, *47376* **93** E1
Biola CA, *1623* **44** C2
Birch Bay WA, *8413* **12** C1
Birch Run MI, *1555* **76** B3
Birch Tree MO, *679* **107** F2
Birchwood Vil. MN, *870* **235** E1
Bird City KS, *447* **42** B1
Bird Island MN, *1042* **66** B4
Birdsboro PA, *5163* **146** B2
Birmingham AL, *212237* **119** F4
Birmingham MI, *20103* **76** C4
Birnamwood WI, *818* **68** B4
Biron WI, *839* **74** A1
Bisbee AZ, *5575* **55** E4
Biscayne Park FL, *3055* **233** B4
Biscoe AR, *476* **117** F2
Biscoe NC, *1700* **122** C1
Bishop CA, *3879* **37** E4
Bishop TX, *3134* **63** F2
Bishopville SC, *3471* **122** B3
Bismarck MO, *1546* **108** A1
Bismarck ND, *61272* **18** C4
Bison SD, *333* **26** A2
Bithlo FL, *8268* **141** D1
Bitter Sprs. AZ, *452* **47** D1
Biwabik MN, *969* **64** C3
Bixby OK, *20884* **106** A4
Blackbird DE, *700* **145** E1
Black Canyon City AZ, *2837* **47** D4
Black Creek NC, *769* **123** E1
Black Creek WI, *1316* **68** C4
Black Diamond WA, *4151* **12** C3
Blackduck MN, *785* **64** A3
Black Eagle MT, *904* **15** F3
Black Earth WI, *1338* **74** A3
Blackfoot ID, *11899* **31** E1
Blackford Co. IN, *12766* **90** A4
Black Forest CO, *13116* **41** E2
Blackhawk SD, *2892* **26** A3
Black Hawk Co. IA, *131090* **73** E4
Black Jack MO, *6929* **256** B1
Black Lick PA, *1462* **92** B4
Blacklick Estates OH, *8682* **206** C3
Black Mtn. NC, *7848* **121** E1
Black River NY, *1348* **79** E1
Black River Falls WI, *3622* **73** F1
Black Rock AR, *662* **107** F4
Black Rock NM, *1323* **48** A3
Blacksburg SC, *1848* **122** A1
Blacksburg VA, *42620* **112** A2
Blackshear GA, *3445* **129** F4
Blackstone MA, *9026* **150** C2
Blackstone VA, *3621* **113** D2
Blackville SC, *2406* **130** B1
Blackwell OK, *7092* **51** E1
Blackwells GA, *2200* **120** C3
Blackwood NJ, *4545* **146** C3
Bladenboro NC, *1750* **123** D3
Bladen Co. NC, *35190* **123** D2
Bladensburg MD, *9148* **270** E3
Blades DE, *1241* **145** E4
Blaine ME, *301* **85** E2
Blaine MN, *57186* **67** D3
Blaine TN, *1856* **110** C4
Blaine WA, *4684* **12** C1
Blaine Co. ID, *21376* **23** D4
Blaine Co. MT, *6491* **16** B2
Blaine Co. NE, *478* **34** C2
Blaine Co. OK, *11943* **51** D2
Blair NE, *7990* **35** F3
Blair OK, *818* **51** D4
Blair WI, *1366* **73** F1
Blair Co. PA, *127089* **92** C4
Blairs VA, *916* **112** C3
Blairstown IA, *692* **87** E1

Baton Rouge LA

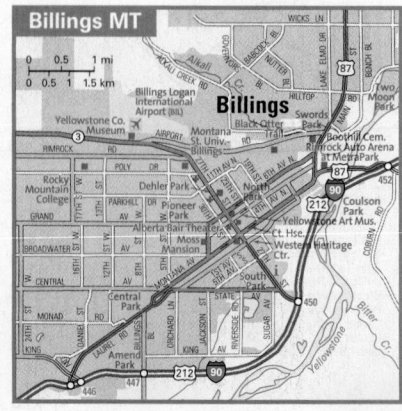

Entries in **bold black** indicate counties or parishes.
Entries in **bold color** indicate cities with detailed inset maps.

Blairstown NJ, *515* **93** F3
Blairsville GA, *652* **121** D2
Blairsville PA, *3412* **92** B4
Blakely GA, *5068* **128** C4
Blakely PA, *6564* **93** F2
Blakes VA, *550* **113** F1
Blanca CO, *385* **41** D4
Blanchard LA, *2899* **124** C2
Blanchard OK, *7670* **51** E3
Blanchard PA, *740* **93** D3
Blanchardville WI, *825* **74** A3
Blanchester OH, *4243* **100** C2
Blanco TX, *1739* **61** D2
Blanco Co. TX, *10497* **61** D1
Bland MO, *539* **97** F4
Bland VA, *409* **112** A2
Bland Co. VA, *6824* **111** F2
Blanding UT, *3375* **40** A4
Blandinsville IL, *651* **87** F4
Blandon PA, *7152* **146** B1
Blasdell NY, *2553* **78** B3
Blauvelt NY, *5689* **148** B3
Blawenburg NJ, *280* **147** D1
Blawnox PA, *1432* **250** C1
Bleckley Co. GA, *13063* **129** E2
Bledsoe Co. TN, *12876* **110** B4
Blennerhassett WV, *3089* **101** E2
Blessing TX, *927* **61** F3
Bliss ID, *318* **30** C1
Bliss Corner MA, *5280* **238** C2
Blissfield MI, *3340* **90** B1
Blocher IN, *600* **100** A3
Bloomdale OH, *678* **90** C2
Bloomer WI, *3539* **67** F3
Bloomfield CT, *20626* **150** A3
Bloomfield IN, *2405* **99** E2
Bloomfield IA, *2640* **87** E3
Bloomfield KY, *838* **100** A4
Bloomfield MO, *1933* **108** B2
Bloomfield NE, *1028* **35** E1
Bloomfield NJ, *47315* **148** B4
Bloomfield NM, *8112* **48** B1
Bloomfield NY, *1361* **78** C3
Bloomfield WI, *3722* **74** C4
Bloomfield Hills MI, *3869* **210** B1
Bloomingburg OH, *938* **100** C1
Bloomingdale FL, *22711* **266** D2
Bloomingdale IL, *22018* **203** B3
Bloomingdale NJ, *7656* **148** A3
Bloomingdale TN, *9888* **111** E3
Blooming Grove NY, *17351* **148** B1
Blooming Grove TX, *821* **59** F3
Blooming Prairie MN, *1996* **73** D2
Bloomington CA, *23851* **229** H2
Bloomington ID, *206* **31** F2
Bloomington IL, *76610* **88** C4
Bloomington IN, *80405* **99** F2
Bloomington MN, *82893* **67** D4
Bloomington TX, *2459* **61** F4
Bloomington WI, *735* **73** F3
Bloomsburg PA, *14855* **93** E3
Bloomsbury NJ, *870* **146** C1
Bloomville OH, *956* **90** C3
Blossburg PA, *1538* **93** D2
Blossom TX, *1494* **116** A4
Blount Co. AL, *57322* **119** F3
Blount Co. TN, *123010* **110** C4
Blountstown FL, *2514* **137** D2
Blountsville AL, *1684* **119** F3
Blountville TN, *3074* **111** E3
Blowing Rock NC, *1241* **111** F4
Bloxom VA, *387* **114** C2
Blue Anchor NJ, *1500* **147** D4
Blue Ash OH, *12114* **100** B2
Blue Bell PA, *6067* **146** C2
Blue Diamond NV, *290* **46** A2
Blue Earth MN, *3353* **72** C2
Blue Earth Co. MN, *64013* **72** C1
Bluefield VA, *5444* **111** F2
Bluefield WV, *10447* **111** F2
Blue Grass IA, *1452* **87** F2
Blue Hill ME, *943* **83** D2
Blue Hill NE, *936* **35** D4
Blue Hills CT, *2901* **150** A3

Biloxi A2
D'Iberville B1
Escatawpa C1
Fontainebleau B2
Gautier C2
Gulfport A1
Helena C1
Latimer B1
Long Beach A2
Moss Pt. C2
New Hope A1
Ocean Sprs. B2
Pascagoula C2
Vancleave C1
Wortham A1

Birmingham AL

Adamsville D1
Alabaster E3
Bayview D1
Bessemer D3
Birmingham E1
Brighton D2
Brookside D1
Cardiff D1
Center Pt. F1
Chalkville F1
Chelsea F3
Concord D2
Edgewater D2
Fairfield D2
Forestdale E1
Fultondale E1
Gardendale E1
Graysville D1
Helena E3
Homewood E2
Hoover E3
Hueytown D2
Indian Sprs. Vil. E3
Irondale F1
Lipscomb D2
Maytown D1
McCalla D3
Midfield D2
Mtn. Brook F2
Mulga D1
Pelham E3
Pleasant Grove D2
Pleasant Hill D3
Republic E1
Shannon E2
Simmsville F3
Summit Farm D3
Sylvan Sprs. D2
Tarrant City E1
Trussville F1
Vestavia Hills E2
Watson E1

Blue Island IL, *23706* **203** D6
Blue Lake CA, *1253* **28** B4
Blue Mound IL, *1158* **98** C1
Blue Mound TX, *2394* **207** A2
Blue Mounds WI, *855* **74** A3
Blue Mtn. MS, *920* **118** C2
Blue Pt. NY, *4773* **149** D4
Blue Rapids KS, *1019* **43** F1
Blue Ridge AL, *1341* **128** A2
Blue Ridge GA, *1290* **120** C2
Blue Ridge TX, *822* **59** F2
Blue Ridge VA, *3084* **112** B1
Blue Ridge Manor KY, *767* **230** F2
Blue River CO, *849* **41** D2
Blue Sprs. MO, *52575* **96** C2
Bluff UT, *258* **40** A4
Bluff City TN, *1733* **111** E3
Bluffdale UT, *7598* **31** E4
Bluffs IL, *715* **98** A1
Bluffton IN, *9897* **90** A3
Bluffton OH, *4125* **90** B3
Bluffton SC, *12530* **130** C3
Bluford IL, *688* **98** C4
Blunt SD, *354* **26** C3
Blythe CA, *20817* **53** F3
Blythe GA, *721* **129** F1
Blytheville AR, *15620* **108** B4
Boalsburg PA, *3722* **92** C3
Boardman OH, *35376* **91** F3
Boardman OR, *3220* **21** E1
Boardman Bridge CT, *600* **148** C1
Boaz AL, *9551* **120** A3
Boaz WV, *1297* **101** F2
Bobtown PA, *757* **102** A1
Boca Grande FL, *700* **140** C4
Boca Raton FL, *84392* **143** F1
Bodega Bay CA, *1077* **36** A3
Bodfish CA, *1956* **45** E4
Boerne TX, *10471* **61** D2
Bogalusa LA, *12232* **134** C1
Bogart GA, *1034* **121** D4
Bogata TX, *1153* **116** A4
Boger City NC, *554* **122** A1
Bogota NJ, *8187* **240** D1
Bogue NC, *684* **115** D4
Bogue Chitto MS, *887* **127** D2
Bohners Lake WI, *2444* **74** C4
Boiling Spr. Lakes NC, *5372* **123** E3
Boiling Sprs. NC, *4647* **121** F1
Boiling Sprs. PA, *3225* **93** D4
Boiling Sprs. SC, *8219* **121** F2
Boise ID, *205671* **22** B4
Boise City OK, *1266* **50** A1
Boise Co. ID, *7028* **22** C4
Bokchito OK, *632* **59** F1
Bokeelia FL, *1780* **142** C1
Bokoshe OK, *512* **116** B1
Boley OK, *1184* **51** F3
Boling TX, *1122* **61** F3
Bolingbrook IL, *73366* **89** D2
Bolivar MO, *10325* **107** D1
Bolivar NY, *1047* **92** C1
Bolivar OH, *994* **91** E3
Bolivar TN, *5417* **118** C1
Bolivar WV, *1045* **144** A2
Bolivar Co. MS, *34145* **118** A4
Bolivia NC, *143* **123** E3
Bollinger Co. MO, *12363* **108** B2
Bolton CT, *5170* **150** A3
Bolton MS, *567* **126** B2
Bolton NC, *691* **123** D3
Bolton Landing NY, *513* **81** D3
Bon Air VA, *16366* **113** E1
Bonaire GA, *800* **129** D2
Bonanza AR, *575* **116** C1
Bonanza OR, *415* **29** D2
Bonaparte IA, *433* **87** E3
Bond Co. IL, *17768* **98** B3
Bondsville MA, *1876* **150** A2
Bonduel WI, *1478* **68** C4
Bondurant IA, *3860* **86** C2
Bonesteel SD, *275* **35** D1
Bonham TX, *10127* **59** F1
Bon Homme Co. SD, *7070* **35** E1
Bonifay FL, *2793* **136** C1
Bonita CA, *12538* **258** C2
Bonita Sprs. FL, *43914* **142** C1
Bonneauville PA, *1800* **103** E1
Bonner MT, *1663* **15** D4
Bonner Co. ID, *40877* **14** B2
Bonners Ferry ID, *2543* **14** B1
Bonner Sprs. KS, *7314* **96** B2
Bonne Terre MO, *6864* **98** A4
Bonnet Shores RI, *2200* **150** C4
Bonneville Co. ID, *104234* **23** F4
Bonney Lake WA, *17374* **262** B5
Bonnieville KY, *255* **110** A1
Bono AR, *2131* **108** A4
Bonsall CA, *3982* **53** D3
Booker TX, *1516* **50** B1
Boomer WV, *615* **101** F4
Boone CO, *339* **41** E3
Boone IA, *12661* **86** C1
Boone NC, *17122* **111** F3
Boone Co. AR, *36903* **107** D3
Boone Co. IL, *54165* **74** B4
Boone Co. IN, *56640* **99** F1
Boone Co. IA, *26306* **86** C1
Boone Co. KY, *118811* **100** B2
Boone Co. MO, *162642* **97** E2
Boone Co. NE, *5505* **35** E3
Boone Co. WV, *24629* **101** E4
Booneville AR, *3990* **116** C1
Booneville KY, *81* **110** C1
Booneville MS, *8743* **119** D2
Boonsboro MD, *3336* **144** A1
Boonton NJ, *8347* **148** A3
Boonville CA, *1035* **36** A2
Boonville IN, *6246* **99** E4
Boonville MO, *8319* **97** D2
Boonville NY, *2072* **79** E2
Boonville NC, *1222* **112** A3
Boothbay ME, *550* **82** C3
Boothbay Harbor ME, *1086* **82** C3
Boothville LA, *854* **134** C4
Bootjack CA, *960* **37** D4
Borden IN, *808* **99** F3
Borden Co. TX, *641* **58** B2
Bordentown NJ, *3924* **147** D2
Borger TX, *13251* **50** B2
Boron CA, *2253* **52** C1
Borrego Sprs. CA, *3429* **53** E3
Boscobel WI, *3231* **73** F3
Bosque Co. TX, *18212* **59** E3
Bosque Farms NM, *3904* **48** C4
Bossier City LA, *61315* **124** C2
Bossier Par. LA, *116979* **125** D1
Boston GA, *1315* **137** E1
Boston MA, *617594* **151** D1
Boswell IN, *778* **89** D4
Boswell OK, *709* **59** F1
Boswell PA, *1277* **92** B4
Botetourt Co. VA, *33148* **112** B1
Bothell WA, *33505* **12** C3
Botkins OH, *1155* **90** B4
Botsford CT, *1000* **149** D2
Bottineau ND, *2211* **18** C1
Bottineau Co. ND, *6429* **18** C1
Botto KY, *550* **110** C2
Boulder CO, *97385* **41** E1
Boulder MT, *1183* **23** E1
Boulder City NV, *15023* **46** B2
Boulder Co. CO, *294567* **41** D1
Boulder Creek CA, *4923* **44** A2
Boundary Co. ID, *10972* **14** B1
Bound Brook NJ, *10402* **147** D1
Bountiful UT, *42552* **31** E4
Bourbon IN, *1810* **89** F2
Bourbon MO, *1632* **97** F4
Bourbon Co. KS, *15173* **96** B4
Bourbon Co. KY, *19985* **100** B4
Bourbonnais IL, *18631* **89** D2
Bourne MA, *1418* **151** E3
Bouse AZ, *996* **54** A1
Boutte LA, *3075* **134** B3
Bovey MN, *804* **64** B3
Bovill ID, *260* **14** B4
Bovina TX, *1868* **49** F4
Bowbells ND, *336* **18** B1
Bow Ctr. NH, *7519* **81** F4
Bowdle SD, *502* **27** D2
Bowdoin Ctr. ME, *425* **82** B3
Bowdoinham ME, *722* **82** B3
Bowdon GA, *2040* **120** B4
Bowen IL, *494* **87** F4

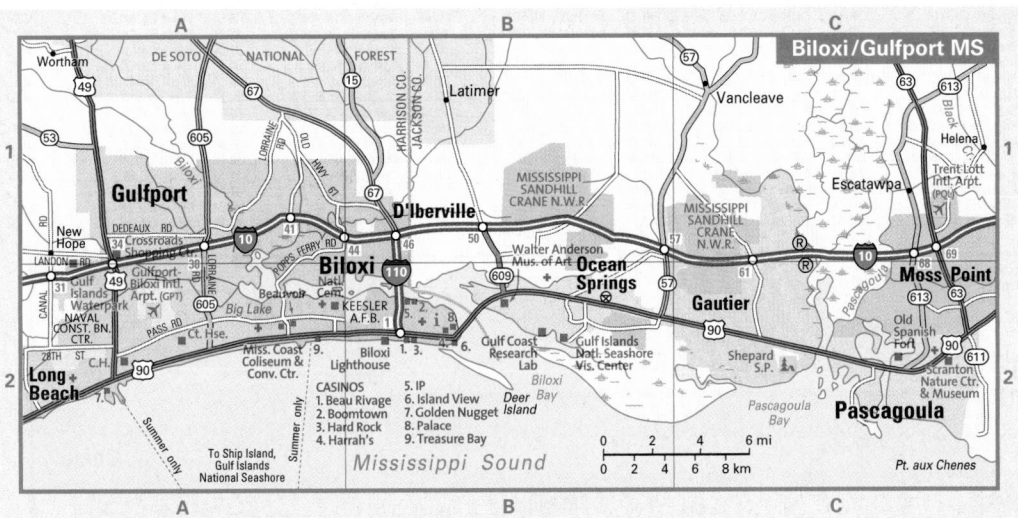

196
Bowers–Burgettstown

Figures after entries indicate population, page number, and grid reference.

Bowers DE, 335 145 F3
Bowie AZ, 449 55 E3
Bowie MD, 54727 144 C3
Bowie TX, 5218 59 E1
Bowie Co. TX, 92565 116 B4
Bowleys Quarters MD, 6755 144 C2
Bowling Green FL, 2930 140 C3
Bowling Green KY, 58067 109 F2
Bowling Green MO, 5334 97 F2
Bowling Green OH, 30028 90 C2
Bowling Green VA, 1111 103 D4
Bowman GA, 862 121 E3
Bowman ND, 1650 25 F1
Bowman SC, 968 130 C1
Bowman Co. ND, 3151 25 F1
Bow Mar CO, 866 209 B4
Boxborough MA, 4996 150 C1
Box Butte Co. NE, 11308 34 A2
Box Elder MT, 87 16 B2
Box Elder SD, 7800 26 A3
Box Elder Co. UT, 49975 31 D3
Boxford MA, 2339 151 F1
Boyce LA, 1004 125 E4
Boyce VA, 589 103 D2
Boyceville WI, 1086 67 E3
Boyd TX, 1207 59 E2
Boyd WI, 552 67 F4
Boyd Co. KY, 49542 101 D4
Boyd Co. NE, 2099 35 D1
Boyden IA, 707 35 F1
Boydton VA, 431 113 D3
Boyertown PA, 4055 146 B2
Boyette FL, 5895 140 C3
Boykins VA, 564 113 E3
Boyle MS, 650 118 A4
Boyle Co. KY, 28432 110 B1
Boyne City MI, 3735 70 B3
Boynton Beach FL, 68217 143 F1
Boys Town NE, 745 245 A2
Bozeman MT, 37280 23 F1
Braceville IL, 793 88 C2
Bracken Co. KY, 8488 100 C3
Brackettville TX, 1688 60 B3
Bradbury CA, 1048 228 E2
Braddock PA, 2159 250 C2
Braddock Hts. MD, 2608 144 A1
Braddock Hills PA, 1880 250 C2
Bradenton FL, 49546 140 B3
Bradenton Beach FL, 1171 140 B3
Bradford AR, 759 117 F1
Bradford IL, 768 88 B2
Bradford NH, 356 81 E4
Bradford OH, 1842 90 B4
Bradford PA, 8770 92 B1
Bradford RI, 1406 150 C4
Bradford TN, 1048 108 C4
Bradford VT, 788 81 E3
Bradford Co. FL, 28520 138 C3
Bradford Co. PA, 62622 93 E2
Bradfordville FL, 1100 137 E2
Bradford Woods PA, 1171 92 A3
Bradley AR, 628 125 D1
Bradley IL, 15895 89 D3
Bradley ME, 1242 83 D1
Bradley WV, 2040 101 F4
Bradley Beach NJ, 4298 147 F2
Bradley Co. AR, 11508 117 E4
Bradley Co. TN, 98963 120 C1
Bradley Jct. FL, 686 140 C3
Bradner OH, 985 90 C2
Brady TX, 5528 58 C4
Braham MN, 1793 67 D2
Braidwood IL, 6191 88 C2
Brainerd MN, 13590 64 B4
Braintree MA, 35744 151 D2
Bramwell WV, 364 111 F1
Branch Co. MI, 45248 90 A1
Branchville AL, 825 119 F4
Branchville NJ, 841 94 A4
Branchville SC, 1024 130 C1
Brandenburg KY, 2643 99 F4
Brandon FL, 103483 140 C2
Brandon MS, 21705 126 B3
Brandon SD, 8785 27 F4
Brandon VT, 1648 81 D3
Brandon WI, 879 74 C2
Brandywine MD, 6719 144 B4
Brandywine Manor PA, 1200 146 B3
Branford CT, 29089 149 D2
Branford FL, 712 138 B3
Branson MO, 10520 107 D3
Brant Beach NJ, 800 147 E4
Brantley AL, 809 128 A4
Brantley Co. GA, 18411 129 F4
Brant Rock MA, 5100 151 E2
Braselton GA, 7511 121 D3
Brasher Falls NY, 669 80 B1
Bratenahl OH, 1197 204 F1
Brattleboro VT, 7414 94 C1
Brawley CA, 24953 53 E4
Braxton Co. WV, 14523 101 F3
Bray OK, 1209 51 E4
Braymer MO, 878 96 C1
Brazil IN, 7912 99 E1
Brazoria TX, 3019 132 A4
Brazoria Co. TX, 313166 132 A4
Brazos Co. TX, 194851 61 F1
Brea CA, 39282 229 F3
Breathitt Co. KY, 13878 111 D1
Breaux Bridge LA, 8139 133 F2
Breckenridge CO, 4540 41 D1
Breckenridge MI, 1328 76 A2
Breckenridge MN, 3386 27 F1
Breckenridge TX, 5780 59 D2
Breckenridge Hills MO, 4746 256 B2
Breckinridge Co. KY, 20059 99 F4
Brecksville OH, 13656 204 F3
Breese IL, 4442 98 B3
Breezy Pt. MD, 800 144 C4
Breezy Pt. MN, 2346 64 B4
Breinigsville PA, 4138 146 B1
Bremen GA, 6227 120 B4
Bremen IN, 4588 89 F2
Bremen KY, 197 109 E1
Bremen OH, 1425 101 D1
Bremer Co. IA, 24276 73 E3
Bremerton WA, 37729 12 C3
Bremond TX, 929 59 F4
Brenham TX, 15716 61 F2
Brent AL, 4947 127 F1
Brent FL, 21804 135 F2
Brentsville VA, 650 144 A4
Brentwood CA, 51481 36 B3
Brentwood MD, 3046 270 E2
Brentwood MO, 8055 256 B2
Brentwood NY, 60664 149 D4
Brentwood PA, 9643 250 B3
Brentwood TN, 37060 109 F4
Bressler PA, 1437 218 C2
Brevard NC, 7609 121 E1
Brevard Co. FL, 543376 141 E2
Brewer ME, 9482 83 D1
Brewerton NY, 4029 79 D3
Brewster MA, 2000 151 F3
Brewster MN, 473 72 A2
Brewster NE, 17 34 C2
Brewster NY, 2390 148 C2
Brewster OH, 2112 91 E3
Brewster WA, 2370 13 E2
Brewster Co. TX, 9232 62 C3
Brewster Hill NY, 2089 148 C1
Brewton AL, 5408 135 F1
Briar TX, 5665 59 E2
Briarcliff TX, 1438 61 D1
Briarcliffe Acres SC, 457 123 D4
Briarcliff Manor NY, 7867 148 B2
Briar Creek PA, 660 93 E3
Briarwood KY, 435 230 F1
Briceville TN, 650 110 C4
Brickerville PA, 1309 146 A2
Bridge City LA, 7706 239 B2
Bridge City TX, 7840 132 C3
Bridgehampton NY, 1756 149 F3
Bridgeport AL, 2418 120 A2
Bridgeport CA, 575 37 E3
Bridgeport CT, 144229 149 D2
Bridgeport IL, 1886 99 D3
Bridgeport MD, 2700 144 A1
Bridgeport MI, 6950 76 B3
Bridgeport NE, 1545 34 A3
Bridgeport NY, 1490 79 E3
Bridgeport PA, 4554 248 A1
Bridgeport TX, 5976 59 E2
Bridgeport WA, 2409 13 E2
Bridgeport WV, 8149 102 A2
Bridger MT, 708 24 B2
Bridgeton MO, 11550 256 B1
Bridgeton NJ, 25349 145 F1
Bridgetown OH, 14407 204 A2
Bridgeview IL, 16446 203 D5
Bridgeville DE, 2048 145 E4
Bridgeville PA, 5148 250 A3
Bridgewater MA, 7841 151 D2
Bridgewater NJ, 44464 147 D1
Bridgewater NY, 470 79 E3
Bridgewater SD, 492 27 E4
Bridgewater VA, 5644 102 C4
Bridgman MI, 2291 89 E1
Bridgton ME, 2071 82 B3
Brielle NJ, 4774 147 E2
Brier WA, 6087 262 B2
Brigantine NJ, 9450 147 F4
Brigham City UT, 17899 31 E3
Bright IN, 5693 100 B2
Brighton AL, 2945 195 D2
Brighton CO, 33352 41 E1
Brighton IL, 2254 98 A2
Brighton IA, 652 87 E2
Brighton MI, 7444 76 B4
Brighton NY, 36609 78 C3
Brighton TN, 2735 118 B1
Brightwaters NY, 3103 149 D4
Brightwood VA, 1001 102 C3
Brilliant AL, 900 119 E3
Brilliant OH, 1482 91 F4
Brillion WI, 3148 74 C1
Brimfield IL, 868 88 B3
Brinckerhoff NY, 2900 148 B1
Brinkley AR, 3188 117 F2
Brinnon WA, 797 12 C3
Brisbane CA, 4282 259 B3
Briscoe Co. TX, 1637 50 B4
Bristol CT, 60477 149 D1
Bristol FL, 996 137 D2
Bristol IN, 1602 89 F1
Bristol NH, 1688 81 F3
Bristol PA, 9726 147 D2
Bristol RI, 22954 151 D3
Bristol SD, 341 27 E2
Bristol TN, 26702 111 E3
Bristol VT, 2030 81 D2
Bristol VA, 17835 111 E3
Bristol WI, 2584 74 C4
Bristol Co. MA, 548285 151 D3
Bristol Co. RI, 49875 151 D3
Bristow OK, 4222 51 F2
Britt IA, 2069 72 C3
Brittany Farms PA, 3695 146 C2
Britton MI, 586 90 B1
Britton SD, 1241 27 E1
Broadalbin NY, 1327 80 C4
Broad Brook CT, 4069 150 A3
Broadmoor CA, 4176 259 B3
Broadus MT, 468 25 E2
Broadview IL, 7932 203 C4
Broadview Hts. OH, 19400 204 F3
Broadwater Co. MT, 5612 15 F4
Broadway NC, 1229 123 D1
Broadway VA, 3691 102 C3
Brock Hall MD, 9552 144 C3
Brockport NY, 8366 78 C3
Brockton MA, 93810 151 D2
Brockton MT, 255 17 E2
Brockway PA, 2072 92 B2
Brocton NY, 1486 78 A4
Brodhead KY, 1211 110 C1
Brodhead WI, 3293 74 B4
Brodheadsville PA, 1800 93 F3
Brogden NC, 2633 123 E1
Broken Arrow OK, 98850 106 A4
Broken Bow NE, 3559 35 D3
Broken Bow OK, 4120 116 B3
Bromley KY, 763 204 A3
Bronson FL, 1113 138 C4
Bronson MI, 2349 90 A1
Bronte TX, 999 58 C3
Bronwood GA, 225 128 C3
Bronx Co. NY, 1385108 148 B4
Brook IN, 997 89 D3
Brookdale SC, 4873 122 A4
Brooke VA, 650 103 D4
Brooke Co. WV, 24069 91 F4
Brookfield CT, 16354 148 C1
Brookfield IL, 18978 203 C5
Brookfield MA, 833 150 B2
Brookfield MO, 4542 97 D1
Brookfield OH, 1288 276 C1
Brookfield WI, 37920 234 B2
Brookfield Ctr. CT, 1800 148 C1
Brookhaven MS, 12513 126 B4
Brookhaven NY, 3451 149 D4
Brookhaven PA, 8006 248 A4
Brookings OR, 6336 28 A2
Brookings SD, 22056 27 F3
Brookings Co. SD, 31965 27 F3
Brookland AR, 1642 108 A4
Brooklandville MD, 2200 193 C1
Brooklawn NJ, 1955 248 C4
Brooklet GA, 1395 130 B2
Brookline MA, 58732 151 D1
Brookline NH, 4991 95 D1
Brooklyn CT, 981 150 B3
Brooklyn IL, 749 256 C2
Brooklyn IN, 1598 99 F1
Brooklyn IA, 1468 87 E1
Brooklyn MI, 1206 90 B1
Brooklyn OH, 11169 204 E2
Brooklyn WI, 1401 74 B3
Brooklyn Ctr. MN, 30104 235 B1
Brooklyn Hts. OH, 1543 204 F2
Brooklyn Park MD, 14373 193 C4
Brooklyn Park MN, 75781 235 B1
Brookneal VA, 1112 112 C2
Brook Park OH, 19212 204 E3
Brookport IL, 984 108 C2
Brooks GA, 524 128 C1
Brooks KY, 2401 100 A4
Brooks ME, 1022 82 C2
Brooks Co. GA, 16243 137 F1
Brooks Co. TX, 7223 63 E3
Brookshire TX, 4702 61 F2
Brookside AL, 1363 195 D1
Brookside DE, 14353 146 B4
Brookside OH, 632 91 F4
Brookside Vil. TX, 1523 220 C4
Brookston IN, 1554 89 E3
Brooksville FL, 7719 140 C1
Brooksville KY, 642 100 C3
Brooksville MS, 1223 127 D1
Brookville IN, 2596 100 A2
Brookville NY, 3465 148 C4
Brookville OH, 5884 100 B1
Brookville PA, 3924 92 B2
Brookwood AL, 1828 127 F1
Broomall PA, 10789 146 C3
Broome Co. NY, 200600 93 F1
Broomfield CO, 55889 41 E1
Broomfield Co. CO, 55889 41 E1
Brooten MN, 743 66 B3
Broussard LA, 8197 133 F2
Broward Co. FL, 1748066 143 E1
Browerville MN, 790 66 B2
Brown City MI, 1325 76 C3
Brown Co. IL, 6937 87 F4
Brown Co. IN, 15242 99 F2
Brown Co. KS, 9984 96 A1
Brown Co. MN, 25893 72 B1
Brown Co. NE, 3145 34 C1
Brown Co. OH, 44846 100 C3
Brown Co. SD, 36531 27 E1
Brown Co. TX, 38106 59 D3
Brown Co. WI, 248007 74 C1
Brown Deer WI, 11999 234 C1
Brownfield TX, 9657 58 A2
Browning MT, 1016 15 E2
Brownsboro TX, 1039 124 A3
Brownsburg IN, 21285 99 F1
Brownsdale MN, 676 73 D2
Browns Mills NJ, 11223 147 D3
Brownstown IL, 759 98 C2
Brownstown IN, 2947 99 F3
Browns Valley MN, 589 27 F1
Brownsville CA, 1069 36 C1
Brownsville KY, 836 109 F2
Brownsville MN, 466 73 F2
Brownsville OR, 1668 20 B3
Brownsville PA, 2331 102 B1
Brownsville TN, 10292 118 C1
Brownsville TX, 175023 63 F4
Brownsville WI, 581 74 C2
Brownton MN, 762 66 C4
Brownville NY, 1119 79 E1
Brownville Jct. ME, 750 84 C4
Brownwood TX, 19288 59 D4
Broxton GA, 1189 129 E4
Broyhill Park VA, 17000 270 B4
Bruce MS, 1939 118 C3
Bruce SD, 204 27 F3
Bruce WI, 779 67 F3
Bruceton TN, 1478 109 D4
Bruceville-Eddy TX, 1475 59 E4
Brule Co. SD, 5255 27 D4
Brundidge AL, 2076 128 B4
Brunson SC, 554 130 B1
Brunswick GA, 15383 139 D1
Brunswick ME, 15175 82 B3
Brunswick MD, 5870 144 A2
Brunswick MO, 858 97 D2
Brunswick OH, 34255 91 E2
Brunswick Co. NC, 107431 123 E3
Brunswick Co. VA, 17434 113 D3
Brush CO, 5463 33 F4
Brush Prairie WA, 2652 20 C1
Brushy OK, 900 116 B1
Brusly LA, 2589 134 A2
Bryan OH, 8545 90 B2
Bryan TX, 76201 61 F1
Bryan Co. GA, 30233 130 B3
Bryan Co. OK, 42416 59 F1
Bryans Road MD, 7244 144 B4
Bryant AR, 16688 117 E2
Bryant SD, 456 27 E3
Bryantville MA, 2600 151 E2
Bryn Athyn PA, 1375 248 D1
Bryn Mawr PA, 3779 146 C3
Bryson TX, 539 59 D2
Bryson City NC, 1424 121 D1
Buchanan GA, 1104 120 B4
Buchanan MI, 4456 89 E1
Buchanan NY, 2230 148 B2
Buchanan VA, 1178 112 B1
Buchanan Co. IA, 20958 73 E4
Buchanan Co. MO, 89201 96 B1
Buchanan Co. VA, 24098 111 F2
Buchanan Dam TX, 1519 61 D1
Buchtel OH, 558 101 E2
Buckeye AZ, 50876 54 B1
Buckeye Lake OH, 2746 101 D1
Buckfield ME, 1723 82 B2
Buckhannon WV, 5639 102 A2
Buckhead Ridge FL, 1450 141 E4
Buckingham PA, 1400 146 C2
Buckingham VA, 133 113 D1
Buckingham Co. VA, 17146 113 D1
Buckland AK, 416 154 B2
Buckley IL, 600 89 D4
Buckley MI, 697 69 F4
Buckley WA, 4354 12 C3
Bucklin KS, 794 42 C4
Bucklin MO, 467 97 D1
Buckner KY, 5837 100 A4
Buckner MO, 3076 96 C2
Bucks Co. PA, 625249 146 C1
Bucksport ME, 2885 83 D2
Bucksport SC, 876 123 D4
Bucoda WA, 562 12 C4
Bucyrus OH, 12362 90 C3
Buda IL, 538 88 B2
Buda TX, 7295 61 E2
Budd Lake NJ, 8968 94 A4
Bude MS, 1063 126 A4
Buellton CA, 4828 52 A2
Buena NJ, 4603 147 D4
Buena WA, 990 13 D4
Buena Park CA, 80530 228 E3
Buena Ventura Lakes FL, 26079 246 C5
Buena Vista CO, 2617 41 D2
Buena Vista GA, 2173 128 C2
Buena Vista MI, 6816 76 B2
Buena Vista VA, 6650 112 C1
Buena Vista Co. IA, 20260 72 B4
Buffalo IN, 692 89 E3
Buffalo IA, 1270 87 F2
Buffalo KY, 498 110 A1
Buffalo MN, 15453 66 C3
Buffalo MO, 3084 107 D1
Buffalo NY, 261310 78 B3
Buffalo ND, 188 19 E4
Buffalo OK, 1299 50 C1
Buffalo SC, 1266 121 F2
Buffalo SD, 330 25 F3
Buffalo TX, 1856 59 F4
Buffalo WV, 1236 101 E3
Buffalo WY, 4585 25 D3
Buffalo Ctr. IA, 905 72 C2
Buffalo City WI, 1023 73 E1
Buffalo Co. NE, 46102 35 D4
Buffalo Co. SD, 1912 27 D3
Buffalo Co. WI, 13587 67 E4
Buffalo Grove IL, 41496 203 C2
Buffalo Lake MN, 733 66 B4
Buford GA, 12225 120 C3
Buhl ID, 4122 30 C1
Buhl MN, 1000 64 C3
Buhler KS, 1327 43 E3
Buies Creek NC, 2942 123 D1
Bullard TX, 2463 124 A3
Bullhead SD, 348 26 C1
Bullhead City AZ, 39540 46 B3
Bullitt Co. KY, 74319 99 F4
Bulloch Co. GA, 70217 130 B2
Bullock Co. AL, 10914 128 B3
Bulls Gap TN, 738 111 D3
Bull Shoals AR, 1950 107 E3
Bull Valley IL, 1077 74 C4
Bulverde TX, 4630 61 D2
Buna TX, 2142 132 C2
Buncombe Co. NC, 238318 111 E4
Bunker Hill IL, 1774 98 B2
Bunker Hill IN, 888 89 F3
Bunker Hill OR, 1444 20 A4
Bunker Hill WV, 700 103 D2
Bunker Hill Vil. TX, 3633 220 B2
Bunkerville NV, 1303 46 B1
Bunkie LA, 4171 133 E1
Bunnell FL, 2676 139 E4
Buras LA, 945 134 C4
Burbank CA, 103340 52 C2
Burbank IL, 28925 203 D5
Burbank WA, 3291 21 E1
Burden KS, 535 43 F4
Bureau Co. IL, 34978 88 B2
Burgaw NC, 3872 123 E2
Burgettstown PA, 1388 91 F4

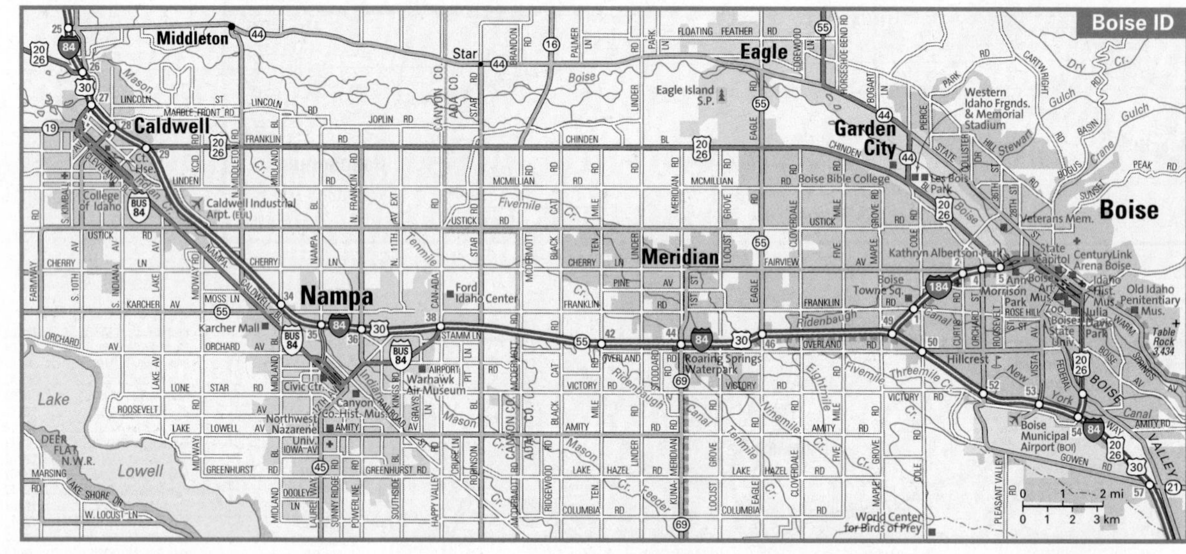
Boise ID
Middleton
Star
Eagle
Caldwell
Eagle Island S.P.
Western Idaho Frgnds. & Memorial Stadium
Garden City
Boise Bible College
College of Idaho
Caldwell Industrial Arpt. (EUL)
Veterans Mem.
Boise
Meridian
State Capitol
CenturyLink Arena Boise
Kathryn Albertson Park
Boise Towne Sq.
Old Idaho Penitentiary
Nampa
Ford Idaho Center
Karcher Mall
Morrison Park
Table Rock 3434
Roaring Springs Waterpark
Warhawk Air Museum
Hillcrest
Canyon Co. Hist. Mus.
Northwest Nazarene Univ.
Deer Flat N.W.R.
Lake Lowell
Boise Municipal Airport (BOI)
World Center for Birds of Prey

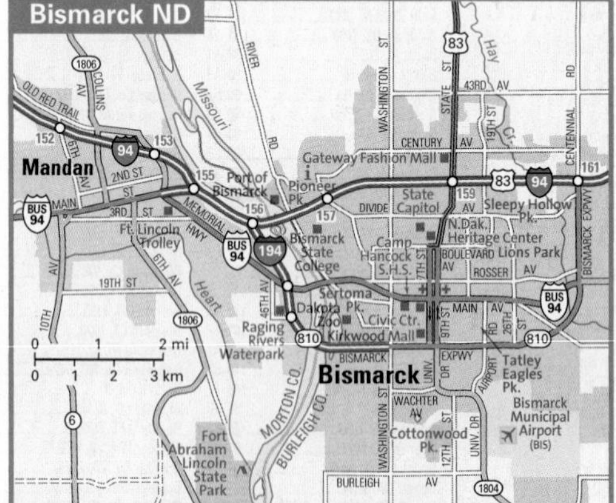
Bismarck ND
Mandan
Missouri
Gateway Fashion Mall
Pioneer Pk.
State Capitol
Sleepy Hollow Pk.
N. Dak. Heritage Center
Camp Hancock S.H.S.
Lions Park
Bismarck State College
Ft. Lincoln Trolley
Heart
Sertoma Pk.
Dakota Zoo
Civic Ctr.
Kirkwood Mall
Raging Rivers Waterpark
Bismarck
Tatley Eagles Pk.
Bismarck Municipal Airport (BIS)
Cottonwood Pk.
Fort Abraham Lincoln State Park

Entries in **bold black** indicate counties or parishes.
Entries in **bold color** indicate cities with detailed inset maps.

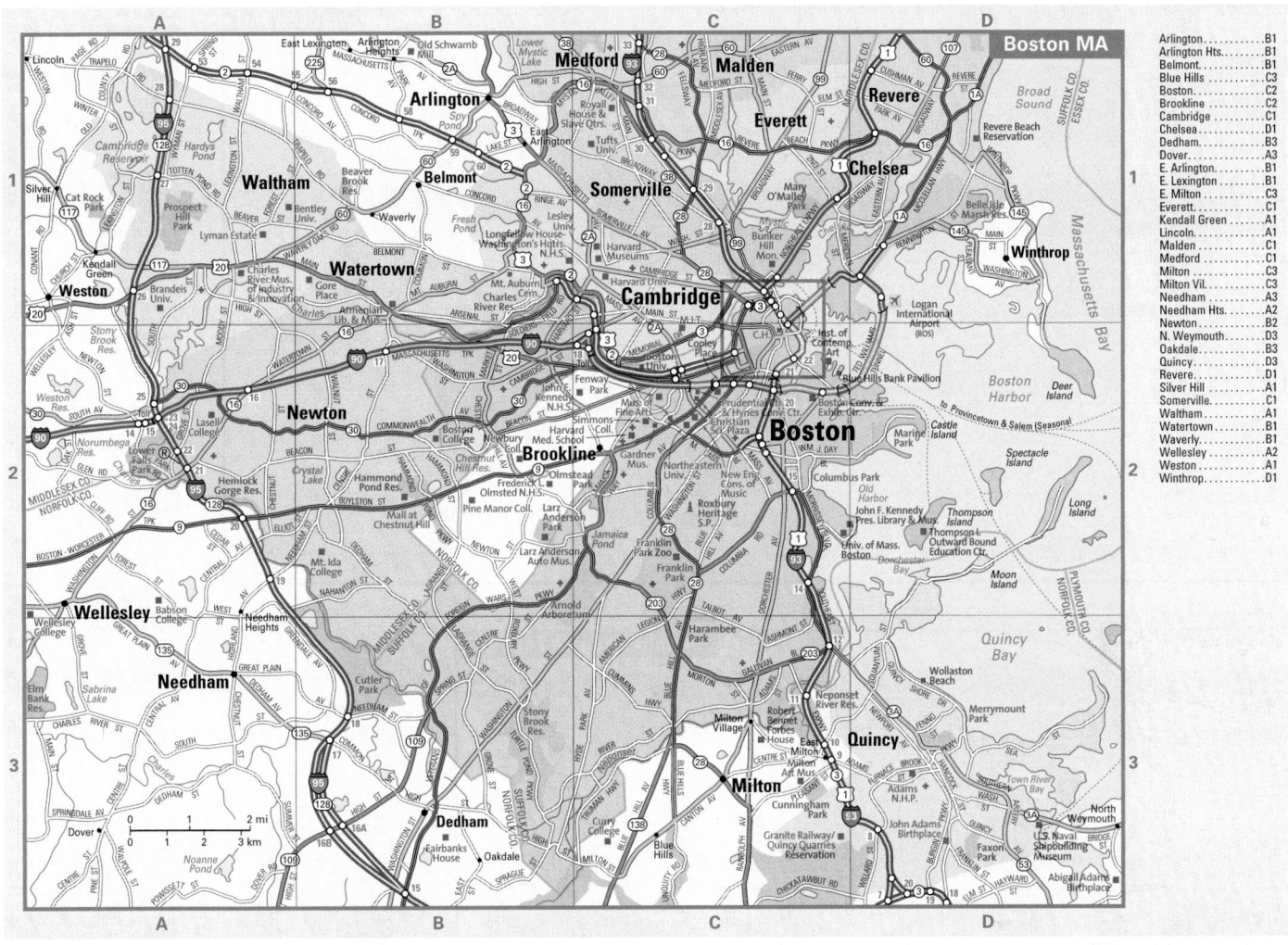

Boston MA

Downtown **Boston MA**

POINTS OF INTEREST

Figures after entries indicate population, page number, and grid reference.

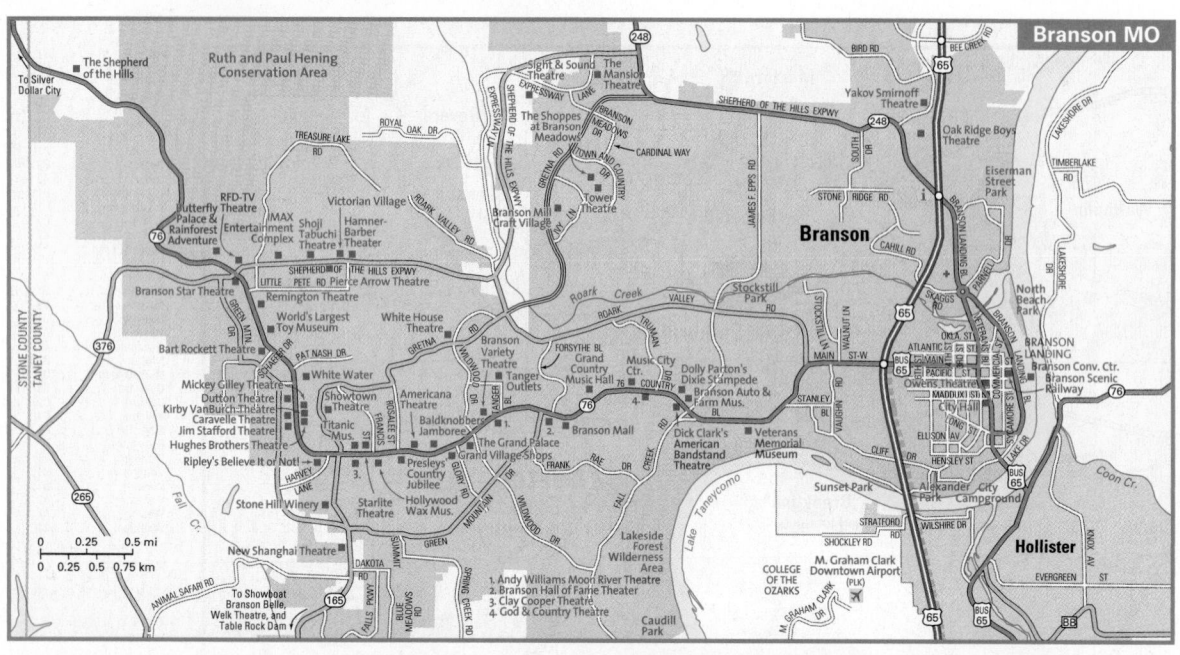

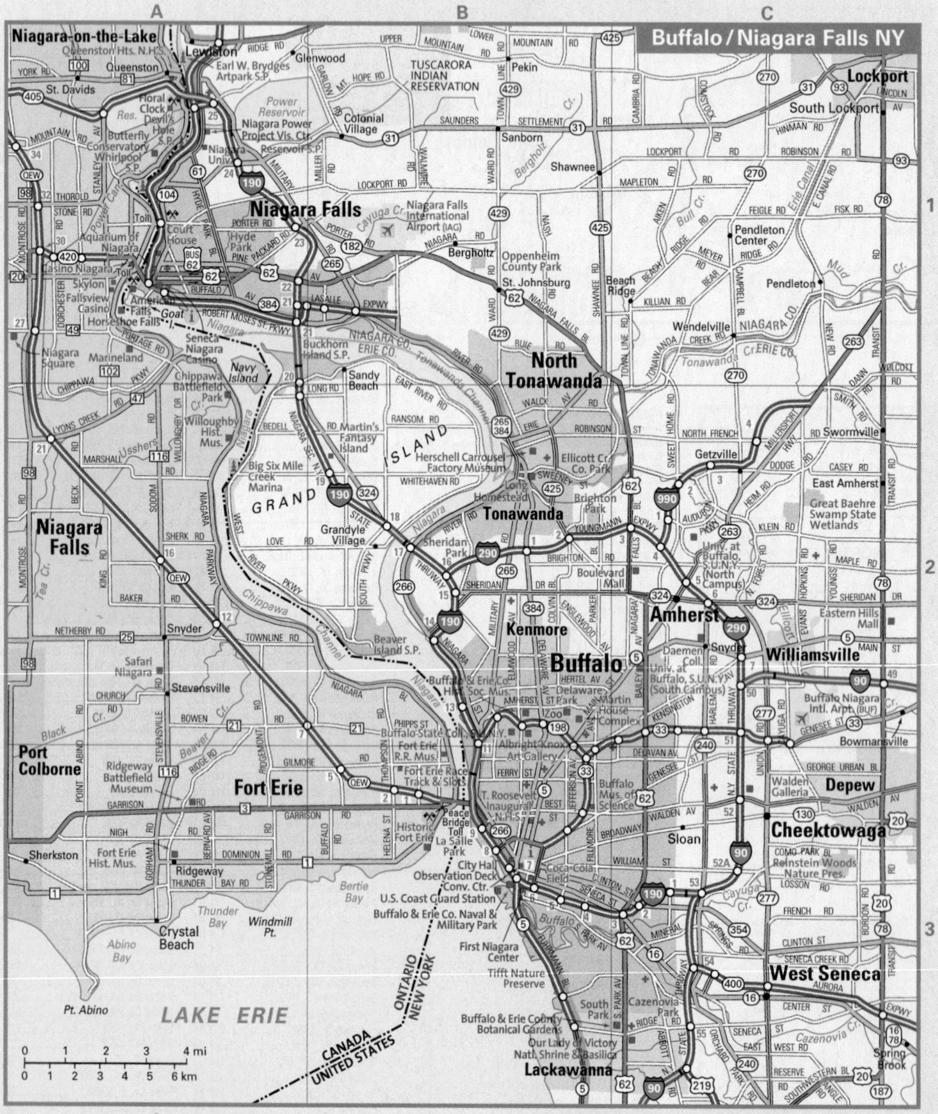

Branson MO

Buffalo / Niagara Falls NY

Map labels — Branson MO:

To Silver Dollar City · The Shepherd of the Hills · Ruth and Paul Hening Conservation Area · Sight & Sound Theatre · The Mansion Theatre · Yakov Smirnoff Theatre · The Shoppes at Branson Meadows · RFD-TV · Butterfly Palace & Rainforest Adventure · IMAX Entertainment Complex · Shoji Tabuchi Theater · Hamner-Barber Theater · Branson · Victorian Village · Branson Mill Craft Village · Tower Theatre · Branson Star Theatre · Remington Theatre · World's Largest Toy Museum · White House Theatre · Mickey Gilley Theatre · Dutton Theatre · Kirby VanBurch Theatre · Caravelle Theatre · Jim Stafford Theatre · Hughes Brothers Theatre · Ripley's Believe it or Not! · White Water · Showtown Theatre · Americana Theatre · Baldknobbers Jamboree · The Grand Palace · Grand Village Shops · Presleys' Country Jubilee · Dick Clark's American Bandstand Theatre · Veterans Memorial Museum · Tanger Outlets · Grand Country Music Hall · Music City Country · Dolly Parton's Dixie Stampede · Branson Auto & Farm Mus. · Branson Mall · Stone Hill Winery · Starlite Theatre · Hollywood Wax Mus. · New Shanghai Theatre · Titanic Mus. · Hollister · Branson Conv. Ctr. · Branson Scenic Railway · Branson Landing · Sunset Park · Lakeside Forest Wilderness Area · College of the Ozarks · M. Graham Clark Downtown Airport (PLK) · Stone County · Taney County

1. Andy Williams Moon River Theatre
2. Branson Hall of Fame Theater
3. Clay Cooper Theatre
4. God & Country Theatre

To Showboat Branson Belle, Welk Theatre, and Table Rock Dam

Map labels — Buffalo / Niagara Falls NY index:

199
Callahan County–Cavalier County

Entries in **bold black** indicate counties or parishes.
Entries in **bold color** indicate cities with detailed inset maps.

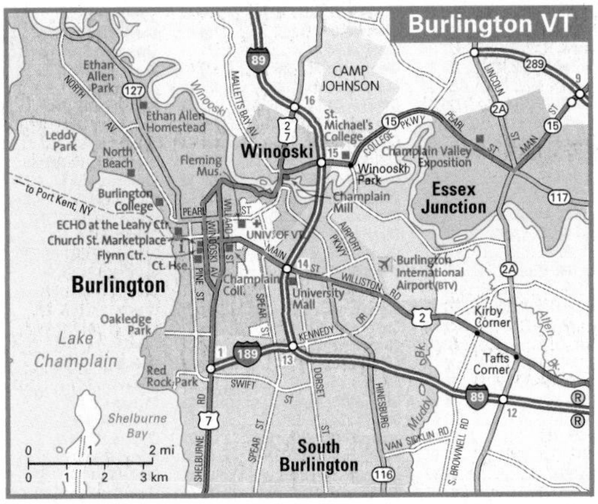
Burlington VT
Burlington
Winooski
Essex Junction
South Burlington
Lake Champlain
Shelburne Bay
CAMP JOHNSON
Ethan Allen Homestead
Burlington Intl. Airport (BTV)
University Mall
Champlain Mill
Champlain Valley Exposition
Church St. Marketplace
Flynn Ctr.
ECHO at the Leahy Ctr.

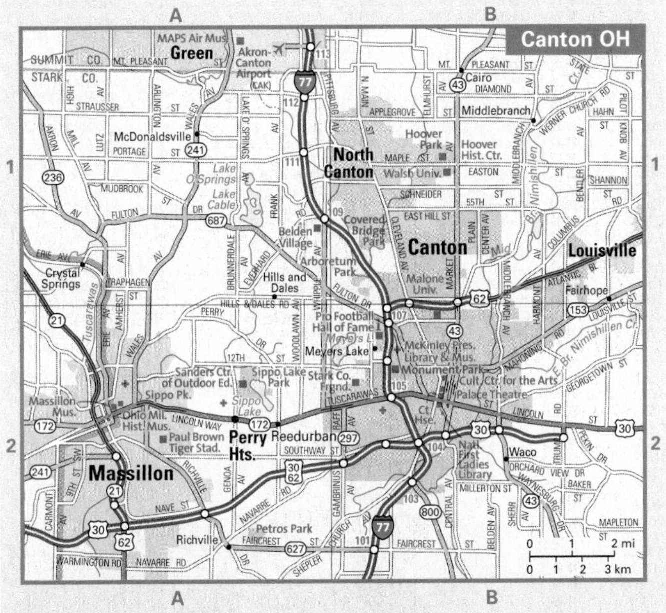
Canton OH
Canton
North Canton
Massillon
Louisville
Green
Perry Hts.
Middlebranch
McDonaldsville
Hills and Dales
Crystal Springs
Belden Village
Richville
Reedurban
Waco
Cairo
Pro Football Hall of Fame
McKinley Pres. Library & Mus.
Akron-Canton Airport (CAK)
MAPS Air Mus.

Cairo B1	Green........A1	McDonaldsville........A1	Perry Hts........A2
Canton........B1	Hills and Dales........A1	Meyers Lake........B2	Reedurban........A2
Crystal Sprs........A1	Louisville........B1	Middlebranch........B1	Richville........A2
Fairhope........B1	Massillon........A2	N. Canton........B1	Waco........B2

Callahan Co. TX, 13544 .... 58 C3
Callaway FL, 14405 .... 136 C2
Callaway NE, 539 .... 34 C3
Callaway Co. MO, 44332 .... 97 E3
Calloway Co. KY, 37191 .... 109 D3
Calmar IA, 978 .... 73 E3
Cal-Nev-Ari NV, 244 .... 46 B3
Calpella CA, 679 .... 36 A2
Calumet MI, 726 .... 65 F3
Calumet OK, 507 .... 51 E3
Calumet City IL, 37042 .... 89 D2
Calumet Co. WI, 48971 .... 74 C1
Calumet Park IL, 7835 .... 203 E6
Calvert TX, 1192 .... 61 F1
Calvert Beach MD, 808 .... 103 E3
Calvert City KY, 2566 .... 109 D2
Calvert Co. MD, 88737 .... 144 C4
Calvert Manor MD, 650 .... 144 B4
Calverton MD, 17724 .... 144 B3
Calverton NY, 6510 .... 149 E3
Calverton Park MO, 1293 .... 256 B1
Camanche IA, 4448 .... 88 A1
Camargo KY, 1081 .... 100 C4
Camarillo CA, 65201 .... 52 B2
Camas WA, 19355 .... 20 C1
Camas Co. ID, 1117 .... 22 C4
Cambria CA, 6032 .... 44 B4
Cambria IL, 1228 .... 108 C1
Cambria WI, 767 .... 74 B2
Cambria Co. PA, 143679 .... 92 B4
Cambridge ID, 328 .... 22 B3
Cambridge IL, 2160 .... 88 A2
Cambridge IA, 827 .... 86 C1
Cambridge MD, 12326 .... 145 D4
Cambridge MA, 105162 .... 151 D1
Cambridge MN, 8111 .... 67 D3
Cambridge NE, 1063 .... 34 C4
Cambridge NY, 1870 .... 81 D4
Cambridge OH, 10635 .... 101 E1
Cambridge VT, 236 .... 81 D1
Cambridge WI, 1457 .... 74 B3
Cambridge City IN, 1870 .... 100 A1
Cambridge Sprs. PA, 2595 .... 92 A1
Camden AL, 2020 .... 127 F3
Camden AR, 12183 .... 117 D4
Camden DE, 3464 .... 145 E2
Camden IN, 611 .... 89 E3
Camden ME, 3570 .... 82 C2
Camden MI, 512 .... 90 A1
Camden NJ, 77344 .... 146 C3
Camden NY, 2231 .... 79 E3
Camden NC, 599 .... 115 E1
Camden OH, 2046 .... 100 B1
Camden SC, 6838 .... 122 B3
Camden TN, 3582 .... 109 D4
Camden Co. GA, 50513 .... 139 D1
Camden Co. MO, 44002 .... 97 D4
Camden Co. NJ, 513657 .... 147 D4
Camden Co. NC, 9980 .... 115 E1
Camden Pt. MO, 474 .... 96 B2
Camdenton MO, 3718 .... 97 D4
Cameron AZ, 885 .... 47 E2
Cameron LA, 406 .... 133 D3
Cameron MO, 9933 .... 96 C1
Cameron SC, 424 .... 122 B4
Cameron TX, 5552 .... 61 E1
Cameron WV, 946 .... 102 A1
Cameron WI, 1783 .... 67 E3
Cameron Co. PA, 5085 .... 92 C2
Cameron Co. TX, 406220 .... 63 F4
Cameron Par. LA, 6839 .... 133 D3
Camilla GA, 5360 .... 129 D4
Camillus NY, 1213 .... 79 D3
Camino CA, 1750 .... 36 C2
Campbell CA, 39349 .... 36 B4
Campbell FL, 2479 .... 141 D2
Campbell MO, 1992 .... 108 B3
Campbell OH, 8235 .... 91 F3
Campbell TX, 638 .... 59 F2
Campbell Co. KY, 90336 .... 100 B3
Campbell Co. SD, 1466 .... 26 C1
Campbell Co. TN, 40716 .... 110 C3
Campbell Co. VA, 54842 .... 112 C2
Campbell Co. WY, 46133 .... 25 E3
Campbell Hall NY, 750 .... 148 A1
Campbellsburg IN, 585 .... 99 F3
Campbellsburg KY, 813 .... 100 A3
Campbellsport WI, 2016 .... 74 C2
Campbellsville KY, 9108 .... 110 A1
Campbellton FL, 230 .... 136 C1
Camp Co. TX, 12401 .... 124 B1
Camp Douglas WI, 601 .... 74 A1
Camp Hill AL, 1014 .... 128 B2
Camp Hill PA, 7888 .... 93 D4
Campion CO, 1832 .... 33 E4
Campobello SC, 502 .... 121 F1
Camp Pt. IL, 1132 .... 87 F4
Camp Sprs. MD, 19096 .... 144 B3
Campti LA, 1056 .... 125 D3
Campton KY, 441 .... 111 D1
Campton NH, 3333 .... 81 F3
Camp Verde AZ, 10873 .... 47 D4
Camp Wood TX, 706 .... 60 C2
Cana VA, 1254 .... 112 A3
Canaan CT, 1212 .... 94 B2
Canaan ME, 300 .... 82 C1
Canaan NH, 524 .... 81 E3
Canaan VT, 392 .... 81 F1
Canadian TX, 2649 .... 50 C2
Canadian Co. OK, 115541 .... 51 E3
Canajoharie NY, 2229 .... 79 F3
Canal Fulton OH, 5479 .... 91 E3
Canal Pt. FL, 367 .... 141 E4
Canal Winchester OH, 7101 .... 101 D1
Canandaigua NY, 10545 .... 78 C3
Canaseraga NY, 550 .... 78 C4
Canastota NY, 4804 .... 79 E3
Canby MN, 1795 .... 27 F3
Canby OR, 15829 .... 20 C2
Candler Co. GA, 10998 .... 129 F2
Cando ND, 1115 .... 19 D2
Candor NY, 851 .... 93 E1
Candor NC, 840 .... 122 C1
Caney KS, 2203 .... 51 F1
Caneyville KY, 608 .... 109 F1
Canfield OH, 7515 .... 91 F3
Canisteo NY, 2270 .... 78 C4
Canistota SD, 656 .... 27 E4
Cannelton IN, 1563 .... 99 E4
Cannon Ball ND, 875 .... 18 C4
Cannon Beach OR, 1690 .... 20 B1
Cannon Co. TN, 13801 .... 110 A4
Cannondale CT, 141 .... 148 C2
Cannon Falls MN, 4083 .... 67 D4
Cannonsburg KY, 856 .... 101 D4
Canon GA, 804 .... 121 E3
Canon City CO, 16400 .... 41 E3
Canonsburg PA, 8992 .... 92 A4
Canterbury DE, 1200 .... 145 E3
Canton CT, 10292 .... 94 C3
Canton GA, 22958 .... 120 C3
Canton IL, 14704 .... 88 A4
Canton KS, 748 .... 43 E3
Canton MA, 21561 .... 151 D2
Canton MS, 13189 .... 126 B2
Canton MO, 2377 .... 87 F4
Canton NY, 6314 .... 80 B2
Canton NC, 4227 .... 121 E1
Canton OH, 73007 .... 91 E3
Canton OK, 625 .... 51 D2
Canton PA, 1976 .... 93 D2
Canton SD, 3057 .... 27 F4
Canton TX, 3581 .... 124 A2
Cantonment FL, 2300 .... 135 F2
Cantua Creek CA, 466 .... 44 C3
Canute OK, 541 .... 51 D3
Canutillo TX, 6321 .... 56 C3
Canyon TX, 13303 .... 50 A3
Canyon City OR, 703 .... 21 F3
Canyon Co. ID, 188923 .... 22 B4
Canyon Day AZ, 1209 .... 55 E1
Canyon Lake CA, 10561 .... 229 J5
Canyon Lake TX, 21262 .... 61 D2
Canyonville OR, 1884 .... 28 B1
Capac MI, 1890 .... 76 C3
Cape Canaveral FL, 9912 .... 141 E2
Cape Carteret NC, 1917 .... 115 D4
Cape Charles VA, 1009 .... 114 B3
Cape Coral FL, 154305 .... 142 C1
Cape Cottage ME, 2300 .... 251 B2
Cape Elizabeth ME, 9068 .... 82 B3
Cape Girardeau MO, 37941 .... 108 B1
Cape Girardeau Co. MO, 75674 .... 108 B1
Cape May NJ, 3607 .... 104 C4
Cape May Co. NJ, 97265 .... 104 C4
Cape May C.H. NJ, 5338 .... 104 C4
Cape Neddick ME, 2568 .... 82 B4
Cape Porpoise ME, 650 .... 82 B4
Cape St. Claire MD, 8747 .... 144 C3
Cape Vincent NY, 726 .... 79 D1
Capitan NM, 1489 .... 57 D1
Capitola CA, 9918 .... 44 B2
Capitol Hts. MD, 4337 .... 270 E3
Capitol Park DE, 700 .... 145 E2
Capron IL, 1376 .... 74 C4
Captain Cook HI, 3429 .... 153 E3
Caraway AR, 1279 .... 108 A4
Carbonado WA, 610 .... 12 C4
Carbon Cliff IL, 2134 .... 208 C2
Carbon Co. MT, 10078 .... 24 B2
Carbon Co. PA, 65249 .... 93 F3
Carbon Co. UT, 21403 .... 39 F1
Carbon Co. WY, 15885 .... 33 D2
Carbondale CO, 6427 .... 40 C2
Carbondale IL, 25902 .... 108 C1
Carbondale KS, 1437 .... 96 A3
Carbondale PA, 8891 .... 93 F2
Carbon Hill AL, 2021 .... 119 E4
Cardiff MD, 650 .... 146 A4
Cardiff NJ, 2100 .... 147 F4
Cardington OH, 2047 .... 90 C4
Cardwell MO, 713 .... 108 A4
Carefree AZ, 3363 .... 54 C1
Carencro LA, 7526 .... 133 F2
Carey ID, 604 .... 23 D4
Carey OH, 3674 .... 90 C3
Caribou ME, 8189 .... 85 D2
Caribou Co. ID, 6963 .... 31 E1
Carleton MI, 2345 .... 90 C1
Carlin NV, 2368 .... 30 B4
Carlinville IL, 5917 .... 98 B2
Carlisle AR, 2214 .... 117 F2
Carlisle IN, 692 .... 99 E3
Carlisle IA, 3876 .... 86 C2
Carlisle KY, 2010 .... 100 C4
Carlisle MA, 4852 .... 150 C1
Carlisle OH, 4915 .... 100 B1
Carlisle PA, 18682 .... 93 D4
Carlisle SC, 436 .... 122 A2
Carlisle Co. KY, 5104 .... 108 C2
Carl Jct. MO, 7445 .... 106 B2
Carlls Corner NJ, 1100 .... 145 F1
Carlsbad CA, 105328 .... 53 D4
Carlsbad NM, 26138 .... 57 E3
Carlsborg WA, 995 .... 12 B2
Carlstadt NJ, 6127 .... 240 C2
Carlton MN, 862 .... 64 C4
Carlton OR, 2007 .... 20 B2
Carlton Co. MN, 35386 .... 64 C4
Carlyle IL, 3281 .... 98 B3
Carlyss LA, 4670 .... 133 D2
Carmel IN, 79191 .... 99 F1
Carmel ME, 2416 .... 82 C1
Carmel NY, 6817 .... 148 C1
Carmel-by-the-Sea CA, 3722 .... 44 B3
Carmel Valley CA, 4407 .... 44 B3
Carmen AZ, 569 .... 55 D4
Carmi IL, 5240 .... 99 D4
Carmichael CA, 61762 .... 255 C2
Carnation WA, 1786 .... 12 C3
Carnegie OK, 1723 .... 51 D3
Carnegie PA, 7972 .... 250 A2
Carnesville GA, 577 .... 121 D3
Carney MD, 29941 .... 193 D1
Carney OK, 647 .... 51 F2
Carneys Pt. NJ, 7382 .... 146 B4
Caro MI, 4229 .... 76 B2
Caroleen NC, 652 .... 121 F1
Carolina RI, 970 .... 150 C4
Carolina Beach NC, 5706 .... 123 E3
Carolina Shores NC, 3048 .... 123 D4
Caroline Co. MD, 33066 .... 145 E4
Caroline Co. VA, 28545 .... 103 E4
Carol Stream IL, 39711 .... 203 B4
Carpendale WV, 977 .... 102 C1
Carpentersville IL, 37691 .... 88 C1
Carpinteria CA, 13040 .... 52 B2
Carrabelle FL, 2778 .... 137 D3
Carrboro NC, 19582 .... 112 C4
Carriere MS, 600 .... 134 C2
Carrier Mills IL, 1653 .... 108 C1
Carrington ND, 2065 .... 19 D3
Carrizo Sprs. TX, 5368 .... 60 C4
Carrizozo NM, 996 .... 56 C1
Carroll IA, 10103 .... 86 B1
Carroll Co. AR, 27446 .... 107 D4
Carroll Co. GA, 110527 .... 120 B4
Carroll Co. IL, 15387 .... 88 B1
Carroll Co. IN, 20155 .... 89 E4
Carroll Co. IA, 20816 .... 86 B1
Carroll Co. KY, 10811 .... 100 A3
Carroll Co. MD, 167134 .... 144 B1
Carroll Co. MS, 10597 .... 118 B4
Carroll Co. MO, 9295 .... 96 C2
Carroll Co. NH, 47818 .... 81 F3
Carroll Co. OH, 28836 .... 91 E3
Carroll Co. TN, 28522 .... 109 D4
Carroll Co. VA, 30042 .... 112 A3
Carrollton AL, 1019 .... 127 E1
Carrollton GA, 24388 .... 120 B4
Carrollton IL, 2484 .... 98 A2
Carrollton KY, 3938 .... 100 A3
Carrollton MI, 6602 .... 76 B2
Carrollton MS, 190 .... 118 B4
Carrollton MO, 3784 .... 96 C2
Carrollton OH, 3241 .... 91 F4
Carrollton TX, 119097 .... 59 F2
Carrolltown PA, 853 .... 92 B4
Carroll Valley PA, 3876 .... 103 D1
Carrollwood FL, 33365 .... 266 C1
Carson CA, 91714 .... 228 D4
Carson IA, 812 .... 86 A2
Carson ND, 293 .... 18 B4
Carson WA, 2279 .... 20 C1
Carson City MI, 1093 .... 76 A3
Carson City NV, 55274 .... 37 D2
Carson Co. TX, 6182 .... 50 B3
Carsonville MI, 527 .... 76 C2
Carter Co. KY, 27720 .... 101 D4
Carter Co. MO, 6265 .... 108 A2
Carter Co. MT, 1160 .... 25 F2
Carter Co. OK, 47557 .... 51 E4
Carter Co. TN, 57424 .... 111 E3
Carteret NJ, 22844 .... 147 E1
Carteret Co. NC, 66469 .... 115 E4
Carter Lake IA, 3785 .... 86 A2
Cartersville GA, 19731 .... 120 B3
Carterville IL, 5496 .... 108 C1
Carterville MO, 1891 .... 106 B2
Carthage AR, 343 .... 117 E3
Carthage IL, 2605 .... 87 F4
Carthage IN, 927 .... 100 A1
Carthage MS, 5075 .... 126 C2
Carthage MO, 14378 .... 106 C2
Carthage NY, 3747 .... 79 E1
Carthage NC, 2205 .... 122 C1
Carthage TN, 2306 .... 110 A3
Carthage TX, 6779 .... 124 C3
Caruthers CA, 2497 .... 44 C3
Caruthersville MO, 6168 .... 108 B4
Carver MA, 11574 .... 151 E3
Carver MN, 3724 .... 66 C4
Carver Co. MN, 91042 .... 66 C4
Cary IL, 18271 .... 88 C1
Cary MS, 313 .... 126 A2
Cary NC, 135234 .... 112 C4
Caryville TN, 2297 .... 110 C3
Casa Blanca AZ, 1388 .... 54 C2
Casa Blanca NM, 669 .... 48 B3
Casa Grande AZ, 48571 .... 54 C2
Cascade CO, 1655 .... 41 E2
Cascade ID, 939 .... 22 B3
Cascade IA, 2159 .... 73 F4
Cascade MD, 1112 .... 103 D1
Cascade MT, 685 .... 15 F3
Cascade WI, 709 .... 74 C2
Cascade Co. MT, 81327 .... 15 F3
Cascade Locks OR, 1144 .... 20 C1
Casco ME, 587 .... 82 B3
Casco WI, 583 .... 69 D4
Caseville MI, 777 .... 76 C1
Casey IL, 2769 .... 99 D2
Casey IA, 426 .... 86 B2
Casey Co. KY, 15955 .... 110 B1
Caseyville IL, 4245 .... 256 D2
Cashion OK, 802 .... 51 E2
Cashmere WA, 3063 .... 13 D3
Cashton WI, 1102 .... 73 F2
Casitas Sprs. CA, 1000 .... 52 B2
Casper WY, 55316 .... 33 D1
Caspian MI, 906 .... 68 C2
Cassadaga FL, 650 .... 141 D1
Cassadaga NY, 634 .... 78 A4
Cass City MI, 2428 .... 76 C2
Cass Co. IL, 13642 .... 98 A1
Cass Co. IN, 38966 .... 89 F3
Cass Co. IA, 13956 .... 86 B2
Cass Co. MI, 52293 .... 89 F1
Cass Co. MN, 28567 .... 64 B4
Cass Co. MO, 99478 .... 96 C3
Cass Co. NE, 25241 .... 35 F3
Cass Co. ND, 149778 .... 19 E3
Cass Co. TX, 30464 .... 124 C1
Casselberry FL, 26241 .... 141 D1
Casselton ND, 2329 .... 19 E4
Cassia Co. ID, 22952 .... 31 D2
Cass Lake MN, 770 .... 64 A3
Cassopolis MI, 1774 .... 89 F1
Cassville MO, 3266 .... 106 C3
Cassville NJ, 900 .... 147 E2
Cassville WV, 701 .... 102 A1
Cassville WI, 947 .... 73 F4
Castaic CA, 19015 .... 52 C2
Castalia OH, 852 .... 91 D2
Castanea PA, 1125 .... 93 D3
Castile NY, 1015 .... 78 B4
Castine ME, 1029 .... 83 D2
Castleberry AL, 583 .... 127 F4
Castle Dale UT, 1630 .... 39 F2
Castleford ID, 226 .... 30 C1
Castle Hayne NC, 1202 .... 123 E3
Castle Hills TX, 4116 .... 257 E2
Castle Rock CO, 48231 .... 41 E2
Castle Rock WA, 1982 .... 20 B1
Castle Shannon PA, 8316 .... 250 B3
Castleton VT, 1485 .... 81 D3
Castleton-on-Hudson NY, 1473 .... 94 B1
Castle Valley UT, 319 .... 40 A3
Castlewood SD, 627 .... 27 F3
Castlewood VA, 2045 .... 111 E2
Castro Co. TX, 8062 .... 50 A4
Castro Valley CA, 61388 .... 259 D3
Castroville CA, 6481 .... 44 B2
Castroville TX, 2680 .... 61 D3
Caswell Co. NC, 23719 .... 112 C3
Catahoula Par. LA, 10407 .... 125 F3
Catalina AZ, 7569 .... 55 D3
Catasauqua PA, 6436 .... 146 B1
Catawba NC, 603 .... 112 A4
Catawba SC, 1343 .... 122 A2
Catawba Co. NC, 154358 .... 122 A1
Catawba Island OH, 850 .... 91 D2
Catawissa PA, 1552 .... 93 E3
Catharpin VA, 600 .... 144 A3
Cathcart WA, 2458 .... 262 B2
Cathedral City CA, 51200 .... 53 E3
Cathlamet WA, 532 .... 20 B1
Catlettsburg KY, 1856 .... 101 D3
Catlin IL, 2040 .... 89 D4
Cato NY, 532 .... 79 D3
Catonsville MD, 41567 .... 144 C2
Catoosa OK, 7151 .... 106 A3
Catoosa Co. GA, 63942 .... 120 B2
Catron Co. NM, 3725 .... 48 A4
Catskill NY, 4081 .... 94 B2
Cattaraugus NY, 1002 .... 78 A4
Cattaraugus Co. NY, 80317 .... 78 A4
Cavalier ND, 1302 .... 19 E1
Cavalier Co. ND, 3993 .... 19 D1

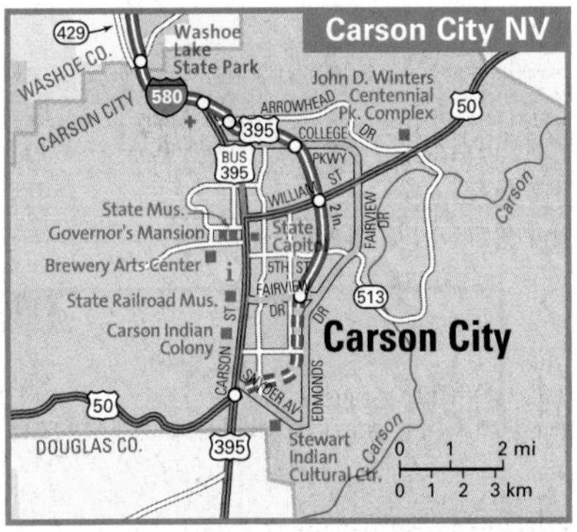
Carson City NV
Carson City
Washoe Lake State Park
John D. Winters Centennial Pk. Complex
State Mus.
Governor's Mansion
Brewery Arts Center
State Railroad Mus.
Carson Indian Colony
Stewart Indian Cultural Ctr.
WASHOE CO.
DOUGLAS CO.

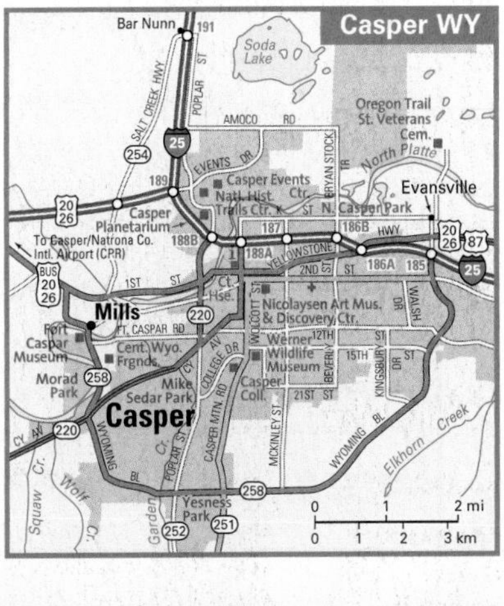
Casper WY
Casper
Mills
Evansville
Bar Nunn
Soda Lake
Oregon Trail St. Veterans Cem.
Casper Events Ctr.
Casper Planetarium
Nicolaysen Art Mus. & Discovery Ctr.
Werner Wildlife Museum
Casper Coll.
Mike Sedar Park
Morad Park
Yesness Park

200
Cave City–Chisago County

Figures after entries indicate population, page number, and grid reference.

Cave City AR, 1904 ... 107 F4
Cave City KY, 2240 ... 110 A2
Cave Creek AZ, 5015 ... 54 C1
Cave Jct. OR, 1883 ... 28 B2
Cave Spr. GA, 1200 ... 120 B3
Cave Spr. VA, 24922 ... 112 B2
Cave Sprs. AR, 1729 ... 106 C3
Cavetown MD, 1473 ... 144 A1
Cawker City KS, 469 ... 43 D1
Cawood KY, 731 ... 111 D2
Cayce SC, 12528 ... 122 A3
Cayucos CA, 2592 ... 44 B4
Cayuga IN, 1162 ... 99 E1
Cayuga NY, 549 ... 79 D3
Cayuga Co. NY, 80026 ... 79 D4
Cayuga Hts. NY, 3729 ... 79 D4
Cazenovia NY, 2835 ... 79 E3
Cecil PA, 2476 ... 92 A4
Cecil Co. MD, 101108 ... 145 E1
Cecilia KY, 572 ... 110 A1
Cecilia LA, 1980 ... 133 F2
Cecilton MD, 663 ... 145 E1
Cedar Bluff AL, 1820 ... 120 A3
Cedar Bluff VA, 1137 ... 111 F2
Cedar Bluffs NE, 610 ... 35 F3
Cedar Brook NJ, 1100 ... 147 D4
Cedarburg WI, 11412 ... 74 C3
Cedar City UT, 28857 ... 39 D4
Cedar Co. IA, 18499 ... 87 F1
Cedar Co. MO, 13982 ... 106 C1
Cedar Co. NE, 8852 ... 35 E1
Cedar Creek NE, 390 ... 35 F3
Cedar Crest NM, 958 ... 48 C3
Cedaredge CO, 2253 ... 40 B2
Cedar Falls IA, 39260 ... 73 D4
Cedar Fort UT, 368 ... 31 E4
Cedar Grove FL, 3397 ... 136 C2
Cedar Grove MD, 950 ... 144 B2
Cedar Grove NJ, 12411 ... 148 A3
Cedar Grove NM, 747 ... 48 C3
Cedar Grove WV, 997 ... 101 F4
Cedar Grove WI, 2113 ... 75 D2
Cedar Hill MO, 1721 ... 98 A4
Cedar Hill TX, 45028 ... 207 C3
Cedar Hills OR, 8300 ... 251 C2
Cedarhurst NY, 6592 ... 241 G5
Cedar Key FL, 702 ... 138 B4
Cedar Lake IN, 11560 ... 89 D2
Cedar Park TX, 48937 ... 61 E1
Cedar Pt. NC, 1279 ... 115 D4
Cedar Rapids IA, 126326 ... 87 E1
Cedar Rapids NE, 382 ... 35 E3
Cedar Sprs. MI, 3509 ... 75 F3
Cedartown GA, 9750 ... 120 B3
Cedar Vale KS, 579 ... 51 F1
Cedarville AR, 1394 ... 116 C1
Cedarville IL, 741 ... 74 B4
Cedarville NJ, 776 ... 145 F2
Cedarville OH, 4019 ... 100 C1
Celebration FL, 7427 ... 141 D1
Celeste TX, 814 ... 59 F2
Celina OH, 10400 ... 90 B4
Celina TN, 1495 ... 110 A3
Celina TX, 6028 ... 59 F2
Celoron NY, 1112 ... 92 B1
Cement OK, 501 ... 51 E3
Cement City MI, 438 ... 90 B1
Centennial CO, 100377 ... 209 C4
Center CO, 2230 ... 41 D4
Center MO, 508 ... 97 F1
Center NE, 94 ... 35 E1
Center ND, 571 ... 18 B3
Center TX, 5193 ... 124 C3
Center Barnstead NH, 500 ... 81 F4
Centerbrook CT, 950 ... 149 E2
Center Brunswick NY, 900 ... 94 B1
Centerburg OH, 1773 ... 91 D4
Center City MN, 628 ... 67 D3
Centereach NY, 31578 ... 149 D3
Centerfield UT, 1367 ... 39 E2
Center Harbor NH, 1096 ... 81 F3
Center Hill FL, 988 ... 140 C1
Center Line MI, 8257 ... 210 C2
Center Moriches NY, 7580 ... 149 D4
Center Ossipee NH, 561 ... 81 F3
Center Pt. AL, 16921 ... 119 F4
Center Pt. IA, 2421 ... 87 E1
Center Pt. TX, 750 ... 61 D2
Centerport NY, 5508 ... 148 C3
Centerton AR, 9515 ... 106 C3
Centerton NJ, 2000 ... 147 D3
Centertown KY, 423 ... 109 E1
Center Valley PA, 1600 ... 146 C1
Centerville GA, 7148 ... 129 D2
Centerville IN, 2552 ... 100 B1
Centerville IA, 5528 ... 87 D3
Centerville LA, 800 ... 133 F3
Centerville MA, 9200 ... 151 F3
Centerville MO, 191 ... 108 A1
Centerville OH, 103 ... 100 B1
Centerville PA, 3263 ... 92 A4
Centerville SC, 6586 ... 121 E3
Centerville SD, 882 ... 35 F1
Centerville TN, 3644 ... 109 E4
Centerville TX, 892 ... 124 A4
Centerville UT, 15335 ... 31 E4
Central AZ, 645 ... 55 E2
Central SC, 5159 ... 121 E2
Central TN, 2279 ... 111 E3
Central Bridge NY, 593 ... 79 F4
Central City AR, 502 ... 116 C1
Central City CO, 663 ... 41 D1
Central City IL, 1172 ... 98 C3
Central City IA, 1257 ... 87 F1
Central City KY, 5978 ... 109 E1
Central City NE, 2934 ... 35 E3
Central City PA, 1124 ... 92 B4
Central Falls RI, 19376 ... 150 C3
Central High OK, 1199 ... 51 E4
Centralia IL, 13032 ... 98 C3
Centralia KS, 512 ... 43 F1
Centralia MO, 4027 ... 97 E2
Centralia WA, 16336 ... 12 B4
Central Islip NY, 34450 ... 149 D4
Central Lake MI, 952 ... 69 F3
Central Park WA, 2685 ... 12 B4
Central Pt. OR, 17169 ... 28 B2
Central Square NY, 1848 ... 79 D3
Central Valley (Woodbury) NY, 1857 ... 148 B2
Central Vil. CT, 1400 ... 150 B3
Central Vil. MA, 600 ... 151 D4
Centre AL, 3489 ... 120 A3
Centre Co. PA, 153990 ... 92 C3
Centre Hall PA, 1265 ... 92 C3
Centreville AL, 2778 ... 127 F1
Centreville IL, 5309 ... 98 A3
Centreville MD, 4285 ... 145 D3
Centreville MI, 1425 ... 89 F1
Centreville MS, 1684 ... 134 A1
Centreville VA, 71135 ... 144 A3
Centuria WI, 948 ... 67 E3
Century FL, 1698 ... 135 F1
Ceres CA, 45417 ... 36 C4
Ceresco NE, 889 ... 35 F3
Cerritos CA, 49041 ... 228 E4
Cerro Gordo IL, 1403 ... 98 C1
Cerro Gordo Co. IA, 44151 ... 73 D3
Chackbay LA, 5177 ... 134 A3
Chadbourn NC, 1856 ... 123 D3
Chadron NE, 5851 ... 34 A1
Chaffee MO, 2955 ... 108 B2
Chaffee Co. CO, 17809 ... 41 D2
Chaffinville MA, 3100 ... 150 B1
Chagrin Falls OH, 4113 ... 91 E2
Chalco NE, 10994 ... 35 F3
Chalfant PA, 800 ... 250 D2
Chalfont PA, 4009 ... 146 C2
Chalkville AL, 3829 ... 195 F1
Challenge CA, 1069 ... 36 C1
Challis ID, 1081 ... 23 D3
Chalmers IN, 508 ... 89 E3
Chalmette LA, 16751 ... 134 B3
Chama NM, 1022 ... 48 C1
Chamberino NM, 919 ... 56 C3
Chamberlain SD, 2387 ... 27 D4
Chamberlayne Farms VA, 5456 ... 254 B1
Chambersburg PA, 20268 ... 103 D1
Chambers Co. AL, 34215 ... 128 B1
Chambers Co. TX, 35096 ... 132 B3
Chamblee GA, 9892 ... 120 C4
Chamisal NM, 310 ... 49 D2
Champaign IL, 81055 ... 88 C4
Champaign Co. IL, 201081 ... 89 D4
Champaign Co. OH, 40097 ... 90 C4
Champion Hts. OH, 6498 ... 91 F2
Champlain NY, 1101 ... 81 D1
Chancellor SD, 264 ... 27 F4
Chandler AZ, 236123 ... 54 C2
Chandler IN, 2887 ... 99 E4
Chandler OK, 3100 ... 51 F2
Chandler TX, 2734 ... 124 A2
Chandler Hts. AZ, 950 ... 54 C2
Chandlerville IL, 553 ... 88 A4
Chanhassen MN, 22952 ... 66 C4
Channahon IL, 12560 ... 88 C2
Channel Lake IL, 1664 ... 74 C4
Channelview TX, 38289 ... 132 B3
Channing TX, 363 ... 50 A2
Chantilly VA, 23039 ... 144 A3
Chanute KS, 9119 ... 106 A1
Chaparral NM, 14631 ... 56 C3
Chapel Hill NC, 57233 ... 112 C4
Chapel Hill TN, 1445 ... 119 F1
Chapin IL, 512 ... 98 A1
Chapin SC, 1445 ... 122 A3
Chaplin KY, 418 ... 100 A4
Chapman KS, 1393 ... 43 F2
Chapmanville WV, 1256 ... 101 E4
Chappaqua NY, 1436 ... 148 B2
Chappell NE, 929 ... 34 A3
Chardon OH, 5148 ... 91 E2
Charenton LA, 1903 ... 133 F3
Chariton IA, 4321 ... 87 D3
Chariton Co. MO, 7831 ... 97 D1
Charlack MO, 1363 ... 256 B2
Charleroi PA, 4120 ... 92 A4
Charles City IA, 7652 ... 73 D3
Charles City VA, 133 ... 113 E1
Charles City Co. VA, 7256 ... 113 E1
Charles Co. MD, 146551 ... 144 B4
Charles Mix Co. SD, 9129 ... 27 D4
Charleston AR, 2494 ... 116 C1
Charleston IL, 21838 ... 99 D2
Charleston ME, 300 ... 82 C1
Charleston MS, 2193 ... 118 B3
Charleston MO, 5947 ... 108 C2
Charleston SC, 120083 ... 131 D2
Charleston TN, 651 ... 120 C1
Charleston UT, 415 ... 31 F4
Charleston WV, 51400 ... 101 E4
Charleston Co. SC, 350209 ... 131 D2
Charlestown IN, 7585 ... 100 A3
Charlestown MD, 1183 ... 145 D1
Charlestown NH, 1152 ... 81 E4
Charlestown RI, 7827 ... 150 C4
Charles Town WV, 5259 ... 103 D2
Charlevoix MI, 2513 ... 69 F3
Charlevoix Co. MI, 25949 ... 70 B3
Charlo MT, 379 ... 15 D3
Charlotte MI, 9074 ... 76 A4
Charlotte NC, 731424 ... 122 A1
Charlotte TN, 1235 ... 109 E4
Charlotte TX, 1715 ... 61 D3
Charlotte Co. FL, 159978 ... 140 C4
Charlotte Co. VA, 12586 ... 113 D2
Charlotte C.H. VA, 543 ... 113 D2
Charlotte Hall MD, 1420 ... 144 C4
Charlotte Harbor FL, 3714 ... 140 C4
Charlottesville VA, 43475 ... 102 C4
Charlton MA, 12981 ... 150 B2
Charlton NY, 3954 ... 94 B1
Charlton City MA, 1400 ... 150 B2
Charlton Co. GA, 12171 ... 138 C1
Charlton Depot MA, 1200 ... 150 B2
Charter Oak CA, 9310 ... 229 F2
Charter Oak IA, 502 ... 86 A1
Chartley MA, 1600 ... 151 D2
Chase KS, 477 ... 43 D3
Chase City VA, 2351 ... 113 D2
Chase Co. KS, 2790 ... 43 F3
Chase Co. NE, 3966 ... 34 B4
Chaska MN, 23770 ... 66 C4
Chassahowitzka FL, 700 ... 140 B1
Chassell MI, 800 ... 65 F4
Chateaugay NY, 833 ... 80 C1
Chatfield MN, 2779 ... 73 E2
Chatham IL, 11500 ... 98 B1
Chatham LA, 557 ... 125 E2
Chatham MA, 1421 ... 151 F3
Chatham NJ, 8962 ... 148 A4
Chatham NY, 1770 ... 94 B2
Chatham VA, 1269 ... 112 C2
Chatham Co. GA, 265128 ... 130 B3
Chatham Co. NC, 63505 ... 112 C4
Chatom AL, 1288 ... 127 D4
Chatsworth GA, 4299 ... 120 C2
Chatsworth IL, 1205 ... 88 C3
Chattahoochee FL, 3652 ... 137 D1
Chattahoochee Co. GA, 11267 ... 128 C2
Chattanooga OK, 461 ... 51 D4
Chattanooga TN, 167674 ... 120 B2
Chattaroy WV, 756 ... 111 E1
Chattooga Co. GA, 26015 ... 120 B3
Chatwood PA, 3600 ... 146 B3
Chaumont NY, 624 ... 79 D1
Chauncey OH, 1049 ... 101 E2
Chautauqua Co. KS, 3669 ... 43 F4
Chautauqua Co. NY, 134905 ... 78 A4
Chauvin LA, 2912 ... 134 B4
Chaves Co. NM, 65645 ... 57 E2
Chazy NY, 565 ... 81 D1
Cheatham Co. TN, 39105 ... 109 E3
Cheat Lake WV, 7988 ... 102 B1
Chebanse IL, 1062 ... 89 D3
Cheboygan MI, 4867 ... 70 C2
Cheboygan Co. MI, 26152 ... 70 C3
Checotah OK, 3335 ... 116 A1
Cheektowaga NY, 75178 ... 78 B3
Chefornak AK, 418 ... 154 B3
Chehalis WA, 7259 ... 12 B4
Chelan WA, 3890 ... 13 E3
Chelan Co. WA, 72453 ... 13 D2
Chelmsford MA, 33802 ... 95 E1
Chelsea AL, 10183 ... 127 F1
Chelsea MA, 35177 ... 151 D1
Chelsea MI, 4944 ... 76 B4
Chelsea NY, 2300 ... 148 B1
Chelsea OK, 1964 ... 106 A3
Chelsea VT, 1250 ... 81 E3
Cheltenham MD, 650 ... 144 C4
Cheltenham PA, 5500 ... 248 C2
Chelyan WV, 776 ... 101 F4
Chemung Co. NY, 88830 ... 93 E1
Chenango Bridge NY, 2883 ... 93 E1
Chenango Co. NY, 50477 ... 79 E4
Chenequa WI, 590 ... 74 C3
Cheney KS, 2094 ... 43 E4
Cheney WA, 10590 ... 13 F3
Cheneyville LA, 625 ... 133 E1
Chenoa IL, 1785 ... 88 C3
Chenoweth OR, 1855 ... 21 D1
Chepachet RI, 1675 ... 150 C3
Cheraw SC, 5851 ... 122 C2
Cheriton VA, 487 ... 114 B3
Cherokee AL, 1048 ... 119 D2
Cherokee IA, 5253 ... 72 A4
Cherokee KS, 714 ... 106 B1
Cherokee OK, 1498 ... 51 D1
Cherokee Co. AL, 25989 ... 120 A3
Cherokee Co. GA, 214346 ... 120 C3
Cherokee Co. IA, 12072 ... 72 A3
Cherokee Co. KS, 21603 ... 106 B2
Cherokee Co. NC, 27444 ... 121 D1
Cherokee Co. OK, 46987 ... 106 B4
Cherokee Co. SC, 55342 ... 121 F2
Cherokee Co. TX, 50845 ... 124 A3
Cherokee Forest SC, 8000 ... 217 A1
Cherokee Vil. AR, 4671 ... 107 F3
Cherry Co. NE, 5713 ... 34 B1
Cherry Creek NY, 461 ... 78 A4
Cherryfield ME, 1157 ... 83 E2
Cherry Grove OH, 4378 ... 204 C3
Cherry Hill NJ, 71045 ... 146 C3
Cherry Hills Vil. CO, 5987 ... 209 C4
Cherryvale KS, 2367 ... 106 A2
Cherryvale SC, 2496 ... 122 B4
Cherry Valley AR, 651 ... 118 A1
Cherry Valley NY, 520 ... 79 F4
Cherryville NC, 5760 ... 122 A1
Chesaning MI, 2394 ... 76 B3
Chesapeake OH, 745 ... 101 D3
Chesapeake VA, 222209 ... 113 F3
Chesapeake WV, 1554 ... 101 F4
Chesapeake Beach MD, 5753 ... 144 C4
Chesapeake City MD, 673 ... 145 E1
Chesapeake Ranch Estates MD, 10519 ... 103 F4
Cheshire CT, 29097 ... 149 D1
Cheshire MA, 514 ... 94 C1
Cheshire Co. NH, 77117 ... 81 E4
Chesilhurst NJ, 1634 ... 147 D4
Chesnee SC, 868 ... 121 F1
Chester CA, 2144 ... 29 D4
Chester CT, 3832 ... 149 E2
Chester IL, 8586 ... 98 B4
Chester MD, 4167 ... 145 D3
Chester MA, 627 ... 94 C2
Chester MT, 847 ... 15 F2
Chester NH, 4768 ... 81 F4
Chester NJ, 1649 ... 94 A4
Chester NY, 3969 ... 148 A2
Chester PA, 33972 ... 146 C3
Chester SC, 5607 ... 122 A2
Chester VT, 1005 ... 81 E4
Chester VA, 20987 ... 113 E1
Chester WV, 2585 ... 91 F3
Chester Co. PA, 498886 ... 146 B3
Chester Co. SC, 33140 ... 122 A2
Chester Co. TN, 17131 ... 119 D1
Chester Depot VT, 850 ... 81 E4
Chesterfield IN, 2547 ... 89 F4
Chesterfield MO, 47484 ... 98 A3
Chesterfield SC, 1472 ... 122 B2
Chesterfield VA, 3558 ... 113 E1
Chesterfield Co. SC, 46734 ... 122 B2
Chesterfield Co. VA, 316236 ... 113 E1
Chester Hts. PA, 2531 ... 146 B3
Chester Hill PA, 883 ... 92 C3
Chesterland OH, 2521 ... 91 E2
Chesterton IN, 13068 ... 89 E2
Chestertown MD, 5252 ... 145 D2
Chestnut Mtn. GA, 650 ... 121 D3
Chestnut Ridge NY, 7916 ... 148 B3
Cheswick PA, 1746 ... 250 D1
Cheswold DE, 1380 ... 145 E2
Chetek WI, 2221 ... 67 E3
Chetopa KS, 1125 ... 106 B2
Chevak AK, 938 ... 154 B3
Cheverly MD, 6173 ... 144 B3
Cheviot OH, 8375 ... 100 B2
Chevy Chase MD, 1953 ... 270 C2
Chevy Chase View MD, 920 ... 270 C1
Chewelah WA, 2607 ... 13 F2
Cheyenne OK, 801 ... 50 C3
Cheyenne WY, 59466 ... 33 E3
Cheyenne Co. CO, 1836 ... 42 A2
Cheyenne Co. KS, 2726 ... 42 B1
Cheyenne Co. NE, 9998 ... 34 A3
Cheyenne Wells CO, 846 ... 42 A2
Cheyney PA, 1600 ... 146 B3
Chicago IL, 2695598 ... 89 D1
Chicago Hts. IL, 30276 ... 89 D2
Chicago Ridge IL, 14305 ... 203 D5
Chichester NH, 2523 ... 81 F4
Chickamauga GA, 3101 ... 120 B2
Chickasaw AL, 6106 ... 135 E1
Chickasaw Co. IA, 12439 ... 73 E3
Chickasaw Co. MS, 17392 ... 118 C4
Chickasha OK, 16036 ... 51 E3
Chico CA, 86187 ... 36 B1
Chico TX, 1002 ... 59 E2
Chicopee MA, 55298 ... 150 A2
Chicora PA, 1043 ... 92 A3
Chicot Co. AR, 11800 ... 125 F1
Chiefland FL, 2245 ... 138 B4
Chilchinbito AZ, 506 ... 47 F1
Chilcoot CA, 387 ... 37 D1
Childersburg AL, 5175 ... 128 A1
Childress TX, 6105 ... 50 C4
Childress Co. TX, 7041 ... 50 C4
Chilhowie VA, 1781 ... 111 F2
Chillicothe IL, 6097 ... 88 B3
Chillicothe MO, 9515 ... 96 C1
Chillicothe OH, 21901 ... 101 D2
Chillicothe TX, 707 ... 50 C4
Chillum MD, 33513 ... 270 D2
Chiloquin OR, 734 ... 28 C1
Chilton WI, 3933 ... 74 C1
Chilton Co. AL, 43643 ... 127 F2
Chimayo NM, 3177 ... 49 D2
China TX, 1160 ... 132 C3
China Grove NC, 3563 ... 122 B1
China Grove TX, 1179 ... 61 D3
Chinchilla PA, 2098 ... 261 E1
Chincoteague VA, 2941 ... 114 C2
Chinle AZ, 4518 ... 47 F2
Chino CA, 77983 ... 229 G3
Chino Hills CA, 74799 ... 229 G3
Chinook MT, 1203 ... 16 B2
Chinook WA, 466 ... 20 B1
Chino Valley AZ, 10817 ... 47 D4
Chipita Park CO, 1709 ... 205 C1
Chipley FL, 3605 ... 136 C1
Chippewa Co. MI, 38520 ... 70 B1
Chippewa Co. MN, 12441 ... 66 A3
Chippewa Co. WI, 62415 ... 67 F3
Chippewa Falls WI, 13661 ... 67 F4
Chippewa Lake OH, 711 ... 91 E3
Chisago City MN, 4967 ... 67 D3
Chisago Co. MN, 53887 ... 67 D3

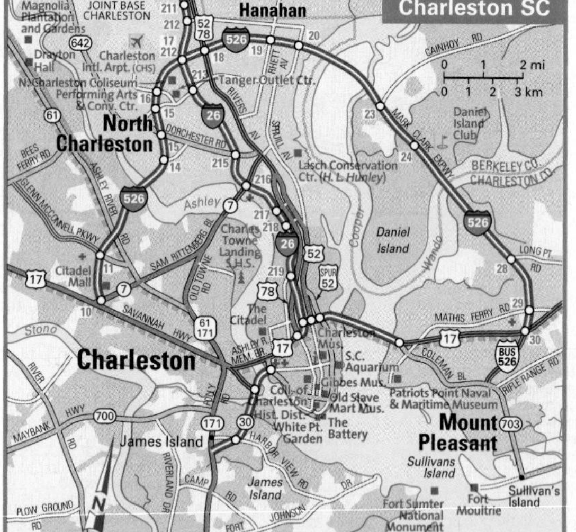

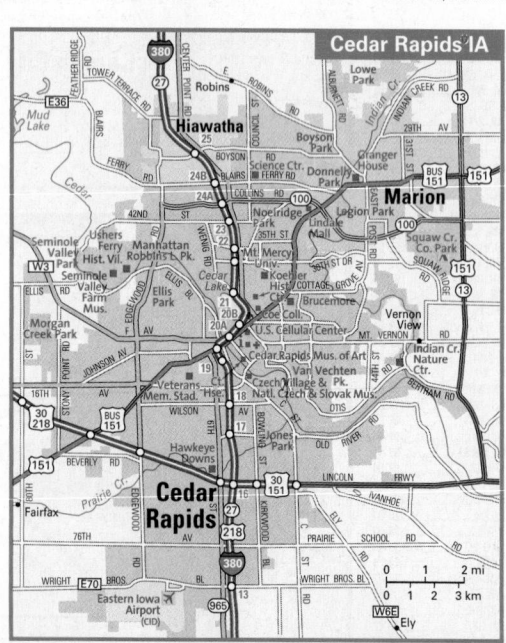

Charleston SC
Hanahan
North Charleston
Charleston
Mount Pleasant
James Island
Sullivans Island
Daniel Island
Magnolia Plantation and Gardens
JOINT BASE CHARLESTON
Drayton Hall
Charleston Intl. Arpt. (CHS)
N. Charleston Coliseum Performing Arts & Conv. Ctr.
Tanger Outlet Ctr.
Citadel Mall
Charles Towne Landing S.H.S.
The Citadel
Charleston Mus.
S.C. Aquarium
Gibbes Mus.
Old Slave Mart Mus.
Coll. of Charleston
Hist. Dist.
White Pt. Garden
The Battery
Patriots Point Naval & Maritime Museum
Fort Sumter National Monument
Fort Moultrie
0 1 2 mi
0 1 2 3 km

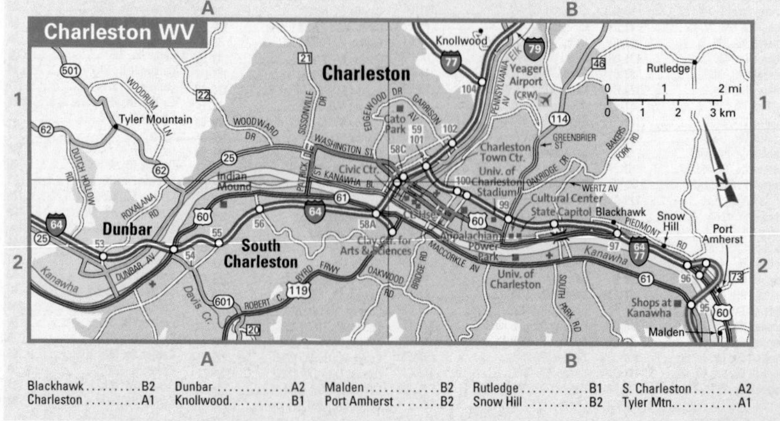

Charleston WV
Charleston
South Charleston
Dunbar
Tyler Mountain
Knollwood
Yeager Airport (CRW)
Rutledge
Charleston Town Ctr.
Univ. of Charleston Stadium
Cultural Center
State Capitol
Blackhawk
Snow Hill
Port Amherst
Shops at Kanawha
Malden
Clay Ctr. for Arts & Sciences
Appalachian Power Park
Univ. of Charleston
Civic Ctr.
Indian Mound
Kanawha
0 1 2 mi
0 1 2 3 km
Blackhawk . . . B2
Charleston . . . A1
Dunbar . . . A2
Knollwood . . . B1
Malden . . . B2
Port Amherst . . . B2
Rutledge . . . B1
Snow Hill . . . B2
S. Charleston . . . A2
Tyler Mtn. . . . A1

Entries in **bold black** indicate counties or parishes.
Entries in **bold color** indicate cities with detailed inset maps.

Charlotte NC

Charlottesville VA

Chattanooga TN

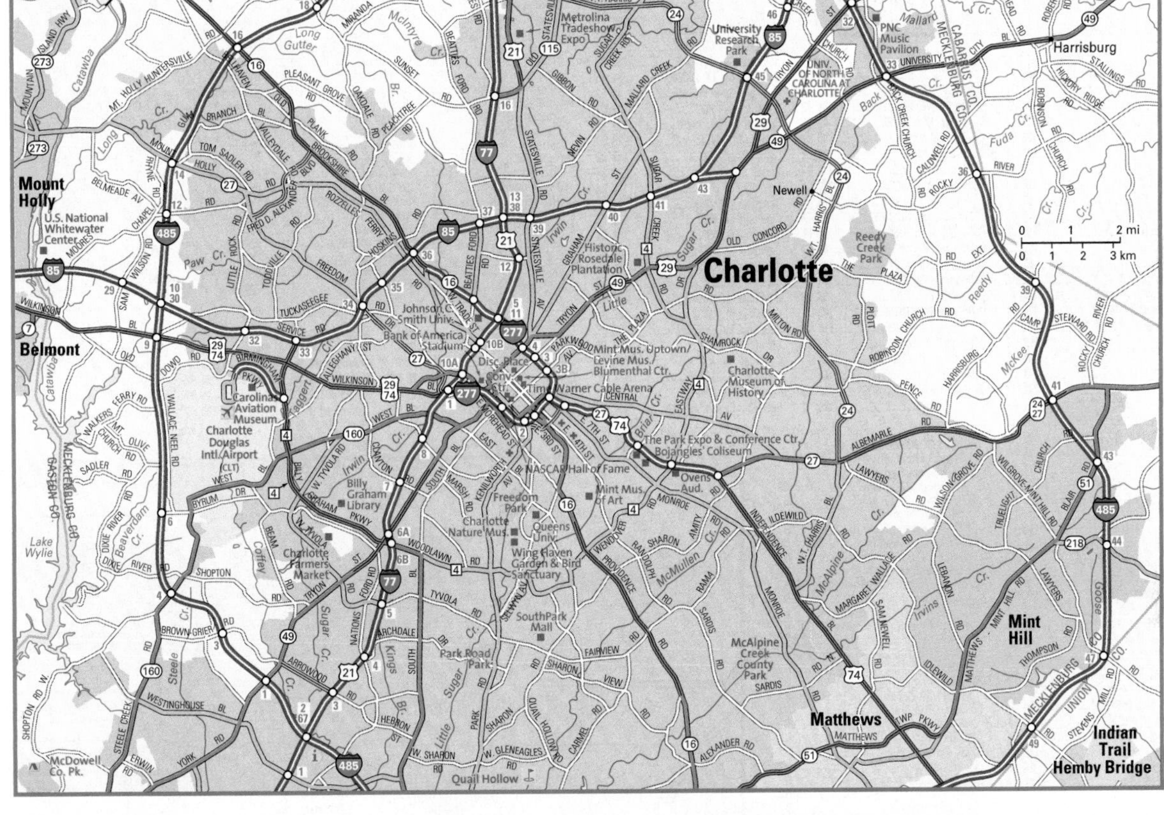

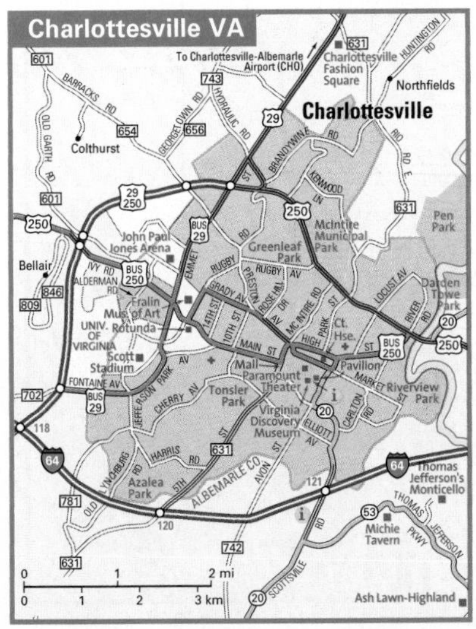

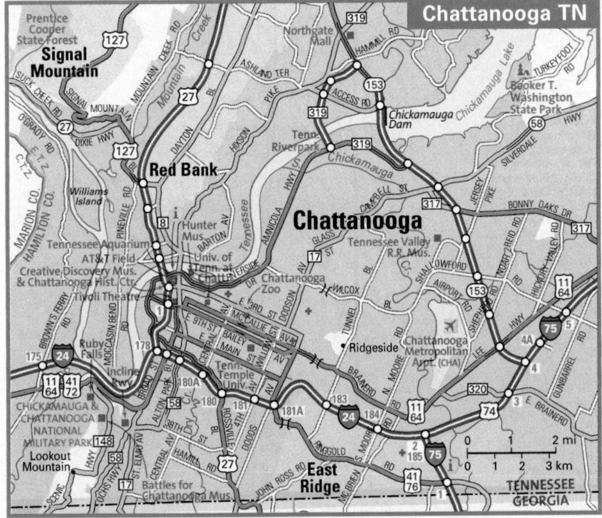

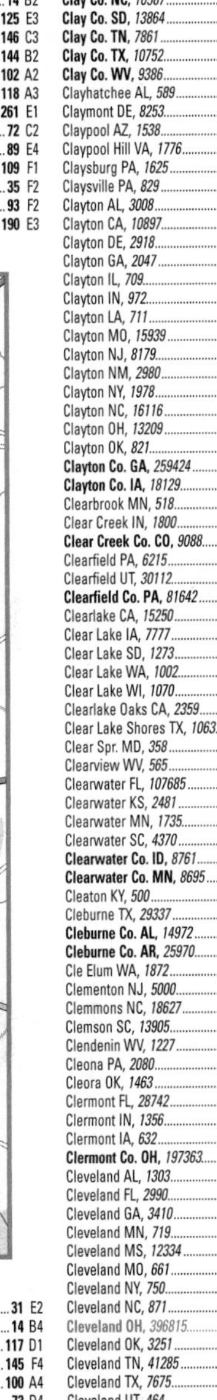

202

Clinton–Columbine Valley

Figures after entries indicate population, page number, and grid reference.

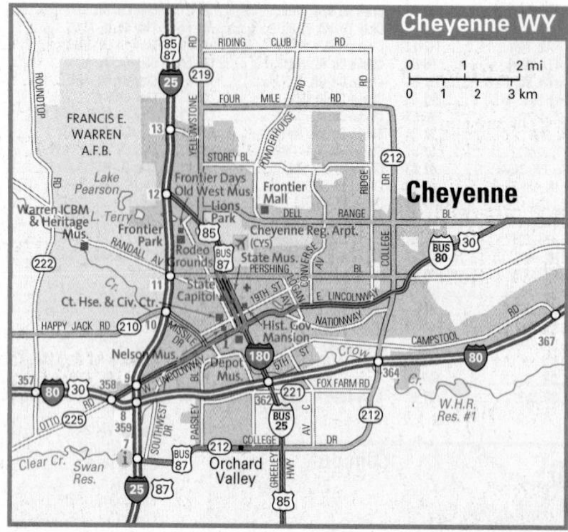

Cheyenne WY

Cheyenne

FRANCIS E. WARREN A.F.B.

Orchard Valley

Collins IA, 495..............87 D1
Collins MS, 2586...........126 C4
Collins Park DE, 8300......274 D3
Collinsville AL, 1983......120 A3
Collinsville IL, 25579......98 B3
Collinsville MS, 1948......127 D2
Collinsville OK, 5606......106 A4
Collinsville TX, 1624.......59 F1
Collinsville VA, 7335......112 B3
Collinwood TN, 982.......119 E1
Colma CA, 1792...........259 B3
Colman SD, 594............27 F4
Colmar Manor MD, 1404...270 E3
Colmesneil TX, 596.......132 C1
Colo IA, 876...............87 D1
Cologne MN, 1519..........66 C4
Cologne NJ, 800..........147 D4
Coloma MI, 1483...........89 F1
Coloma WI, 5099...........68 C2
Colome SD, 296............34 C1
Colon MI, 1173............90 A1
Colona IL, 5099...........88 A2
Colonia NJ, 17795........147 A4
Colonial Beach VA, 3542...103 E4
Colonial Hts. TN, 6934....111 E3
Colonial Hts. VA, 17411...113 E2
Colonial Park PA, 13229...218 C1
Colonie NY, 7793..........94 B1
Colony KS, 408............96 A4
Colorado City AZ, 4821.....46 C1
Colorado City CO, 2193.....41 E3
Colorado City TX, 4146.....58 B3
Colorado Co. TX, 20874....61 F2
Colorado Sprs. CO, 416427..41 E3
Colquitt GA, 1992.........137 D1
Colquitt Co. GA, 45498....137 F1
Colstrip MT, 2214..........25 D1
Colton CA, 52154.........229 A2
Colton SD, 687............27 F4
Columbia AL, 128..........128 B4
Columbia CA, 2297.........37 D3
Columbia CT, 4971.........149 F1
Columbia IL, 9707..........98 A3
Columbia KY, 4110.........110 B2
Columbia LA, 390..........125 E3
Columbia MD, 6582........126 B4
Columbia MO, 108500.......97 C3
Columbia MS, 6582........126 B4
Columbia NC, 891.........113 F4
Columbia PA, 10400.......103 E1
Columbia SC, 129272......122 A3
Columbia TN, 34681.......119 F1
Columbia Beach MD, 700...144 C3

CHICAGO MAP INDEX

Addison..............C4
Algonquin............A2
Alsip................D6
Arlington Hts........C2
Aurora...............A5
Bannockburn..........C2
Barrington...........A2
Barrington Hills.....A2
Batavia..............A4
Bedford Park.........D5
Bellwood.............C4
Bensenville..........C4
Berkeley.............C4
Berwyn...............C4
Bloomingdale.........B3
Blue Island..........D6
Bolingbrook..........B6
Bridgeview...........C5
Broadview............C4
Brookfield...........C4
Buffalo Grove........C2
Burbank..............D5
Burnham..............E6
Burr Ridge...........C5
Burtons Bridge.......A1
Calumet City.........E6
Calumet Park.........E6
Carol Stream.........B4
Carpentersville......A2
Cary.................A2
Chicago..............E4
Chicago Ridge........D5
Cicero...............C4
Clarendon Hills......C5
Crest Hill...........B6
Crestwood............D6
Crystal Lake.........A1
Darien...............C5
Deerfield............D2
Deer Park............B2
Des Plaines..........C3
Diamond Lake.........B1
Dixmoor..............D6
Dolton...............E6
Downers Grove........C5
E. Dundee............A2
Elgin................A3
Elk Grove Vil........C3

Elmhurst.............C4
Elmwood Park.........D4
Evanston.............D3
Evergreen Park.......D5
Forest Lake..........B1
Forest Park..........D4
Forest View..........D5
Fox River Grove......A2
Franklin Park........C4
Geneva...............A4
Glencoe..............D2
Glendale Hts.........B4
Glen Ellyn...........B4
Glenview.............D3
Golf.................D3
Grayslake............B1
Green Oaks...........C1
Hanover Park.........B3
Harvey...............E6
Harwood Hts..........D4
Hawthorn Woods.......B1
Hazel Crest..........E6
Hickory Hills........D5
Highland Park........D1
Highwood.............D1
Hillside.............C4
Hinsdale.............C5
Hodgkins.............C5
Hoffman Estates......B3
Holiday Hills........A1
Homer Glen...........C6
Hometown.............D5
Indian Creek.........C1
Indian Head Park.....C5
Inverness............B2
Island Lake..........A1
Itasca...............B3
Ivanhoe..............B1
Justice..............C5
Kenilworth...........D2
Kildeer..............B2
Knollwood............C1
La Grange............C5
La Grange Park.......C5
Lake Barrington......A2
Lake Bluff...........D1
Lake Forest..........D1
Lake in the Hills....A2
Lakemoor.............A1
Lake Zurich..........B2
Lemont...............B6

Libertyville.........C1
Lincolnshire.........C2
Lincolnwood..........D3
Lisle................B4
Lockport.............B6
Lombard..............B4
Long Grove...........C2
Lyons................D5
Markham..............D6
Maywood..............C4
McCook...............D5
McHenry..............A1
Medinah..............B3
Melrose Park.........C4
Merrionette Park.....D6
Mettawa..............C1
Midlothian...........D6
Montgomery...........A5
Morton Grove.........D3
Mount Prospect.......C3
Mundelein............B1
Naperville...........B5
Niles................D3
Norridge.............D4
N. Aurora............A5
N. Barrington........B2
N. Chicago...........C1
Northbrook...........D2
Northfield...........D2
Northlake............C4
N. Riverside.........D4
Oak Brook............C4
Oakbrook Terrace.....C4
Oak Forest...........D6
Oak Lawn.............D5
Oak Park.............D4
Oakwood Hills........A1
Orland Hills.........C6
Orland Park..........C6
Oswego...............A6
Palatine.............B2
Palos Hts............D5
Palos Hills..........D5
Palos Park...........C6
Park Ridge...........C3
Phoenix..............D6
Plainfield...........A6
Port Barrington......A1
Posen................D6
Prairie Grove........A1
Prospect Hts.........C2

Riverdale............E6
River Forest.........D4
River Grove..........D4
Riverside............D4
Riverwoods...........C2
Robbins..............D6
Rolling Meadows......B3
Romeoville...........B6
Rondout..............C1
Roselle..............B4
Rosemont.............C3
St. Charles..........A4
Schaumburg...........C3
Schiller Park........C3
Skokie...............D3
Sleepy Hollow........A2
S. Barrington........A2
S. Elgin.............A3
S. Holland...........D6
Stickney.............D5
Stone Park...........C4
Streamwood...........B3
Summit...............D5
Tinley Park..........D6
Tower Lakes..........B1
Trout Valley.........A1
Valley View..........A3
Vernon Hills.........C1
Villa Park...........C4
Volo.................B1
Warrenville..........B5
Wauconda.............B1
Wayne................A4
Westchester..........C4
Westmont.............C5
Wheaton..............B4
Wheeling.............C2
Willowbrook..........C5
Willow Sprs..........C5
Wilmette.............D3
Winfield.............B4
Winnetka.............D2
Wood Dale............B3
Woodridge............B5
Worth................D6

Columbia City IN, 8750....89 F2
Columbia City OR, 1946....20 C1
Columbia Co. AR, 24552...125 D1
Columbia Co. FL, 67537...138 C2
Columbia Co. GA, 124053..121 F4
Columbia Co. NY, 63096...94 B2
Columbia Co. OR, 49351....20 B1
Columbia Co. PA, 67295....93 E3
Columbia Co. WA, 4078.....13 F4
Columbia Co. WI, 56833....74 B3
Columbia Falls MT, 4688....15 D2
Columbia Hts. MN, 19496...235 C2

Columbiana AL, 4197......127 F3
Columbiana Co. OH, 107841..91 F3
Columbiana OH, 6384.......91 F3
Columbiaville MI, 787......76 B3
Columbiaville NY, 1200.....94 B2
Columbine Valley CO, 1256..209 B4

POINTS OF INTEREST
900 North Michigan Avenue Shops..B1
Adler Planetarium &
 Astronomy Museum............C3
Art Institute of Chicago..........B2
Auditorium Building..............B2
Bank of America Theatre..........B2
Buckingham Fountain..............B2
Cadillac Palace Theatre..........B2
Centennial Fountain & Arc........B2
Chicago Architecture Foundation..B2
Chicago Board of Trade...........B2
Chicago Ctr. for the Perform. Arts..A2
Chicago Children's Museum........C1
Chicago Cultural Center..........B2
Chicago Fire Marker..............A3
Chicago Mercantile Exchange......A2
Chicago Place....................B1
Chicago Stock Exchange...........B2
Chicago Theatre..................B2
Chicago Yacht Club...............C2
City Hall........................B2
Civic Opera House................A2
Cloud Gate.......................B2
Crown Fountain...................B2
Daley Plaza......................B2
Dearborn Station.................B3
East-West University.............B3
The Field Museum.................C3
Ford Center for the Performing Arts..B2
Goodman Theatre..................B2
Harris Theater...................B2
Harold Washington Library Center..B2
James R. Thompson Center.........B2
Jane Addams' Hull House Mus......A3
John G. Shedd Aquarium...........C3
John Hancock Center..............B1
Merchandise Mart.................B1
Monadnock Building...............B2
Moody Bible Institute............B1
Mus. of Broadcast Communications..B1
Mus. of Contemporary Art.........B1
Mus. of Contemporary Photography..B3
Navy Pier........................C1
Newberry Library.................B1
New Maxwell Street Market........A3
Northwestern Univ. (Chi. Campus)..C1
Petrillo Band Shell..............B2
Pritzker Pavilion................B2
River East Plaza.................B2
The Shops at North Bridge........B1
Smith Museum of Stained Glass
 Windows........................C1
Soldier Field....................C3
Spertus Museum...................B3
Symphony Center..................B2
Tribune Tower....................B1
Trump Intl. Tower & Tower........B1
Union Station....................A2
Univ. of Illinois at Chicago.....A3
Water Tower......................B1
Water Tower Place................B1
Willis Tower.....................A2
Wrigley Building.................B1

Downtown Chicago IL

RIVER NORTH

NEAR NORTH

THE LOOP

GREEK TOWN

PRINTER'S ROW

LITTLE ITALY

LAKE MICHIGAN

Chicago Harbor

Outer Harbor

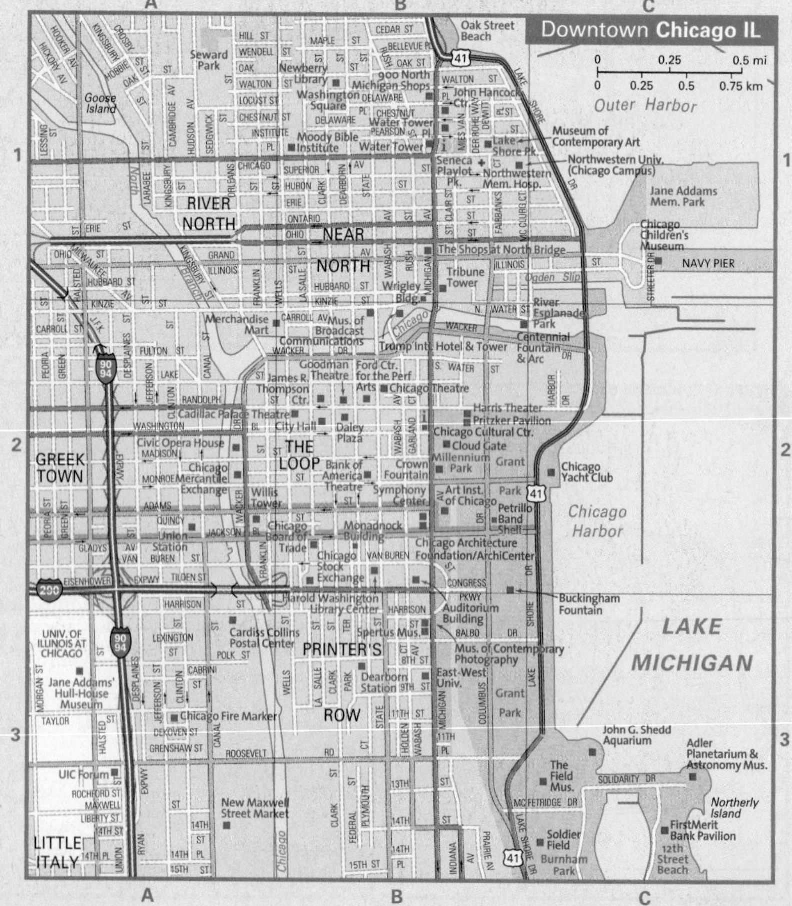

Entries in **bold black** indicate counties or parishes.
Entries in **bold color** indicate cities with detailed inset maps.

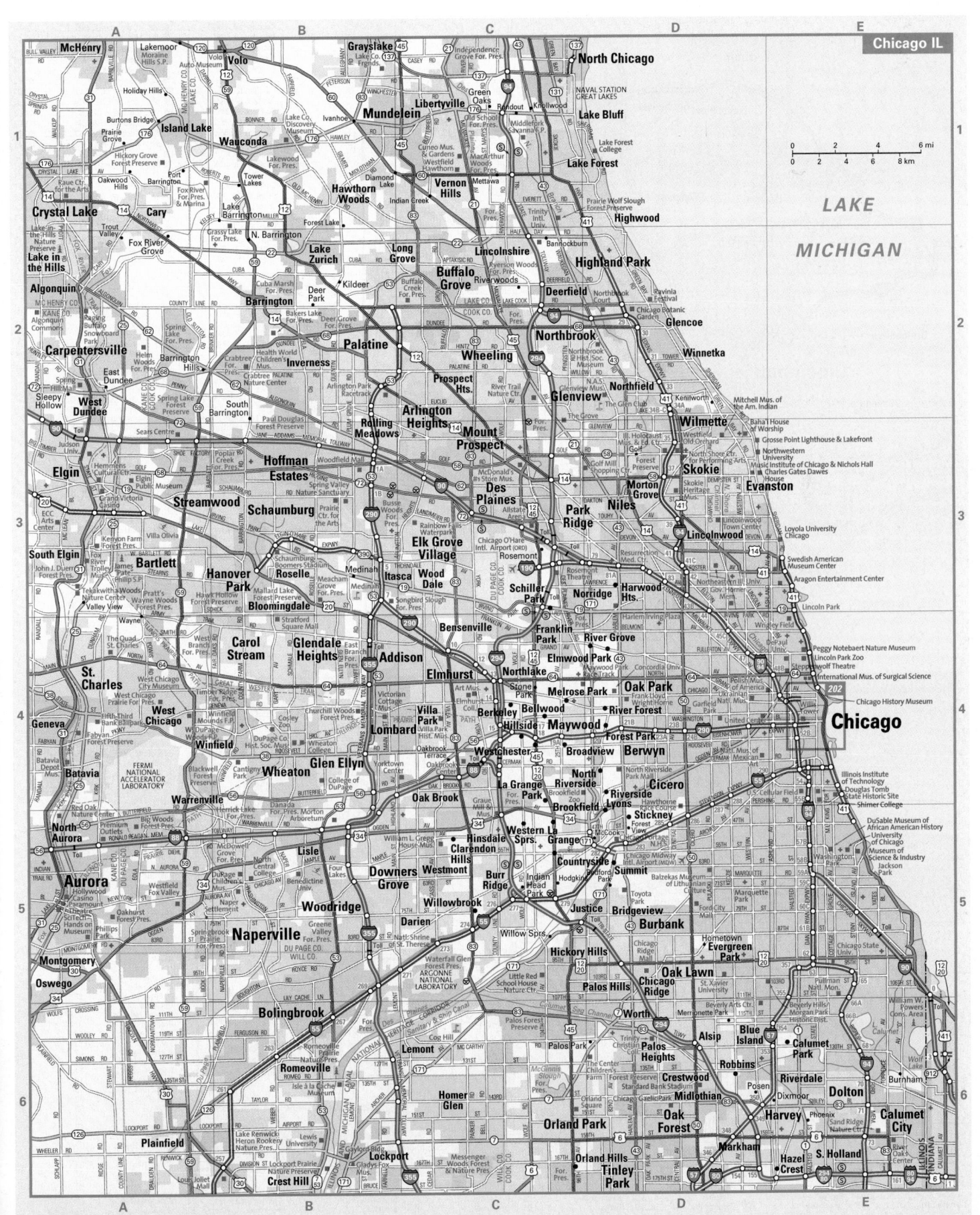

204

Columbus–Concord

Figures after entries indicate population, page number, and grid reference.

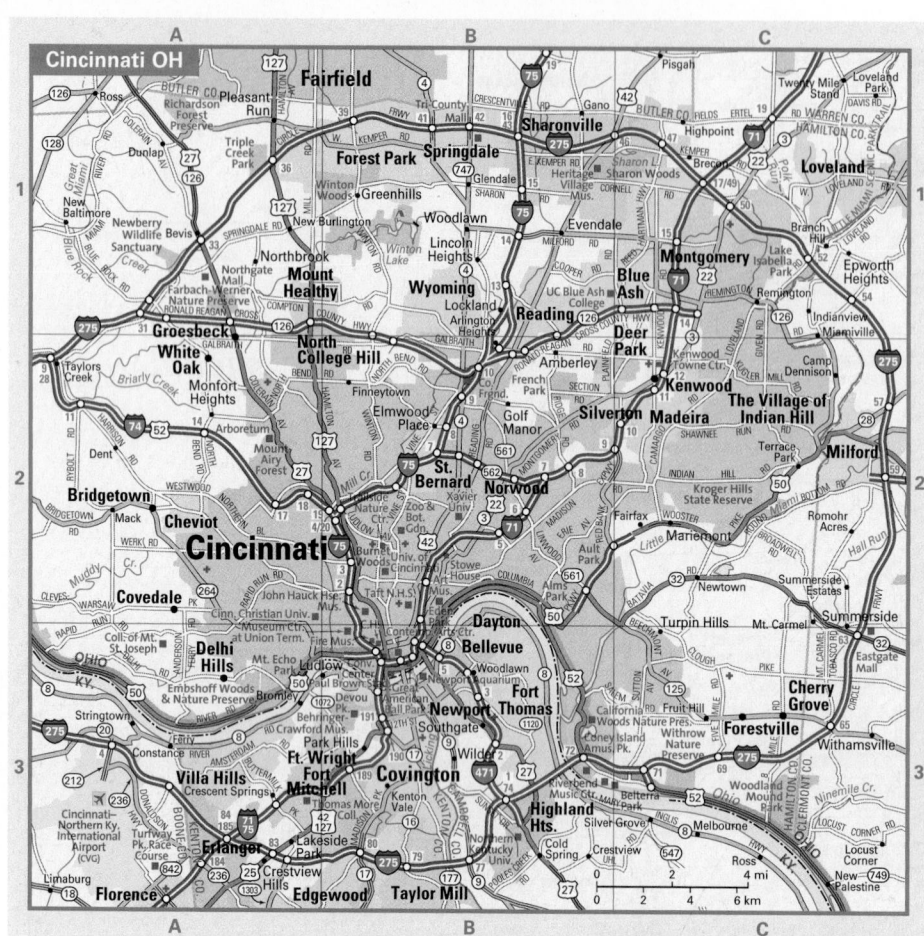

Cincinnati OH

Cleveland OH

LAKE ERIE

Cleveland

Entries in **bold black** indicate counties or parishes.
Entries in **bold color** indicate cities with detailed inset maps.

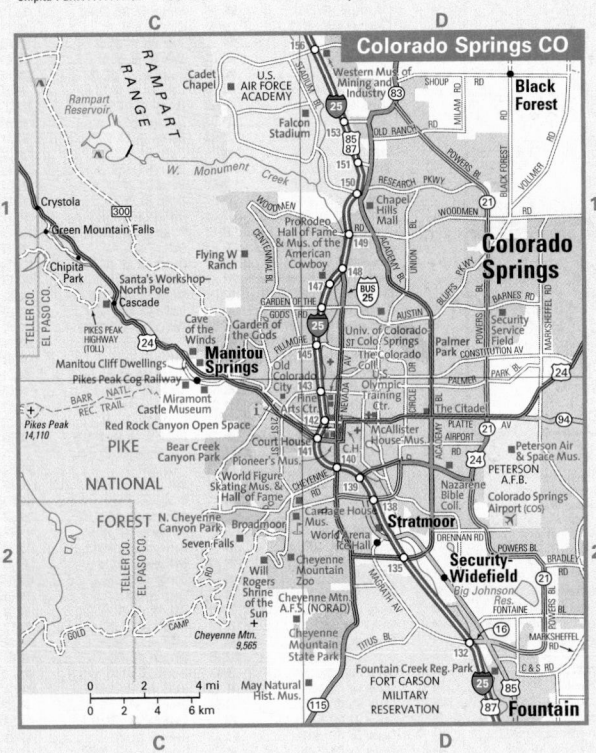

Colorado Springs CO

Colorado Springs

Black Forest

Manitou Springs

Stratmoor

Security-Widefield

Fountain

Columbia SC

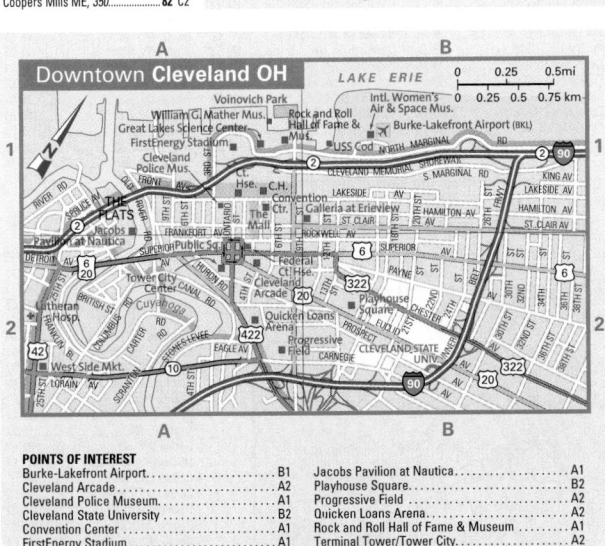

Columbus GA

Columbus

Phenix City

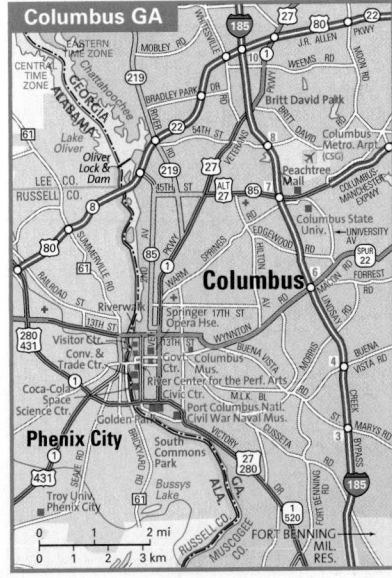

Figures after entries indicate population, page number, and grid reference.

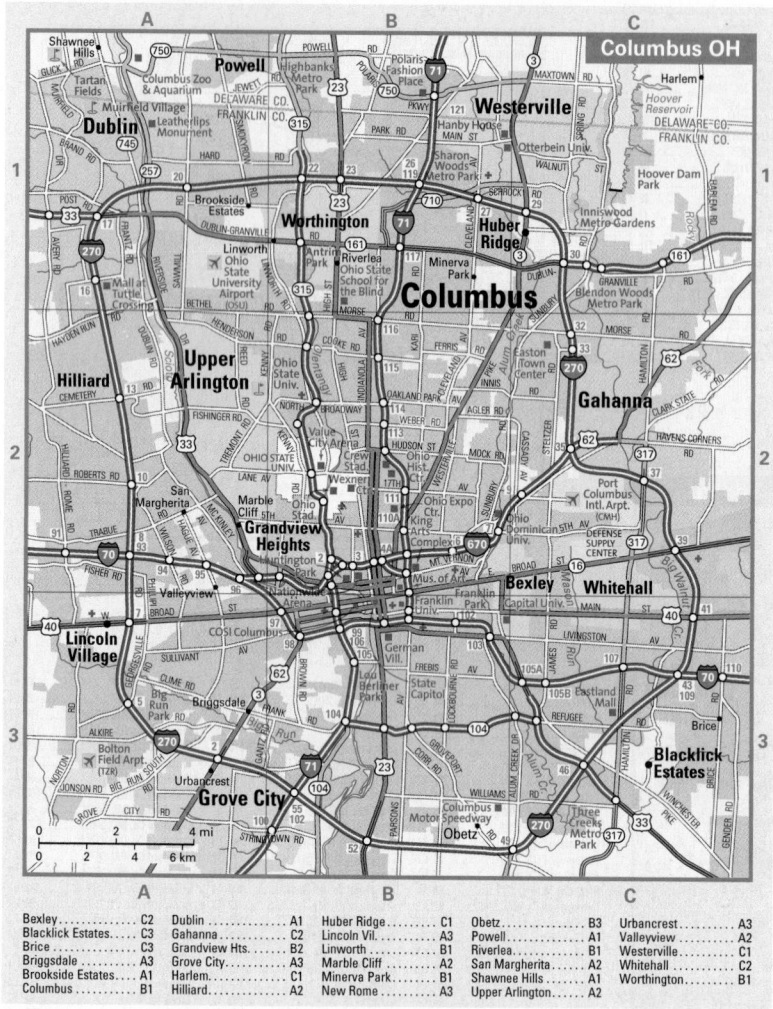

Columbus OH

City index (Columbus OH inset):

Bexley	C2	Dublin	A1	Huber Ridge	C1	Obetz	B3	Urbancrest	A3
Blacklick Estates	C3	Gahanna	C2	Lincoln Vil.	A3	Powell	A1	Valleyview	A2
Brice	C3	Grandview Hts.	B2	Linworth	B1	Riverlea	B1	Westerville	C1
Briggsdale	A3	Grove City	A3	Marble Cliff	A2	San Margherita	A1	Whitehall	C2
Brookside Estates	A1	Harlem	C1	Minerva Park	B1	Shawnee Hills	A1	Worthington	B1
Columbus	B1	Hilliard	A2	New Rome	A3	Upper Arlington	A2		

Crescent City IL, 615, ... 89 D3
Crescent Sprs. KY, 3801 .... 204 A3
Cresco IA, 3868, ... 73 E2
Cresson PA, 1711, ... 92 B4
Cressona PA, 1651, ... 146 A1
Crested Butte CO, 1487, ... 40 C2
Crest Hill IL, 20837, ... 89 D2
Crestline CA, 10770, ... 53 D2
Crestline OH, 4630, ... 91 D3
Creston IA, 7834, ... 86 B3
Creston OH, 2171, ... 91 E3

Crestview FL, 20978, ... 136 B1
Crestview KY, 475, ... 204 B3
Crestview Hills KY, 3148, ... 204 A3
Cridersville OH, 1852, ... 90 B3
Crimora VA, 2209, ... 102 C4
Cripple Creek CO, 1189, ... 41 E2
Crisfield MD, 2726, ... 103 F4
Crisp Co. GA, 23439, ... 129 D3
Crittenden KY, 3815, ... 100 B3
Crittenden Co. AR, 50902, ... 118 B1
Crittenden Co. KY, 9315, ... 109 D2
Crivitz WI, 984, ... 68 C3
Crocker MO, 1110, ... 97 E4
Crockett CA, 3094, ... 259 C1
Crockett Co. TN, 14586, ... 108 C4
Crockett Co. TX, 3719, ... 60 A1
Crofton KY, 749, ... 109 E2
Crofton MD, 27348, ... 144 C3
Crofton NE, 726, ... 35 E1
Croghan NY, 618, ... 79 D2
Crompond NY, 2292, ... 148 B2
Cromwell CT, 13594, ... 149 E1
Crook Co. OR, 20978, ... 21 D3
Crook Co. WY, 7083, ... 25 F3
Crooked Lake Park FL, 1722, ... 141 D3
Crooks SD, 1269, ... 27 F4
Crookston MN, 7891, ... 19 F3
Crooksville OH, 2534, ... 101 E1
Crosby MN, 2386, ... 64 B4
Crosby ND, 1070, ... 18 A1
Crosby TX, 2299, ... 132 B3
Crosby Co. TX, 6059, ... 58 A1
Crosbyton TX, 1741, ... 58 B1
Cross City FL, 1728, ... 137 F3
Cross Co. AR, 17870, ... 118 A1
Crossett AR, 5507, ... 125 F1
Cross Hill SC, 507, ... 122 A3
Cross Keys NJ, 3600, ... 146 C4
Crosslake MN, 2194, ... 64 B4
Cross Plains TN, 1714, ... 109 E3
Cross Plains TX, 982, ... 59 D3
Cross Plains WI, 3538, ... 74 B3
Cross Roads TX, 959, ... 59 F2
Crossville AL, 1862, ... 120 A3
Crossville IL, 745, ... 99 D4
Crossville TN, 10795, ... 110 B4
Crosswicks NJ, 900, ... 147 D2
Croswell MI, 2447, ... 76 C3

Crothersville IN, 1591, ... 99 F4
Croton Falls NY, 1200, ... 148 C1
Croton-on-Hudson NY, 8070, ... 148 B1
Crow Agency MT, 1616, ... 24 C1
Crowder MS, 712, ... 118 B3
Crowder OK, 430, ... 116 A1
Crowell TX, 948, ... 58 C1
Crowley LA, 13265, ... 133 E2
Crowley TX, 12838, ... 59 E2
Crowley Co. CO, 5823, ... 41 F3
Crown Hts. NY, 2840, ... 148 B1
Crown Pt. IN, 27317, ... 89 D2
Crown Pt. LA, 650, ... 134 B3
Crownpoint NM, 2278, ... 48 B2
Crown Pt. NY, 2119, ... 81 D3
Crownsville MD, 1757, ... 144 C3
Cutchogue NY, 3349, ... 149 E3
Cruger MS, 386, ... 126 B1

Crump TN, 1428, ... 119 D1
Crystal MN, 22151, ... 235 B2
Crystal NH, 311, ... 48 A2
Crystal Beach FL, 4000, ... 266 A1
Crystal City MO, 4855, ... 98 A4
Crystal City TX, 7138, ... 60 C4
Crystal Falls MI, 1469, ... 68 C2
Crystal Lake CT, 1945, ... 150 A3
Crystal Lake IL, 40743, ... 88 C1
Crystal Lakes OH, 1486, ... 100 C1
Crystal River FL, 3108, ... 140 B1
Crystal Sprs. FL, 1327, ... 140 C2
Crystal Sprs. MS, 5044, ... 126 B3
Cuba IL, 1294, ... 88 A4
Cuba MO, 3356, ... 97 F4
Cuba NM, 731, ... 48 C2
Cuba NY, 1575, ... 92 C1
Cuba City WI, 2086, ... 74 A4
Cudahy CA, 23805, ... 228 D3
Cudahy WI, 18267, ... 75 D3
Cuddebackville NY, 750, ... 148 A1
Cudjoe Key FL, 1763, ... 143 D4
Cuero TX, 6841, ... 61 E3
Culberson Co. TX, 2398, ... 57 E4
Culbertson MT, 714, ... 17 F2
Culbertson NE, 595, ... 34 C4
Culdesac ID, 380, ... 14 B4
Cullen LA, 1163, ... 125 D1
Cullman AL, 14775, ... 119 F3
Cullman Co. AL, 80406, ... 119 F3
Culloden WV, 3061, ... 101 D3
Cullowhee NC, 6228, ... 121 D1
Culpeper VA, 16379, ... 103 D3
Culpeper Co. VA, 46689, ... 103 D3
Culver IN, 1353, ... 89 E2
Culver OR, 1357, ... 21 D3
Culver City CA, 38883, ... 228 C3
Cumberland IN, 5169, ... 99 F1
Cumberland KY, 2237, ... 111 D2
Cumberland MD, 20859, ... 102 C1
Cumberland NC, 4400, ... 123 D2
Cumberland WI, 393, ... 113 D1
Cumberland WI, 2170, ... 67 E3
Cumberland Ctr. ME, 2499, ... 82 B3
Cumberland Co. IL, 11048, ... 99 D3
Cumberland Co. KY, 6856, ... 110 A2
Cumberland Co. ME, 281674, ... 82 B3
Cumberland Co. NJ, 156898, ... 145 F2
Cumberland Co. NC, 319431, ... 123 D2
Cumberland Co. PA, 235406, ... 103 D1
Cumberland Co. TN, 56053, ... 110 B4
Cumberland Co. VA, 10052, ... 113 D1
Cumberland Foreside ME, 500, ... 82 B3
Cumberland Hill RI, 7934, ... 150 C2
Cumby TX, 777, ... 124 A1
Cuming Co. NE, 9139, ... 35 F2
Cumming GA, 5430, ... 120 C3
Cunningham KS, 454, ... 43 D4
Cupertino CA, 58302, ... 36 B4
Curlew FL, 5900, ... 266 A1
Currituck NC, 125, ... 115 E1
Currituck Co. NC, 23547, ... 115 E1
Curry Co. NM, 48376, ... 49 F4
Curry Co. OR, 22364, ... 28 A2
Curtis NE, 939, ... 34 C4
Curwensville PA, 2542, ... 92 B3
Cushing OK, 7826, ... 51 F2
Cushing TX, 612, ... 124 B3
Cushman AR, 452, ... 107 F4
Cusseta GA, 11267, ... 128 C3
Custer Co. CO, 4255, ... 41 E3
Custer Co. ID, 4368, ... 23 D3
Custer Co. MT, 11696, ... 25 E1
Custer Co. NE, 10939, ... 34 C3
Custer Co. OK, 27469, ... 51 D2
Custer Co. SD, 8216, ... 25 F4
Cut and Shoot TX, 1070, ... 132 A2
Cut Bank MT, 2869, ... 15 E1
Cutchogue NY, 3349, ... 149 E3
Cuthbert GA, 3873, ... 128 C3
Cutler CA, 5000, ... 45 D3
Cutler Ridge FL, 24781, ... 143 E3
Cutlerville MI, 14370, ... 75 F3
Cut Off LA, 5976, ... 134 B3

Cutten CA, 3108, ... 28 A4
Cuyahoga Co. OH, 1280122, ... 91 E2
Cuyahoga Falls OH, 49652, ... 91 E3
Cuyahoga Hts. OH, 638, ... 204 F2
Cygnet OH, 597, ... 90 C2
Cynthiana IN, 545, ... 99 D4
Cynthiana KY, 6402, ... 100 B4
Cypress CA, 47802, ... 228 E4
Cypress Quarters FL, 1215, ... 141 E4
Cyril OK, 1059, ... 51 E3

D

Dacono CO, 4152, ... 41 E1
Dacula GA, 4442, ... 121 D3
Dade City FL, 6437, ... 140 C2
Dade Co. GA, 16633, ... 120 B2
Dade Co. MO, 7883, ... 106 C1
Dadeville AL, 3230, ... 128 B2
Daggett CA, 600, ... 53 D1
Daggett Co. UT, 1059, ... 32 A4
Dagsboro DE, 805, ... 145 F4
Dahlgren VA, 2653, ... 103 E4
Dahlonega GA, 5242, ... 120 C3
Daisetta TX, 966, ... 132 B2
Dakota Co. MN, 398552, ... 67 D4
Dakota Co. NE, 21006, ... 35 F2
Dale IN, 1593, ... 99 E4
Dale City VA, 65969, ... 144 A4
Dale Co. AL, 50251, ... 128 B4
Daleville IN, 1647, ... 89 F4
Daleville VA, 2557, ... 112 B1
Dalhart TX, 7930, ... 50 A2
Dallas NC, 4488, ... 122 A1
Dallas OR, 14583, ... 20 B2
Dallas PA, 2804, ... 93 E2
Dallas TX, 1197816, ... 59 F2
Dallas Ctr. IA, 1623, ... 86 C2
Dallas City IL, 945, ... 87 F3
Dallas Co. AL, 43820, ... 127 F3
Dallas Co. AR, 8116, ... 117 E4
Dallas Co. IA, 66135, ... 86 C2
Dallas Co. MO, 16777, ... 107 D1
Dallas Co. TX, 2368139, ... 59 F2
Dallastown PA, 4049, ... 103 E1
Dalton GA, 33128, ... 120 B2
Dalton MA, 6892, ... 94 C1
Dalton OH, 1830, ... 91 E3
Dalton PA, 1234, ... 93 F2
Dalton City IL, 544, ... 98 C1
Dalton Gardens ID, 2335, ... 14 B3
Dalworthington Gardens TX, 2259, ... 207 B3
Daly City CA, 101123, ... 36 B4
Dalzell SC, 3059, ... 122 B3
Damariscotta ME, 1142, ... 82 C3
Damariscotta Mills MD, 82, ... 144 B2
Damascus MD, 15257, ... 144 B2
Damascus OR, 10539, ... 20 C2
Damascus VA, 814, ... 111 F3
Dana IN, 608, ... 99 E1
Dana Pt. CA, 33351, ... 52 C3
Danboro PA, 1500, ... 146 C2
Danbury CT, 80893, ... 148 C2
Danbury NC, 189, ... 112 A3
Danbury TX, 1715, ... 132 A3
Dandridge TN, 2812, ... 111 D4
Dane WI, 995, ... 74 B3
Dane Co. WI, 488073, ... 74 B3
Danforth IL, 604, ... 89 D3
Dania Beach FL, 29639, ... 143 F2
Daniel MD, 650, ... 144 B4
Daniels Co. MT, 1751, ... 17 E1
Danielson CT, 4051, ... 150 B3
Danielsville GA, 560, ... 121 D3
Dannemora NY, 3936, ... 80 C1
Dansville NY, 4719, ... 78 C4
Dante VA, 649, ... 111 E2
Danube MN, 505, ... 66 B4
Danvers IL, 1154, ... 88 B4

Danvers MA, 26493, ... 151 F1
Danville AR, 2409, ... 117 D2
Danville CA, 42039, ... 36 B4
Danville IL, 33027, ... 89 D4
Danville IN, 9001, ... 99 F1
Danville KY, 16218, ... 110 B1
Danville NH, 4387, ... 95 E1
Danville OH, 1044, ... 91 D4
Danville PA, 4699, ... 93 E3
Danville VT, 383, ... 81 E2
Danville VA, 43055, ... 112 C3
Danville WV, 691, ... 101 E4
Daphne AL, 21570, ... 135 E2
Darby MT, 720, ... 23 D1
Darby PA, 10687, ... 146 C3
Dardanelle AR, 4745, ... 117 D1
Dardenne Prairie MO, 11494, ... 98 A3
Dare Co. NC, 33920, ... 115 F2
Dares Beach MD, 1400, ... 144 C4
Darien CT, 20732, ... 148 C3
Darien GA, 1975, ... 130 B4
Darien IL, 22086, ... 203 C5
Darien WI, 1580, ... 74 C4
Darke Co. OH, 52959, ... 100 B1
Darlington IN, 843, ... 89 E4
Darlington SC, 6289, ... 122 C3
Darlington WI, 2451, ... 74 A4
Darlington Co. SC, 68681, ... 122 B3
Darmstadt IN, 1407, ... 99 D4
Darnestown MD, 6802, ... 144 B2
Darrington WA, 1347, ... 12 C2
Dasher GA, 912, ... 137 F1
Dassel MN, 1469, ... 66 C3
Dauphin PA, 791, ... 93 D4
Dauphin Co. PA, 268100, ... 93 D4
Dauphin Island AL, 1238, ... 135 E2
Davenport FL, 2888, ... 141 D2
Davenport IA, 99685, ... 88 A2
Davenport ND, 252, ... 19 E4
Davenport OK, 814, ... 51 F2
Davenport WA, 1734, ... 13 F3
David City NE, 2906, ... 35 F3
Davidson NC, 10944, ... 122 A1
Davidson Co. NC, 162878, ... 112 B4
Davidson Co. TN, 626681, ... 109 F4
Davidsville PA, 1130, ... 92 B4
Davie FL, 91992, ... 143 E2
Davie Co. NC, 41240, ... 112 A4
Daviess Co. IN, 29818, ... 99 E3
Daviess Co. KY, 96656, ... 109 E1
Daviess Co. MO, 8433, ... 96 C1
Davis CA, 65622, ... 36 B3
Davis IL, 677, ... 74 B4
Davis OK, 2683, ... 51 F4
Davis WV, 660, ... 102 B2
Davis Co. IA, 8753, ... 87 E3
Davis Co. UT, 306479, ... 31 E3
Davison Co. SD, 19504, ... 27 E4
Davy WV, 420, ... 111 F1
Dawes Co. NE, 9182, ... 34 A1
Dawson GA, 4540, ... 128 C3
Dawson MN, 1540, ... 27 F2
Dawson TX, 807, ... 59 F3
Dawson Co. GA, 22330, ... 120 C3
Dawson Co. MT, 8966, ... 17 F3
Dawson Co. NE, 24326, ... 35 D4
Dawson Co. TX, 13833, ... 58 A2
Dawson Sprs. KY, 2764, ... 109 E2
Dawsonville GA, 2536, ... 120 C3
Day Co. SD, 5710, ... 27 E2
Dayton ID, 463, ... 31 E2
Dayton IN, 1420, ... 89 E4
Dayton IA, 837, ... 72 C4
Dayton KY, 5338, ... 204 B2
Dayton MN, 4671, ... 66 C3
Dayton NV, 8964, ... 37 D2
Dayton NJ, 7063, ... 147 D1
Dayton OH, 141527, ... 100 B1
Dayton OR, 2534, ... 20 B2
Dayton TN, 7191, ... 120 B1
Dayton TX, 7242, ... 132 B3
Dayton VA, 1530, ... 102 C3
Dayton WA, 2526, ... 13 F4
Dayton WY, 757, ... 24 C2
Daytona Beach FL, 61005, ... 139 E4
Daytona Beach Shores FL, 4247, ... 139 E4
Dayville CT, 1600, ... 150 B3
Deadwood SD, 1270, ... 25 F3
Deaf Smith Co. TX, 19372, ... 49 F3
Deal NJ, 750, ... 147 E2
Deale MD, 4945, ... 144 C3
Deal Island MD, 471, ... 103 F4
Dearborn MI, 98153, ... 76 C4
Dearborn MO, 496, ... 96 B1
Dearborn Co. IN, 50047, ... 100 B2
Dearborn Hts. MI, 57774, ... 210 B3
Dearing KS, 431, ... 106 A2
DeArmanville AL, 700, ... 120 A4
Deary ID, 506, ... 14 B4
Deaver WY, 178, ... 24 B2
De Baca Co. NM, 2022, ... 49 E4
DeBary FL, 19320, ... 141 D1
De Beque CO, 504, ... 40 B2
Decatur AL, 55683, ... 119 F2
Decatur GA, 18335, ... 120 C4
Decatur IL, 76122, ... 98 C1
Decatur IN, 9405, ... 90 A3
Decatur MI, 1819, ... 89 F1

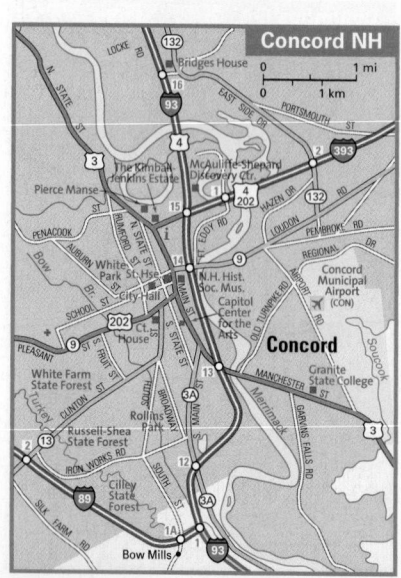

Concord NH

Bridges House
McAuliffe-Shepard Discovery Ctr.
Pierce Manse
The Kimball Jenkins Estate
N.H. Hist. Soc. Mus.
Capitol Center for the Arts
Concord Municipal Airport (CON)
N.H. State House
White Farm State Forest
Russell-Shea State Forest
Granite State College
Rollins Park
Cilley State Forest
Concord
Bow Mills

Corpus Christi TX

Nueces Bay
Mus. of Sci & History
Asian Cultures Museum
Whataburger Field
U.S.S. Lexington
Texas State Aquarium
Art Mus. of South Texas
American Bank Center
C.H. & Ct. Hse.
Gulf Coast Racing
Corpus Christi Intl. Arpt. (CRP)
Corpus Christi Bay
La Palmera Mall
Texas A&M University Corpus Christi
Corpus Christi
Cayo del Oso
N.A.S. CORPUS CHRISTI & ARMY DEPOT
P22

0 1 2 3 mi
0 1 2 3 4 km

Entries in **bold black** indicate counties or parishes.
Entries in **bold color** indicate cities with detailed inset maps.

Dallas/Fort Worth TX

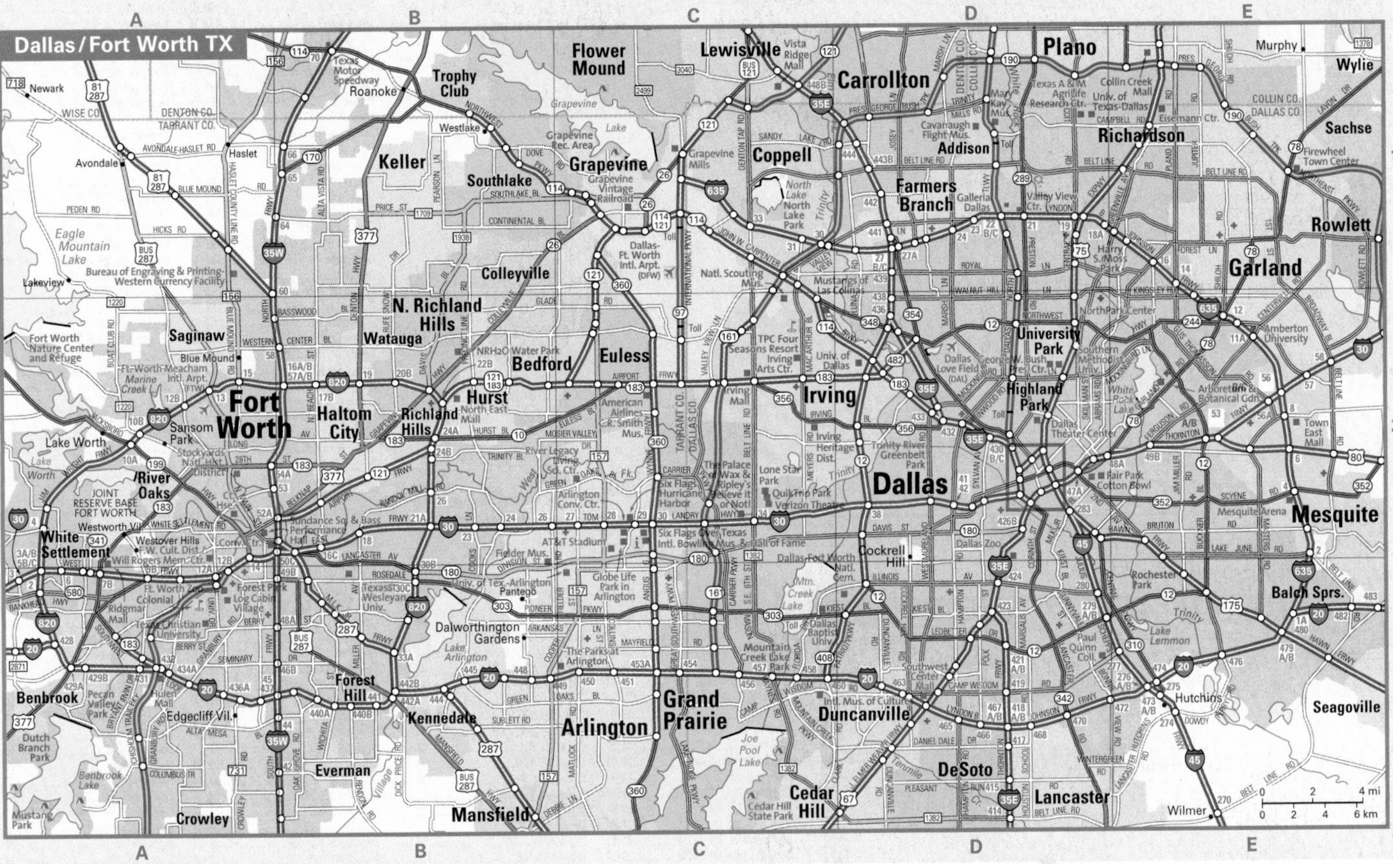

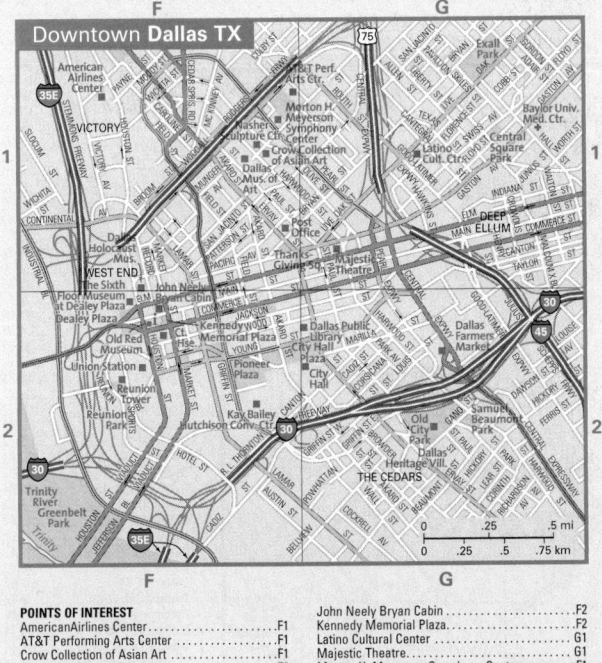

Downtown Dallas TX

POINTS OF INTEREST

AmericanAirlines Center.............F1	John Neely Bryan Cabin.............F2
AT&T Performing Arts Center.............F1	Kennedy Memorial Plaza.............F2
Crow Collection of Asian Art.............F1	Latino Cultural Center.............G1
Dallas Convention Center.............F2	Majestic Theatre.............G1
Dallas Heritage Village.............G2	Morton H. Meyerson Symphony Center.............F1
Dallas Holocaust Museum.............F1	Nasher Sculpture Center.............F1
Dallas Museum of Art.............F1	Old Red Museum.............F2
Dallas Public Library.............G2	Reunion Arena.............F2
Farmers Market.............G2	Reunion Tower.............F2
	The Sixth Floor Museum at Dealey Plaza.............F2

Figures after entries indicate population, page number, and grid reference.

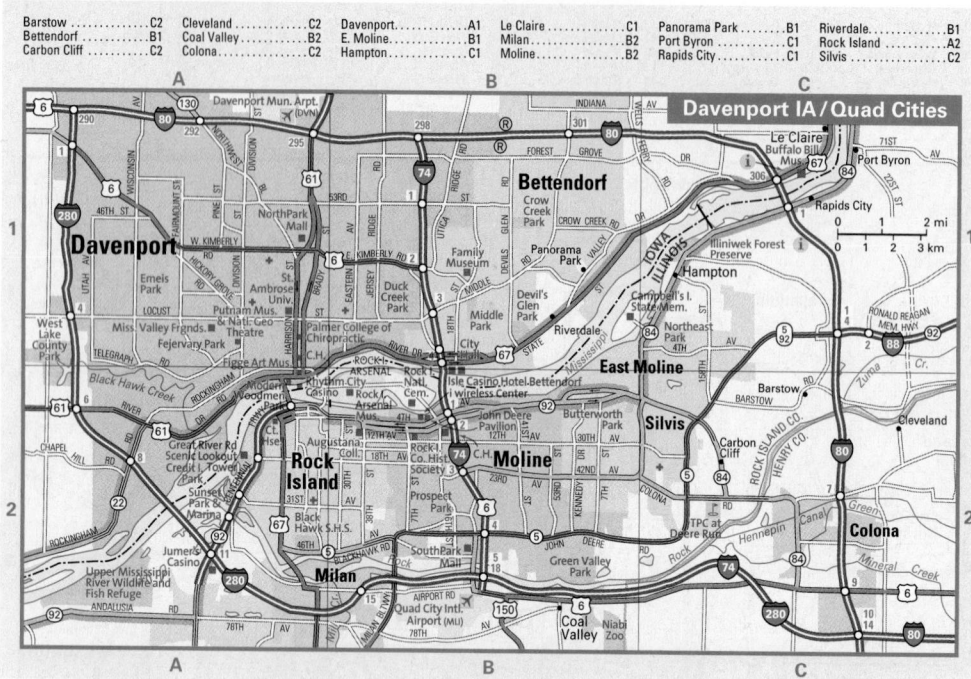

Davenport IA / Quad Cities

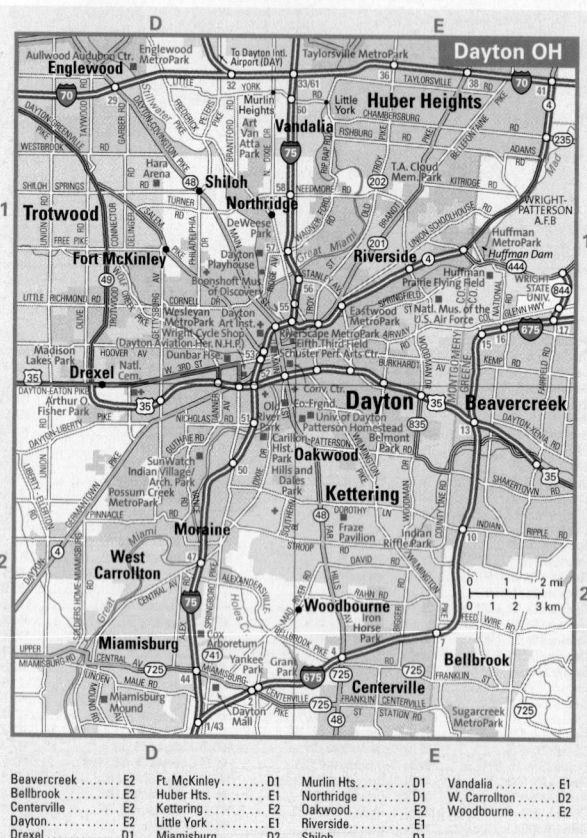

Dayton OH

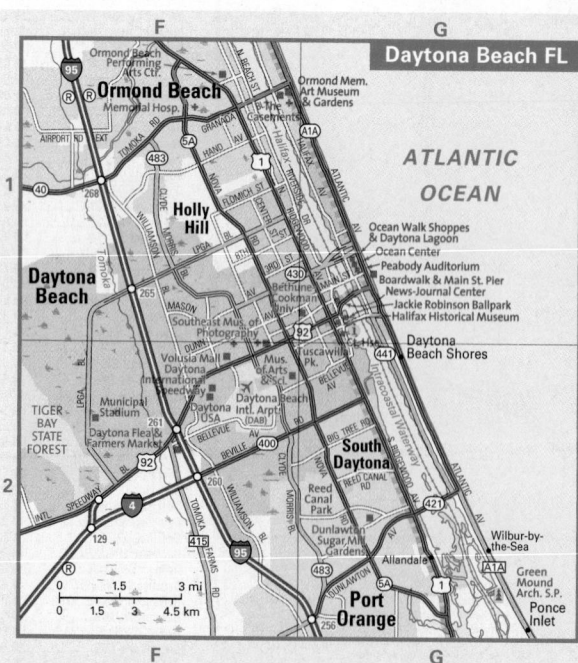

Daytona Beach FL

Entries in **bold black** indicate counties or parishes.
Entries in **bold color** indicate cities with detailed inset maps.

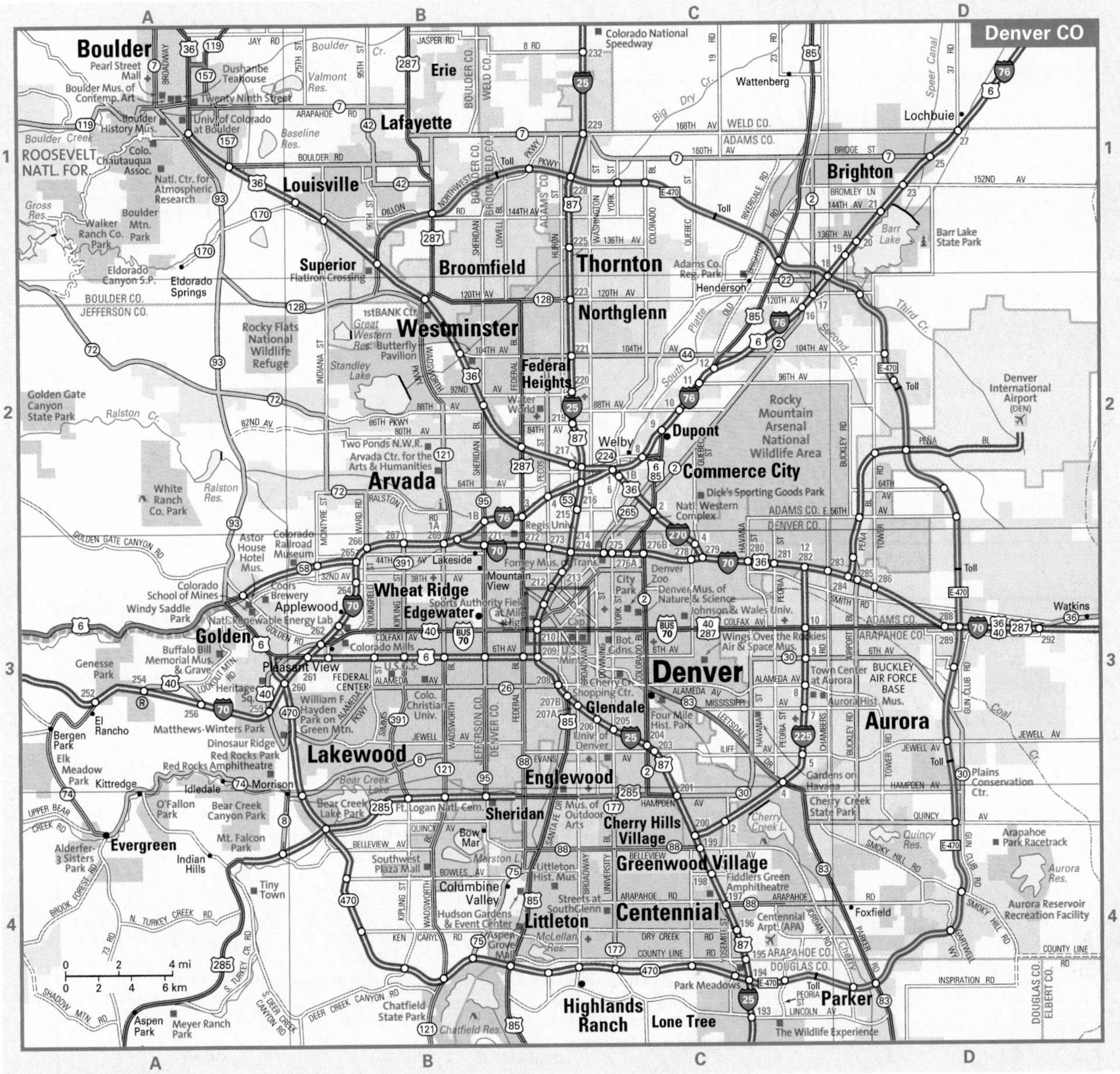

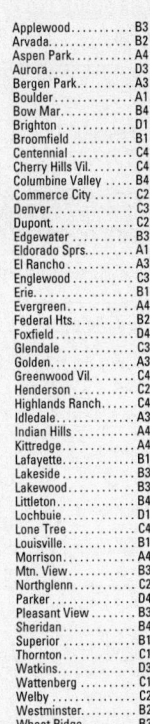

Denver CO

Applewood B3
Arvada B2
Aspen Park A4
Aurora D3
Bergen Park A3
Boulder A1
Bow Mar B4
Brighton D1
Broomfield B1
Centennial C4
Cherry Hills Vil. C4
Columbine Valley B4
Commerce City C2
Denver C3
Dupont C2
Edgewater B3
Eldorado Sprs. A1
El Rancho A3
Englewood C3
Erie B1
Evergreen A4
Federal Hts. B2
Foxfield D4
Glendale C3
Golden A3
Greenwood Vil. C4
Henderson C2
Highlands Ranch C4
Idledale A3
Indian Hills A4
Kittredge A4
Lafayette B1
Lakeside B3
Lakewood B3
Littleton B4
Lochbuie D1
Lone Tree C4
Louisville B1
Morrison A4
Mtn. View B3
Northglenn C2
Parker D4
Pleasant View B4
Sheridan B3
Superior B1
Thornton C1
Watkins D3
Wattenberg C1
Welby C2
Westminster B2
Wheat Ridge B3

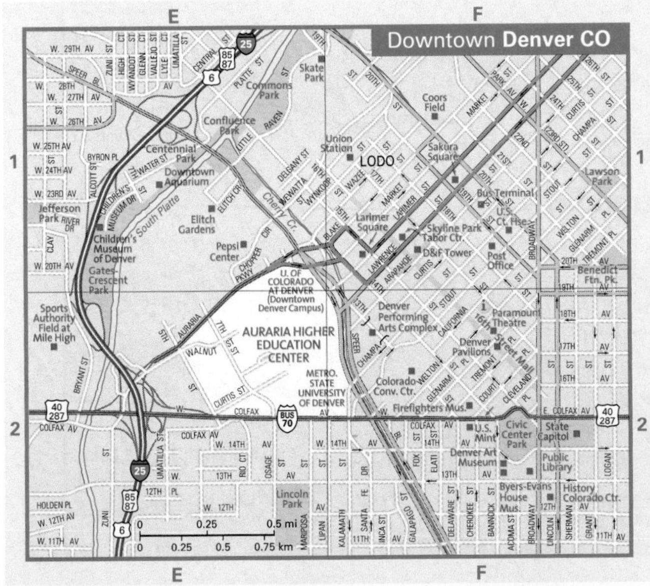

Downtown **Denver CO**

POINTS OF INTEREST

16th Street Mall E1
Auraria Higher Education Center E2
Bus Terminal F1
Byers-Evans House F2
Children's Museum of Denver E1
Colorado Convention Center F2
Colorado History Museum F2
Coors Field F1
D&F Tower F2
Denver Art Museum F2
Denver Pavilions F2
Denver Performing Arts Complex F2
Downtown Aquarium E1
Elitch Gardens E1
Firefighters Museum F2
Invesco Field at Mile High E2
Larimer Square F1
LoDo F1
Metropolitan State Coll. of Denver E2
Paramount Theatre F2
Pepsi Center E1
Post Office F2
Public Library F2
Sakura Square F1
Skate Park F1
State Capitol F2
Tabor Center F1
Union Station F1
U.S. Court House F2
U.S. Mint F2
Univ. of Colorado at Denver
  (Downtown Denver Campus) E2

Figures after entries indicate population, page number, and grid reference.

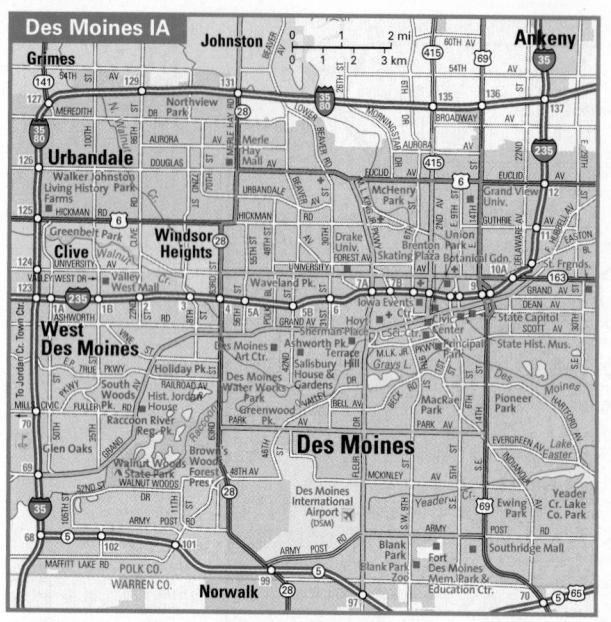

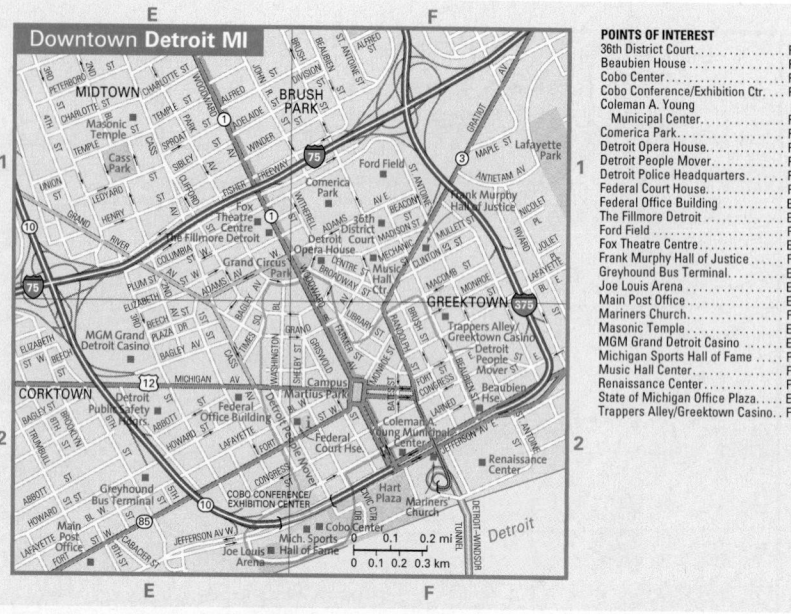

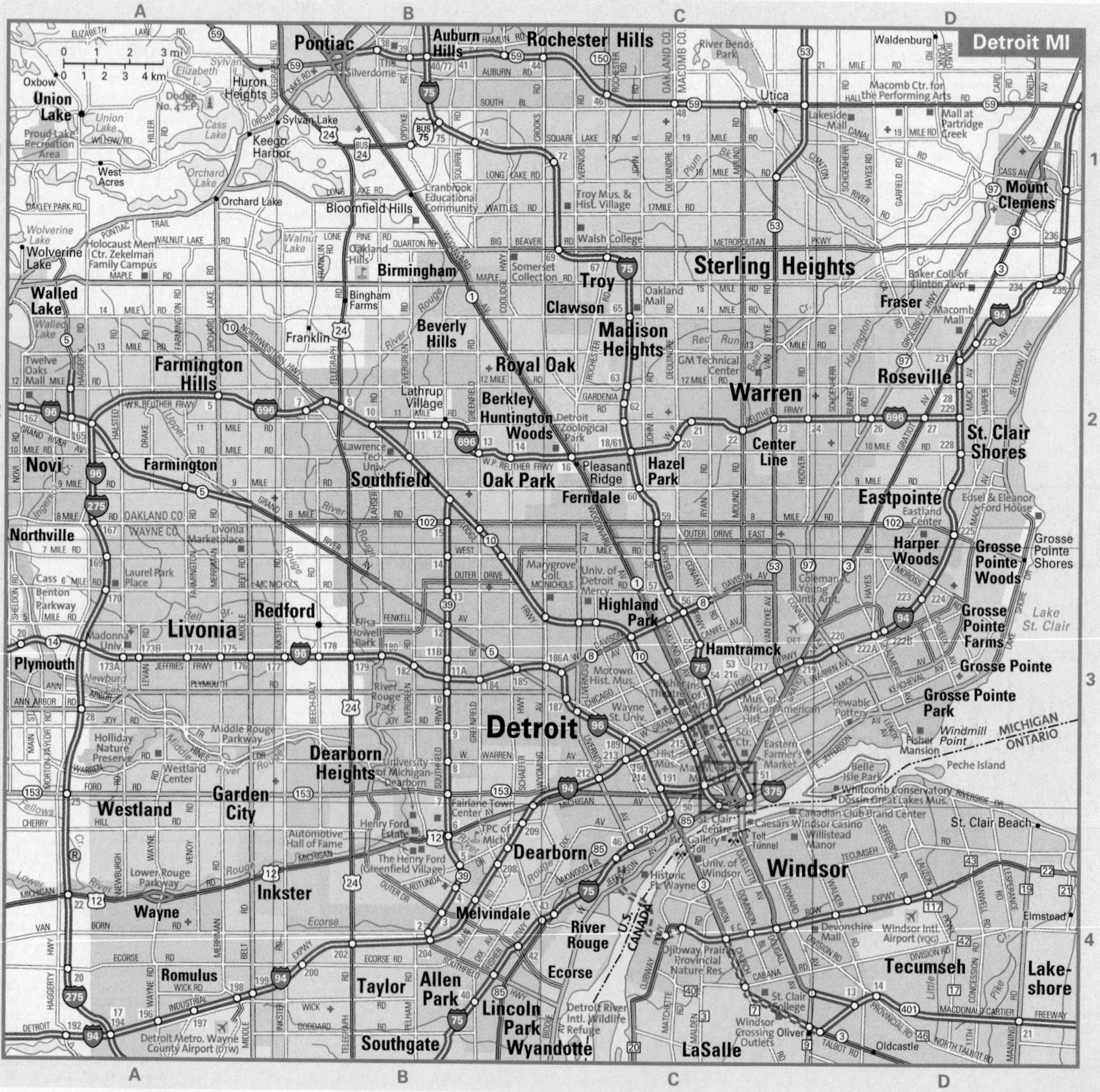

Entries in **bold black** indicate counties or parishes.
Entries in **bold color** indicate cities with detailed inset maps.

Durant OK, 15856 .... 59 F1
Durham CA, 5518 .... 36 B1
Durham CT, 2933 .... 149 E1
Durham NH, 10345 .... 82 A4
Durham NC, 228330 .... 112 C4
Durham OR, 1351 .... 251 C3
Durham Co. NC, 267587 .... 112 C4
Duryea PA, 4917 .... 93 F2
Dushore PA, 608 .... 93 E2
Duson LA, 1716 .... 133 E2
Dustin OK, 395 .... 51 F3
Dutchess Co. NY, 297488 .... 148 C1
Dutch Neck NJ, 4400 .... 147 D2
Dutton MT, 316 .... 15 F2
Duval Co. FL, 864263 .... 139 D2
Duval Co. TX, 11782 .... 63 E2
Duvall WA, 6695 .... 12 C3
Duxbury MA, 1802 .... 151 E2
Duxbury VT, 1289 .... 81 E2
Dwaar Kill NY, 1400 .... 148 A1
Dwarf KY, 550 .... 111 D1
Dwight IL, 4260 .... 88 C3
Dyer AR, 876 .... 116 C1
Dyer IN, 16390 .... 89 D2
Dyer TN, 2341 .... 108 C4
Dyer Co. TN, 38335 .... 108 C4
Dyersburg TN, 17145 .... 108 C4
Dyersville IA, 4058 .... 73 F4
Dyess AR, 410 .... 118 B1
Dysart IA, 1379 .... 87 E1

E

Eads CO, 609 .... 42 A3
Eagan MN, 64206 .... 235 D4
Eagar AZ, 4885 .... 48 A4
Eagle CO, 6508 .... 40 C1
Eagle ID, 19908 .... 22 B4
Eagle NE, 1024 .... 35 F4
Eagle WI, 1950 .... 74 C3
Eagle Bend MN, 535 .... 66 B1
Eagle Butte SD, 1318 .... 26 B2
Eagle Co. CO, 52197 .... 40 C1
Eagle Grove IA, 3583 .... 72 C4
Eagle Lake FL, 2255 .... 140 C2
Eagle Lake ME, 625 .... 85 D1
Eagle Lake MN, 2422 .... 72 C1
Eagle Lake TX, 3639 .... 61 F2
Eagle Mtn. UT, 21415 .... 31 E4
Eagle Nest NM, 290 .... 49 D1
Eagle Pass TX, 26248 .... 60 B4
Eagle Pt. OR, 8469 .... 28 C2
Eagle River MI, 71 .... 65 F3
Eagle River WI, 1398 .... 68 B2
Eagleton Vil. TN, 5052 .... 110 C4
Eagleville PA, 4800 .... 146 C2
Eagleville TN, 604 .... 109 F4
Earle AR, 2414 .... 118 A1
Earlham IA, 1450 .... 86 C2
Earlimart CA, 8537 .... 45 D4
Earlington KY, 1413 .... 109 E2
Earlsboro OK, 628 .... 51 F3
Earlville IL, 1701 .... 88 C2
Earlville IA, 812 .... 73 F4
Earlville NY, 872 .... 79 E4
Earlville PA, 800 .... 146 B2
Early IA, 557 .... 72 A4
Early TX, 2762 .... 59 D4
Early Co. GA, 11008 .... 128 C4
Earlysville VA, 750 .... 102 C4
Earth TX, 1065 .... 50 A4
Easley SC, 19993 .... 121 E2
E. Alton IL, 6301 .... 98 A3
E. Arcadia NC, 487 .... 123 E3
E. Arlington VT, 750 .... 81 D4
E. Atlantic Beach NY, 2049 .... 241 G5
E. Aurora NY, 6236 .... 78 B4
E. Bank WV, 959 .... 101 F4
E. Barre VT, 826 .... 81 E2
E. Barrington NH, 400 .... 81 F4
E. Baton Rouge Par. LA, 440171 .... 134 A1
E. Bend NC, 612 .... 112 A3
E. Berlin PA, 1521 .... 103 E1
E. Bernard TX, 2272 .... 61 F2
E. Bernstadt KY, 716 .... 110 C2
E. Bethel MN, 11626 .... 67 D3
E. Blackstone MA, 1600 .... 150 C2
E. Brady PA, 942 .... 92 A3
E. Brewster MA, 850 .... 151 F3
E. Brewton AL, 2478 .... 135 F1
E. Bridgewater MA, 12974 .... 151 D2
E. Brookfield MA, 1323 .... 150 B2
E. Brooklyn CT, 1638 .... 150 B3
E. Brunswick NJ, 47512 .... 147 E1
E. Butler PA, 732 .... 92 A3
E. Camden AR, 931 .... 117 E4
E. Canton OH, 1591 .... 91 E3
E. Carbon UT, 1301 .... 39 F1
E. Carroll Par. LA, 7759 .... 126 A2
Eastchester NY, 19554 .... 148 B3
E. Chicago IN, 29698 .... 89 D2
E. Cleveland OH, 17843 .... 91 E2
E. Dennis MA, 2753 .... 151 F3
E. Douglas MA, 2557 .... 150 C2
E. Dublin GA, 2441 .... 129 E2
E. Dubuque IL, 1704 .... 73 F4
E. Duke OK, 424 .... 50 C4
E. Dundee IL, 2860 .... 203 A2
E. Ellijay GA, 546 .... 120 C2
E. End AR, 6998 .... 117 E2
E. Falmouth MA, 6038 .... 151 E4
E. Feliciana Par. LA, 20267 .... 134 A1
E. Flat Rock NC, 4995 .... 121 E1
E. Freehold NJ, 4894 .... 147 E2
E. Freetown MA, 1200 .... 151 D3
E. Gaffney SC, 3085 .... 121 F1
E. Galesburg IL, 812 .... 88 A3
Eastgate WA, 4958 .... 262 B3
E. Glacier Park MT, 363 .... 15 D2
E. Glastonbury CT, 1400 .... 149 E1
E. Glenville NY, 6616 .... 94 B1
E. Grand Forks MN, 8601 .... 19 E2
E. Grand Rapids MI, 10694 .... 215 B2
E. Greenbush NY, 4487 .... 188 E3
E. Greenville PA, 2951 .... 146 B1
E. Greenwich RI, 13146 .... 150 C3
E. Gull Lake MN, 1004 .... 64 A4
E. Haddam CT, 550 .... 149 E1
Eastham MA, 5453 .... 151 F3
E. Hampton CT, 2691 .... 149 E1
Easthampton MA, 16053 .... 150 A1
E. Hampton NY, 1083 .... 149 F3
E. Hanover NJ, 11426 .... 148 A3
E. Hardwick VT, 300 .... 81 E2
E. Hartford CT, 51252 .... 150 A3
E. Harwich MA, 4872 .... 151 F3
E. Haven CT, 29257 .... 149 D2
E. Helena MT, 1984 .... 15 E4
E. Highland Park VA, 14796 .... 254 B1
E. Holden ME, 475 .... 83 D1
E. Hope ID, 210 .... 14 B2
E. Ithaca NY, 2231 .... 79 D4
E. Jordan MI, 2351 .... 69 F3
Eastlake OH, 18577 .... 91 E2
Eastland TX, 3960 .... 59 D3
Eastland Co. TX, 18583 .... 59 D3
E. Lansdowne PA, 2668 .... 248 B3
E. Lansing MI, 48579 .... 76 A4
E. Lebanon ME, 650 .... 82 A4
E. Liverpool OH, 11195 .... 91 F3
E. Longmeadow MA, 15720 .... 150 A2
E. Los Angeles CA, 126496 .... 228 D3
Eastman GA, 4962 .... 129 E3
E. Marion MA, 550 .... 151 E3
E. Marion NY, 926 .... 149 E2
E. McKeesport PA, 2126 .... 250 D3
E. Meadow NY, 38132 .... 148 C4
E. Middlebury VT, 425 .... 81 D3
E. Middletown NY, 5000 .... 148 A1
E. Millcreek UT, 21385 .... 257 B2
E. Millinocket ME, 1567 .... 85 D4
E. Moline IL, 21302 .... 88 A2
E. Montpelier VT, 80 .... 81 E2
E. Moriches NY, 5249 .... 149 E4
E. Mtn. TX, 580 .... 124 B2
E. Naples FL, 23000 .... 142 C2
E. Nassau NY, 587 .... 94 B1
E. Newark NJ, 2406 .... 240 B3
E. Newnan GA, 1321 .... 128 C1
E. Northport ME, 350 .... 82 C2
E. Northport NY, 20217 .... 148 C3
E. Olympia WA, 900 .... 12 C4
Easton CA, 2083 .... 44 C3
Easton CT, 7488 .... 148 C2
Easton ME, 1249 .... 85 E2
Easton MD, 15945 .... 145 D3
Easton PA, 26800 .... 93 F3
Easton TX, 510 .... 124 B2
E. Orange NJ, 64270 .... 148 A4
E. Orleans MA, 6341 .... 151 F3
Eastover NC, 3628 .... 123 D1
Eastover SC, 813 .... 122 B4
E. Palatka FL, 1654 .... 139 D3
E. Palestine OH, 4721 .... 91 F3
E. Palo Alto CA, 28155 .... 259 D5
E. Patchogue NY, 22469 .... 149 D4
E. Peoria IL, 23402 .... 88 B3
E. Petersburg PA, 4506 .... 146 A2
E. Pittsburgh PA, 1822 .... 250 D2
Eastpoint FL, 2337 .... 137 D3
E. Point GA, 33712 .... 120 C4
Eastpointe MI, 32442 .... 210 D2
Eastport ME, 1331 .... 83 F1
Eastport NY, 1831 .... 149 E3
E. Poultney VT, 400 .... 81 D3
E. Prairie MO, 3176 .... 108 C2
E. Prospect PA, 905 .... 103 E1
E. Providence RI, 47037 .... 150 C3
E. Quincy CA, 2489 .... 36 C1
E. Quogue NY, 4757 .... 149 E3
E. Randolph NY, 620 .... 92 B1
E. Ridge TN, 20979 .... 120 B2
E. Rochester NY, 6587 .... 254 G2
E. Rockaway NY, 9818 .... 147 F1
E. Rockingham NC, 3736 .... 122 C2
E. Rutherford NJ, 8913 .... 240 C2
E. St. Louis IL, 27006 .... 98 A3
E. Sandwich MA, 3940 .... 151 E3
E. Setauket NY, 15931 .... 149 D3
E. Shoreham NY, 6666 .... 149 D3
Eastsound WA, 750 .... 12 C1
E. Spencer NC, 1534 .... 112 A4
E. Stroudsburg PA, 9840 .... 93 F3
E. Swanzey NH, 475 .... 95 D1
E. Syracuse NY, 3084 .... 265 B2
E. Tawakoni TX, 883 .... 59 F2
E. Tawas MI, 2808 .... 76 B1
E. Texas PA, 6000 .... 146 B1
E. Thermopolis WY, 254 .... 24 C4
E. Troy WI, 4281 .... 74 C4
E. Vassalboro ME, 300 .... 82 C2
Eastview MD, 650 .... 144 B1
Eastview TN, 705 .... 119 D2
E. Village CT, 1500 .... 149 D2
Eastville VA, 305 .... 114 B3
E. Wareham MA, 1700 .... 151 E3
E. Washington PA, 2234 .... 92 A4
E. Wenatchee WA, 13190 .... 13 D3
E. Wilton ME, 550 .... 82 B2
E. Winthrop ME, 650 .... 82 B2
Eastwood LA, 4093 .... 125 D2
E. York PA, 8777 .... 275 F1
Eaton CO, 4365 .... 33 E4
Eaton IN, 1805 .... 90 A4
Eaton OH, 8407 .... 100 B1
Eaton Co. MI, 107759 .... 76 A4
Eaton Estates OH, 1222 .... 91 D2
Eaton Park FL, 3000 .... 266 E2
Eaton Rapids MI, 5214 .... 76 A4
Eatons Neck NY, 1406 .... 148 C3
Eatonton GA, 6480 .... 129 E1
Eatontown NJ, 12709 .... 147 E2
Eatonville FL, 2159 .... 246 C1
Eatonville WA, 2758 .... 12 C4
Eau Claire MI, 625 .... 89 F1
Eau Claire WI, 65883 .... 67 F4
Eau Claire Co. WI, 98736 .... 67 F4
Ebensburg PA, 3351 .... 92 B4
Eccles WV, 362 .... 111 F1
Echo OR, 699 .... 21 E1
Echols Co. GA, 4034 .... 138 B1
Eclectic AL, 1001 .... 128 A2
Economy PA, 8970 .... 92 A3
Ecorse MI, 9512 .... 210 C4
Ecru MS, 895 .... 118 C3
Ector TX, 695 .... 59 F1
Ector Co. TX, 137130 .... 57 F3
Edcouch TX, 3161 .... 63 E4
Eddington ME, 2052 .... 83 D1
Eddy Co. NM, 53829 .... 57 E2
Eddy Co. ND, 2385 .... 19 D3
Eddystone PA, 2410 .... 248 A4
Eddyville IA, 1024 .... 87 D2
Eddyville KY, 2554 .... 109 D2
Eden ID, 405 .... 31 D1
Eden MD, 823 .... 103 F4
Eden NY, 3516 .... 78 A4
Eden NC, 15527 .... 112 B3
Eden TX, 2766 .... 58 C4
Eden WI, 875 .... 74 C2
Eden WY, 281 .... 32 A2
Eden Prairie MN, 60797 .... 235 A4
Edenton NC, 5004 .... 113 F4
Eden Valley MN, 1042 .... 66 B3
Edenville NY, 650 .... 148 A2
Edgar NE, 498 .... 35 E4
Edgar WI, 1479 .... 68 A4
Edgar Co. IL, 18576 .... 99 D1
Edgard LA, 2441 .... 134 B3
Edgartown MA, 3779 .... 151 E4
Edgecliff Vil. TX, 2776 .... 207 A3
Edgecombe Co. NC, 56552 .... 113 E4
Edgefield SC, 4750 .... 121 F4
Edgefield Co. SC, 26985 .... 121 F4
Edgeley ND, 563 .... 19 D4
Edgemere MD, 8669 .... 144 C2
Edgemont SD, 774 .... 25 F4
Edgemoor DE, 5677 .... 146 B4
Edgerton KS, 1671 .... 96 B3
Edgerton MN, 1189 .... 27 F4
Edgerton MO, 546 .... 96 B2
Edgerton OH, 2012 .... 90 A2
Edgerton WI, 5461 .... 74 B3
Edgerton WY, 195 .... 25 D4
Edgewater AL, 883 .... 195 D2
Edgewater CO, 5170 .... 209 B3
Edgewater FL, 20750 .... 139 E4
Edgewater NJ, 11513 .... 240 D2
Edgewater Park NJ, 7968 .... 147 D3
Edgewood FL, 2503 .... 246 C3
Edgewood IN, 1913 .... 89 F4
Edgewood IA, 864 .... 73 F4
Edgewood KY, 8575 .... 204 B3
Edgewood MD, 25562 .... 145 D1
Edgewood NM, 3735 .... 48 C3
Edgewood OH, 4432 .... 91 F1
Edgewood PA, 3118 .... 250 C2
Edgewood TX, 1441 .... 124 A2
Edgewood WA, 9387 .... 262 B5
Edina MN, 47941 .... 67 D4
Edina MO, 1176 .... 87 E4
Edinboro PA, 6438 .... 92 A1
Edinburg IL, 1078 .... 98 B1
Edinburg NJ, 900 .... 147 D2
Edinburg ND, 196 .... 19 E2
Edinburg TX, 77100 .... 63 E4
Edinburg VA, 1041 .... 102 C3
Edinburgh IN, 4480 .... 99 F2
Edison GA, 1531 .... 128 C4
Edison NJ, 99967 .... 147 E1
Edisto Beach SC, 414 .... 130 C2
Edmond OK, 81405 .... 51 E2
Edmonds WA, 39709 .... 12 C3
Edmondson AR, 427 .... 118 B1
Edmonson Co. KY, 12161 .... 109 F2
Edmonston MD, 1445 .... 270 E2
Edmonton KY, 1595 .... 110 A2
Edmore MI, 1201 .... 76 A2
Edmore ND, 182 .... 19 D2
Edmunds Co. SD, 4071 .... 27 D2
Edmundson MO, 834 .... 256 B1
Edna KS, 442 .... 106 A2
Edna TX, 5499 .... 61 F3
Edon OH, 834 .... 90 A2
Edwards CO, 10266 .... 40 C1
Edwards MS, 1034 .... 126 A2
Edwardsburg MI, 1259 .... 89 F1
Edwards Co. IL, 6721 .... 99 D4
Edwards Co. KS, 3037 .... 43 D4
Edwards Co. TX, 2002 .... 60 B2
Edwardsville IL, 24293 .... 98 B3
Edwardsville KS, 4340 .... 96 B2
Edwardsville PA, 4816 .... 261 A1
Effingham IL, 12328 .... 98 C2
Effingham KS, 546 .... 96 A1
Effingham Co. GA, 52250 .... 130 B2
Effingham Co. IL, 34242 .... 98 C2
Effort PA, 2269 .... 93 F3
Egan SD, 278 .... 27 F3
Egg Harbor City NJ, 4243 .... 147 D4
Egypt PA, 2391 .... 189 A1
Ehrenberg AZ, 1470 .... 53 F3
Ehrhardt SC, 545 .... 130 C1
Ekalaka MT, 332 .... 25 F1
Elaine AR, 636 .... 118 A3
Elam PA, 2000 .... 146 B3
Elba AL, 3940 .... 128 A4
Elba NY, 676 .... 78 B3
Elberfeld IN, 625 .... 99 E4
Elberta AL, 1498 .... 135 F2
Elberta MI, 372 .... 69 E4
Elberta UT, 256 .... 39 E1
Elbert Co. CO, 23086 .... 41 E2
Elbert Co. GA, 20166 .... 121 E3
Elberton GA, 4653 .... 121 E3
Elbow Lake MN, 1176 .... 27 F1
Elbridge NY, 1058 .... 79 D3
Elburn IL, 5602 .... 88 C1
El Cajon CA, 99478 .... 53 D4
El Campo TX, 11602 .... 61 F3
El Cenizo TX, 249 .... 63 D2
El Centro CA, 42598 .... 53 E4
El Cerrito CA, 4590 .... 229 H4
El Cerrito CA, 23549 .... 259 B2
Eldersburg MD, 30531 .... 144 B1
Eldon IA, 927 .... 87 E3
Eldon MO, 4567 .... 97 E4
Eldon OK, 368 .... 106 B4
Eldora IA, 2732 .... 73 D4
El Dorado AR, 18884 .... 125 E1
Eldorado IL, 4122 .... 109 D1
El Dorado KS, 13021 .... 43 F4
Eldorado OK, 446 .... 50 C4
Eldorado TX, 1951 .... 60 B1
El Dorado Co. CA, 181058 .... 36 C2
Eldorado Sprs. CO, 585 .... 209 A1
El Dorado Sprs. MO, 3593 .... 96 C4
Eldred PA, 825 .... 92 C1
Eldridge IA, 5651 .... 88 A2
Eleanor WV, 1518 .... 101 E3
Electra TX, 2791 .... 59 D1
Electric City WA, 968 .... 13 E2
Eleele HI, 2390 .... 152 B1
Elephant Butte NM, 1431 .... 56 B2
Eleva WI, 670 .... 67 F4
Elfers FL, 13986 .... 140 B2
Elfrida AZ, 459 .... 55 E4
Elgin AZ, 161 .... 55 D4
Elgin IL, 108188 .... 88 C1
Elgin IA, 683 .... 73 E3
Elgin MN, 1089 .... 73 E1
Elgin NE, 661 .... 35 E2
Elgin ND, 642 .... 18 B4
Elgin OK, 2156 .... 51 D4
Elgin OR, 1711 .... 21 F1
Elgin SC, 1311 .... 122 A3
Elgin SC, 2426 .... 122 B2
Elgin TX, 8135 .... 61 E1
El Granada CA, 5467 .... 259 B5
Elida OH, 1905 .... 90 B3
Elihu KY, 650 .... 110 B2
Elizabeth CO, 1358 .... 41 E2
Elizabeth IL, 761 .... 74 A4
Elizabeth LA, 532 .... 133 E1
Elizabeth NJ, 124969 .... 148 A4
Elizabeth PA, 1493 .... 92 A4
Elizabeth WV, 823 .... 101 F2
Elizabeth City NC, 18683 .... 113 F3
Elizabeth Lake CA, 1756 .... 52 C2
Elizabethton TN, 14176 .... 111 E3
Elizabethtown IL, 299 .... 109 D1
Elizabethtown KY, 28531 .... 110 A1

Duluth MN

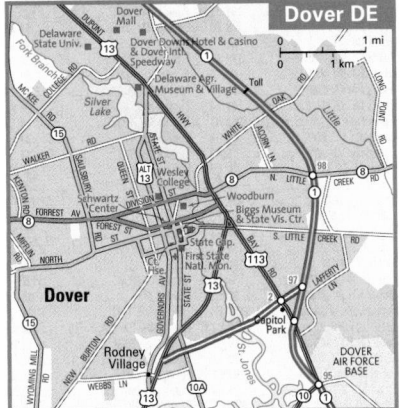

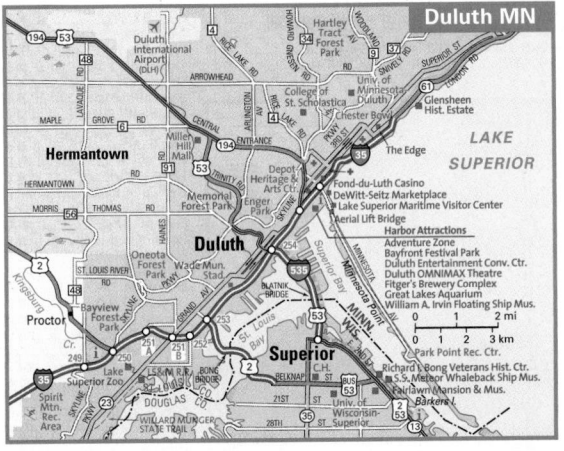

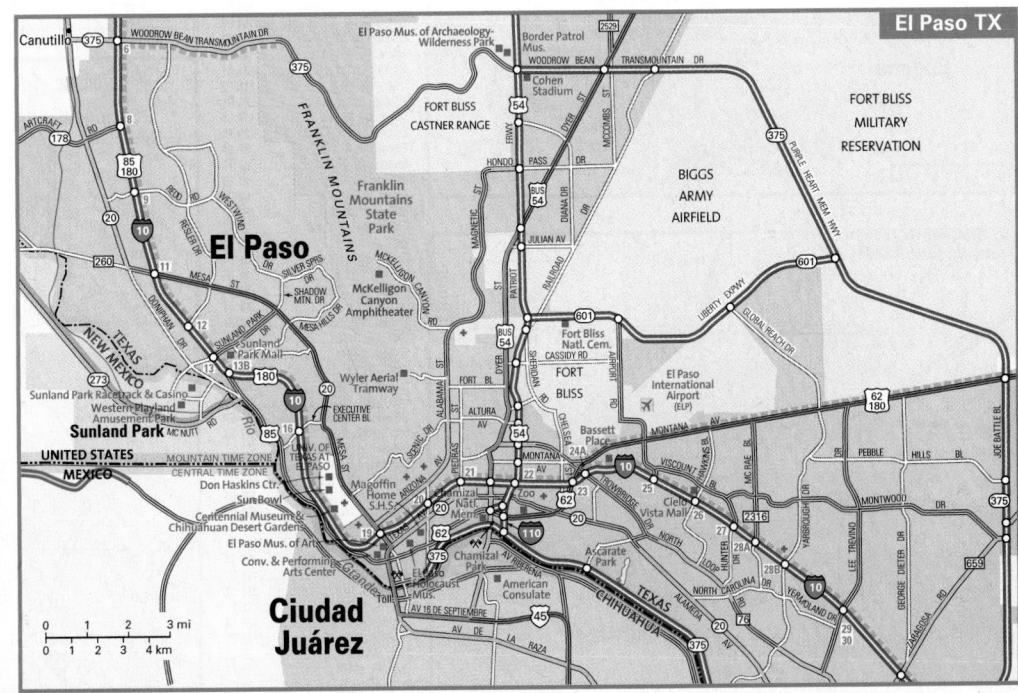

212
Elizabethtown – Ewing

Figures after entries indicate population, page number, and grid reference.

Elizabethtown NY, 754 81 D2
Elizabethtown NC, 3583 123 D2
Elizabethtown PA, 11545 93 E4
Elizabethville PA, 1510 93 D4
El Jebel CO, 3801 40 C2
Elkader IA, 1273 73 F3
Elk City OK, 11693 50 C3
Elk Co. KS, 2882 43 F4
Elk Co. PA, 31946 92 B2
Elk Grove CA, 153015 36 C3
Elk Grove Vil. IL, 33127 203 C3
Elkhart IN, 50949 89 F2
Elkhart KS, 2205 50 A1
Elkhart TX, 1371 124 A4
Elkhart Co. IN, 197559 89 F2
Elkhart Lake WI, 967 74 C2
Elkhorn CA, 1565 236 E2
Elk Horn IA, 662 86 B2
Elkhorn WI, 10084 74 C4
Elkhorn City KY, 982 111 E1
Elkin NC, 4001 112 A3
Elkins AR, 2648 106 C4
Elkins WV, 7094 102 A3
Elkland PA, 1821 93 D1
Elkmont AL, 434 119 F2
Elk Mound WI, 878 67 E4
Elko NV, 18297 30 B4
Elko Co. NV, 48818 30 C3
Elko New Market MN, 4110 67 D4
Elk Pt. SD, 1963 35 F1
Elk Rapids MI, 1642 69 F4
Elkridge MD, 15593 144 C2
Elk Ridge UT, 2436 39 E1
Elk River MN, 22974 66 C3
Elk Run Hts. IA, 1117 73 E4
Elkton KY, 2062 109 E2
Elkton MD, 15443 145 E1
Elkton MI, 808 76 C2
Elkton SD, 736 27 F3
Elkton TN, 578 119 F2
Elkton VA, 2726 102 C3
Elkview WV, 1222 101 F3
Elkville IL, 928 98 B4
El Lago TX, 2706 132 B3
Ellaville GA, 1812 129 D3
Ellenboro NC, 873 121 F1
Ellenboro WV, 363 101 F2
Ellendale DE, 381 145 F3
Ellendale MN, 691 72 C2
Ellendale ND, 1394 27 D1
Ellensburg WA, 18174 13 D4
Ellenton FL, 4275 266 B4
Ellenville NY, 4135 94 A3
Ellerbe NC, 1054 122 C2
Ellerslie MD, 572 102 C1
Ellettsville IN, 6378 99 F2
Ellicott NY, 2200 78 B4
Ellicott City MD, 65834 144 C2
Ellijay GA, 1619 120 C2
Ellington CT, 12921 150 A3
Ellington MO, 987 108 A2
Ellinwood KS, 2131 43 D3
Elliott Co. KY, 7852 101 D4
Ellis KS, 2062 42 C2
Ellis Co. KS, 28452 43 D2
Ellis Co. OK, 4151 50 C2
Ellis Co. TX, 149610 59 F3
Ellisport WA, 1200 262 A4
Elliston MT, 219 15 E4
Elliston VA, 902 112 B2
Ellisville MS, 4448 126 C4
Ellisville MO, 9133 256 A2
Elloree SC, 692 122 B4
Ellsworth IA, 531 72 C4
Ellsworth KS, 3120 43 E2
Ellsworth ME, 7741 83 D2
Ellsworth MI, 349 69 F3
Ellsworth MN, 463 27 F4
Ellsworth PA, 1027 92 A4
Ellsworth WI, 3284 67 E4
Ellsworth Co. KS, 6497 43 E3
Ellwood City PA, 7921 91 F3
Elma IA, 546 73 D3
Elma NY, 2571 78 B3
Elma WA, 3107 12 B4
Elm City NC, 1298 113 D4
Elm Creek NE, 901 35 D4
Elmendorf TX, 1488 61 D3
Elmer NJ, 1395 145 F1
Elm Grove WI, 5934 234 B2
Elmhurst IL, 44121 89 D1
Elmira NY, 29200 93 D1
El Mirage AZ, 31797 249 A1
Elmira Hts. NY, 4097 93 D1
Elm Mott TX, 1200 59 E4
Elmo UT, 418 39 F2
Elmont NY, 33198 148 C4
Elmont VA, 500 113 E1
El Monte CA, 113475 228 E2
Elmore MN, 663 72 C2
Elmore OH, 1410 90 C2
Elmore City OK, 697 51 E4
Elmore Co. AL, 79303 128 A2
Elmore Co. ID, 27038 22 B4
Elm Sprs. AR, 1535 106 C3
Elmville CT, 1300 150 B3
Elmwood IL, 2097 88 A3
Elmwood NE, 634 35 F4
Elmwood WI, 817 67 E4
Elmwood Park IL, 24883 203 D4
Elmwood Park NJ, 19403 240 C1
Elmwood Place OH, 2188 204 B2
Elnora IN, 640 99 E3
Elnora NY, 2700 94 B1
Elon NC, 9419 112 C4
Eloy AZ, 16631 54 C2
El Paso IL, 2810 88 B3
El Paso TX, 649121 56 C4
El Paso Co. CO, 622263 41 E2
El Paso Co. TX, 800647 56 C4
El Portal FL, 2325 233 B4
El Prado NM, 400 49 D1
El Reno OK, 16749 51 E3
El Rio CA, 7198 52 B2
El Rito NM, 808 48 C2
Elroy WI, 1442 74 A2
Elsa TX, 5660 63 E4
Elsah IL, 673 98 A2
Elsberry MO, 1934 98 A2
El Segundo CA, 16654 228 C3
Elsie MI, 966 76 A3
Elsinore UT, 847 39 E3
Elsmere DE, 6131 146 B4
Elsmere KY, 8451 100 B2
Elsmere NY, 3200 188 D3
El Sobrante CA, 12669 259 C1
Elton LA, 1128 133 E2
Elvaton MD, 3500 193 C5
Elverson PA, 1225 146 B2
Elwood IL, 2279 89 D2
Elwood IN, 8614 89 F4
Elwood KS, 1224 96 B1
Elwood NE, 707 34 C4
Elwood NJ, 1437 147 D4
Elwood UT, 1034 31 E3
Ely IA, 1776 87 E1
Ely MN, 3460 64 C2
Ely NV, 4255 38 B2
Elyria OH, 54533 91 D2
Elysburg PA, 2194 93 E3
Elysian MN, 652 72 C1
Emanuel Co. GA, 22598 129 F2
Emerado ND, 414 19 E2
Emerald Isle NC, 3655 115 D4
Emerson GA, 1470 120 C3
Emerson NE, 840 35 F2
Emerson NJ, 7401 148 B3
Emery SD, 447 27 E4
Emery UT, 288 39 E2
Emery Co. UT, 10976 39 F2
Emery Mills ME, 350 82 A4
Emeryville CA, 10080 259 C2
Emigsville PA, 2672 103 E1
Emily MN, 813 64 B4
Eminence KY, 2498 100 A4
Eminence MO, 600 107 F2
Emlenton PA, 625 92 A2
Emmaus PA, 11211 146 B1
Emmet AR, 518 117 D4
Emmet Co. IA, 10302 72 B3
Emmet Co. MI, 32694 70 B3
Emmetsburg IA, 3904 72 B3
Emmett ID, 6557 22 B4
Emmitsburg MD, 2814 103 D1
Emmonak AK, 762 154 B2
Emmons Co. ND, 3550 18 C4
Emmorton MD, 4000 145 D1
Emory TX, 1239 124 A1
Emory VA, 1251 111 F2
Empire CO, 282 41 D1
Empire LA, 993 134 C4
Empire NV, 217 29 E4
Empire City OK, 955 51 E4
Emporia KS, 24916 43 F3
Emporia VA, 5927 113 E3
Emporium PA, 2073 92 C2
Emsworth PA, 2449 250 A1
Encampment WY, 450 33 D3
Encinal TX, 559 60 C4
Encinitas CA, 59518 53 D4
Enderlin ND, 886 19 E4
Endicott NY, 13392 93 E1
Endicott WA, 289 13 F4
Endwell NY, 11446 93 E1
Energy IL, 1146 108 C1
Enfield CT, 45441 150 A2
Enfield IL, 596 99 D4
Enfield NH, 1540 81 E3
Enfield NC, 2532 113 E4
Enfield Ctr. NH, 600 81 E3
England AR, 2825 117 E2
Englewood CO, 30255 41 E1
Englewood FL, 14863 140 C4
Englewood NJ, 27147 148 B3
Englewood OH, 13465 100 B1
Englewood TN, 1532 120 C1
Englewood Beach FL, 1000 140 C4
Englewood Cliffs NJ, 5281 240 D1
English IN, 645 99 F4
Englishtown NJ, 1847 147 E2
Enhaut PA, 1007 218 C2
Enid OK, 49379 51 E1
Enigma GA, 1278 129 E4
Enka NC, 1500 121 E1
Ennis MT, 838 23 E2
Ennis TX, 18513 59 F3
Enoch UT, 5803 39 D4
Enochville NC, 2925 122 B1
Enola PA, 6111 218 A1
Enon OH, 2415 100 C1
Enoree SC, 665 121 F2
Enosburg Falls VT, 1329 81 D1
Ensley FL, 20602 135 F2
Ensor KY, 500 109 E1
Enterprise AL, 26562 128 B4
Enterprise KS, 855 43 F2
Enterprise MS, 526 127 D3
Enterprise OR, 1940 22 A2
Enterprise UT, 605 38 C4
Enterprise WV, 961 102 A2
Entiat WA, 1112 13 D3
Enumclaw WA, 10669 12 C3
Ephraim UT, 6135 39 E2
Ephrata PA, 13394 146 A2
Ephrata WA, 7664 13 E3
Epping NH, 1681 81 F4
Epps LA, 854 125 F2
Epworth IA, 1860 73 F4
Epworth Hts. OH, 3300 204 C1
Equality IL, 595 109 D1
Erath LA, 2114 133 F3
Erath Co. TX, 37890 59 D3
Erda UT, 4642 31 E4
Erial NJ, 6200 146 C4
Erick OK, 1052 50 C3
Erie CO, 18135 209 B1
Erie IL, 1602 88 A2
Erie KS, 1150 106 A1
Erie PA, 101786 92 A1
Erie Co. NY, 919040 78 B4
Erie Co. OH, 77079 91 D2
Erie Co. PA, 280566 92 A1
Erin TN, 1324 109 E3
Erlanger KY, 18082 100 B2
Erwin NC, 4405 123 D1
Erwin TN, 6097 111 E4
Erwinville LA, 2192 134 A2
Escalante UT, 797 39 E4
Escalon CA, 7132 36 C4
Escambia Co. AL, 38319 136 A1
Escambia Co. FL, 297619 135 F1
Escanaba MI, 12616 69 D2
Escatawpa MS, 3722 195 C1
Escobares TX, 1188 63 D4
Escondido CA, 143911 53 D4
Esko MN, 1869 64 C4
Eskridge KS, 534 43 F2
Esmeralda Co. NV, 783 37 F4
Espanola NM, 10224 49 D2
Espanong NJ, 2700 148 A3
Esparto CA, 3108 36 B2
Espy PA, 1642 93 E3
Essex CT, 6783 149 E2
Essex IA, 798 86 A3
Essex MD, 39262 144 C2
Essex MA, 1471 151 F1
Essex MO, 472 108 B2
Essex Co. MA, 743159 151 F1
Essex Co. NJ, 783969 148 A3
Essex Co. NY, 39370 80 C3
Essex Co. VT, 6306 81 F1
Essex Co. VA, 11151 103 E4
Essex Fells NJ, 2113 240 A2
Essex Jct. VT, 9271 81 D2
Essexville MI, 3478 76 B2
Estacada OR, 2695 20 C2
Estancia NM, 1655 49 D4
Estelle LA, 16377 239 C2
Estelline SD, 768 27 F3
Estell Manor NJ, 1735 104 C3
Ester AK, 2422 154 C2
Estero FL, 22612 142 C1
Estes Park CO, 5858 33 E4
Estherville IA, 6360 72 B2
Estherwood LA, 889 133 E2
Estill SC, 2040 130 B2
Estill Co. KY, 14672 110 C1
Estill Sprs. TN, 2055 120 A1
Estral Beach MI, 418 90 C1
Ethan SD, 331 27 E4
Ethel MS, 418 126 C1
Ethete WY, 1553 32 B1
Ethridge TN, 465 119 E1
Etna CA, 737 28 B3
Etna PA, 3451 250 C1
Etna Green IN, 586 89 F2
Etowah NC, 6944 121 E1
Etowah TN, 3490 120 C1
Etowah Co. AL, 104430 120 A3
Ettrick VA, 6682 113 E2
Ettrick WI, 524 73 F1
Eubank KY, 319 110 B2
Euclid OH, 48920 91 E2
Eudora AR, 2269 126 A1
Eudora KS, 6136 96 B3
Eufaula AL, 13137 128 B3
Eufaula OK, 2813 116 A1
Eugene OR, 156185 20 B4
Euharlee GA, 4136 120 B3
Euless TX, 51277 207 C2
Eunice LA, 10398 133 E2
Eunice NM, 2922 57 F3
Eupora MS, 2197 118 C4
Eureka CA, 27191 28 A4
Eureka IL, 5295 88 B3
Eureka KS, 2633 43 F4
Eureka MO, 10189 98 A3
Eureka MT, 1037 14 C1
Eureka NV, 610 38 A1
Eureka SD, 868 27 D1
Eureka UT, 669 39 E1
Eureka Co. NV, 1987 30 B4
Eureka Mill SC, 1476 122 A2
Eureka Sprs. AR, 2073 106 C3
Eustace TX, 991 59 F3
Eustis FL, 18558 140 C1
Eustis NE, 401 34 C4
Eutaw AL, 2934 127 E2
Eva AL, 519 119 F3
Evadale TX, 1483 132 C2
Evangeline Par. LA, 33984 133 E1
Evans CO, 18537 33 E4
Evans GA, 29011 121 F4
Evans WV, 750 101 E3
Evans City PA, 1833 92 A3
Evans Co. GA, 11000 130 B3
Evansdale IA, 4751 73 E4
Evans Mills NY, 621 79 E1
Evanston IL, 74486 89 D1
Evanston WY, 12359 31 F3
Evansville IL, 701 98 B4
Evansville IN, 117429 99 D4
Evansville MN, 612 66 A2
Evansville WI, 5012 74 B4
Evansville WY, 2544 33 D1
Evaro MT, 322 15 D4
Evart MI, 1903 75 F1
Evarts KY, 962 111 D2
Eveleth MN, 3718 64 C3
Evendale OH, 2767 204 B1
Evening Shade AR, 432 107 F4
Everett MA, 41667 197 C1
Everett PA, 1834 102 C1
Everett WA, 103019 12 C2
Everglades City FL, 479 143 D2
Evergreen AL, 3944 127 F4
Evergreen CO, 9038 41 D1
Evergreen MT, 7616 15 D2
Evergreen Park IL, 19852 203 D5
Everly IA, 603 72 A3
Everman TX, 6108 207 B3
Everson PA, 793 92 A4
Everson WA, 2481 12 C1
Evesboro NJ, 2400 147 D3
Ewa Beach HI, 14955 152 A3
Ewa Villages HI, 6108 152 A3
Ewing NE, 387 35 E2
Ewing NJ, 35790 147 D2

Erie PA
LAKE ERIE
Presque Isle Lighthouse
Presque Isle State Park
Lawrence Park
Perry Monument
Warner Theatre
Wesleyville
Erie Maritime Mus./U.S. Brig Niagara
Mus. of Erie Co. History
Presque Isle Bay
Waldameer Park & Water World
Watson-Curtze Mansion
Gannon Univ.
Erie
Mercyhurst Univ.
Glenwood Pk.
Belle Valley
Erie Intl. Arpt.-Tom Ridge Field
Erie Zoo
Presque Isle Downs and Casino
L. Erie Coll. of Osteopathic Med.
Asbury Woods Nature Ctr.
Kearsarge
Millcreek Mall
Weis Library
Five Points

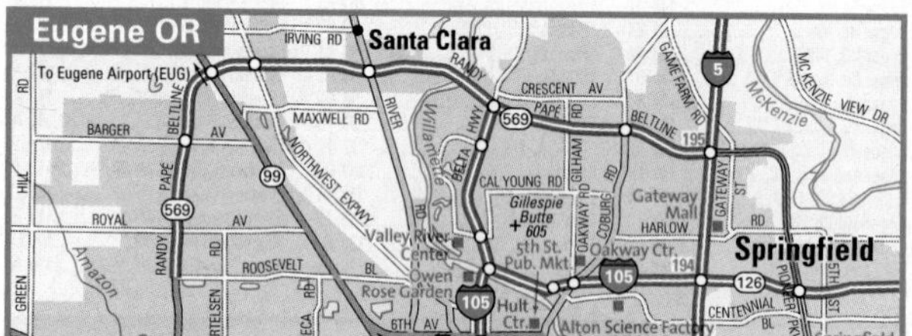
Eugene OR
To Eugene Airport (EUG)
Santa Clara
Gateway Mall
Valley River Center
Owen Rose Garden
Springfield
Alton Science Factory
Mus. of Nat. & Cult. Hist.
Springfield Museum
Eugene
Historical Museum
Westmoreland Park
New Hope Christian College
UNIV. OF OREGON
Civic Stadium
Hendricks Park
Amazon Park
Mount Pisgah Arboretum
Morse Ranch Park
Glenwood

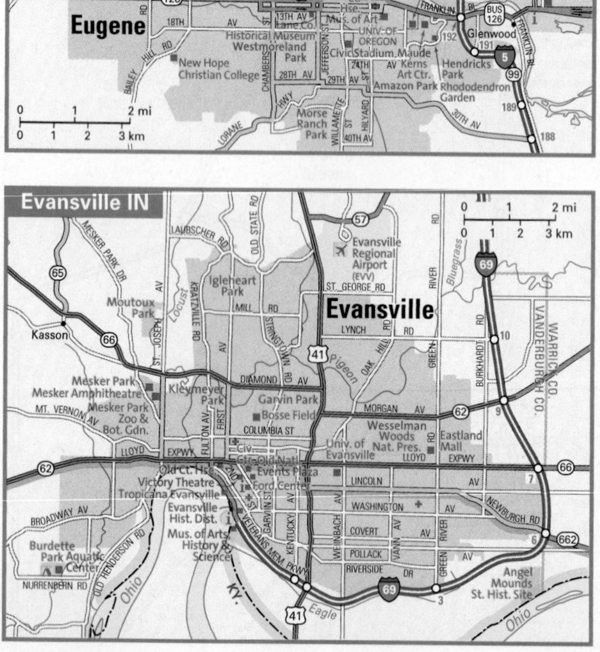
Evansville IN
Evansville Regional Airport (EVV)
Igleheart Park
Evansville
Moutoux Park
Kasson
Mesker Park
Mesker Amphitheatre
Mesker Park Zoo & Bot. Gdn.
Kleymeyer Park
Garvin Park
Bosse Field
Wesselman Woods Nat. Pres.
Univ. of Evansville
Eastland Mall
Old Ct. Hse.
Victory Theatre
Tropicana Evansville
Evansville Hist. Dist.
Mus. of Arts, History & Science
Burdette Park Aquatic Center
Angel Mounds St. Hist. Site
Ohio

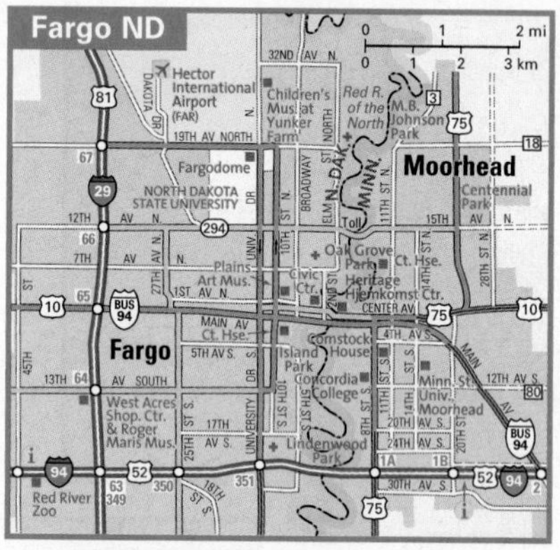
Fargo ND
Hector International Airport (FAR)
Children's Mus. at Yunker Farm
Red R. of the North
M.B. Johnson Park
Moorhead
Fargodome
NORTH DAKOTA STATE UNIVERSITY
Centennial Park
Plains Art Mus.
Oak Grove Park
Heritage Hjemkomst Ctr.
Fargo
Island Park
Comstock House
Concordia College
Minn. St. Univ. Moorhead
West Acres Shop. Ctr. & Roger Maris Mus.
Lindenwood Park
Red River Zoo

Fayetteville AR
Springdale
Shiloh Mus.
Arts Ctr. of the Ozarks
Arkansas & Missouri R.R.
Tontitown
Randal Tyson Park
Lake Fayetteville Park
Northwest Arkansas Mall
Botanical Gdn. of the Ozarks
Johnson
Lake Fayetteville
Ark. Music Pavilion
Fayetteville
County Fairgrounds
UNIV. OF ARKANSAS
Razorback Stad.
Bud Walton Arena
Hist. Dist.
Walton Arts Ctr.
Fayetteville Natl. Cem.
Combs Park
Lake Sequoyah
Farmington

213
Ewing–Foley

Entries in **bold black** indicate counties or parishes.
Entries in **bold color** indicate cities with detailed inset maps.

Ewing VA, 439 111 D3
Excel AL, 723 127 F4
Excelsior Sprs. MO, 11084 96 C2
Exeter CA, 10334 45 D3
Exeter MO, 772 106 C3
Exeter NE, 591 35 E4
Exeter NH, 9242 82 A4
Exeter PA, 5652 261 C1
Exeter RI, 6425 150 C4
Exira IA, 840 86 B2
Exmore VA, 1460 114 B3
Experiment GA, 2894 129 D1
Exton PA, 4842 146 B3
Eyota MN, 1977 73 E1

F

Fabens TX, 8257 56 C4
Factoryville PA, 1158 93 F2
Fairacres NM, 824 56 B3
Fairbank IA, 1113 73 E4
Fairbanks AK, 31535 154 C2
Fairbanks FL, 750 138 C3
Fairbanks ME, 700 82 B1
Fair Bluff NC, 951 123 D3
Fairborn OH, 32352 100 C1
Fairburn GA, 12950 120 C4
Fairbury IL, 3757 88 C3
Fairbury NE, 3942 43 E1
Fairchance PA, 1975 102 B1
Fairchild WI, 550 67 F4
Fairchilds TX, 763 132 A4
Fairfax CA, 7441 36 B3
Fairfax DE, 2300 274 E1
Fairfax IA, 2123 87 E1
Fairfax MN, 1235 66 B4
Fairfax MO, 638 86 A4
Fairfax OH, 1699 204 C2
Fairfax OK, 1380 51 F1
Fairfax SC, 2025 130 B1
Fairfax VT, 3765 81 D1
Fairfax VA, 22565 144 A3
Fairfax Co. VA, 1081726 144 A3
Fairfield AL, 11117 119 F4
Fairfield CA, 105321 36 B3
Fairfield CT, 59404 149 D2
Fairfield ID, 416 22 C4
Fairfield IL, 5154 99 D4
Fairfield IA, 9464 87 E3
Fairfield ME, 2638 82 C2
Fairfield MT, 708 15 E3
Fairfield NE, 387 35 E4
Fairfield NJ, 7466 240 A1
Fairfield OH, 42510 100 B2
Fairfield TX, 2951 59 F4
Fairfield WA, 612 14 B3
Fairfield Bay AR, 2338 117 E1
Fairfield Co. CT, 916829 149 D2
Fairfield Co. OH, 146156 101 D1
Fairfield Co. SC, 23956 122 A3
Fairfield Glade TN, 6989 110 B4
Fairgrove MI, 563 76 B2
Fair Grove MO, 1393 107 D1
Fairhaven MA, 16112 151 D3
Fair Haven MI, 1500 76 C4
Fair Haven NJ, 6121 147 E2
Fair Haven NY, 745 79 D3
Fair Haven VT, 2269 81 D3
Fairhope AL, 15326 135 E2
Fairland IN, 315 99 F1
Fairland MD, 23681 144 B2
Fairland OK, 1057 106 B2
Fair Lawn NJ, 32457 148 B3
Fairlawn OH, 7437 188 A1
Fairlawn VA, 2367 112 A2
Fairlea WV, 1747 112 A1
Fairless Hills PA, 8466 147 D2
Fairmead CA, 1447 44 C2
Fairmont MN, 10666 72 B2
Fairmont NE, 560 35 E4
Fairmont NC, 2663 123 D3
Fairmont WV, 18704 102 A2
Fairmont City IL, 2635 256 C2
Fairmount GA, 720 120 C3
Fairmount IL, 642 99 D1
Fairmount IN, 2954 89 F4
Fairmount MD, 457 103 F4
Fairmount NY, 10224 79 D3
Fairmount ND, 367 27 F1
Fairmount TN, 2825 120 B1
Fairmount Hts. MD, 1494 270 E3
Fair Oaks CA, 30912 255 C1
Fair Oaks GA, 8225 120 C4
Fair Oaks Ranch TX, 5986 61 D2
Fair Plain MI, 7631 89 E1
Fairplains NC, 2120 111 F3
Fairplay CO, 679 41 D2
Fairport NY, 5353 78 C3
Fairport Harbor OH, 3109 91 E1
Fairton NJ, 1264 145 F1
Fairview AL, 446 119 F3
Fairview GA, 6769 120 B2
Fairview MI, 600 70 C4
Fairview MT, 840 17 F2
Fairview NJ, 13835 148 B3
Fairview NC, 2678 121 E1
Fairview NC, 3300 122 B1
Fairview OK, 2579 51 D2
Fairview OR, 8920 20 C2
Fairview PA, 198 91 F1
Fairview TN, 7720 109 E4
Fairview TX, 7248 59 F2
Fairview UT, 1247 39 E1
Fairview WV, 408 102 A1
Fairview WY, 275 31 F1
Fairview Hts. IL, 17078 98 B3
Fairview Park IN, 1386 99 E1
Fairview Park OH, 16826 204 D2
Fairview Shores FL, 10239 246 C1
Fairway KS, 3882 224 B3
Faison NC, 961 123 E1
Faith NC, 807 122 B1
Faith SD, 421 26 B2
Falconer NY, 2420 92 B1
Falcon Hts. MN, 5321 235 C2
Falfurrias TX, 4981 63 E3
Falkville AL, 1279 119 F3
Fall Branch TN, 1291 111 E3
Fallbrook CA, 30534 53 D3
Fall City WA, 1993 12 C3
Fall Creek WI, 1315 67 F4
Falling Waters WV, 876 103 D1
Fallon NV, 8606 37 E1
Fallon Co. MT, 2890 17 F4
Fall River MA, 88857 151 D3
Fall River WI, 1712 74 B2
Fall River Co. SD, 7094 33 F1
Fall River Mills CA, 573 29 D3
Falls Church VA, 12332 144 B3
Falls City NE, 4325 86 A4
Falls City OR, 947 20 B2
Falls City TX, 611 61 E3
Falls Co. TX, 17866 59 F4
Falls Creek PA, 1037 92 B3
Fallston MD, 8958 144 C1
Fallston NC, 607 122 A1
Falmouth KY, 2169 100 B3
Falmouth MA, 3799 151 E4
Falmouth VA, 4274 103 D4
Falmouth Foreside ME, 1511 82 B3
Fancy Farm KY, 458 108 C2
Fannett TX, 2252 132 C3
Fannin Co. GA, 23682 120 C2
Fannin Co. TX, 33915 59 F1
Fanning Sprs. FL, 764 138 B3
Fanwood NJ, 7318 147 E1
Fargo ND, 105549 19 F4
Far Hills NJ, 919 148 A4
Faribault MN, 23352 73 D1
Faribault Co. MN, 14553 72 C2
Farley IA, 1537 73 F4
Farmer City IL, 2037 88 C4
Farmers Branch TX, 28616 207 D1
Farmersburg IN, 1118 99 E2
Farmers Mills NY, 800 148 C1
Farmersville CA, 10588 45 D3
Farmersville IL, 724 98 B2
Farmersville OH, 1009 100 B1
Farmersville PA, 991 189 B1
Farmersville TX, 3301 59 F2
Farmerville LA, 3860 125 E2
Farmingdale ME, 1970 82 C2
Farmingdale NJ, 1329 147 E2
Farmingdale NY, 8189 148 C4
Farmington AR, 5974 106 C4
Farmington CT, 24941 94 C3
Farmington IL, 2448 88 A3
Farmington IA, 664 87 E3
Farmington ME, 4288 82 B1
Farmington MI, 10372 210 A2
Farmington MN, 21086 67 D4
Farmington MS, 2186 119 D2
Farmington MO, 16240 108 A1
Farmington NH, 3885 81 F4
Farmington NM, 45877 48 B1
Farmington UT, 18275 31 E3
Farmington WV, 375 102 A1
Farmington Hills MI, 79740 210 A2
Farmingville NY, 15481 149 D3
Farmland IN, 1333 90 A4
Farmville NC, 4654 115 C2
Farmville VA, 8216 113 D2
Farragut IA, 485 86 A3
Farragut TN, 20676 110 C4
Farrell PA, 5111 91 F2
Farr West UT, 5928 244 A1
Farson WY, 313 32 A2
Farwell MI, 871 76 A2
Farwell TX, 1363 49 F4
Faulk Co. SD, 2364 27 D2
Faulkner Co. AR, 113237 117 E1
Faulkton SD, 736 27 D2
Fauquier Co. VA, 65203 144 A4
Favoretta FL, 650 139 E4
Fayette AL, 4619 119 E4
Fayette IA, 1338 73 E3
Fayette MS, 1614 126 A4
Fayette MO, 2688 97 D2
Fayette OH, 1283 90 B2
Fayette Co. AL, 17241 119 E4
Fayette Co. GA, 106567 120 C4
Fayette Co. IL, 22140 98 C2
Fayette Co. IN, 24277 100 A1
Fayette Co. IA, 20880 73 E4
Fayette Co. KY, 295803 100 B4
Fayette Co. OH, 29030 100 C1
Fayette Co. PA, 136606 102 B1
Fayette Co. TN, 38413 118 C1
Fayette Co. TX, 24554 61 E2
Fayette Co. WV, 46039 101 F4
Fayetteville AR, 73580 106 C4
Fayetteville GA, 15945 120 C4
Fayetteville NY, 4373 79 E3
Fayetteville NC, 200564 123 D2
Fayetteville PA, 3128 103 D1
Fayetteville TN, 6827 119 F1
Fayetteville WV, 2892 101 F4
Fearrington Vil. NC, 2339 112 C4
Feasterville PA, 3074 248 D1
Federal Hts. CO, 11467 209 B2
Federalsburg MD, 2739 145 E4
Federal Way WA, 89306 12 C3
Felicity OH, 818 100 C3
Felida WA, 7385 20 C1
Fellowship NJ, 4900 147 D3
Fellsmere FL, 5197 141 E3
Felton CA, 4057 236 D1
Felton DE, 1298 145 E3
Fennimore WI, 2497 73 F3
Fennville MI, 1398 75 E4
Fenton MI, 11756 76 B4
Fenton MO, 4022 256 A3
Fentress Co. TN, 17959 110 B3
Fenwick Island DE, 379 114 C1
Ferdinand IN, 2157 99 E4
Fergus Co. MT, 11586 16 B3
Fergus Falls MN, 13138 19 F4
Ferguson KY, 924 110 B2
Ferguson MO, 21203 256 B1
Fernandina Beach FL, 11487 139 D1
Fernan Lake Vil. ID, 186 14 B3
Ferndale CA, 1371 28 A4
Ferndale MD, 16746 193 C4
Ferndale MI, 19900 210 C2
Ferndale PA, 1636 146 C1
Ferndale WA, 11415 12 C1
Fernley NV, 19368 37 E1
Fern Park FL, 7704 246 C1
Ferrell NJ, 1100 146 C4
Ferrellsburg WV, 500 101 E4
Ferrelview MO, 451 96 B2
Ferriday LA, 3511 125 F4
Ferris TX, 2436 59 F3
Ferron UT, 1626 39 E2
Ferrum VA, 2043 112 B2
Ferry Co. WA, 7551 13 F2
Ferry Pass FL, 28921 135 F2
Ferrysburg MI, 2892 75 E3
Fertile MN, 842 19 F3
Fessenden ND, 479 18 C3
Festus MO, 11602 98 A4
Fieldale VA, 879 112 B3
Fielding UT, 455 31 E2
Fieldsboro NJ, 540 147 D2
Fife WA, 9173 262 B5
Fife Lake MI, 443 69 F4
Filer ID, 2508 30 C1
Fillmore CA, 15002 52 B2
Fillmore IN, 533 99 E1
Fillmore UT, 2435 39 D2
Fillmore Co. MN, 20866 73 E2
Fillmore Co. NE, 5890 35 E4
Fincastle KY, 817 230 F1
Fincastle VA, 353 112 B1
Findlay IL, 683 98 C1
Findlay OH, 41202 90 C3
Finley ND, 445 19 E3
Finley WA, 6012 21 E1
Finney Co. KS, 36776 42 B3
Finneytown OH, 12741 204 B2
Fircrest WA, 6497 262 A5
Firebaugh CA, 7549 44 C2
Firth ID, 477 23 E4
Firth NE, 590 35 F4
Firthcliffe NY, 4949 148 B1
Fisher IL, 1881 88 C4
Fisher Co. TX, 3974 58 B2
Fishers IN, 76794 99 F1
Fishersville VA, 7462 102 C4
Fishkill NY, 2171 148 B1
Fishkill Plains NY, 900 148 B1
Fiskdale MA, 2583 150 B2
Fitchburg MA, 40318 95 D1
Fitchburg WI, 25260 74 B3
Fitchville CT, 750 149 F1
Fitzgerald GA, 9053 129 E4
Fitzwilliam NH, 2396 95 D1
Five Corners MA, 2100 151 D2
Flagler CO, 561 41 F2
Flagler Beach FL, 4484 139 E4
Flagler Co. FL, 95696 139 D3
Flagstaff AZ, 65870 47 E3
Flagtown NJ, 3000 147 D1
Flanagan IL, 1110 88 C3
Flanders NY, 4472 149 E3
Flanders (E. Lyme) CT, 18459 149 F2
Flandreau SD, 2341 27 F3
Flasher ND, 232 18 B4
Flathead Co. MT, 90928 14 C2
Flat Lick KY, 960 110 C2
Flatonia TX, 1383 61 E2
Flat Rock MI, 9878 90 C1
Flat Rock NC, 1690 112 A3
Flat Rock NC, 3114 121 E1
Flatwoods KY, 7423 101 D3
Flatwoods WV, 277 102 A3
Fleetwood PA, 4085 146 B1
Fleming CO, 408 34 A4
Fleming Co. KY, 14348 100 C4
Fleming-Neon KY, 770 111 E2
Flemingsburg KY, 2658 100 C3
Flemington NJ, 4581 147 D1
Flemington PA, 1330 93 D3
Fletcher NC, 7187 121 E1
Fletcher OK, 1177 51 D4
Flint MI, 102434 76 B3
Flint TX, 1200 124 A3
Flippin AR, 1355 107 E3
Flohrville MD, 950 144 B1
Flomaton AL, 1440 135 F1
Floodwood MN, 528 64 C4
Flora IL, 5070 98 C3
Flora IN, 2036 89 E4
Flora MS, 1886 126 B2
Florala AL, 1980 136 B1
Floral City FL, 5217 140 C1
Floral Park NY, 15863 241 G3
Flora Vista NM, 2191 48 B1
Flordell Hills MO, 822 256 C1
Florence AL, 39319 119 E2
Florence AZ, 25536 54 C2
Florence CA, 60197 228 D3
Florence CO, 3881 41 E3
Florence KS, 465 43 F3
Florence KY, 29951 100 B2
Florence MS, 4141 126 B3
Florence MT, 765 15 D4
Florence NJ, 4426 147 D2
Florence OR, 8466 20 B4
Florence SC, 37056 122 C3
Florence SD, 374 27 E2
Florence TX, 1136 61 E1
Florence WI, 592 68 C2
Florence Co. SC, 136885 122 C3
Florence Co. WI, 4423 68 C2
Floresville TX, 6448 61 D3
Florham Park NJ, 11696 148 A4
Florida NY, 2833 148 A2
Florida City FL, 11245 143 E3
Florien LA, 633 125 D4
Florin CA, 47513 36 C3
Florissant MO, 52158 98 A3
Flourtown PA, 4538 248 B1
Flovilla GA, 653 129 D1
Flower Hill NY, 4665 241 G2
Flower Mound TX, 64669 207 C1
Flowery Branch GA, 5679 121 D3
Flowood MS, 7823 126 B3
Floyd VA, 425 112 B2
Floydada TX, 3038 58 B1
Floyd Co. GA, 96317 120 B3
Floyd Co. IN, 74578 99 F4
Floyd Co. IA, 16303 73 D3
Floyd Co. KY, 39451 111 E1
Floyd Co. TX, 6446 50 B4
Floyd Co. VA, 15279 112 A2
Flushing MI, 8389 76 B3
Flushing OH, 879 91 F4
Fluvanna Co. VA, 25691 113 D1
Flying Hills PA, 2568 146 A2
Foard Co. TX, 1336 58 C1
Fogelsville PA, 950 146 B1
Folcroft PA, 6606 248 B4
Foley AL, 14618 135 E2
Foley MN, 2603 66 C2

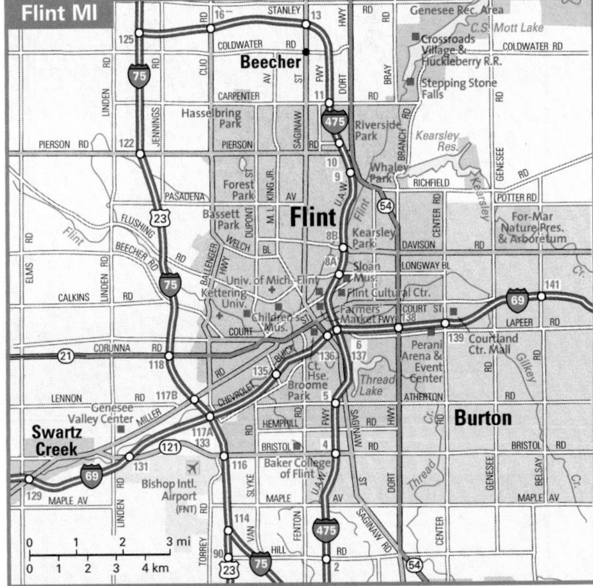
Flint MI
Beecher
Flint
Burton
Swartz Creek
Bishop Intl. Airport (FNT)

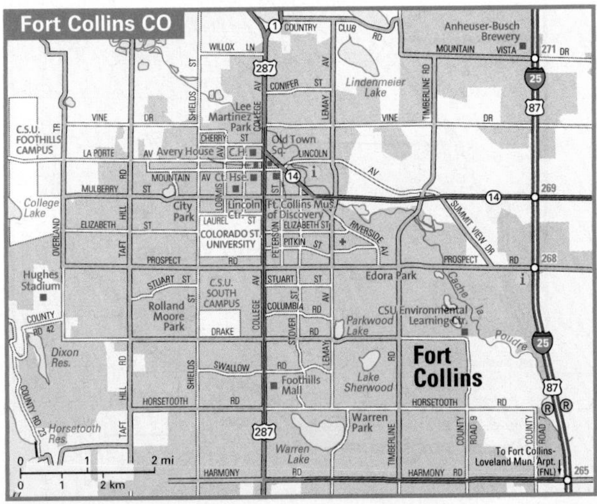
Fort Collins CO
Fort Collins
C.S.U. Foothills Campus
Colorado State University
Horsetooth Res.

Figures after entries indicate population, page number, and grid reference.

Fort Myers FL

Frankfort KY

Fresno CA

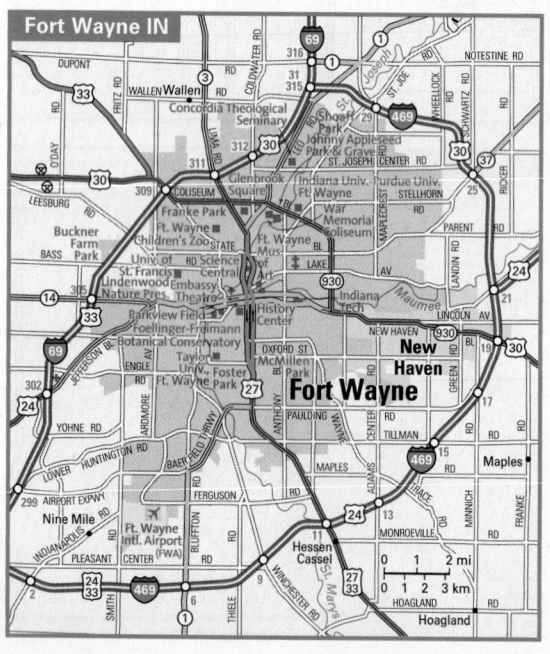

Fort Wayne IN

Entries in **bold black** indicate counties or parishes.
Entries in **bold color** indicate cities with detailed inset maps.

Franklin Co. ME, 30768 82 B1
Franklin Co. MA, 71372 150 A1
Franklin Co. MS, 8118 126 A4
Franklin Co. MO, 101492 97 F3
Franklin Co. NE, 3225 43 D1
Franklin Co. NY, 51599 80 C2
Franklin Co. NC, 60619 113 D4
Franklin Co. OH, 1163414 101 D1
Franklin Co. PA, 149618 103 D1
Franklin Co. TN, 41052 120 A1
Franklin Co. TX, 10605 124 B1
Franklin Co. VT, 47746 81 D1
Franklin Co. VA, 56159 112 B2
Franklin Co. WA, 78163 13 F4
Franklin Furnace OH, 1660 101 D3
Franklin Grove IL, 1021 88 B1
Franklin Par. LA, 20767 125 F2
Franklin Park IL, 18333 203 C4
Franklin Park PA, 13470 92 A3
Franklin Sprs. GA, 952 121 E3
Franklin Square NY, 29320 241 G4
Franklinton LA, 3857 134 B1
Franklinton NC, 2023 113 D4
Franklinville NJ, 1500 145 F1
Franklinville NY, 1740 78 B4
Franklinville NC, 1164 112 B4
Frankston TX, 1229 124 A3
Frankton IN, 1862 89 F4
Frannie WY, 157 24 B2
Fraser CO, 1224 41 D1
Fraser MI, 14480 210 D2
Frazee MN, 1350 19 F4
Frazer MT, 362 17 E2
Frazeysburg OH, 1326 91 D4
Frazier Park CA, 2691 52 B1
Frederic WI, 1137 67 E2
Frederica DE, 774 145 E3
Frederick CO, 8679 41 E1
Frederick MD, 65239 144 A1
Frederick OK, 3940 51 D4
Frederick SD, 199 27 D1
Frederick Co. MD, 233385 144 A1
Frederick Co. VA, 78305 102 C2
Fredericksburg IA, 931 73 E3
Fredericksburg PA, 1357 92 A2
Fredericksburg PA, 987 93 E4
Fredericksburg TX, 10530 61 D2
Fredericksburg VA, 24286 103 D4
Fredericktown MO, 3985 108 A1
Fredericktown OH, 2493 91 D4
Fredonia AZ, 1314 47 D1
Fredonia KS, 2482 106 A1
Fredonia KY, 401 109 D2
Fredonia NY, 11230 78 A4
Fredonia PA, 502 91 F2
Fredonia WI, 2160 74 C2
Freeborn Co. MN, 31255 72 C2
Freeburg IL, 4354 98 B3
Freeburg PA, 575 93 D3
Freedom CA, 3070 44 B2
Freedom WI, 1500 74 C1
Freehold NJ, 12052 147 E2
Freeland MI, 6969 76 B2
Freeland PA, 3531 93 E3
Freeland WA, 2045 262 A1
Freeman MO, 482 96 B3
Freeman SD, 1306 27 E4
Freemansburg PA, 2636 146 C1
Freeport FL, 1787 136 B2
Freeport IL, 25638 74 B4
Freeport ME, 1485 82 B3
Freeport NY, 42860 147 F1
Freeport PA, 1813 92 A3
Freeport TX, 12049 133 E4
Freer TX, 2818 63 E2
Freestone Co. TX, 19816 59 F4
Freetown IN, 385 99 F2
Freetown NY, 2400 149 F3
Freeville NY, 520 79 D4
Freewood Acres NJ, 3100 147 E2
Fremont CA, 214089 36 B4
Fremont IN, 2138 90 A1
Fremont IA, 743 87 E2
Fremont MI, 4081 75 F2
Fremont NE, 26397 35 F3
Fremont NH, 4283 81 F4
Fremont NC, 1255 123 E1
Fremont OH, 16734 90 C2
Fremont WI, 679 74 B1
Fremont Co. CO, 46824 41 D3
Fremont Co. ID, 13242 23 F3
Fremont Co. IA, 7441 86 A3
Fremont Co. WY, 40123 32 C1
Fremont Hills MO, 826 107 D2
Frenchburg KY, 486 100 C4
French Camp CA, 3376 36 C4
French Lick IN, 1807 99 F3
French Settlement LA, 1116 134 A2
Frenchtown MT, 1825 15 D4
Frenchtown NJ, 1373 146 C1
Frenchville ME, 1225 85 D1
Fresno CA, 494665 44 C3
Fresno TX, 19069 220 B4
Fresno Co. CA, 930450 37 E4
Frewsburg NY, 1906 92 B1
Friant CA, 509 44 C2
Friars Pt. MS, 1200 118 A3
Friday Harbor WA, 2162 12 B2
Fridley MN, 27208 67 D3
Friedens PA, 1523 102 C1
Friedensburg PA, 858 146 A1
Friend NE, 1027 35 E4
Friendly MD, 9250 144 B4
Friendship ME, 1204 82 C3
Friendship NY, 1218 92 C1
Friendship TN, 668 108 C4
Friendship WI, 725 74 A1
Friendsville MD, 491 102 B1
Friendsville TN, 913 110 C4
Friendswood TX, 35805 132 B4
Fries VA, 484 112 A3
Frio Co. TX, 17217 60 C3
Friona TX, 4123 49 F4
Frisco CO, 2683 41 D1
Frisco TX, 116989 59 F2
Frisco City AL, 1309 127 F4
Fritch TX, 2117 50 B2
Froid MT, 185 17 F2
Fromberg MT, 438 24 B2
Frontenac FL, 1900 232 A1
Frontenac KS, 3437 106 B1
Frontenac MO, 3482 256 B2
Frontier ND, 214 19 F4
Frontier Co. NE, 2756 34 C4
Fronton TX, 180 63 D4
Front Royal VA, 14440 102 C3
Frost TX, 643 59 F3
Frostburg MD, 9002 102 C1
Frostproof FL, 2992 141 D3
Fruita CO, 12646 40 B2
Fruit Cove FL, 29362 139 D2
Fruit Hts. UT, 4701 31 E3
Fruit Hill OH, 3755 204 C3
Fruitland ID, 4684 22 A4
Fruitland IA, 977 87 F2
Fruitland MD, 4866 103 F4
Fruitland NM, 650 48 B1
Fruitland Park FL, 4078 140 C1
Fruitport MI, 1093 75 E3
Fruitville FL, 13224 266 C5
Fryeburg ME, 1631 81 F3
Fulda MN, 1318 72 A2
Fullerton CA, 135161 52 C3
Fullerton MD, 10100 193 D2
Fullerton NE, 1307 35 E3
Fulshear TX, 1134 132 A3
Fulton IL, 3481 88 A1
Fulton KY, 2445 108 C3
Fulton MD, 2049 144 B2
Fulton MS, 3961 119 D3
Fulton MO, 12790 97 E3
Fulton NY, 11896 79 D3
Fulton TX, 1358 61 E4
Fulton Co. AR, 12245 107 F3
Fulton Co. GA, 920581 120 C3
Fulton Co. IL, 37069 88 A4
Fulton Co. IN, 20836 89 F3
Fulton Co. KY, 6813 108 C3
Fulton Co. NY, 55531 79 F3
Fulton Co. OH, 42698 90 B2
Fulton Co. PA, 14845 103 D1
Fultondale AL, 8380 119 F4
Fultonville NY, 784 79 F3
Fuquay-Varina NC, 17937 123 D1
Furnas Co. NE, 4959 42 C1
Fyffe AL, 1018 120 A3

G

Gabbs NV, 269 37 F2
Gackle ND, 310 19 D4
Gadsden AL, 36856 120 A3
Gadsden AZ, 678 53 F4
Gadsden TN, 470 108 C4
Gadsden Co. FL, 46389 137 D2
Gaffney SC, 12414 121 F2
Gage Co. NE, 22311 35 F4
Gahanna OH, 33248 101 D1
Gail TX, 231 58 B2
Gainesboro TN, 962 110 A3
Gaines Co. TX, 17526 57 F2
Gainesville FL, 124354 138 C3
Gainesville GA, 33804 121 D3
Gainesville MO, 773 107 E3
Gainesville TX, 16002 59 E1
Gainesville VA, 11481 144 A3
Gaithersburg MD, 59933 144 B2
Galatia IL, 933 108 C1
Galax VA, 7042 112 A3
Galena AK, 470 154 C2
Galena IL, 3429 74 A4
Galena IN, 1818 99 F4
Galena KS, 3085 106 B2
Galena MO, 440 107 D2
Galena Park TX, 10887 220 C3
Galesburg IL, 32195 88 A3
Galesburg MI, 2009 75 F4
Gales Ferry CT, 1162 149 F1
Galesville WI, 1481 73 F1
Galeton PA, 1149 92 C1
Galeville NY, 4617 265 A1
Galien MI, 549 89 E1
Galilee RI, 700 150 C4
Galion OH, 10512 91 D3
Galisteo NM, 253 49 D3
Gallatin MO, 1786 96 C1
Gallatin TN, 30278 109 F3
Gallatin Co. IL, 5589 109 D1
Gallatin Co. KY, 8589 100 B3
Gallatin Co. MT, 89513 23 F2
Gallatin Gateway MT, 856 23 F1
Gallaway TN, 680 118 B1
Gallia Co. OH, 30934 101 E3
Galliano LA, 7676 134 B4
Gallipolis OH, 3641 101 E3
Gallitzin PA, 1668 92 B4
Gallup NM, 21678 48 A3
Galt CA, 23647 36 C3
Galva IL, 2589 88 A2
Galva KS, 870 43 E3
Galveston IN, 1311 89 F3
Galveston KY, 450 111 E1
Galveston TX, 47743 132 B4
Galveston Co. TX, 291309 132 B4
Gamaliel KY, 376 110 A3
Gambell AK, 681 154 A2
Gamber MD, 1000 144 B1
Gambier OH, 2391 91 D4
Gamewell NC, 4051 111 F4
Ganado AZ, 1210 47 F2
Ganado TX, 2003 61 F3
Gang Mills NY, 4185 93 D1
Gann Valley SD, 14 27 D3
Gansevoort NY, 800 81 D4
Gantt SC, 14229 217 A2
Gap PA, 1931 146 A3
Garber OK, 822 51 E1
Gardena CA, 58829 228 C4
Garden City AL, 492 119 F3
Garden City CO, 234 33 E4
Garden City GA, 8778 130 B3
Garden City ID, 10972 22 B4
Garden City KS, 26658 42 B3
Garden City MI, 27692 210 A3
Garden City MO, 1642 96 C3
Garden City NY, 22371 241 G3
Garden City SC, 9209 123 D4
Garden City TX, 334 58 A3
Garden City UT, 562 31 F2
Garden City South NY, 4024 241 G4
Garden Co. NE, 2057 34 A3
Gardendale AL, 13893 119 F4
Gardendale MI, 800 76 C3
Gardendale TX, 1574 58 A3
Garden Grove CA, 170883 228 E4
Garden Home OR, 6674 251 C2
Garden Plain KS, 849 43 E4
Garden Ridge TX, 3259 61 D2
Garden View PA, 2503 93 D2
Gardenville PA, 1000 146 C1
Gardiner ME, 5800 82 C2
Gardiner MT, 875 23 F2
Gardiner NY, 950 148 B1
Gardner IL, 1463 88 C2
Gardner KS, 19123 96 B3
Gardner MA, 20228 95 D1
Gardnertown NY, 4373 148 B1
Gardnerville NV, 5656 37 D2
Garfield AR, 502 106 C3
Garfield NJ, 30487 148 B3
Garfield TX, 1698 61 E2
Garfield WA, 597 14 B4
Garfield Co. CO, 56389 40 B1
Garfield Co. MT, 1206 17 D3
Garfield Co. NE, 2049 35 D2
Garfield Co. OK, 60580 51 E1
Garfield Co. UT, 5172 39 E3
Garfield Co. WA, 2266 14 A4
Garfield Hts. OH, 28849 91 E2
Garibaldi OR, 779 20 B2
Garland NC, 625 123 D2
Garland TX, 226876 59 F2
Garland UT, 2400 31 E2
Garland Co. AR, 96024 117 D2
Garnavillo IA, 745 73 F3
Garner IA, 3129 72 C3
Garner KY, 600 111 D1
Garner NC, 25745 113 D4
Garnett KS, 3415 96 A4
Garrard Co. KY, 16912 110 C1
Garretson SD, 1166 27 F4
Garrett IN, 6286 90 A2
Garrett KY, 1200 111 E1
Garrett Co. MD, 30097 102 B2
Garrett Park MD, 992 270 C1
Garrettsville OH, 2325 91 F2
Garrison KY, 866 101 D3
Garrison MD, 8823 193 A1
Garrison ND, 1453 18 B3
Garrison TX, 895 124 B3
Garrisonville VA, 2700 144 A4
Garvin Co. OK, 27576 51 E4
Garwin IA, 527 87 D1
Gary IN, 80294 89 D2
Gary SD, 227 27 F2
Gary WV, 968 111 F1
Garysburg NC, 1057 113 E3
Garyville LA, 2811 134 B3
Garza Co. TX, 6461 58 B2
Gas KS, 564 96 A4
Gas City IN, 5965 89 F4
Gasconade Co. MO, 15222 97 F3
Gasport NY, 1248 78 B3
Gassaway WV, 908 101 F3
Gassville AR, 2078 107 E3
Gaston IN, 871 89 F4
Gaston NC, 1152 113 E3
Gaston OR, 637 20 B2
Gaston SC, 1645 122 A4
Gaston Co. NC, 206086 122 A1
Gastonia NC, 71741 122 A1
Gate City VA, 2034 111 E3
Gates NY, 4910 78 C3
Gates OR, 471 20 C3
Gates TN, 647 108 B4
Gates Co. NC, 12197 113 F3
Gates Mills OH, 2270 204 G1
Gatesville NC, 321 113 F3
Gatesville TX, 15751 59 E4
Gatlinburg TN, 3944 111 D4
Gauley Bridge WV, 614 101 F4
Gautier MS, 18572 135 D2
Gayle Mill SC, 913 122 A2
Gaylord MI, 3645 70 C3
Gaylord MN, 2305 66 C4
Gaylordsville CT, 750 148 C1
Gays Mills WI, 491 73 F3
Gayville SD, 407 35 E1
Gearhart OR, 1462 20 B1
Geary OK, 1280 51 D3
Geary Co. KS, 34362 43 F2
Geauga Co. OH, 93389 91 E2
Geddes SD, 208 35 D1
Geistown PA, 2467 92 B4
Gem Co. ID, 16719 22 B3
Genesee ID, 955 14 B4
Genesee MI, 1800 76 B3
Genesee Co. MI, 425790 76 B3
Genesee Co. NY, 60079 78 B3
Geneseo IL, 6586 88 A2
Geneseo NY, 8031 78 C4
Geneva AL, 4452 136 C1
Geneva FL, 2940 141 D1
Geneva IL, 21495 88 C1
Geneva IN, 1293 90 A3
Geneva NE, 2217 35 E4
Geneva NY, 13261 79 D3
Geneva OH, 6215 91 F1
Geneva WA, 2321 12 C1
Geneva Co. AL, 26790 136 C1
Geneva-on-the-Lake OH, 1288 91 F1
Genoa IL, 5193 88 C1
Genoa NE, 1003 35 E3
Genoa OH, 2336 90 C2
Genoa City WI, 3042 74 C4
Genola UT, 1370 39 E1
Gentry AR, 3158 106 B3
Gentry Co. MO, 6738 86 B4
George IA, 1080 72 A2
George WA, 501 13 E4
George Co. MS, 22578 135 D1
Georgetown CA, 2367 36 C2
Georgetown CO, 1034 41 D1
Georgetown CT, 1805 148 C2
Georgetown DE, 6422 145 F4
Georgetown GA, 11823 128 C3
Georgetown ID, 476 31 F1
Georgetown IL, 404 99 D1
Georgetown IN, 2876 99 F4
Georgetown KY, 29098 100 B4
Georgetown MA, 8183 151 F1
Georgetown OH, 4331 100 C3
Georgetown PA, 174 146 A3
Georgetown PA, 2200 261 A2
Georgetown SC, 9163 131 E1
Georgetown TX, 47400 61 E1
Georgetown Co. SC, 60158 122 C4
George West TX, 2445 61 D4
Georgia Ctr. VT, 375 81 D1
Georgiana AL, 1738 127 F4
Gerald MO, 1345 97 F3
Geraldine AL, 896 120 A3
Geraldine MT, 261 16 A3
Gerber CA, 1060 36 B1
Gering NE, 8500 33 F2
Gerlach NV, 206 29 E4
Germania NJ, 750 147 D4
Germantown IL, 1269 98 B3
Germantown MD, 86395 144 B2
Germantown NY, 845 94 B2
Germantown OH, 5547 100 B1
Germantown TN, 38844 118 B1
Germantown WI, 19749 74 C3
Germantown Hills IL, 3438 88 B3
Geronimo OK, 1268 51 D4
Geronimo TX, 1032 61 E2
Gerrardstown WV, 550 103 D2
Gervais OR, 2464 20 B2
Gettysburg OH, 513 90 B4
Gettysburg PA, 7620 103 E1
Gettysburg SD, 1162 26 C2
Geyserville CA, 862 36 A2
Ghent KY, 323 100 A3
Ghent NY, 564 94 B2
Ghent OH, 5261 188 A1
Gholson TX, 1061 59 E4
Giants Neck CT, 1000 149 F2
Gibbon MN, 772 66 B4
Gibbon NE, 1833 35 D4
Gibbsboro NJ, 2274 147 D3
Gibbstown NJ, 3739 146 C3
Gibraltar MI, 4656 90 C1
Gibsland LA, 979 125 D2
Gibson GA, 663 129 F1
Gibson MD, 650 145 D1
Gibson NC, 540 122 C2
Gibsonburg OH, 2581 90 C2
Gibson City IL, 3407 88 C4
Gibson Co. IN, 33503 99 E4
Gibson Co. TN, 49683 108 C4
Gibsonton FL, 14234 140 C3
Gibsonville NC, 6410 112 B4
Giddings TX, 4881 61 F2
Gideon MO, 1093 108 B3
Gifford FL, 9590 141 E3
Gifford IL, 975 89 D4
Gig Harbor WA, 7126 12 C3
Gila Bend AZ, 1922 54 B2
Gila Co. AZ, 53597 55 D1
Gilbert AZ, 208453 54 C2
Gilbert IA, 1082 86 C1
Gilbert LA, 521 125 F3
Gilbert MN, 1799 64 C3
Gilbert SC, 565 122 A4
Gilbert WV, 450 111 F1
Gilbertsville PA, 4832 146 B2
Gilbertville IA, 712 73 E4
Gilbertville MA, 1000 150 B1
Gilby ND, 237 19 E2
Gilchrist Co. FL, 16939 138 C3
Gilcrest CO, 1034 33 E4
Giles Co. TN, 29485 119 F1
Giles Co. VA, 17286 112 A1
Gilford NH, 7126 81 F3
Gilford Park NJ, 8700 147 E3
Gillespie IL, 3319 98 B2
Gillespie Co. TX, 24837 61 D1
Gillett AR, 691 117 F3
Gillett WI, 1386 68 C4
Gillette WY, 29087 25 E3
Gilliam Co. OR, 1871 21 D2
Gilman IL, 1814 89 D3
Gilman IA, 509 87 D1
Gilman VT, 375 81 F2
Gilmer TX, 4905 124 B2
Gilmer Co. GA, 28292 120 C2
Gilmer Co. WV, 8693 101 F2
Gilmore City IA, 504 72 B4
Gilpin Co. CO, 5441 41 D1
Gilroy CA, 48821 44 B2
Gilt Edge TN, 477 118 B1
Ginger Blue MO, 61 106 B3
Girard IL, 2103 98 B2
Girard KS, 2789 106 B1
Girard OH, 9958 91 F2
Girard PA, 3104 91 F1
Girardville PA, 1519 93 E3
Gisela AZ, 570 47 E4
Glacier Co. MT, 13399 15 E1
Gladbrook IA, 945 87 D1
Gladden AZ, 400 54 B1
Glades Co. FL, 12884 141 D4
Glade Spr. VA, 1456 111 F2
Gladewater TX, 6441 124 B2
Gladstone MI, 4973 69 D2
Gladstone MO, 25410 96 B2
Gladstone ND, 239 18 A4
Gladstone OR, 11497 251 D3
Gladwin MI, 2933 76 A1
Gladwin Co. MI, 25692 76 A1
Glandorf OH, 1001 90 B3
Glasco KS, 498 43 E2
Glasco NY, 2099 94 B2
Glascock Co. GA, 3082 129 F1
Glasford IL, 1022 88 B4
Glasgow DE, 14303 145 E1
Glasgow KY, 14028 110 A2
Glasgow MO, 1103 97 D2
Glasgow MT, 3250 17 D2
Glasgow VA, 1133 112 C1
Glasgow WV, 905 101 F4
Glasgow Vil. MO, 5429 256 C1
Glassboro NJ, 18579 146 C4
Glasscock Co. TX, 1226 58 A3
Glassmanor MD, 17295 270 D5
Glassport PA, 4483 250 C3
Glastonbury CT, 33089 150 A3
Gleason TN, 1445 108 C3
Glenaire MO, 545 224 C2
Glen Allen AL, 510 119 E4
Glen Allen VA, 14774 254 B1
Glen Alpine NC, 1517 111 F4
Glenarden MD, 6000 144 B3
Glenburn ND, 380 18 B2
Glenburn PA, 953 93 F2
Glen Burnie MD, 67639 144 C2
Glen Carbon IL, 12934 98 B3
Glencoe AL, 5160 120 A4
Glencoe IL, 8723 89 D1
Glencoe MN, 5631 66 C4
Glencoe OK, 601 51 F2
Glen Cove ME, 375 82 C2
Glen Cove NY, 26964 148 C3
Glendale AZ, 226721 54 C1
Glendale CA, 191719 52 C2
Glendale CO, 4184 209 C3
Glendale MO, 5925 256 B2
Glendale OH, 2155 204 B1
Glendale OR, 874 28 B1
Glendale RI, 800 150 C2
Glendale UT, 381 39 D4
Glen Dale WV, 1526 101 F1
Glendale WI, 12872 234 C1
Glendale Hts. IL, 34208 203 B4
Glendive MT, 4935 17 F3
Glendo WY, 205 33 E1
Glendora CA, 50073 229 F2
Glendora NJ, 4750 146 C3
Glen Elder KS, 445 43 D1
Glen Ellen CA, 784 36 B3
Glen Ellyn IL, 27450 203 B4
Glen Gardner NJ, 1704 104 C1
Glenham NY, 4300 148 B1
Glen Lyon PA, 1873 93 E2
Glen Mills MA, 750 151 F1

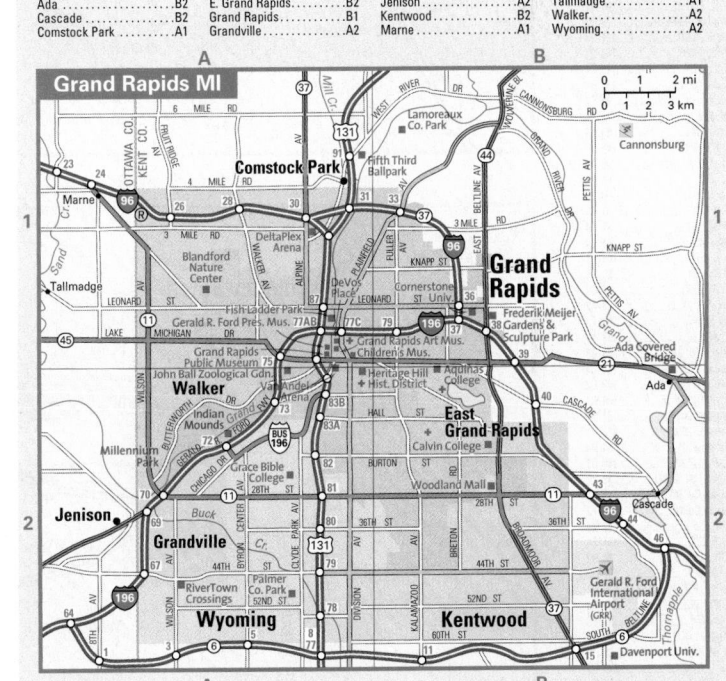

216

Glenmoor–Gray Summit

Figures after entries indicate population, page number, and grid reference.

Glenmoor OH, 1987 ..... 91 F3
Glenmora LA, 1342 ..... 133 E1
Glennallen AK, 483 ..... 154 C3
Glenn Co. CA, 28122 ..... 36 B1
Glen Dale MD, 13466 ..... 144 C3
Glen Hts. TX, 11278 ..... 59 F3
Glenns Ferry ID, 1319 ..... 30 C1
Glenville GA, 3569 ..... 130 A3
Glenolden PA, 7153 ..... 146 C4
Glenpool OK, 10808 ..... 51 F2
Glen Raven NC, 2750 ..... 112 C4
Glen Ridge NJ, 7527 ..... 240 B2
Glen Rock NJ, 11601 ..... 148 B3
Glen Rock PA, 2025 ..... 103 E1
Glenrock WY, 2576 ..... 33 D1
Glen Rose TX, 2444 ..... 59 E3
Glen St. Mary FL, 437 ..... 138 C2
Glens Falls NY, 14700 ..... 81 D4
Glenside PA, 8384 ..... 146 C2
Glen Ullin ND, 807 ..... 18 B4
Glenview IL, 44692 ..... 203 D2
Glenview KY, 531 ..... 230 E1
Glenview Hills KY, 319 ..... 230 E1
Glenville MN, 643 ..... 73 D2
Glenville WV, 1537 ..... 101 F3
Glenwood AR, 2228 ..... 117 D3
Glenwood GA, 747 ..... 129 F3
Glenwood IA, 5269 ..... 86 A3
Glenwood MD, 650 ..... 144 B2
Glenwood MN, 2564 ..... 66 B2
Glenwood UT, 464 ..... 39 E2
Glenwood City WI, 1242 ..... 67 E3
Glenwood Sprs. CO, 9614 ..... 40 C1
Glidden IA, 1146 ..... 86 B1
Glide OR, 1795 ..... 20 B4
Globe AZ, 7532 ..... 55 D1
Glorieta NM, 430 ..... 49 D3
Gloster MS, 960 ..... 126 A4
Gloucester MA, 28789 ..... 151 F1
Gloucester VA, 2269 ..... 113 F1
Gloucester City NJ, 11456 ..... 146 C3
Gloucester Co. NJ, 288288 ..... 146 C4
Gloucester Co. VA, 36858 ..... 113 F1
Gloucester Pt. VA, 9402 ..... 113 F2
Glouster OH, 1791 ..... 101 E1
Gloversville NY, 15665 ..... 79 F3
Gloverville SC, 2831 ..... 121 F4
Glyndon MD, 1200 ..... 144 C1
Glyndon MN, 1394 ..... 19 F4
Glynn Co. GA, 79626 ..... 130 B4
Gnadenhutten OH, 1288 ..... 91 E4
Gobles MI, 829 ..... 75 F4
Goddard KS, 4344 ..... 43 E4
Godeffroy NY, 650 ..... 148 A1
Godfrey IL, 17982 ..... 98 A4
Godley IL, 601 ..... 88 C2
Godley TX, 1009 ..... 59 E3
Goessel KS, 539 ..... 43 E3
Goffstown NH, 3196 ..... 81 E4
Gogebic Co. MI, 16427 ..... 65 E4
Golconda IL, 668 ..... 109 D1
Golconda NV, 214 ..... 30 A3
Gold Bar WA, 2075 ..... 12 C2
Gold Beach OR, 2253 ..... 28 A2
Golden CO, 18867 ..... 41 E1
Golden IL, 644 ..... 87 F4
Golden Beach FL, 919 ..... 233 C3
Golden Beach MD, 3796 ..... 144 C4
Golden Bridge NY, 1578 ..... 148 C2
Golden City MO, 765 ..... 106 C1
Goldendale WA, 3407 ..... 21 D1
Golden Gate FL, 23961 ..... 142 C1
Golden Meadow LA, 2101 ..... 134 B4
Goldenrod FL, 12039 ..... 246 D1
Golden Valley MN, 20371 ..... 235 B2
Golden Valley Co. MT, 884 ..... 16 B4
Golden Valley Co. ND, 1680 ..... 17 F3
Goldfield IA, 635 ..... 72 C4
Goldfield NV, 268 ..... 37 F4
Gold Hill OR, 1220 ..... 28 B2
Goldonna LA, 430 ..... 125 D3
Goldsboro NC, 36437 ..... 123 E1
Goldsboro PA, 952 ..... 93 D4
Goldsby OK, 1801 ..... 51 E3
Goldthwaite TX, 1878 ..... 59 D4
Goleta CA, 29888 ..... 52 B2
Golf Manor OH, 3611 ..... 204 B2
Goliad TX, 1908 ..... 61 E4
Goliad Co. TX, 7210 ..... 61 E4
Gonzales CA, 8187 ..... 44 B3
Gonzales LA, 9781 ..... 134 A2
Gonzales TX, 7237 ..... 61 E3
Gonzales Co. TX, 19807 ..... 61 E3
Gonzalez FL, 13273 ..... 135 F2
Goochland VA, 861 ..... 113 D1
Goochland Co. VA, 21717 ..... 113 D1
Goodfield IL, 860 ..... 88 B3
Good Hope AL, 2264 ..... 119 F3
Goodhue MN, 735 ..... 73 D1
Goodhue Co. MN, 46183 ..... 73 D1
Gooding ID, 3567 ..... 30 C1
Gooding Co. ID, 15464 ..... 30 C1
Goodland IN, 1043 ..... 89 D3
Goodland KS, 4489 ..... 42 B2
Goodlettsville TN, 15921 ..... 109 F3
Goodman MS, 1386 ..... 126 B1
Goodman MO, 1248 ..... 106 B3
Goodrich MI, 1860 ..... 76 B3
Goodsprings NV, 229 ..... 46 A2
Good Thunder MN, 583 ..... 72 C1
Goodview MN, 4036 ..... 73 E1
Goodwater AL, 1475 ..... 128 A1
Goodwell OK, 1293 ..... 50 B1

Goodyear AZ, 65275 ..... 54 C1
Goose Creek SC, 35938 ..... 131 D1
Gordo AL, 1750 ..... 127 E1
Gordon AR, 1071 ..... 106 C4
Goshen CA, 3006 ..... 45 D3
Goshen IN, 31719 ..... 89 F2
Goshen KY, 909 ..... 100 A3
Goshen MD, 1300 ..... 144 B2
Goshen NY, 5454 ..... 148 A2
Goshen OH, 6636 ..... 20 B4
Goshen UT, 921 ..... 39 E1
Goshen VA, 361 ..... 102 B4
Goshen Co. WY, 13249 ..... 33 F2
Gosnell AR, 3548 ..... 108 B4
Gosport IN, 826 ..... 99 E2
Gotha FL, 1915 ..... 246 A2

Gorman NC, 1011 ..... 112 C4
Gorman TX, 1083 ..... 59 D3
Gordon AL, 332 ..... 137 D1
Gordon GA, 2017 ..... 129 E1
Gordon NE, 1612 ..... 34 A1
Gordon PA, 763 ..... 93 E3
Gordon Co. GA, 55186 ..... 120 B3
Gordonsville TN, 1213 ..... 110 A4
Gordonsville VA, 1496 ..... 102 C4
Gordonville PA, 508 ..... 146 A3
Gore OK, 977 ..... 116 B1
Goreville IL, 1049 ..... 108 C1
Gorham ME, 6882 ..... 82 B3
Gorham NH, 1600 ..... 81 F2
Gorham NY, 617 ..... 78 C4

Gothenburg NE, 3574 ..... 34 C4
Gould AR, 837 ..... 117 F3
Goulding FL, 4102 ..... 247 B1
Goulds FL, 10103 ..... 143 E3
Gouldtown NJ, 2300 ..... 145 F1
Gouverneur NY, 3949 ..... 79 E1
Gove KS, 80 ..... 42 C2
Gove Co. KS, 2695 ..... 42 C2
Gowanda NY, 2709 ..... 78 A4
Gower MO, 1526 ..... 96 B1
Gowrie IA, 1037 ..... 72 B4
Grabill IN, 1053 ..... 90 A2
Grace ID, 915 ..... 31 F1
Graceville FL, 2278 ..... 136 C1
Graceville MN, 577 ..... 27 F1
Grady AR, 449 ..... 117 F3

Grady Co. GA, 25011 ..... 137 E1
Grady Co. OK, 52431 ..... 51 E4
Graettinger IA, 844 ..... 72 B3
Graford TX, 584 ..... 59 D2
Grafton IL, 674 ..... 98 A2
Grafton MA, 17765 ..... 150 C1
Grafton ND, 4284 ..... 19 E2
Grafton OH, 6636 ..... 91 D2
Grafton WV, 5164 ..... 102 A2
Grafton WI, 11459 ..... 74 C3
Grafton Co. NH, 89118 ..... 81 F2
Graham KY, 475 ..... 109 E2
Graham NC, 14153 ..... 112 C4
Graham TX, 8903 ..... 59 D2
Grandview WA, 10862 ..... 21 E1
Granbury TX, 7978 ..... 59 E3
Granby CO, 1864 ..... 41 D1
Granby CT, 11088 ..... 150 A1
Granby MA, 1368 ..... 150 A1
Granby MO, 2134 ..... 106 C2
Grand Bay AL, 3672 ..... 135 E2
Grand Blanc MI, 8276 ..... 76 B3
Grand Canyon AZ, 2047 ..... 47 D2
Grand Coteau LA, 947 ..... 133 F2
Grand Coulee WA, 988 ..... 13 E1
Grand Co. CO, 14843 ..... 41 D1
Grand Co. UT, 9225 ..... 40 A2
Grandfield OK, 1038 ..... 51 D4
Grand Forks ND, 52838 ..... 19 E2
Grand Forks Co. ND, 66861 ..... 19 E3
Grand Haven MI, 10412 ..... 75 E3
Grandin NJ, 1400 ..... 147 D1
Grand Island NE, 48520 ..... 35 E4
Grand Isle LA, 1296 ..... 134 B4
Grand Isle VT, 1955 ..... 81 D1
Grand Isle Co. VT, 6970 ..... 81 D1
Grand Jct. CO, 58566 ..... 40 B2
Grand Jct. IA, 824 ..... 86 C1
Grand Lake CO, 471 ..... 33 D4
Grand Ledge MI, 7786 ..... 76 A4
Grand Marais MN, 1351 ..... 65 D3
Grand Meadow MN, 1139 ..... 73 D2
Grand Mound IA, 642 ..... 88 A1
Grand Prairie TX, 175396 ..... 207 C3
Grand Rapids MI, 188040 ..... 75 F3
Grand Rapids MN, 10869 ..... 64 B3

Grand Rapids OH, 965 ..... 90 B2
Grand Ridge FL, 892 ..... 137 D1
Grand Rivers KY, 382 ..... 109 D2
Grand Saline TX, 3136 ..... 124 A2
Grand Terrace CA, 12040 ..... 229 J3
Grand Tower IL, 605 ..... 108 B1
Grandview CO, 600 ..... 40 B4
Grand View ID, 452 ..... 30 B1
Grandview IN, 749 ..... 99 E4
Grandview IA, 556 ..... 87 F2
Grandview MO, 24475 ..... 96 B3
Grandview TX, 1561 ..... 59 E3
Grandview WA, 561 ..... 101 F3
Grandview Hts. OH, 6536 ..... 206 B2
Grandville MI, 15378 ..... 75 F3
Grandy NC, 1000 ..... 115 F1
Granger IN, 30465 ..... 89 F1
Granger IA, 1244 ..... 86 C2
Granger TX, 1419 ..... 61 E1
Granger WA, 3246 ..... 13 E4
Grangeville ID, 3141 ..... 22 B1
Granite UT, 1932 ..... 257 B3
Granite City IL, 29849 ..... 98 A3
Granite Falls MN, 2897 ..... 66 A4
Granite Falls NC, 4722 ..... 111 F4
Granite Falls WA, 3364 ..... 12 C2
Granite Quarry NC, 2930 ..... 122 B1
Granite Shoals TX, 4910 ..... 61 D1
Granite Sprs. NY, 2300 ..... 148 B2
Graniteville SC, 2614 ..... 121 F4
Graniteville VT, 784 ..... 81 E2
Grannis AR, 554 ..... 116 C3
Grant AL, 896 ..... 120 A2
Grant MN, 4096 ..... 67 D3
Grant NE, 1165 ..... 34 B4
Grant City MO, 859 ..... 86 B4
Grant Co. AR, 17853 ..... 117 E3
Grant Co. IN, 70061 ..... 89 F3
Grant Co. KS, 7829 ..... 42 B4
Grant Co. KY, 24662 ..... 100 B2
Grant Co. MN, 6018 ..... 27 F1
Grant Co. NE, 614 ..... 34 B1
Grant Co. NM, 29514 ..... 55 F2
Grant Co. ND, 2394 ..... 18 B4
Grant Co. OK, 4527 ..... 51 E1
Grant Co. OR, 7445 ..... 21 F3
Grant Co. SD, 7356 ..... 27 F2
Grant Co. WA, 89120 ..... 13 E3
Grant Co. WV, 11937 ..... 102 B2

Grand Rapids WI, 51208 ..... 73 E3
Grant Hollow NY, 700 ..... 188 E1
Grant Par. LA, 22309 ..... 125 E3
Grant Park IL, 1331 ..... 89 D2
Grants NM, 9182 ..... 48 B3
Grantsburg WI, 1341 ..... 67 D2
Grantsdale MT, 750 ..... 23 D1
Grants Pass OR, 34533 ..... 28 B2
Grantsville MD, 766 ..... 102 B1
Grantsville UT, 8893 ..... 31 E4
Grantsville WV, 561 ..... 101 F3
Grant Town WV, 613 ..... 102 A1
Grantville GA, 3041 ..... 128 C1
Grantville PA, 1000 ..... 93 E4
Granville IL, 1427 ..... 88 B2
Granville NY, 2543 ..... 81 D4
Granville ND, 241 ..... 18 C2
Granville OH, 5646 ..... 91 D4
Granville Co. NC, 59916 ..... 113 D3
Grapeland TX, 1489 ..... 124 A4
Grapeview WA, 954 ..... 12 C3
Grapevine TX, 46334 ..... 59 E2
Grasonville MD, 3425 ..... 145 D3
Grass Lake MI, 1173 ..... 76 B4
Grass Valley CA, 12860 ..... 36 C2
Graterford PA, 1400 ..... 146 B2
Gratiot Co. MI, 42476 ..... 76 A3
Gratis OH, 881 ..... 100 B1
Graton CA, 1707 ..... 36 A3
Graves Co. KY, 37121 ..... 108 C3
Gravette AR, 2325 ..... 106 B3
Grawn MI, 772 ..... 69 F4
Gray GA, 3276 ..... 129 D1
Gray KY, 650 ..... 110 C2
Gray LA, 5584 ..... 134 A3
Gray ME, 884 ..... 82 B3
Gray TN, 1222 ..... 111 E3
Gray Co. KS, 6006 ..... 42 C4
Gray Co. TX, 22535 ..... 50 B3
Gray Court SC, 795 ..... 121 F2
Grayland WA, 953 ..... 12 B4
Grayling MI, 1884 ..... 70 C4
Graymoor-Devondale KY, 2870 ..... 230 E1
Grays Harbor Co. WA, 72797 ..... 12 B3
Grayslake IL, 20957 ..... 74 C4
Grayson GA, 2666 ..... 121 D1
Grayson KY, 4217 ..... 101 D4
Grayson LA, 532 ..... 125 E3
Grayson Co. KY, 25746 ..... 109 F1
Grayson Co. TX, 120877 ..... 59 F1
Grayson Co. VA, 15533 ..... 111 F3
Gray Summit MO, 2701 ..... 98 A3

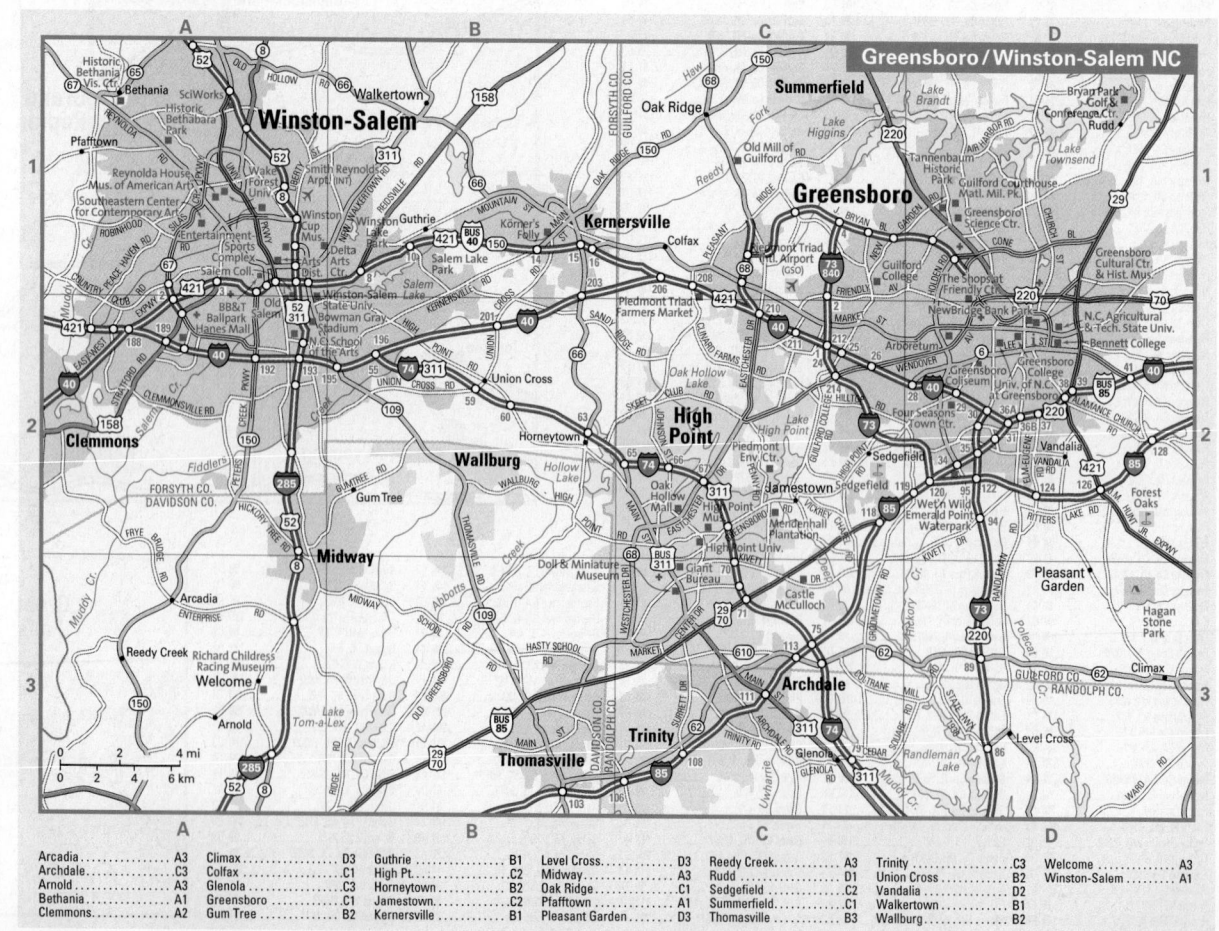

Green Bay WI

Howard
Hobart
Ashwaubenon
Green Bay
Allouez
Bellevue
De Pere

Greensboro / Winston-Salem NC

Winston-Salem
Summerfield
Oak Ridge
Greensboro
Bethania
Walkertown
Kernersville
Colfax
Clemmons
Wallburg
High Point
Jamestown
Sedgefield
Midway
Archdale
Trinity
Thomasville
Pleasant Garden
Welcome

217
Graysville–Harrisburg

Entries in **bold black** indicate counties or parishes.
Entries in **bold color** indicate cities with detailed inset maps.

Graysville AL, 2165 119 F4
Graysville TN, 1502 120 B1
Grayville IL, 1666 99 D4
Greasewood AZ, 547 47 F3
Great Barrington MA, 2231 94 B2
Great Bend KS, 15995 43 D3
Great Bend NY, 843 79 E1
Great Bend PA, 734 93 F1
Great Falls MT, 58505 15 F3
Great Falls SC, 1979 122 A2
Great Falls VA, 15427 144 B3
Great Meadows NJ, 303 94 A4
Great Mills MD, 2600 103 E4
Great Neck NY, 9989 148 B4
Great Neck Estates NY, 2761 241 G3
Great Neck Gardens NY, 1186 241 G2
Great Neck Plaza NY, 6707 241 G2
Great River NY, 1489 149 D4
Greece NY, 14519 78 C3
Greeley CO, 92889 33 E4
Greeley NE, 466 35 D3
Greeley Co. KS, 1247 42 B3
Greeley Co. NE, 2538 35 D3
Greeleyville SC, 438 122 B4
Green OH, 25699 91 E3
Green OR, 7515 28 B1
Greenacres CA, 5566 45 D4
Greenacres FL, 37573 143 F1
Greenback TN, 1064 110 C4
Green Bay WI, 104057 68 C4
Greenbelt MD, 23068 144 B3
Greenbrier AR, 4706 117 E1
Greenbrier TN, 6433 109 F3
Greenbrier Co. WV, 35480 102 A4
Greenbush MA, 550 151 E2
Greenbush MN, 719 19 F1
Greencastle IN, 10326 99 E1
Greencastle PA, 3996 103 D1
Green City MO, 657 87 D4
Green Co. KY, 11258 110 A1
Green Co. WI, 36842 74 B4
Green Cove Sprs. FL, 6908 139 D3
Green Creek NJ, 1300 104 C4
Greendale IN, 4520 100 B2
Greendale MO, 651 256 B2
Greendale WI, 14046 234 C3
Greene IA, 1130 73 D3
Greene ME, 4076 82 B2
Greene NY, 1580 79 E4
Greene Co. AL, 9045 127 E2
Greene Co. AR, 42090 108 A3
Greene Co. GA, 15994 121 E4
Greene Co. IL, 13886 98 A2
Greene Co. IN, 33165 99 E2
Greene Co. IA, 9336 86 B1
Greene Co. MS, 14400 127 D4
Greene Co. MO, 275174 107 D1
Greene Co. NY, 49221 94 A2
Greene Co. NC, 21362 115 C3
Greene Co. OH, 161573 100 C1
Greene Co. PA, 38686 102 A1
Greene Co. TN, 68831 111 D3
Greene Co. VA, 18403 102 C4
Greenevers NC, 634 123 E2
Greeneville TN, 15062 111 D4
Greenfield CA, 3991 44 B3
Greenfield IL, 1071 98 A2
Greenfield IN, 20602 99 F1
Greenfield IA, 1982 86 B2
Greenfield MA, 17456 94 C1
Greenfield MO, 1371 106 C1
Greenfield NH, 375 95 D1
Greenfield OH, 4639 100 C2
Greenfield TN, 2182 108 C4
Greenfield WI, 36720 234 C3
Green Forest AR, 2761 107 D3
Green Harbor MA, 2609 151 E2
Green Haven MD, 24287 144 C2
Green Haven NY, 3000 148 C1
Green Hill TN, 6618 109 F3
Greenhills OH, 3615 204 B1
Green Island NY, 2620 188 E2
Green Lake WI, 960 74 B2
Green Lake Co. WI, 19051 74 B2
Greenland AR, 1259 106 C4
Greenland NH, 3549 82 A4
Green Lane PA, 508 146 B2
Greenleaf ID, 846 22 A4
Greenlee Co. AZ, 8437 55 E2
Greenmount MD, 600 144 B1
Green Mtn. Falls CO, 640 205 C1
Green Oaks IL, 3866 203 C1
Green Park MO, 2622 256 B3
Green Pond NJ, 1400 148 A3
Greenport NY, 2197 149 E3
Green River UT, 952 39 F2
Green River WY, 12515 32 A3
Greensboro AL, 2497 127 E2
Greensboro FL, 602 137 D2
Greensboro GA, 3359 121 D4
Greensboro MD, 1931 145 E3
Greensboro NC, 269666 112 B4
Greensboro Bend VT, 232 81 E2
Greensburg IN, 11492 100 A2
Greensburg KS, 777 43 D4
Greensburg KY, 2163 110 A2
Greensburg LA, 718 134 B1
Greensburg PA, 14892 92 A4
Green Sprs. OH, 1368 90 C2
Greensville Co. VA, 12243 113 E2
Greentown IN, 2415 89 F4
Greentown OH, 3804 91 E3
Green Tree PA, 4432 250 B2
Greenup IL, 1513 99 D2
Greenup KY, 1188 101 D3
Greenup Co. KY, 36910 101 D3
Green Valley AZ, 21391 55 D3
Green Valley CA, 600 52 C2
Green Valley IL, 709 88 B4
Green Valley MD, 12262 144 B2
Greenview IL, 778 88 B4
Green Vil. PA, 1100 103 D1
Greenville AL, 8135 128 A3
Greenville CA, 1129 36 C1
Greenville DE, 2326 146 B3
Greenville FL, 843 137 F2
Greenville GA, 876 128 C1
Greenville IL, 7000 98 B3
Greenville IN, 595 99 F4
Greenville KY, 4312 109 E2
Greenville ME, 1257 84 C4
Greenville MI, 8481 75 F3
Greenville MS, 34400 126 A1
Greenville MO, 511 108 A2
Greenville NH, 1108 95 D1
Greenville NY, 7116 94 B2
Greenville NC, 84554 115 D2
Greenville OH, 13227 90 A4
Greenville PA, 5919 91 F2
Greenville RI, 8658 150 C3
Greenville SC, 58409 121 E2
Greenville TX, 25557 59 F2
Greenville VA, 832 102 B4
Greenville WI, 950 74 C1
Greenville Co. SC, 451225 121 E2
Greenville Jct. ME, 850 84 C4
Greenwich CT, 12942 148 C3
Greenwich NY, 1777 81 D4
Greenwich OH, 1476 91 D3
Greenwood AR, 8952 116 C1
Greenwood DE, 973 145 E3
Greenwood FL, 686 137 D1
Greenwood IN, 49791 99 F1
Greenwood LA, 3219 124 C2
Greenwood MS, 15205 118 B4
Greenwood MO, 5221 96 B3
Greenwood NE, 568 35 F3
Greenwood SC, 23222 121 F3
Greenwood WI, 1026 68 A4
Greenwood Co. KS, 6689 43 F3
Greenwood Co. SC, 69661 121 F3
Greenwood Lake NY, 3154 148 A2
Greenwood Vil. CO, 13925 209 C4
Greer SC, 25515 121 F2
Greer Co. OK, 6239 50 C3
Greers Ferry AR, 891 117 E1
Gregg Co. TX, 121730 124 B2
Gregory SD, 1295 35 D1
Gregory TX, 1907 63 F2
Gregory Co. SD, 4271 35 D1
Greilickville MI, 1530 69 F4
Grenada MS, 13092 118 B4
Grenada Co. MS, 21906 118 B4
Gresham OR, 105594 20 C2
Gresham WI, 586 68 C4
Gresham Park GA, 7432 190 E4
Gretna FL, 1460 137 D2
Gretna LA, 17736 134 B3
Gretna NE, 4441 35 F3
Gretna VA, 1267 112 C2
Greybull WY, 1847 24 C3
Gridley CA, 6584 36 B2
Gridley IL, 1432 88 C3
Gridley KS, 341 96 A4
Griffin GA, 23643 129 D1
Griffith IN, 16893 89 D2
Grifton NC, 2617 115 D3
Griggs Co. ND, 2420 19 D3
Griggsville IL, 1226 98 A1
Grimes AL, 558 128 B4
Grimes IA, 8246 86 C2
Grimes Co. TX, 26604 132 A2
Grinnell IA, 9218 87 D1
Griswold IA, 1036 86 B2
Groesbeck OH, 6788 204 A2
Groesbeck TX, 4328 59 F4
Groom TX, 574 50 B3
Grosse Pointe MI, 5421 210 D3
Grosse Pointe Farms MI, 9479 210 D3
Grosse Pointe Park MI, 11555 210 D3
Grosse Pointe Shores MI, 3008 210 D3
Grosse Pointe Woods MI, 16135 76 C4
Grosse Tete LA, 647 133 F2
Grosvenor Dale CT, 700 150 B2
Groton CT, 10389 149 F2
Groton MA, 1124 95 D1
Groton NY, 2363 79 D4
Groton SD, 1458 27 E2
Groton VT, 437 81 E2
Groton Long Pt. CT, 518 149 F2
Grottoes VA, 2668 102 C4
Grove OK, 6623 106 B3
Grove City FL, 1804 140 C4
Grove City MN, 635 66 B3
Grove City OH, 35575 101 D1
Grove City PA, 8322 92 A2
Grove Hill AL, 1570 127 E4
Groveland CA, 601 37 D4
Groveland FL, 8729 140 C1
Groveland MA, 2800 95 E1
Groveport OH, 5363 101 D1
Grover NC, 708 122 A1
Grover Beach CA, 13156 52 A1
Groves TX, 16144 132 C3
Groveton NH, 1118 81 F2
Groveton TX, 1057 132 B1
Groveton VA, 14598 144 B4
Grovetown GA, 11216 121 F4
Grubbs AR, 386 107 F4
Gruetli-Laager TN, 1813 120 A1
Grundy VA, 1021 111 E2
Grundy Ctr. IA, 2706 73 D4
Grundy Co. IL, 50063 88 C2
Grundy Co. IA, 12453 73 D4
Grundy Co. MO, 10261 86 C4
Grundy Co. TN, 13703 120 A1
Gruver TX, 1194 50 B2
Guadalupe AZ, 5523 249 C3
Guadalupe CA, 7080 52 A1
Guadalupe Co. NM, 4687 49 E4
Guadalupe Co. TX, 131533 61 E3
Guerneville CA, 4534 36 A3
Guernsey WY, 1147 33 E2
Guernsey Co. OH, 40087 91 E4
Gueydan LA, 1398 133 E3
Guilderland NY, 35303 188 C2
Guildhall VT, 268 81 F2
Guilford CT, 22307 149 E2
Guilford ME, 903 82 C1
Guilford MD, 12918 193 A5
Guilford Co. NC, 488406 112 B4
Guin AL, 2376 119 E4
Gulf Breeze FL, 5763 135 F2
Gulf Co. FL, 15863 137 D3
Gulfport FL, 12029 140 B3
Gulfport MS, 67793 135 D2
Gulf Shores AL, 9741 135 E2
Gulf Stream FL, 786 143 F1
Gun Barrel City TX, 5672 59 F3
Gunnison CO, 5854 40 C3
Gunnison MS, 452 118 A4
Gunnison UT, 3285 39 E2
Gunnison Co. CO, 15324 40 C2
Gunter TX, 1498 59 F1
Guntersville AL, 8197 120 A3
Guntown MS, 2083 119 D3
Gurdon AR, 2212 117 D4
Gurley AL, 801 119 F2
Gurn Spr. NY, 600 80 C4
Gustavus AK, 442 155 D4
Gustine CA, 5520 36 C4
Guthrie KY, 1419 109 E3
Guthrie OK, 10191 51 E2
Guthrie TX, 160 58 C1
Guthrie Ctr. IA, 1569 86 B2
Guthrie Co. IA, 10954 86 B2
Guthriesville PA, 1800 146 B3
Guttenberg IA, 1919 73 F4
Guttenberg NJ, 11176 240 D2
Guymon OK, 11442 50 B1
Guys TN, 466 119 D2
Guyton GA, 1684 130 B2
Gwinn MI, 1917 69 D1
Gwinner ND, 753 27 E1
Gwinnett Co. GA, 805321 121 D4
Gwynn VA, 602 113 F1
Gypsum CO, 6477 40 C1
Gypsum KS, 405 43 E2

H

Haakon Co. SD, 1937 26 B3
Habersham Co. GA, 43041 121 D2
Hacienda Hts. CA, 54038 228 E3
Hackberry LA, 1261 133 D3
Hackensack NJ, 43010 148 B3
Hackett AR, 812 116 C1
Hackettstown NJ, 9724 94 A4
Hackleburg AL, 1516 119 E3
Haddam CT, 7635 149 E1
Haddonfield NJ, 11593 146 C3
Haddon Hts. NJ, 7473 248 D4
Hadley MA, 4793 150 A1
Hadley NY, 1009 80 C4
Hagaman NY, 1292 80 C4
Hagan GA, 996 129 F3
Hagerhill KY, 900 111 D1
Hagerman ID, 872 30 C1
Hagerman NM, 1257 57 E2
Hagerstown IN, 1787 100 A1
Hagerstown MD, 39662 144 A1
Hahira GA, 2737 137 F1
Hahnville LA, 3344 134 B3
Haiku HI, 8118 153 D1
Hailey ID, 7960 22 C4
Haileyville OK, 813 116 A2
Haines AK, 1713 155 D3
Haines OR, 416 21 F2
Haines City FL, 20535 141 D2
Hainesport NJ, 2200 147 D3
Halaula HI, 469 153 E2
Halawa HI, 14014 152 C3
Hale Ctr. TX, 2252 58 A1
Hale Co. AL, 15760 127 E2
Hale Co. TX, 36273 58 A1
Haledon NJ, 8318 148 B3
Haleiwa HI, 3970 152 A2
Hales Corners WI, 7692 74 C3
Haleyville AL, 4173 119 E3
Halfmoon NY, 18474 188 E1
Half Moon NC, 8352 115 D4
Half Moon Bay CA, 11324 36 B4
Halfway MD, 10701 144 A1
Halfway OR, 288 22 A2
Halifax MA, 7500 151 D2
Halifax NC, 234 113 E3
Halifax PA, 841 93 D4
Halifax VA, 1309 112 C2
Halifax Co. NC, 54691 113 E4
Halifax Co. VA, 36241 112 C2
Haliimaile HI, 964 153 D1
Hallam PA, 2673 103 E1
Hallandale Beach FL, 37113 143 F2
Hall Co. GA, 179684 121 D3
Hall Co. NE, 58607 35 D4
Hall Co. TX, 3353 50 B4
Hallettsville TX, 2550 61 F3
Halliday ND, 188 18 A3
Hallock MN, 981 19 E1
Hallowell ME, 2381 82 C2
Halls TN, 2255 108 C4
Hallsburg TX, 507 59 F4
Halls Crossroads TN, 2100 110 C4
Halls Gap KY, 450 110 B1
Hallstead PA, 1303 93 F1
Hallsville MO, 1491 97 E2
Hallsville TX, 3577 124 B2
Halsey OR, 904 20 B3
Halstad MN, 597 19 F3
Halstead KS, 2085 43 E3
Haltom City TX, 42409 207 B2
Hamblen Co. TN, 62544 111 D3
Hamburg AR, 2857 125 F1
Hamburg IA, 1187 86 A3
Hamburg MN, 513 66 C4
Hamburg NJ, 3277 148 A2
Hamburg NY, 9409 78 B4
Hamburg PA, 4289 146 A1
Hamden CT, 58180 149 D2
Hamden OH, 879 101 D2
Hamel IL, 816 98 B3
Hamilton AL, 6885 119 D3
Hamilton GA, 1016 128 C2
Hamilton IL, 2951 87 F4
Hamilton IN, 1532 90 A2
Hamilton MI, 1300 75 F4
Hamilton MO, 1809 96 C1
Hamilton MT, 4348 23 D1
Hamilton NY, 4239 79 E3
Hamilton NC, 408 113 E4
Hamilton OH, 62477 100 B2
Hamilton RI, 2500 150 C4
Hamilton TX, 3095 59 E4
Hamilton VA, 506 144 A2
Hamilton City CA, 1759 36 B1
Hamilton Co. FL, 14799 138 C2
Hamilton Co. IL, 8457 98 C4
Hamilton Co. IN, 274569 99 F1
Hamilton Co. IA, 15673 72 C4
Hamilton Co. KS, 2690 42 A3
Hamilton Co. NE, 9124 35 E4
Hamilton Co. NY, 4836 79 F2
Hamilton Co. OH, 802374 100 B2
Hamilton Co. TN, 336463 120 B1
Hamilton Co. TX, 8517 59 D4
Hamilton Square NJ, 12784 147 D2
Ham Lake MN, 15296 67 D3
Hamler OH, 576 90 B2
Hamlet IN, 800 89 E2
Hamlet NC, 6495 122 C2
Hamlin TX, 2124 58 C2
Hamlin WV, 1142 101 E4
Hamlin Co. SD, 5903 27 E3
Hammon OK, 568 50 C3
Hammond IL, 509 98 C1
Hammond IN, 80830 89 D2
Hammond LA, 20019 134 B2
Hammond WI, 1922 67 E4
Hammondsport NY, 661 78 C4
Hammondville AL, 488 120 A2
Hammonton NJ, 14791 147 D4
Hamorton PA, 1400 146 B3
Hampden ME, 4343 83 D1
Hampden Co. MA, 463490 150 A2
Hampden Sydney VA, 1450 113 D2
Hampshire IL, 5563 88 C1
Hampshire Co. MA, 158080 94 C2
Hampshire Co. WV, 23964 102 C2
Hampstead MD, 6323 144 B1
Hampstead NH, 8523 95 E1
Hampton AR, 1324 117 E4
Hampton FL, 500 138 C3
Hampton GA, 6987 129 D1
Hampton IL, 1863 208 C1
Hampton IA, 4461 73 D4
Hampton MD, 5052 193 C1
Hampton NE, 423 35 E4
Hampton NH, 9656 95 E1
Hampton NJ, 1401 104 C1
Hampton PA, 632 103 E1
Hampton SC, 2808 130 B2
Hampton TN, 1300 111 E3
Hampton VA, 137436 113 F2
Hampton Bays NY, 13603 149 E3
Hampton Beach NH, 2275 95 E1
Hampton Co. SC, 21090 130 B2
Hampton Park NY, 950 149 E3
Hamtramck MI, 22423 210 C3
Hana HI, 1235 153 E1
Hanahan SC, 17997 131 D1
Hanamaulu HI, 3835 152 B1
Hanapepe HI, 2638 152 B1
Hanceville AL, 2982 119 F3
Hancock MD, 1545 102 C1
Hancock MI, 4634 65 F3
Hancock MN, 765 66 A3
Hancock NH, 204 81 E4
Hancock NY, 1031 93 F1
Hancock Co. GA, 9429 129 E1
Hancock Co. IL, 19104 87 F4
Hancock Co. IN, 70002 100 A1
Hancock Co. IA, 11341 72 C3
Hancock Co. KY, 8565 109 F1
Hancock Co. ME, 54418 83 D1
Hancock Co. MS, 43929 134 C2
Hancock Co. OH, 74782 90 B3
Hancock Co. TN, 6819 111 D3
Hancock Co. WV, 30676 91 F4
Hand Co. SD, 3431 27 D3
Hanford CA, 53967 45 D3
Hankinson ND, 919 27 F1
Hanley Hills MO, 2101 256 B2
Hanna WY, 841 33 D2
Hanna City IL, 1225 88 B3
Hannibal MO, 17916 97 F1
Hannibal NY, 555 79 D3
Hanover CT, 700 149 F1
Hanover IL, 844 74 A4
Hanover IN, 3546 100 A3
Hanover KS, 682 43 F1
Hanover MA, 13164 151 E2
Hanover MN, 2938 66 C3
Hanover NH, 8636 81 E3
Hanover NJ, 13731 148 A3
Hanover OH, 921 91 D4
Hanover PA, 15289 103 E1
Hanover VA, 252 113 E1
Hanover Co. VA, 99863 103 D4
Hanover Park IL, 37973 203 B3
Hansen ID, 1144 30 C1
Hansford Co. TX, 5613 50 B2
Hanson KY, 742 109 E1
Hanson MA, 2118 151 D2
Hanson Co. SD, 3331 27 E4
Hapeville GA, 6373 190 D5
Happy TX, 678 50 A4
Happy Camp CA, 1190 28 B2
Happy Valley OR, 13903 251 D2
Harahan LA, 9277 239 B2
Haralson Co. GA, 28780 120 B4
Harbert MI, 1619 89 E1
Harbeson DE, 375 145 F4
Harbor OR, 2391 28 A2
Harbor Beach MI, 1703 76 C2
Harbor Bluffs FL, 2860 266 A2
Harbor Hills NY, 575 241 G2
Harbor Hills OH, 1509 101 D1
Harbor Sprs. MI, 1194 70 B3
Harbour Hts. FL, 2987 140 C4
Hardee Co. FL, 27731 140 C3
Hardeeville SC, 2952 130 B3
Hardeman Co. TN, 27253 118 C1
Hardeman Co. TX, 4139 50 C4
Hardin IL, 967 98 A2
Hardin KY, 615 109 D2
Hardin MO, 569 96 C2
Hardin MT, 3505 24 C1
Hardin TX, 819 132 B2
Hardin Co. IL, 4320 109 D1
Hardin Co. IA, 17534 73 D4
Hardin Co. KY, 105543 110 A1
Hardin Co. OH, 32058 90 C3
Hardin Co. TN, 26026 119 D1
Hardin Co. TX, 54635 132 C2
Harding Co. NM, 695 49 E2
Harding Co. SD, 1255 25 F1
Hardinsburg KY, 2343 109 F1
Hardwick GA, 3930 129 E1
Hardwick VT, 1345 81 E2
Hardy AR, 772 107 F3
Hardy Co. WV, 14025 102 C2
Harewood Park MD, 3400 145 D1
Harford Co. MD, 244826 144 C1
Hargill TX, 877 63 E4
Harker Hts. TX, 26700 59 E4
Harkers Island NC, 1207 115 E4
Harlan IA, 5106 86 A2
Harlan KY, 1745 111 D2
Harlan Co. KY, 29278 111 D2
Harlan Co. NE, 3423 35 D4
Harlem FL, 2658 141 D4
Harlem GA, 2666 129 F1
Harlem MT, 808 16 C2
Harleysville PA, 9286 146 C2
Harleyville SC, 677 130 C1
Harlingen TX, 64849 63 F4
Harlowton MT, 997 16 B4
Harmon Co. OK, 2922 50 C4
Harmony IN, 656 99 E1
Harmony MN, 1020 73 E2
Harmony NC, 531 112 A4
Harmony PA, 890 92 A3
Harmony RI, 985 150 C3
Harnett Co. NC, 114678 123 D1
Harney Co. OR, 7422 21 E4
Harold KY, 1400 111 E1
Harper KS, 1473 43 E4
Harper TX, 1192 60 C1
Harper Co. KS, 6034 43 E4
Harper Co. OK, 3685 50 C1
Harpersville AL, 1637 128 A1
Harper Woods MI, 14236 210 D2
Harrah OK, 5095 51 E3
Harrah WA, 625 13 D4
Harriman NY, 2424 148 B2
Harriman TN, 6350 110 B4
Harrington DE, 3562 145 E3
Harrington ME, 882 83 E2
Harrington WA, 424 13 F3
Harris MN, 1132 67 D3
Harrisburg AR, 2288 118 A1
Harrisburg IL, 9017 109 D1
Harrisburg NE, 100 33 F3

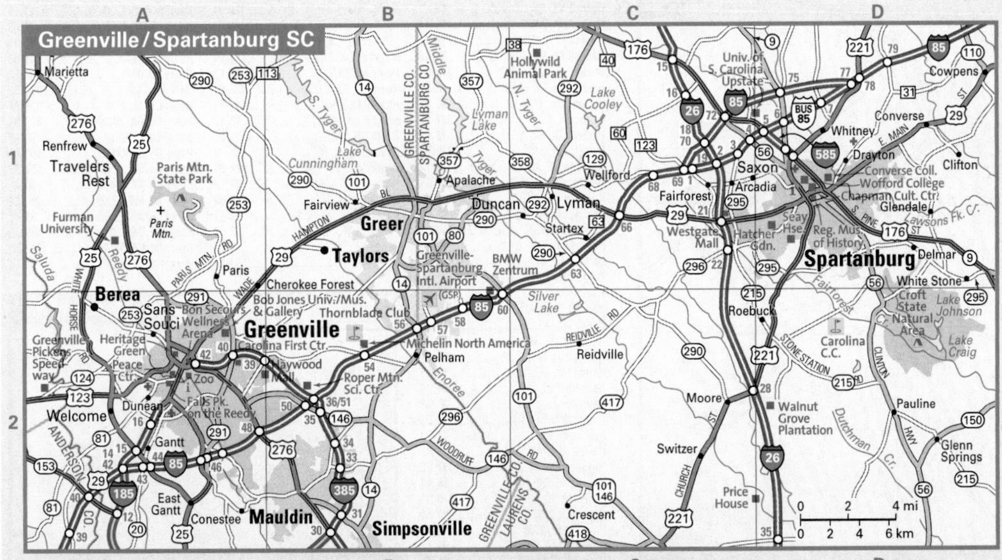

Greenville / Spartanburg SC
A
B
C
D
1
2
Marietta
Renfrew
Travelers Rest
Paris Mtn. State Park
Furman University
Paris Mtn.
Cunningham
Lake
Fairview
Greer
Taylors
Paris
Cherokee Forest
Berea
Sans Souci
Bob Jones Univ./Mus. & Gallery
Bon Secours Wellness Arena
Greenville
Heritage Green
Greenville-Pickens Speedway
Carolina First Ctr.
Haywood Mall
Roper Mtn. Sci. Ctr.
Zoo
Falls Pk. on the Reedy
Dunean
Welcome
Gantt
East Gantt
Conestee
Mauldin
Simpsonville
Thornblade Club
Greenville-Spartanburg Intl. Airport
BMW Zentrum
Michelin North America
Pelham
Silver Lake
Reidville
Apalache
Duncan
Lyman
Startex
Wellford
Lyman Lake
Lake Cooley
Hollywild Animal Park
Fairforest
Saxon
Arcadia
Westgate Mall
Hatcher Gdn.
Seay Hse.
Reg. Mus. of History
Spartanburg
Converse
Drayton
Converse Coll.
Wofford College
Chapman Cult. Ctr.
Glendale
Whitney
Clifton
Cowpens
Univ. of S. Carolina Upstate
Delmar
White Stone
Croft State Natural Area
Lake Johnson
Lake Craig
Carolina C.C.
Roebuck
Moore
Pauline
Walnut Grove Plantation
Glenn Springs
Switzer
Price House
Crescent
GREENVILLE CO.
SPARTANBURG CO.
0 2 4 mi
0 2 4 6 km

Apalache B1
Arcadia C1
Berea A2
Cherokee Forest A1
Clifton D1
Conestee A2
Converse D1
Cowpens D1
Crescent C2
Delmar D1
Drayton D1
Duncan C1
Dunean A2
E. Gantt A2
Fairforest C1
Fairview B1
Gantt A2
Glendale D1
Glenn Sprs. D2
Greenville A2
Greer B1
Lake Forest A2
Lyman C1
Marietta A1
Mauldin B2
Moore C2
Paris A1
Pauline D2
Pelham B2
Reidville C2
Renfrew A1
Roebuck D2
Sans Souci A2
Saxon C1
Simpsonville B2
Spartanburg D1
Startex C1
Switzer C2
Taylors B1
Travelers Rest A1
Welcome A2
Wellford C1
White Stone D1
Whitney D1

218
Harrisburg–Henryetta

Figures after entries indicate population, page number, and grid reference.

Entry		
Harrisburg NC, 11526	122	B1
Harrisburg OR, 3567	20	B3
Harrisburg PA, 49528	93	D4
Harrisburg SD, 4089	27	F4
Harris Co. GA, 32024	128	C2
Harris Co. TX, 4092459	132	A3
Harrison AR, 12943	107	D3
Harrison GA, 489	129	F2
Harrison ID, 203	14	B3
Harrison ME, 2315	82	B2
Harrison MI, 2114	76	A1
Harrison NE, 251	33	F1
Harrison NJ, 13620	148	B4
Harrison NY, 27472	148	C3
Harrison OH, 9897	100	B2
Harrison TN, 7769	120	B1
Harrisonburg LA, 348	125	F3
Harrisonburg VA, 48914	102	C3
Harrison Co. IN, 39364	99	F4
Harrison Co. IA, 14928	86	A1

Harrisburg PA (map legend):

Bressler		C2
Camp Hill		A2
Colonial Park		C1
Eberlys Mill		A2
Edgemont		B1
Enhaut		C2
Enola		A1
Estherton		B1
Fair Acres		B2
Good Hope		A1
Green Lane Farms		A2
Harrisburg		B1
Highland Park		B2
Highspire		C2
Lawnton		C1
Lemoyne		B2
Marsh Run		C2
Mechanicsburg		A2
New Cumberland		B2
Oakleigh		C2
Oberlin		C2
Paxtang		B1
Paxtang Manor		C1
Paxtonia		C1
Penbrook		B1
Progress		B1
Reesers Summit		C2
Rossmoyne		A2
Rossmoyne Manor		A2
Rutherford Hts.		C1
Shiremanstown		A2
Steelton		B2
Summerdale		A1
W. Enola		A1
W. Fairview		A1
White Hill		A2
Wormleysburg		B2

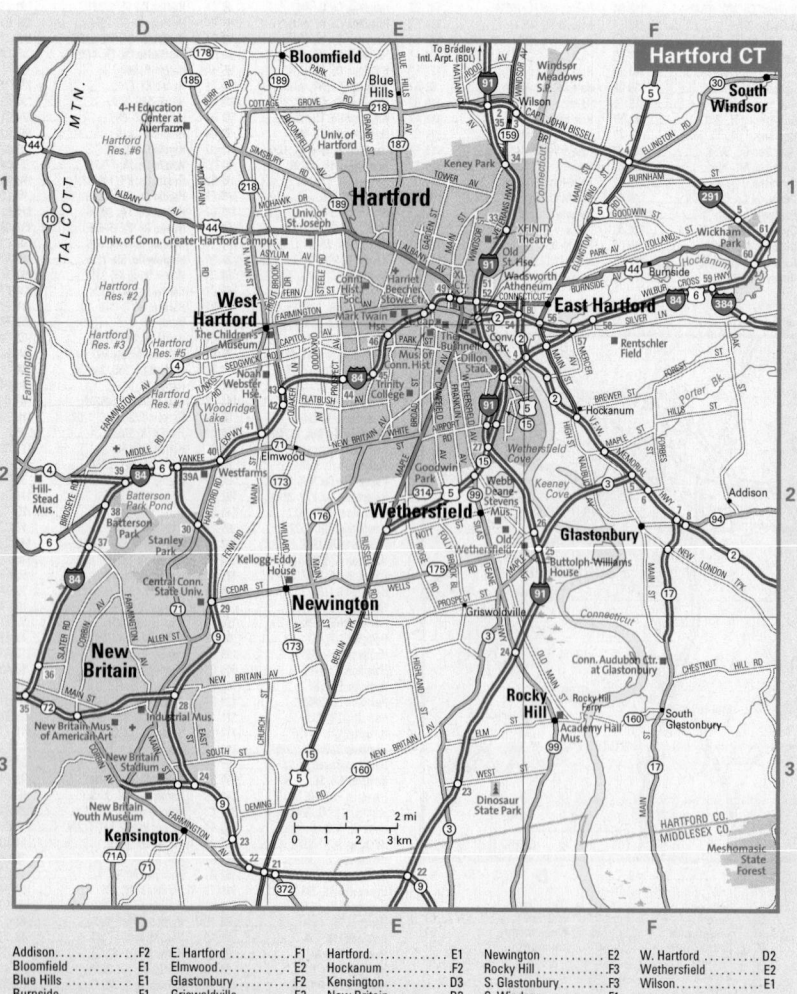

Harrisburg PA

Hartford CT

Hartford CT (map legend):

Addison		F2
Bloomfield		E1
Blue Hills		E1
Burnside		F1
E. Hartford		F1
Elmwood		E2
Glastonbury		F2
Griswoldville		E2
Hartford		E1
Hockanum		F1
Kensington		D3
New Britain		D3
Newington		E2
Rocky Hill		E2
S. Glastonbury		F3
S. Windsor		F1
W. Hartford		D2
Wethersfield		E2
Wilson		E1

Entry		
Harrison Co. KY, 18846	100	B3
Harrison Co. MS, 187105	134	C2
Harrison Co. OH, 8957	91	E4
Harrison Co. OH, 15864	91	E4
Harrison Co. TX, 65631	124	B2
Harrison Co. WV, 69099	102	A2
Harrisonville MO, 10019	96	B3
Harristown IL, 1367	98	C1
Harrisville MI, 493	71	D4
Harrisville NH, 961	95	D1
Harrisville NY, 628	79	E1
Harrisville PA, 897	92	A3
Harrisville RI, 1605	150	C2
Harrisville UT, 5567	31	E3
Harrisville WV, 1876	101	F2
Harrodsburg KY, 8340	110	B1
Harrogate TN, 4389	110	C3
Harrold SD, 124	27	D3
Hart MI, 2126	75	E2
Hart TX, 1114	50	A4
Hart Co. GA, 25213	121	E3
Hart Co. KY, 18199	110	A2
Hartford AL, 2624	136	C1
Hartford AR, 642	116	C2
Hartford CT, 124775	150	A3
Hartford IL, 1429	98	A3
Hartford IA, 771	86	C2
Hartford KS, 371	43	F3
Hartford KY, 2672	109	E1
Hartford MI, 2688	89	F1
Hartford SD, 2534	27	F4
Hartford WV, 614	101	E2
Hartford WI, 14223	74	C3
Hartford City IN, 6220	90	A4
Hartford Co. CT, 894014	150	A3
Hartington NE, 1554	35	E1
Hartland ME, 813	82	C1
Hartland VT, 380	81	E3
Hartland WI, 9110	74	C3
Hartley IA, 1672	72	A3
Hartley Co. TX, 6062	50	A4
Hartman AR, 519	116	C1
Harts WV, 656	101	E4
Hartselle AL, 14255	119	F4
Hartshorne OK, 2125	116	A2
Hartsville SC, 7764	122	B3
Hartsville TN, 7870	109	F3
Hartville MO, 613	107	E2
Hartville OH, 2944	91	E3
Hartwell GA, 4469	121	E3
Harvard IL, 9447	74	C4
Harvard MA, 6520	150	C1
Harvard NE, 1013	35	E4
Harvest AL, 5281	119	F2
Harvey IL, 25282	203	E6
Harvey LA, 20348	239	C2
Harvey MI, 1393	69	D1
Harvey ND, 1783	18	C3
Harvey Co. KS, 34684	43	E3
Harveysburg OH, 546	100	C2
Harveys Lake PA, 2791	93	E2
Harwich MA, 1798	151	F3
Harwich Port MA, 1644	151	F3
Harwinton CT, 5571	94	C3
Harwood ND, 718	19	F4
Harwood Hts. IL, 8612	203	D3
Hasbrouck Hts. NJ, 11842	240	C1
Haskell AR, 3990	117	E3
Haskell OK, 2007	106	A4
Haskell TX, 3322	58	C2
Haskell Co. KS, 4256	42	B4
Haskell Co. OK, 12769	116	B1
Haskell Co. TX, 5899	58	C2
Haskins OH, 1188	90	C2
Haslet TX, 1517	207	A1
Haslett MI, 19220	76	A4
Hastings FL, 580	139	D3
Hastings MI, 7350	75	F4
Hastings MN, 22172	67	D4
Hastings NE, 24907	35	E4
Hastings PA, 1278	92	B3
Hatboro PA, 7360	146	C2
Hatch NM, 1648	56	B2
Hatfield AR, 413	116	C3
Hatfield IN, 813	99	E4
Hatfield MA, 1318	150	A1
Hatfield PA, 3290	146	C2
Hatley MS, 482	119	D4
Hatteras NC, 504	115	F3
Hattiesburg MS, 45989	126	C4
Hatton ND, 763	19	E3
Haubstadt IN, 1577	99	D4
Haughton LA, 3454	125	D2
Hauppauge NY, 20882	149	D3
Hauser ID, 678	14	B3
Hauula HI, 4148	152	A2
Havana FL, 1754	137	E2
Havana IL, 3301	88	A4
Havelock NC, 20735	115	D4
Haven KS, 1237	43	E4
Haverhill FL, 1873	143	F1
Haverhill MA, 60879	95	E1
Haverhill NH, 4697	81	E3
Haverstraw NY, 11910	148	B2
Havertown PA, 22300	248	B3
Haviland KS, 701	43	D4
Havre de Grace MD, 12952	145	D1
Hawaiian Gardens CA, 14254	228	E4
Hawaiian Ocean View HI, 4437	153	F4

Entry		
Hawaiian Paradise Park HI, 11404	153	F3
Hawaii Co. HI, 185079	153	E2
Hawarden IA, 2546	35	F1
Hawesville KY, 945	99	E4
Hawi HI, 1081	153	E2
Hawkins TX, 1278	124	B2
Hawkins Co. TN, 56833	111	D3
Hawkinsville GA, 4589	129	E3
Hawley MN, 2067	19	F4
Hawley PA, 1211	93	F2
Hawley TX, 634	58	C2
Hawleyville CT, 800	148	C1
Haw River NC, 2298	112	C4
Hawthorne CA, 84293	228	D3
Hawthorne FL, 1417	138	C3
Hawthorne NV, 3269	37	E3
Hawthorne NY, 18791	148	B3
Hawthorne NY, 4586	148	B3
Hawthorn Woods IL, 7663	203	B1
Haxtun CO, 946	34	A4
Hayden AL, 444	119	F4
Hayden AZ, 662	55	D2
Hayden CO, 1810	32	C4
Hayden ID, 13294	14	B3
Hayden Lake ID, 574	14	B3
Haydenville MA, 700	150	A1
Hayes LA, 780	133	E2
Hayes Ctr. NE, 214	34	B4
Hayes Co. NE, 967	34	B4
Hayesville NC, 311	121	D2
Hayesville OR, 19936	20	B2
Hayfield MN, 1340	73	D2
Hayfork CA, 2368	28	B4
Haymarket VA, 1782	144	A3
Haynesville LA, 2327	125	D1
Haynesville VA, 550	103	E4
Hayneville AL, 932	128	A3
Hays KS, 20510	43	D2
Hays MT, 843	16	C2
Hays NC, 1851	112	A3
Hays Co. TX, 157107	61	D2
Hay Sprs. NE, 570	34	A1
Haysville KS, 10826	43	E4
Hayti MO, 2939	108	B3
Hayti SD, 381	27	F3
Hayti Hts. MO, 626	108	B3
Hayward CA, 144186	36	B4
Hayward WI, 2318	67	F2
Haywood Co. NC, 59036	111	D4
Haywood Co. TN, 18787	108	C4
Hazard KY, 4456	111	D2
Hazardville CT, 4599	150	A2
Hazel KY, 410	109	D3
Hazel Crest IL, 14100	203	E6
Hazel Green AL, 3630	119	F2
Hazel Green WI, 1256	74	A4
Hazel Park MI, 16422	210	C2
Hazelton ID, 753	31	D1
Hazelton ND, 235	18	C4
Hazelwood MO, 25703	256	B1
Hazen AR, 1468	117	F2
Hazen ND, 2411	18	B3
Hazlehurst GA, 4226	129	F3
Hazlehurst MS, 4009	126	B3
Hazleton IA, 823	73	E4
Hazleton PA, 25340	93	E3
Hazlettville DE, 450	145	E2
Headland AL, 4510	136	C1
Head of the Harbor NY, 1472	149	D3
Healdsburg CA, 11254	36	B3
Healdton OK, 2788	51	E4
Healy AK, 1021	154	C2
Heard Co. GA, 11834	128	B1
Hearne TX, 4459	61	F1
Heart Butte MT, 582	15	E2
Heath OH, 10310	101	D1
Heathcote NJ, 5821	147	D1
Heath Sprs. SC, 790	122	B2
Heathsville VA, 142	103	E4
Heavener OK, 3414	116	B2
Hebbronville TX, 4558	63	E2
Hebbville MD, 10900	193	A2
Heber AZ, 2722	47	E4
Heber CA, 4275	53	E4

Entry		
Heber City UT, 11362	31	F1
Heber Sprs. AR, 7165	117	E1
Hebron CT, 9198	150	A3
Hebron IL, 1216	74	C4
Hebron IN, 3724	89	E2
Hebron KY, 5929	100	B2
Hebron MD, 1084	103	F3
Hebron NE, 1579	43	E1
Hebron ND, 747	18	B4
Hebron OH, 2336	101	D1
Hebron Estates KY, 1087	100	A4
Hecla SD, 227	27	E1
Hector AR, 450	117	D1
Hector MN, 1151	66	B4
Hedrick IA, 764	87	E2
Hedwig Vil. TX, 2557	220	B2
Heeia HI, 4463	152	A3
Heflin AL, 3480	120	A4
Heidelberg MS, 718	127	D3
Heidelberg PA, 1244	250	A3
Heilwood PA, 711	92	B3
Helena AL, 16793	127	F1
Helena AR, 6323	118	A2
Helena GA, 2883	129	E3
Helena MS, 1184	195	C1
Helena MT, 28190	15	E4
Helena OK, 1403	51	D1
Helenwood TN, 865	110	B3
Hellertown PA, 5898	146	C1
Helmetta NJ, 2178	147	E1
Helotes TX, 7341	61	D2
Helper UT, 2201	39	F1
Hemet CA, 78657	53	D3
Hemingford NE, 803	34	A2
Hemingway SC, 459	122	C4
Hemlock MI, 1466	76	B2
Hemphill TX, 1198	124	C1
Hemphill Co. TX, 3807	50	C2
Hempstead NY, 53891	148	C4
Hempstead TX, 5770	62	A1
Hempstead Co. AR, 22609	116	C4
Henagar AL, 2344	120	A2
Henderson KY, 28757	109	E1
Henderson LA, 1674	133	F2
Henderson NE, 991	35	E4
Henderson NV, 257729	46	B2
Henderson NC, 15368	113	D3
Henderson TN, 6309	119	D1
Henderson TX, 13712	124	B3
Henderson Co. NC, 106740	121	E1
Henderson Co. KY, 46250	109	E1
Henderson Co. NC, 106740	121	E1
Henderson Co. TN, 27769	108	C4
Henderson Co. TX, 78532	124	A2
Hendersonville NC, 13137	121	E1
Hendersonville TN, 51372	109	F3
Hendricks MN, 713	27	F3
Hendricks Co. IN, 145448	99	F1
Hendron KY, 4687	108	C2
Hendry Co. FL, 39140	143	D1
Henefer UT, 766	31	F3
Henlopen Acres DE, 122	145	F4
Hennepin IL, 757	88	B2
Hennepin Co. MN, 1152425	66	C3
Hennessey OK, 2131	51	E2
Henniker NH, 1747	81	F4
Henning MN, 802	64	A4
Henning TN, 945	108	B4
Henrico Co. VA, 306335	113	E1
Henrietta NY, 42581	78	C3
Henrietta TX, 3141	59	D1
Henry IL, 2464	88	B3
Henry SD, 267	27	E2
Henry TN, 464	109	D3
Henry Co. AL, 17302	128	B4
Henry Co. GA, 203922	129	D1
Henry Co. IL, 50486	88	A2
Henry Co. IN, 49462	100	A1
Henry Co. IA, 20145	87	F3
Henry Co. KY, 15416	100	A3
Henry Co. MO, 22272	96	C4
Henry Co. OH, 28215	90	B2
Henry Co. TN, 32330	109	D3
Henry Co. VA, 54151	112	B3
Henryetta OK, 5927	51	F3

Helena MT

Entries in **bold black** indicate counties or parishes.
Entries in **bold color** indicate cities with detailed inset maps.

Honolulu HI

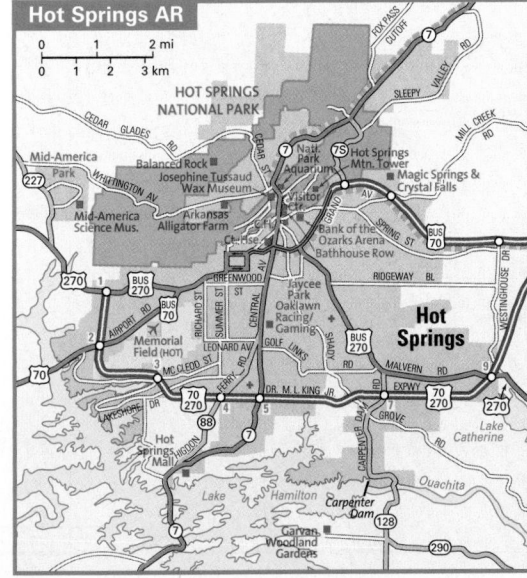

Honolulu

PACIFIC OCEAN

WAIKIKI

Māmala Bay

Hot Springs AR

Figures after entries indicate population, page number, and grid reference.

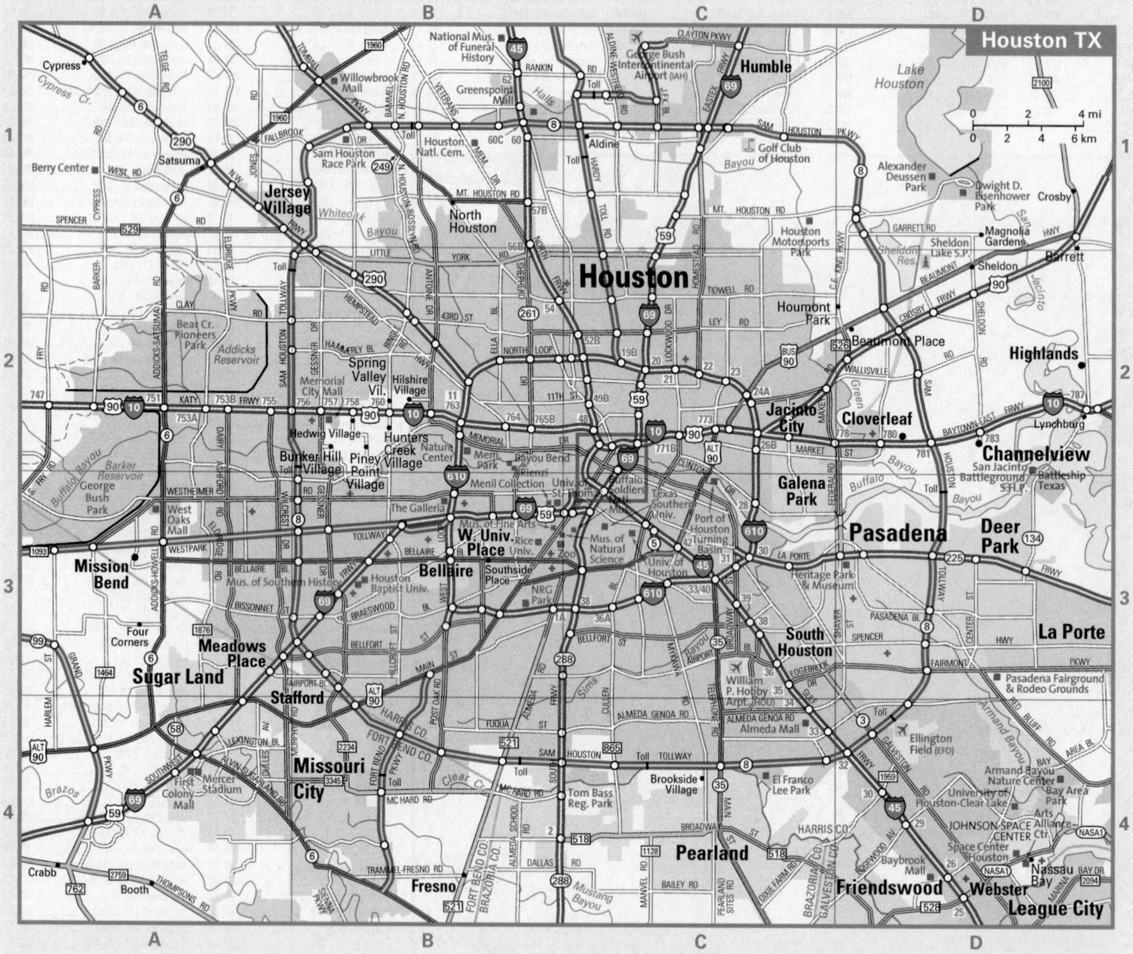

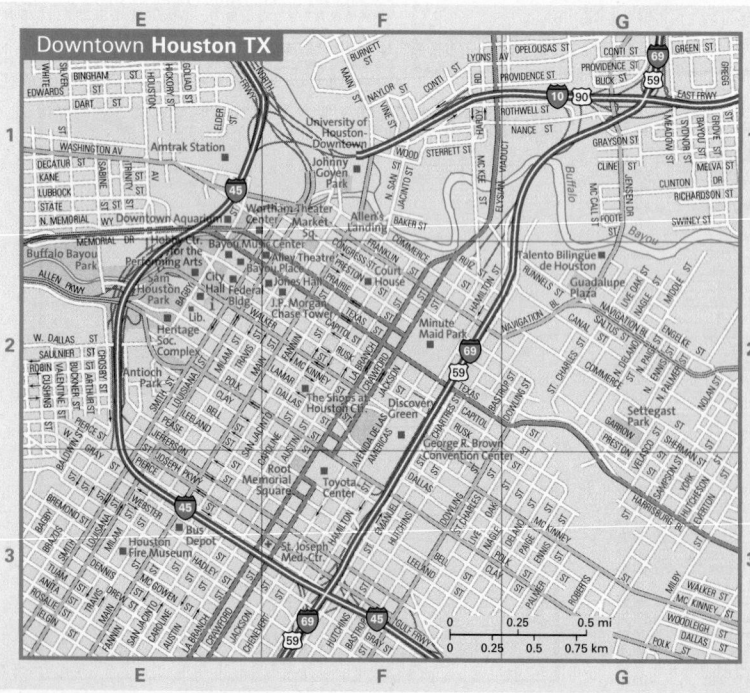

Houston TX

Downtown Houston TX

Entries in **bold black** indicate counties or parishes.
Entries in **bold color** indicate cities with detailed inset maps.

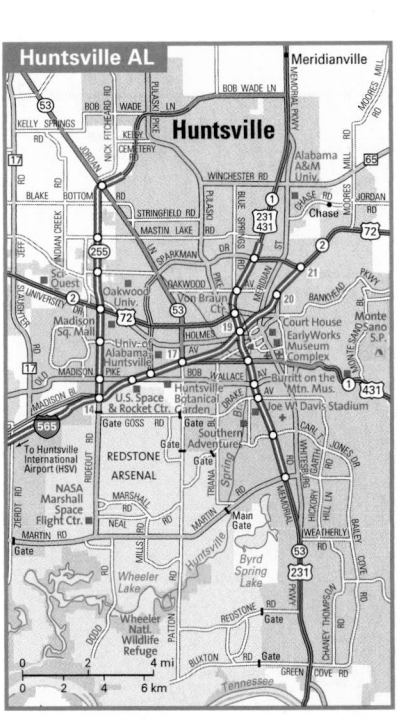

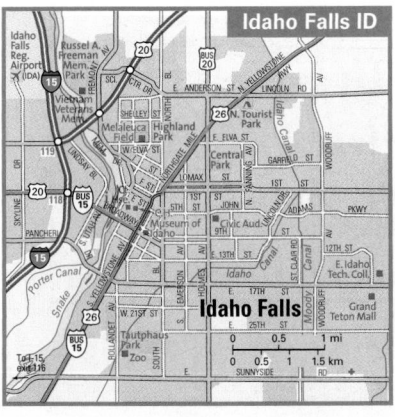

Indianapolis IN

Zionsville, Eagle Village, Home Place, Carmel, Fishers, Royalton, Williams Creek, Meridian Hills, Holliday Park, North Crows Nest, Crows Nest, Rocky Ripple, Spring Hills, Lawrence, Indianapolis, Speedway, Clermont, Wynnedale, Marian Univ., Riverside Park, Avon, Plainfield, Beech Grove, Southport, Homecroft, Camby, Friendswood, West Newton, Southwestway Park

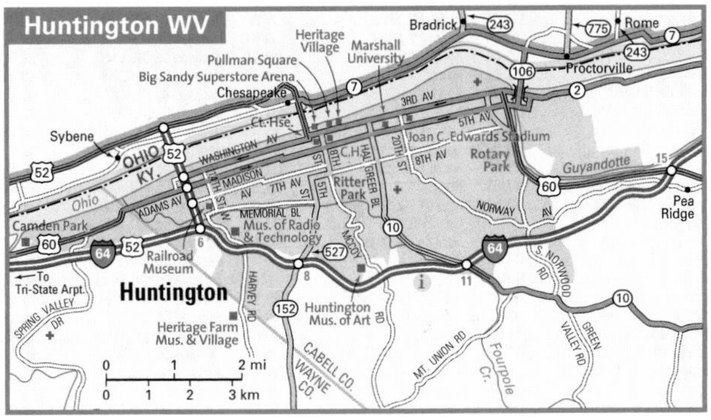

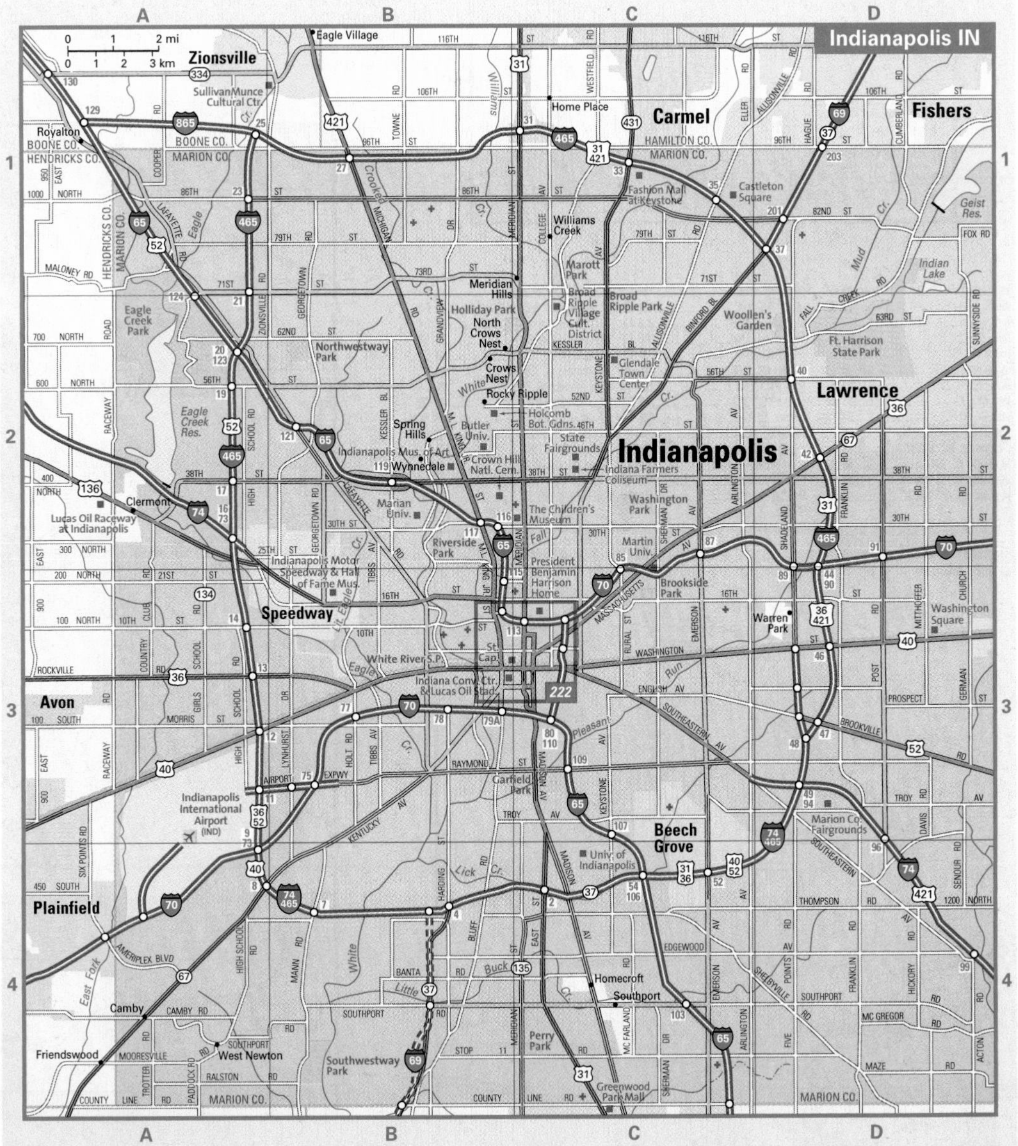

Figures after entries indicate population, page number, and grid reference.

POINTS OF INTEREST

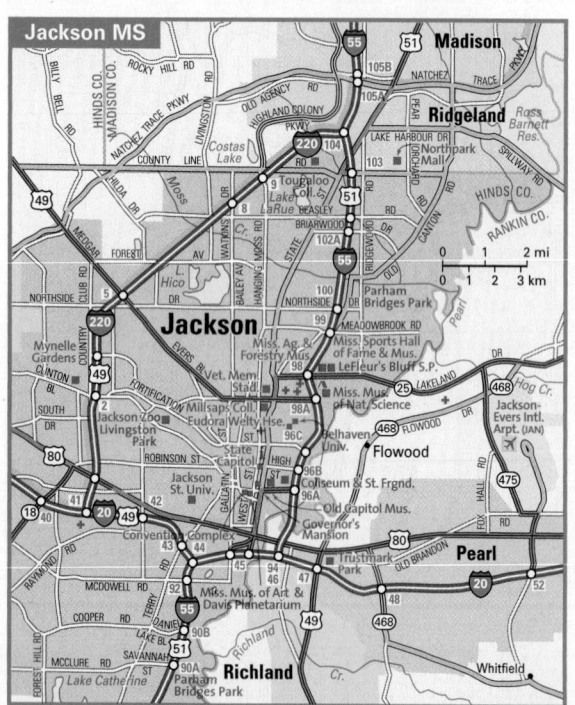

Downtown Indianapolis IN

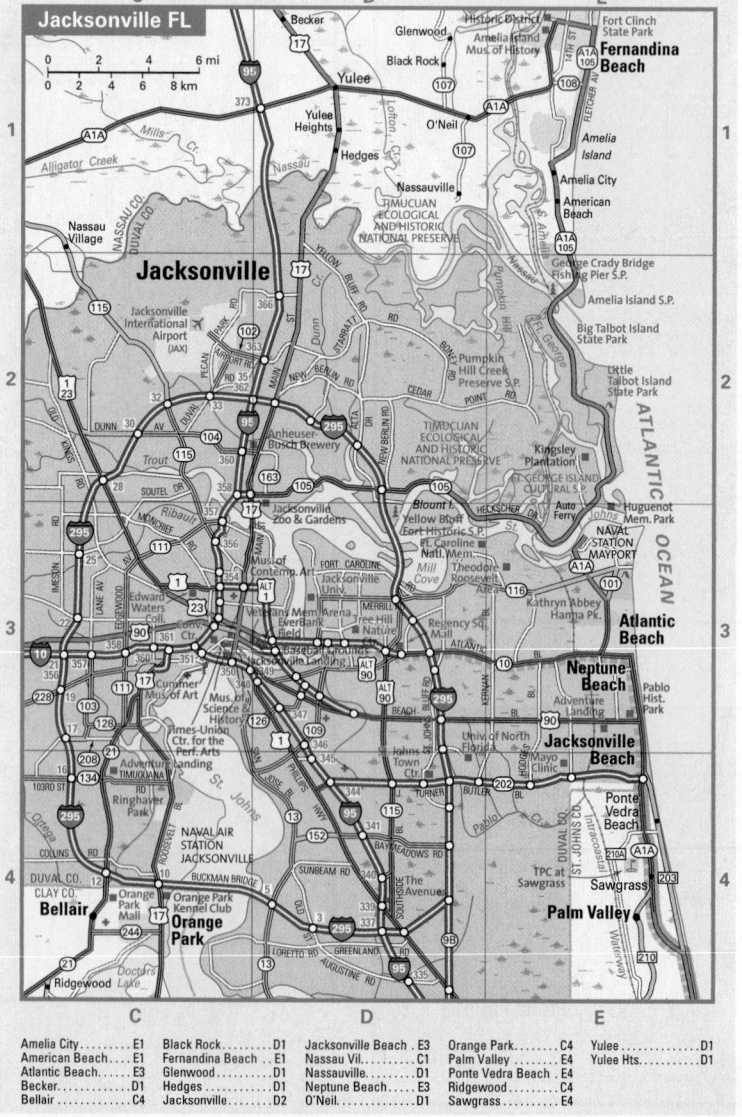

Jacksonville FL

Jackson MS

223
Jacksonville–Keysville

Entries in **bold black** indicate counties or parishes.
Entries in **bold color** indicate cities with detailed inset maps.

Jacksonville NC, 70145 ... 115 D4
Jacksonville OR, 2785 ... 28 B2
Jacksonville PA, 637 ... 92 B4
Jacksonville TX, 14544 ... 124 A3
Jacksonville VT, 223 ... 94 C1
Jacksonville Beach FL, 21362 ... 139 D2
Jacobstown NJ, 950 ... 147 D2
Jacobus PA, 1841 ... 103 E1
Jaffrey NH, 2757 ... 95 D1
Jal NM, 2047 ... 57 F3
Jamaica Beach TX, 983 ... 132 B4
Jamesburg NJ, 5915 ... 147 E2
James City NC, 5899 ... 115 D3
James City Co. VA, 67009 ... 113 F1
Jamesport MO, 524 ... 96 C1
Jamesport NY, 1710 ... 149 E3
Jamestown CA, 3433 ... 37 D3
Jamestown IN, 958 ... 99 E1
Jamestown KS, 286 ... 43 E1
Jamestown KY, 1794 ... 110 B2
Jamestown MI, 750 ... 75 F3
Jamestown NY, 31146 ... 92 B1
Jamestown NC, 3382 ... 112 B4
Jamestown ND, 15427 ... 19 D4
Jamestown OH, 1993 ... 100 C1
Jamestown PA, 617 ... 91 F2
Jamestown RI, 5405 ... 150 C4
Jamestown TN, 1959 ... 110 B3
James Town WY, 536 ... 32 A3
Jamesville NC, 491 ... 113 F4
Jamul CA, 6163 ... 53 D4
Jane Lew WV, 409 ... 102 A2
Janesville CA, 1408 ... 29 D4
Janesville IA, 930 ... 73 D4
Janesville MN, 2256 ... 72 C1
Janesville WI, 63575 ... 74 B4
Jarales NM, 2475 ... 48 C4
Jarratt VA, 638 ... 113 E2
Jarrell TX, 984 ... 61 E1
Jarrettsville MD, 2916 ... 144 C1
Jasmine Estates FL, 18989 ... 140 B2
Jasonville IN, 2222 ... 99 E2
Jasper AL, 14352 ... 119 E4
Jasper AR, 466 ... 107 D4
Jasper FL, 4546 ... 138 B2
Jasper GA, 3684 ... 120 C3
Jasper IN, 15038 ... 99 E4
Jasper MN, 633 ... 27 F4
Jasper MO, 931 ... 106 C1
Jasper OR, 700 ... 20 B4
Jasper TN, 3279 ... 120 A2
Jasper TX, 7590 ... 132 C1
Jasper Co. GA, 13900 ... 129 D1
Jasper Co. IL, 9698 ... 99 D2
Jasper Co. IN, 33478 ... 89 E3
Jasper Co. IA, 36842 ... 87 D2
Jasper Co. MS, 17062 ... 126 C3
Jasper Co. MO, 117404 ... 106 C2
Jasper Co. SC, 24777 ... 130 C3
Jasper Co. TX, 35710 ... 132 C1
Jay FL, 533 ... 135 F1
Jay ME, 4985 ... 82 B2
Jay OK, 2448 ... 106 B3
Jay Co. IN, 21253 ... 90 A4
Jayton TX, 534 ... 58 B2
Jeanerette LA, 5530 ... 133 F3
Jean Lafitte LA, 1903 ... 134 B3
Jeannette PA, 9654 ... 92 A4
Jeddito AZ, 293 ... 47 F2
Jeff Davis Co. GA, 15068 ... 129 F3
Jeff Davis Co. TX, 2342 ... 62 B2
Jefferson GA, 9432 ... 121 D3
Jefferson IA, 4345 ... 86 B1
Jefferson LA, 11193 ... 239 B1
Jefferson MA, 1600 ... 150 B1
Jefferson NC, 1611 ... 111 F3
Jefferson OH, 3120 ... 91 F1
Jefferson OR, 3098 ... 20 B3
Jefferson PA, 631 ... 103 E1
Jefferson SC, 753 ... 122 B2
Jefferson SD, 547 ... 35 F1
Jefferson TX, 2106 ... 124 C2
Jefferson WI, 7973 ... 74 B3
Jefferson City MO, 43079 ... 97 E3
Jefferson City MT, 472 ... 15 E4
Jefferson City TN, 8047 ... 111 D4
Jefferson Co. AL, 658466 ... 119 F4
Jefferson Co. AR, 77435 ... 117 F3
Jefferson Co. CO, 534543 ... 41 E1
Jefferson Co. FL, 14761 ... 137 E2
Jefferson Co. GA, 16930 ... 129 F1
Jefferson Co. ID, 26140 ... 23 E4
Jefferson Co. IL, 38827 ... 98 C4
Jefferson Co. IN, 32428 ... 100 A3
Jefferson Co. IA, 16843 ... 87 E3
Jefferson Co. KS, 19126 ... 96 A2
Jefferson Co. KY, 741096 ... 100 A4
Jefferson Co. MS, 7726 ... 126 A3
Jefferson Co. MO, 218733 ... 98 A4
Jefferson Co. MT, 11406 ... 23 E1
Jefferson Co. NE, 7547 ... 35 F4
Jefferson Co. NY, 116229 ... 79 E2
Jefferson Co. OH, 69709 ... 91 F4
Jefferson Co. OK, 6472 ... 59 E1
Jefferson Co. OR, 21720 ... 20 C3
Jefferson Co. PA, 45200 ... 92 B2
Jefferson Co. TN, 51407 ... 111 D4
Jefferson Co. TX, 252273 ... 132 C3
Jefferson Co. WA, 29872 ... 12 B3
Jefferson Co. WV, 53498 ... 103 D2
Jefferson Co. WI, 83686 ... 74 C3
Jefferson Davis Co. MS, 12487 ... 126 B4
Jefferson Davis Par. LA, 31594 ... 133 E2
Jefferson Hts. NY, 1094 ... 94 B2
Jefferson Hills PA, 10619 ... 92 A4
Jefferson Par. LA, 432552 ... 134 B3
Jeffersontown KY, 26595 ... 100 A4
Jefferson Valley NY, 14142 ... 148 B2
Jeffersonville GA, 1035 ... 129 E2
Jeffersonville IN, 44953 ... 100 A4
Jeffersonville KY, 1506 ... 100 C4
Jeffersonville OH, 1203 ... 100 C1
Jeffersonville PA, 10200 ... 248 A1
Jeffersonville VT, 729 ... 81 D1
Jellico TN, 2355 ... 110 C3
Jemez Pueblo NM, 1788 ... 48 C3
Jemez Sprs. NM, 250 ... 48 C2
Jemison AL, 2585 ... 127 F1
Jena LA, 3398 ... 125 E4
Jenison MI, 16538 ... 75 F3
Jenkins KY, 2203 ... 111 E2
Jenkins Co. GA, 8340 ... 129 F2
Jenkintown PA, 4422 ... 146 C2
Jenks OK, 16924 ... 51 F2
Jennerstown PA, 695 ... 92 B4
Jennings FL, 878 ... 137 F2
Jennings LA, 10383 ... 133 E2
Jennings MO, 14712 ... 256 B1
Jennings Co. IN, 28525 ... 100 A3
Jenny Lind AR, 650 ... 116 C1
Jensen Beach FL, 11707 ... 141 E4
Jerauld Co. SD, 2071 ... 27 D3
Jericho NY, 13567 ... 148 C4
Jericho VT, 1329 ... 81 D2
Jermyn PA, 2169 ... 93 F2
Jerome AZ, 444 ... 47 D4
Jerome ID, 10890 ... 30 C1
Jerome PA, 1017 ... 92 B4
Jerome Co. ID, 22374 ... 31 D1
Jersey City NJ, 247597 ... 148 B4
Jersey Co. IL, 22985 ... 98 A2
Jersey Shore PA, 4361 ... 93 D2
Jersey Vil. TX, 7620 ... 132 A3
Jerseyville IL, 8465 ... 98 A2
Jerseyville NJ, 1000 ... 147 E2
Jerusalem RI, 800 ... 150 C4
Jessamine Co. KY, 48586 ... 100 B4
Jessup MD, 7137 ... 144 C2
Jessup PA, 4676 ... 93 F2
Jesup GA, 10214 ... 130 A4
Jesup IA, 2520 ... 73 E4
Jetmore KS, 867 ... 42 C3
Jewell IA, 1215 ... 72 C4
Jewell KS, 432 ... 43 E1
Jewell Co. KS, 3077 ... 43 E1
Jewett OH, 692 ... 91 F4
Jewett TX, 1167 ... 59 F4
Jewett City (Griswold) CT, 3487 ... 149 F1
Jim Hogg Co. TX, 5300 ... 63 E3
Jim Thorpe PA, 4781 ... 93 F3
Jim Wells Co. TX, 40838 ... 63 E2
Joanna SC, 1539 ... 121 F3
Joaquin TX, 824 ... 124 C3
Jo Daviess Co. IL, 22678 ... 74 A4
John Day OR, 1744 ... 21 F3
Johns Island SC, 650 ... 131 D2
Johnson AR, 3354 ... 106 C4
Johnson VT, 1443 ... 81 E2
Johnsonburg PA, 2483 ... 92 B2
Johnson City KS, 1495 ... 42 B4
Johnson City NY, 15174 ... 93 E1
Johnson City OR, 566 ... 251 D3
Johnson City TN, 63152 ... 111 E3
Johnson City TX, 1656 ... 61 D1
Johnson Co. AR, 25540 ... 117 D1
Johnson Co. GA, 9980 ... 129 F2
Johnson Co. IL, 12582 ... 108 C1
Johnson Co. IN, 139654 ... 99 F2
Johnson Co. IA, 130882 ... 87 F2
Johnson Co. KS, 544179 ... 96 B3
Johnson Co. KY, 23356 ... 111 D1
Johnson Co. MO, 52595 ... 96 C3
Johnson Co. NE, 5217 ... 35 F4
Johnson Co. TN, 18244 ... 111 F3
Johnson Co. TX, 150934 ... 59 E3
Johnson Co. WY, 8569 ... 25 D4
Johnson Creek WI, 2738 ... 74 C3
Johnsonville SC, 1480 ... 122 C4
Johnston IA, 17278 ... 86 C2
Johnston SC, 2362 ... 121 F4
Johnston City IL, 3543 ... 108 C1
Johnston Co. NC, 168878 ... 113 D4
Johnston Co. OK, 10957 ... 51 F4
Johnstown CO, 9887 ... 33 E4
Johnstown NY, 8743 ... 79 F3
Johnstown OH, 4632 ... 91 D4
Johnstown PA, 20978 ... 92 B4
Joiner AR, 576 ... 118 B1
Joliet IL, 147433 ... 89 D2
Joliet MT, 595 ... 24 B2
Jollyville TX, 16151 ... 61 E1
Jones OK, 2692 ... 51 E3
Jonesboro AR, 67263 ... 108 A4
Jonesboro GA, 4724 ... 120 C4
Jonesboro IL, 1821 ... 108 C1
Jonesboro IN, 1756 ... 89 F4
Jonesboro LA, 4704 ... 125 E3
Jonesborough TN, 5051 ... 111 E3
Jonesburg MO, 768 ... 97 F3
Jones Co. GA, 28669 ... 129 D1
Jones Co. IA, 20638 ... 87 F1
Jones Co. MS, 67761 ... 126 C4
Jones Co. NC, 10153 ... 115 D3
Jones Co. SD, 1006 ... 26 C4
Jones Co. TX, 20202 ... 58 C2
Jones Creek TX, 2020 ... 132 A4
Jonesport ME, 1408 ... 83 E2
Jonestown MS, 1298 ... 118 A3
Jonestown PA, 64 ... 93 E4
Jonestown TX, 1834 ... 61 E1
Jonesville LA, 2265 ... 125 F4
Jonesville MI, 2258 ... 90 B1
Jonesville NC, 2285 ... 112 A3
Jonesville SC, 911 ... 121 F2
Jonesville VT, 375 ... 81 D2
Jonesville VA, 1034 ... 111 D3
Joplin MO, 50150 ... 106 B2
Joplin MT, 157 ... 15 F2
Joppatowne MD, 12616 ... 145 D1
Jordan MN, 5470 ... 66 C4
Jordan MT, 343 ... 17 D3
Jordan NY, 1368 ... 79 D3
Joseph OR, 1081 ... 22 A2
Joseph City AZ, 1386 ... 47 F3
Josephine TX, 812 ... 59 F2
Josephine Co. OR, 82713 ... 28 B2
Joshua TX, 5910 ... 59 E3
Joshua Tree CA, 7414 ... 53 E2
Jourdanton TX, 3871 ... 61 D3
Juab Co. UT, 10246 ... 39 D1
Judith Basin Co. MT, 2072 ... 16 A3
Judsonia AR, 2019 ... 117 F1
Julesburg CO, 1225 ... 34 A3
Juliaetta ID, 579 ... 14 B4
Julian CA, 1502 ... 53 D4
Julian NC, 600 ... 112 B4
Jumpertown MS, 480 ... 119 D2
Junction TX, 2574 ... 60 C1
Junction UT, 191 ... 39 E3
Junction City AR, 581 ... 125 E1
Junction City KS, 23353 ... 43 F2
Junction City KY, 2241 ... 110 B1
Junction City LA, 582 ... 125 E1
Junction City OH, 819 ... 101 E1
Junction City OR, 5392 ... 20 B3
Juneau AK, 31275 ... 155 E4
Juneau WI, 2814 ... 74 C2
Juneau Co. WI, 26664 ... 74 A1
Juniata NE, 755 ... 35 D4
Juniata Co. PA, 24636 ... 93 D3
Junior WV, 520 ... 102 A2
Juno Beach FL, 3176 ... 141 F4
Jupiter FL, 55156 ... 141 F4
Jupiter Island FL, 817 ... 141 F4
Jurupa Valley CA, 94235 ... 229 H3
Justice IL, 12926 ... 203 D5
Justin TX, 3246 ... 59 E2
Justus PA, 950 ... 261 E1

K

Kaaawa HI, 1379 ... 152 A2
Kaanapali HI, 1045 ... 153 D1
Kadoka SD, 654 ... 26 B4
Kahaluu HI, 4738 ... 152 A3
Kahoka MO, 2078 ... 87 E4
Kahuku HI, 2614 ... 152 A2
Kahului HI, 26337 ... 153 D1
Kaibab AZ, 124 ... 47 D1
Kaibito AZ, 1522 ... 47 E1
Kailua HI, 38635 ... 152 B3
Kailua-Kona HI, 11975 ... 153 E3
Kake AK, 557 ... 155 E4
Kalaheo HI, 4595 ... 152 B1
Kalama WA, 2344 ... 20 C1
Kalamazoo MI, 74262 ... 75 F4
Kalamazoo Co. MI, 250331 ... 75 F4
Kalaoa HI, 9644 ... 153 E3
Kalaupapa HI, ... 152 C3
Kalawao Co. HI, 90 ... 152 C3
Kaleva MI, 470 ... 75 F1
Kalida OH, 1542 ... 90 B3
Kalihiwai HI, 428 ... 152 B1
Kalispell MT, 19927 ... 15 D2
Kalkaska MI, 2020 ... 69 F4
Kalkaska Co. MI, 17153 ... 70 B4
Kalona IA, 2363 ... 87 E2
Kamas UT, 1811 ... 31 F4
Kamiah ID, 1295 ... 22 B1
Kanab UT, 4312 ... 47 D1
Kanabec Co. MN, 16239 ... 67 D2
Kanarraville UT, 355 ... 39 D4
Kanawha IA, 652 ... 72 C3
Kanawha WV, 500 ... 101 F2
Kanawha Co. WV, 193063 ... 101 F4
Kandiyohi MN, 491 ... 66 B3
Kandiyohi Co. MN, 42239 ... 66 B3
Kane PA, 3730 ... 92 B2
Kane Co. IL, 515269 ... 88 C1
Kane Co. UT, 7125 ... 39 E4
Kaneohe HI, 34597 ... 152 A3
Kankakee IL, 27537 ... 89 D3
Kankakee Co. IL, 113449 ... 89 D2
Kannapolis NC, 42625 ... 122 B1
Kanopolis KS, 492 ... 43 E2
Kanosh UT, 474 ... 39 D2
Kansas IL, 787 ... 99 D1
Kansas OK, 802 ... 106 B3
Kansas City KS, 145786 ... 96 B2
Kansas City MO, 459787 ... 96 B2
Kapaa HI, 10699 ... 152 B1
Kapaau HI, 1734 ... 153 E2
Kaplan LA, 4600 ... 133 E3
Karlstad MN, 760 ... 19 F2
Karnak IL, 499 ... 108 C2
Karnes City TX, 3042 ... 61 E3
Karnes Co. TX, 14824 ... 61 E3
Karns TN, 1500 ... 110 C4
Kasigluk AK, 569 ... 154 B3
Kasota MN, 675 ... 72 C1
Kasson IN, 1500 ... 99 D4
Kasson MN, 5931 ... 73 D1
Kathleen FL, 6332 ... 140 C2
Kathleen GA, 650 ... 129 D2
Katonah NY, 1679 ... 148 C2
Katy TX, 14102 ... 132 A3
Kauai Co. HI, 67091 ... 152 B1
Kaufman TX, 6703 ... 59 F2
Kaufman Co. TX, 103350 ... 59 F3
Kaukauna WI, 15462 ... 74 C1
Kaumakani HI, 749 ... 152 B1
Kaunakakai HI, 3425 ... 152 C3
Kawkawlin MI, 1600 ... 76 B2
Kaycee WY, 263 ... 25 D4
Kay Co. OK, 46562 ... 51 E1
Kayenta AZ, 5189 ... 47 F1
Kaysville UT, 27300 ... 31 E3
Keaau HI, 2253 ... 153 F3
Kealakekua HI, 2019 ... 153 E3
Keams Canyon AZ, 304 ... 47 F2
Keansburg NJ, 10105 ... 147 E1
Kearney MO, 8381 ... 96 B2
Kearney NE, 30787 ... 35 D4
Kearney Co. NE, 6489 ... 35 D4
Kearneysville WV, 650 ... 103 D2
Kearns UT, 35731 ... 257 A2
Kearny AZ, 1950 ... 55 D2
Kearny NJ, 40684 ... 148 B4
Kearny Co. KS, 3977 ... 42 B3
Keauhou HI, 3549 ... 153 E3
Keavy KY, 450 ... 110 C2
Kechi KS, 1909 ... 43 E4
Keedysville MD, 1152 ... 144 A1
Keegan ME, 550 ... 85 E1
Keego Harbor MI, 2970 ... 210 A1
Keene NH, 23409 ... 95 D1
Keene TX, 6106 ... 59 E3
Keener NC, 567 ... 123 E2
Keenesburg CO, 1127 ... 41 E1
Keeseville NY, 1815 ... 81 D2
Keewatin MN, 1068 ... 64 B3
Keiser AR, 759 ... 108 B4
Keith Co. NE, 8368 ... 34 B3
Keithsburg IL, 609 ... 87 F3
Keizer OR, 36478 ... 20 B2
Kekaha HI, 3537 ... 152 B1
Keller TX, 39627 ... 59 E2
Kellogg ID, 2120 ... 14 B3
Kellogg IA, 599 ... 87 D1
Kellyville OK, 1150 ... 51 F2
Kelseyville CA, 3353 ... 36 B2
Kelso MO, 586 ... 108 B2
Kelso WA, 11925 ... 20 B1
Kemah TX, 1773 ... 132 B3
Kemblesville PA, 1000 ... 146 B4
Kemmerer WY, 2656 ... 31 F2
Kemp TX, 1154 ... 59 F3
Kemper Co. MS, 10456 ... 127 D2
Kempner TX, 1089 ... 59 E4
Kenai AK, 7100 ... 154 C3
Kenansville NC, 855 ... 123 E2
Kenbridge VA, 1257 ... 113 D2
Kendall FL, 75371 ... 143 E2
Kendall NY, 750 ... 78 B3
Kendall Co. IL, 114736 ... 88 C2
Kendall Co. TX, 33410 ... 61 D2
Kendall Park NJ, 9339 ... 147 D1
Kendallville IN, 9862 ... 90 A2
Kendrick FL, 600 ... 138 C4
Kendrick ID, 303 ... 14 B4
Kenedy TX, 3296 ... 61 E3
Kenedy Co. TX, 416 ... 63 F3
Kenefick TX, 563 ... 132 B2
Kenesaw NE, 880 ... 35 D4
Kenilworth IL, 2513 ... 203 D2
Kenilworth NJ, 7914 ... 240 A4
Kenilworth PA, 1907 ... 146 B2
Kenly NC, 1339 ... 123 E1
Kenmare ND, 1096 ... 18 B1
Kenmore NY, 15423 ... 78 A3
Kenmore WA, 20460 ... 262 B2
Kennebec SD, 240 ... 26 C4
Kennebec Co. ME, 122151 ... 82 B2
Kennebunk ME, 5214 ... 82 B4
Kennebunkport ME, 1238 ... 82 B4
Kennedale TX, 6763 ... 207 B3
Kennedy AL, 447 ... 119 D4
Kenner LA, 66702 ... 134 B3
Kennesaw GA, 29783 ... 120 C3
Kenneth City FL, 4980 ... 266 A3
Kennett MO, 10932 ... 108 B3
Kennett Square PA, 6072 ... 146 B3
Kennewick WA, 73917 ... 21 E1
Keno OR, 650 ... 28 C2
Kenosha WI, 99218 ... 75 D4
Kenosha Co. WI, 166426 ... 74 C4
Kenova WV, 3216 ... 101 D4
Kensett AR, 1648 ... 117 F1
Kensington CA, 5077 ... 259 C2
Kensington CT, 8459 ... 149 E1
Kensington KS, 473 ... 43 D1
Kensington MD, 2213 ... 270 C1
Kensington NY, 1161 ... 241 G2
Kensington Park FL, 3901 ... 266 C5
Kent CT, 2962 ... 94 B3
Kent OH, 28904 ... 91 E3
Kent WA, 92411 ... 12 C3
Kent City MI, 1057 ... 75 F3
Kent Co. DE, 162310 ... 145 E3
Kent Co. MD, 20197 ... 145 D2
Kent Co. MI, 602622 ... 75 F3
Kent Co. RI, 166158 ... 150 C3
Kent Co. TX, 808 ... 58 B2
Kentfield CA, 6485 ... 259 A1
Kentland IN, 1748 ... 89 D3
Kenton DE, 261 ... 145 E2
Kenton KY, 375 ... 100 B3
Kenton OH, 8262 ... 90 C3
Kenton TN, 1281 ... 108 C3
Kenton Co. KY, 159720 ... 100 B2
Kentwood LA, 2198 ... 134 B1
Kentwood MI, 48707 ... 75 F3
Kenvil NJ, 3009 ... 148 A3
Kenwood MD, 9800 ... 193 D2
Kenwood OH, 6981 ... 204 C2
Kenwood Beach MD, 600 ... 144 C4
Kenyon MN, 1815 ... 73 D1
Keokuk IA, 10780 ... 87 F4
Keokuk Co. IA, 10511 ... 87 E2
Keosauqua IA, 1006 ... 87 E3
Keota IA, 1009 ... 87 E2
Keota OK, 564 ... 116 B1
Kerens TX, 1573 ... 59 F3
Kerhonkson NY, 1684 ... 94 A3
Kerkhoven MN, 759 ... 66 B3
Kerman CA, 13544 ... 44 C3
Kermit TX, 5708 ... 57 F3
Kern Co. CA, 839631 ... 45 D4
Kernersville NC, 23123 ... 112 B4
Kernville CA, 1395 ... 45 E4
Kerr Co. TX, 49625 ... 60 C2
Kerrville TX, 22347 ... 60 C2
Kersey CO, 1454 ... 33 E4
Kershaw SC, 1803 ... 122 B2
Kershaw Co. SC, 61697 ... 122 B3
Keshena WI, 1262 ... 68 C4
Ketchikan AK, 8050 ... 155 E4
Ketchum ID, 2689 ... 22 C4
Kettering OH, 56163 ... 100 B1
Kettle Falls WA, 1595 ... 13 F1
Kettleman City CA, 1439 ... 44 C3
Kevil KY, 376 ... 108 C2
Kewanee IL, 12916 ... 88 A2
Kewanna IN, 613 ... 89 E3
Kewaskum WI, 4004 ... 74 C2
Kewaunee WI, 2952 ... 75 D1
Kewaunee Co. WI, 20574 ... 69 D4
Keweenaw Co. MI, 2156 ... 65 F3
Keya Paha Co. NE, 824 ... 35 D1
Key Biscayne FL, 12344 ... 143 F2
Key Colony Beach FL, 797 ... 143 D4
Keyes CA, 5601 ... 36 C4
Key Largo FL, 10433 ... 143 E3
Keyport NJ, 7240 ... 147 E1
Keys OK, 565 ... 106 B4
Keyser WV, 5439 ... 102 C2
Keystone CO, 1079 ... 41 D1
Keystone IA, 622 ... 87 E1
Keystone SD, 337 ... 25 F4
Keystone WV, 282 ... 111 F1
Keystone Hts. FL, 1350 ... 139 D3
Keysville VA, 832 ... 113 D2

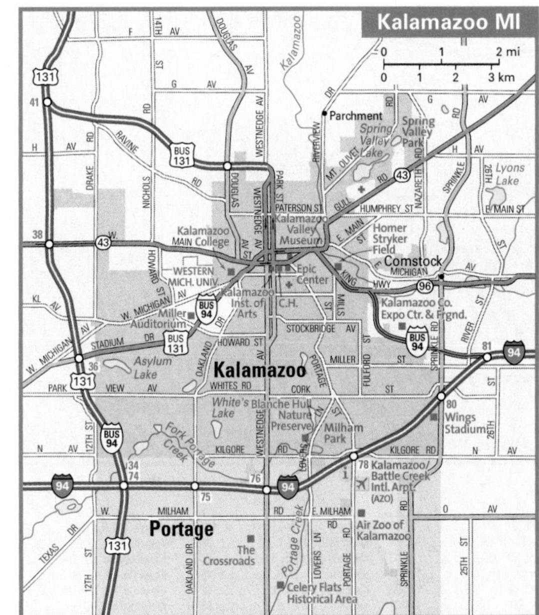

Kalamazoo MI
0 1 2 mi
0 1 2 3 km
Parchment
Kalamazoo
Portage
Comstock
Kalamazoo Valley Museum
Western Mich. Univ.
Kalamazoo Co. Expo Ctr. & Frgnd.
Kalamazoo/Battle Creek Intl. Arpt. (AZO)
Air Zoo of Kalamazoo
Celery Flats Historical Area

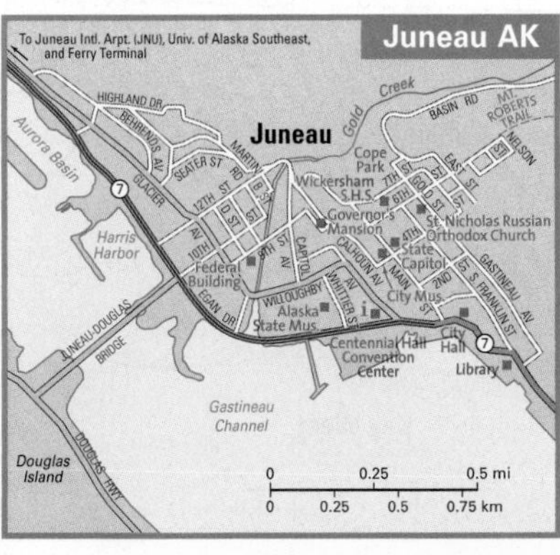

Juneau AK
To Juneau Intl. Arpt. (JNU), Univ. of Alaska Southeast, and Ferry Terminal
Juneau
Gastineau Channel
Douglas Island
Harris Harbor
Alaska State Mus.
Centennial Hall Convention Center
0 0.25 0.5 mi
0 0.25 0.5 0.75 km

Figures after entries indicate population, page number, and grid reference.

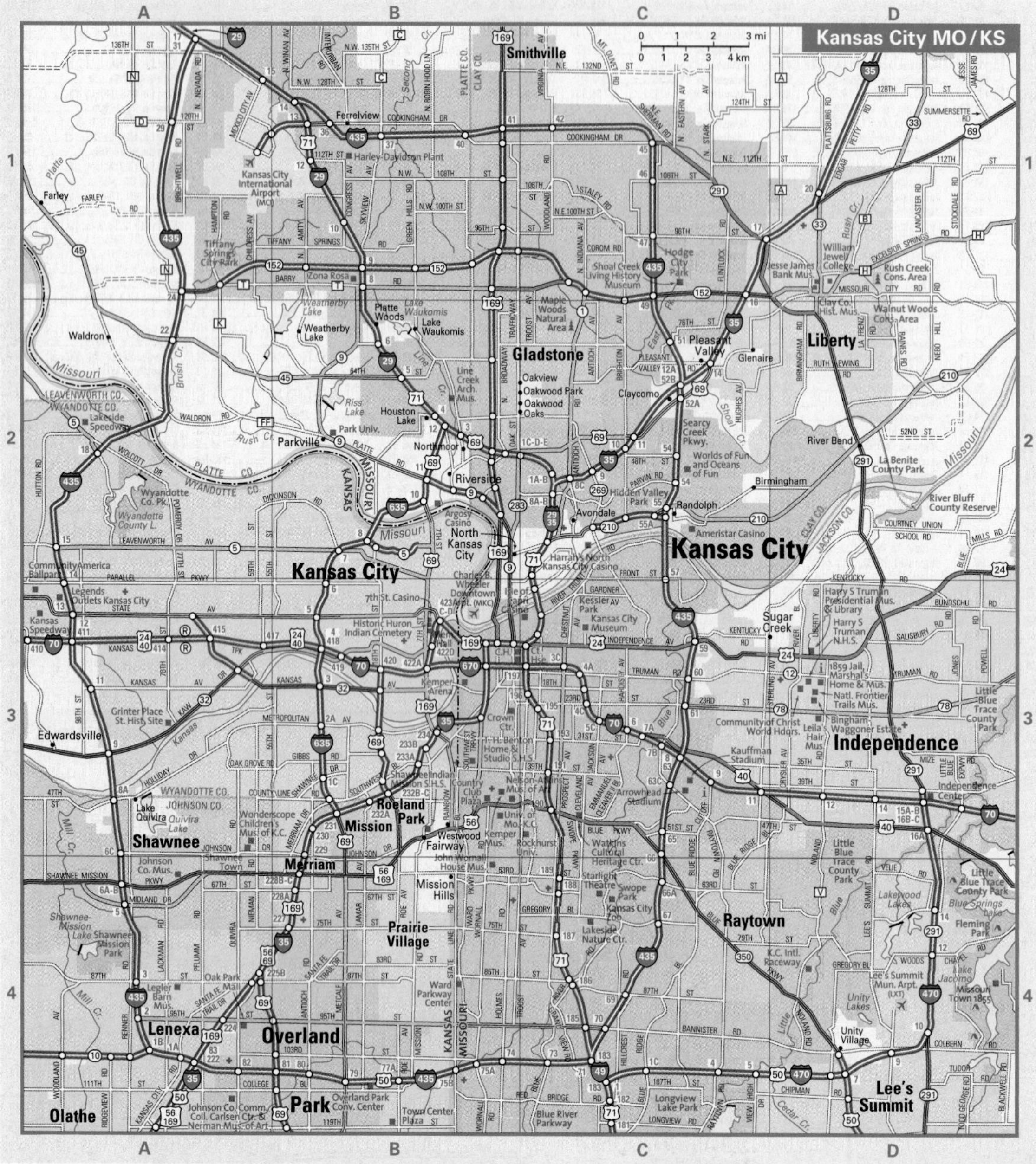

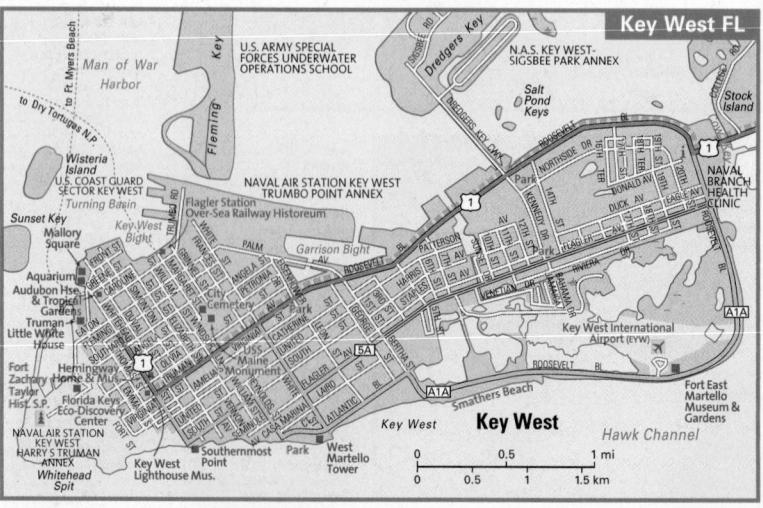

Kansas City MO/KS

Key West FL

Entries in **bold black** indicate counties or parishes.
Entries in **bold color** indicate cities with detailed inset maps.

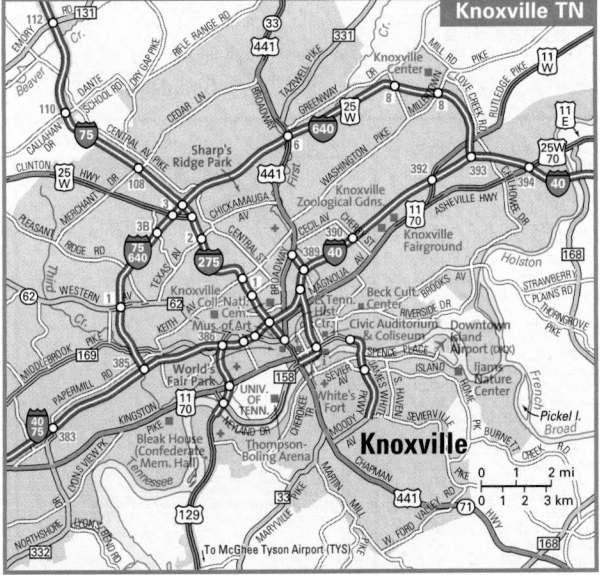

Knoxville TN

Lafayette LA

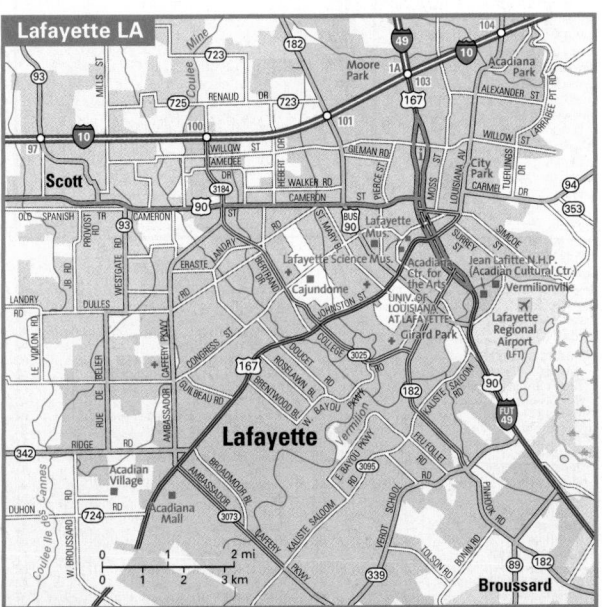

Lancaster PA

Bird in Hand C2
E. Petersburg A1
Lancaster B2
Landisville A1
Leacock C1
Leola C1
Millersville A2
Mountville A2
Neffsville B1
Rohrerstown A2
Salunga A1
Smoketown C2

Lansing MI

Figures after entries indicate population, page number, and grid reference.

Las Vegas NV

Las Vegas Strip NV

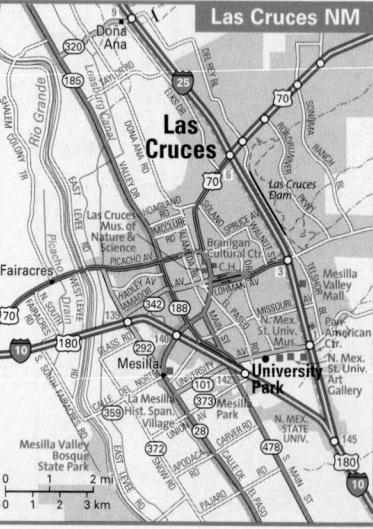

Las Cruces NM

Entries in **bold black** indicate counties or parishes.
Entries in **bold color** indicate cities with detailed inset maps.

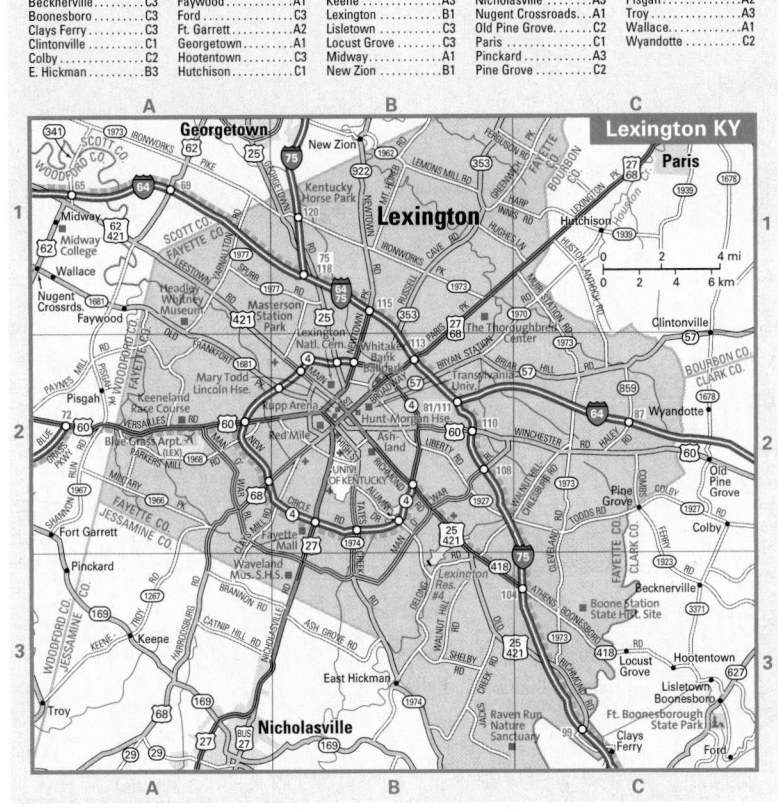

Becknerville C3	Faywood A1	Keene A3	Nicholasville A3	Pisgah A2
Boonesboro C3	Ford C2	Lexington B1	Nugent Crossroads .. A1	Troy A1
Clays Ferry C3	Ft. Garrett A2	Lisletown C3	Old Pine Grove C2	Wallace A1
Clintonville C1	Georgetown A1	Locust Grove C3	Paris C1	Wyandotte C2
Colby C2	Hootentown A1	Midway A1	Pinckard A3	
E. Hickman B3	Hutchison C1	New Zion B1	Pine Grove C2	

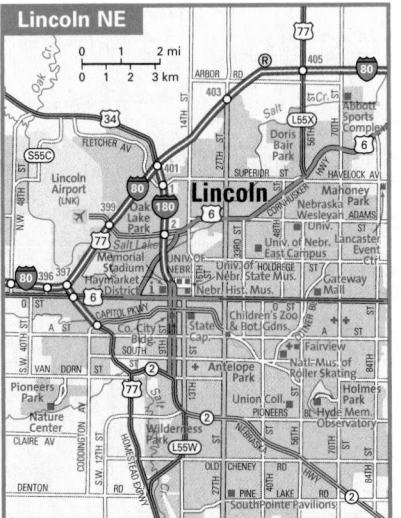

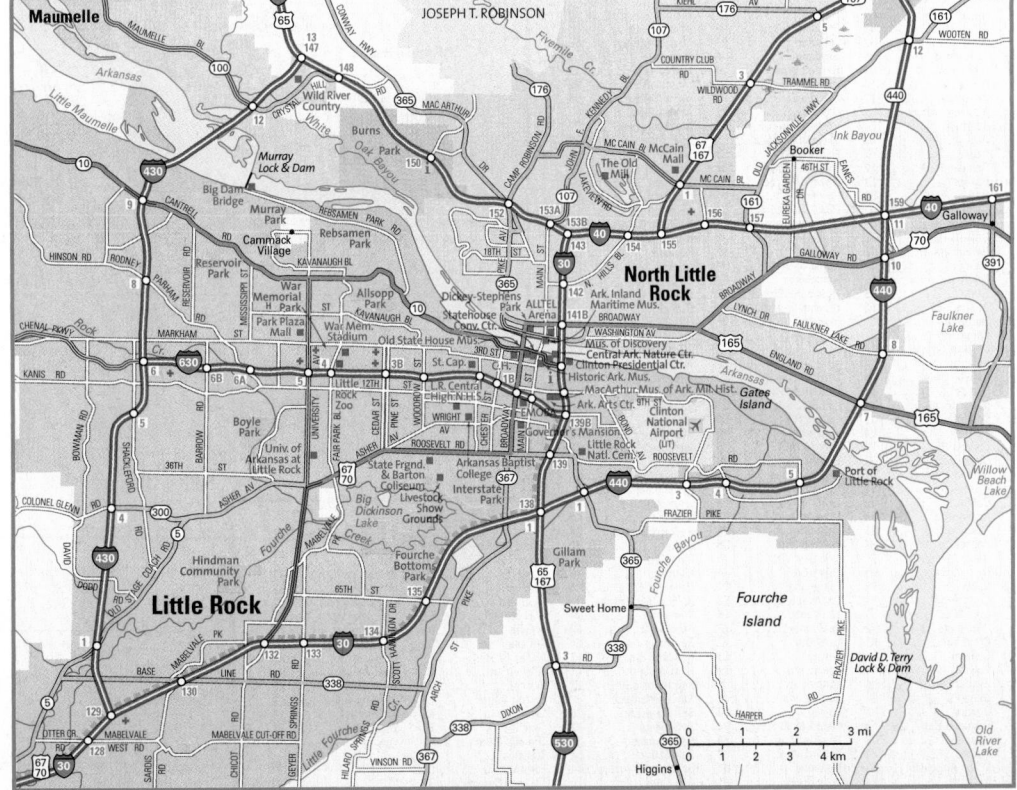

Lebanon OH, 20033 .... 100 B2	Leicester MA, 10970 .... 150 B1	Lepanto AR, 1893 .... 118 B1
Lebanon OR, 15518 .... 20 B3	Leigh NE, 405 .... 35 E3	Le Roy IL, 3560 .... 88 C4
Lebanon PA, 25477 .... 93 E2	Leighton AL, 728 .... 119 E2	LeRoy KS, 561 .... 96 A4
Lebanon TN, 26190 .... 109 F3	Leipsic DE, 183 .... 145 E2	Le Roy MN, 929 .... 73 D2
Lebanon VA, 3424 .... 111 E2	Leipsic OH, 2093 .... 90 B3	Le Roy NY, 4391 .... 78 B3
Lebanon Co. PA, 133568 .... 93 E4	Leisure City TN, 22655 .... 143 E3	Leslie AR, 441 .... 107 E4
Lebanon Jct. KY, 1813 .... 100 A4	Leisuretowne NJ, 3582 .... 147 D3	Leslie MI, 1851 .... 76 A4
Lebec CA, 1468 .... 52 B1	Leitchfield KY, 6699 .... 109 F1	**Leslie Co. KY**, 11310 .... 111 D2
Lecanto FL, 5882 .... 140 B1	Leitersburg MD, 573 .... 103 D1	Lesslie SC, 3112 .... 122 A4
Lecompte LA, 1227 .... 133 E1	Leithsville PA, 1200 .... 146 C1	Lester Prairie MN, 1730 .... 66 C4
Lecompton KS, 625 .... 96 A2	Leland IL, 977 .... 88 C2	Le Sueur MN, 4058 .... 72 C1
Ledbetter KY, 1683 .... 109 D2	Leland MS, 4481 .... 126 A1	**Le Sueur Co. MN**, 27703 .... 72 C1
Ledgewood NJ, 1100 .... 148 A3	Leland NC, 13527 .... 123 E3	**Letcher Co. KY**, 24519 .... 111 D2
Ledyard Ctr. CT, 15172 .... 149 F1	Le Mars IA, 9826 .... 35 F1	Leupp AZ, 951 .... 47 D3
Lee MA, 2051 .... 94 C2	Lemay MO, 16645 .... 256 B3	Levant ME, 2171 .... 83 D1
Leechburg PA, 2156 .... 92 A3	Lemmon SD, 1227 .... 26 B1	Levant UT, 841 .... 39 E1
Lee Co. AL, 140247 .... 128 B2	Lemmon Valley NV, 5040 .... 37 D1	Level Plains AL, 2085 .... 128 B4
Lee Co. AR, 10424 .... 118 A2	Lemon Grove CA, 25320 .... 53 D4	Levelland TX, 13542 .... 57 F1
Lee Co. FL, 618754 .... 141 E3	Lemont IL, 16000 .... 89 D2	**Levy Co. FL**, 40801 .... 138 C4
Lee Co. GA, 28298 .... 129 D4	Lemont PA, 2270 .... 92 C3	Lewes DE, 2747 .... 145 F3
Lee Co. IL, 36031 .... 88 B2	Lemoore CA, 24531 .... 44 C3	**Lewis and Clark Co. MT**, 63395 .... 15 E3
Lee Co. IA, 35862 .... 87 F3	Lemoyne PA, 4553 .... 218 B2	Lewisburg KY, 810 .... 109 E2
Lee Co. KY, 7887 .... 110 C1	Lena IL, 2912 .... 74 A4	Lewisburg OH, 1820 .... 100 B1
Lee Co. MS, 82910 .... 119 D3	**Lenawee Co. MI**, 99892 .... 90 B1	Lewisburg PA, 5792 .... 93 D3
Lee Co. NC, 57866 .... 123 D1	Lenexa KS, 48190 .... 96 B2	Lewisburg TN, 11100 .... 119 F1
Lee Co. SC, 19220 .... 122 B3	Lennon MI, 511 .... 76 B3	Lewisburg WV, 3830 .... 112 A1
Lee Co. TX, 16612 .... 61 F1	Lennox CA, 22753 .... 228 C4	**Lewis Co. ID**, 3821 .... 22 B1
Lee Co. VA, 25587 .... 111 D3	Lennox SD, 2111 .... 27 F4	**Lewis Co. KY**, 13870 .... 100 C3
Leeds AL, 11773 .... 119 F4	Lenoir NC, 18228 .... 111 F4	**Lewis Co. MO**, 10211 .... 87 F4
Leeds ND, 427 .... 19 D2	Lenoir City TN, 8642 .... 110 C4	**Lewis Co. NY**, 27087 .... 79 E2
Leeds UT, 820 .... 39 D4	**Lenoir Co. NC**, 59495 .... 115 D3	**Lewis Co. TN**, 12161 .... 119 E1
Leelanau Co. MI, 21708 .... 69 F4	Lenox GA, 873 .... 129 E4	**Lewis Co. WA**, 75455 .... 12 C4
Leesburg AL, 1027 .... 120 A3	Lenox IA, 1407 .... 86 B3	**Lewis Co. WV**, 16372 .... 102 A4
Leesburg FL, 20117 .... 140 C1	Lenox MA, 5077 .... 94 B2	Lewisport KY, 1670 .... 99 E4
Leesburg GA, 2896 .... 129 D4	Lenwood CA, 3543 .... 53 D1	Lewis Run PA, 617 .... 92 B1
Leesburg IN, 555 .... 89 F2	Lenzburg IL, 521 .... 98 B4	Lewiston CA, 1193 .... 28 B1
Leesburg NJ, 1500 .... 145 F2	Leo-Cedarville IN, 3603 .... 90 A2	Lewiston ID, 31894 .... 14 B4
Leesburg OH, 1314 .... 100 C1	Leola AR, 501 .... 117 E3	Lewiston ME, 36592 .... 82 B2
Leesburg VA, 42616 .... 144 A2	Leola PA, 7214 .... 146 A2	Lewiston MI, 1392 .... 76 A1
Leesport PA, 1918 .... 146 A1	Leola SD, 457 .... 27 D1	Lewiston MN, 1620 .... 73 F1
Lee's Summit MO, 91364 .... 96 B3	Leominster MA, 40759 .... 150 C1	Lewiston NY, 2701 .... 78 A3
Leesville LA, 6612 .... 133 D1	Leon IA, 1977 .... 86 C3	Lewiston Woodville NC, 549 .... 113 E4
Leeton MO, 566 .... 96 C3	Leon KS, 704 .... 43 F4	Lewiston UT, 1766 .... 31 E2
Leetonia OH, 1959 .... 91 F3	Leonard ND, 223 .... 19 E4	Lewistown IL, 2384 .... 88 A4
Leflore Co. MS, 32317 .... 118 B4	Leonard TX, 1990 .... 59 F1	Lewistown MD, 600 .... 144 A1
Le Flore Co. OK, 50384 .... 116 B2	Leonardo NJ, 2147 .... 147 E1	Lewistown MO, 534 .... 87 F4
Lefors TX, 497 .... 50 B3	Leonardtown MD, 2930 .... 103 E4	Lewistown MT, 5901 .... 16 B4
Le Grand CA, 1659 .... 37 D4	Leonardville KS, 449 .... 43 F2	Lewistown PA, 8338 .... 93 D4
Le Grand IA, 938 .... 87 D1	**Leon Co. FL**, 275487 .... 137 E2	Lewisville AR, 1280 .... 125 D1

Lawnton PA, 3813 .... 218 C1	Lawson MO, 2473 .... 96 C2	Lehi UT, 47407 .... 31 E4	**Leon Co. TX**, 16801 .... 124 A4	Lewisville ID, 458 .... 23 E4
Lawrence IN, 46001 .... 99 F1	Lawtell LA, 1198 .... 133 E2	Lehigh IA, 416 .... 72 C4	Leonia NJ, 8937 .... 240 D1	Lewisville NC, 12639 .... 112 A4
Lawrence KS, 87643 .... 96 A2	Lawtey FL, 730 .... 138 C3	Lehigh Acres FL, 86784 .... 143 D1	Leon Valley TX, 10151 .... 61 D2	Lewisville TX, 95290 .... 59 F2
Lawrence MA, 76377 .... 95 E1	Lawton IA, 908 .... 35 F1	**Lehigh Co. PA**, 349497 .... 93 F3	Leonville LA, 1084 .... 133 F2	Lexington AL, 735 .... 119 E2
Lawrence MI, 996 .... 89 F1	Lawton MI, 1900 .... 89 F1	Lehighton PA, 5500 .... 93 F3	Leoti KS, 1534 .... 42 B3	Lexington GA, 228 .... 121 E4
Lawrence NY, 6483 .... 147 F1	Lawton OK, 96867 .... 51 D4			
Lawrenceburg IN, 5042 .... 100 B2	Laysville CT, 1100 .... 149 F2			
Lawrenceburg KY, 10505 .... 100 B4	Layton UT, 67311 .... 31 E3			
Lawrenceburg TN, 10428 .... 119 E1	Laytonville CA, 1227 .... 36 A1			
Lawrence Co. AL, 34339 .... 119 E3	Leachville AR, 1993 .... 108 A4			
Lawrence Co. AR, 17415 .... 107 F4	Leacock PA, 6625 .... 146 A2			
Lawrence Co. IL, 16833 .... 99 D3	Lea Co. NM, 64727 .... 57 F2			
Lawrence Co. IN, 46134 .... 99 F3	Lead SD, 3124 .... 25 D3			
Lawrence Co. KY, 15860 .... 101 D4	Leadville CO, 2602 .... 41 D2			
Lawrence Co. MS, 12929 .... 126 B4	Leadwood MO, 1282 .... 98 A4			
Lawrence Co. MO, 38634 .... 106 C2	League City TX, 83560 .... 132 B4			
Lawrence Co. OH, 62450 .... 101 D3	Leake Co. MS, 23805 .... 126 C2			
Lawrence Co. PA, 91108 .... 91 F3	Leakesville MS, 898 .... 135 E1			
Lawrence Co. SD, 24097 .... 25 F3	Leakey TX, 425 .... 60 C2			
Lawrence Co. TN, 41869 .... 119 E1	Lealman FL, 19879 .... 266 B3			
Lawrenceville AL, 28546 .... 120 C4	Leander TX, 26521 .... 61 E1			
Lawrenceville IL, 4348 .... 99 D3	Leander FL, 618 .... 128 C4			
Lawrenceville PA, 581 .... 93 D1	Leary GA, 666 .... 129 D4			
Lawrenceville VA, 1438 .... 113 D2	Leavenworth KS, 35251 .... 96 B2			
	Leavenworth WA, 1965 .... 13 D3			
Leavenworth Co. KS, 76227 .... 96 B2	Lebanon IN, 15792 .... 89 E4			
Leavittsburg OH, 1973 .... 276 A1	Lebanon KY, 5539 .... 110 B1			
Leawood KS, 682 .... 106 B2	Lebanon MO, 14474 .... 107 E1			
Leawood MO, 3583 .... 145 E2	Lebanon NH, 13151 .... 81 E3			
Lebanon IL, 4418 .... 98 B3	Lebanon NJ, 1358 .... 147 D1			

Figures after entries indicate population, page number, and grid reference.

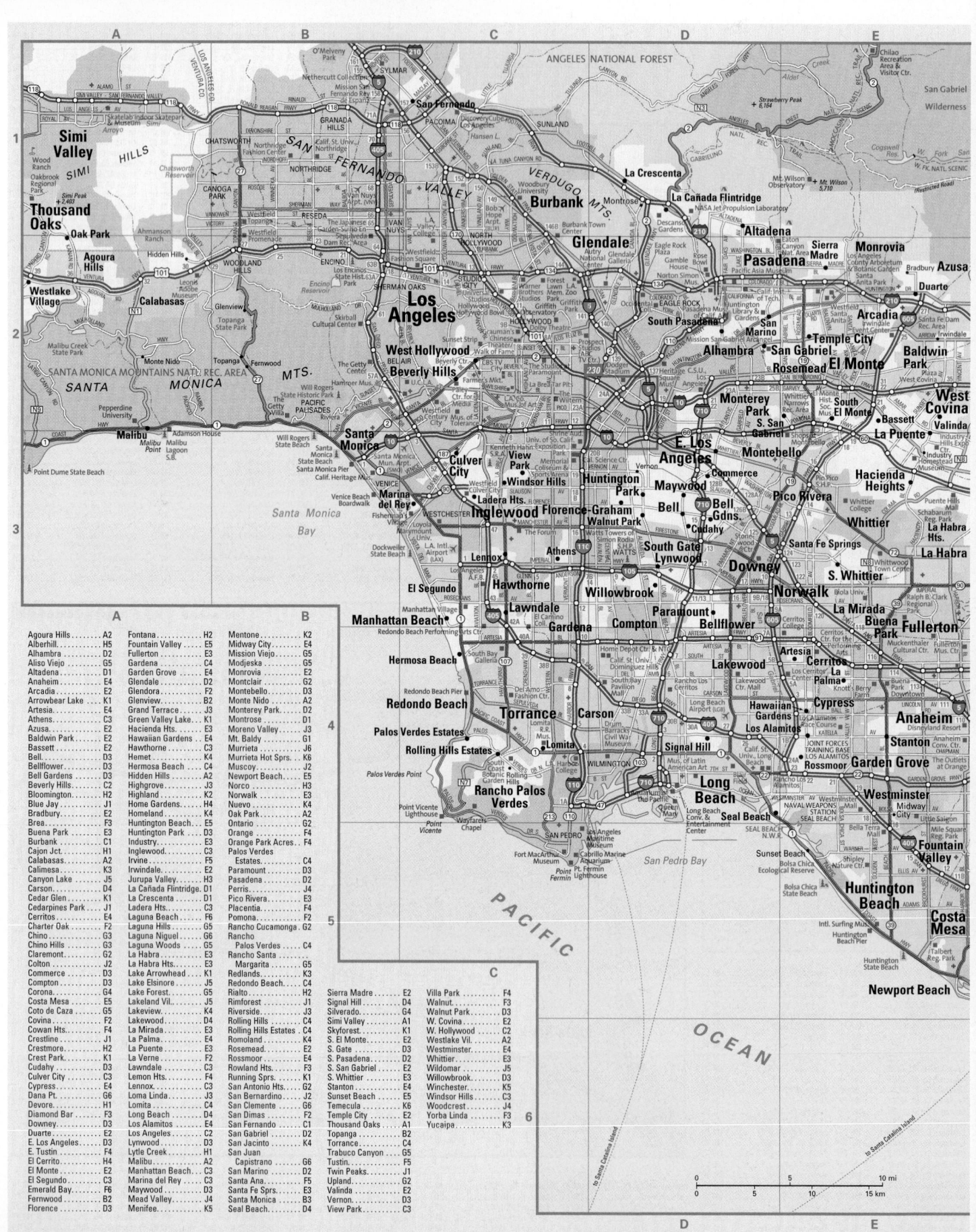

Entries in **bold black** indicate counties or parishes.
Entries in **bold color** indicate cities with detailed inset maps.

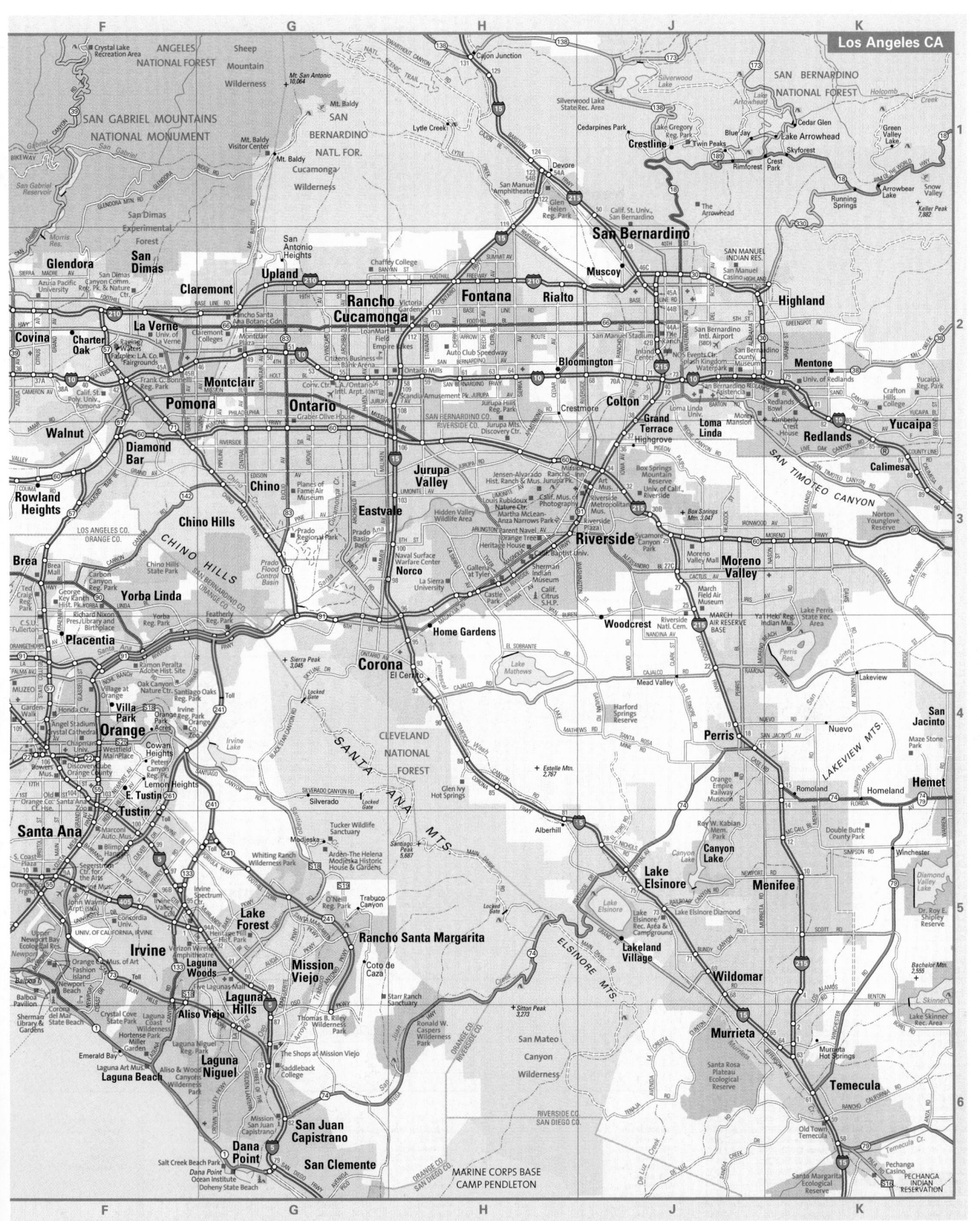

Los Angeles CA

Figures after entries indicate population, page number, and grid reference.

POINTS OF INTEREST

Angels Flight..........A1	Flower District..........A2	Museum of Neon Art..........A2
Bradbury Building..........A1	GRAMMY Museum..........A2	Music Center..........A1
California Plaza..........A1	Japanese American Natl. Museum..........B1	NOKIA Theatre..........A2
Cathedral of Our Lady of the Angels..........A1	Jewelry District..........A2	Olvera Street..........B1
Chinese American Museum..........B1	L.A. Center Studios..........A2	Post Office..........B1
City Hall..........B1	L.A. Live..........A2	STAPLES Center..........A2
Convention Center..........A2	Library..........A2	The Geffen Contemporary at MOCA..........B1
Court House..........A1	Mt. St. Mary's College..........A2	Union Station..........B1
Dodger Stadium..........B1	Museum of Contemporary Art	Walt Disney Concert Hall..........A1
El Pueblo de Los Angeles Hist. Mon...B1	(MOCA)..........A1	

Downtown Los Angeles CA

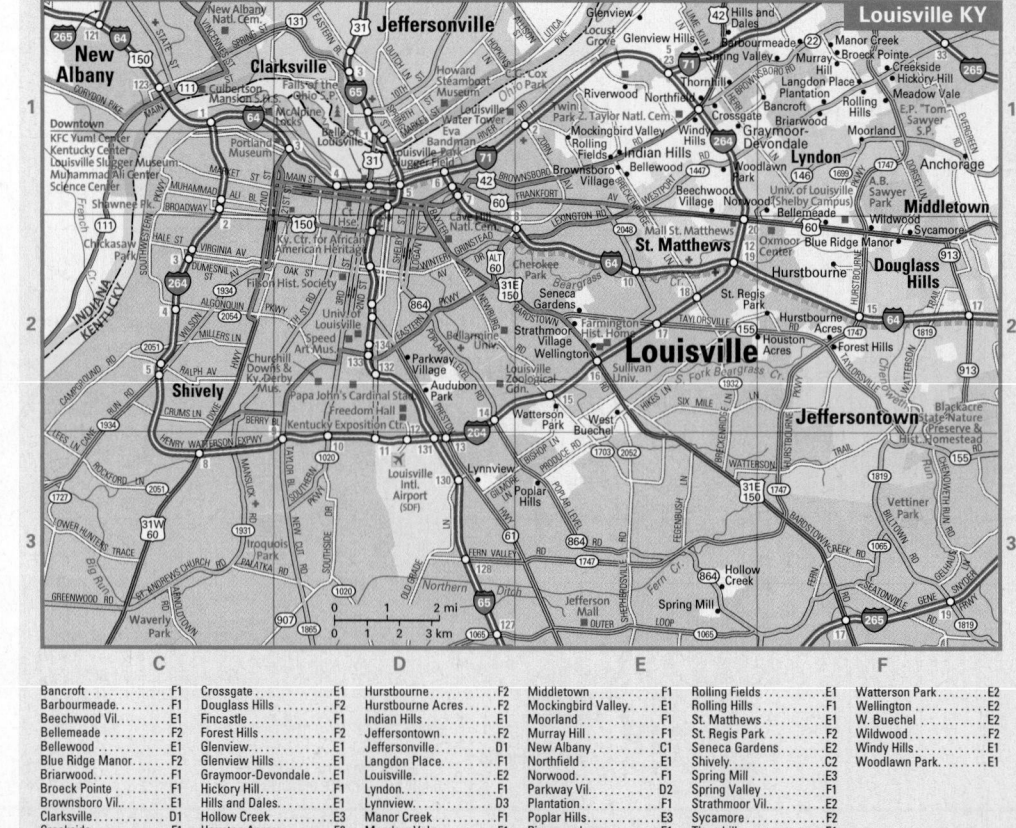

Lincoln Hts. OH, 3286..........204 B1	Lionville PA, 6189..........146 B3
Lincolnia VA, 22855..........270 B4	Lipscomb AL, 2210..........195 D2
Lincoln Par. LA, 46735..........125 E2	Lipscomb TX, 37..........50 C2
Lincoln Park CO, 3546..........41 E3	**Lipscomb Co. TX,** 3302..........50 C2
Lincoln Park MI, 38144..........90 C1	Lisbon IA, 2152..........87 F1
Lincoln Park NJ, 10521..........148 A3	Lisbon ME, 9077..........82 B3
Lincolnshire IL, 7275..........203 C2	Lisbon NH, 980..........81 E2
Lincolnton GA, 1566..........121 E4	Lisbon ND, 2154..........19 E4
Lincolnton NC, 10486..........122 A1	Lisbon OH, 2821..........91 F3
Lincoln Vil. OH, 9032..........206 A3	Lisbon Falls ME, 4100..........82 B3
Lincolnville SC, 1139..........131 D1	Lisle IL, 22390..........203 B5
Lincolnville Ctr. ME, 325..........82 C3	Lisman AL, 539..........127 D3
Lincolnwood IL, 12590..........203 D3	Lisman AL, 539..........127 D3
Lincroft NJ, 6135..........147 E2	Litchfield CT, 1258..........94 C3
Lind WA, 564..........13 F4	Litchfield IL, 6939..........98 B2
Linda CA, 17773..........36 C2	Litchfield ME, 3110..........82 B2
Lindale GA, 4191..........120 B3	Litchfield MN, 6726..........66 B3
Lindale TX, 4818..........124 A2	Litchfield MI, 1369..........90 A1
Lindcove CA, 406..........45 D3	**Litchfield Co. CT,** 189927..........94 B3
Linden AL, 2123..........127 E2	Litchfield Park AZ, 5476..........249 A2
Linden CA, 1784..........36 C3	Lithia Sprs. GA, 15491..........120 C4
Linden IN, 759..........89 E4	Lithonia GA, 1924..........120 C4
Linden MI, 3991..........76 B3	Lithopolis OH, 1106..........101 D1
Linden NJ, 40499..........147 E1	Lititz PA, 9369..........146 A2
Linden TN, 908..........119 E1	Little Canada MN, 9773..........235 D2
Linden TX, 1988..........124 C1	Little Chute WI, 10449..........74 C1
Linden WI, 549..........74 A3	Little Compton RI, 3492..........151 D4
Lindenhurst IL, 14462..........74 C4	Little Creek DE, 224..........145 E2
Lindenhurst NY, 27253..........148 C4	Little Cypress TX, 1800..........132 C2
Lindenwold NJ, 17613..........146 C3	Little Eagle SD, 319..........26 C1
Lindon UT, 10070..........31 D1	Little Elm TX, 25898..........59 F2
Lindsay CA, 11768..........45 D3	Little Falls MN, 8343..........66 C2
Lindsay OK, 2840..........51 E4	Little Falls NJ, 11694..........148 A3
Lindsay TX, 1018..........59 E1	Little Falls NY, 4946..........79 F3
Lindsborg KS, 3458..........43 E3	Little Ferry NJ, 10626..........240 C2
Lindstrom MN, 4442..........67 D3	Littlefield TX, 6372..........58 A1
Linesville PA, 1040..........91 F2	Little Flock AR, 2585..........106 C3
Lineville AL, 2395..........128 B1	Littlefork MN, 647..........64 B2
Lingle WY, 468..........33 F2	Little Heaven DE, 1400..........145 E3
Linglestown PA, 6334..........93 E3	Little River KS, 557..........43 E3
Linn KS, 410..........43 F1	Little River SC, 8960..........123 E2
Linn MO, 1459..........97 E3	Little River-Academy TX, 1961..........61 E1
Linn TX, 801..........63 E3	Little Rock AR, *193524*..........117 E2
Linn Co. IA, 211226..........87 E1	**Little River Co. AR,** 13171..........116 C4
Linn Co. KS, 9656..........96 B4	Littlerock CA, 1377..........52 C2
Linn Co. MO, 12761..........97 D1	Little Silver NJ, 5950..........147 E2
Linn Co. OR, 116672..........20 C3	Littlestown PA, 4434..........103 E1
Linneus MO, 278..........97 D1	Littleton CO, 41737..........41 E1
Linn Valley KS, 804..........96 B4	Littleton NH, 4412..........81 F2
Lino Lakes MN, 20216..........235 D2	Littleton NC, 674..........113 D3
Linthicum MD, 10324..........193 C4	Little Valley NY, 1143..........92 B1
Linton IN, 5413..........99 E2	Live Oak CA, 17158..........36 C2
Linton ND, 1097..........26 C1	Live Oak CA, 17158..........236 D1
Linwood KS, 700..........89 F4	Live Oak FL, 6850..........138 B2
Linwood KS, 375..........96 B3	Live Oak TX, 13131..........61 D2
Linwood MI, 1200..........76 B2	**Live Oak Co. TX,** 11531..........61 D4
Linwood NJ, 7092..........147 F4	Livermore CA, 80968..........36 B4

Livermore KY, 1365..........109 E1	
Livermore Falls ME, 1594..........82 B2	
Liverpool NY, 2347..........265 E1	
Liverpool PA, 955..........93 D4	
Livingston AL, 3485..........127 D2	
Livingston CA, 13058..........36 C4	
Livingston IL, 858..........98 B4	
Livingston LA, 1769..........134 A2	
Livingston MT, 7044..........23 F1	
Livingston NJ, 29366..........148 A4	
Livingston TN, 4058..........110 A3	
Livingston TX, 5335..........132 B1	
Livingston Co. IL, 38950..........88 C3	
Livingston Co. KY, 9519..........109 D2	
Livingston Co. MI, 180967..........76 B3	
Livingston Co. MO, 15195..........96 C1	
Livingston Co. NY, 65393..........78 C3	
Livingston Manor NY, 1221..........94 A2	
Livingston Par. LA, 128026..........134 B2	
Livonia LA, 1442..........133 F2	
Livonia MI, 96942..........76 B4	
Livonia NY, 1409..........78 C3	
Llangollen Estates DE, 5600..........145 E1	
Llano TX, 3232..........61 D1	
Llano Co. TX, 19301..........61 D1	
Loa UT, 572..........39 E3	
Loami IL, 745..........98 B1	
Lobelville TN, 897..........109 E4	
Lochbuie CO, 4726..........209 D1	
Lochearn MD, 25333..........144 C2	
Loch Lynn Hts. MD, 552..........102 B2	
Loch Sheldrake NY, 800..........94 A3	
Lockeford CA, 3233..........36 C3	
Lockesburg AR, 739..........116 C4	
Lockhart AL, 516..........136 C1	
Lockhart FL, 13060..........246 B1	
Lockhart TX, 12698..........61 E2	
Lock Haven PA, 9772..........93 D3	
Lockland OH, 3449..........204 B1	
Lockney TX, 1842..........50 B4	
Lockport IL, 24839..........89 D2	
Lockport LA, 2578..........134 B3	
Lockport NY, 21165..........78 B3	
Lockwood MO, 936..........106 C1	
Locust NC, 2930..........122 B1	
Locust Fork AL, 1186..........119 F4	
Locust Grove GA, 5402..........129 D1	
Locust Grove OK, 1423..........106 B3	
Locust Valley NY, 3406..........148 C3	
Lodge Grass MT, 428..........24 C2	
Lodge Pole MT, 265..........16 C2	
Lodi CA, 62134..........36 C3	
Lodi NJ, 24136..........240 C1	
Lodi OH, 2746..........91 D3	
Lodi WI, 3050..........74 B3	

Lexington IL, 2060..........88 C3	Lilydale MN, 623..........235 D3
Lexington KY, *295803*..........100 B4	Lily Lake IL, 993..........88 C1
Lexington MA, 31394..........151 E1	Lima MT, 221..........23 E3
Lexington MI, 1178..........76 C3	Lima NY, 2139..........78 C3
Lexington MN, 2049..........235 C1	Lima OH, 38771..........90 B3
Lexington MO, 4726..........96 C2	Lima PA, 2735..........248 A4
Lexington MS, 1731..........126 B1	Lime Lake NY, 867..........78 B4
Lexington NC, 18931..........112 B4	Limeport PA, 1100..........146 C1
Lexington OH, 4822..........91 D3	Limerick ME, 2240..........82 A3
Lexington OK, 2152..........51 E3	Limerick PA, 850..........146 B2
Lexington SC, 17870..........122 A3	Limestone ME, 1075..........85 E1
Lexington TN, 7652..........109 D4	**Limestone Co. AL,** 82782..........119 F2
Lexington TX, 1177..........61 E1	**Limestone Co. TX,** 23384..........59 F4
Lexington VA, 7042..........112 C1	Limon CO, 1880..........41 F2
Lexington Co. SC, 262391..........122 A4	Lincoln AL, 6266..........120 A4
Lexington Park MD, 11626..........103 F4	Lincoln AR, 2249..........106 B4
Libby MT, 2628..........14 C2	Lincoln CA, 42819..........36 C2
Liberal KS, 20525..........50 B1	Lincoln DE, 950..........145 F3
Liberal MO, 759..........106 B1	Lincoln ID, 3647..........23 E4
Liberty IL, 516..........97 F1	Lincoln IL, 14504..........88 B4
Liberty IN, 2133..........100 B1	Lincoln KS, 1297..........43 E2
Liberty KY, 2168..........110 B1	Lincoln ME, 2894..........85 D4
Liberty ME, 300..........82 C2	Lincoln MA, 6362..........197 A1
Liberty MS, 728..........134 A1	Lincoln MT, 1013..........15 E4
Liberty MO, 29149..........96 B2	Lincoln MO, 1190..........97 D4
Liberty NY, 4392..........94 A3	Lincoln NE, *258379*..........35 F4
Liberty NC, 2656..........112 B4	Lincoln ND, 2406..........18 C4
Liberty PA, 2551..........250 C3	Lincoln Beach OR, 2045..........20 B2
Liberty SC, 3269..........121 E2	Lincoln City OR, 7930..........20 B2
Liberty TN, 310..........110 A4	**Lincoln Co. AR,** 14134..........117 F3
Liberty TX, 8397..........132 B3	**Lincoln Co. CO,** 5467..........41 F2
Liberty Ctr. OH, 1180..........90 B2	**Lincoln Co. GA,** 7996..........121 E4
Liberty City TX, 2351..........124 B2	**Lincoln Co. ID,** 5208..........31 D1
Liberty Corner NJ, 1700..........147 D1	**Lincoln Co. KS,** 3241..........43 E2
Liberty Co. FL, 8365..........137 D2	**Lincoln Co. KY,** 24742..........110 B1
Liberty Co. GA, 63453..........130 B3	**Lincoln Co. ME,** 34457..........82 C2
Liberty Co. MT, 2339..........15 F1	**Lincoln Co. MN,** 5896..........27 F3
Liberty Co. TX, 75643..........132 B2	**Lincoln Co. MS,** 34869..........126 B4
Liberty Hill TX, 967..........61 E1	**Lincoln Co. MO,** 52566..........97 F2
Liberty Lake WA, 7591..........14 B3	**Lincoln Co. MT,** 19687..........14 C2
Libertyville IL, 20315..........74 C4	**Lincoln Co. NE,** 36288..........34 C3
Licking MO, 3124..........107 F1	**Lincoln Co. NV,** 5345..........38 B4
Licking Co. OH, 166492..........91 D4	**Lincoln Co. NM,** 20497..........49 D4
Lidgerwood ND, 652..........27 E1	**Lincoln Co. NC,** 76126..........122 A1
Lido Beach NY, 2897..........147 F1	**Lincoln Co. OK,** 34273..........51 F2
Lighthouse Pt. FL, 10344..........143 F1	**Lincoln Co. OR,** 46034..........20 B3
Ligonier IN, 4405..........89 F2	**Lincoln Co. SD,** 44828..........35 F1
Ligonier PA, 1573..........92 B4	**Lincoln Co. TN,** 33361..........119 F1
Lihue HI, 6455..........152 B1	**Lincoln Co. WA,** 10570..........13 F3
Lilburn MO, 1190..........108 B3	**Lincoln Co. WV,** 21720..........101 E4
Lilburn GA, 11596..........120 C4	**Lincoln Co. WI,** 28743..........68 A3
Lillington NC, 3194..........123 D1	**Lincoln Co. WY,** 18106..........32 A2
Lily PA, 963..........92 B4	Lincolndale NY, 1521..........148 C2
Lily KY, 1200..........110 C2	

Louisville KY

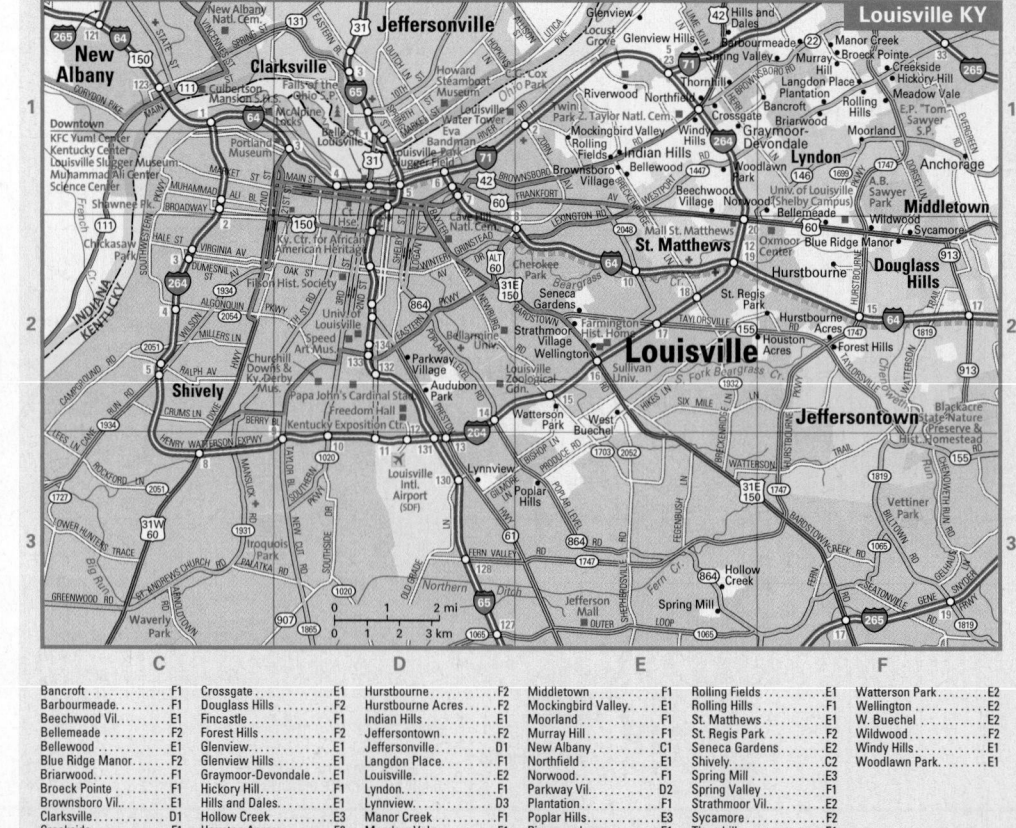

Bancroft..........F1	Crossgate..........E1	Hurstbourne..........F2	Middletown..........F1	Rolling Fields..........E1	Watterson Park..........E2
Barbourmeade..........F1	Douglass Hills..........F1	Hurstbourne Acres..........F2	Mockingbird Valley..........E1	Rolling Hills..........F1	Wellington..........E2
Beechwood Vil...........E1	Fincastle..........F1	Indian Hills..........E1	Moorland..........F1	St. Matthews..........E1	W. Buechel..........E2
Bellemeade..........E1	Forest Hills..........F1	Jeffersontown..........F1	Murray Hill..........E1	St. Regis Park..........F1	Wildwood..........F1
Bellewood..........E1	Glenview..........E1	Jeffersonville..........D1	New Albany..........C1	Seneca Gardens..........E2	Windy Hills..........E1
Blue Ridge Manor..........F1	Glenview Hills..........E1	Langdon Place..........F1	Northfield..........E1	Shively..........C2	Woodlawn Park..........E1
Briarwood..........E1	Graymoor-Devondale..........E1	Louisville..........E2	Norwood..........F1	Spring Mill..........F1	
Broeck Pointe..........E1	Hickory Hill..........F1	Lyndon..........F1	Parkway Vil...........D2	Spring Valley..........E1	
Brownsboro Vil...........E1	Hills and Dales..........E1	Lynnview..........D3	Plantation..........F1	Strathmoor Vil...........E2	
Clarksville..........D1	Hollow Creek..........E3	Manor Creek..........F1	Poplar Hills..........E3	Sycamore..........E1	
Creekside..........F1	Houston Acres..........F2	Meadow Vale..........F1	Riverwood..........E1	Thornhill..........E1	

Entries in **bold black** indicate counties or parishes.
Entries in **bold color** indicate cities with detailed inset maps.

Logan IA, 1534 ....86 A2
Logan KS, 589 ....42 C1
Logan NM, 1042 ....49 F3
Logan OH, 7152 ....101 D1
Logan UT, 48174 ....31 E2
Logan WV, 1779 ....101 E4
Logan Co. AR, 22353 ....116 C1
Logan Co. CO, 22709 .....34 A4
Logan Co. IL, 30005 ......98 B1
Logan Co. KS, 2756 ....42 B2
Logan Co. KY, 26835 ....109 F2
Logan Co. ND, 1990 ....18 C4
Logan Co. NE, 763 ....34 C3
Logan Co. OH, 45858 .....90 B4
Logan Co. OK, 41848 ......51 E2
Logan Co. WV, 36743 ....101 E4

Lone Oak KY, 454 ....108 C2
Lone Oak TX, 598 ....59 F2
Lone Pine CA, 2035 ....45 E3
Lone Rock WI, 888 ....74 A3
Lone Star LA, 1400 ....239 A2
Lone Star TX, 1581 ....124 B1
Lone Tree CO, 10218 .....209 C4
Lone Tree IA, 1300 ....87 F2
Lone Wolf OK, 438 ....51 D3
Long Beach CA, 462257 ...52 C3
Long Beach IN, 1179 ......89 E1
Long Beach MD, 1821 ....103 E4
Long Beach MS, 14792 ...135 D2
Long Beach NY, 33275 ...147 F1
Long Beach WA, 1392 .....12 B4
Longboat Key FL, 6888 ...140 B3

Lorain Co. OH, 301356 ....91 D2
Loraine TX, 602 ....58 B3
Lorane PA, 4236 ....146 B2
Lordsburg NM, 2797 ......55 F3
Loreauville LA, 887 ......133 F3
Lorena TX, 1691 ....59 E4
Lorenzo TX, 1147 ....58 A1
Loretto KY, 713 ....110 A1
Loretto MN, 650 ....66 C3
Loretto PA, 1302 ....92 B4
Loretto TN, 1714 ....119 E2
Loris SC, 2396 ....123 D3
Lorton VA, 18610 ....144 B4

Loughman FL, 2680 ....141 D2
Louisa KY, 2467 ....101 D4
Louisa VA, 1555 ....103 D4
Louisa Co. IA, 11387 ....87 F2
Louisa Co. VA, 33153 .....103 D4
Louisburg KS, 4315 ....96 B3
Louisburg NC, 3359 ......113 D4
Louise TX, 995 ....61 F3
Louisiana MO, 3364 ....97 F2
Louisville AL, 519 ....128 B3
Louisville CO, 18376 ......41 E1
Louisville GA, 2493 ......129 F1
Louisville KY, 597337 ....100 A4
Louisville MS, 6631 ......126 C1
Louisville NE, 1106 ....35 F3
Louisville OH, 9186 ....91 E3
Louisville TN, 2439 ......110 C4
Loup City NE, 1029 ....35 D3
Loup Co. NE, 632 ....35 D2
Love Co. OK, 9423 ....59 E1
Lovelady TX, 649 ....132 A1
Loveland CO, 66859 ....33 E4
Loveland OH, 12081 ......100 B2
Loveland Park OH, 1523 ..204 C1
Lovell WY, 2360 ....24 C2
Lovelock NV, 1894 ....29 F4
Loves Park IL, 23996 .....74 B4
Lovettsville VA, 1613 ...144 A2
Loveville MD, 650 ....103 E4
Lovilia IA, 538 ....87 D3
Loving NM, 1413 ....57 E2
Loving Co. TX, 82 ....57 E2
Lovingston VA, 520 ......112 C1
Lovington IL, 1130 ....98 C1
Lovington NM, 11009 ......57 F2
Lowden IA, 789 ....87 F1
Lowell AR, 7327 ....106 C3
Lowell IN, 9276 ....89 E2
Lowell MA, 106519 ....95 E1
Lowell MI, 3783 ....75 F3
Lowell NC, 3526 ....122 A1
Lowell OH, 549 ....101 F1
Lowell OR, 1045 ....20 C4
Lowellville OH, 1155 ....91 F3
Lower Brule SD, 613 ....27 D3
Lower Lake CA, 1294 ......36 B2
Lowesville NC, 2945 .....122 A1
Low Moor VA, 258 ....112 B1
Lowry City MO, 640 ....96 C4
Lowville NY, 3470 ....79 E2
Loxley AL, 1632 ....135 E2
Loyal WI, 1261 ....68 A4
Loyalhanna PA, 3428 ......92 B4
Loyal KY, 1461 ....111 D2
Loyalton CA, 862 ....37 D1
Lubbock TX, 229573 ......58 A1
Lubbock TX, 278831 ....58 A1
Lubec ME, 349 ....83 F1
Lubeck WV, 1311 ....101 E2
Lucama NC, 1108 ....113 D4
Lucas KS, 393 ....43 D2
Lucas OH, 615 ....91 D3
Lucas TX, 5166 ....59 F2
Lucas Co. IA, 8898 ....87 D3
Lucas Co. OH, 441815 .....90 C2
Lucasville OH, 2757 ......101 D3
Luce Co. MI, 6631 ....69 F1
Lucedale MS, 2923 ....135 E1
Lucerne CA, 2412 ....36 B2
Lucerne WY, 535 ....24 C4
Lucernemines PA, 937 ....92 B4
Luck WI, 1119 ....67 E3
Luckey OH, 1012 ....90 C2
Ludington MI, 8076 ....75 E1
Ludingtonville NY, 1000 .148 C1
Ludlow KY, 4407 ....204 B3
Ludlow MA, 21103 ....150 A2
Ludlow VT, 811 ....81 E4
Ludowici GA, 1703 ....130 B4
Lufkin TX, 35067 ....124 B4
Lugoff SC, 7434 ....122 B3
Lukachukai AZ, 1701 ......48 A1
Lula GA, 2758 ....121 D3
Luling LA, 12119 ....239 A2
Luling TX, 5411 ....61 E2
Lumber City GA, 1328 ...129 F3
Lumberport WV, 876 .....102 A2
Lumberton MS, 2086 .....134 C1
Lumberton NJ, 12331 ....147 D3
Lumberton NC, 21542 ...123 D2
Lumberton TX, 11943 ....132 C2
Lumpkin GA, 2741 ....128 C3
Lumpkin Co. GA, 29966 ..120 C3
Luna Co. NM, 25095 ....56 A3
Luna Pier MI, 1436 ....90 C1
Lunenburg MA, 1760 ......95 D1
Lunenburg VT, 1328 ......81 E2
Lunenburg VA, 165 ......113 D2
Lunenburg Co. VA, 12914 .113 D2
Lupton AZ, 25 ....48 A3
Luray VA, 4895 ....102 C3
Lusby MD, 1835 ....103 F3
Lusk WY, 1567 ....33 E1
Lutcher LA, 3559 ....134 B3
Luther OK, 2741 ....51 E2
Luthersville GA, 874 ....128 C1
Luttrell TN, 1074 ....110 C3
Lutz FL, 19344 ....140 B2
Luverne AL, 2800 ....128 A3

Luverne MN, 4745 ....27 F4
Luxemburg WI, 2515 ......69 D4
Luxora AR, 1178 ....108 B4
Luzerne PA, 2845 ....261 B1
Luzerne Co. PA, 320918 ...93 E3
Lycoming Co. PA, 116111 ...93 D2
Lydia LA, 952 ....133 F3
Lydick IN, 1300 ....89 E2
Lyerly GA, 540 ....120 B3
Lyford TX, 2611 ....63 F4
Lykens PA, 1779 ....93 E4
Lyle MN, 551 ....73 D2
Lyle WA, 499 ....21 D1
Lyman NE, 341 ....33 F3
Lyman SC, 3243 ....121 F2
Lyman WA, 438 ....12 C2
Lyman WY, 2115 ....32 A3
Lyman Co. SD, 3755 ....26 C4
Lyman MS, 350 ....135 D2
Lynbrook NY, 19427 .....147 F1
Lynch KY, 747 ....111 D2
Lynchburg MS, 2437 .....118 B2
Lynchburg OH, 1499 ....100 C2
Lynchburg SC, 373 ......122 B3
Lynchburg TN, 6362 .....119 F1
Lynchburg VA, 75568 ...112 C1
Lynch Hts. DE, 593 ......145 F3
Lyndeborough NH, 888 ...95 D1
Lyndell PA, 1000 ....146 B3
Lynden WA, 11951 ....12 C1
Lyndhurst NJ, 19290 ....240 C2
Lyndhurst OH, 14001 ...204 G2
Lyndhurst VA, 1490 .....102 C3

Lyndon KS, 1052 ....96 A3
Lyndon KY, 11002 ....230 F1
Lyndon NY, 4600 ....265 B2
Lyndon VT, 5448 ....81 E2
Lyndon Ctr. VT, 1200 .....81 E2
Lyndonville NY, 838 ......78 B3
Lyndonville VT, 1207 .....81 E2
Lyndora PA, 6685 ....92 A3
Lynn AL, 659 ....119 E3
Lynn IN, 1097 ....90 A4
Lynn Haven FL, 18493 ..136 C2
Lynn MA, 90329 ....151 D1
Lynn TX, 5915 ....58 A2
Lynn Co. TX, 5915 ....58 A2
Lynnview KY, 914 ....230 D1
Lynnwood WA, 35836 ....12 C3
Lynwood CA, 69772 .....228 D3
Lyon MS, 350 ....118 A3
Lyon Co. IA, 11581 ....27 F4
Lyon Co. KS, 33690 ....43 F3
Lyon Co. KY, 8314 ....109 D2
Lyon Co. MN, 25857 ....27 E2
Lyon Co. NV, 51980 ....37 E2
Lyons CO, 2033 ....33 E4
Lyons GA, 4367 ....129 F3
Lyons IL, 10729 ....203 D5
Lyons IN, 742 ....99 E2
Lyons KS, 3739 ....43 E3
Lyons MI, 851 ....75 F3
Lyons NE, 851 ....35 F3
Lyons NY, 3619 ....79 D3
Lyons VA, 562 ....90 B2

Lyons OR, 1161 ....20 C3
Lyons Falls NY, 566 ......79 E2
Lyons Plain CT, 2100 ....148 C2
Lytle TX, 2492 ....61 D3

M

Mabank TX, 3035 ....59 F3
Mabel MN, 780 ....73 E2
Maben MS, 871 ....118 C4
Mableton GA, 37115 ....120 C4
Mabscott WV, 1408 ....111 F1
Mabton WA, 2286 ....21 E1
Macclenny FL, 6374 .....138 C2
Macedon NY, 1523 ....78 C3
Macedonia OH, 11188 ....91 E2
Machesney Park IL, 23499 ..74 B4
Machias ME, 1274 ....83 E1
Machias NY, 471 ....78 B4
Mack OH, 11585 ....204 A2
Mackay ID, 517 ....23 D4
Mackinac Co. MI, 11113 ...70 C1
Mackinac Island MI, 492 ..70 C2
Mackinaw IL, 1950 ....88 B4
Mackinaw City MI, 806 ...70 C2
Macksville KS, 549 ....43 D3
Macomb IL, 19288 ....88 A4
Macomb Co. MI, 840978 ...76 C4
Macon AR, 1100 ....117 D2
Macon Co. AL, 91351 .....129 D2
Macon IL, 1138 ....98 C1
Macon MS, 2768 ....127 D1
Macon MO, 5471 ....97 E1

Lubbock TX

Macon GA

Manchester NH

Fitchburg A2
Madison A1
Maple Bluff B1

McFarland B2
Middleton A1
Monona B2

Shorewood Hills A2
Sun Prairie B1
Waunakee A1

Madison WI

Logandale NV, 800 ....46 B1
Logansport IN, 18396 .....89 E3
Logansport LA, 1555 ....124 C1
Loganville GA, 10458 ...121 D4
Loganville PA, 1240 .....103 E1
Log Cabin TX, 714 ....59 F3
Log Lane Vil. CO, 873 ....33 F4
Loleta CA, 783 ....28 A4
Lolita TX, 555 ....61 F3
Lolo MT, 3892 ....15 D4
Loma Linda CA, 23261 ..229 J3
Loma Linda MO, 725 ....106 B2
Loma Rica CA, 2368 ......36 C2
Lombard IL, 43165 ....203 B4
Lometa TX, 856 ....59 D4
Lomira WI, 2430 ....74 C2
Lomita CA, 20256 ....228 C4
Lompoc CA, 42434 ....52 A2
Lonaconing MD, 1214 ...102 C1
London AR, 1039 ....117 D1
London KY, 7993 ....110 C2
London OH, 9904 ....100 C1
Londonderry NH, 11051 ..95 E1
Londonderry VT, 1709 ....81 D4
Londontowne MD, 7579 .144 C3
Lone Grove OK, 5054 .....51 E4
Lone Jack MO, 1050 ....96 C3

Long Branch NJ, 30719 ..147 F2
Long Co. GA, 14464 ....130 B3
Long Creek IL, 1328 ....98 C1
Long Grove IA, 808 ....88 A1
Long Grove IL, 8043 ......203 C2
Los Angeles CA, 3792621 ..52 C2
Long Lake MN, 1768 ......66 C4
Longmeadow MA, 15784 .150 A2
Longmont CO, 86270 ......41 E1
Long Pond PA, 1500 .....151 E3
Longport NJ, 895 ....147 F4
Long Prairie MN, 3458 ....66 B2
Longton KS, 348 ....43 F4
Long Valley NJ, 1907 ....148 A4
Long View NC, 4871 .....111 F4
Longview TX, 80455 .....124 B2
Longview WA, 36648 ......20 B1
Longwood FL, 13657 ....141 D1
Lonoke AR, 4245 ....117 F2
Lonoke Co. AR, 68356 ...117 F2
Lonsdale MN, 3674 ....67 D4
Lookout Mtn. GA, 1602 ...120 B2
Lookout Mtn. TN, 1832 ..120 B2
Loomis CA, 6430 ....36 C3
Loomis NE, 382 ....35 D4
Lorain OH, 64097 ....91 D2

Los Alamos NM, 12019 ....48 C2
Los Alamos Co. NM, 17950 .48 C2
Los Altos CA, 28976 ......36 B4
Los Altos Hills CA, 7922 ..259 C6
Los Angeles Co. CA, 9818605 ..52 C2
Los Banos CA, 35972 .....44 B2
Los Chavez NM, 5446 .....48 C4
Los Fresnos TX, 5542 .....63 F4
Los Gatos CA, 29413 ......36 B4
Los Indios TX, 1083 ....63 F4
Los Lunas NM, 14835 .....48 C4
Los Molinos CA, 2037 .....36 B1
Los Olivos CA, 1132 ....52 A2
Los Osos CA, 14276 ....44 B4
Los Padillas NM, 1800 ....48 C3
Los Ranchos de Albuquerque
NM, 6024 ....48 C3
Lost Creek WV, 496 ......102 A2
Lost Hills CA, 2412 ....44 C4
Lost Nation IA, 446 ....87 F1
Lott TX, 759 ....59 F4
Loudon NH, 5381 ....110 C4
Loudon TN, 4856 ....110 C4
Loudonville NY, 10800 ....94 B1
Loudonville OH, 2641 .....91 D3
Loudoun Co. VA, 312311 ..144 A2

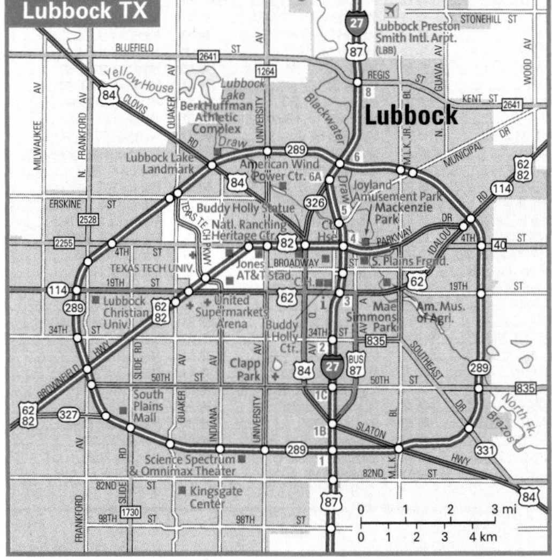

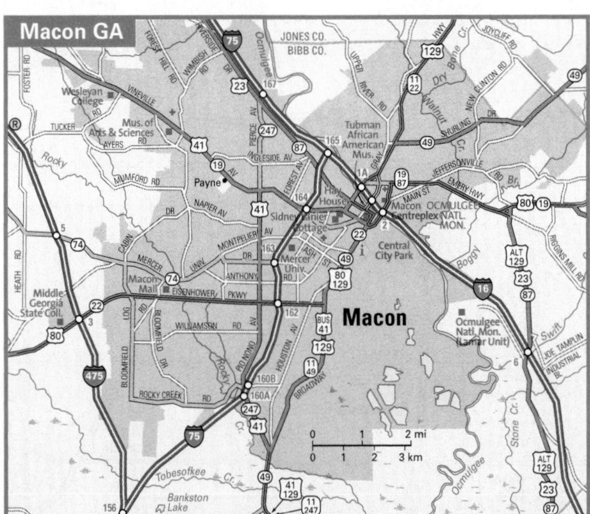

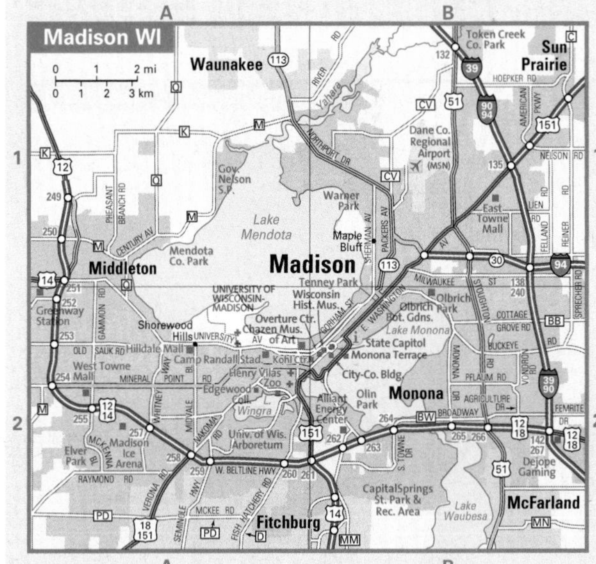

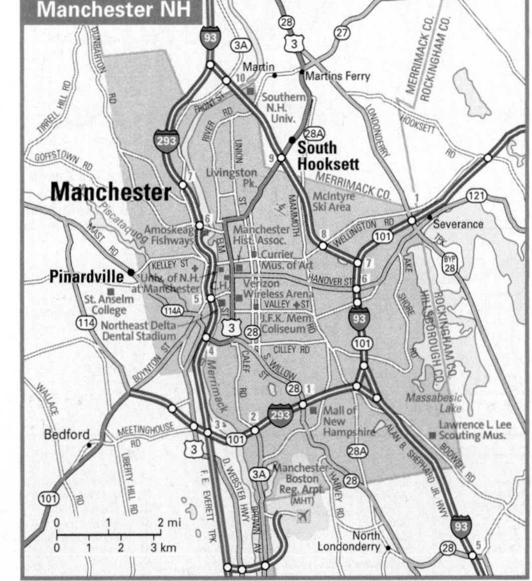

Figures after entries indicate population, page number, and grid reference.

Macon Co. AL, *21452* **128** B3
Macon Co. GA, *14740* **129** D2
Macon Co. IL, *110768* **98** C1
Macon Co. MO, *15566* **97** D1
Macon Co. NC, *33922* **121** D1
Macon Co. TN, *22248* **110** A3
Macoupin Co. IL, *47765* **98** B2
Macungie PA, *3074* **146** B1
Macy NE, *1023* **35** F2
Madawaska ME, *2967* **85** D1
Maddock ND, *382* **19** D2
Madeira OH, *8726* **204** C2
Madeira Beach FL, *4263* **140** B3
Madelia MN, *2308* **72** B1
Madera CA, *61416* **44** C2
Madera Co. CA, *150865* **44** C2
Madill OK, *3770* **51** F4
Madison AL, *42938* **119** F2
Madison AR, *769* **118** A2
Madison CT, *18812* **149** E2
Madison FL, *2843* **137** F2
Madison GA, *3979* **121** D4
Madison IL, *3891* **98** A3
Madison IN, *11967* **100** A3
Madison KS, *701* **43** F3
Madison ME, *2630* **82** B1
Madison MN, *1551* **27** F2
Madison MS, *24149* **126** B2
Madison MO, *554* **97** E2
Madison NE, *2438* **35** E2
Madison NJ, *15845* **148** A4
Madison NC, *2246* **112** B3
Madison OH, *3184* **91** F1
Madison SD, *6474* **27** F3
Madison VA, *229* **102** C4
Madison WV, *3076* **101** E4
Madison WI, *233209* **74** B3
Madison Co. AL, *334811* **119** F2
Madison Co. AR, *15717* **106** C4
Madison Co. FL, *19224* **137** F2
Madison Co. GA, *28120* **121** E3
Madison Co. ID, *37536* **23** F4
Madison Co. IL, *269282* **98** B3
Madison Co. IN, *131636* **89** F4
Madison Co. IA, *15679* **86** C2
Madison Co. KY, *82916* **110** C1
Madison Co. MS, *95203* **126** B2
Madison Co. MO, *12226* **108** A1
Madison Co. MT, *7691* **23** E2
Madison Co. NE, *34876* **35** E2
Madison Co. NY, *73442* **79** E4
Madison Co. NC, *20764* **111** E4
Madison Co. OH, *43435* **100** C1
Madison Co. TN, *98294* **108** C4
Madison Co. TX, *13664* **61** F1
Madison Co. VA, *13308* **102** C3
Madison Hts. MI, *29694* **210** C2
Madison Hts. VA, *11285* **112** C1
Madison Lake MN, *1017* **72** C1
Madison Par. LA, *12093* **126** A3
Madisonville KY, *19591* **109** E1
Madisonville LA, *748* **134** B2
Madisonville TN, *4577* **120** C1
Madisonville TX, *4396* **61** F1
Madras OR, *6046* **21** D3
Madrid IA, *2543* **86** C1
Madrid NY, *757* **80** B1
Maeser UT, *3601* **32** A4
Magalia CA, *11310* **36** C1
Magazine AR, *847* **116** C1
Magdalena NM, *938* **48** B4
Magee MS, *4408* **126** C3
Maggie Valley NC, *1150* **121** E1
Magna UT, *26505* **257** A2
Magnolia AR, *11577* **125** D1
Magnolia DE, *225* **145** E2
Magnolia MS, *2420* **134** B1
Magnolia NJ, *4341* **248** D4
Magnolia NC, *939* **123** E2
Magnolia OH, *978* **91** E3
Magnolia TX, *1393* **132** A2
Magoffin Co. KY, *13333* **111** D1
Mahanoy City PA, *4162* **93** E3
Mahaska Co. IA, *22381* **87** D2
Mahnomen MN, *1214* **19** F3
Mahnomen Co. MN, *5413* **19** F3
Mahomet IL, *7258* **88** C4
Mahoning Co. OH, *238823* **91** F3
Mahopac NY, *8369* **148** C2
Mahtomedi MN, *7676* **235** E1
Mahwah NJ, *25890* **148** B3
Maiden NC, *3310* **122** A1
Maili HI, *9488* **152** A3
Maine NY, *1000* **93** E1
Maineville OH, *975* **100** B2
Maitland FL, *15751* **141** D1
Maize KS, *3420* **43** E4
Majestic KY, *600* **111** E1
Major Co. OK, *7527* **51** D2
Makaha HI, *8278* **152** A3
Makakilo City HI, *18248* **152** A3
Makawao HI, *7184* **153** D1
Makena HI, *99* **153** D1
Malabar FL, *2757* **141** E2
Malad City ID, *2095* **31** E2
Malaga CA, *947* **44** C3
Malaga NJ, *1700* **145** F1
Malakoff TX, *2324* **59** F3
Malcolm NE, *382* **35** F4
Malden MA, *59450* **151** D1
Malden MO, *4275* **108** B3
Malden WV, *750* **200** B2
Malheur Co. OR, *31313* **22** A4
Malibu CA, *12645* **52** B2
Malin OR, *805* **29** D2
Mallory WV, *1654* **111** F1
Malone FL, *2088* **137** D1
Malone NY, *5911* **80** C1
Malone WA, *475* **12** B4
Malta ID, *193* **31** D2
Malta IL, *1164* **88** C1
Malta MT, *1997* **16** C2
Malta NY, *2100* **94** B1
Malta OH, *671* **101** E1
Maltby WA, *10830* **262** B2
Malvern AL, *1448* **136** C1
Malvern AR, *10318* **117** D3
Malvern IA, *1142* **86** A3
Malvern OH, *1189* **91** E3
Malvern PA, *2998* **146** B3
Malverne NY, *8514* **241** G4
Mamaroneck NY, *18929* **148** C3
Mammoth AZ, *1426* **55** D2
Mammoth Hot Sprs. WY, *263* **23** F2
Mammoth Lakes CA, *8234* **37** E4
Mammoth Spr. AR, *977* **107** F3
Mamou LA, *3242* **133** E2
Man WV, *759* **111** F1
Manahawkin NJ, *2303* **147** E4
Manasquan NJ, *5897* **147** E2
Manassa CO, *991* **41** D4
Manassas VA, *37821* **144** A4
Manassas Park VA, *14273* **144** A3
Manatee Co. FL, *322833* **140** C3
Manawa WI, *1371* **74** B1
Mancelona MI, *1390* **70** B4
Manchaca TX, *1133* **61** E2
Manchaug MA, *850* **150** C2
Manchester CT, *30577* **150** A3
Manchester GA, *4230* **128** C2
Manchester IA, *5179* **73** F4
Manchester KY, *1255* **110** C2
Manchester ME, *2465* **82** B2
Manchester MD, *4808* **103** E1
Manchester MI, *2091* **90** B1
Manchester MO, *18094* **256** A3
Manchester NH, *109565* **81** F4
Manchester NY, *1709* **78** C3
Manchester OH, *2023* **100** C3
Manchester PA, *2763* **93** E4
Manchester TN, *10102* **120** A1
Manchester VT, *749* **81** D4
Manchester WA, *5413* **262** A3
Manchester-by-the-Sea MA, *5228* **151** F1
Manchester Ctr. VT, *2120* **81** D4
Mancos CO, *1336* **40** B4
Mandan ND, *18331* **18** C4
Mandaree ND, *596* **18** A3
Manderson SD, *626* **26** A4
Mandeville AR, *700* **116** C4
Mandeville LA, *11560* **134** B2
Mangham LA, *672* **125** F2
Mango FL, *11313* **266** C2
Mangonia Park FL, *1888* **141** F4
Mangum OK, *3010* **50** C3
Manhasset NY, *8080* **148** C4
Manhasset Hills NY, *3592* **241** G3
Manhattan IL, *7051* **89** D2
Manhattan KS, *52281* **43** F2
Manhattan MT, *1520* **23** F1
Manhattan Beach CA, *35135* **228** C3
Manheim PA, *4858* **93** E4
Manila AR, *3342* **108** B4
Manila UT, *310* **32** A3
Manilla IA, *776* **86** A1
Manistee MI, *6226* **75** E1
Manistee Co. MI, *24733* **70** A4
Manistique MI, *3097* **69** E2
Manito IL, *1642* **88** B4
Manitou Beach MI, *2019* **90** B1
Manitou Sprs. CO, *4992* **41** E2
Manitowoc WI, *33736* **75** D1
Manitowoc Co. WI, *81442* **75** D1
Mankato KS, *869* **43** E1
Mankato MN, *39309* **72** C1
Manlius NY, *4704* **79** E3
Manly IA, *1323* **73** D3
Mannford OK, *3076* **51** F2
Manning IA, *1500* **86** B1
Manning ND, *74* **18** A3
Manning SC, *4108* **122** B4
Mannington WV, *2063* **102** A1
Mannsville OK, *863* **51** F4
Manokotak AK, *442* **154** B3
Manomet MA, *2900* **151** E3
Manor PA, *3239* **92** A4
Manor TX, *5037* **61** E1
Manorhaven NY, *6556* **241** G2
Manorville NY, *14314* **149** D3
Mansfield AR, *1139* **116** C2
Mansfield IL, *906* **88** C4
Mansfield LA, *5001* **124** C3
Mansfield MA, *7360* **151** D2
Mansfield MO, *1296* **107** E2
Mansfield OH, *47821* **91** D3
Mansfield PA, *3625* **93** D1
Mansfield TX, *56368* **59** E3
Mansfield Ctr. CT, *947* **150** B3
Mansfield Four Corners CT, *700* **150** B3
Manson IA, *1690* **72** B4
Manson WA, *1468* **13** E2
Mansura LA, *1419* **133** F1
Mantachie MS, *1144* **119** D3
Manteca CA, *67096* **36** C4
Manteno IL, *9204* **89** D2
Manteo NC, *1434* **115** F2
Manti UT, *3276* **39** E2
Manton MI, *1287* **75** F1
Mantorville MN, *1197* **73** D1
Mantua OH, *1043* **91** E2
Mantua UT, *687* **31** E3
Mantua VA, *7135* **270** A4
Manvel ND, *360* **19** E2
Manvel TX, *5179* **132** A4
Manville NJ, *10344* **147** D1
Manville RI, *3800* **150** C2
Many LA, *2853* **125** D4
Many Farms AZ, *1348* **47** F2

Bellwood A1
Bonaventure B2
Cape Canaveral B2
Cocoa A2
Cocoa Beach B2
Cocoa West A2
Frontenac A1
Georgiana B2
Indialantic B3
Indian Harbour Beach B3
La Grange A1
Malabar B3
Melbourne A3
Melbourne Beach B3
Melbourne Vil. B3
Merritt Island B2
Mims A1
Palm Bay B3
Palm Shores B3
Pineda B2
Port St. John A1
Rockledge A2
Satellite Beach B3
Sharpes A2
S. Patrick Shores ... B3
Titusville A1
Viera A2
W. Melbourne B3

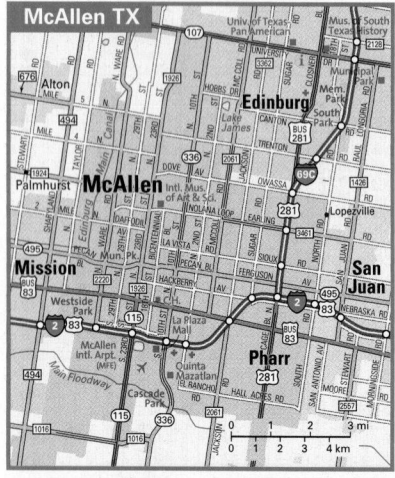

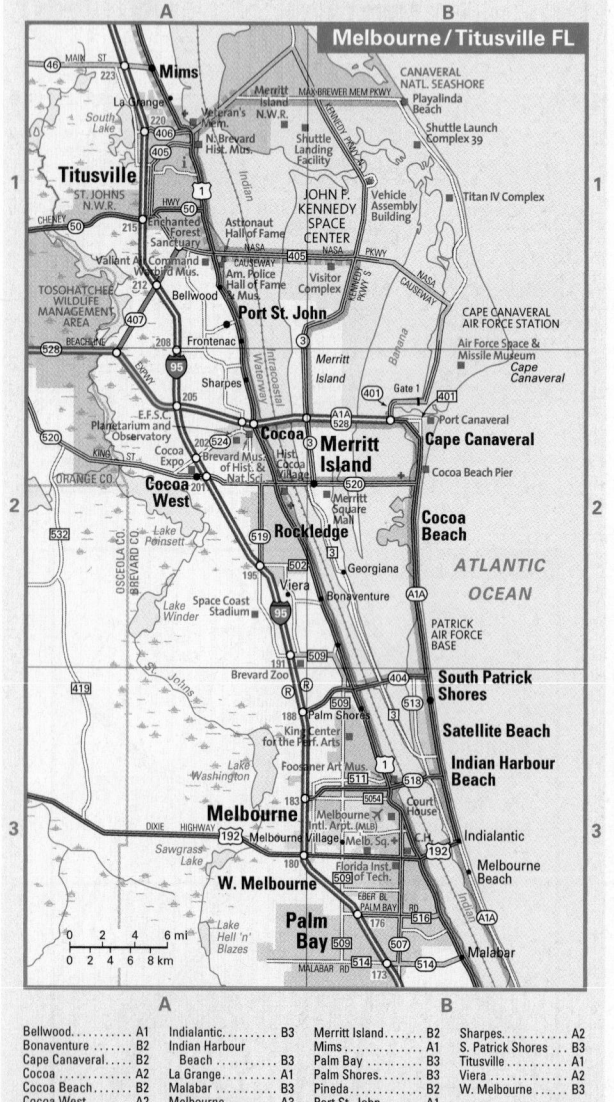

Entries in **bold black** indicate counties or parishes.
Entries in **bold color** indicate cities with detailed inset maps.

Miami / Fort Lauderdale FL

(Detailed inset map of the Miami / Fort Lauderdale metropolitan area, including Boca Raton, Deerfield Beach, Pompano Beach, Coral Springs, Margate, Tamarac, North Lauderdale, Lauderhill, Sunrise, Plantation, Weston, Davie, Cooper City, Pembroke Pines, Miramar, Fort Lauderdale, Oakland Park, Wilton Manors, Hollywood, Hallandale Beach, Aventura, North Miami Beach, North Miami, Opa-locka, Miami Gardens, Hialeah, Hialeah Gardens, Doral, Miami, Miami Springs, Miami Beach, Sweetwater, West Miami, Westchester, Kendale Lakes, South Miami, Coral Gables, Kendall, Pinecrest, Richmond Hts., Palmetto Bay, Perrine, Goulds, Cutler Bay, Key Biscayne, and Biscayne National Park, with the Atlantic Ocean to the east.)

Scale: 0 – 2 – 4 – 6 mi / 0 – 3 – 6 – 9 km

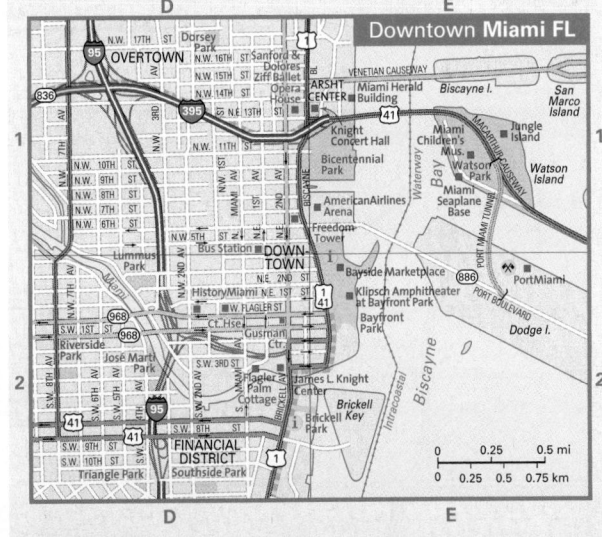

Downtown Miami FL

(Inset map of Downtown Miami, including Overtown, Downtown, Financial District, Brickell, Biscayne I., San Marco Island, Watson Island, and PortMiami.)

Scale: 0 – 0.25 – 0.5 mi / 0 – 0.25 – 0.5 – 0.75 km

Figures after entries indicate population, page number, and grid reference.

Milwaukee WI

Milwaukee WI

Downtown Milwaukee WI

Downtown Milwaukee WI

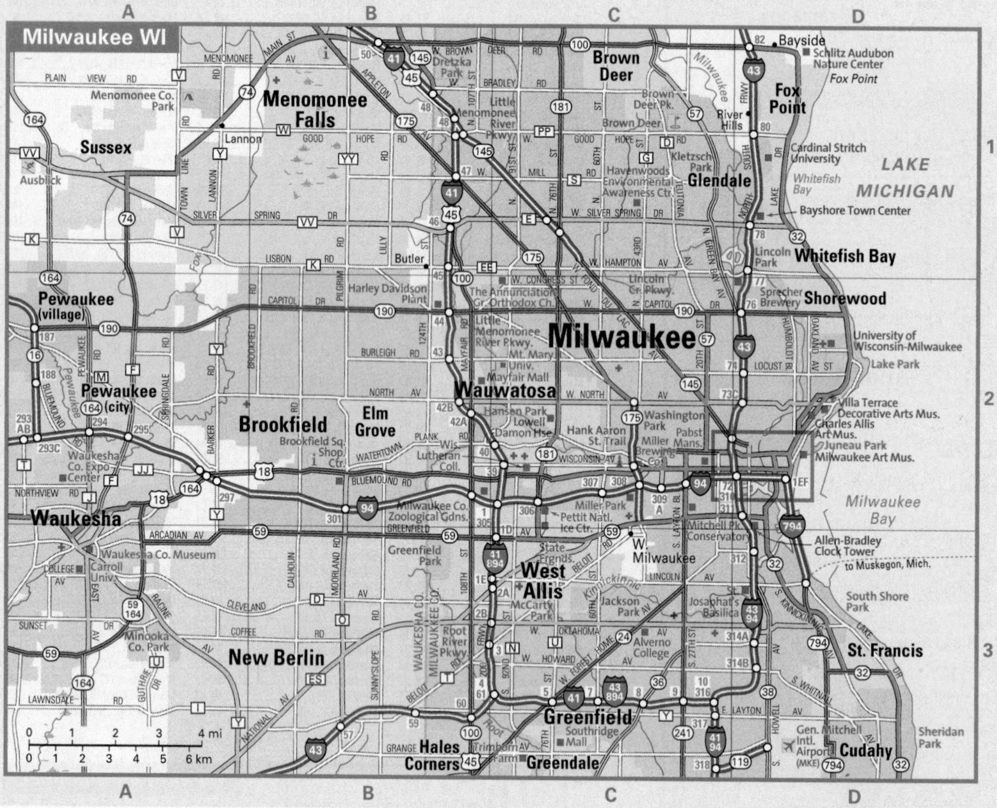

Entries in **bold black** indicate counties or parishes.
Entries in **bold color** indicate cities with detailed inset maps.

Minneapolis / St Paul MN

Figures after entries indicate population, page number, and grid reference.

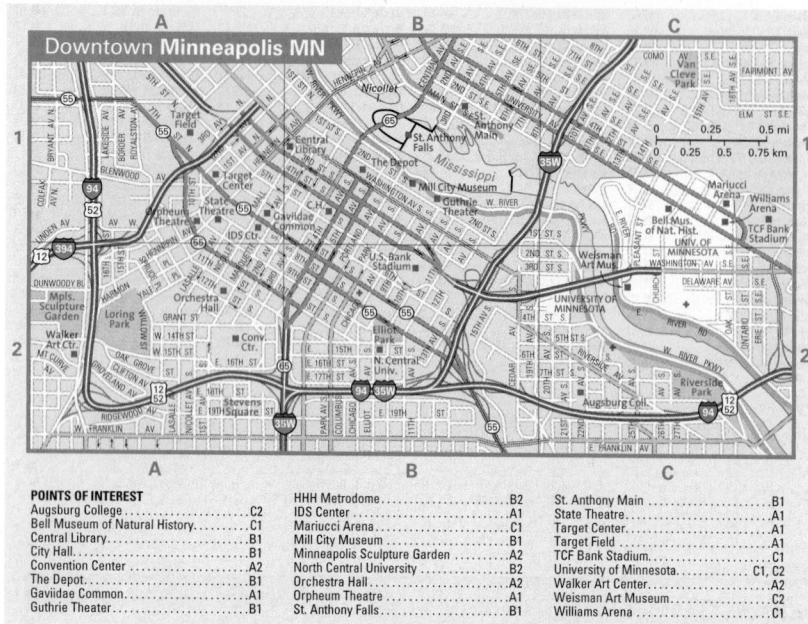

Downtown Minneapolis MN

Monterey Bay CA

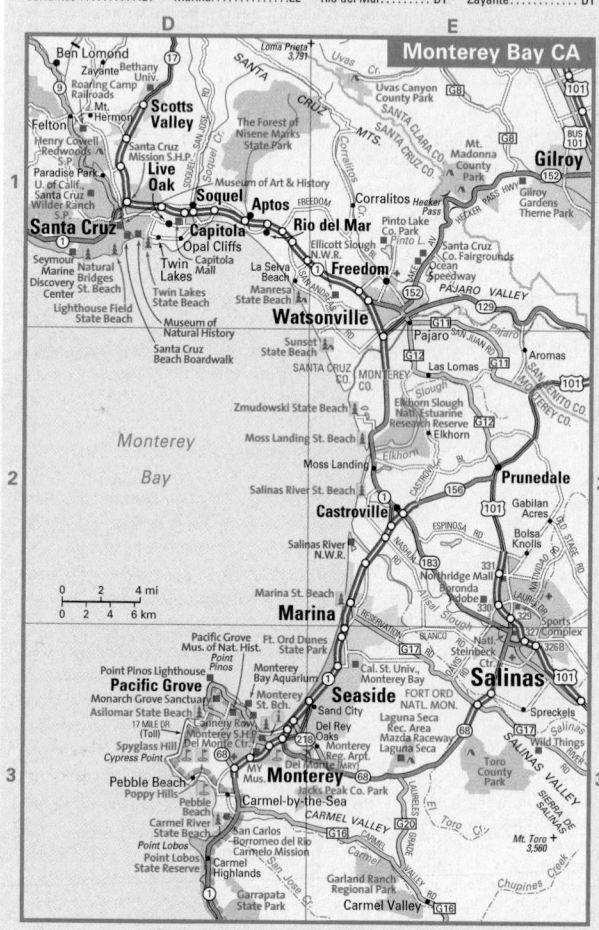

Missoula MT

Mobile AL

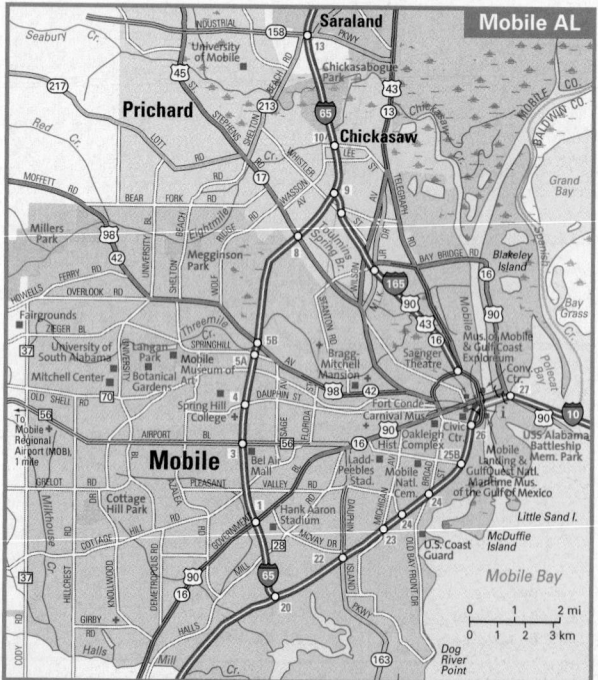

Montgomery AL

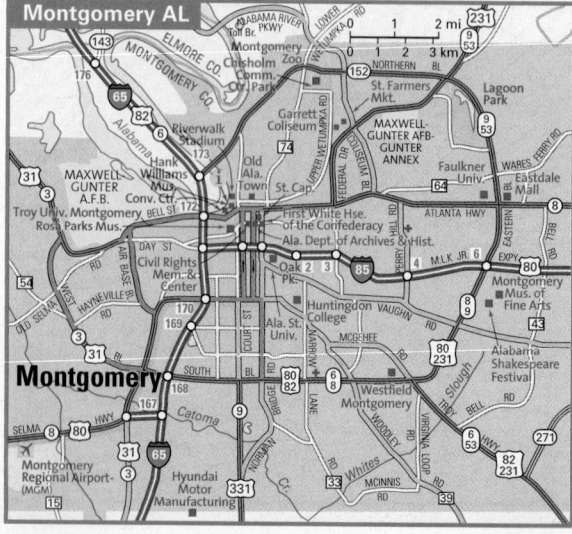

Entries in **bold black** indicate counties or parishes.
Entries in **bold color** indicate cities with detailed inset maps.

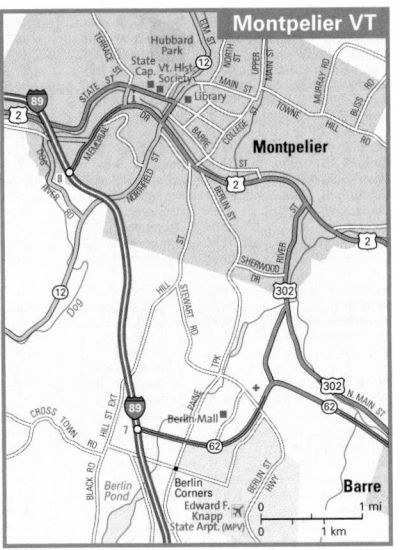

Montpelier VT

Montpelier

Barre

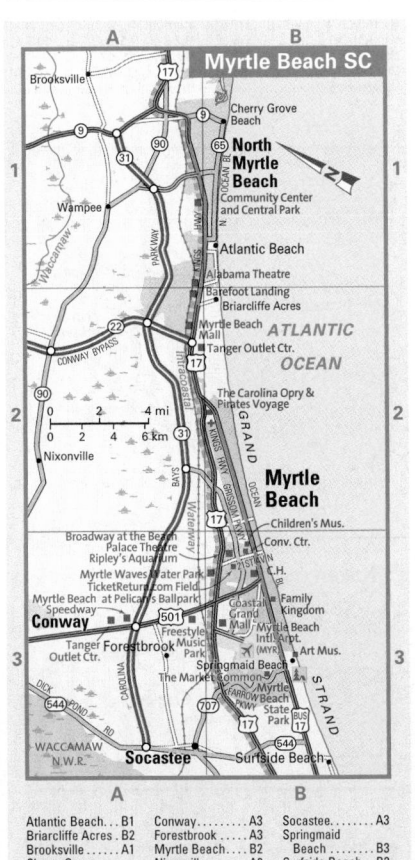

Myrtle Beach SC

North Myrtle Beach

Myrtle Beach

Conway

Socastee

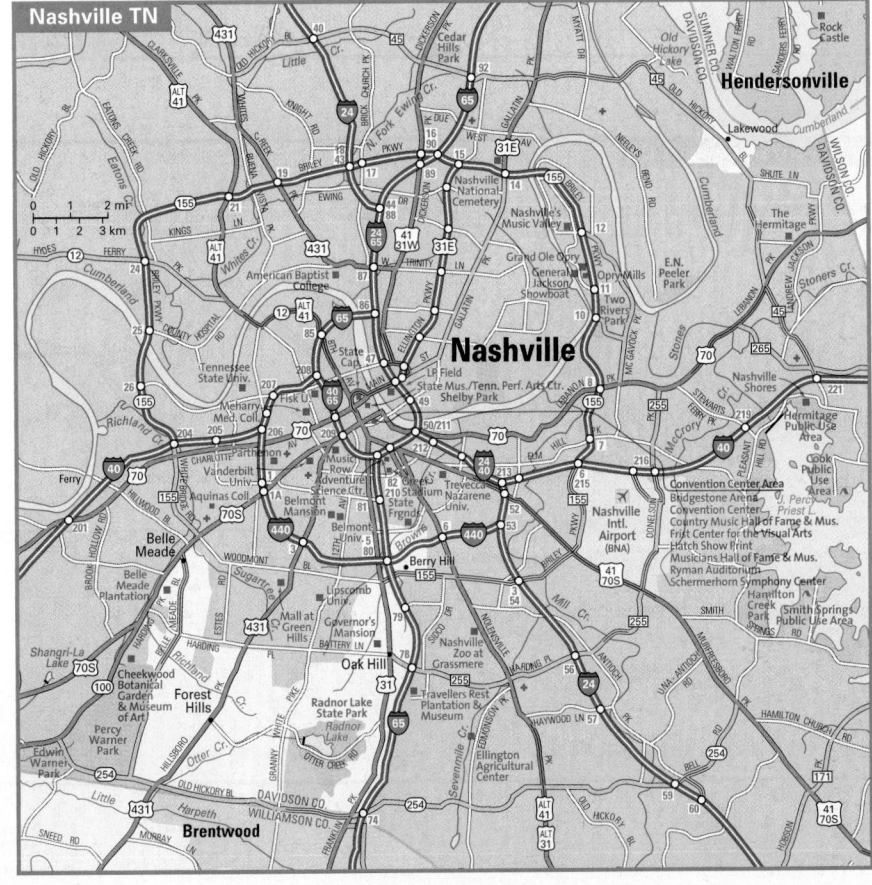

Nashville TN

Hendersonville

Nashville

Brentwood

Figures after entries indicate population, page number, and grid reference.

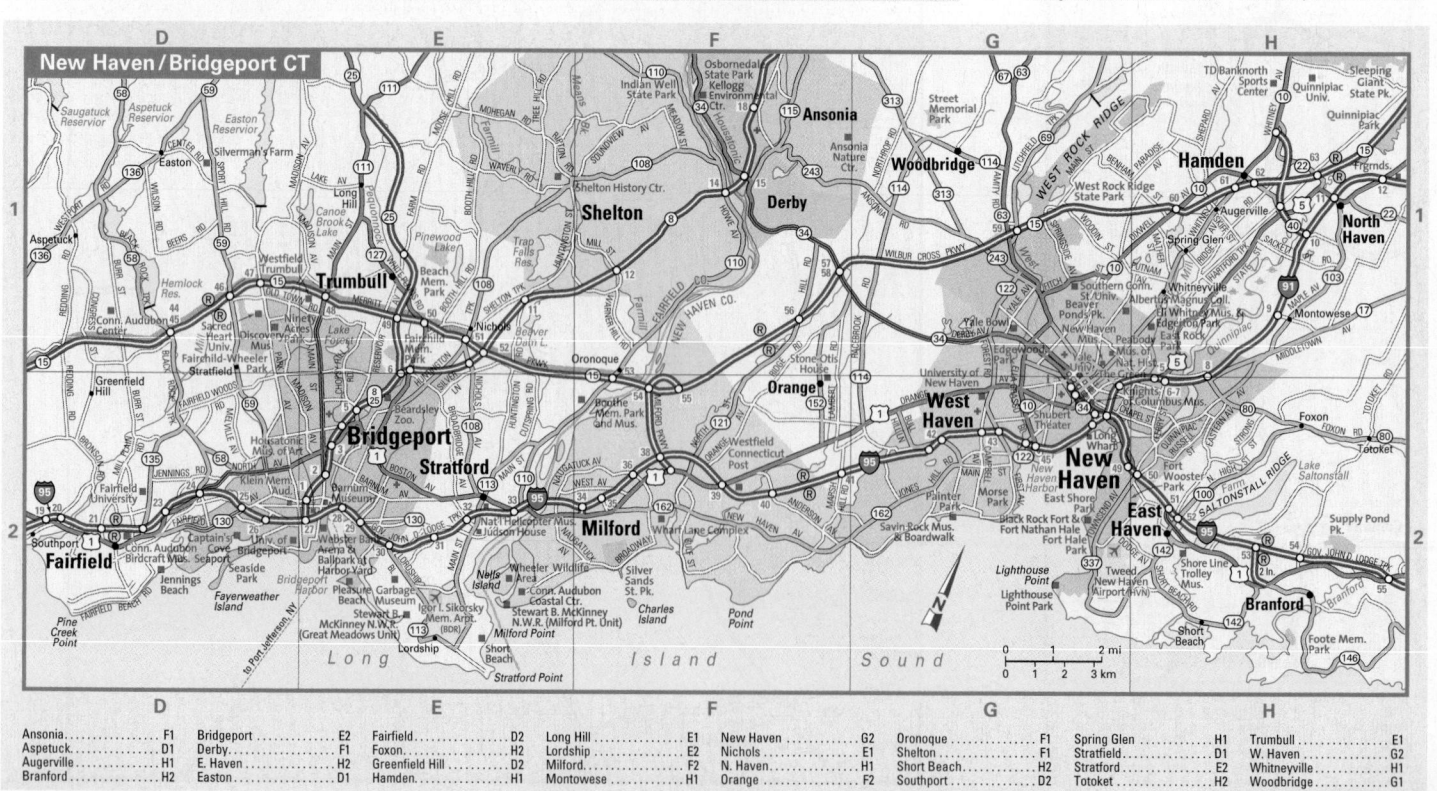

Entries in **bold black** indicate counties or parishes.
Entries in **bold color** indicate cities with detailed inset maps.

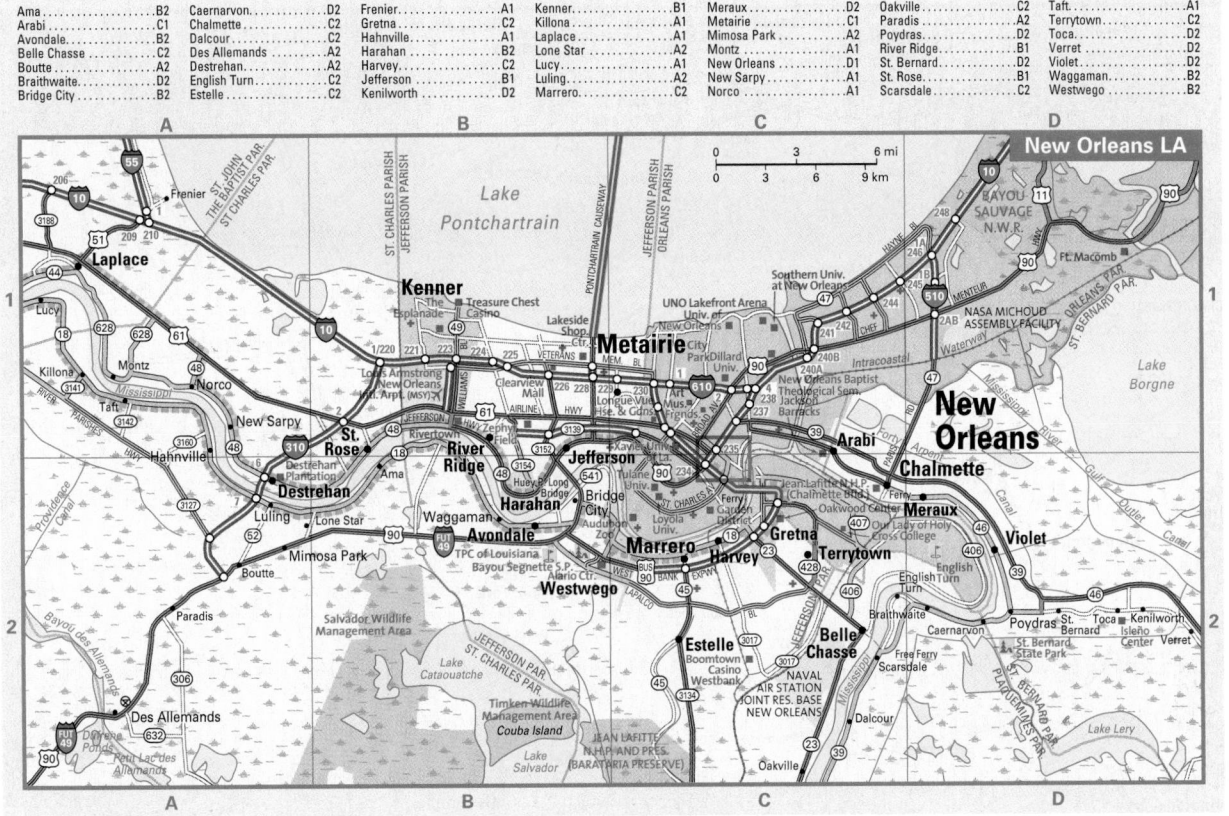

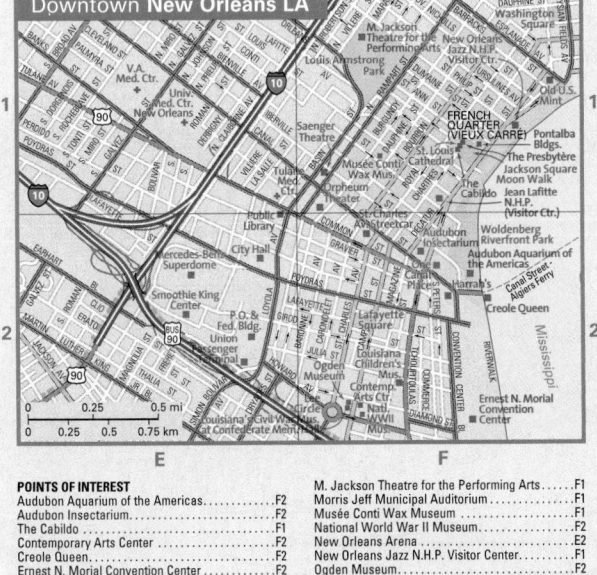

POINTS OF INTEREST

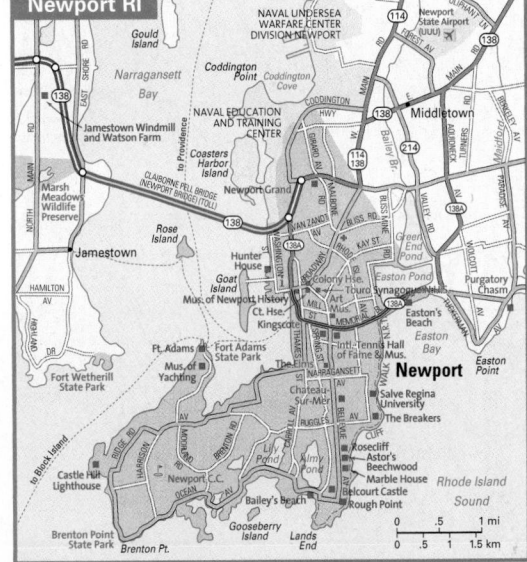

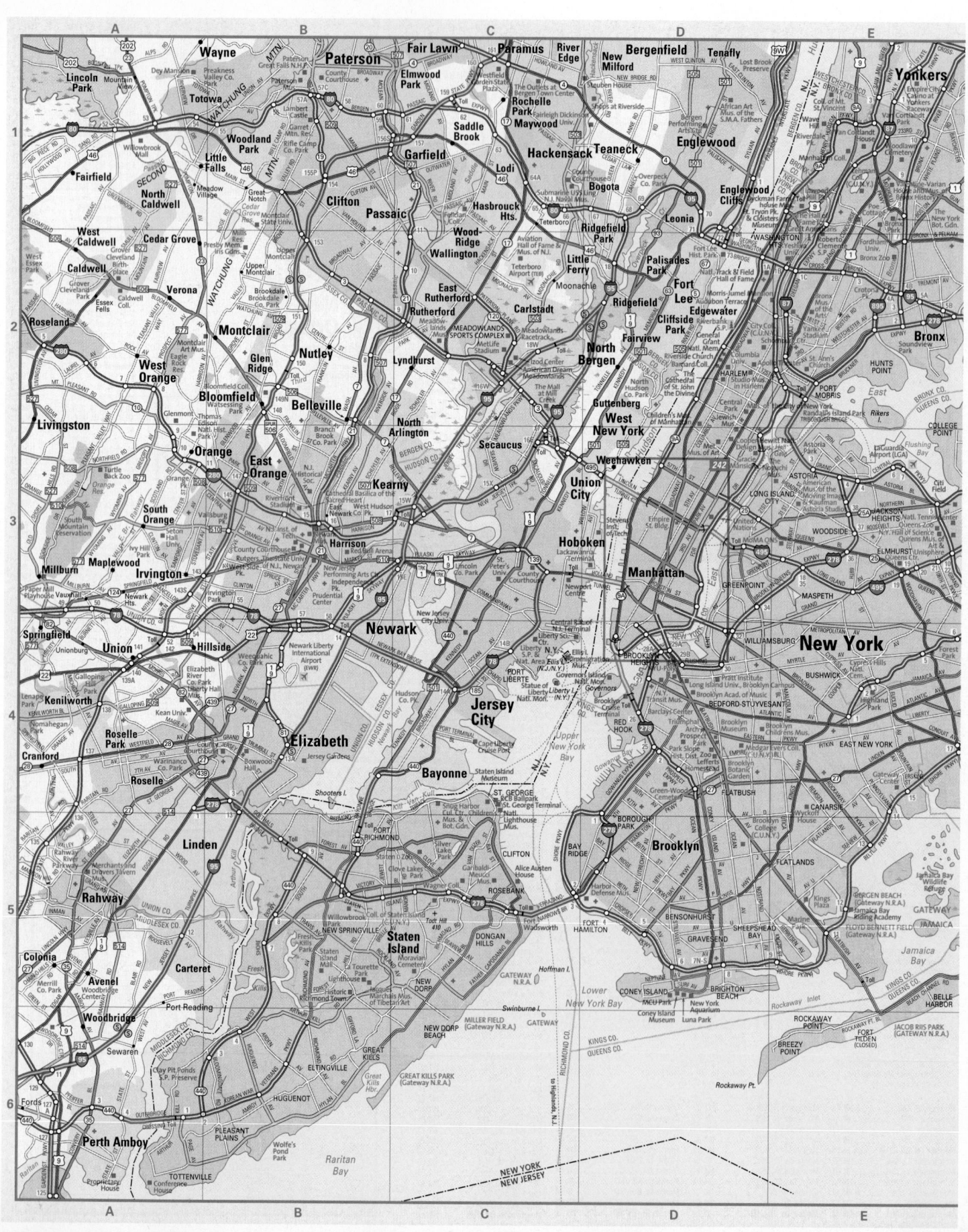

Entries in **bold black** indicate counties or parishes.
Entries in **bold color** indicate cities with detailed inset maps.

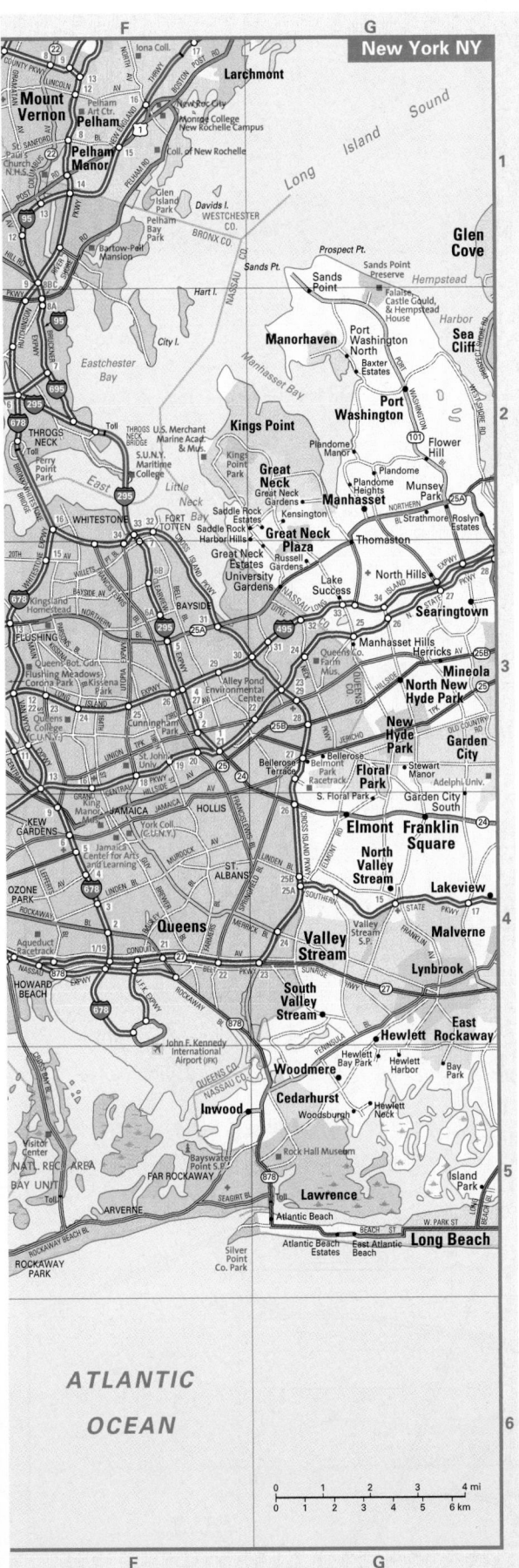

New York NY

Atlantic Beach	G5	Fairview	D2
Atlantic Beach Estates	G5	Floral Park	G3
Avenel	A5	Flower Hill	G2
Baxter Estates	G2	Fords	C3
Bayonne	C4	Ft. Lee	D2
Bay Park	G4	Franklin Square	G3
Bellerose	G3	Garden City	G3
Bellerose Terrace	G3	Garden City South	G4
Belleville	B2	Garfield	C1
Bergenfield	D1	Glen Cove	G1
Bloomfield	B2	Glen Ridge	B2
Bogota	D1	Great Neck	G2
Brookdale	B2	Great Neck Estates	G3
Caldwell	A2	Great Neck Gardens	G2
Carlstadt	C2	Great Neck Plaza	G2
Carteret	A5	Great Notch	B1
Cedar Grove	A2	Guttenberg	D2
Cedarhurst	G4	Hackensack	C1
Cliffside Park	D2	Harbor Hills	G2
Clifton	C1	Harrison	C1
Colonia	A5	Hasbrouck Hts.	C1
Cranford	A4	Herricks	G3
E. Atlantic Beach	G5	Hewlett	G4
E. Newark	B3	Hewlett Bay Park	G5
E. Orange	B3	Hewlett Harbor	G5
E. Rockaway	G4	Hewlett Neck	G5
E. Rutherford	C2	Hillside	A4
Edgewater	D2	Hoboken	D2
Elizabeth	B4	Inwood	F5
Elmont	G3	Irvington	A3
Elmwood Park	C1	Island Park	G4
Englewood	D1	Jersey City	C2
Englewood Cliffs	D1	Kearny	B3
Essex Fells	A2	Kenilworth	A4
Fairfield	A1	Kensington	G2
Fair Lawn	C1	Kings Pt.	G2

Lake Success	G3	N. Hills	G3
Lakeview	G4	N. New Hyde Park	G3
Larchmont	F1	N. Valley Stream	G4
Lawrence	G5	Nutley	B2
Leonia	D1	Orange	A3
Lincoln Park	A1	Palisades Park	D2
Linden	A5	Paramus	C1
Little Falls	A1	Passaic	B1
Little Ferry	C2	Paterson	B1
Livingston	A2	Pelham	F1
Lodi	C1	Pelham Manor	F1
Long Beach	G5	Perth Amboy	A5
Lynbrook	G4	Plandome	G2
Lyndhurst	C2	Plandome Hts.	G2
Malverne	G4	Plandome Manor	G2
Manhasset	G3	Port Reading	A5
Manhasset Hills	G3	Port Washington	G2
Manorhaven	G2	Port Washington North	G2
Maplewood	A3	Rahway	A5
Maywood	C1	Ridgefield	D2
Meadow Vil.	A1	Ridgefield Park	D1
Millburn	A3	River Edge	C1
Mineola	G3	Rochelle Park	C1
Montclair	B2	Roseland	A2
Moonachie	C2	Roselle	A4
Mtn. View	A1	Roselle Park	A4
Mt. Vernon	F1	Roslyn Estates	G2
Munsey Park	G2	Russell Gardens	G3
Newark	B4	Rutherford	C2
Newark Hts.	A3	Saddle Brook	C1
New Hyde Park	G3	Saddle Rock	G2
New Milford	D1	Saddle Rock Estates	G2
New York	E4	Sands Pt.	G1
N. Arlington	C2	Sea Cliff	G1
N. Bergen	D2	Searingtown	G3
N. Caldwell	A1	Secaucus	C3

Sewaren	A6
S. Floral Park	G4
S. Orange	A3
S. Valley Stream	G4
Springfield	A4
Stewart Manor	G3
Strathmore	G2
Teaneck	D1
Tenafly	D1
Teterboro	C1
Thomaston	G3
Totowa	A1
Union	A4
Unionburg	A4
Union City	C3
University Gardens	G3
Upper Montclair	B2
Valley Stream	G4
Vauxhall	A3
Verona	A2
Wallington	C2
Wayne	A1
Weehawken	D3
W. Caldwell	A2
W. New York	D2
W. Orange	A2
Woodbridge	A6
Woodland Park	B1
Woodmere	G5
Wood-Ridge	C2
Woodsburgh	G5
Yonkers	E1

242
New Castle–New Lenox

Figures after entries indicate population, page number, and grid reference.

Manhattan **New York NY**

Entries in **bold black** indicate counties or parishes.
Entries in **bold color** indicate cities with detailed inset maps.

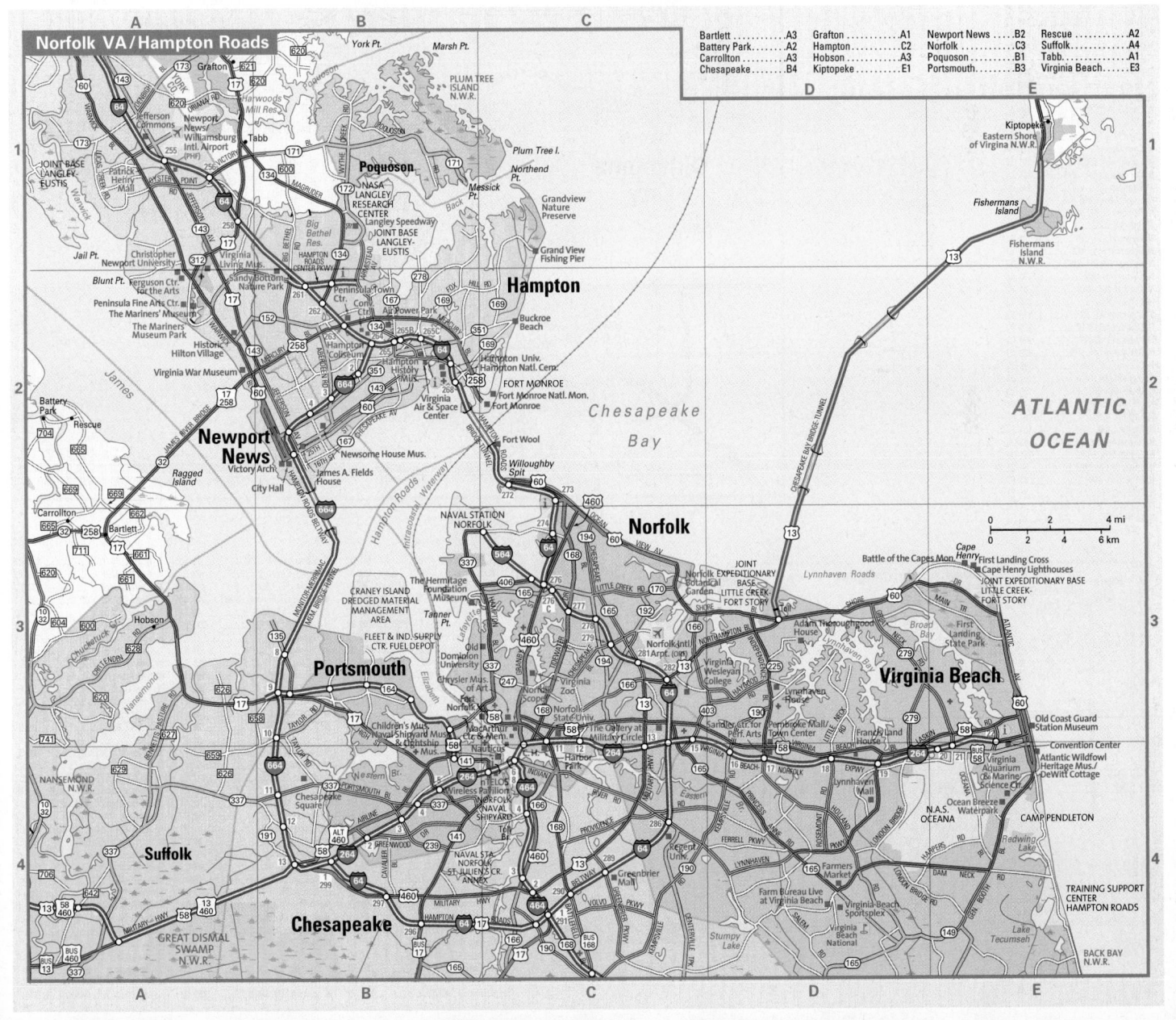

244
North Acton–North Wilkesboro

Figures after entries indicate population, page number, and grid reference.

Oklahoma City OK

Arcadia..........F1
Bethany..........D2
Choctaw..........F2
Del City..........E2
Edmond..........E1
Forest Park..........E2
Jones..........F1
Lake Aluma..........E2
Midwest City..........F2
Moore..........E3
Mustang..........C3
Newcastle..........D4
Nichols Hills..........D2
Nicoma Park..........F2
Norman..........E4
Oklahoma City..........C3
Piedmont..........C1
Richland..........C1
Smith Vil...........E2
Spencer..........E2
The Village..........D1
Valley Brook..........E3
Warr Acres..........D2
Woodlawn Park..........D2
Yukon..........C2

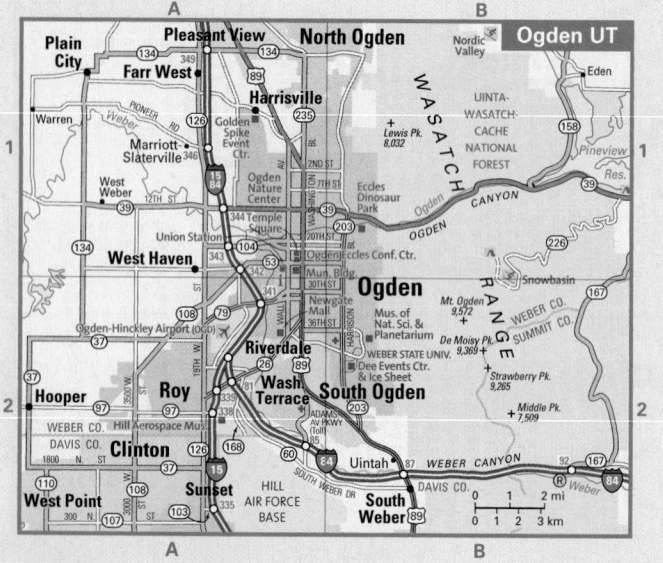

Ogden UT

Clinton..........A2
Eden..........B1
Farr West..........A1
Harrisville..........A1
Hooper..........A2
Marriott-Slaterville..........A2
N. Ogden..........B1
Ogden..........B2
Plain City..........A1
Pleasant View..........A1
Riverdale..........A2
Roy..........A2
S. Ogden..........A2
S. Weber..........A2
Sunset..........A2
Uintah..........B2
Warren..........A1
Washington Terrace..........A2
W. Haven..........A1
W. Point..........A1
W. Weber..........A1

Entries in **bold black** indicate counties or parishes.
Entries in **bold color** indicate cities with detailed inset maps.

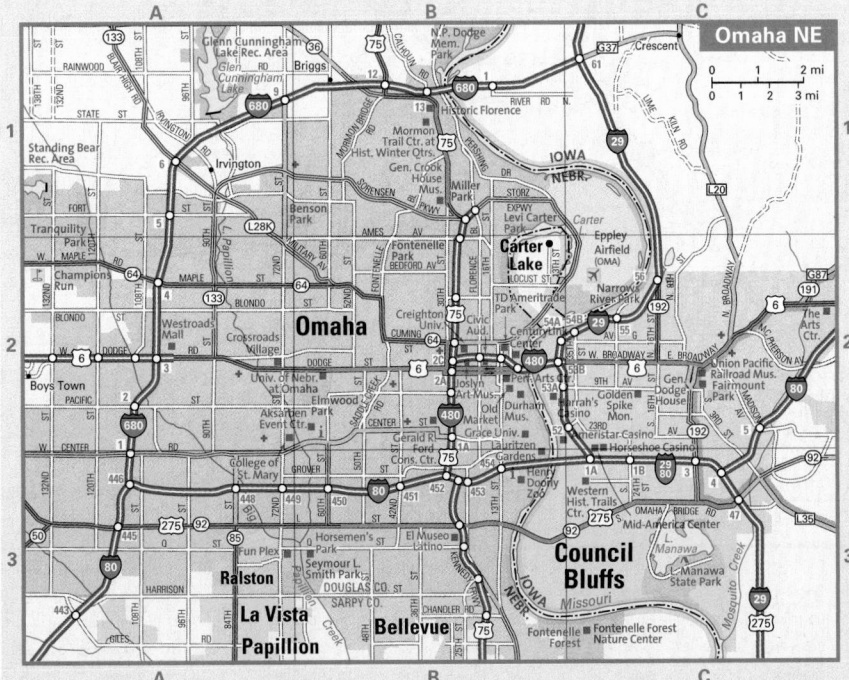

Olympia WA

Tumwater · Lacey · Olympia

Omaha NE

Council Bluffs

La Vista

Papillion

Bellevue

Ralston

246
Ossineke–Palm Springs

Figures after entries indicate population, page number, and grid reference.

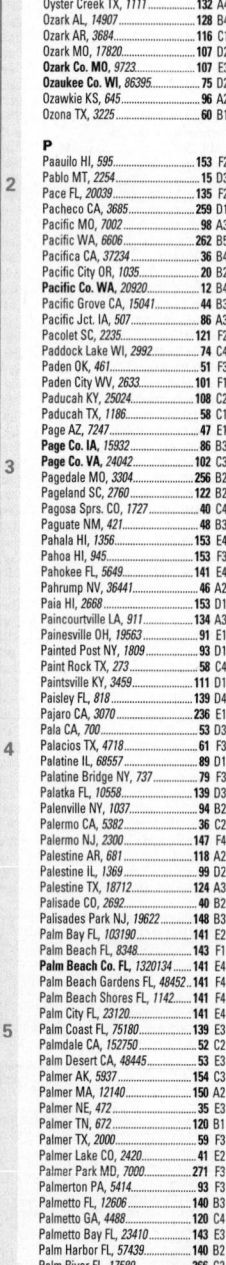

Entries in **bold black** indicate counties or parishes.
Entries in **bold color** indicate cities with detailed inset maps.

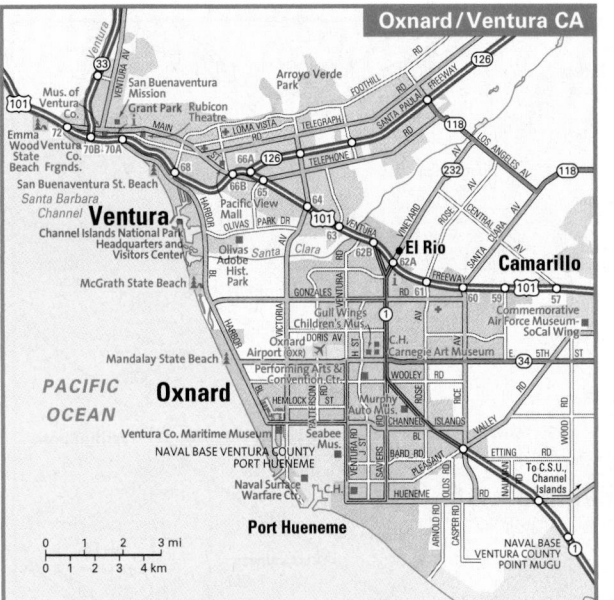

Oxnard/Ventura CA

Palm Springs CA

Pensacola FL

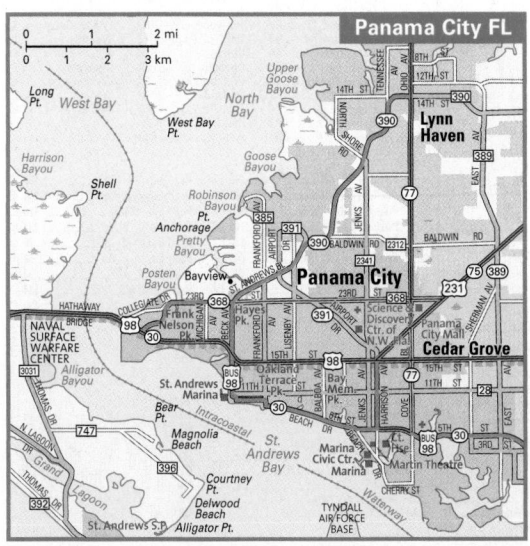

Panama City FL

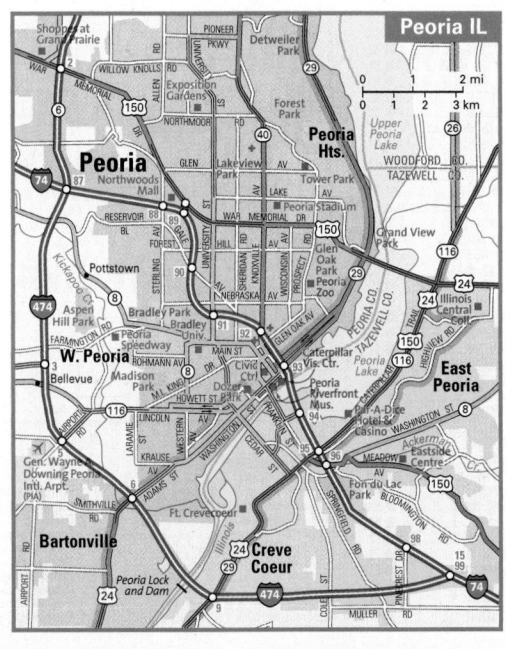

Peoria IL

248

Patterson Gardens–Pearl River

Figures after entries indicate population, page number, and grid reference.

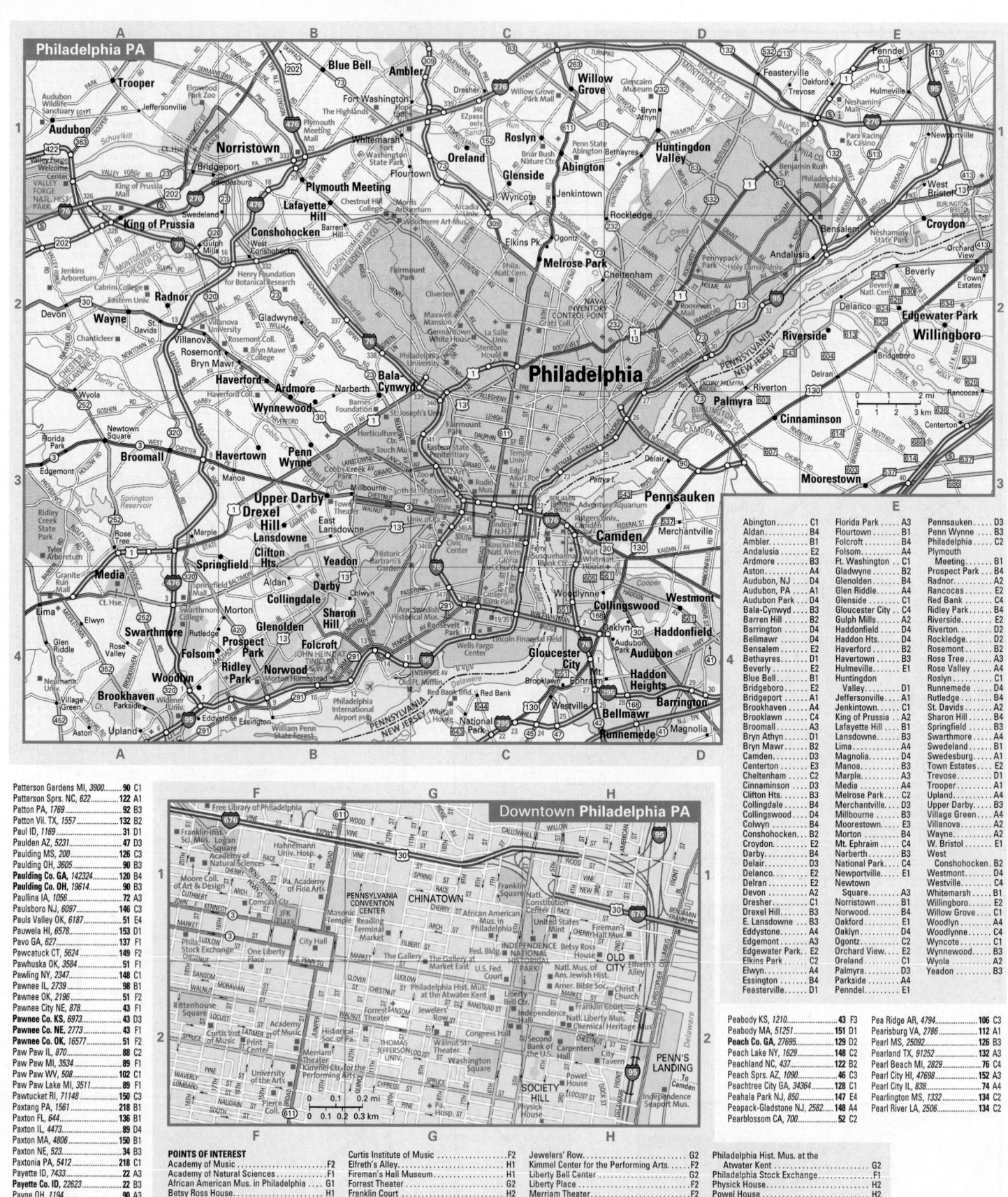

Entries in **bold black** indicate counties or parishes.
Entries in **bold color** indicate cities with detailed inset maps.

POINTS OF INTEREST

Arizona Center F1
Arizona Science Center F2
Arizona State Capitol E2
Arizona State Fairgrounds E1
Arizona Veterans Memorial Coliseum E1
Chase Field F2
Children's Museum F2
City Hall F2
Convention Center F2
Dodge Theatre E2
Heard Museum F1
Herberger Theater Center F1
Heritage Square F2
Orpheum Theatre E2
Phoenix Art Museum F1
Phoenix Museum of History F2
Symphony Hall F2
US Airways Center F2

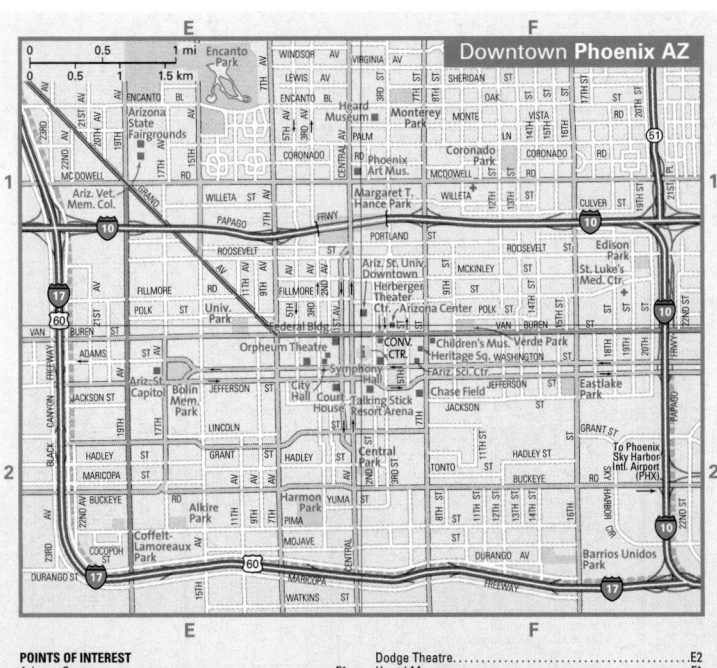

Pierre SD

Figures after entries indicate population, page number, and grid reference.

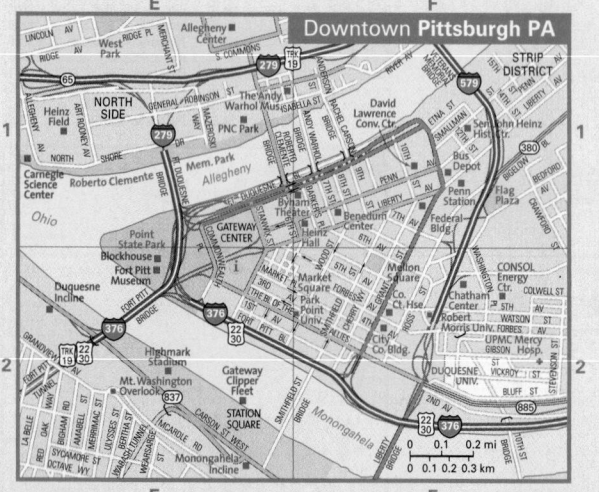

Pittsburgh PA

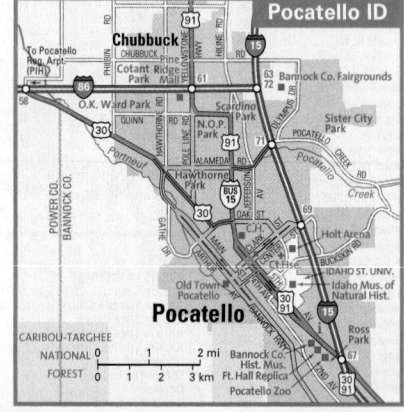

Downtown Pittsburgh PA

Pocatello ID

Entries in **bold black** indicate counties or parishes.
Entries in **bold color** indicate cities with detailed inset maps.

Portland ME

Providence RI

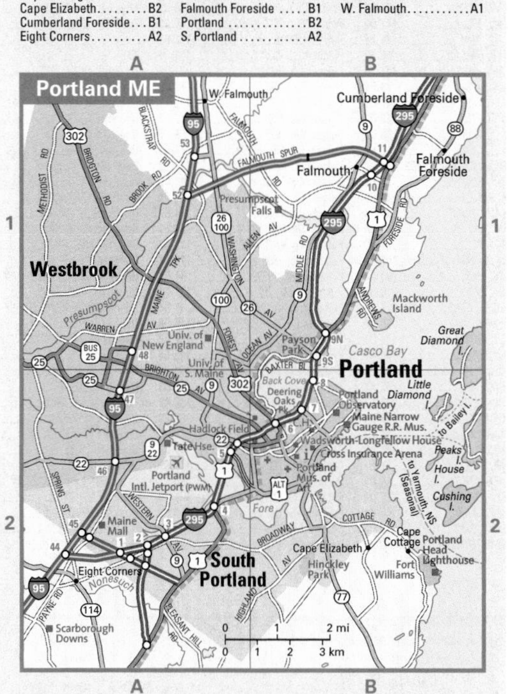

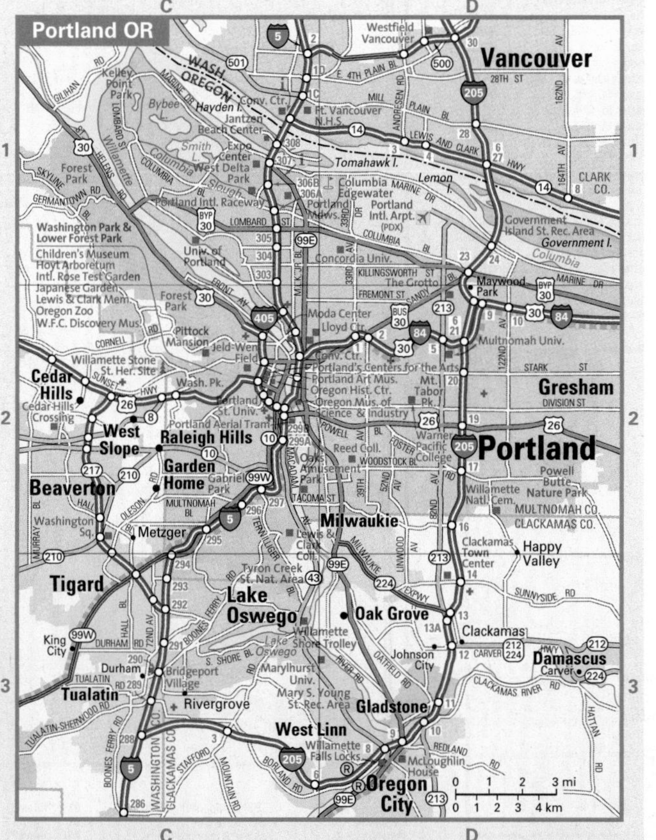

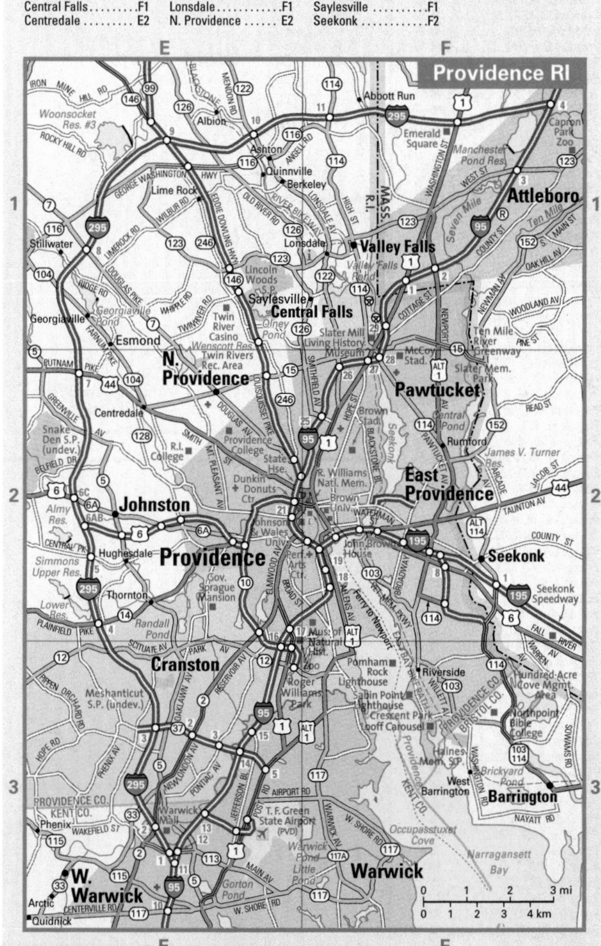

Figures after entries indicate population, page number, and grid reference.

Provo UT

Pleasant Grove
Lindon
Orem
Provo
Springville
Vineyard
Lakeview
Provo Canyon
Bridal Veil Falls
UINTA-WASATCH-CACHE NATIONAL FOR.
Cooling Pond
Shops at Riverwoods
Orem City Ctr.
Heritage Mus.
Utah Valley University
L.D.S. Temple
BRIGHAM YOUNG UNIV.
Earth Sci. Mus.
7-Peaks Resort & Ice Arena
Reg. Govt. Ctr.
Powell Brent Brown Ballpark
Powell Slough Waterfowl Mgmt. Area
Utah Lake State Park
D.U.P. Mus.
Covey Ctr. for the Arts
Provo Municipal Airport (PVU)
Provo Towne Centre
Buckley Mtn. 9,502
Provo Bay
2 mi
3 km

Pueblo CO

Pueblo
COLORADO STATE UNIV. PUEBLO
Pueblo Mall
Pueblo Memorial Airport (PUB)
Pueblo Weisbrod Aircraft Mus. & Intl. B-24 Mem. Mus.
Baxter
Pueblo Zoo
El Pueblo History Mus.
Union Av. Hist. District
Rosemount Mus.
Southeastern Colo. Heritage Ctr.
Sangre de Cristo Arts and Conf. Ctr.
City Park
Colorado St. Frgnd.
Arkansas
Lake Minnequa
Lombard Village
2 mi
3 km

Racine/Kenosha WI

Wind Point
Wingspread
Caledonia
Johnson Park
John H. Batten Intl. Arpt. (RAC)
North Bay
Prairie Performing Arts Center
Racine Zoo
North Beach Park
Mount Pleasant
Wustum Museum
Racine
Racine Art Museum
Racine Heritage Museum
DeKoven Center
Golden Rondelle Theater
Sturtevant
Pritchard Park
Regency Mall
Elmwood Park
RACINE CO.
KENOSHA CO.
Petrifying Springs Pk.
UNIV. OF WIS.-PARKSIDE
Somers
LAKE MICHIGAN
Carthage College
Kenosha Regional Airport (ENW)
Kenosha
Kenosha History Center
Kenosha Public Mus.
Rhode Center for the Arts
Eichelman Park
Mun. Bldg.
Southport Plaza
Kemper Center & Anderson Arts Center
Southport Park
Pleasant Prairie
2 mi
3 km

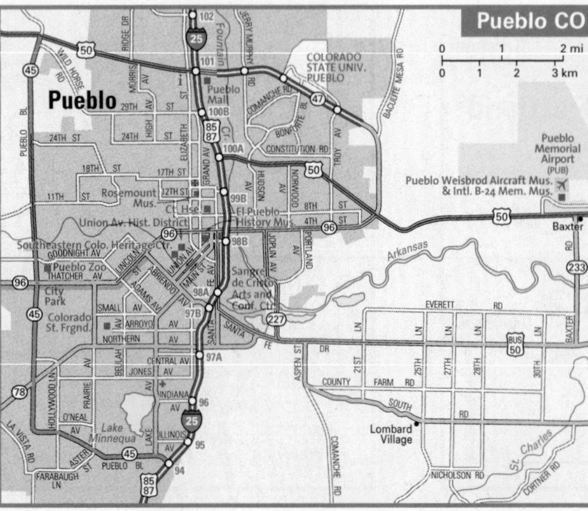

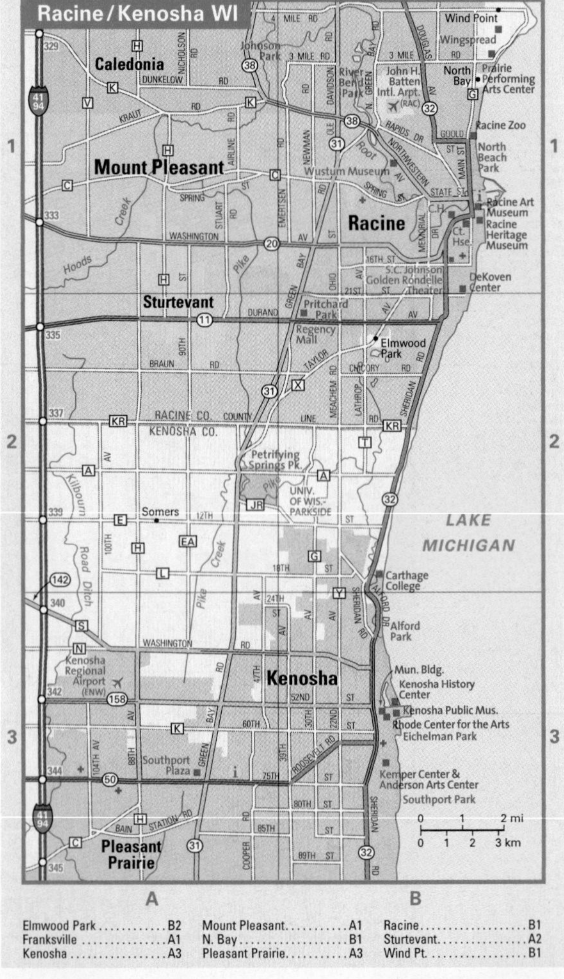

Entries in **bold black** indicate counties or parishes.
Entries in **bold color** indicate cities with detailed inset maps.

Raleigh / Durham / Chapel Hill NC

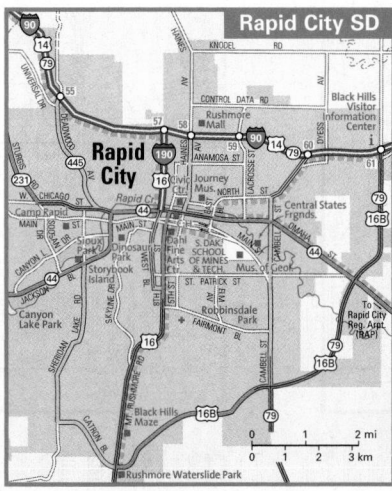

Rapid City SD

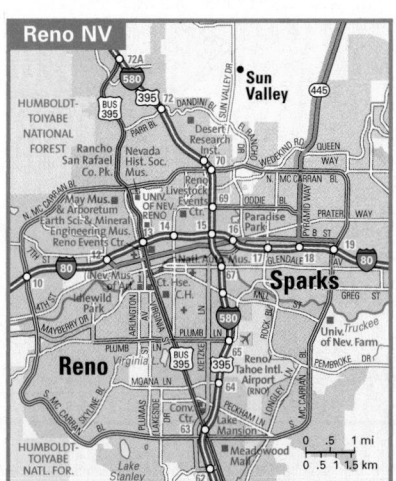

Reno NV

Figures after entries indicate population, page number, and grid reference.

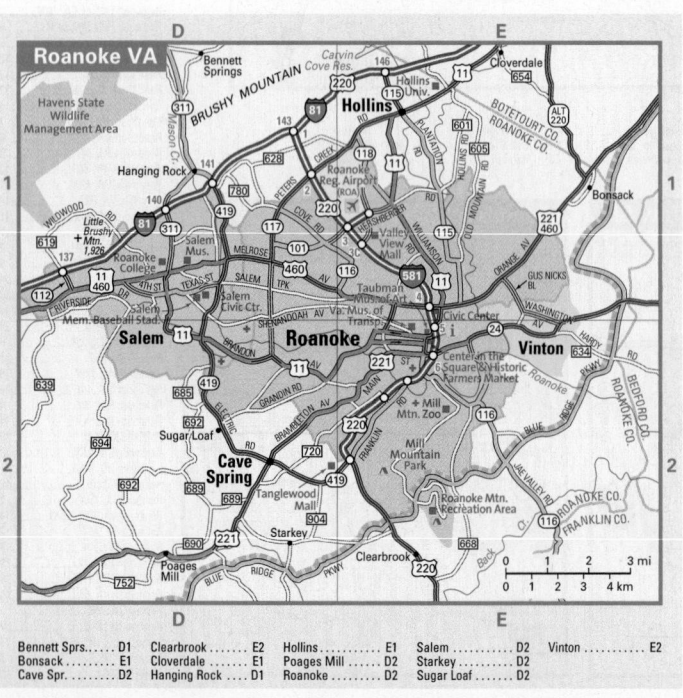

Richmond VA

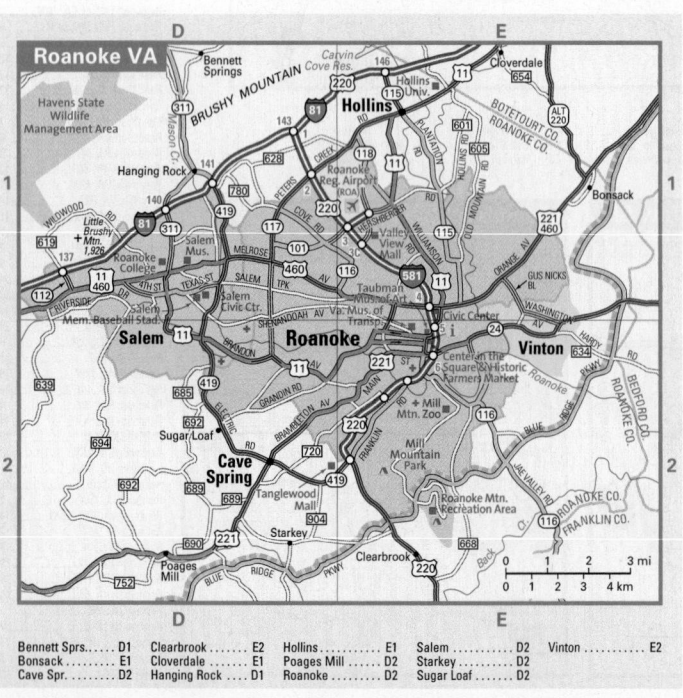

Roanoke VA

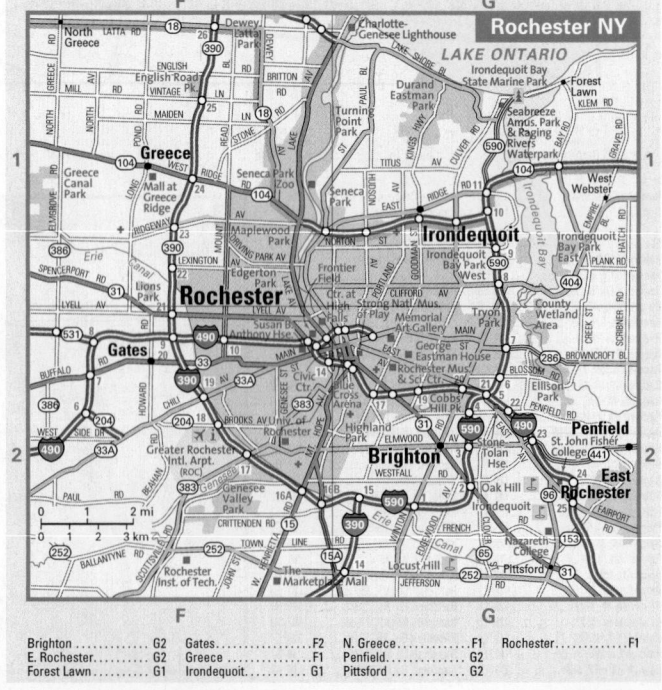

Rochester NY

Entries in **bold black** indicate counties or parishes.
Entries in **bold color** indicate cities with detailed inset maps.

Riverdale ND, 205............... 18 B3
Riverdale UT, 8426............. 244 A2
Riverdale Park MD, 6956..... 270 E2
River Edge NJ, 11340......... 240 C1
River Falls AL, 526............. 128 A4
River Falls WI, 15000........... 67 D4
River Forest IL, 11172........ 203 D4
River Grove IL, 10227........ 203 D4
Rivergrove OR, 289............ 251 C3
Riverhead NY, 13299.......... 149 E3
River Hills WI, 1597........... 234 D1
River Oaks TX, 7427........... 207 A2
River Ridge LA, 13494........ 239 B1
Riverside AL, 2208............. 120 A4
Riverside CA, 303871.......... 53 D2

Riverside IL, 8875.............. 203 D4
Riverside IA, 993................. 87 F2
Riverside MO, 2937............ 224 B2
Riverside NJ, 7765............. 147 D3
Riverside NY, 497............... 149 E3
Riverside PA, 381................. 93 E3
Riverside Co. CA, 2189641.... 53 E3
Riverton IL, 3455................. 98 B1
Riverton KS, 929................ 106 B2
Riverton NJ, 2779.............. 146 E3
Riverton UT, 38753............. 31 E4
Riverton WY, 10615............. 32 B1
Riverview FL, 71050........... 140 C2
Riverview MO, 2856............ 256 C1
Riverwood KY, 446............. 230 E1
Riverwoods IL, 3660........... 203 C2
Rives Jct. MI, 650................ 76 A4
Rivesville WV, 934.............. 102 A1
Riviera Beach FL, 32488..... 141 E4
Riviera Beach MD, 12677.... 144 C2
Roachdale IN, 926............... 99 E1
Roaming Shores OH, 1508.... 91 F2
Roane Co. TN, 54181.......... 110 B4
Roane Co. WV, 14926...... 101 F3
Roan Mtn. TN, 1360............ 111 E3
Roanoke AL, 6074.............. 128 B4
Roanoke IL, 2065................ 88 B3
Roanoke IN, 1722............... 90 A4
Roanoke TX, 5962.............. 207 B1
Roanoke VA, 97032............ 112 B2
Roanoke Co. VA, 92376.... 112 A1
Roanoke Rapids NC, 15754... 113 E3
Roaring Spr. PA, 2585.......... 92 C4
Robards KY, 515................ 109 E1
Robbins IL, 5337................ 203 D6
Robbins NC, 1097.............. 122 C1
Robbinsdale MN, 13953...... 235 B2
Robbinsville NC, 3401........ 147 D2
Robbinsville NC, 620.......... 121 D1
Robersonville NC, 1488...... 113 E4
Roberta GA, 1007............... 129 D2
Robert Lee TX, 1049............ 58 B3
Roberts ID, 580.................... 23 E4
Roberts WI, 1651.................. 67 E4
Roberts Co. SD, 10149...... 27 F1
Roberts Co. TX, 929.......... 50 B2
Robertsdale AL, 5276......... 135 E2
Robertson Co. KY, 2282.... 100 C3
Robertson Co. TN, 66283... 109 F3
Robertson Co. TX, 16622... 61 E1
Robertsville NJ, 11297........ 147 E2
Robeson Co. NC, 134168... 123 D2
Robesonia PA, 2061........... 146 A2
Robins IA, 3142................... 87 E1

Robinson IL, 7713.............. 99 D2
Robinson TX, 10509............ 59 E4
Robstown TX, 11487........... 63 F2
Roby TX, 643........................ 58 B2
Rochdale MA, 1400............. 150 B2
Rochelle GA, 1174.............. 129 E3
Rochelle IL, 9574................ 88 B1
Rochelle Park NJ, 6070...... 240 C1
Rochester IL, 3689............... 98 B1
Rochester IN, 6218............... 89 F3
Rochester MN, 106769......... 73 D1
Rochester NH, 29752........... 81 F4
Rochester NY, 210565......... 79 D3
Rochester PA, 3657............. 91 F3
Rochester VT, 812................. 81 D3
Rochester WA, 2388............. 12 B4

Rochester WI, 3682............. 74 C4
Rochester Hills MI, 70995.... 76 C4
Rock MA, 850...................... 151 D3
Rockaway NJ, 6438............ 148 A3
Rockaway Beach MO, 841.... 107 D3
Rockaway Beach OR, 1312.... 20 B1
Rockbridge Co. VA, 22307... 102 B4
Rockcastle Co. KY, 17056... 110 C2
Rock Co. MN, 9687............. 27 F4
Rock Co. NE, 1526.............. 35 D2
Rock Co. WI, 160331.......... 74 B4
Rock Creek MN, 1628.......... 67 D2
Rock Creek OH, 529............ 91 F2
Rockdale MD, 16100............ 144 B3
Rockdale TX, 5595............... 61 E1
Rockdale Co. GA, 85215.... 120 C4
Rockfall CT, 1561................ 149 D3
Rock Falls IL, 9266.............. 88 B1
Rockford AL, 477................. 128 A4
Rockford IL, 152871............. 74 B4
Rockford IA, 860................... 73 D3
Rockford MN, 5719............... 75 F3
Rockford OH, 1120............... 90 A3
Rockford TN, 856................ 110 C4
Rockingham NC, 9558........ 122 C2
Rockingham Co. NH, 295223... 81 F4
Rockingham Co. NC, 93663... 112 C3
Rockingham Co. VA, 76314... 102 C3
Rock Island IL, 39018.......... 88 A2
Rock Island OK, 646........... 116 B1
Rock Island WA, 788............ 13 E3
Rock Island Co. IL, 147546... 88 A2
Rockland ID, 295.................. 31 E1
Rockland ME, 7297............... 82 C2
Rockland MA, 17489........... 151 D2
Rockland MA, 5272............... 73 F1
Rockland Co. NY, 311687... 148 B2
Rockledge GA, 1120............ 120 A3
Rockledge FL, 24926.......... 141 E2
Rockledge PA, 2543............ 248 D2
Rocklin CA, 56974............... 36 C2
Rock Mills AL, 600.............. 128 B3
Rock Pt. AZ, 642................... 47 F1
Rockport AR, 755................ 117 D3
Rockport IN, 2270................. 99 E4
Rockport KY, 3209.............. 109 E1
Rockport ME, 4966............. 151 F1

Rock Port MO, 1318............. 86 A4
Rockport TX, 8766............... 61 E4
Rock Rapids IA, 2549........... 27 F4
Rocksprings TX, 1182.......... 60 B2
Rock Sprs. WY, 23036......... 32 B3
Rockton IL, 7685.................. 74 B4
Rockvale CO, 487................. 41 E3
Rock Valley IA, 3354............ 35 F1
Rockville CT, 7474.............. 150 A3
Rockville IN, 2607................. 99 E1
Rockville MD, 61209........... 144 B2
Rockville MN, 2448............... 66 C3
Rockville RI, 425................. 150 C4
Rockwall TX, 37490............. 59 F2
Rockwall Co. TX, 78337.... 59 F2

Rockwell AR, 3780.............. 117 D3
Rockwell IA, 1039................. 73 D3
Rockwell NC, 2108.............. 122 B1
Rockwell City IA, 1709......... 72 B4
Rockwood MI, 3289............. 90 C1
Rockwood PA, 890............... 92 A4
Rockwood TN, 5562............ 110 B4
Rocky Ford CO, 3957............ 41 F3
Rocky Hill CT, 18760.......... 149 E1
Rocky Hill NJ, 682.............. 147 D1
Rocky Mount NC, 57477...... 113 E4
Rocky Mount VA, 4799........ 112 B2
Rocky Pt. NY, 14014........... 149 D3
Rocky Ridge UT, 733............ 39 E1
Rocky Ripple IN, 606.......... 221 B2
Rocky River OH, 20213....... 204 E2
Rocky Top TN, 1781............ 110 C3
Rodeo CA, 8679.................. 259 C1
Roebuck SC, 2200.............. 121 F2
Roeland Park KS, 6731....... 224 B3
Roessleville NY, 10800....... 188 D2
Roff OK, 725........................ 51 F4
Roger Mills Co. OK, 3647... 50 C2
Rogers AR, 55964.............. 106 C3
Rogers MN, 8597................. 66 C3
Rogers TX, 1218................... 59 E4
Rogers City MI, 2827............ 71 D3
Rogers Co. OK, 86905..... 106 A3
Rogersville AL, 1257........... 119 E2
Rogersville MO, 3073......... 107 D2
Rogersville TN, 4420.......... 111 D3
Rogue River OR, 2131........... 28 B3
Rohnert Park CA, 40971....... 36 B3
Roland IA, 1284................... 86 C1
Roland OK, 3169................ 116 B1
Rolesville NC, 3786............ 113 D4
Rolette ND, 594................... 18 C1
Rolette Co. ND, 13937...... 18 C1
Rolfe IA, 584........................ 72 B3
Rolla KS, 442........................ 50 B1
Rolla MO, 19559.................. 97 F4
Rolla ND, 1280..................... 18 C1
Rolling Fields KY, 646......... 230 E1
Rolling Fork MS, 2143........ 126 A1
Rolling Hills CA, 1860......... 228 C4
Rolling Hills KY, 959.......... 230 E1
Rolling Hills WY, 440............ 33 D1
Rolling Hills Estates CA, 8067... 228 C4
Rolling Meadows IL, 24099... 203 B3
Rolling Prairie IN, 582.......... 89 E2
Rollingstone MN, 664........... 73 E1
Rollinsford NH, 2527............ 82 A4
Roma TX, 9765..................... 63 D4
Romancoke MD, 800........... 145 D3
Roman Forest TX, 1538...... 132 B2
Rome GA, 36303................. 120 B3
Rome IL, 1738....................... 88 B3

Rome NY, 23725................... 79 E3
Rome City IN, 1361.............. 90 A2
Romeo CO, 404..................... 41 D4
Romeo MI, 3596.................. 76 C4
Romeoville IL, 39680........... 89 D2
Romney WV, 1848............... 102 C2
Romoland CA, 1684........... 229 K4
Romulus MI, 23989............. 90 C1
Rومona KY, 1349................. 94 B3
Roncevalle NY, 1765........... 112 A1
Roncommon MI, 1075........... 76 C4
Rooks Co. KS, 5181............. 43 D2
Roosevelt NJ, 882............... 147 E2
Roosevelt Co. MT, 10425.... 17 E2
Roosevelt Co. NM, 19846... 49 F4
Roosevelt Park MI, 3831....... 75 E3
Roper NC, 611..................... 113 F4
Ropesville TX, 434................ 58 A1
Rosamond CA, 18150.......... 52 C1
Rosamond CA, 18150.......... 52 C1
Rosaryville MD, 18150........ 144 C4
Rosburg WA, 317.................. 12 B4
Roscoe IL, 10785................. 74 B4
Roscoe NY, 541..................... 94 A2
Roscoe SD, 329.................... 27 D2
Roscoe TX, 1322.................. 58 B3
Roscommon MI, 1075............ 76 C4
Roscommon Co. MI, 24449... 76 A1
Roseau MN, 2633.................. 19 F1
Roseau Co. MN, 15629...... 19 F1
Rosebud SD, 1587................ 34 C1
Rosebud TX, 1412............... 59 F4
Rosebud Co. MT, 9233...... 17 D4
Roseburg OR, 21181............ 28 B1
Rose City MI, 653................. 76 B3
Rose City TX, 502.................. 61 F2
Rosedale IN, 725.................. 99 E1
Rosedale LA, 793................ 133 F2
Rosedale MD, 19257........... 144 C2
Rosedale MS, 1873............ 118 A4
Rosedale Beach DE, 750..... 145 F3
Rose Haven MD, 1400........ 144 C4
Rose Hill KS, 3931............... 43 F4
Rose Hill NC, 1626............. 123 E2
Rose Hill VA, 711.................. 111 D3
Rose Hill VA, 20226............ 270 C5
Roseland FL, 1472.............. 141 E3
Roseland LA, 1123.............. 134 B1
Roseland NJ, 5819.............. 240 A2
Roselawn IN, 4131................ 89 D3
Roselle IL, 22763............... 203 B4
Roselle NJ, 21085.............. 147 E1
Roselle Park NJ, 13297...... 147 E1

Rose Lodge OR, 1894........... 20 B2
Rosemead CA, 53764......... 228 E2
Rosemont CA, 22681.......... 255 C3
Rosemont IL, 4202.............. 203 C3
Rosemont MN, 21874......... 235 B4
Rosemount OH, 2112.......... 101 D3
Rosenberg TX, 30618......... 132 A3
Rosendale NY, 1349............. 94 B3
Rosendale WI, 1063............. 74 C2
Rosenhayn NJ, 1098........... 145 F1
Rosepine LA, 1692.............. 133 D1
Roseto PA, 1567................... 93 F3
Rose Valley PA, 913........... 248 A4
Roseville CA, 118788............ 36 C2
Roseville IL, 989.................. 88 A3
Roseville MI, 47299............. 210 D2
Roseville MN, 33660........... 235 C2
Roseville OH, 1852.............. 101 E1
Roseville Park DE, 6200...... 146 B4
Rosholt SD, 423.................... 27 F1
Rosiclare IL, 1160............... 109 D1
Roslyn NY, 16900............... 248 C1
Roslyn SD, 183..................... 27 E2
Roslyn WA, 893..................... 13 D3
Roslyn Estates NY, 1251...... 241 G2
Rosman NC, 576................ 121 E1
Ross CA, 2415..................... 259 A1
Ross OH, 3417.................... 100 B3
Ross Co. OH, 78064.......... 101 D2
Rossford OH, 6293.............. 267 B2
Rossiter PA, 646................... 92 B3
Rossmoor CA, 10244.......... 228 E4
Rossmoor NJ, 2466............ 147 E2
Rossville GA, 4105............. 120 B2
Rossville IL, 1331................. 89 D4
Rossville IN, 1653............... 89 E4
Rossville KS, 1151................ 43 F2
Rossville MD, 15147........... 193 E2
Rossville TN, 1082............. 118 C1
Rossville VA, 539................ 103 D2
Roswell GA, 88346............ 120 C3
Roswell NM, 48366.............. 57 E1
Rotan TX, 1508..................... 58 B2
Rothsay MN, 493.................. 19 F4
Rothschild WI, 5269............. 68 B4
Rotonda FL, 8759................ 140 C4
Rotterdam NY, 20652.......... 94 B1
Rotterdam Jct. NY, 918......... 94 B1
Rougemont NC, 978........... 112 C3
Rough Rock AZ, 4747............ 47 F1
Round Hill VA, 539.............. 103 D2
Round Lake NY, 623............. 94 B1
Round Mtn. NV, 550.............. 37 F2
Round Pond ME, 325............ 82 C3
Round Rock TX, 99887......... 61 E1
Roundup MT, 1788................ 16 C4
Rouses Pt. NY, 2209............. 81 D1

Routt Co. CO, 23509............. 32 C4
Rouzerville PA, 917............. 103 D1
Rowan Co. KY, 23333...... 100 C4
Rowan Co. NC, 138428..... 112 A4
Rowland NC, 1037.............. 122 C3
Rowland Hts. CA, 48993...... 229 F3
Rowlesburg WV, 584.......... 102 B2
Rowlett TX, 56199............... 207 E1
Rowley MA, 1416............... 151 F1
Roxana DE, 375.................. 145 F4
Roxboro NC, 8362.............. 112 C3
Roxie MS, 497..................... 126 A4
Roxton TX, 650.................... 116 A4
Roy NM, 234......................... 49 E3
Roy UT, 36884...................... 31 E3
Royal Ctr. IN, 861................ 89 E3
Royal City WA, 2140............. 13 E4
Royal Oak MD, 750............ 145 D3
Royal Oak MI, 57236............ 76 C4
Royal Palm Beach FL, 34140... 141 E4
Royal Pines NC, 4272......... 121 E1
Royalton IL, 1151.................. 98 C4
Royalton MN, 1242............... 66 C2
Royersford PA, 4752.......... 146 B2
Royse City TX, 9349............. 59 F2
Royston GA, 2582............... 121 E3
Rubonia FL, 1700................ 266 B4
Ruch OR, 840........................ 28 B3
Rudyard MT, 258................... 15 F2
Rugby ND, 2876..................... 18 C2
Ruidoso NM, 7751................. 57 D2
Ruidoso Downs NM, 2815.... 57 D2
Rule TX, 636........................... 58 C2
Ruleville MS, 3007.............. 118 A4
Rumford ME, 4218................. 82 B2
Rumson NJ, 7122................ 147 F2
Runaway Bay TX, 1286......... 59 E2
Runge TX, 1031..................... 61 E3
Runnels Co. TX, 10501..... 58 C3
Runnemede NJ, 8468........ 146 C3
Running Sprs. CA, 4862..... 229 K1
Rupert ID, 5554..................... 31 D1
Rupert WV, 942................... 102 A4
Rural Hall NC, 2937............ 112 B3
Rural Retreat VA, 1483........ 111 F2
Rural Valley PA, 876............. 92 B3
Rush City MN, 3079.............. 67 D2
Rush Co. IN, 17392.......... 100 A1
Rush Co. KS, 3307............. 43 D3
Rushford MN, 1731............... 73 E2
Rushford Vil. MN, 807.......... 73 E2
Rushmere VA, 1018............. 113 F2
Rush Sprs. OK, 1231............. 51 E4
Rush Valley UT, 447.............. 31 E4
Rushville IL, 3192.............. 88 A4
Rushville IN, 6341............... 100 A1
Rushville NE, 890.................. 34 A1

Rockford IL

Sacramento CA

Arcade....................... B2	Citrus Hts........................ C1	Foothill Farms................... C1	Rio Linda........................ B1	W. Sacramento................. A3
Arden....................... B2	Fair Oaks....................... C1	N. Highlands................... B1	Rosemont....................... C2	
Carmichael................. C2	Florin.......................... B3	Rancho Cordova............... C2	Sacramento..................... A2	

Figures after entries indicate population, page number, and grid reference.

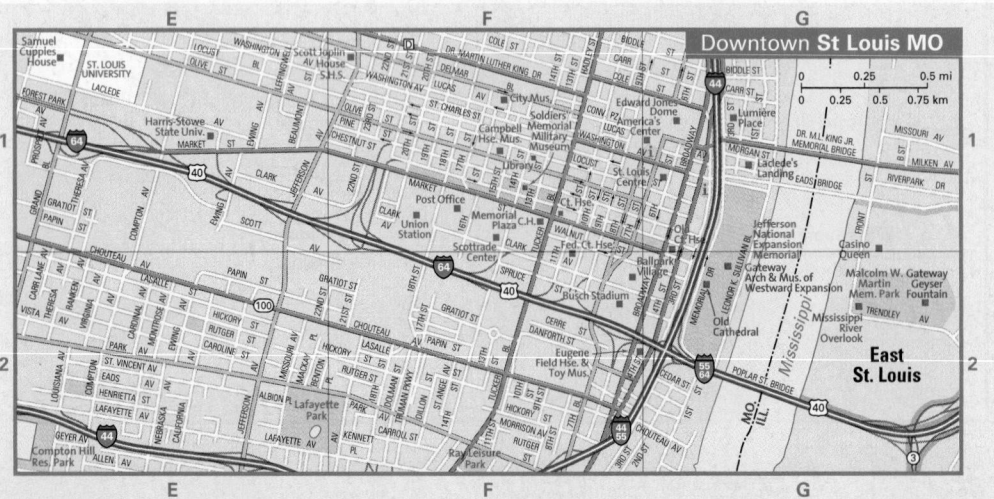

Entries in **bold black** indicate counties or parishes.
Entries in **bold color** indicate cities with detailed inset maps.

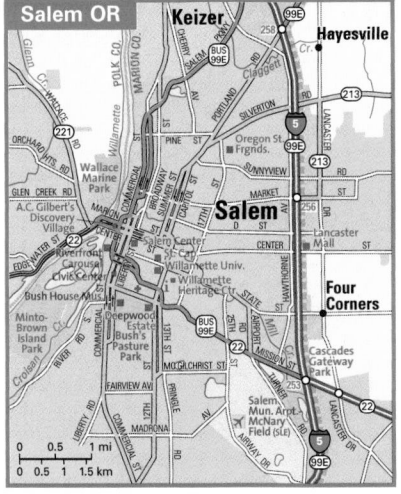

Salem OR

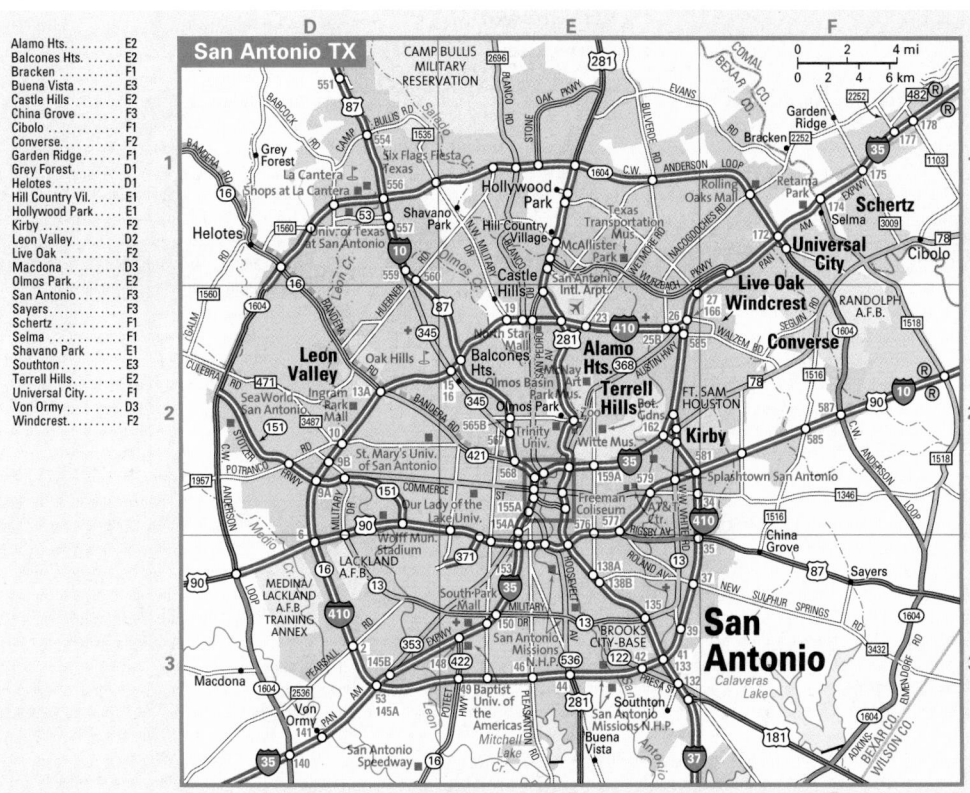

San Antonio TX

Salt Lake City UT

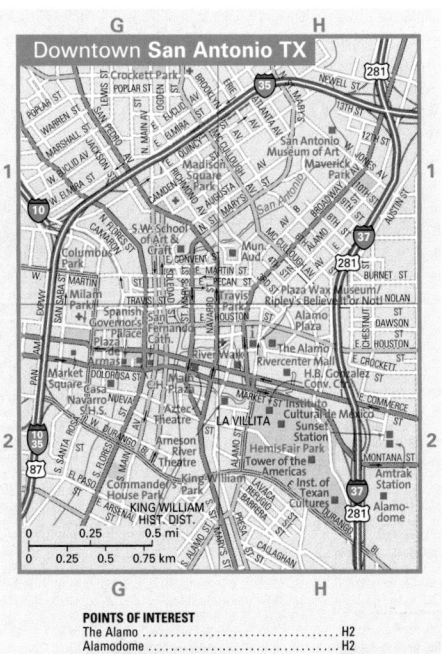

Downtown San Antonio TX

POINTS OF INTEREST

258

St Charles County–Saluda County

Figures after entries indicate population, page number, and grid reference.

Bonita C2	El Cajon C1	La Mesa C2	San Diego C2	Sunnyside C2
Chula Vista B3	Imperial Beach B3	Lemon Grove C2	Santee C1	Tijuana, MX C3
Coronado A2	Lakeside C1	National City B2	Spring Valley C2	

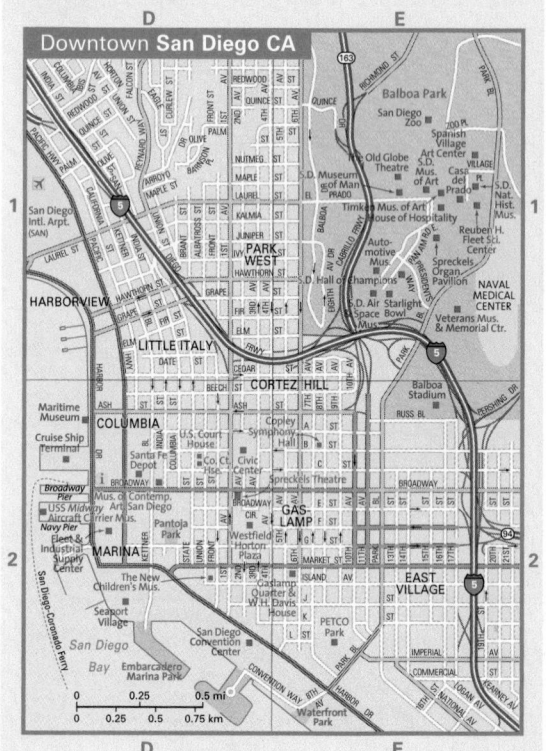

POINTS OF INTEREST

Automotive Museum E1	San Diego Hall of Champions E1
Balboa Park E1	San Diego International Airport D1
Balboa Stadium E1	San Diego Museum of Art E1
Casa del Prado E1	San Diego Museum of Man E1
Civic Center D2	San Diego Natural History Museum E1
Copley Symphony Hall E2	San Diego Zoo E1
County Court House D2	Santa Fe Depot D2
Gaslamp Quarter & W. H. Davis House E2	Seaport Village D2
The Globe Theatres E1	Spanish Village Art Center E1
House of Hospitality E1	Spreckels Organ Pavilion E1
Maritime Museum D2	Spreckels Theatre D2
Museum of Contemporary Art, San Diego ... D2	Starlight Bowl E1
The New Children's Museum D2	Timken Museum of Art E1
PETCO Park E2	USS Midway Aircraft Carrier Museum D2
Reuben H. Fleet Science Center E1	Veterans Museum & Memorial Center E1
San Diego Aerospace Museum E1	Westfield Horton Plaza D2
San Diego Convention Center D2	

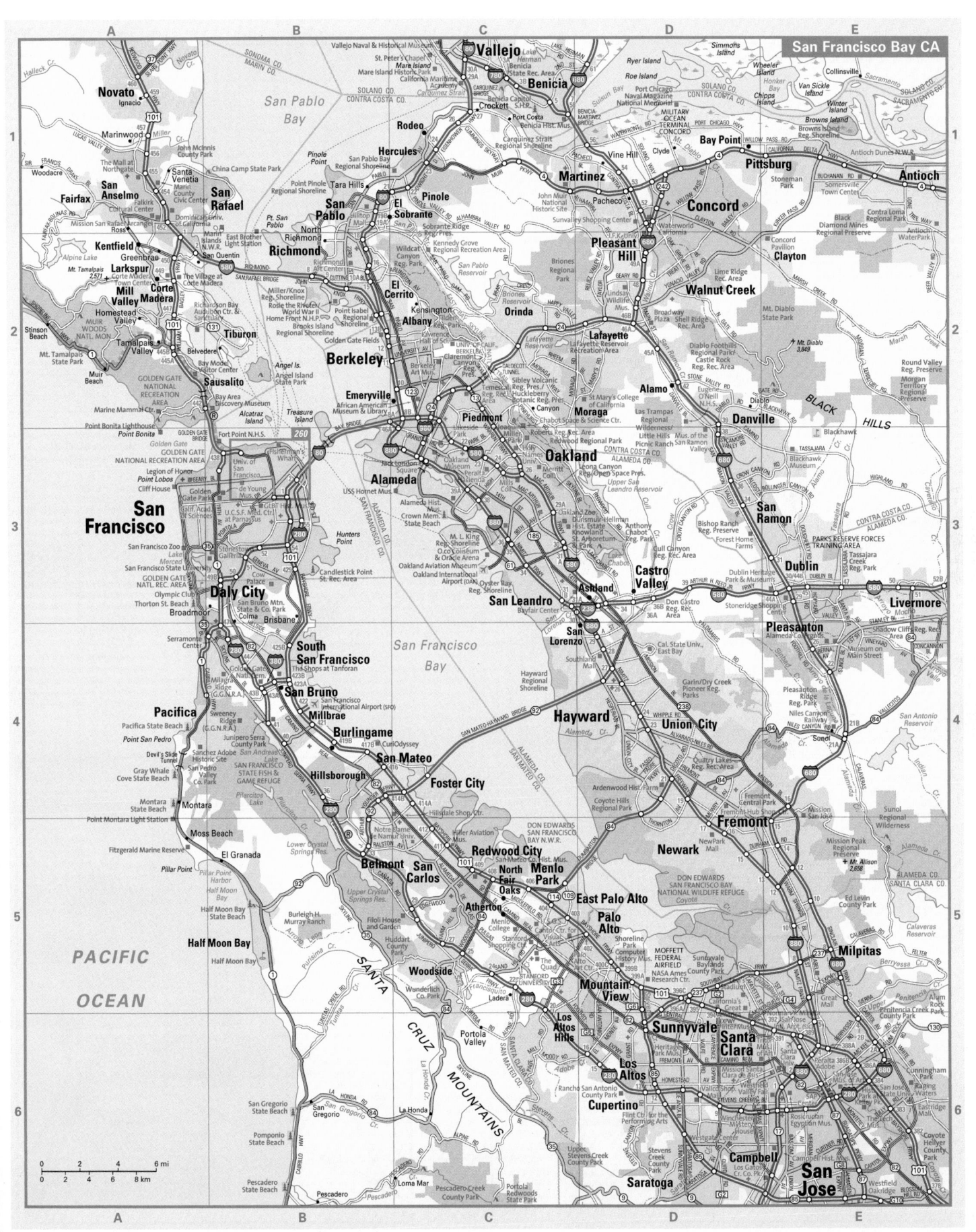

San Francisco Bay CA

Figures after entries indicate population, page number, and grid reference.

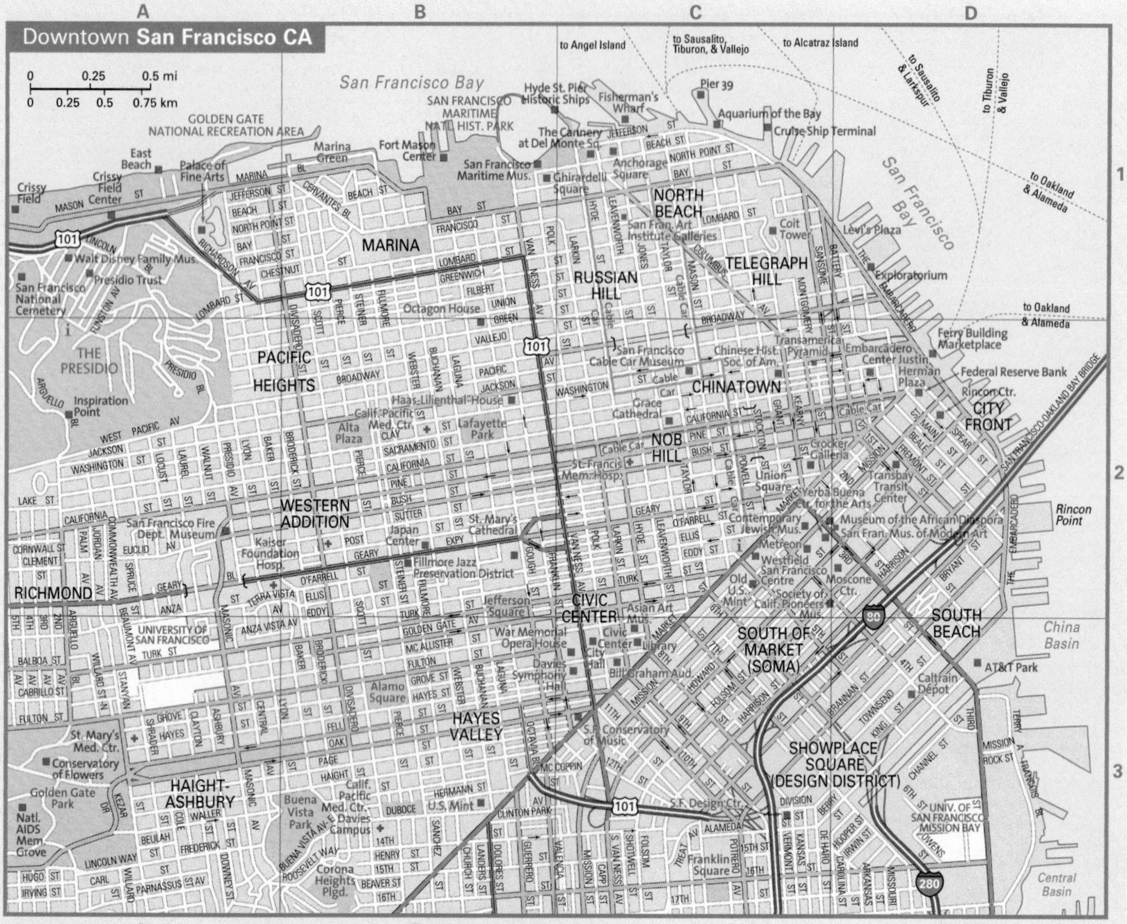

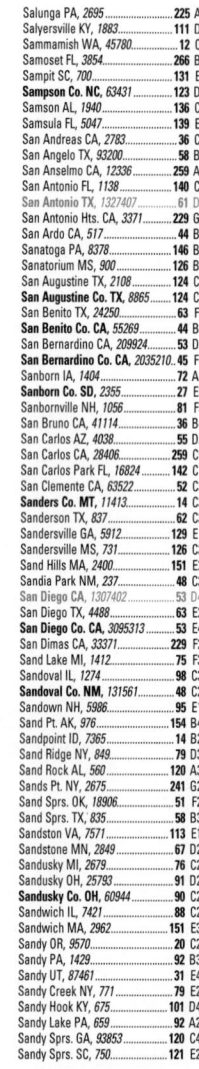

Downtown San Francisco CA

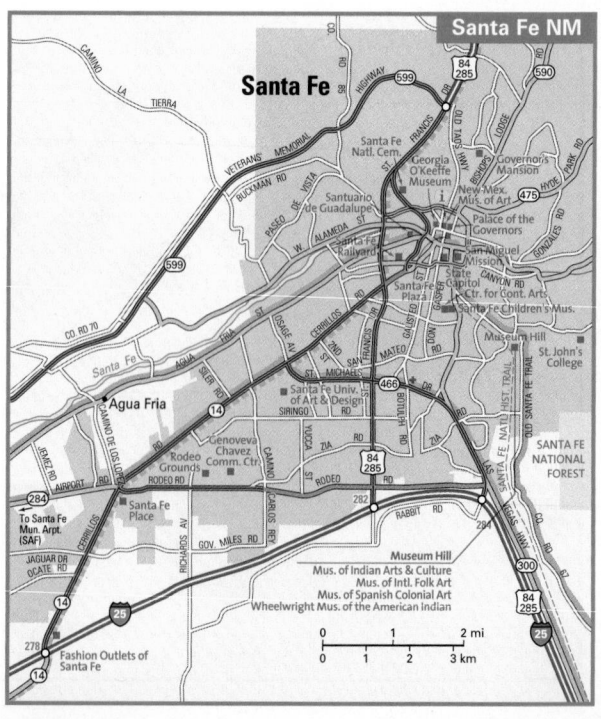

POINTS OF INTEREST

Anchorage Square C1
Ansel Adams Center for Photography D2
Aquarium of the Bay C1
Asian Art Museum C3
AT&T Park D3
Bill Graham Auditorium C3
Caltrain Depot D3
The Cannery at Del Monte Square C1
Chinese Historical Society of America C2
City Hall C3
Coit Tower C1
Conservatory of Flowers A3
Contemporary Jewish Mus. C2
Crissy Field A1
Crissy Field Center A1
Crocker Galleria C2
Cruise Ship Terminal C1
Davies Symphony Hall C3
East Beach A1
Embarcadero Center D2
Exploratorium/ Palace of Fine Arts A1
Fillmore Jazz Preservation District B2
Ferry Building Marketplace D2
Fisherman's Wharf C1
Fort Mason Center B1
Ghirardelli Square B1
Golden Gate Natl. Rec. Area A1
Golden Gate Park A3
Grace Cathedral C2
Haas-Lilienthal House B2
Hyde Street Pier Historic Ships . C1
Inspiration Point A2
Japan Center B2
Levi's Plaza D1
Library C3
Metreon C2
Moscone Center D2
Museum of the African Diaspora C2
National AIDS Memorial Grove . A3
Octagon House B2
Old U.S. Mint C2
Pier 39 . . . . C1
The Presidio A2
Presidio Trust A1
Rincon Center D2
St. Mary's Cathedral B2
San Francisco Art Institute Galleries C1
San Francisco Cable Car Mus. . . C2
San Francisco Cons. of Music . . C3
San Francisco Design Center . . . C3
San Francisco Fire Dept. Mus. . . A2
San Francisco Maritime Mus. . . B1
San Francisco Maritime Natl. Hist. Park B1
San Francisco Museum of Modern Art D2
San Francisco Natl. Cemetery . . A1
Soc. of Calif. Pioneers Mus. . . . C2
Transamerica Pyramid C2
Transbay Terminal D2
U.S. Mint B3
Univ. of San Francisco A3
Univ. of San Francisco-Mission Bay D3
Walt Disney Family Mus. A1
War Memorial Opera House . . . C3
Westfield San Francisco Centre C2
Yerba Buena Center for the Arts C2

Salunga PA, *2695* **225** A1
Salyersville KY, *1883* **111** D1
Sammamish WA, *45780* **12** C3
Samoset FL, *3854* **266** B4
Sampit SC, *700* **131** E1
Sampson Co. NC, *63431* **123** D1
Samson AL, *1940* **136** C1
Samsula FL, *5047* **139** E4
San Andreas CA, *2783* **36** C3
San Angelo TX, *93200* **58** B4
San Anselmo CA, *12336* **259** A1
San Antonio FL, *1138* **140** C2
San Antonio TX, *1327407* 61 D3
San Antonio Hts. CA, *3371* **229** G2
San Ardo CA, *517* **44** B3
Sanatoga PA, *8378* **146** B2
Sanatorium MS, *900* **126** B3
San Augustine TX, *2108* **124** C4
San Augustine Co. TX, *8865* **124** C4
San Benito TX, *24250* **63** F4
San Benito Co. CA, *55269* **44** B3
San Bernardino CA, *209924* **53** D2
San Bernardino Co. CA, *2035210* . . **45** F4
Sanborn IA, *1404* **72** A3
Sanborn Co. SD, *2355* **27** E3
Sanbornville NH, *1056* **81** F3
San Bruno CA, *41114* **36** B4
San Carlos AZ, *4038* **55** D2
San Carlos CA, *28406* **259** C5
San Carlos Park FL, *16824* **142** C1
San Clemente CA, *63522* **52** C3
Sanders Co. MT, *11413* **14** C3
Sanderson TX, *837* **62** C3
Sandersville GA, *5912* **129** E1
Sandersville MS, *731* **126** C3
Sand Hills MA, *2400* **151** E2
Sandia Park NM, *237* **48** C3
San Diego CA, *1307402* 53 D4
San Diego TX, *4488* **63** E2
San Diego Co. CA, *3095313* **53** E4
San Dimas CA, *33371* **229** F2
Sand Lake MI, *1412* **75** F3
Sandoval IL, *1274* **98** C3
Sandoval Co. NM, *131561* **48** C2
Sandown NH, *5986* **95** E1
Sand Pt. AK, *976* **154** B4
Sandpoint ID, *7365* **14** B2
Sand Ridge NY, *849* **79** D3
Sand Rock AL, *560* **120** A3
Sands Pt. NY, *2675* **241** G2
Sand Sprs. OK, *18906* **51** F2
Sand Sprs. TX, *835* **58** B3
Sandston VA, *7571* **113** E1
Sandstone MN, *2849* **67** D2
Sandusky MI, *2679* **76** C2
Sandusky OH, *25793* **91** D2
Sandusky Co. OH, *60944* **90** C2
Sandwich IL, *7421* **88** C2
Sandwich MA, *2962* **151** E3
Sandy OR, *9570* **20** C2
Sandy PA, *1429* **92** B3
Sandy UT, *87461* **31** E4
Sandy Creek NY, *771* **79** E2
Sandy Hook KY, *675* **101** D4
Sandy Lake PA, *659* **92** A2
Sandy Sprs. GA, *93853* **120** C4
Sandy Sprs. SC, *750* **121** E2

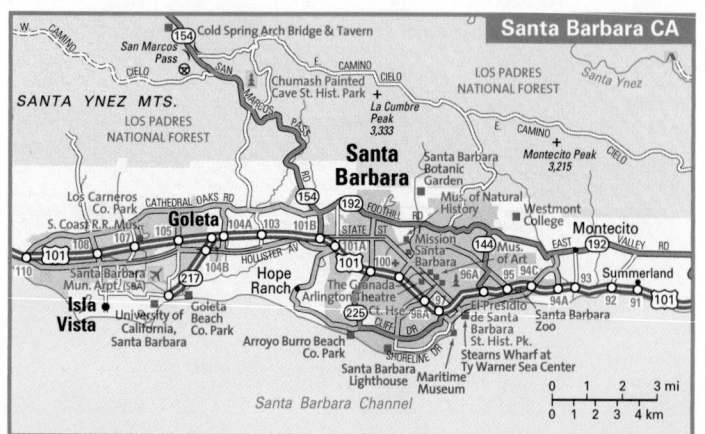

Entries in **bold black** indicate counties or parishes.
Entries in **bold color** indicate cities with detailed inset maps.

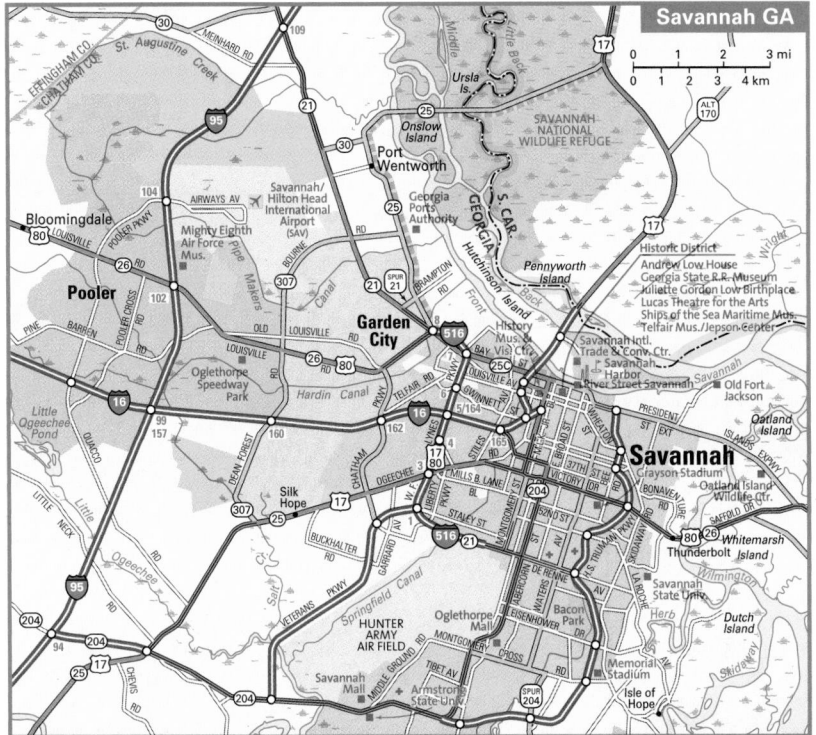

Savannah GA

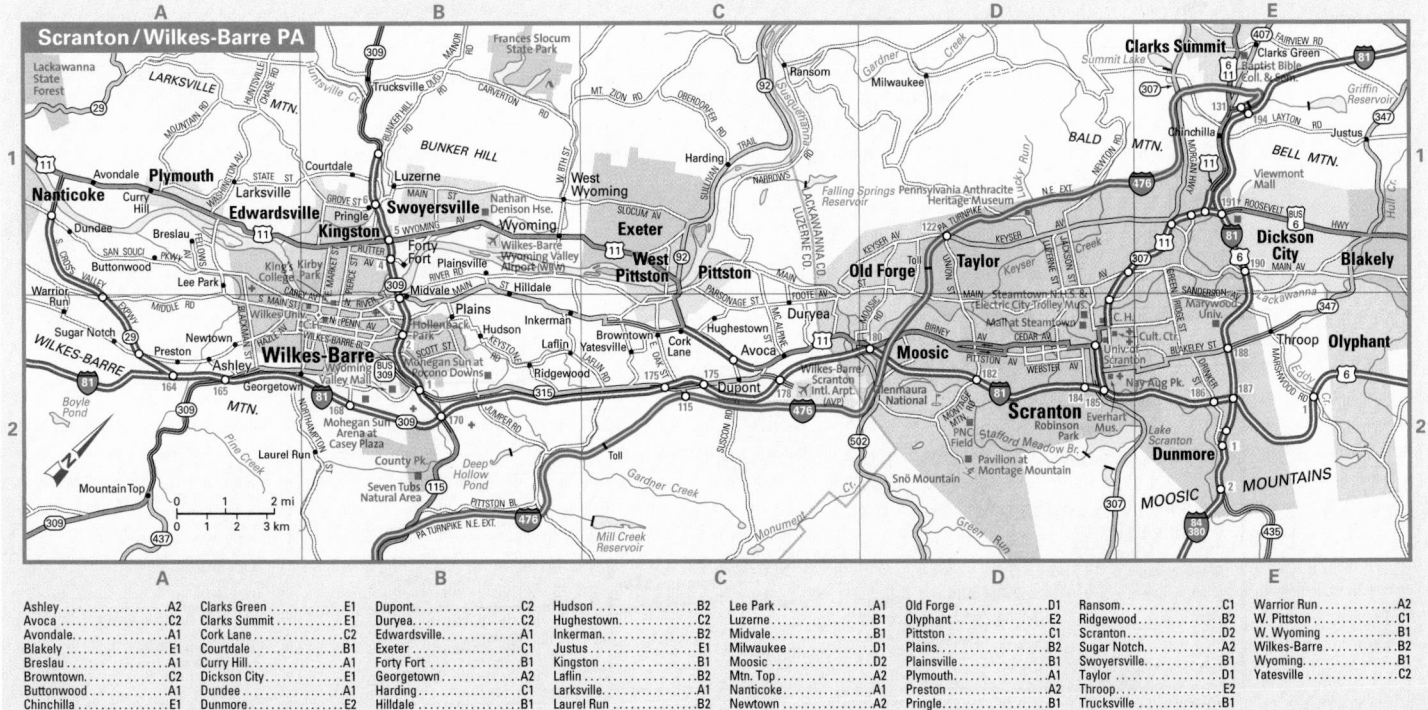

Scranton / Wilkes-Barre PA

262
Scranton–Seneca Gardens

Figures after entries indicate population, page number, and grid reference.

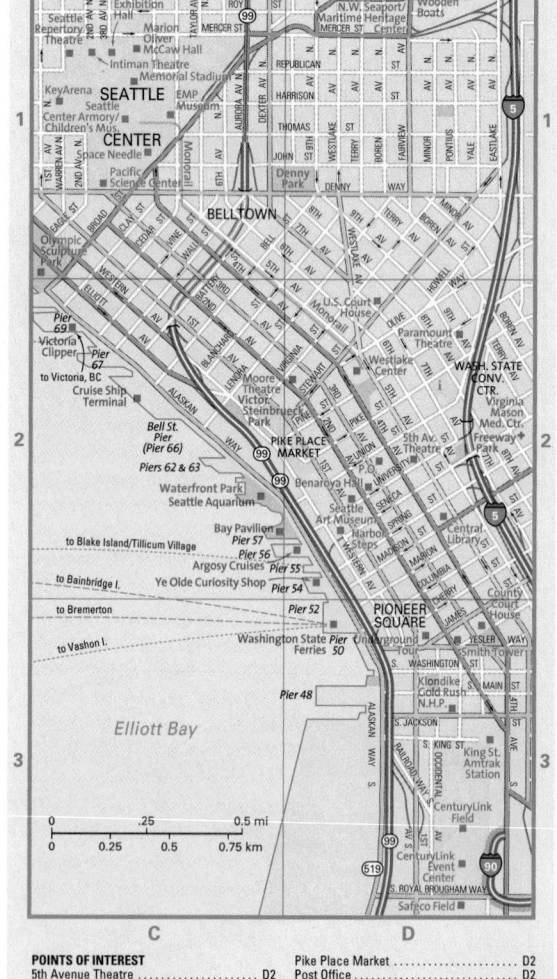

Seattle/Tacoma WA

Downtown Seattle WA

Entries in **bold black** indicate counties or parishes.
Entries in **bold color** indicate cities with detailed inset maps.

Shreveport LA

Sioux Falls SD

South Bend IN

Spokane WA

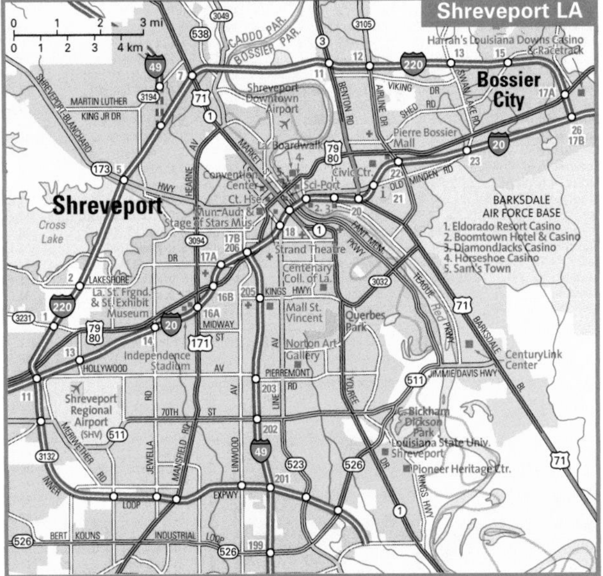

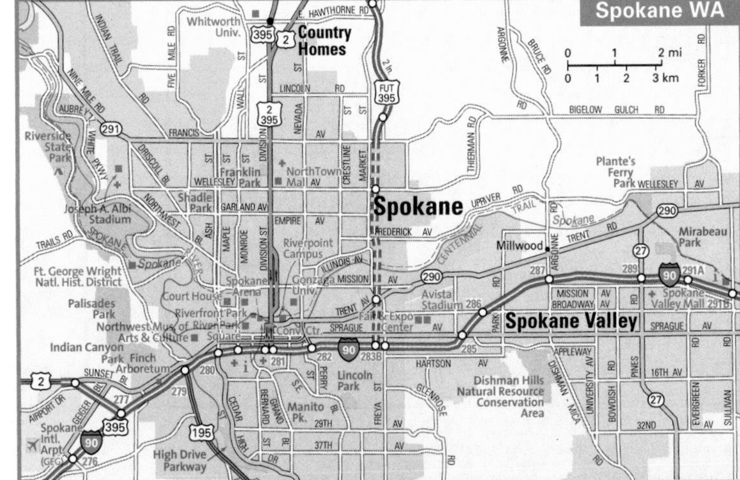

264
Slater–South Lebanon

Figures after entries indicate population, page number, and grid reference.

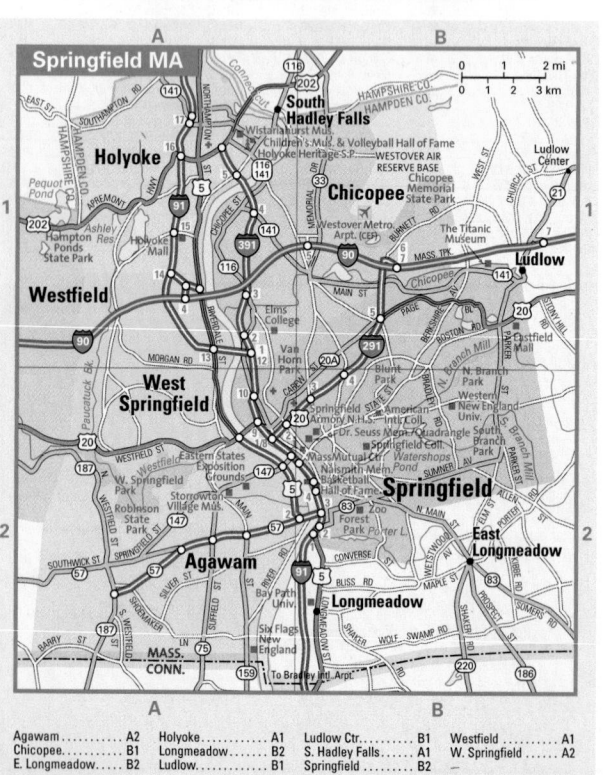

Springfield IL

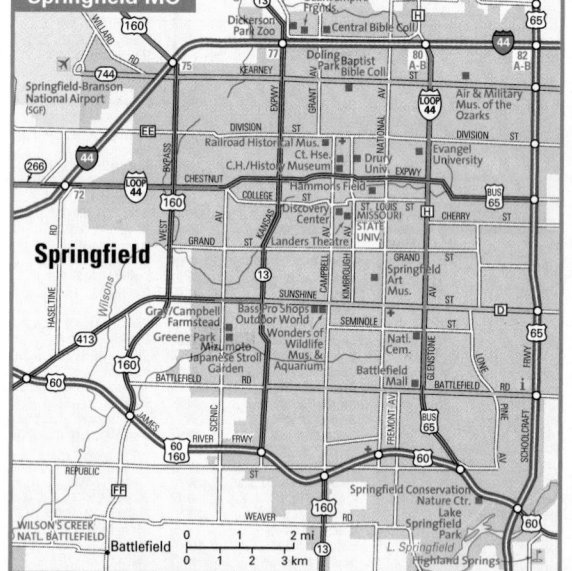

Springfield MO

Springfield MA

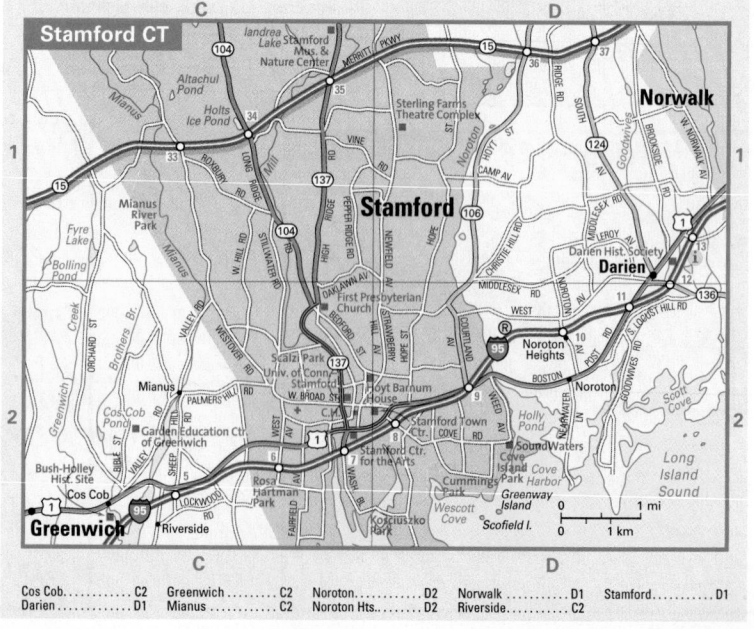

Stamford CT

Entries in **bold black** indicate counties or parishes.
Entries in **bold color** indicate cities with detailed inset maps.

Bayberry..............A1
Collamer..............B1
DeWitt..............B2
E. Syracuse..............B2
Fairmount..............A2
Franklin Park..............B1

Galeville..............A1
Jamesville..............B2
Lakeland..............A1
Liverpool..............A1
Lyndon..............B2
Mattydale..............B1

Nedrow..............A2
N. Syracuse..............B1
Onondaga Hill..............A2
Solvay..............A2
Split Rock..............A2
Syracuse..............A2

Taunton..............A2
Westvale..............A2

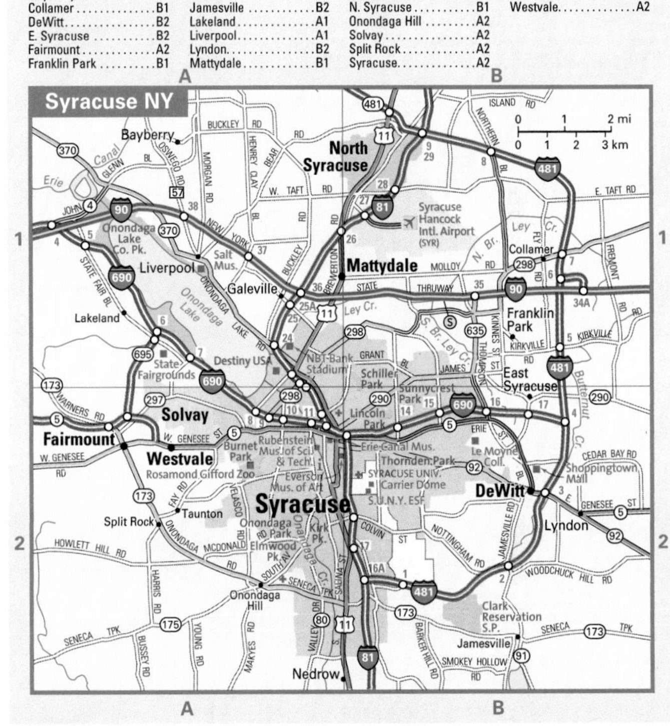

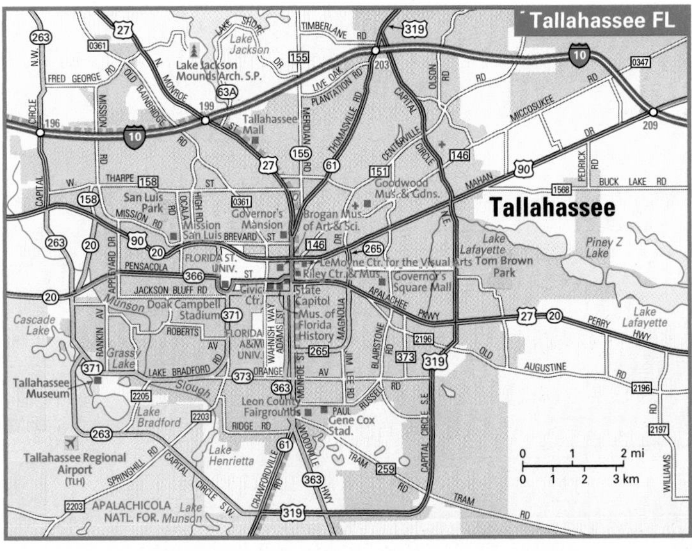

Figures after entries indicate population, page number, and grid reference.

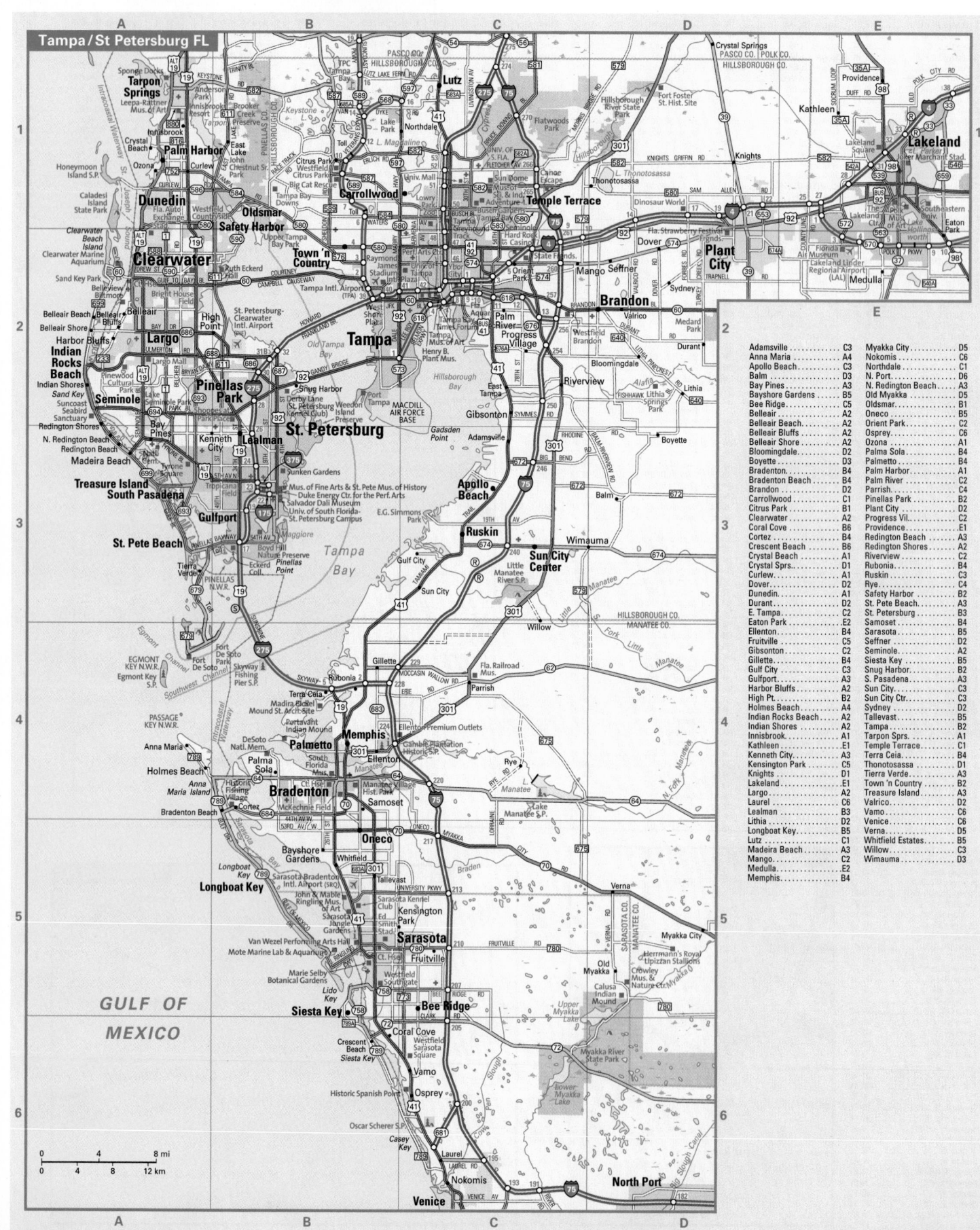

Tampa/St Petersburg FL

GULF OF MEXICO

0   4   8 mi
0   4   8   12 km

Entries in **bold black** indicate counties or parishes.
Entries in **bold color** indicate cities with detailed inset maps.

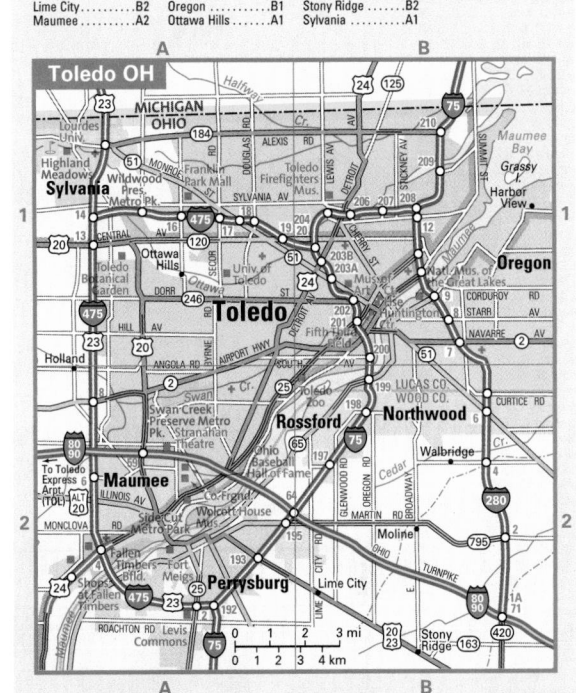

Toledo OH

Harbor View.....B1	Moline.......B2	Perrysburg.....A2	Toledo.......A1
Holland.......A2	Northwood......B2	Rossford.......B2	Walbridge......B2
Lime City.....B2	Oregon.......B1	Stony Ridge.....B2	
Maumee.......A2	Ottawa Hills...A1	Sylvania.......A1	

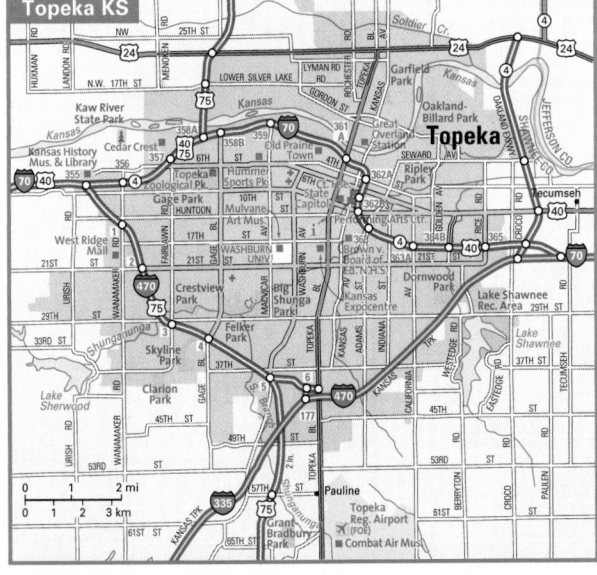

Topeka KS

268

Terre Hill–Troy

Figures after entries indicate population, page number, and grid reference.

Terre Hill PA, 1295	146 A2	Tice FL, 4470	142 C1	Tilden IL, 934	98 B4	Timmonsville SC, 2320	122 C3	Tipton IA, 3221	87 F1	Topsfield MA, 2717	151 F1	Trempealeau Co. WI, 28816	67 F4

Terre Hill PA, 1295.............146 A2
Terrell TX, 15816..................59 F2
Terrell Co. GA, 9315.............128 C4
Terrell Co. TX, 984.................60 A1
Terrell Hills TX, 4878............257 E2
Terry MS, 1063...................126 B3
Terry MT, 605........................17 A4
Terry Co. TX, 12651...............57 F2
Terrytown LA, 23319.............134 B3
Terrytown NE, 1198................33 F2
Terryville CT, 5387...............149 D1
Terryville NY, 11849.............149 D3
Tesuque NM, 925....................49 D2
Teton ID, 735.........................23 H4
Teton Co. ID, 10170................23 H4
Teton Co. MT, 6073.................15 E3
Teton Co. WY, 21294..............24 A3
Tetonia ID, 269......................23 H4
Teutopolis IL, 1530.................98 C2
Tewksbury MA, 28961..............95 E1
Texarkana AR, 29919.............116 C4
Texarkana TX, 36411.............116 C4
Texas MA, 1300....................150 B2
Texas City TX, 45099.............132 B4
Texas Co. MO, 26008.............107 D3
Texas Co. OK, 20640...............50 A1
Texhoma OK, 926....................50 A1
Texico NM, 1130.....................49 F4
Thatcher AZ, 4865..................55 E2
Thaxton MS, 643...................118 C3
Thayer IL, 693........................98 B1
Thayer KS, 497......................106 A1
Thayer MO, 2243...................107 F3
Thayer Co. NE, 5228................35 E4
Thayne WY, 366......................31 H1
The Colony TX, 36328..............59 F2
The Dalles OR, 13620..............21 D2
Thedford NE, 188....................34 C2
The Hills TX, 2472...................61 E1
Theodore AL, 6811.................135 E2
The Pinery CO, 10517..............41 E1
The Plains OH, 3080...............101 E2
Theresa NY, 863.....................79 E1
Theresa WI, 1262....................74 C2
Thermal CA, 2865....................53 E3
Thermalito CA, 6646................36 C1
Thermopolis WY, 3009.............24 C4
The Village OK, 8929................51 E3
The Vil. of Indian Hill OH, 5785....204 C2
The Woodlands TX, 93847.......132 A2
Thibodaux LA, 14566.............134 A3
Thief River Falls MN, 8573.......19 F2
Thiells NY, 5032....................148 B2
Thiensville WI, 3235................74 C3
Thomas OK, 1181....................51 D2
Thomas WV, 586....................102 B2
Thomasboro IL, 1126...............88 C4
Thomas Co. GA, 44720...........137 E1
Thomas Co. KS, 7900...............42 B2
Thomas Co. NE, 647................34 C2
Thomaston CT, 1910...............149 D1
Thomaston GA, 9170..............128 C3
Thomaston ME, 1875...............82 C3
Thomaston NY, 2617...............241 G3
Thomasville AL, 4209..............127 E3
Thomasville GA, 18413...........137 E1
Thomasville NC, 26757...........112 B4
Thompson IA, 502....................72 C2
Thompson ND, 986..................19 E3
Thompson Falls MT, 1313.........14 C3
Thompson's Sta. TN, 2194......109 F4
Thompsontown PA, 697............93 D4
Thompsonville CT, 8577..........150 B4
Thompsonville IL, 543..............98 C4
Thompsonville MI, 441.............69 F4
Thomson GA, 6778................121 E4
Thomson IL, 588.....................88 A1
Thonotosassa FL, 13014........140 C2
Thoreau NM, 1865...................48 B3
Thorndale PA, 3407...............146 B3
Thorndale TX, 1336.................61 E1
Thorne Bay AK, 471...............155 E4
Thornton AR, 407...................117 E4
Thornton CA, 1131..................36 C3
Thornton CO, 118772..............41 E1
Thornton TX, 526....................59 F4
Thorntown IN, 1520.................89 E4
Thornville OH, 991..................101 D1
Thornwood NY, 3759..............148 B2
Thorofare NJ, 1940................146 C3
Thorp WI, 1621.......................67 F4
Thorsby AL, 1980...................127 F1
Thousand Oaks CA, 126683......52 B2
Thousand Palms CA, 7715.......53 E3
Thrall TX, 839........................61 E1
Three Bridges NJ, 850...........147 E1
Three Forks MT, 1869..............23 F1
Three Oaks MI, 1622...............89 E1
Three Pts. AZ, 5581................55 D3
Three Rivers CA, 2182.............45 D3
Three Rivers MA, 2939...........150 A2
Three Rivers MI, 7811.............89 F1
Three Rivers TX, 1848.............61 D4
Three Way TN, 1709...............108 C4
Throckmorton TX, 828.............59 D2
Throckmorton Co. TX, 1641......59 D2
Throop PA, 4088....................261 E2
Thurmont MD, 6170................144 A1
Thurston OH, 604...................101 D1
Thurston Co. NE, 6940.............35 F2
Thurston Co. WA, 252264........12 C4
Tiana NY, 2200.....................149 E3
Tiburon CA, 8962...................259 B2

Tice FL, 4470.......................142 C1
Tickfaw LA, 694....................134 B2
Ticonderoga NY, 3382..............81 D3
Tidioute PA, 688.....................92 B2
Tierra Amarilla NM, 382............48 C1
Tierra Verde FL, 3721.............266 A3
Tieton WA, 1191.....................13 D4
Tiffin IA, 1947........................87 E1
Tiffin OH, 17963.....................90 C3
Tift Co. GA, 40118.................129 E4
Tifton GA, 16350...................129 E4
Tigard OR, 48035....................20 C2
Tigerton WI, 741.....................68 B4
Tignall GA, 546.....................121 E4
Tijeras NM, 541......................48 C3
Tiki Island TX, 968.................132 B4

Tilden IL, 934.........................98 B4
Tilden NE, 953........................35 E2
Tilden TX, 261........................61 D4
Tilghman MD, 784..................145 D4
Tillamook OR, 4935.................20 B2
Tillamook Co. OR, 25250..........20 B1
Tillmans Corner AL, 17398......135 E2
Tillman Co. OK, 7992...............51 D4
Tillson NY, 1586......................94 B3
Tilton IL, 2724........................89 D4
Tilton NH, 3567......................81 F4
Tiltonsville OH, 1372................91 F4
Timber Lake SD, 443................26 C2
Timberlake VA, 12183.............112 C1
Timberon NM, 348...................57 D2
Timberville VA, 2522...............102 C3

Timmonsville SC, 2320...........122 C3
Timpson TX, 1155..................124 C3
Tinley Park IL, 56703...............89 D2
Tinton Falls NJ, 17892............147 E2
Tioga LA, 1500.....................125 E4
Tioga ND, 1230.......................18 A2
Tioga PA, 666.........................93 D1
Tioga TX, 803.........................59 F1
Tioga Co. NY, 51125................93 E1
Tioga Co. PA, 41981................93 D1
Tionesta PA, 483.....................92 A2
Tippah Co. MS, 22232.............118 C3
Tipp City OH, 9689.................100 B1
Tippecanoe Co. IN, 172780......89 E4
Tipton CA, 2543......................45 D3
Tipton IN, 5106.......................89 D4

Tipton IA, 3221.......................87 F1
Tipton MO, 3262.....................97 D3
Tipton PA, 1083......................92 C4
Tipton Co. IN, 15936................89 F4
Tipton Co. TN, 61081..............118 B3
Tiptonville TN, 4464...............108 B3
Tishomingo OK, 3034...............51 F4
Tishomingo Co. MS, 19593.....119 D2
Tiskilwa IL, 829......................88 B2
Titonka IA, 476.......................72 C3
Titus Co. TX, 32334...............124 B1
Titusville FL, 43761................141 E1
Titusville NJ, 800...................147 D2
Titusville PA, 5601...................92 A2
Tiverton RI, 7557...................151 D4
Tivoli NY, 1118.......................94 B2
Toano VA, 1400.....................113 F1
Toast NC, 1450......................112 A3
Tobaccoville NC, 2441............112 A3
Toccoa GA, 8491...................121 D2
Todd Co. KY, 12460................109 E2
Todd Co. MN, 24895................66 B1
Todd Co. SD, 9612..................34 C1
Togiak AK, 817......................154 B3
Tohatchi NM, 808....................48 A3
Tok AK, 1258.........................155 D2
Toledo IL, 1238.......................99 D2
Toledo IA, 2341......................87 D1
Toledo OH, 287208..................90 C2
Toledo OR, 3465......................20 B3
Toledo WA, 725.......................12 C4
Tolland CT, 13146..................150 A3
Tolland Co. CT, 152691...........149 E1
Tolles CT, 650.......................149 D1
Tolleson AZ, 6545..................249 A3
Tolono IL, 3447.......................99 D1
Toluca IL, 1414.......................88 B3
Tomah WI, 9093......................74 A1
Tomahawk WI, 3397.................68 B3
Tomball TX, 10753.................132 A2
Tom Bean TX, 1045.................59 F1
Tome NM, 1867.......................48 C3
Tom Green Co. TX, 110224.......58 C4
Tomkins Cove NY, 1460...........148 B2
Tompkins Co. NY, 101564........79 D4
Tompkinsville KY, 2402...........110 A3
Toms River NJ, 88791............147 E3
Tonalea AZ, 549......................47 E2
Tonasket WA, 1032..................13 E1
Tonawanda NY, 15130.............78 A3
Tonganoxie KS, 4996...............96 B2
Tonica IL, 768........................88 B2
Tonkawa OK, 3216..................51 E1
Tonopah NV, 2478...................37 F3
Tontitown AR, 2460................106 C4
Tooele UT, 31605....................31 D4
Tooele Co. UT, 58218...............31 D4
Tool TX, 2240.........................59 F3
Toole Co. MT, 5324..................15 F1
Toombs Co. GA, 27223...........129 E2
Toomsboro GA, 472................129 E2
Topeka IN, 1153.....................89 F2
Topeka KS, 127473..................96 A2
Toppenish WA, 8949................13 D4

Topsfield MA, 2717................151 F1
Topsham ME, 5931..................82 B3
Topton PA, 2069....................146 B1
Toquerville UT, 1370................39 D4
Tornillo TX, 1568....................56 C4
Toronto OH, 5091....................91 F4
Toronto SD, 212......................27 F3
Torrance CA, 145438...............52 C3
Torrance Co. NM, 16383...........49 D4
Torreon NM, 326......................48 B2
Torreon NM, 244......................48 C4
Torrington CT, 36383...............94 C3
Torrington WY, 6501................33 F2
Totowa NJ, 10804..................240 A1
Toughkenamon PA, 1492.........146 B3
Towaco NJ, 2700....................148 A3
Towanda KS, 1450..................43 F4
Towanda PA, 2919..................93 E1
Towaoc CO, 1087....................40 B4
Tower MN, 500........................64 C3
Tower City ND, 253..................19 E4
Tower City PA, 1346.................93 E4
Tower Hill IL, 611.....................98 C2
Town Creek AL, 1283...............203 B1
Town and Country MO, 10815...256 A2
Town Creek AL, 1110...............119 E2
Towner ND, 533......................18 C2
Towner Co. ND, 2246................19 D1
Town Line NY, 2367.................78 B3
Town 'n Country FL, 78442......266 B2
Town of Pines IN, 708..............89 E2
Towns Co. GA, 10471.............121 D2
Townsend DE, 2049................145 E1
Townsend MA, 1128.................95 D1
Townsend MT, 1878.................15 F4
Towson MD, 55197.................144 C1
Tracy CA, 82922......................36 C4
Tracy MN, 2163.......................72 A1
Tracy City TN, 1481................120 A1
Tracyton WA, 5233.................262 A3
Traer IA, 1703........................87 E1
Trafalgar IN, 1101....................99 F2
Trafford AL, 646.....................119 F4
Trafford PA, 3174...................250 D3
Trail Creek IN, 2052.................89 E2
Traill Co. ND, 8121...................19 E3
Trainer PA, 1828....................146 C3
Tramway NC, 750...................122 C1
Tranquility CA, 799..................44 C3
Transylvania Co. NC, 33090.....121 D1
Trappe MD, 1077...................145 D4
Trappe PA, 3509....................146 B2
Trapper Creek AK, 481............154 C3
Traskwood AR, 518................117 E3
Travelers Rest SC, 4576.........121 E2
Traver CA, 713........................45 D3
Traverse City MI, 14674...........69 F4
Traverse Co. MN, 3558............27 F1
Travis Co. TX, 1024266............61 E1
Treasure Co. MT, 718...............17 D4
Treasure Island FL, 6705.........140 B3
Trego Co. KS, 3001..................42 C2
Tremont IL, 2236.....................88 B4
Tremont PA, 1752...................146 A1
Tremonton UT, 7647................31 E3

Trempealeau Co. WI, 28816.....67 F4
Trent SD, 232.........................27 F4
Trenton FL, 1999...................138 C3
Trenton GA, 2301...................120 B2
Trenton IL, 2715......................98 B3
Trenton KY, 384.....................109 E3
Trenton MI, 18853...................90 C1
Trenton MO, 6001....................86 C4
Trenton NE, 560......................42 B1
Trenton NJ, 84913.................147 D2
Trenton OH, 11869.................100 B1
Trenton TN, 4264...................108 C4
Trenton TX, 635......................59 F1
Trent Woods NC, 4155............115 D3
Treutlen Co. GA, 6885............129 E2
Trevorton PA, 1834..................93 E3
Trevose PA, 3550...................146 C2
Trexlertown PA, 1988..............146 B1
Treynor IA, 919.......................86 A2
Trezevant TN, 859..................108 C4
Triadelphia WV, 811.................91 F4
Triana AL, 496.......................119 F2
Triangle VA, 8188...................144 A4
Tribes Hill NY, 1003.................94 B3
Tribune KS, 741......................42 B3
Tri-City OR, 3931.....................28 B1
Trigg Co. KY, 14339...............109 D3
Tri-Lakes IN, 1421...................90 A2
Trilby FL, 419........................140 C1
Trimble CO, 650......................40 B4
Trimble Co. KY, 8809..............100 A3
Trimont MN, 747.....................72 B2
Trinidad CA, 311......................28 A4
Trinidad CO, 9096....................41 E4
Trinidad TX, 886.....................59 F3
Trinity AL, 2095......................119 F2
Trinity NC, 6614.....................112 B4
Trinity TX, 2647.....................132 A1
Trinity Co. CA, 13786...............28 B4
Trinity Co. TX, 14585.............132 B1
Trion GA, 1827......................120 B2
Tripoli IA, 1313.......................73 E4
Tripp SD, 647.........................35 E1
Tripp Co. SD, 5644..................26 C4
Triumph LA, 216....................134 B4
Trona CA, 18..........................45 E4
Trooper PA, 5744...................146 C2
Trophy Club TX, 8024.............207 B1
Tropic UT, 530........................39 E4
Trotwood OH, 24431...............100 B1
Troup TX, 1869......................124 B3
Troup Co. GA, 67044..............128 C1
Trousdale Co. TN, 7870..........109 F3
Trout Creek MT, 242................14 C2
Troutdale OR, 15962...............20 C2
Troutdale VA, 178...................111 F3
Trout Lake WA, 557..................21 D1
Troutman NC, 2383.................112 A4
Trout Valley IL, 537................203 A1
Troutville VA, 431...................112 B1
Trowbridge Park MI, 2176........69 D1
Troy AL, 18033......................128 A3
Troy ID, 862...........................14 B4
Troy IL, 9888.........................98 B3
Troy KS, 1010.........................96 B1

Trenton NJ

Bakersville B1	Fallsington A2	Mercerville B1	Trenton A2
Ewing A1	Lawrenceville B1	Morrisville A2	W. Trenton A1
Ewingville A1	Lewisville B1	Slackwood B1	White Horse B2

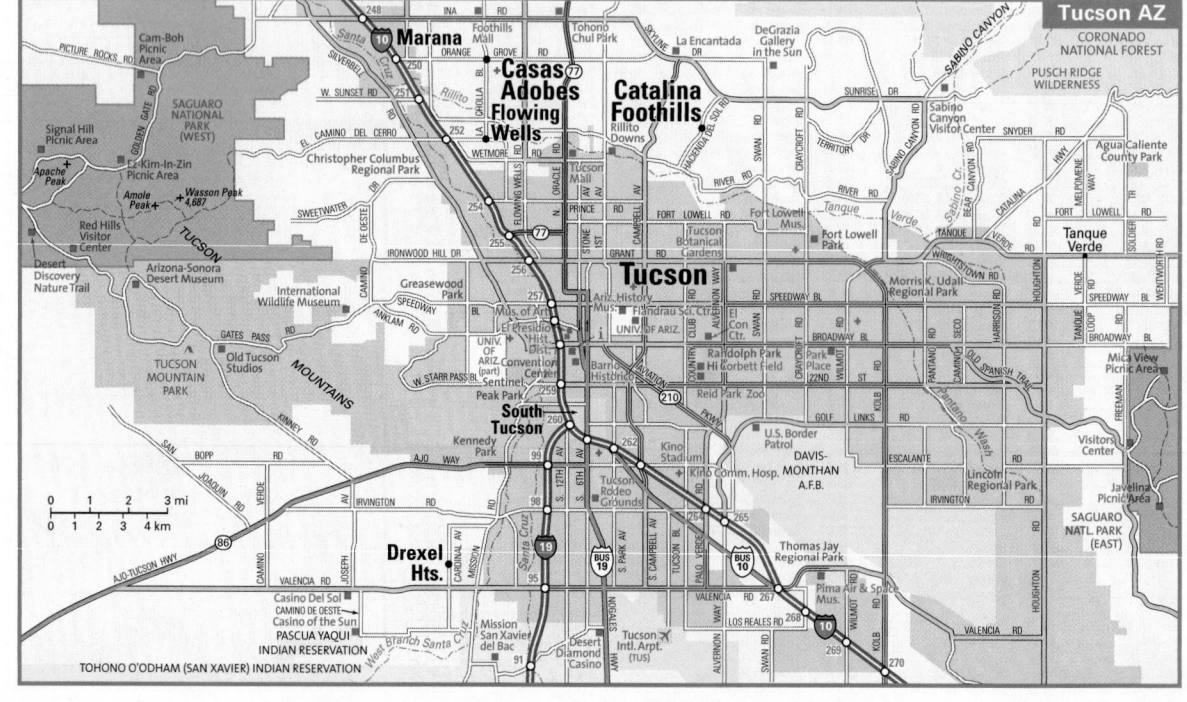

Entries in **bold black** indicate counties or parishes.
Entries in **bold color** indicate cities with detailed inset maps.

Tulsa OK

OSAGE INDIAN RESERVATION

Sand Springs

Tulsa

Oakhurst

Catoosa

Broken Arrow

Sapulpa

Jenks

Bixby

Vicksburg MS

VICKSBURG NATIONAL MILITARY PARK

Vicksburg

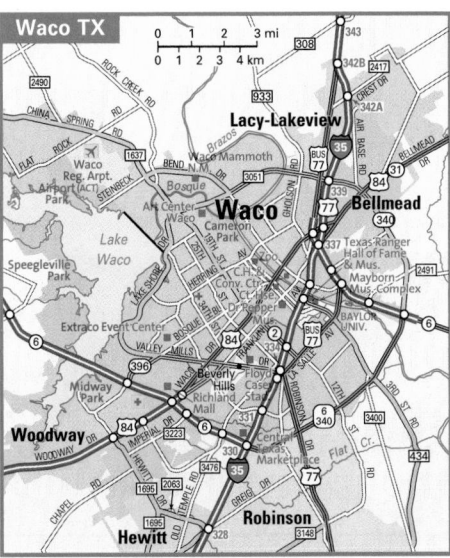

Waco TX

Lacy-Lakeview

Bellmead

Waco

Woodway

Hewitt

Robinson

Figures after entries indicate population, page number, and grid reference.

Washington DC

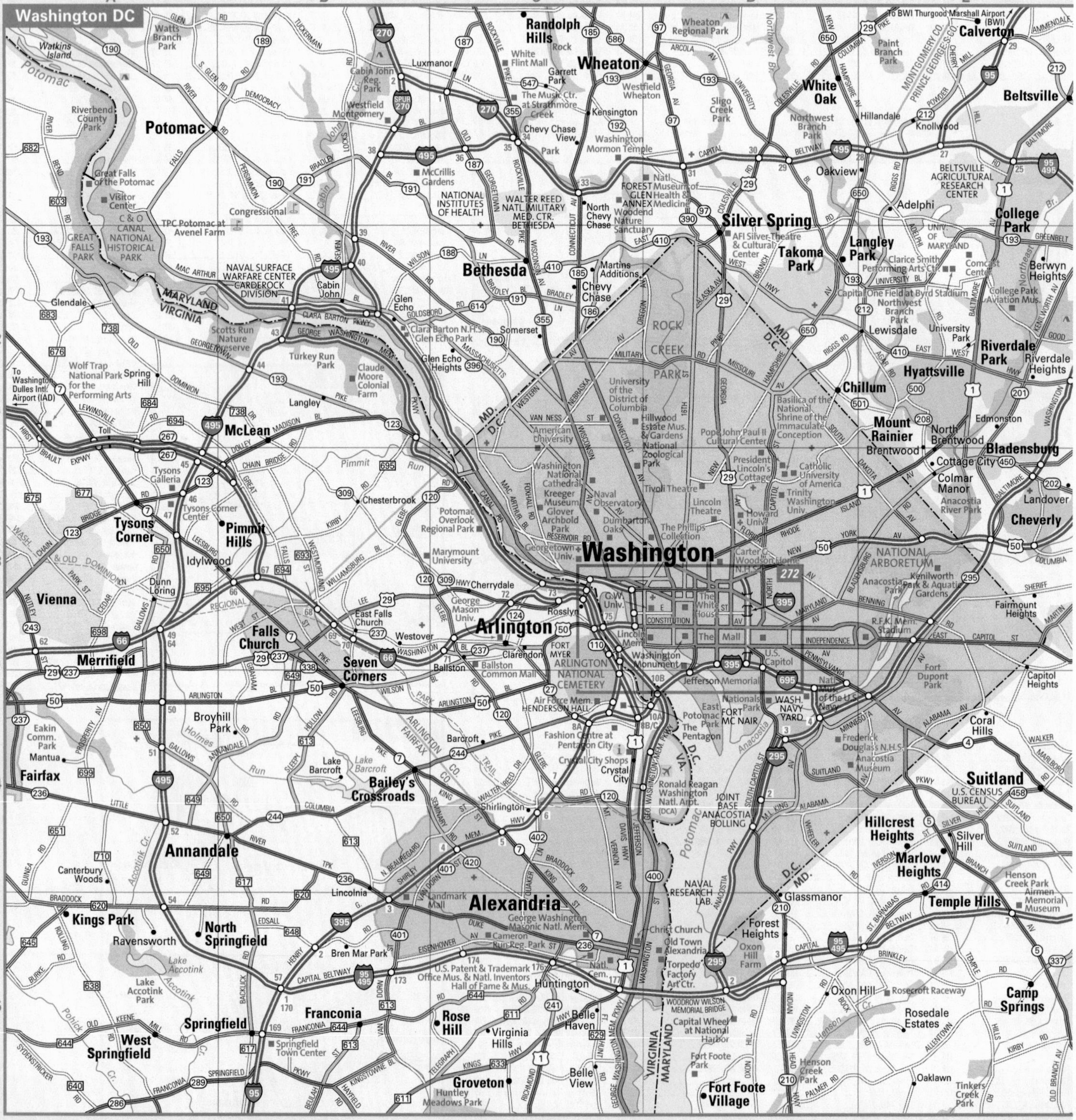

271
Vermont–Waynesboro

Entries in **bold black** indicate counties or parishes.
Entries in **bold color** indicate cities with detailed inset maps.

Vermont IL, *667* **88** A4
Vermontville MI, *759* **76** A4
Vernal UT, *9089* **32** A4
Verndale MN, *602* **64** A4
Vernon AL, *2000* **119** D4
Vernon CT, *29179* **150** A3
Vernon FL, *687* **136** C2
Vernon IN, *318* **100** A2
Vernon MI, *783* **76** B3
Vernon NY, *1172* **79** E3
Vernon TX, *11002* **51** D4
Vernon VT, *2141* **94** C1
Vernon Co. MO, *21159* **96** C4
Vernon Co. WI, *29773* **73** F2
Vernon Hills IL, *25113* **203** C1
Vernonia OR, *2151* **20** B1
Vernon Par. LA, *52334* **125** D4
Vernon Valley NJ, *1626* **148** A2
Vero Beach FL, *15220* **141** E3
Verona MS, *3006* **119** D3
Verona MO, *619* **106** C2
Verona NJ, *13332* **148** A3
Verona NC, *700* **115** D4
Verona PA, *2474* **250** D1
Verona VA, *4239* **102** C4
Verona WI, *10619* **74** B3
Verplanck NY, *1729* **148** B2
Versailles CT, *750* **149** F1
Versailles IN, *2113* **100** A2
Versailles KY, *8568* **100** B4

Versailles MO, *2482* **97** D3
Versailles OH, *2687* **90** B4
Vesper WI, *584* **68** A4
Vestal NY, *3900* **93** E1
Vestal Ctr. NY, *850* **93** E1
Vestavia Hills AL, *34033* **119** F4
Vevay IN, *1683* **100** A3
Vian OK, *1466* **116** B1
Viborg SD, *782* **35** F1
Viburnum MO, *693* **107** F1
Vici OK, *699* **51** D2
Vicksburg MI, *2906* **89** F1
Vicksburg MS, *23856* **126** A2
Victor CO, *397* **41** E2
Victor ID, *1928* **23** F4
Victor IA, *893* **87** E1
Victor MT, *745* **15** D4
Victor NY, *2696* **78** C3
Victoria KS, *1214* **43** D2
Victoria MN, *7345* **66** C4
Victoria TX, *62592* **61** F3
Victoria VA, *1725* **113** D2
Victoria Co. TX, *86793* **61** F3
Victorville CA, *115903* **53** D2
Victory Gardens NJ, *1520* **148** A3
Vidalia GA, *10473* **129** F3
Vidalia LA, *4299* **125** F4
Vidor TX, *10579* **132** C2
Vienna GA, *4011* **129** D3
Vienna IL, *1434* **108** C1
Vienna LA, *386* **125** E2
Vienna MO, *610* **97** E4
Vienna VA, *15687* **144** B3
Vienna WV, *10749* **101** E2
View Park CA, *10958* **228** C3
Vigo Co. IN, *107848* **99** E2
Vilano Beach FL, *2678* **139** E3
Vilas Co. WI, *21430* **68** B2
Village Green NY, *3891* **79** D3
Village Green PA, *7822* **248** A4
Villages of Oriole FL, *4758* **143** F1
Villa Grove IL, *2537* **99** D1
Villa Hills KY, *7489* **204** A3
Villa Park CA, *5812* **229** F4
Villa Park IL, *21904* **203** C4
Villa Rica GA, *13956* **120** B4
Villa Ridge MO, *2636* **98** A3
Villas NJ, *9483* **104** C4
Ville Platte LA, *7430* **133** E1
Villisca IA, *1252* **86** B3
Vilonia AR, *3815* **117** E1
Vimy Ridge AR, *600* **117** E2
Vinalhaven ME, *1235* **83** D3
Vincennes IN, *18423* **99** D3
Vincent AL, *1988* **128** A1
Vincent CA, *15922* **52** C2
Vincentown NJ, *750* **147** D3
Vinco PA, *1305* **92** B4
Vine Grove KY, *4520* **110** A1
Vine Hill CA, *3761* **259** D1
Vineland MN, *1001* **66** C1
Vineland NJ, *60724* **145** F1
Vinemont AL, *425* **119** F3
Vineyard Haven MA, *2114* **151** E4
Vinings GA, *9734* **190** C2
Vinita OK, *5743* **106** B3
Vinita Park MO, *1880* **256** B2
Vinton CA, *387* **37** D1
Vinton IA, *5257* **87** E1
Vinton LA, *3212* **133** D2
Vinton TX, *1971* **56** C3
Vinton VA, *8098* **112** B2
Vinton Co. OH, *13435* **101** E2
Viola DE, *157* **145** E3
Viola IL, *955* **88** A2
Viola WI, *699* **73** F2
Violet LA, *4973* **134** C3
Virden IL, *3425* **98** B2
Virgin UT, *596* **39** D4
Virginia IL, *1611* **98** A1
Virginia MN, *8712* **64** C3
Virginia Beach VA, *437994* **114** B4
Virginia City MT, *190* **23** E2
Virginia City NV, *855* **37** D2
Virginia Gardens FL, *2375* **233** A4
Viroqua WI, *4362* **73** F2
Visalia CA, *124442* **45** D3
Vista CA, *93834* **53** D3
Vivian LA, *3671* **124** C1
Volcano HI, *2575* **153** F4
Volga SD, *1768* **27** F3
Volin SD, *161* **35** E1
Voluntown CT, *2631* **149** F1
Volusia Co. FL, *494593* **139** E4
Vonore TN, *1474* **120** C1
Voorheesville NY, *2789* **94** B1

W

Wabash IN, *10666* **89** F3
Wabasha MN, *2521* **73** E1
Wabasha Co. MN, *21676* **73** E1
Wabash Co. IL, *11947* **99** D3
Wabash Co. IN, *32888* **89** F3
Wabasso FL, *609* **141** E3
Wabasso MN, *696* **72** A1
Wabaunsee Co. KS, *7053* **43** F2
Waco TX, *124805* **59** E4
Waconia MN, *10697* **66** C4
Waddington NY, *972* **80** B1
Wade MS, *1074* **135** D2
Wade NC, *556* **123** D1
Wadena MN, *4088* **64** A4
Wadena Co. MN, *13843* **64** A4
Wadesboro NC, *5813* **122** B2
Wading River NY, *7719* **149** D3
Wadley AL, *751* **128** B1
Wadley GA, *2061* **129** F1
Wadsworth NV, *834* **37** D1
Wadsworth OH, *21567* **91** E3
Waelder TX, *1065* **61** E2
Wagener SC, *797* **122** A4
Waggaman LA, *10015* **239** B2
Wagner SD, *1566* **35** E1
Wagoner OK, *8323* **106** A4
Wagoner Co. OK, *73085* **106** A4
Wagon Mound NM, *314* **49** E2
Wagontown PA, *1100* **146** B3
Wagram NC, *840* **122** C2
Wahiawa HI, *17821* **152** A2
Wahkiakum Co. WA, *3978* **12** B4
Wahoo NE, *4508* **35** F3
Wahpeton ND, *7766* **27** F1
Waialua HI, *3860* **152** A2
Waianae HI, *13177* **152** A3
Waiehu HI, *8841* **153** D1
Waihee HI, *7310* **153** D1
Waikane HI, *778* **152** A2
Waikapu HI, *2965* **153** D1
Waikoloa Vil. HI, *6362* **153** E3
Wailua HI, *2254* **152** B1
Wailuku HI, *15313* **153** D1
Waimalu HI, *13730* **152** A3
Waimanalo HI, *5451* **152** B3
Waimanalo Beach HI, *4481* **152** B3
Waimea HI, *1855* **152** B1
Waimea (Kamuela) HI, *9212* **153** E2
Wainscott NY, *650* **149** F3
Wainwright AK, *556* **154** C1
Waipahu HI, *38216* **152** A3
Waipio Acres HI, *5236* **152** A3
Waite Park MN, *6715* **66** C3
Waitsburg WA, *1217* **13** F4
Waitsfield VT, *164* **81** D2
Wakarusa IN, *1758* **89** F2
Wakeby MA, *1600* **151** E3
Wake Co. NC, *900993* **113** D4
WaKeeney KS, *1862* **42** C2
Wakefield KS, *980* **43** F2
Wakefield MA, *24932* **151** D1
Wakefield MI, *1851* **65** E4
Wakefield NE, *1451* **35** F2
Wakefield RI, *8487* **150** C4
Wakefield VA, *11275* **113** F2
Wake Forest NC, *30117* **113** D4
Wakeman OH, *1047* **91** D2
Wake Vil. TX, *5492* **124** C1
Wakonda SD, *321* **35** F1
Wakulla Co. FL, *30776* **137** E2
Walbridge OH, *3019* **267** B2
Walcott IA, *1629* **87** F2
Walden CO, *608* **33** D4
Walden NY, *6978* **148** B1
Walden TN, *1898* **120** B1
Waldo AR, *1372* **125** D1
Waldo FL, *1015* **138** C3
Waldoboro ME, *1233* **82** C2
Waldo Co. ME, *38786* **82** C2
Waldorf MD, *67752* **144** B4
Waldport OR, *2033* **20** B3
Waldron AR, *3618* **116** C2
Waldron IN, *804* **100** A2
Waldron MI, *538* **90** B1
Wales MA, *1737* **150** B2
Wales WI, *2549* **74** C3
Waleska GA, *644* **120** C3
Walford IA, *1463* **87** E1
Walhalla ND, *996* **19** E1
Walhalla SC, *4263* **121** E2
Walker IA, *791* **73** E4
Walker LA, *6138* **134** A2
Walker MI, *23537* **75** F3
Walker MN, *941* **64** A3
Walker Co. AL, *67023* **119** E4
Walker Co. GA, *68756* **120** B2
Walker Co. TX, *67861* **132** A1
Walker Mill MD, *11302* **271** F4
Walkersville MD, *5800* **144** A1
Walkerton IN, *2144* **89** E2
Walkertown NC, *4675* **112** B4
Walker Valley NY, *853* **148** A1
Walkerville MT, *675* **23** E1
Wall PA, *580* **250** D3
Wall SD, *766* **26** B3
Wallace ID, *784* **14** B3
Wallace NC, *3880* **123** E2
Wallace VA, *550* **111** E3
Wallace Co. KS, *1485* **42** B2
Walla Walla WA, *31731* **21** F1
Walla Walla Co. WA, *58781* **21** F1
Wallburg MI, *3047* **112** B4
Walled Lake MI, *6999* **210** A2
Waller TX, *2326* **61** F2
Waller Co. TX, *43205* **132** A3
Wallingford CT, *44736* **149** D1
Wallingford VT, *830* **81** D4
Wallington NJ, *11335* **148** B3
Wallis TX, *1252* **61** F2
Wallkill NY, *2288* **148** B1
Wall Lake IA, *819* **72** B4
Wallowa OR, *808* **22** A1
Wallowa Co. OR, *7008* **22** A1
Walnut CA, *29172* **229** F3
Walnut IL, *1416* **88** B2
Walnut IA, *785* **86** A2
Walnut MS, *771* **118** C2
Walnut Cove NC, *1425* **112** B3
Walnut Creek CA, *64173* **36** B4
Walnut Creek NC, *835* **123** E1
Walnut Grove AL, *698* **120** A3
Walnut Grove CA, *1542* **36** C3
Walnut Grove GA, *1330* **121** D4
Walnut Grove MN, *871* **72** A1
Walnut Grove MS, *1911* **126** C2
Walnut Grove MO, *665* **106** C1
Walnut Grove TN, *864* **109** F3
Walnut Hill TN, *2394* **111** E3
Walnut Park CA, *15966* **228** D3
Walnutport PA, *2070* **93** F3
Walnut Ridge AR, *4890* **108** A4
Walnut Sprs. TX, *827* **59** E3
Walpole MA, *5918* **151** D2
Walpole NH, *605* **81** E4
Walsenburg CO, *3068* **41** E4
Walsh CO, *546* **42** A4
Walsh Co. ND, *11119* **19** E2
Walterboro SC, *5398* **130** C1
Walterhill TN, *401* **109** F4
Walters OK, *2551* **51** D4
Walthall MS, *144* **118** C4
Walthall Co. MS, *15443* **134** B1
Waltham MA, *60632* **151** D1
Walthill NE, *780* **35** F2
Walthourville GA, *4111* **130** B3
Walton IN, *1049* **89** F3
Walton KY, *3635* **100** B3
Walton NY, *3088* **93** F1
Walton Co. FL, *55043* **136** B2
Walton Co. GA, *83768* **121** D4
Walton Hills OH, *2281* **204** G3
Walworth WI, *2816* **74** C4
Walworth Co. SD, *5438* **26** C2
Walworth Co. WI, *102228* **74** C4
Wamac IL, *1185* **98** C3
Wamego KS, *4372* **43** F2
Wampsville NY, *543* **79** E3
Wamsutter WY, *451* **32** C3
Wanakah NY, *3199* **78** A4
Wanamassa NJ, *4532* **147** E2
Wanamingo MN, *1086* **73** D1
Wanaque NJ, *11116* **148** A3
Wanatah IN, *1048* **89** E2
Wanblee SD, *725* **26** B4
Wanchese NC, *1642* **115** F2
Wapakoneta OH, *9867* **90** B4
Wapanucka OK, *438* **51** F4
Wapato WA, *4997* **13** D4
Wapella IL, *558* **88** C4
Wapello IA, *2067* **87** F2
Wapello Co. IA, *35625* **87** D3
Waples TX, *800* **59** E3
Wappingers Falls NY, *5522* **148** B1
War WV, *862* **111** F1
Ward AR, *4067* **117** F2
Ward Co. ND, *61675* **18** B2
Ward Co. TX, *10658* **57** F4
Warden WA, *2692* **13** E4
Wardner ID, *188* **14** B3
Wardsville MO, *1506* **97** E3
Ware MA, *6170* **150** B1
Ware Co. GA, *36312* **129** F4
Wareham MA, *21221* **151** E3
Ware Shoals SC, *2170* **121** F3
Waretown NJ, *1569* **147** E3
Warm Beach WA, *2437* **12** C2
Warm Sprs. GA, *485* **128** C1
Warm Sprs. OR, *2945* **21** D3
Warm Sprs. VA, *123* **102** B4
Warner NH, *444* **81** F4
Warner OK, *1641* **116** A1
Warner SD, *457* **27** D2
Warner Robins GA, *66588* **129** D2
Warr Acres OK, *10043* **244** D2
Warren AR, *6003* **117** E4
Warren IL, *1428* **74** A4
Warren IN, *1239* **90** A3
Warren ME, *3794* **82** C2
Warren MA, *1405* **150** B2
Warren MI, *134056* **76** C4
Warren MN, *1563* **19** F2
Warren OH, *41557* **91** F2
Warren PA, *9710* **92** B1
Warren RI, *10611* **151** D3
Warren Co. GA, *5834* **129** F1
Warren Co. IL, *17707* **88** A3
Warren Co. IN, *8508* **89** D4
Warren Co. IA, *46225* **86** C2
Warren Co. KY, *113792* **109** F2
Warren Co. MS, *48773* **126** A2
Warren Co. MO, *32513* **97** F3
Warren Co. NJ, *108692* **93** F3
Warren Co. NY, *65707* **80** C3
Warren Co. NC, *20972* **113** D3
Warren Co. OH, *212693* **100** C2
Warren Co. PA, *41815* **92** B1
Warren Co. TN, *39839* **110** A4
Warren Co. VA, *37575* **103** D2
Warren Glen NJ, *650* **146** C1
Warren Park IN, *1480* **99** F1
Warrensburg IL, *1210* **98** C1
Warrensburg MO, *18838* **96** C3
Warrensburg NY, *3103* **80** C4
Warrensville PA, *1100* **93** D2
Warrensville Hts. OH, *13542* **204** G2
Warrenton GA, *1937* **129** F1
Warrenton MO, *7880* **97** F3
Warrenton NC, *862* **113** D3
Warrenton OR, *4989* **20** B1
Warrenton VA, *9611* **103** D3
Warrenville IL, *13140* **203** A4
Warrick Co. IN, *59689* **99** E4
Warrington FL, *14531* **135** F2
Warrington PA, *5400* **146** C2
Warrior AL, *3176* **119** F4
Warrior Run PA, *584* **261** A2
Warroad MN, *1781* **64** A1
Warsaw IL, *1607* **87** F4
Warsaw IN, *13559* **89** F2
Warsaw KY, *1615* **100** B3
Warsaw MN, *627* **72** C1
Warsaw MO, *2127* **97** D4
Warsaw NY, *3473* **78** B4
Warsaw NC, *3054* **123** E2
Warsaw OH, *682* **91** D4
Warsaw VA, *1512* **103** E4
Warson Woods MO, *1962* **256** B2
Wartburg TN, *918* **110** B4
Wartrace TN, *651* **120** A1
Warwick NY, *6731* **148** A2
Warwick RI, *82672* **150** C3
Wasatch Co. UT, *23530* **31** F4
Wasco CA, *25545* **45** D4
Wasco OR, *410* **21** D1
Wasco Co. OR, *25213* **21** D2
Waseca MN, *9410* **72** C1
Waseca Co. MN, *19136* **72** C1
Washakie Co. WY, *8533* **24** C4
Washburn IL, *1155* **88** B3
Washburn IA, *876* **73** E4
Washburn ME, *997* **85** D2
Washburn ND, *1246* **18** B3
Washburn WI, *2117* **65** D4
Washburn Co. WI, *15911* **67** E2
Washington CT, *600* **148** C1
Washington DC, *601723* **144** B3
Washington GA, *4134* **121** E4
Washington IL, *15134* **88** B3
Washington IN, *11509* **99** E3
Washington IA, *7266* **87** E2
Washington KS, *1131* **43** F1
Washington LA, *964* **133** F2
Washington MO, *13982* **97** F3
Washington NJ, *6461* **93** F3
Washington NC, *9744* **115** D3
Washington OK, *618* **51** E3
Washington PA, *13663* **91** F4
Washington UT, *18761* **46** C1
Washington VT, *1047* **81** E2
Washington VA, *135* **103** D3
Washington WV, *1175* **101** E2
Washington Co. AL, *17581* **127** E4
Washington Co. AR, *203065* **106** B4
Washington Co. CO, *4814* **34** A4
Washington Co. FL, *24896* **136** C2
Washington Co. GA, *21187* **129** E1
Washington Co. ID, *10198* **22** A3
Washington Co. IL, *14716* **98** B4
Washington Co. IN, *28262* **99** F3
Washington Co. IA, *21704* **87** E2
Washington Co. KS, *5799* **43** E1
Washington Co. KY, *11717* **110** B1
Washington Co. ME, *32856* **83** E1
Washington Co. MD, *147430* **103** D1
Washington Co. MN, *238136* **67** D3
Washington Co. MS, *51137* **126** A1
Washington Co. MO, *25195* **97** F4
Washington Co. NE, *20234* **35** F3
Washington Co. NY, *63216* **81** D4
Washington Co. NC, *13228* **113** F4
Washington Co. OH, *61778* **101** E2
Washington Co. OK, *50976* **106** A2
Washington Co. OR, *529710* **20** B2
Washington Co. PA, *207820* **92** A4
Washington Co. RI, *126979* **150** C4
Washington Co. TN, *122979* **111** E3
Washington Co. TX, *33718* **61** F2
Washington Co. UT, *138115* **38** C4
Washington Co. VT, *59534* **81** E2
Washington Co. VA, *54876* **111** F3
Washington Co. WI, *131887* **74** C2
Washington C.H. OH, *14192* **100** C1
Washington Crossing NJ, *950* **147** D2
Washington Crossing PA, *1300* **147** D2
Washington Hts. NY, *1689* **148** A1
Washington Par. LA, *47168* **134** B1
Washington Park IL, *4196* **256** D2
Washington Terrace UT, *9067* **244** A2
Washingtonville NY, *5899* **148** B1
Washingtonville OH, *801* **91** F3
Washita Co. OK, *11629* **51** D3
Washoe Co. NV, *421407* **29** E4
Washougal WA, *14095* **20** C2
Washtenaw Co. MI, *344791* **90** B1
Wasilla AK, *7831* **154** C3
Waskom TX, *2160* **124** C2
Wataga IL, *843* **88** A3
Watauga TN, *458* **111** E3
Watauga TX, *23497* **207** B2
Watauga Co. NC, *51079* **111** F3
Watchung NJ, *5801* **147** E1
Waterboro ME, *6214* **82** B3
Waterbury CT, *110366* **149** D1
Waterbury VT, *1763* **81** D2
Waterbury Ctr. VT, *850* **81** E2
Waterford CA, *8456* **36** C4
Waterford CT, *2887* **149** F2
Waterford MI, *73150* **76** B4
Waterford NY, *1990* **188** E1
Waterford PA, *1517* **92** A1
Waterford WI, *5368* **74** C4
Waterford Works NJ, *1000* **147** D4
Waterloo IL, *9811* **98** A4
Waterloo IN, *2242* **90** A2
Waterloo IA, *68406* **73** E4
Waterloo MD, *900* **144** C2
Waterloo NE, *848* **35** F3
Waterloo NY, *5171* **79** D3
Waterloo WI, *3333* **74** B3
Waterman IL, *1506* **88** C1
Water Mill NY, *1559* **149** E3
Waterproof LA, *688* **125** F3
Watertown CT, *3574* **149** D1
Watertown FL, *2829* **138** C2
Watertown MA, *31915* **151** D1
Watertown MN, *4205* **66** C4
Watertown NY, *27023* **79** E1
Watertown SD, *21482* **27** F2
Watertown TN, *1477* **109** F4
Watertown WI, *23861* **74** C3
Water Valley MS, *3392* **118** B3
Waterville KS, *680* **43** F1
Waterville ME, *15722* **82** C2
Waterville MN, *1868* **72** C1
Waterville NY, *1583* **79** E3
Waterville OH, *5523* **90** C2
Waterville WA, *1138* **13** E3
Watervliet MI, *1735* **89** F1
Watervliet NY, *10254* **188** E2
Watford City ND, *1744* **18** A3
Wathena KS, *1364* **96** B1
Watkins MN, *962* **66** C3
Watkins Glen NY, *1859* **79** D4
Watkinsville GA, *2832* **121** D4
Watonga OK, *5111* **51** D2
Watonwan Co. MN, *11211* **72** B1
Watseka IL, *5255* **89** D3
Watson IL, *754* **98** C2
Watson LA, *1047* **134** A2
Watsontown PA, *2351* **93** D3
Watsonville CA, *51199* **44** B2
Watterson Park KY, *976* **230** E2
Waubay SD, *576* **27** E2
Wauchula FL, *5001* **140** C3
Wauconda IL, *13603* **203** B1
Waukee IA, *13790* **86** C2
Waukegan IL, *89078* **75** D4
Waukesha WI, *70718* **74** C3
Waukesha Co. WI, *389891* **74** C3
Waukomis OK, *1286* **51** E2
Waukon IA, *3897* **73** E3
Waunakee WI, *12097* **74** B3
Wauneta NE, *577* **34** B4
Waupaca WI, *6069* **74** B1
Waupaca Co. WI, *52410* **68** B4
Waupun WI, *11340* **74** C2
Wauregan CT, *1205* **150** B3
Waurika OK, *2064* **51** E4
Wausa NE, *634* **35** E1
Wausau WI, *39106* **68** B4
Wausaukee WI, *575* **68** C3
Wauseon OH, *7332* **90** B2
Waushara Co. WI, *24496* **74** B1
Wautoma WI, *2218* **74** B1
Wauwatosa WI, *46396* **234** C2
Wauzeka WI, *711* **73** F3
Waveland MS, *6435* **134** C2
Waverly FL, *767* **141** D2
Waverly IL, *1307* **98** B1
Waverly IA, *9874* **73** D4
Waverly KS, *592* **96** A3
Waverly MN, *1357* **66** C3
Waverly MO, *849* **96** C2
Waverly NE, *3277* **35** F4
Waverly NY, *4444* **93** E1
Waverly OH, *4408* **101** D2
Waverly TN, *4105* **109** D4
Waverly VA, *2149* **113** E2
Waverly Hall GA, *735* **128** C2
Waxahachie TX, *29621* **59** F3
Waxhaw NC, *9859* **122** B2
Waycross GA, *14649* **129** F4
Wayland IA, *966* **87** E2
Wayland MA, *12994* **150** C1
Wayland MI, *4079* **75** F4
Wayland NY, *1865* **78** C4
Waymart PA, *1341* **93** F2
Wayne IL, *2431* **203** A4
Wayne MI, *17593* **210** A4
Wayne NE, *5660* **35** F2
Wayne NJ, *53918* **148** A3
Wayne OH, *887* **90** C2
Wayne OK, *688* **51** E3
Wayne PA, *1000* **146** C3
Wayne WV, *1413* **101** D4
Wayne City IL, *1032* **98** C4
Wayne Co. GA, *30099* **130** A4
Wayne Co. IL, *16760* **98** C3
Wayne Co. IN, *68917* **100** A1
Wayne Co. IA, *6403* **87** D3
Wayne Co. KY, *20813* **110** B3
Wayne Co. MI, *1820584* **76** B4
Wayne Co. MS, *20747* **127** D4
Wayne Co. MO, *13521* **108** A2
Wayne Co. NE, *9595* **35** F2
Wayne Co. NY, *93772* **79** D3
Wayne Co. NC, *122623* **123** E1
Wayne Co. OH, *114520* **91** E3
Wayne Co. PA, *52822* **93** F1
Wayne Co. TN, *17021* **119** E1
Wayne Co. UT, *2778* **39** F3
Wayne Co. WV, *42481* **101** E4
Wayne Lakes OH, *718* **100** B1
Waynesboro GA, *5766* **129** F1
Waynesboro MS, *5043* **127** D4
Waynesboro PA, *10568* **103** D1
Waynesboro TN, *2449* **119** E1

272

Waynesboro–Wentzville

Figures after entries indicate population, page number, and grid reference.

POINTS OF INTEREST

Arena Stage E4
Arlington Natl. Cemetery A4
Arthur M. Sackler Gallery C2
Art Museum of the Americas C2
Arts & Industries Building E3
Blair House C2
Bureau of Engraving & Printing D3
Cathedral of St. Matthew the Apostle C1
Corcoran Gallery of Art C2
Daughters of the American Revolution
  Constitution Hall C2
Decatur House C1
Dept. of Agriculture D3
Dept. of Commerce D2
Dept. of Education E3
Dept. of Energy E3
Dept. of Housing and
  Urban Development E3
Dept. of Justice D2
Dept. of Labor F2
Dept. of State C2
Dept. of the Interior C2

Dept. of the Treasury D2
Dept. of Transportation E3
Dept. of Veterans Affairs D1
District of Columbia Court House E2
District of Columbia War Memorial C3
Donald W. Reynolds Center for
  American Art & Portraiture E2
The Ellipse D2
Environmental Protection Agency D2
Fish Wharf D4
Folger Shakespeare Library G3
Ford's Theatre Natl. Hist. Site E2
Franklin Delano Roosevelt Memorial C3
Freer Gallery of Art D3
Friendship Archway E1
Gallaudet Univ. G1
George Mason Memorial C4
Georgetown Univ. Law Center F2
George Washington Univ. B2
Government Printing Office F1
Hirshhorn Mus. & Sculpture Garden E3
Ice Skating Rink E2
Internal Revenue Service E2

International Spy Museum E2
James Madison Building G3
J. Edgar Hoover FBI Building E2
John Adams Building G3
John Ericsson Memorial B3
John F. Kennedy Center for the
  Performing Arts B2
John F. Kennedy Gravesite A4
Judiciary Square E2
Korean War Veterans Memorial C3
Koshland Science Museum E2
Lafayette Square D2
Lansburgh Theatre E2
L'Enfant Plaza E3
Library of Congress G3
Lincoln Memorial B3
Lyndon B. Johnson Memorial Grove B4
Marine Corps War Memorial
  (Iwo Jima Memorial) A3
Martin Luther King, Jr.
  Memorial Library E2
NASA E4

Natl. Air & Space Museum E3
The Natl. Archives E2
Natl. Building Museum E2
Natl. Gallery of Art East Building E3
Natl. Gallery of Art West Building E2
Natl. Geographic Society &
  Explorers Hall D1
Natl. Mus. of African Art E3
Natl. Mus. of American Hist. E2
Natl. Mus. of Natural Hist. E2
Natl. Mus. of the American Indian E3
Natl. Mus. of Women in the Arts D1
Natl. Portrait Gallery E2
Natl. Postal Museum F2
Natl. Theatre E2
Natl. WWII Memorial C3
Navy-Merchant Marine Memorial C4
The Netherlands Carillon A3
Newseum E2
Octagon House C2
Old Post Office Pavilion D2
Old Stone House B1
Organization of American States C2

Reflecting Pool C3
Renwick Gallery D2
Ronald Reagan Building and
  Intl. Trade Center D2
Seabees of the United States
  Navy Memorial A3
Sewall-Belmont House G2
The Shops at Georgetown Park A1
Sidney Harman Hall E2
Signers of the Declaration of
  Independence Memorial C3
Smithsonian American Art Museum E2
Smithsonian Institution Castle E3
The Supreme Court G3
Taft Memorial Carillon F2
Theodore Roosevelt Memorial A2
Thomas Jefferson Building G3
Thomas Jefferson Memorial D4
Union Station F2
United Spanish War
  Veterans Memorial A3
U.S. Botanic Garden F3
U.S. Capitol F3

U.S. Capitol Visitor Center F3
U.S. Claims Court D1
U.S. District Court House E2
U.S. Grant Memorial F3
U.S. Holocaust Memorial Museum D3
U.S. Navy Memorial &
  Naval Heritage Center E2
U.S. Postal Service Headquarters E3
Verizon Center E2
Vietnam Veterans Memorial C3
Vietnam Women's Memorial C3
Warner Theatre D2
Washington Convention Center E1
The Washington Design Center D1
Washington Harbour A1
Washington Monument D3
Washington Post D1
The White House D2
Women in Military Service for
  America Memorial A4
Zero Milestone D2

Entries in **bold black** indicate counties or parishes.
Entries in **bold color** indicate cities with detailed inset maps.

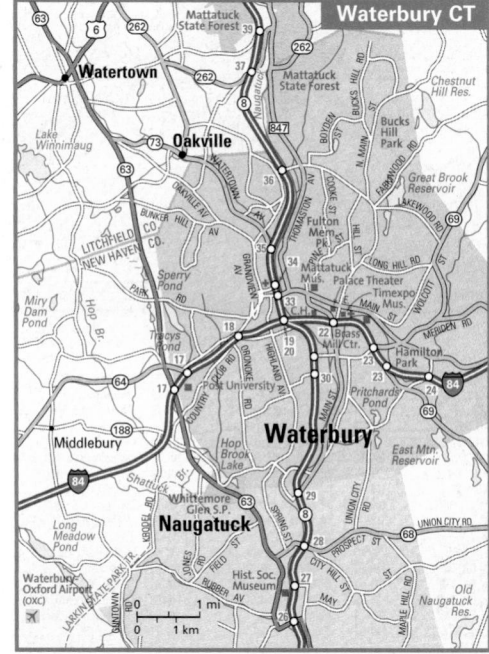

Waterbury CT

Downtown Washington DC

Wichita KS

274
Wexford County–Winneconne

Figures after entries indicate population, page number, and grid reference.

Wexford Co. MI, 32735 ... 69 F4
Weyauwega WI, 1900 ... 74 B1
Weyers Cave VA, 2473 ... 102 C4
Weymouth MA, 53743 ... 151 D2
Wharton NJ, 6522 ... 148 A3
Wharton OH, 358 ... 90 C3
Wharton TX, 8832 ... 61 F3
Wharton Co. TX, 41280 ... 61 F3
What Cheer IA, 646 ... 87 E2
Whatcom Co. WA, 201140 ... 12 C1
Whately MA, 425 ... 150 A1
Wheatfield IN, 853 ... 89 E2
Wheatland CA, 3456 ... 36 C2
Wheatland IN, 480 ... 99 E3
Wheatland IA, 764 ... 87 F1
Wheatland WY, 3627 ... 33 E2
Wheatland Co. MT, 2168 ... 16 B4
Wheatley AR, 355 ... 118 A2
Wheaton IL, 52894 ... 89 D1
Wheaton MD, 48284 ... 144 B3
Wheaton MN, 1424 ... 27 F1
Wheaton MO, 696 ... 106 C2
Wheat Ridge CO, 30166 ... 209 B3
Wheeler MS, 300 ... 119 D2
Wheeler OR, 414 ... 20 B1
Wheeler TX, 1592 ... 50 C3
Wheeler Co. GA, 7421 ... 129 E3
Wheeler Co. NE, 818 ... 35 D2
Wheeler Co. OR, 1441 ... 21 E3
Wheeler Co. TX, 5410 ... 50 C3
Wheelersburg OH, 6437 ... 101 D3
Wheeling IL, 37648 ... 89 D1
Wheeling WV, 28486 ... 91 F4
Wheelwright KY, 780 ... 111 E1
Wheelwright MA, 425 ... 150 B1
Whigham GA, 471 ... 137 E1
Whippany NJ, 3800 ... 148 A3
Whispering Pines NC, 2928 ... 122 C1
Whitaker PA, 1271 ... 250 C2
Whitakers NC, 744 ... 113 E4
White GA, 670 ... 120 C3
White SD, 485 ... 27 F3
White Bear Lake MN, 23797 ... 235 D1
White Bird ID, 91 ... 22 B1
White Bluff TN, 3206 ... 109 E4
White Castle LA, 1883 ... 134 A2
White Ctr. WA, 13495 ... 262 B4
White City FL, 3719 ... 141 E3
White City KS, 618 ... 43 F2
White City OR, 7975 ... 28 B2
White Cloud MI, 1408 ... 75 F2
White Co. AR, 77076 ... 117 F1
White Co. GA, 27144 ... 121 D2
White Co. IL, 14665 ... 99 D4
White Co. IN, 24643 ... 89 E3
White Co. TN, 25841 ... 110 A4
White Deer TX, 1000 ... 50 B3
White Earth MN, 580 ... 19 F3
Whiteface TX, 449 ... 57 F1
Whitefield NH, 1142 ... 81 F2
Whitefish MT, 6357 ... 15 D2
Whitefish Bay WI, 14110 ... 234 D1
Whiteford MD, 700 ... 146 A4
White Hall AL, 858 ... 127 F2
White Hall AR, 5526 ... 117 E3
White Hall IL, 2520 ... 98 A2
Whitehall MI, 2706 ... 75 E2
Whitehall MT, 1038 ... 23 E1
Whitehall NY, 2614 ... 81 D3
Whitehall OH, 18062 ... 206 C2
Whitehall PA, 14268 ... 146 B1
Whitehall PA, 13944 ... 250 B3
Whitehall VA, 250 ... 102 C4
White Hall VA, 300 ... 103 D2
White Hall WV, 648 ... 102 A2
Whitehall WI, 1558 ... 73 F1
White Haven PA, 1097 ... 93 F3
White Horse NJ, 9494 ... 147 D2
White Horse PA, 475 ... 146 A3
White Horse Beach MA, 2300 ... 151 E3
Whitehouse OH, 4149 ... 90 B2
White House TN, 10255 ... 109 F3
Whitehouse TX, 7660 ... 124 B3
White House Sta. NJ, 2089 ... 147 D1
White Island Shores MA, 2106 ... 151 E3
White Lake NY, 475 ... 94 A3
White Lake NC, 802 ... 123 D2
White Lake SD, 372 ... 27 D4
Whiteland IN, 4169 ... 99 F1
Whitelaw WI, 757 ... 75 D1
White Marsh MD, 9513 ... 193 E2
White Marsh VA, 600 ... 113 F1
White Oak MD, 17403 ... 270 D1
White Oak OH, 19167 ... 204 A2
White Oak PA, 7862 ... 92 A4
White Oak TX, 6469 ... 124 B2
White Pigeon MI, 1522 ... 89 F1
White Pine MI, 474 ... 65 E4
White Pine TN, 2196 ... 111 D4
White Pine Co. NV, 10030 ... 38 B1
White Plains KY, 884 ... 109 E2
White Plains MD, 3600 ... 144 B4
White Plains NY, 56853 ... 148 B3
White Plains NC, 1074 ... 112 A3
Whiteriver AZ, 4104 ... 55 E1
White River SD, 581 ... 26 C4
White River Jct. VT, 2286 ... 81 E3
White Rock NM, 5725 ... 48 C2
Whiterocks UT, 289 ... 32 A4
White Salmon WA, 2224 ... 21 D1
Whitesboro NY, 3772 ... 79 E3
Whitesboro TX, 3793 ... 59 F1
Whitesburg GA, 588 ... 120 B4
Whitesburg KY, 2139 ... 111 D2
White Settlement TX, 16116 ... 207 A2
White Shield ND, 336 ... 18 B3
Whiteside Co. IL, 58498 ... 88 A1
White Sprs. FL, 777 ... 138 C2
White Stone VA, 352 ... 113 F1
White Sulphur Sprs. MT, 939 ... 15 F4
White Sulphur Sprs. WV, 2444 ... 112 B1
Whitesville KY, 552 ... 109 F1
Whitesville NY, 400 ... 92 C1
Whitesville WV, 514 ... 101 F4
White Swan WA, 793 ... 13 D4
Whiteville NC, 5394 ... 123 D3
Whiteville TN, 4638 ... 118 C1
Whitewater KS, 718 ... 43 E3
Whitewater WI, 14390 ... 74 C3
Whitewood SD, 927 ... 25 F3
Whitewright TX, 1604 ... 59 F1
Whitfield FL, 2882 ... 140 B3
Whitfield Co. GA, 102599 ... 120 B2
Whiting IN, 4997 ... 89 D2
Whiting IA, 762 ... 35 F2
Whiting NJ, 1800 ... 147 E3
Whiting WI, 1724 ... 68 B4
Whitinsville MA, 6704 ... 150 C2
Whitley City KY, 1170 ... 110 C3
Whitley Co. IN, 33292 ... 89 F3
Whitley Co. KY, 35637 ... 110 C2
Whitman MA, 14489 ... 151 D2
Whitman Co. WA, 44776 ... 14 A4
Whitmire SC, 1441 ... 121 F3
Whitmore Lake MI, 6423 ... 76 B4
Whitmore Vil. HI, 4499 ... 152 A2
Whitney TX, 2087 ... 59 E3
Whitney Pt. NY, 964 ... 79 E4
Whitsett NC, 590 ... 112 B4
Whittemore IA, 504 ... 72 B3
Whittemore MI, 384 ... 76 B1
Whittier CA, 85331 ... 52 C2
Whitwell TN, 1699 ... 120 B1
Why AZ, 167 ... 54 B3
Wibaux MT, 589 ... 17 F4
Wibaux Co. MT, 1017 ... 17 F4
Wichita KS, 382368 ... 43 E4
Wichita Co. KS, 2234 ... 42 B3
Wichita Co. TX, 131500 ... 59 D1
Wichita Falls TX, 104553 ... 59 D1
Wickenburg AZ, 6363 ... 54 B1
Wickes AR, 754 ... 116 C3
Wickett TX, 498 ... 57 F4
Wickford RI, 1900 ... 150 C4
Wickliffe KY, 688 ... 108 C2
Wickliffe OH, 12750 ... 91 E2
Wicomico Church VA, 250 ... 113 F1
Wicomico Co. MD, 98733 ... 114 C1
Widefield CO, 29845 ... 205 D2
Wiggins CO, 893 ... 33 F4
Wiggins MS, 4390 ... 135 D1
Wilbarger Co. TX, 13535 ... 58 C1
Wilber NE, 1855 ... 35 F4
Wilberforce OH, 2271 ... 100 C1
Wilbraham MA, 3915 ... 150 A2
Wilbur WA, 884 ... 13 F3
Wilbur Park MO, 471 ... 256 B3
Wilburton OK, 2843 ... 116 A2
Wilcox NE, 358 ... 35 D4
Wilcox PA, 383 ... 92 B2
Wilcox Co. AL, 11670 ... 127 F3
Wilcox Co. GA, 9255 ... 129 E3
Wilder ID, 1533 ... 22 A4
Wilder KY, 3035 ... 204 B3
Wilder VT, 1690 ... 81 E3
Wilderness VA, 300 ... 103 D4
Wildomar CA, 32176 ... 53 D3
Wild Rose WI, 725 ... 74 B1
Wildwood FL, 6709 ... 140 C1
Wildwood MO, 35517 ... 98 A3
Wildwood NJ, 5325 ... 104 C4
Wildwood TX, 1235 ... 132 C2
Wildwood Crest NJ, 3270 ... 104 C4
Wiley CO, 405 ... 42 A3
Wilhoit AZ, 868 ... 47 D4
Wilkes-Barre PA, 41498 ... 93 E2
Wilkesboro NC, 3413 ... 111 F4
Wilkes Co. GA, 10593 ... 121 E4
Wilkes Co. NC, 69340 ... 112 A3
Wilkeson WA, 477 ... 12 C3
Wilkin Co. MN, 6576 ... 19 F4
Wilkinsburg PA, 15930 ... 250 C2
Wilkinson Co. GA, 9563 ... 129 E2
Wilkinson Co. MS, 9878 ... 125 F4
Willacoochee GA, 1391 ... 129 E4
Willacy Co. TX, 22134 ... 63 F3
Willamina OR, 2025 ... 20 B2
Willard MO, 5288 ... 107 D2
Willard NM, 253 ... 49 D4
Willard OH, 6236 ... 91 D3
Willard UT, 1772 ... 31 E3
Willards MD, 958 ... 114 C1
Will Co. IL, 677560 ... 89 D2
Willcox AZ, 3757 ... 55 E3
Willernie MN, 507 ... 235 E1
Williams AZ, 3023 ... 47 D3
Williams CA, 5123 ... 36 B2
Williams IA, 344 ... 72 C4
Williams OR, 1072 ... 28 B2
Williams Bay WI, 2564 ... 74 C4
Williamsburg CO, 662 ... 41 E3
Williamsburg FL, 7646 ... 246 B4
Williamsburg IA, 3068 ... 87 E2
Williamsburg KS, 397 ... 96 A3
Williamsburg KY, 5245 ... 110 C3
Williamsburg MA, 550 ... 150 A1
Williamsburg NM, 449 ... 56 B2
Williamsburg OH, 2490 ... 100 C2
Williamsburg PA, 1254 ... 92 C4
Williamsburg VA, 14068 ... 113 F2
Williamsburg Co. SC, 34423 ... 122 C4
Williams Co. ND, 22398 ... 17 F2
Williams Co. OH, 37642 ... 90 A2
Williams Creek IN, 407 ... 221 C1
Williamsfield IL, 578 ... 88 A3
Williamson NY, 2495 ... 78 C3
Williamson WV, 3191 ... 111 E1
Williamson Co. IL, 66357 ... 108 C1
Williamson Co. TN, 183182 ... 109 F4
Williamson Co. TX, 422679 ... 61 E1
Williamsport IN, 1898 ... 89 D4
Williamsport MD, 2137 ... 103 D1
Williamsport OH, 1023 ... 101 D1
Williamsport PA, 29381 ... 93 D2
Williamston MI, 3854 ... 76 A4
Williamston NC, 5511 ... 113 E4
Williamston SC, 3934 ... 121 E2
Williamstown KY, 3925 ... 100 B3
Williamstown MA, 4325 ... 94 C1
Williamstown NJ, 15567 ... 146 C4
Williamstown NY, 475 ... 79 E2
Williamstown PA, 1387 ... 93 E4
Williamstown VT, 1162 ... 81 E2
Williamstown WV, 2908 ... 101 F2
Williamsville DE, 350 ... 114 C1
Williamsville IL, 1476 ... 98 B1
Williamsville MS, 400 ... 126 C1
Williamsville NY, 5300 ... 198 C2
Willimantic CT, 17737 ... 150 B3
Willingboro NJ, 36530 ... 147 D3
Willis TX, 5662 ... 132 A2
Willisburg KY, 282 ... 110 B1
Williston FL, 2768 ... 138 C4
Williston MD, 155 ... 145 E3
Williston ND, 14716 ... 17 F2
Williston OH, 487 ... 90 C2
Williston SC, 3139 ... 130 B1
Williston TN, 395 ... 118 C1
Williston VT, 8698 ... 81 D2
Willisville IL, 633 ... 98 B4
Willis Wharf VA, 475 ... 114 B3
Willits CA, 4888 ... 36 A2
Willmar MN, 19610 ... 66 B3
Willoughby OH, 22268 ... 91 E2
Willoughby Hills OH, 9485 ... 204 G1
Willow AK, 2102 ... 154 C3
Willowbrook CA, 35983 ... 228 D3
Willowbrook IL, 8540 ... 203 C5
Willow City ND, 163 ... 18 C2
Willow Creek CA, 1710 ... 28 B4
Willow Creek MT, 210 ... 23 E1
Willow Grove PA, 15726 ... 146 C2
Willowick OH, 14171 ... 91 E2
Willow Lake SD, 263 ... 27 E3
Willow Park TX, 3982 ... 59 E2
Willows CA, 6166 ... 36 B1
Willows MD, 900 ... 144 C4
Willow Sprs. IL, 5524 ... 203 C5
Willow Sprs. MO, 2184 ... 107 E2
Willow Street PA, 7578 ... 146 A3
Willsboro NY, 753 ... 81 D2
Willshire OH, 397 ... 90 A3
Wills Pt. TX, 3524 ... 59 F2
Willwood WY, 100 ... 24 B3
Wilmar AR, 511 ... 117 F4
Wilmer AL, 500 ... 135 E1
Wilmer TX, 3682 ... 207 E3
Wilmerding PA, 2190 ... 250 D3
Wilmette IL, 27087 ... 89 D1
Wilmington DE, 70851 ... 146 B4
Wilmington IL, 142 ... 88 C2
Wilmington NC, 106476 ... 123 E3
Wilmington OH, 12520 ... 100 C2
Wilmington VT, 463 ... 94 C1
Wilmington Island GA, 15138 ... 130 C3
Wilmington Manor DE, 7889 ... 274 D3
Wilmore KY, 3686 ... 100 B4
Wilmot AR, 550 ... 125 F1
Wilmot SD, 492 ... 27 F2
Wilsall MT, 178 ... 23 F1
Wilson AR, 903 ... 118 B1
Wilson KS, 781 ... 43 D2
Wilson LA, 595 ... 134 A1
Wilson NY, 1264 ... 78 B3
Wilson NC, 49167 ... 113 D4
Wilson OK, 1724 ... 51 E4
Wilson PA, 7896 ... 93 F3
Wilson TX, 489 ... 58 A2
Wilson WY, 1482 ... 23 F4
Wilson Co. KS, 9409 ... 106 A1
Wilson Co. NC, 81234 ... 113 E4
Wilson Co. TN, 113993 ... 109 F3
Wilson Co. TX, 42918 ... 61 E3
Wilson's Mills NC, 2277 ... 123 D1
Wilsonville AL, 1827 ... 128 A1
Wilsonville IL, 586 ... 98 B2
Wilsonville OR, 19509 ... 20 C2
Wilton AL, 687 ... 127 F1
Wilton AR, 374 ... 116 C4
Wilton CA, 5363 ... 36 C3
Wilton CT, 17960 ... 148 C2
Wilton IA, 2802 ... 87 F2
Wilton ME, 2198 ... 82 B2
Wilton NH, 1163 ... 95 D1
Wilton NY, 600 ... 80 C4
Wilton ND, 711 ... 18 C3
Wilton WI, 504 ... 73 F2
Wilton Manors FL, 11632 ... 233 C2
Wimauma FL, 6373 ... 140 C3
Wimberley TX, 2626 ... 61 D2
Wimbledon ND, 216 ... 19 D3
Winamac IN, 2490 ... 89 E3
Winchendon MA, 4213 ... 95 D1
Winchester CA, 2534 ... 53 D3
Winchester ID, 340 ... 22 B1
Winchester IL, 1593 ... 98 A1
Winchester IN, 4935 ... 90 A4
Winchester KS, 551 ... 96 A2
Winchester KY, 18368 ... 100 B4
Winchester MA, 21374 ... 151 D1
Winchester MO, 1547 ... 256 A2
Winchester NH, 1733 ... 94 C1
Winchester OH, 1051 ... 100 C3
Winchester OK, 516 ... 51 F2
Winchester TN, 8530 ... 120 A1
Winchester VA, 26203 ... 103 D2
Winchester Bay OR, 382 ... 20 A4
Windber PA, 4138 ... 92 B4
Windcrest TX, 5364 ... 61 D2
Winder GA, 14099 ... 121 D3
Windermere FL, 2462 ... 141 D1
Windfall IN, 708 ... 89 F4
Wind Gap PA, 2720 ... 93 F3
Windham CT, 23733 ... 149 F1
Windham NH, 13592 ... 95 E1
Windham OH, 2209 ... 91 F2
Windham Co. CT, 118428 ... 150 B3
Windham Co. VT, 44513 ... 81 E4
Wind Lake WI, 5342 ... 74 C3
Windom MN, 4646 ... 72 B2
Window Rock AZ, 2712 ... 48 A2
Wind Pt. WI, 1723 ... 75 D4
Windsor CA, 26801 ... 36 B3
Windsor CO, 18644 ... 33 E4
Windsor CT, 28778 ... 150 A3
Windsor IL, 1187 ... 98 C2
Windsor MO, 2901 ... 96 C3
Windsor NY, 916 ... 93 F1
Windsor NC, 3630 ... 113 F4
Windsor PA, 1319 ... 103 E1
Windsor VT, 2066 ... 81 E4
Windsor VA, 2626 ... 113 F2
Windsor WI, 3573 ... 74 B3
Windsor Co. VT, 56670 ... 81 E3
Windsor Hts. WV, 423 ... 91 F4
Windsor Hills CA, 10958 ... 228 C3
Windsor Locks CT, 12498 ... 150 A2
Windthorst TX, 409 ... 59 D1
Windy Hills KY, 2385 ... 230 E1
Winfall NC, 594 ... 113 F3
Winfield AL, 4717 ... 119 E4
Winfield IL, 9080 ... 203 B4
Winfield IN, 4383 ... 89 D2
Winfield IA, 1134 ... 87 F3
Winfield KS, 12301 ... 43 F4
Winfield MO, 1404 ... 98 A2
Winfield TN, 967 ... 110 C3
Winfield TX, 524 ... 124 B1
Winfield WV, 2301 ... 101 E3
Wingate NC, 3491 ... 122 B2
Wingdale NY, 1500 ... 148 C1
Wingo KY, 632 ... 108 C3
Winifred MT, 208 ... 16 B3
Wink TX, 940 ... 57 F4
Winkelman AZ, 353 ... 55 D2
Winkler Co. TX, 7110 ... 57 F3
Winlock WA, 1339 ... 12 B4
Winnebago IL, 3101 ... 74 B4
Winnebago MN, 1437 ... 72 C2
Winnebago NE, 774 ... 35 F2
Winnebago Co. IL, 295266 ... 74 B4
Winnebago Co. IA, 10866 ... 72 C2
Winnebago Co. WI, 166994 ... 74 C1
Winneconne WI, 2383 ... 74 C1

Five Forks ... A1
Gloucester Pt. ... C2
Hayes ... C1
Lackey ... C2
Newport News ... C2
Scotland ... A2
Wicomico ... C1
Williamsburg ... A1
Yorktown ... C2

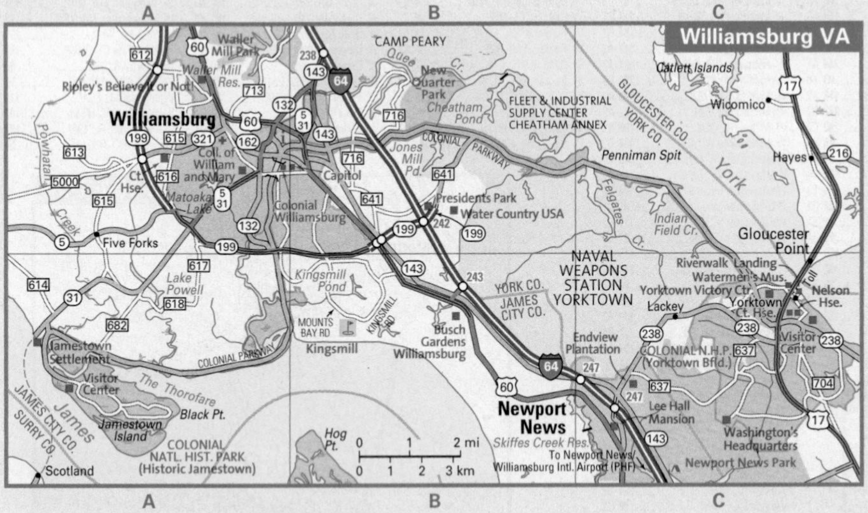
Williamsburg VA
A
B
C
1
2
Williamsburg
Ripley's Believe It or Not!
Waller Mill Park
Waller Mill Res.
CAMP PEARY
New Quarter Park
FLEET & INDUSTRIAL SUPPLY CENTER CHEATHAM ANNEX
Cheatham Pond
Catlett Islands
GLOUCESTER CO.
YORK CO.
Wicomico
Penniman Spit
York
Hayes
Col. of William and Mary
Capitol
Colonial Williamsburg
Matoaka Lake
Jones Mill Pd.
Presidents Park
Water Country USA
Indian Field Cr.
Gloucester Point
Five Forks
Powhatan
Lake Powell
Kingsmill Pond
Kingsmill
MOUNTS BAY RD
Busch Gardens Williamsburg
NAVAL WEAPONS STATION YORKTOWN
YORK CO.
JAMES CITY CO.
Riverwalk Landing
Watermen's Mus.
Yorktown Victory Ctr.
Lackey
Yorktown Ct. Hse.
Nelson Hse.
Visitor Center
COLONIAL N.H.P. (Yorktown Bfld.)
Jamestown Settlement
Visitor Center
The Thorofare
Jamestown Island
Black Pt.
James
JAMES CITY CO.
SURRY CO.
Scotland
COLONIAL NATL. HIST. PARK (Historic Jamestown)
Hog Pt.
COLONIAL PARKWAY
Endview Plantation
Newport News
Lee Hall Mansion
Washington's Headquarters
Skiffes Creek Res.
To Newport News/ Williamsburg Intl. Airport (PHF)
Newport News Park
0 1 2 mi
0 1 2 3 km

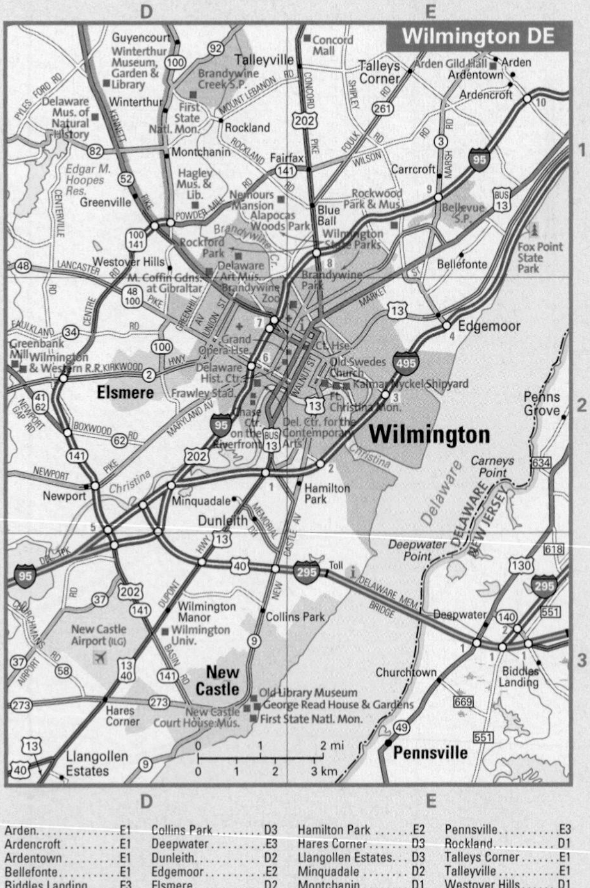
Wilmington DE
D
E
1
2
3
Guyencourt
Winterthur Museum, Garden & Library
Winterthur
Talleyville
Brandywine Creek S.P.
Concord Mall
Talleys Corner
Arden Gild Hall
Arden
Ardentown
Ardencroft
Delaware Mus. of Natural History
First State Natl. Mon.
Rockland
Montchanin
Fairfax
Carrcroft
Edgar M. Hoopes Res.
Greenville
Hagley Mus. & Lib.
Nemours Mansion
Alapocas Woods Park
Blue Ball
Rockwood Park & Mus.
Bellevue S.P.
Westover Hills
Rockford Park
Delaware Art Mus.
Brandywine Park
Brandywine Zoo
Bellefonte
Fox Point State Park
M. Coffin Gdns. at Gibraltar
Grand Opera Hse.
Ct. Hse.
Edgemoor
Greenbank Mill
Wilmington & Western R.R.
Delaware Hist. Ctr.
Old Swedes Church
Kalmar Nyckel Shipyard
Elsmere
Frawley Stad.
Christina Mon.
Del. Ctr. for the Contemporary Arts
Wilmington
Penns Grove
Carneys Point
Newport
Christina
Minquadale
Hamilton Park
Dunleith
Delaware
DELAWARE
NEW JERSEY
Deepwater Point
Deepwater
Wilmington Manor
Wilmington Univ.
Collins Park
New Castle Airport (ILG)
New Castle
Old Library Museum
George Read House & Gardens
First State Natl. Mon.
Hares Corner
New Castle Court House Mus.
Churchtown
Biddles Landing
Llangollen Estates
Pennsville
0 1 2 mi
0 1 2 3 km

Arden ... E1
Ardencroft ... E1
Ardentown ... E1
Bellefonte ... E1
Biddles Landing ... E3
Blue Ball ... E1
Carrcroft ... E1
Churchtown ... E3
Collins Park ... D3
Deepwater ... E3
Dunleith ... D2
Edgemoor ... E2
Elsmere ... D2
Fairfax ... E1
Greenville ... D1
Guyencourt ... D1
Hamilton Park ... E2
Hares Corner ... D3
Llangollen Estates ... D3
Minquadale ... D2
Montchanin ... D1
New Castle ... D3
Newport ... D2
Penns Grove ... E2
Pennsville ... E3
Rockland ... D1
Talleys Corner ... E1
Talleyville ... E1
Westover Hills ... D1
Wilmington ... E2
Wilmington Manor ... D3
Winterthur ... D1

Entries in **bold black** indicate counties or parishes.
Entries in **bold color** indicate cities with detailed inset maps.

Worcester MA

Wilmington NC

Yakima WA

York PA

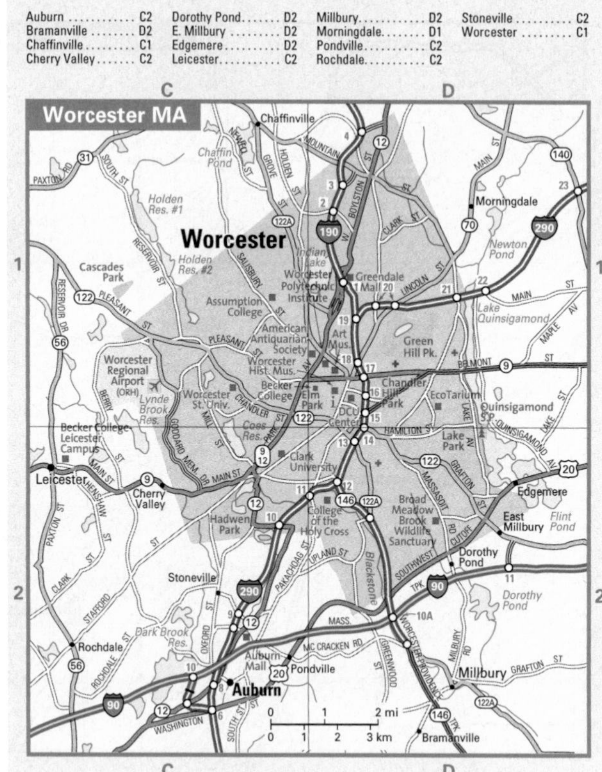

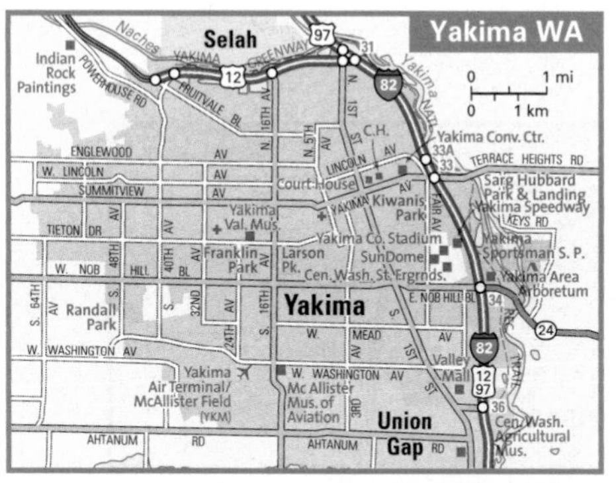

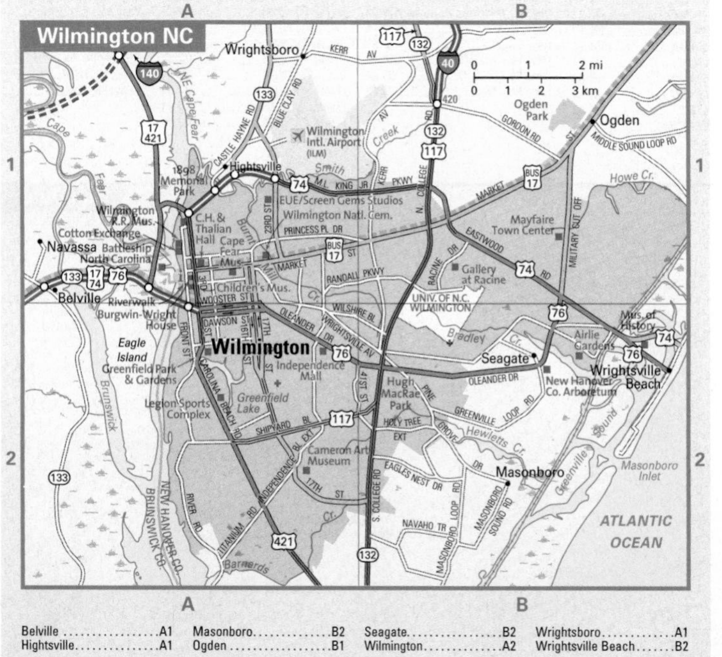

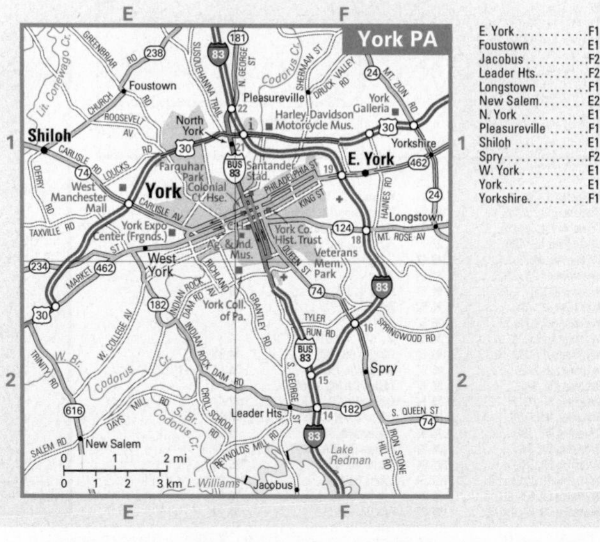

Figures after entries indicate population, page number, and grid reference.

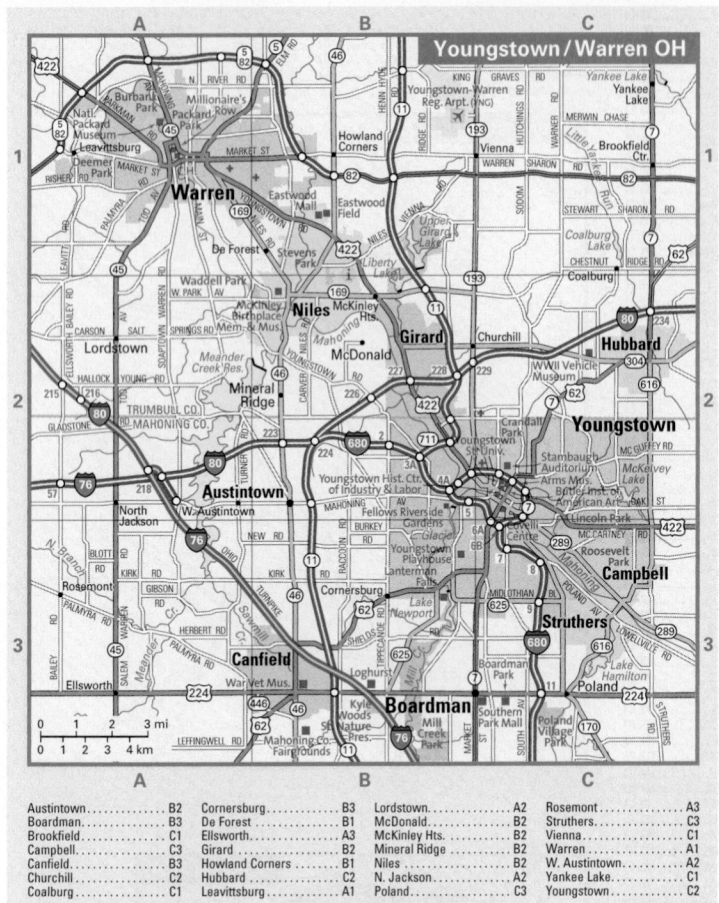

Austintown B2
Boardman B3
Brookfield C1
Campbell C3
Canfield B3
Churchill C2
Coalburg C1
Cornersburg B3
De Forest B1
Ellsworth A3
Girard B2
Howland Corners B1
Hubbard C2
Leavittsburg A1
Lordstown A2
McDonald B2
McKinley Hts. B2
Mineral Ridge B2
Niles B2
N. Jackson A2
Poland C3
Rosemont A3
Struthers C3
Vienna C1
Warren A1
W. Austintown A2
Yankee Lake C1
Youngstown C2

Yuma AZ

San Juan PR

Wymore NE, *1457* 43 F1
Wynantskill NY, *3276* 188 E2
Wyncote PA, *3044* 248 C1
Wyndmere ND, *429* 27 F1
Wynne AR, *8367* 118 A1
Wynnewood OK, *2212* 51 E4
Wynona OK, *437* 51 F1
Wyocena WI, *768* 74 B2
Wyodak WY, *125* 25 E3
Wyola MT, *215* 24 C2
Wyoming DE, *1313* 145 E2
Wyoming IL, *1429* 88 B3
Wyoming IA, *515* 87 F1
Wyoming MI, *72125* 75 F3
Wyoming MN, *7791* 67 D3
Wyoming NY, *434* 78 B3
Wyoming OH, *8428* 204 B1
Wyoming PA, *3073* 261 B1
Wyoming RI, *270* 150 C4
Wyoming Co. NY, *42155* 78 B4
Wyoming Co. PA, *28276* 93 E2
Wyoming Co. WV, *23796* 111 F1
Wyomissing PA, *10461* 146 A2
Wythe Co. VA, *29235* 112 A2
Wytheville VA, *8211* 112 A2

X

Xenia IL, *391* 98 C3
Xenia OH, *25719* 100 C1

Y

Yachats OR, *690* 20 B3
Yacolt WA, *1566* 20 C1
Yadkin Co. NC, *38406* 112 A3
Yadkinville NC, *2959* 112 A4
Yah-ta-hey NM, *590* 48 A2
Yakima WA, *91067* 13 D4
Yakima Co. WA, *243231* 13 D4
Yakutat AK, *662* 155 D3
Yalaha FL, *1364* 140 C1
Yale MI, *1955* 76 C3
Yale OK, *1227* 51 F2
Yalesville CT, *3600* 149 D1
Yalobusha Co. MS, *12678* 118 B3
Yamhill OR, *1024* 20 B2
Yamhill Co. OR, *99193* 20 B2
Yampa CO, *429* 40 C1
Yancey Co. NC, *17818* 111 E4
Yanceyville NC, *2039* 112 C3
Yankeetown FL, *502* 138 C4
Yankton SD, *14454* 35 E1
Yankton Co. SD, *22438* 35 E1
Yaphank NY, *5945* 149 D3
Yardley PA, *2434* 147 D2
Yardville NJ, *7186* 147 D2
Yarmouth ME, *5869* 82 B3
Yarmouth MA, *24807* 151 F3
Yarmouth Port MA, *5320* 151 F3
Yarnell AZ, *649* 47 D4
Yarrow Pt. WA, *1001* 262 B3
Yates Ctr. KS, *1417* 96 A4
Yates City IL, *693* 88 A3
Yates Co. NY, *25348* 78 C4
Yatesville GA, *357* 129 D1
Yatesville PA, *607* 261 C2
Yavapai Co. AZ, *211033* 47 D4
Yazoo City MS, *11403* 126 B2
Yazoo Co. MS, *28065* 126 B2
Yeadon PA, *11443* 146 C3
Yeagertown PA, *1050* 93 D3
Yell Co. AR, *22185* 117 D2
Yellow House PA, 475 ..... 146 B2
Yellow Medicine Co. MN, *10438* . 66 A4
Yellow Sprs. MD, *1100* 144 A1
Yellow Sprs. OH, *3487* 100 C1
Yellowstone Co. MT, *147972* 24 C1
Yellville AR, *1204* 107 E3
Yelm WA, *6848* 12 C4
Yemassee SC, *1027* 130 C2
Yerington NV, *3048* 37 E2
Yerkes KY, *500* 111 D2
Yermo CA, *900* 53 D1
Yoakum TX, *5815* 61 E3
Yoakum Co. TX, *7879* 57 F2
Yoder WY, *151* 33 F2
Yoe PA, *1018* 103 E1
Yolo CA, *450* 36 B2
Yolo Co. CA, *200849* 36 B2
Yoncalla OR, *1047* 20 B4
Yonkers NY, *195976* 148 B3
Yorba Linda CA, *64234* 229 F3
York AL, *2538* 127 D2
York NE, *7766* 35 E4
York NY, *450* 78 C3
York PA, *43718* 103 E1
York SC, *7736* 122 A2
York Beach ME, *1400* 82 B4
York Co. ME, *197131* 82 B4
York Co. NE, *13665* 35 E4
York Co. PA, *434972* 103 E1
York Co. SC, *226073* 122 A2
York Co. VA, *65464* 113 F2
York Harbor ME, *3033* 82 B4
York Haven PA, *709* 93 E4
Yorkshire NY, *1180* 78 B4
Yorkshire VA, *7541* 144 A3
York Sprs. PA, *574* 103 E1
Yorktown IN, *9405* 89 F4
Yorktown NY, *36318* 148 B2
Yorktown TX, *2092* 61 E3
Yorktown VA, *195* 113 F2
Yorktown Hts. NY, *1781* 148 B2
York Vil. ME, *2000* 82 B4
Yorkville IL, *16921* 88 C2
Yorkville OH, *1079* 91 F4
Young AZ, *666* 47 E4
Young Co. TX, *18550* 59 D2
Young Harris GA, *899* 121 D2
Youngstown NY, *1935* 78 A3
Youngstown OH, *66982* 91 F3
Youngstown PA, *326* 92 B4
Youngsville LA, *8105* 133 F2
Youngsville NC, *1157* 113 D4
Youngsville PA, *1729* 92 B1
Youngtown AZ, *6156* 249 A1
Youngwood PA, *3050* 92 A4
Yountville CA, *2933* 36 B3
Ypsilanti MI, *19435* 90 C1
Yreka CA, *7765* 28 C2
Yuba City CA, *64925* 36 C2
Yuba Co. CA, *72155* 36 C2
Yucaipa CA, *51367* 53 D2
Yucca Valley CA, *20700* 53 E2
Yukon OK, *22709* 51 E3
Yulee FL, *11491* 139 D2
Yuma AZ, *93064* 53 F4
Yuma CO, *3524* 42 A1
Yuma Co. AZ, *195751* 54 A2
Yuma Co. CO, *10043* 34 A4
Yutan NE, *1174* 35 F3

Z

Zacata VA, *450* 103 E4
Zachary LA, *14960* 134 A1
Zanesville IN, *600* 90 A3
Zanesville OH, *25487* 101 E1
Zap ND, *237* 18 B3
Zapata TX, *5089* 63 D3
Zapata Co. TX, *14018* 63 D3
Zavala Co. TX, *11677* 60 C3
Zavalla TX, *713* 132 C1
Zearing IA, *554* 87 D1
Zeb OK, *497* 106 B4
Zebulon GA, *1174* 128 C1
Zebulon KY, *700* 111 E1
Zebulon NC, *4433* 113 D4
Zeeland MI, *5504* 75 F3
Zeigler IL, *1801* 98 C4
Zelienople PA, *3812* 92 A3
Zephyr Cove NV, *565* 37 D2
Zephyrhills FL, *13288* 140 C2
Zia Pueblo NM, *737* 48 C3
Ziebach Co. SD, *2801* 26 B2
Zillah WA, *2964* 13 E4
Zimmerman MN, *5228* 66 C3
Zion IL, *24413* 75 D4
Zion KY, *550* 109 E1
Zion PA, *2030* 92 C3
Zion Crossroads VA, 375 ..... 102 C4
Zionsville IN, *14160* 99 F1
Zolfo Sprs. FL, *1827* 140 C3
Zumbrota MN, *3252* 73 D1
Zuni Pueblo NM, *6302* 48 A3
Zwolle LA, *1759* 125 D4

PUERTO RICO

Aceitunas PR, *1436* 187 D1
Adjuntas PR, *4406* 187 D1
Aguada PR, *3212* 187 D1
Aguadilla PR, *13310* 187 D1
Aguas Buenas PR, *4204* 187 E1
Aguilita PR, *4747* 187 E1
Aibonito PR, *8249* 187 E1
Añasco PR, *5075* 187 D1
Arecibo PR, *44191* 187 E1
Arroyo PR, *6396* 187 E1
Bajadero PR, *3710* 187 E1
Barceloneta PR, *3785* 187 E1
Barranquitas PR, *2695* 187 E1
Bayamón PR, *185996* 187 E1
Betances PR, *876* 187 D1
Boquerón PR, *1218* 187 D1
Cabo Rojo PR, *9803* 187 D1
Caguas PR, *82243* 187 E1
Camuy PR, *3704* 187 D1
Canóvanas PR, *7297* 187 F1
Carolina PR, *157832* 187 F1
Cataño PR, *28140* 187 E1
Cayey PR, *16680* 187 E1
Cayuco PR, *1120* 187 D1
Ceiba PR, *5633* 187 F1
Ceiba PR, *3698* 187 E1
Ciales PR, *2591* 187 E1
Cidra PR, *5109* 187 E1
Coamo PR, *11522* 187 E1
Coco PR, *5758* 187 E1
Comerío PR, *4020* 187 E1
Comunas PR, *1900* 187 F1
Coquí PR, *3293* 187 E1
Corazón PR, *2131* 187 E1
Corozal PR, *10160* 187 E1
Coto Norte PR, *1604* 187 E1
Daguao PR, *1604* 187 F1
Dorado PR, *13258* 187 E1
Duque PR, *1320* 187 F1
El Mangó PR, *1482* 187 F1
Esperanza PR, *1219* 187 F1
Fajardo PR, *28930* 187 F1
Florida PR, *4711* 187 E1
Guánica PR, *7254* 187 D1
Guayabal PR, *2036* 187 E1
Guayama PR, *22691* 187 E1
Guayanilla PR, *3949* 187 D1
Guaynabo PR, *75443* 187 E1
Gurabo PR, *7609* 187 F1
Hatillo PR, *4439* 187 D1
Hormigueros PR, *12443* 187 D1
Humacao PR, *18629* 187 F1
Isabela PR, *11255* 187 D1
Jagual PR, *1062* 187 E1
Jayuya PR, *2759* 187 E1
Jobos PR, *2479* 187 E1
Juana Diaz PR, *7916* 187 E1
Juncos PR, *7564* 187 F1
La Parguera PR, *1044* 187 D1
La Plena PR, *865* 187 E1
Lajas PR, *4586* 187 D1
Lares PR, *4917* 187 D1
Las Marías PR, *2049* 187 D1
Las Marías PR, *998* 187 D1
Las Piedras PR, *5883* 187 F1
Levittown PR, *26960* 187 E1
Loíza PR, *3875* 187 F1
Los Llanos PR, *2118* 187 E1
Luquillo PR, *7761* 187 F1
Manatí PR, *14011* 187 E1
Maricao PR, *868* 187 D1
Maunabo PR, *1668* 187 F1
Mayagüez PR, *70463* 187 D1
Moca PR, *3861* 187 D1
Mora PR, *1583* 187 D1
Morovis PR, *2032* 187 E1
Naguabo PR, *4443* 187 F1
Naranjito PR, *1655* 187 E1
Orocovis PR, *722* 187 E1
Palmarejo PR, *1087* 187 D1
Palomas PR, *1742* 187 D1
Patillas PR, *4333* 187 E1
Peñuelas PR, *5859* 187 D1
Playita PR, *2192* 187 F1
Pole Ojea PR, *1695* 187 D1
Ponce PR, *132502* 187 E1
Potala Pastillo PR, *3092* 187 E1
Puerto Real PR, *5983* 187 D1
Punta Santiago PR, *4964* 187 F1
Quebrada PR, *995* 187 D1
Quebradillas PR, *5282* 187 D1
Rafael Capó PR, *1700* 187 D1
Rincón PR, *1456* 187 D1
Río Grande PR, *12677* 187 F1
Sabana Eneas PR, *1576* 187 D1
Sabana Grande PR, *8179* 187 D1
Sabana Hoyos PR, *1783* 187 E1
Salinas PR, *4771* 187 E1
San Antonio PR, *7574* 187 E1
San Antonio PR, *2300* 187 D1
San Germán PR, *10989* 187 D1
San Isidro PR, *6828* 187 F1
San Juan PR, *381931* 187 E1
San Lorenzo PR, *8037* 187 F1
San Sebastián PR, *9622* 187 D1
Santa Isabel PR, *5976* 187 E1
Santo Domingo PR, *3156* 187 D1
Tallaboa PR, *925* 187 D1
Toa Alta PR, *3713* 187 E1
Trujillo Alto PR, *48437* 187 E1
Utuado PR, *8397* 187 E1
Vázquez PR, *1890* 187 E1
Vega Alta PR, *10266* 187 E1
Vega Baja PR, *25905* 187 E1
Vieques PR, *3316* 187 F1
Villalba PR, *3384* 187 E1
Yabucoa PR, *6047* 187 F1
Yauco PR, *17186* 187 D1
Yaurel PR, *1050* 187 E1

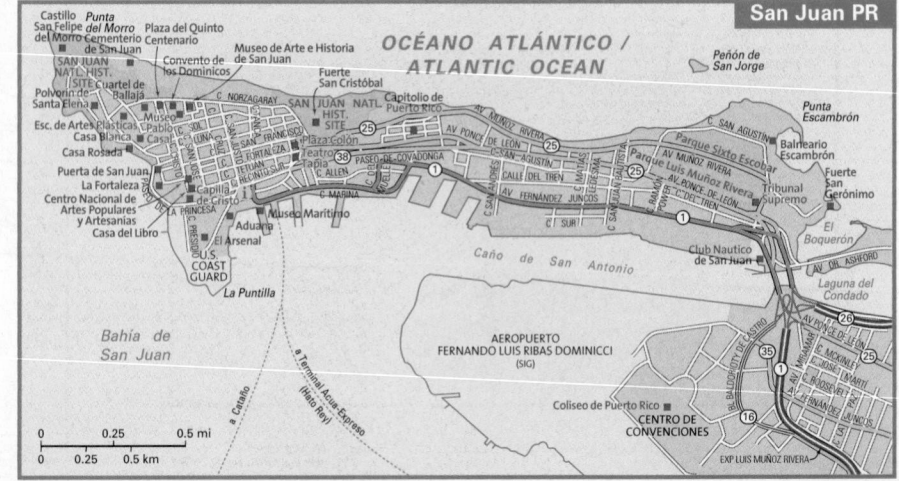

Entries in **bold color** indicate cities with detailed inset maps.

CANADA

Abbotsford BC, 115463 ... 163 D3
Aberdeen SK, 534 ... 165 F1
Acton ON, 7767 ... 172 C2
Acton Vale QC, 7299 ... 175 D3
Adstock QC, 1629 ... 175 E2
Airdrie AB, 20382 ... 164 C2
Air Ronge SK, 955 ... 160 B3
Beauharnois QC, 6387 ... 174 C3
Beaumont AB, 7006 ... 159 D4
Beaumont QC, 2153 ... 175 E1
Beaupré QC, 2761 ... 175 E1
Beausejour MB, 2772 ... 167 F3
Beauval SK, 843 ... 159 F2
Beaverlodge AB, 2110 ... 157 F1
Beaverton ON, 3065 ... 173 D1
Bécancour QC, 11051 ... 175 D2
Blanc-Sablon QC, 1201 ... 183 D1
Blenheim ON, 4795 ... 172 B4
Blind Bay BC, 2464 ... 163 F1
Blind River ON, 3969 ... 170 B3
Blue Mts. ON, 6116 ... 172 C1
Bluewater ON, 6919 ... 172 B2
Blyth ON, 987 ... 172 B2
Bobcaygeon ON, 2854 ... 173 E1
Bois-Blanc NB, 857 ... 179 D2

Ajax ON, 73753 ... 173 D2
Aklavik NT, 632 ... 155 D1
Alban ON, 1084 ... 170 C3
Albanel QC, 2455 ... 176 B3
Alberta Beach AB, 762 ... 158 C4
Alberton PE, 1115 ... 179 E3
Aldergrove BC, 11910 ... 163 D3
Alexandria ON, 3369 ... 174 B3
Alfred ON, 1348 ... 174 B3
Alix AB, 825 ... 164 C2
Allan SK, 679 ... 165 F2
Alliston ON, 9679 ... 172 C1
Alma QC, 25918 ... 176 C3
Almonte ON, 4659 ... 174 A3
Altona MB, 3434 ... 167 E4
Amherst NS, 9470 ... 180 C1
Amherstburg ON, 20339 ... 172 A4
Amos QC, 13044 ... 171 E1
Amqui QC, 6473 ... 178 B1
Ange-Gardien QC, 1994 ... 175 D3
Angus ON, 9722 ... 172 C1
Annapolis Royal NS, 550 ... 180 B3
Antigonish NS, 4754 ... 181 E1
Arborg MB, 959 ... 167 E3
Arcola SK, 532 ... 166 C4
Armagh QC, 1603 ... 175 F1
Armstrong BC, 4256 ... 164 A3
Arnold's Cove NL, 1024 ... 183 E4
Arnprior ON, 7192 ... 174 A3
Arthur ON, 2284 ... 172 C2
Asbestos QC, 6580 ... 175 E3
Ascot Corner QC, 2342 ... 175 E3
Ashcroft BC, 1788 ... 163 E1
Asquith SK, 574 ... 165 F2
Assiniboia SK, 2483 ... 166 A4
Athabasca AB, 2415 ... 159 D3
Athens ON, 1026 ... 174 A4
Atholville NB, 1381 ... 178 C2
Atikokan ON, 3560 ... 168 C4
Aurora ON, 40167 ... 173 D2
Austin QC, 1201 ... 175 D3
Avondale NL, 701 ... 183 E4
Ayer's Cliff QC, 1102 ... 175 D3
Aylesford NS, 807 ... 180 C2
Aylmer ON, 7126 ... 172 C3
Aylmer QC, 36085 ... 174 B3
Ayr ON, 3636 ... 172 C3
Baddeck NS, 907 ... 181 F1
Badger NL, 906 ... 183 D3
Baie-Comeau QC, 23079 ... 177 D2
Baie-du-Febvre QC, 1135 ... 175 D2
Baie-Ste-Anne NB, 1600 ... 179 D3
Baie-St-Paul QC, 7290 ... 176 C4
Baie Verte NL, 1492 ... 183 D2
Balcarres SK, 622 ... 166 B3
Balgonie SK, 1239 ... 166 B3
Balmoral NB, 1836 ... 178 C2
Bancroft ON, 4089 ... 171 E4
Banff AB, 7135 ... 164 B3
Barraute QC, 2010 ... 171 E2
Barrhead AB, 4213 ... 158 C3
Barrie ON, 103710 ... 173 D1
Barry's Bay ON, 1259 ... 171 E4
Bas-Caraquet NB, 1689 ... 179 D2
Bashaw AB, 825 ... 164 C1
Bassano AB, 1320 ... 165 D3
Bathurst NB, 12924 ... 179 D2
Battleford SK, 3820 ... 159 F4
Bay Bulls NL, 1014 ... 183 F4
Bayfield ON, 909 ... 172 B2
Bay Roberts NL, 5237 ... 183 E4
Beachburg ON, 870 ... 174 A3
Beamsville ON, 9047 ... 173 D3
Beauceville QC, 6261 ... 175 E2
Bedford NS ... 181 D3
Bedford QC, 2667 ... 175 D4
Beechville NS, 2312 ... 181 D3
Beeton ON, 3822 ... 173 D2
Behchokò NT, 1894 ... 155 F2
Beiseker AB, 838 ... 164 C2
Bella Bella BC, 1253 ... 156 C4
Belledune NB, 1923 ... 178 C2
Bellefeuille QC, 14066 ... 174 C3
Belleville ON, 45986 ... 173 E1
Belmont ON, 1819 ... 172 B3
Beloeil QC, 19053 ... 175 D3
Benito MB, 415 ... 166 C2
Bentley AB, 1035 ... 164 C2
Beresford NB, 4414 ... 179 D2
Berthierville QC, 3939 ... 175 D2
Bertrand NB, 1269 ... 179 D2
Berwick NS, 2282 ... 180 C2
Betsiamites QC, 1625 ... 178 A1
Bible Hill NS, 5741 ... 181 D2
Bienfait SK, 786 ... 166 C4
Biggar SK, 2243 ... 165 F2
Big River SK, 741 ... 159 F3
Binscarth MB, 445 ... 166 C3
Birch Hills SK, 957 ... 160 B4
Birchy Bay NL, 612 ... 183 E2
Birtle MB, 715 ... 167 D3
Bishop's Falls NL, 3688 ... 183 D3
Black Diamond AB, 1866 ... 164 C3
Blackfalds AB, 3042 ... 164 C2
Black Lake QC, 4109 ... 175 E2
Blacks Hbr. NB, 1082 ... 180 A2
Blackville NB, 1015 ... 179 D3
Blaine Lake SK, 508 ... 160 B4
Blainville QC, 36029 ... 174 C3
Blairmore AB, 1993 ... 164 C4
Boischatel QC, 4303 ... 175 E1
Boissevain MB, 1495 ... 167 D4
Bolton ON, 20553 ... 173 D2
Bon Accord AB, 1532 ... 159 D4
Bonaventure QC, 2756 ... 179 D2
Bonavista NL, 4021 ... 183 E3
Bonnyville AB, 5709 ... 159 E3
Borden-Carleton PE, 798 ... 179 E4
Bothwell ON, 1002 ... 172 B3
Botwood NL, 3221 ... 183 D2
Bouctouche NB, 2426 ... 179 D4
Bourget ON, 1005 ... 174 B3
Bowden AB, 1174 ... 164 C2
Bowen Island BC, 2957 ... 163 D3
Bow Island AB, 1704 ... 165 D4
Bowmanville ON, 32556 ... 173 D2
Bowser BC, 1307 ... 162 C3
Bowsman MB, 320 ... 166 C2
Boyle AB, 836 ... 159 D3
Bracebridge ON, 13751 ... 171 D4
Bradford ON, 16978 ... 173 D2
Bradford-W. Gwillimbury ON, 22228 ... 173 D1
Bragg Creek AB, 678 ... 164 C3
Brampton ON, 325428 ... 173 D2
Brandon MB, 39716 ... 167 D4
Brant ON, 31669 ... 172 C3
Brantford ON, 86417 ... 172 C3
Brantville NB, 1153 ... 179 D3
Bridgenorth ON, 2279 ... 173 E1
Bridgetown NS, 1035 ... 180 B3
Bridgewater NS, 7621 ... 180 C3
Brigham QC, 2250 ... 175 D3
Brighton ON, 9449 ... 173 E2
Brigus NL, 784 ... 183 E4
Bristol NB, 719 ... 178 B4

Broadview SK, 669 ... 166 C3
Brochet MB, 226 ... 161 D1
Brockville ON, 21375 ... 174 B4
Bromont QC, 4808 ... 175 D3
Bromptonville QC, 5571 ... 175 E3
Brooklin ON, 5789 ... 173 D2
Brooklyn NS, 1078 ... 180 C4
Brooks AB, 11604 ... 165 D3
Brookside NS, 1286 ... 181 D3
Brownsburg-Chatham QC, 6770 ... 174 C3
Bruderheim AB, 1202 ... 159 D4
Bruno SK, 571 ... 166 B2
Brussels ON, 1143 ... 172 B2
Buchans NL, 877 ... 183 D3
Buckingham QC, 11668 ... 174 B3
Buffalo Creek BC, 701 ... 157 F4
Buffalo Lake AB, 722 ... 157 F1
Buffalo Narrows SK, 1137 ... 159 F2
Burford ON, 1841 ... 172 C3
Burgeo NL, 1782 ... 182 C4
Burin NL, 2470 ... 183 E4
Burk's Falls ON, 940 ... 171 D4
Burlington ON, 150836 ... 173 D3
Burnaby BC, 193954 ... 163 D3
Burns Lake BC, 1942 ... 157 D2
Burnt Islands NL, 801 ... 182 C4
Bury QC, 1171 ... 175 E3
Cabano QC, 3213 ... 178 A2
Cache Creek BC, 1056 ... 163 E1
Caledon ON, 50595 ... 172 C2
Caledon East ON, 1974 ... 172 C2
Caledonia ON, 8582 ... 172 C3
Caledon Vil. ON, 1651 ... 172 C2
Calgary AB, 878866 ... 164 C3
Calmar AB, 1902 ... 159 D4
Cambridge NS, 723 ... 180 C2
Cambridge ON, 110372 ... 172 C3
Cambridge-Narrows NB, 654 ... 180 B1
Campbellford ON, 3675 ... 173 E1
Campbell River BC, 28456 ... 162 B2
Campbellton NB, 7798 ... 178 C2
Camperville MB, 524 ... 167 D2
Camrose AB, 14854 ... 159 D4
Canal Flats BC, 709 ... 164 B3
Candle Lake SK, 503 ... 160 B4
Canmore AB, 10792 ... 164 B3
Canning NS, 811 ... 180 C2
Cannington ON, 2007 ... 173 D1
Canora SK, 2200 ... 166 C2
Canso NS, 992 ... 181 F2
Cantley QC, 5898 ... 174 B3
Cap-aux-Meules QC, 1659 ... 179 F3
Cap-Chat QC, 2913 ... 178 C1
Cap-de-la-Madeleine QC, 32534 ... 175 D2
Cape Breton Reg. Mun. NS, 105968 ... 181 F1
Cape St. George NL, 926 ... 182 C3
Caplan QC, 2010 ... 179 D2
Cap-Pele NB, 2266 ... 179 E4
Capreol ON, 3471 ... 170 C3
Cap-St-Ignace QC, 3204 ... 175 F1
Cap-Santé QC, 2571 ... 175 E1
Caraquet NB, 4442 ... 179 D2
Carberry MB, 1513 ... 167 D4
Carbonear NL, 4759 ... 183 E4
Cardigan PE, 382 ... 179 F4
Cardinal ON, 1739 ... 174 B4
Cardston AB, 3475 ... 164 C4
Carleton Place ON, 9083 ... 174 A3
Carleton-St-Omer QC, 4010 ... 178 C2
Carlisle ON, 2180 ... 172 C2
Carlyle SK, 1260 ... 166 C4
Carmacks YT, 431 ... 155 D3
Carman MB, 2831 ... 167 E4
Carmanville NL, 798 ... 183 E2
Carnduff SK, 1017 ... 166 C4
Caronport SK, 1040 ... 166 A3
Carrot River SK, 1017 ... 160 C4
Carseland AB, 662 ... 164 C3
Carstairs AB, 2254 ... 164 C2
Cartwright MB, 304 ... 167 D4
Cartwright NL, 629 ... 183 F1
Casselman ON, 2910 ... 174 B3
Cassidy BC, 978 ... 162 C3
Castlegar BC, 7002 ... 164 A4
Castor AB, 935 ... 165 D2
Catalina NL, 995 ... 183 E3
Causapscal QC, 2634 ... 178 B1
Cavendish PE, 267 ... 179 E4
Cawston BC, 1013 ... 163 F3
Cayuga ON, 1643 ... 172 C3
Cedar BC, 4440 ... 162 C3
Central Saanich BC, 15348 ... 163 D4
Centreville NS, 1047 ... 180 C2
Centreville-Wareham-Trinity NL, 1146 ... 183 E3
Chalk River ON, 975 ... 171 E3
Chambly QC, 20342 ... 175 D3
Chambord QC, 1693 ... 176 B3
Champlain QC, 1623 ... 175 D2
Chandler QC, 2817 ... 179 D1
Channel-Port aux-Basques NL, 4637 ... 182 C4
Chapais QC, 1795 ... 176 A2
Chapleau ON, 2832 ... 170 B2
Charlesbourg QC, 70310 ... 175 E1
Charlie Lake BC, 1727 ... 158 A2
Charlo NB, 1449 ... 178 C2
Charlottetown PE, 32245 ... 179 E4
Charny QC, 10507 ... 175 E1
Chase BC, 2460 ... 163 F1
Châteauguay QC, 41003 ... 174 C3
Château-Richer QC, 3442 ... 175 E1
Chatham ON, 44156 ... 172 B4
Chatham-Kent ON, 107341 ... 172 A4
Chemainus BC, 2706 ... 162 C3
Chertsey QC, 4112 ... 174 C2
Chesley ON, 1880 ... 172 B1
Chester NS, 1590 ... 180 C3
Chestermere AB, 3414 ... 164 C3
Chesterville ON, 1498 ... 174 B4
Chéticamp NS ... 181 E3
Chetwynd BC, 2591 ... 157 E1
Chibougamau QC, 7922 ... 176 A2
Chicoutimi QC, 60008 ... 176 C3
Chilliwack BC, 62927 ... 163 E3
Chipman NB, 1432 ... 178 C4
Christina Lake BC, 1035 ... 164 A4
Churchbridge SK, 796 ... 166 C3
Chute-aux-Outardes QC, 1968 ... 177 D2
Clair NB, 863 ... 178 A3
Clairmont AB, 1481 ... 157 F1
Clarence-Rockland ON, 19612 ... 174 B3
Clarenville NL, 5104 ... 183 E3
Claresholm AB, 3622 ... 164 C4
Clarington ON, 69834 ... 173 D2
Clarke's Beach NL, 1257 ... 183 E4
Clark's Hbr. NS, 944 ... 180 B4
Clermont QC, 3078 ... 176 C4
Clinton ON, 3117 ... 172 B2

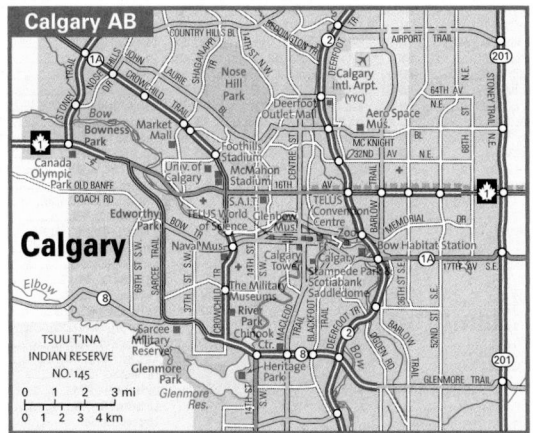

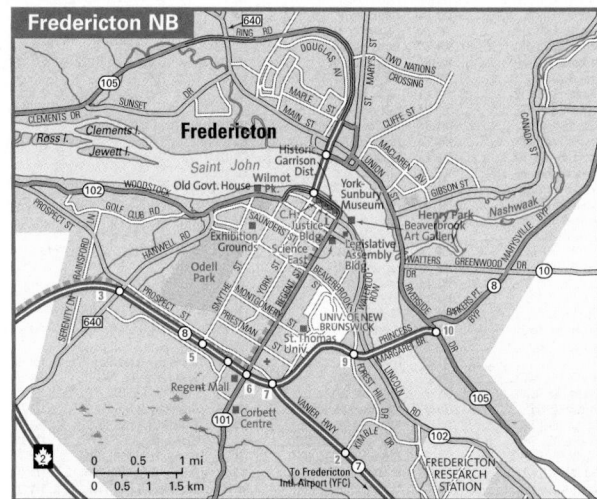

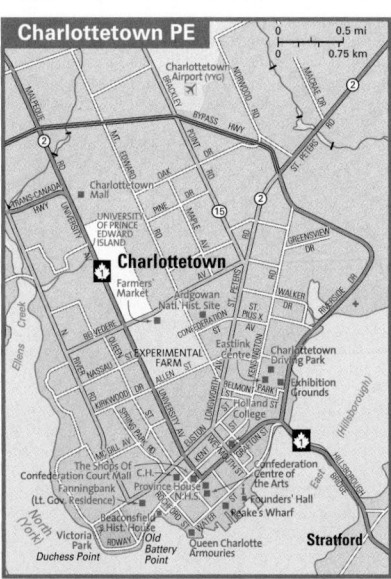

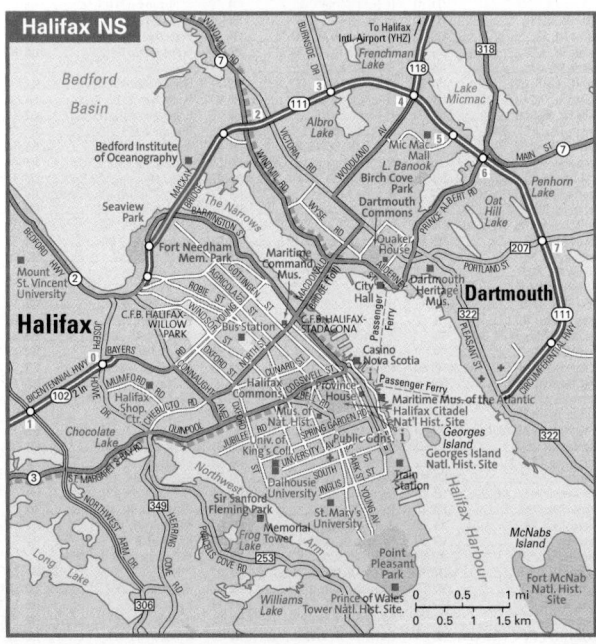

278
Clyde River – L'Islet

Figures after entries indicate population, page number, and grid reference.

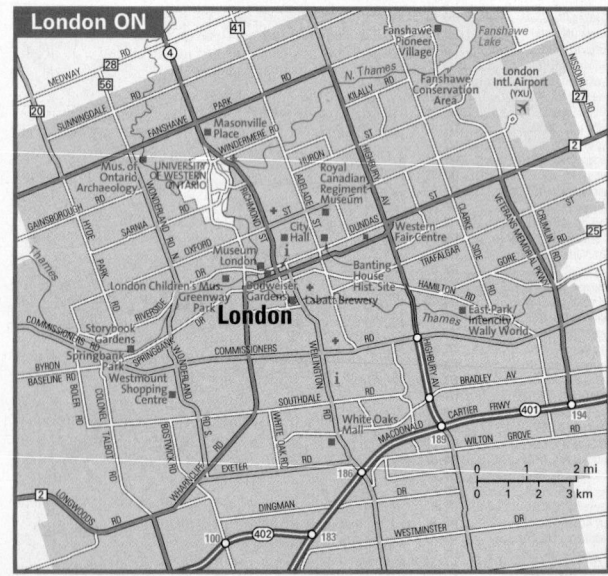

Entries in **bold color** indicate cities with detailed inset maps.

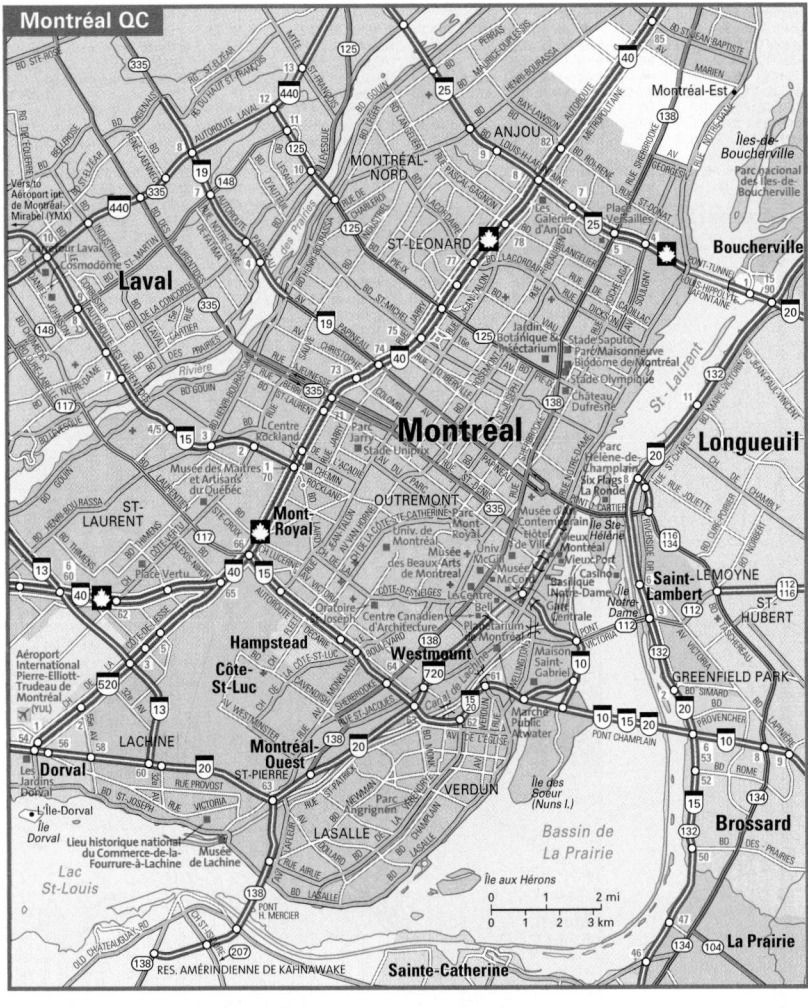

Montréal QC

Ottawa ON

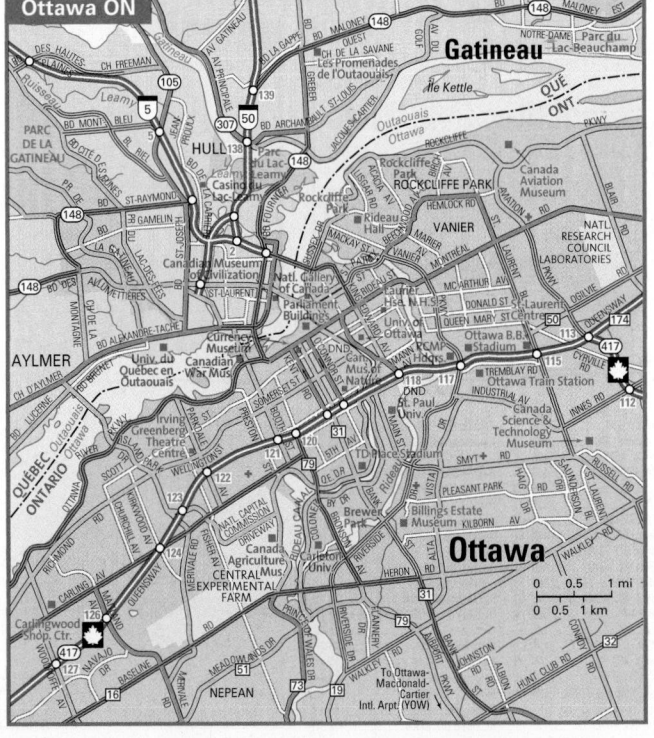

Figures after entries indicate population, page number, and grid reference.

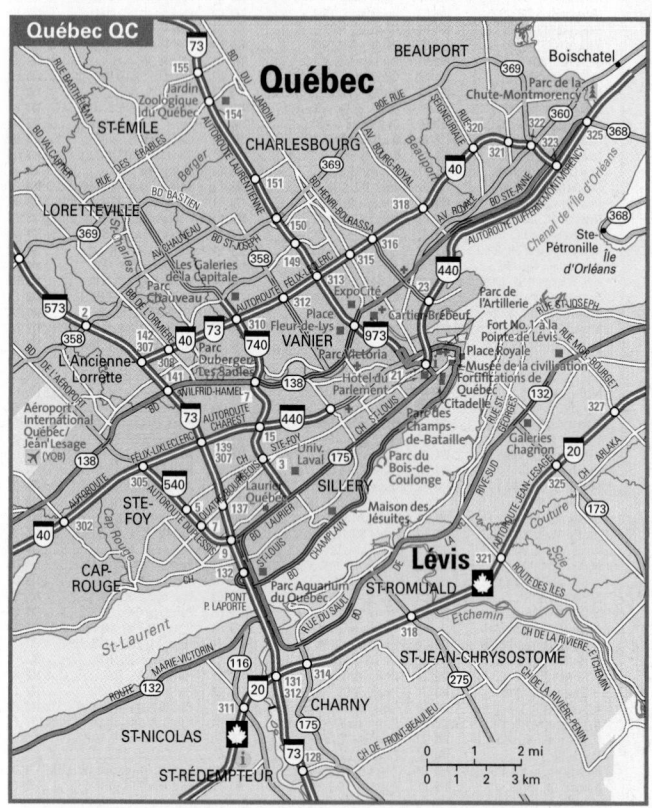

Québec QC

Québec

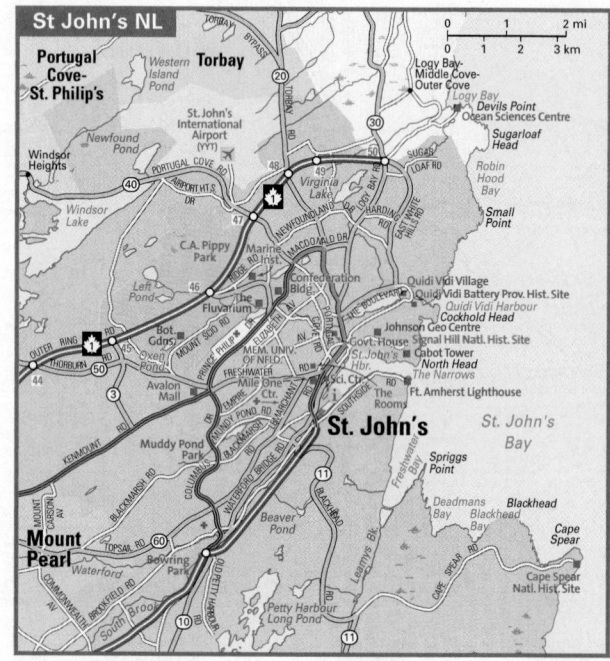

St John's NL

Regina SK

Regina

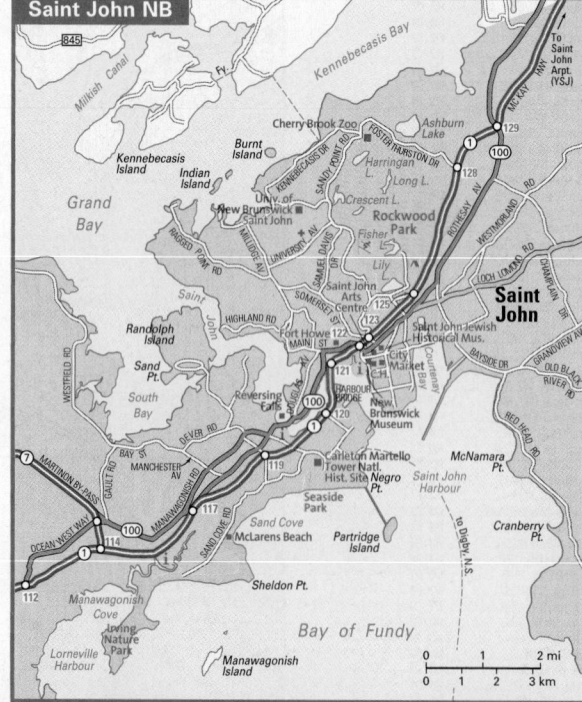

Saint John NB

Saskatoon SK

Saskatoon

Entries in **bold color** indicate cities with detailed inset maps.

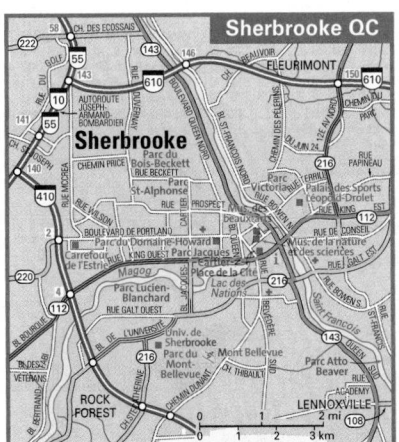

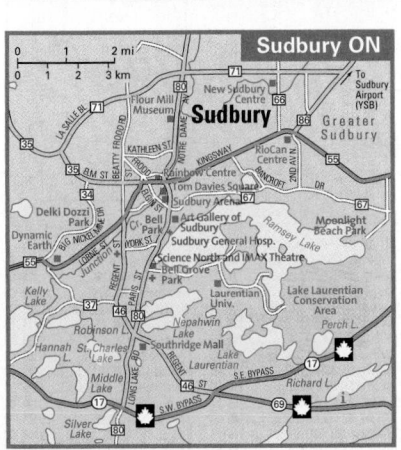

Downtown Toronto ON

Figures after entries indicate population, page number, and grid reference.

Vancouver BC

Victoria BC

Winnipeg MB

Entries in **bold color** indicate cities with detailed inset maps.

México MX

Cancún MX

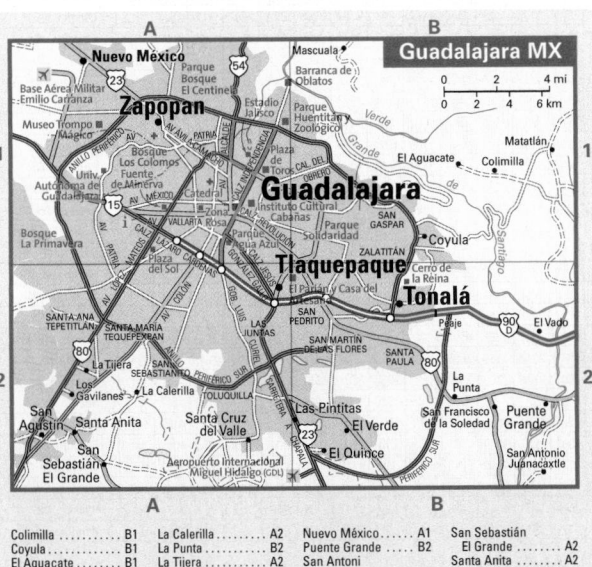

Guadalajara MX

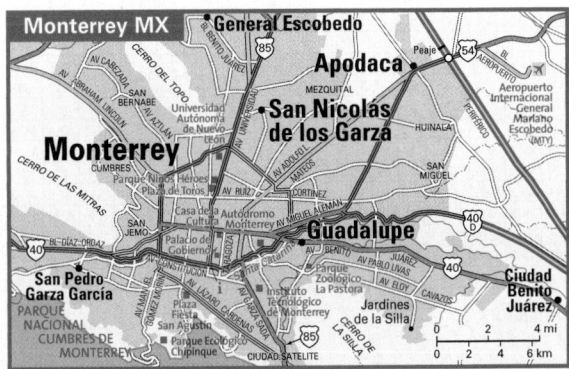

Monterrey MX

City to City Distance Chart

Miles

	Albuquerque, NM	Amarillo, TX	Anchorage, AK	Atlanta, GA	Baltimore, MD	Billings, MT	Birmingham, AL	Bismarck, ND	Boise, ID	Boston, MA	Buffalo, NY	Calgary, AB	Charleston, SC	Charleston, WV	Charlotte, NC	Cheyenne, WY	Chicago, IL	Cincinnati, OH	Cleveland, OH	Columbus, OH	Dallas, TX	Denver, CO	Des Moines, IA	Detroit, MI	El Paso, TX	Halifax, NS	Houston, TX	Indianapolis, IN	Jackson, MS	Jacksonville, FL	Kansas City, MO	Las Vegas, NV	Little Rock, AR	Los Angeles, CA	Louisville, KY
Albany, NY	2095	1811	4421	1010	333	2083	1093	1675	2526	172	292	2512	913	634	771	1789	832	730	484	621	1680	1833	1155	571	2326	877	1768	795	1331	1094	1282	2586	1354	2859	832
Albuquerque, NM		286	3563	1490	1902	991	1274	1333	966	2240	1808	1498	1793	1568	1649	538	1352	1409	1619	1476	754	438	1091	1608	263	2945	994	1298	1157	1837	894	578	900	806	1320
Amarillo, TX			3734	1206	1618	988	991	1398	1266	1957	1524	1669	1510	1285	1365	534	1069	1126	1335	1192	470	434	808	1324	438	2662	711	1014	874	1517	610	864	617	1092	1036
Anchorage, AK				4304	4297	2601	4253	2724	2745	4592	4133	2065	4495	4093	4348	3056	3584	3890	3935	3946	4087	3300	3421	3872	4002	4821	4328	3771	4294	4652	3547	3356	3929	3403	3886
Atlanta, GA					679	1889	150	1559	2218	1100	910	2395	317	503	238	1482	717	476	726	577	792	1403	967	735	1437	1805	800	531	386	344	801	2067	528	2237	419
Baltimore, MD						1959	795	1551	2401	422	370	2388	583	352	441	1665	708	521	377	420	1399	1690	1031	532	2045	1128	1470	600	1032	763	1087	2445	1072	2705	602
Billings, MT							1839	413	626	2254	1796	536	2157	1755	2012	455	1246	1552	1597	1608	1433	554	1007	1534	1255	2806	1673	1432	1836	2237	1088	965	1530	1239	1547
Birmingham, AL								1509	2170	1215	909	2346	466	578	389	1434	667	475	725	576	647	1356	919	734	1292	1921	678	481	241	494	753	1852	381	2092	369
Bismarck, ND									1039	1846	1388	794	1749	1347	1604	594	838	1144	1189	1200	1342	693	675	1126	1597	2398	1582	1024	1548	1906	801	1378	1183	1702	1139
Boise, ID										2697	2239	735	2520	2182	2375	737	1708	1969	2040	2036	1711	833	1369	1977	1206	3249	1952	1852	2115	2566	1376	760	1808	1033	1933
Boston, MA											462	2683	1003	741	861	1961	1003	862	654	760	1819	2004	1326	741	2465	714	1890	940	1453	1184	1427	2757	1493	3046	964
Buffalo, NY												2224	899	431	695	1502	545	442	197	333	1393	1546	868	277	2039	1167	1513	508	1134	1080	995	2299	1066	2572	545
Calgary, AB													2586	2184	2441	991	1675	1981	2026	2037	2114	1234	1512	1963	1936	2912	2355	1862	2385	2743	1638	1291	2020	1565	1977
Charleston, SC														468	204	1783	907	622	724	637	1109	1705	1204	879	1754	1708	1110	721	703	238	1102	2371	900	2554	610
Charleston, WV															265	1445	506	209	255	168	1072	1367	802	410	1718	1446	1192	320	816	649	764	2122	745	2374	251
Charlotte, NC																1637	761	476	520	433	1031	1559	1057	675	1677	1566	1041	575	625	385	956	2225	754	2453	464
Cheyenne, WY																	972	1233	1304	1300	979	100	633	1241	801	2513	1220	1115	1382	1829	640	843	1076	1116	1197
Chicago, IL																		302	346	359	936	1015	337	283	1543	1555	1108	184	750	1065	532	1768	662	2042	299
Cincinnati, OH																			253	105	958	1200	599	261	1605	1567	1079	116	700	803	597	1955	632	2215	106
Cleveland, OH																				144	1208	1347	669	171	1854	1359	1328	319	950	904	806	2100	882	2374	356
Columbus, OH																					1059	1266	665	192	1706	1465	1179	176	801	818	663	2021	733	2281	207
Dallas, TX																						887	752	1218	647	2524	241	913	406	1049	554	1331	327	1446	852
Denver, CO																							676	1284	701	2556	1127	1088	1290	1751	603	756	984	1029	1118
Des Moines, IA																								606	1283	1878	992	481	931	1315	194	1429	567	1703	595
Detroit, MI																									1799	1278	1338	318	960	1060	795	2037	891	2310	366
El Paso, TX																										3171	758	1489	1051	1642	1085	717	974	801	1499
Halifax, NS																											2595	1646	2158	1889	2133	3309	2198	3583	1669
Houston, TX																												839	445	884	795	1474	447	1558	972
Indianapolis, IN																													675	879	485	1843	587	2104	112
Jackson, MS																														598	747	1735	269	1851	594
Jacksonville, FL																															1148	2415	873	2441	766
Kansas City, MO																																1358	382	1632	516
Las Vegas, NV																																	1478	274	1874
Little Rock, AR																																		1706	526
Los Angeles, CA																																			2126

Kilometers

	Albany, NY	Albuquerque, NM	Amarillo, TX	Anchorage, AK	Atlanta, GA	Baltimore, MD	Billings, MT	Birmingham, AL	Bismarck, ND	Boise, ID	Boston, MA	Buffalo, NY	Calgary, AB	Charleston, SC	Charleston, WV	Charlotte, NC	Cheyenne, WY	Chicago, IL	Cincinnati, OH	Cleveland, OH	Columbus, OH	Dallas, TX	Denver, CO	Des Moines, IA	Detroit, MI	El Paso, TX	Halifax, NS	Houston, TX	Indianapolis, IN	Jackson, MS	Jacksonville, FL	Kansas City, MO	Las Vegas, NV	Little Rock, AR	Los Angeles, CA	Louisville, KY
Albuquerque, NM	3371																																			
Amarillo, TX	2914	460																																		
Anchorage, AK	7113	5733	6008																																	
Atlanta, GA	1625	2397	1940	6925																																
Baltimore, MD	536	3060	2603	6914	1093																															
Billings, MT	3352	1595	1590	4185	3039	3152																														
Birmingham, AL	1759	2050	1595	6843	241	1279	2959																													
Bismarck, ND	2695	2145	2249	4383	2508	2496	665	2428																												
Boise, ID	4064	1554	2037	4417	3569	3863	1007	3492	1672																											
Boston, MA	277	3604	3149	7389	1770	679	3627	1955	2970	4339																										
Buffalo, NY	470	2909	2452	6650	1464	595	2890	1463	2233	3603	743																									
Calgary, AB	4042	2410	2685	3323	3854	3842	862	3775	1278	1183	4317	3578																								
Charleston, SC	1469	2885	2430	7232	510	938	3471	750	2814	4055	1614	1446	4161																							
Charleston, WV	1020	2523	2068	6586	809	566	2824	930	2167	3511	1192	693	3514	753																						
Charlotte, NC	1241	2653	2196	6996	383	710	3237	626	2581	3821	1385	1118	3928	328	426																					
Cheyenne, WY	2879	866	859	4917	2385	2679	732	2307	956	1186	3155	2417	1595	2869	2325	2634																				
Chicago, IL	1339	2175	1720	5767	1154	1139	2005	1073	1348	2748	1614	877	2695	1459	814	1224	1564																			
Cincinnati, OH	1175	2267	1812	6259	766	838	2497	764	1841	3168	1387	711	3187	1001	336	766	1984	486																		
Cleveland, OH	779	2605	2148	6331	1168	607	2570	1167	1913	3282	1052	317	3260	1165	410	837	2098	557	407																	
Columbus, OH	999	2375	1918	6349	928	676	2587	927	1931	3276	1223	536	3278	1025	270	697	2092	578	169	232																
Dallas, TX	2703	1213	756	6576	1274	2251	2306	1041	2159	2753	2927	2241	3401	1784	1725	1659	1575	1506	1541	1944	1704															
Denver, CO	2949	705	698	5310	2257	2719	891	2182	1115	1340	3224	2488	1986	2743	2200	2508	161	1633	1931	2167	2037	1427														
Des Moines, IA	1858	1755	1300	5504	1556	1659	1620	1479	1086	2203	2134	1397	2433	1937	1290	1701	1018	542	964	1076	1070	1210	1088													
Detroit, MI	919	2587	2130	6230	1183	856	2468	1181	1812	3181	1192	446	3158	1414	660	1086	1997	455	420	275	309	1960	2066	975												
El Paso, TX	3743	423	705	6439	2312	3290	2019	2079	2570	1940	3966	3281	3115	2822	2764	2698	1289	2483	2582	2983	2745	1041	1128	2064	2895											
Halifax, NS	1411	4739	4283	7757	2904	1815	4515	3091	3858	5228	1149	1878	4685	2748	2327	2520	4043	2502	2521	2187	2357	4061	4113	3022	2056	5102										
Houston, TX	2845	1599	1144	6964	1287	2365	2692	1091	2545	3141	3041	2434	3789	1786	1918	1675	1963	1783	1736	2137	1897	388	1813	1596	2153	1220	4175									
Indianapolis, IN	1279	2088	1632	6068	854	965	2304	774	1648	2980	1512	817	2996	1160	515	925	1794	296	187	513	283	1469	1751	774	512	2396	2648	1350								
Jackson, MS	2142	1862	1406	6909	621	1660	2954	388	2491	3403	2338	1825	3837	1131	1313	1006	2224	1207	1126	1529	1289	653	2076	1498	1545	1691	3472	716	1086							
Jacksonville, FL	1760	2956	2441	7485	553	1228	3599	795	3067	4129	1905	1738	4413	383	1044	619	2943	1714	1292	1455	1316	1688	2817	2116	1706	2642	3039	1422	1414	962						
Kansas City, MO	2063	1438	981	5707	1289	1749	1751	1212	1289	2214	2296	1601	2636	1773	1229	1538	1030	856	961	1297	1067	891	970	312	1279	1746	3432	1279	780	1202	1847					
Las Vegas, NV	4161	930	1390	5400	3326	3934	1553	2980	2217	1223	4436	3699	2077	3815	3414	3580	1356	2845	3146	3379	3252	2142	1216	2299	3278	1154	5324	2372	2965	2792	3886	2185				
Little Rock, AR	2179	1448	993	6322	850	1725	2462	613	1903	2909	2402	1715	3250	1448	1199	1213	1731	1065	1017	1419	1179	526	1583	912	1434	1567	3537	719	944	433	1405	615	2378			
Los Angeles, CA	4600	1297	1757	5475	3599	4352	1994	3366	2739	1662	4901	4138	2518	4109	3820	3947	1796	3286	3564	3820	3670	2327	1656	2740	3717	1289	5765	2507	3385	2978	3928	2626	441	2745		
Louisville, KY	1339	2124	1667	6253	674	969	2489	594	1833	3110	1551	877	3181	981	404	747	1926	481	171	573	333	1371	1799	957	589	2412	2685	1564	180	956	1232	830	3015	846	3421	
Memphis, TN	1953	1662	1207	6570	626	1501	2615	388	2151	3144	2177	1492	3498	1223	975	988	1958	867	793	1194	956	750	1796	1158	1210	1789	3311	943	747	339	1179	862	2592	225	2959	621
México, MX	4520	2352	2051	8061	2821	3899	3641	2624	3952	3985	4574	4058	4737	3319	3541	3208	2911	3421	3360	3760	3522	1815	2750	3002	3776	1926	5709	1535	3287	2249	2956	2684	2846	2344	2981	3187
Miami, FL	2315	3467	2951	7997	1064	1784	4109	1307	3578	4639	2460	2293	4925	938	1599	1175	3455	2224	1836	2011	1871	2200	3329	2626	2254	3152	3595	1932	1924	1472	555	2359	4397	1915	4439	1744
Milwaukee, WI	1495	2294	1837	5651	1308	1295	1891	1228	1234	2813	1770	1033	2579	1614	967	1379	1628	143	640	713	730	1625	1697	608	611	2602	2658	1920	449	1344	1866	922	2909	1202	3350	634
Minneapolis, MN	2003	2154	1697	5110	1817	1804	1350	1736	693	2357	2280	1541	2039	2122	1477	1887	1418	658	1149	1223	1241	1607	1487	396	1121	2462	3168	1995	959	1852	2376	710	2698	1310	3139	1144
Mobile, AL	2162	2162	1780	7258	534	1630	3249	415	2840	3704	2306	1874	4187	1033	1347	920	2526	1485	1176	1578	1339	1028	2378	1794	1595	1981	1981	761	1186	301	660	1496	3092	735	3268	1006
Montréal, QC	370	3495	3038	6607	1997	907	3368	2074	2711	4079	504	639	3535	1842	1323	1614	2895	1353	1311	946	1167	2851	2965	1874	907	3802	1150	3044	1403	2436	2132	2187	4177	2327	4616	1480
Nashville, TN	1614	2008	1553	6534	389	1152	2652	312	2116	3179	1828	1152	3463	874	636	639	1995	763	452	854	615	1096	1870	1167	870	2137	2962	1289	462	681	948	899	2938	571	3305	282
New Orleans, LA	2317	2053	1598	7207	761	1837	3146	565	2790	3595	2515	2018	4135	1260	1490	1147	2417	1504	1319	1722	1482	845	2267	1797	1736	1799	3649	579	1329	298	895	1500	2983	732	3084	1149
New York, NY	243	3242	2785	7062	1398	309	3297	1585	2640	4008	346	644	3990	1244	829	1015	2824	1282	1023	750	861	2557	2895	1804	1001	3596	1480	2671	1150	1968	1533	1934	4106	2031	4537	1189
Oklahoma City, OK	2492	879	422	6245	1519	2179	1974	1173	1828	2423	2726	2031	3070	2008	1644	1773	1244	1298	1389	1726	1496	336	1096	879	1709	1186	3862	722	1210	985	2077	560	1809	571	2175	1245
Omaha, NE	2079	1566	1168	5409	1591	1879	1455	1514	991	1986	2354	1617	2338	2076	1532	1841	800	763	1184	1297	1290	1076	870	219	1195	1989	3242	1464	994	1504	2150	302	2082	917	2521	1133
Orlando, FL	1987	3112	2595	7641	708	1455	3754	951	3223	4283	2130	1965	4570	610	1271	845	3099	1868	1480	1681	1541	1844	2972	2270	1899	2796	3266	1577	1569	1117	227	2003	4042	1559	4084	1389
Ottawa, ON	486	3392	2936	6455	1866	842	3265	1971	2608	3977	665	536	3384	1780	1221	1483	2793	1252	1208	845	1064	2748	2862	1772	805	3701	1324	2941	1302	2333	2069	2085	4074	2224	4515	1377
Philadelphia, PA	359	3144	2689	7010	1258	167	3249	1443	2592	3961	516	666	3939	1102	730	874	2776	1236	927	703	763	2415	2806	1755	953	3455	1651	2529	1054	1826	1393	1836	4023	1891	4441	1091
Phoenix, AZ	4121	750	1212	5776	3006	3807	1929	2772	2674	1598	4354	3659	2454	3514	3274	3390	1615	2927	3018	3355	3125	1733	1455	2507	3337	695	5490	1911	2838	2385	3334	2188	459	2200	594	2874
Pittsburgh, PA	780	2687	2230	6526	1088	396	2766	1228	2109	3477	953	349	3455	1033	349	705	2293	751	470	219	306	2005	2349	1273	470	3046	2087	2198	595	1590	1323	1379	3564	1480	3984	634
Portland, ME	434	3762	3305	7546	1926	837	3784	2113	3128	4497	172	901	4475	1772	1350	1543	3313	1772	1545	1208	1381	3084	3382	2291	1348	4124	872	3199	1670	2494	2061	2454	4594	2558	5059	1709
Portland, OR	4753	2245	2727	3902	4259	4553	1430	4182	2093	695	5030	4291	1371	4743	4199	4508	1876	3438	3858	3973	3965	3443	2029	2893	3870	2843	5918	3831	3669	4093	4817	2904	1911	3599	1562	3800
Québec, QC	582	3734	3279	6846	2209	1120	3607	2314	2951	4320	624	879	3775	2055	1564	1826	3136	1595	1564	1187	1406	3091	3205	2114	1147	4043	940	3284	1644	2676	2344	2428	4417	2566	4858	1720
Raleigh, NC	1028	2867	2412	7157	637	497	3395	880	2739	4014	1173	1033	4085	449	504	254	2829	1385	840	914	776	1913	2703	1862	1165	2951	2307	1928	1028	1260	740	1733	3797	1430	4164	907
Rapid City, SD	2816	1353	1347	4795	2431	2616	610	2354	515	1496	3091	2354	1472	2935	2288	2700	491	1469	1961	2034	2051	1733	650	1012	1932	1778	3979	2121	1772	2346	2991	1142	1665	1759	2106	1955
Reno, NV	4420	1641	2101	4843	3926	4220	1545	3849	2208	692	4697	3958	2069	4410	3866	4175	1543	3105	3525	3640	3632	3110	1696	2560	3537	2116	5585	3334	3335	3760	4484	2571	711	3266	835	3467
Richmond, VA	776	3018	2563	7065	848	245	3303	1091	2647	4016	920	780	3994	689	518	465	2832	1290	853	758	832	2106	2716	1812	1009	3146	2055	2140	1031	1471	980	1746	3932	1582	4315	920
St. Louis, MO	1667	1691	1234	6113	883	1353	2158	806	1694	2619	1900	1205	3041	1368	824	1133	1435	473	563	901	671	1022	1376	702	883	1998	3036	1389	385	813	1442	405	2590	669	2986	425
Salt Lake City, UT	3578	1004	1551	4729	3083	3379	882	3006	1545	550	3854	3115	1406	3569	3025	3334	702	2262	2682	2796	2790	2269	854	1717	2695	1390	4742	2655	2492	2917	3643	1728	671	2425	1112	2624
San Antonio, TX	3142	1316	825	6833	1609	2689	2414	1413	2573	2833	3366	2679	3511	2108	2162	1997	1683	2043	1981	2383	2143	436	1522	1623	2397	895	4500	322	1908	1036	1744	1307	2047	965	2182	1810
San Diego, CA	4697	1327	1788	5673	3485	4383	2095	3252	2840	1763	4932	4235	2619	3995	3850	3870	1897	3387	3595	3921	3701	2212	1757	2841	3818	1175	5866	2393	3414	2864	3813	2727	542	2740	200	3450
San Francisco, CA	4769	1788	2248	4940	4212	4570	1892	3977	2814	1039	5044	4307	2409	4721	4216	4439	1892	3453	3873	3987	3981	2940	2045	2907	3886	1900	5932	3118	3685	3591	4541	2919	925	3237	619	3817
Seattle, WA	4664	2354	2837	3623	4352	4465	1313	4275	1977	805	4940	4203	1093	4784	4137	4549	1986	3318	3810	3883	3900	3553	2138	2932	3781	3128	5828	3940	3619	4203	4911	3012	2021	3709	1847	3804
Tampa, FL	2076	3136	2619	7664	732	1545	3778	975	3247	4307	2220	2053	4592	698	1360	935	3123	1892	1504	1772	1667	1868	2996	2294	1921	2821	3355	1601	1593	1141	315	2026	4064	1583	4108	1413
Toronto, ON	644	2962	2505	6595	1541	909	2835	1541	2179	3546	917	171	3524	1619	864	1290	2362	821	779	488	708	2319	2433	1342	375	3269	1681	2512	870	1903	1910	1654	3644	1794	4084	948
Vancouver, BC	4878	2570	3052	3430	4566	4679	1527	4491	2191	1018	5155	4417	899	4998	4352	4763	2201	3533	4024	4098	4116	3768	2354	3147	3995	3358	6043	4156	3834	4418	5126	3229	2237	3924	2077	4018
Washington, DC	594	3051	2594	6903	1023	61	3142	1220	2486	3854	737	618	3831	867	557	639	2669	1128	832	595	669	2191	2713	1649	846	3231	1873	2306	959	1603	1158	1743	3928	1667	4348	959
Wichita, KS	2367	1138	681	5921	1591	2053	1717	1348	1503	2166	2600	1905	2814	2077	1533	1842	986	1171	1263	1601	1371	591	838	628	1583	1445	3736	978	1084	1241	2151	309	2053	747	2434	1134
Winnipeg, MB	2730	2587	2285	4385	2542	2531	1324	2463	668	2336	3006	2269	1313	2850	2203	2615	1821	1384	1876	1948	1966	2193	1892	1121	1847	3010	3361	2581	1685	2526	3102	1324	3012	1939	3453	1870

Milles

	Memphis, TN	México, MX	Miami, FL	Milwaukee, WI	Minneapolis, MN	Mobile, AL	Montréal, QC	Nashville, TN	New Orleans, LA	New York, NY	Oklahoma City, OK	Omaha, NE	Orlando, FL	Ottawa, ON	Philadelphia, PA	Phoenix, AZ	Pittsburgh, PA	Portland, ME	Portland, OR	Québec, QC	Raleigh, NC	Rapid City, SD	Reno, NV	Richmond, VA	St. Louis, MO	Salt Lake City, UT	San Antonio, TX	San Diego, CA	San Francisco, CA	Seattle, WA	Tampa, FL	Toronto, ON	Vancouver, BC	Washington, DC	Wichita, KS	Winnipeg, MB
Albany, NY	1214	2809	1439	929	1245	1344	230	1003	1440	151	1549	1292	1235	302	223	2561	485	270	2954	362	639	1750	2747	482	1036	2224	1953	2919	2964	2899	1290	400	3032	369	1471	1697
Albuquerque, NM	1033	1462	2155	1426	1339	1344	2172	1248	1276	2015	546	973	1934	2108	1954	466	1670	2338	1395	2321	1782	841	1020	1876	1051	624	818	825	1111	1463	1949	1841	1597	1896	707	1608
Amarillo, TX	750	1275	1834	1142	1055	1106	1888	965	993	1731	262	726	1613	1825	1671	753	1386	2054	1695	2038	1499	837	1306	1593	767	964	513	1111	1397	1763	1628	1557	1897	1612	423	1420
Anchorage, AK	4083	5010	4970	3512	3176	4511	4106	4061	4479	4389	3881	3362	4749	4012	4357	3590	4056	4690	2425	4255	4448	2980	3010	4391	3799	2939	4247	3526	3070	2252	4763	4099	2132	4290	3680	2725
Atlanta, GA	389	1753	661	813	1129	332	1241	242	473	869	944	989	440	1160	782	1868	676	1197	2647	1373	396	1511	2440	527	549	1916	1000	2166	2618	2705	455	958	2838	636	989	1580
Baltimore, MD	933	2423	1109	805	1121	1013	564	716	1142	192	1354	1168	904	523	104	2366	246	520	2830	696	309	1626	2623	152	841	2100	1671	2724	2840	2775	960	565	2908	38	1276	1573
Billings, MT	1625	2263	2554	1175	839	2019	2093	1648	1955	2049	1227	904	2333	2029	2019	1199	1719	2352	889	2242	2110	379	960	2053	1341	548	1500	1302	1176	816	2348	1762	949	1953	1067	823
Birmingham, AL	241	1631	812	763	1079	258	1289	194	351	985	729	941	591	1225	897	1723	763	1313	2599	1438	547	1463	2392	678	501	1868	878	2021	2472	2657	606	958	2791	758	838	1531
Bismarck, ND	1337	2456	2224	767	431	1765	1685	1315	1734	1641	1136	616	2003	1621	1611	1662	1311	1944	1301	1834	1702	320	1372	1645	1053	960	1599	1765	1749	1229	2018	1354	1362	1545	934	415
Boise, ID	1954	2477	2883	1748	1465	2302	2535	1976	2234	2491	1506	1234	2662	2472	2462	993	2161	2795	432	2685	2495	930	430	2496	1628	342	1761	1096	646	500	2677	2204	633	2395	1346	1452
Boston, MA	1353	2843	1529	1100	1417	1433	313	1136	1563	215	1694	1463	1324	413	321	2706	592	107	3126	388	729	1921	2919	572	1181	2395	2092	3065	3135	3070	1380	570	3204	458	1616	1868
Buffalo, NY	927	2522	1425	642	958	1165	397	716	1254	400	1262	1005	1221	333	414	2274	217	560	2667	546	642	1463	2460	485	749	1936	1665	2632	2677	2612	1276	106	2745	384	1184	1410
Calgary, AB	2174	2944	3061	1603	1267	2602	2197	2152	2570	2480	1908	1453	2840	2103	2448	1525	2147	2781	852	2346	2539	915	1286	2482	1890	874	2182	1628	1497	679	2854	2190	559	2381	1749	816
Charleston, SC	760	2063	583	1003	1319	642	1145	543	783	773	1248	1290	379	1106	685	2184	642	1101	2948	1277	279	1824	2741	428	850	2218	1310	2483	2934	2973	434	1006	3106	539	1291	1771
Charleston, WV	606	2201	994	601	918	837	822	395	926	515	1022	952	790	759	454	2035	217	839	2610	972	313	1422	2403	322	512	1880	1344	2393	2620	2571	845	537	2705	346	953	1369
Charlotte, NC	614	1994	730	857	1173	572	1003	397	713	631	1102	1144	525	922	543	2107	438	959	2802	1135	158	1678	2595	289	704	2072	1241	2405	2759	2827	581	802	2960	397	1145	1625
Cheyenne, WY	1217	1809	2147	1012	881	1570	1799	1240	1502	1755	773	497	1926	1736	1725	1004	1425	2059	1166	1949	1758	305	959	1760	892	436	1046	1179	1176	1234	1941	1468	1368	1659	613	1132
Chicago, IL	539	2126	1382	89	409	923	841	474	935	797	807	474	1161	778	768	1819	467	1101	2137	991	861	913	1930	802	294	1406	1270	2105	2146	2062	1176	510	2196	701	728	860
Cincinnati, OH	493	2088	1141	398	714	731	815	281	820	636	863	736	920	751	576	1876	292	960	2398	972	522	1219	2191	530	350	1667	1231	2234	2407	2368	935	484	2501	517	785	1166
Cleveland, OH	742	2337	1250	443	760	981	588	531	1070	466	1073	806	1045	525	437	2085	136	751	2469	738	568	1264	2262	471	560	1738	1481	2437	2478	2413	1101	303	2547	370	995	1211
Columbus, OH	594	2189	1163	454	771	832	725	382	921	535	930	802	958	661	474	1942	190	858	2464	874	482	1275	2257	517	417	1734	1332	2300	2474	2424	1036	440	2558	416	852	1222
Dallas, TX	466	1128	1367	1010	999	639	1772	681	525	1589	209	669	1146	1708	1501	1077	1246	1917	2140	1921	1189	1077	1933	1309	635	1410	271	1375	1827	2208	1161	1441	2342	1362	367	1363
Denver, CO	1116	1709	2069	1055	924	1478	1843	1162	1409	1799	681	541	1847	1779	1744	904	1460	2102	1261	1992	1680	404	1054	1688	855	531	946	1092	1271	1329	1862	1512	1463	1686	521	1176
Des Moines, IA	720	1866	1632	378	246	1115	1165	725	1117	1121	546	136	1411	1101	1091	1558	791	1424	1798	1314	1157	629	1591	1126	436	1067	1009	1766	1807	1822	1426	834	1956	1025	390	697
Detroit, MI	752	2347	1401	380	697	991	564	541	1079	622	1062	743	1180	500	592	2074	292	838	2405	713	724	1201	2198	627	549	1675	1490	2373	2415	2350	1194	233	2483	526	984	1148
El Paso, TX	1112	1197	1959	1617	1530	1231	2363	1328	1118	2235	737	1236	1738	2300	2147	432	1893	2563	1767	2513	1834	1105	1315	1955	1242	864	556	730	1181	1944	1753	2032	2087	2008	898	1871
Halifax, NS	2058	3548	2234	1652	1969	1231	715	1841	2268	920	2400	2015	2030	823	1026	3412	1297	542	3678	584	1434	2473	3471	1277	1887	2947	2797	3646	3687	3622	2085	1045	3756	1164	2322	2089
Houston, TX	586	954	1201	1193	1240	473	1892	801	360	1660	449	910	980	1828	1572	1188	1366	1988	2381	2041	1198	1318	2072	1330	863	1650	200	1487	1938	2449	995	1561	2583	1433	608	1604
Indianapolis, IN	464	2043	1196	279	596	737	872	287	826	715	752	618	975	809	655	1764	370	1038	2280	1022	639	1101	2073	641	239	1549	1186	2122	2290	2249	990	541	2383	596	674	1047
Jackson, MS	211	1398	915	835	1151	187	1514	423	185	1223	612	935	694	1450	1135	1482	988	1550	2544	1663	783	1458	2337	914	505	1813	644	1780	2232	2612	709	1183	2746	996	771	1570
Jacksonville, FL	733	1837	345	1160	1477	410	1325	589	556	953	1291	1336	141	1286	866	2072	822	1281	2994	1457	460	1859	2787	609	896	2264	1084	2370	2822	3052	196	1187	3186	720	1337	1928
Kansas City, MO	536	1668	1466	573	441	930	1359	559	932	1202	348	188	1245	1296	1141	1360	857	1525	1805	1509	1077	710	1598	1085	252	1074	812	1695	1814	1872	1259	1028	2007	1083	192	823
Las Vegas, NV	1611	1769	2733	1808	1677	1922	2596	1826	1854	2552	1124	1294	2512	2532	2500	285	2215	2855	1188	2745	2360	1035	442	2444	1610	417	1272	337	575	1256	2526	2265	1390	2441	1276	1872
Little Rock, AR	140	1457	1190	747	814	457	1446	355	455	1262	355	570	969	1382	1175	1367	920	1590	2237	1595	889	1093	2030	983	416	1507	600	1703	2012	2305	984	1115	2439	1036	464	1205
Los Angeles, CA	1839	1853	2759	2082	1951	2031	2869	2054	1917	2820	1352	1567	2538	2806	2760	369	2476	3144	971	3019	2588	1309	519	2682	1856	691	1356	124	385	1148	2553	2538	1291	2702	1513	2146
Louisville, KY	386	1981	1084	394	711	625	920	175	714	739	774	704	863	856	678	1786	394	1062	2362	1069	564	1215	2155	572	264	1631	1125	2144	2372	2364	878	589	2497	596	705	1162
Memphis, TN		1595	1051	624	940	395	1306	215	396	1123	487	724	830	1243	1035	1500	780	1451	2382	1456	749	1247	2175	843	294	1652	739	1841	2144	2440	845	975	2574	896	597	1359
México, MX			2154	2200	2113	1426	2900	1810	1313	2619	1323	1783	1933	2838	2525	1484	2375	2941	2819	3051	2151	2365	2367	2283	1825	2135	853	1683	2233	2996	1948	2570	3139	2386	1481	2477
Miami, FL				1478	1794	727	1671	907	874	1299	1609	1654	232	1631	1211	2390	1167	1627	3312	1803	805	2176	3105	954	1214	2581	1401	2688	3140	3370	274	1532	3504	1065	1655	2246
Milwaukee, WI					337	1019	939	569	1020	894	880	514	1257	875	865	1892	564	1198	2063	1088	956	842	1970	899	367	1446	1343	2145	2186	1991	1272	607	2124	799	769	789
Minneapolis, MN						1335	1255	886	1337	1211	793	383	1573	1192	1181	1805	881	1515	1727	1405	1273	606	1839	1216	621	1315	1257	2014	2055	1654	1588	924	1788	1115	637	452
Mobile, AL							1575	450	146	1203	799	1119	506	1481	1115	1662	1019	1531	2731	1707	730	1641	2545	861	688	2000	673	1960	2411	2799	521	1214	2933	970	958	1787
Montréal, QC								1094	1632	383	1625	1300	1466	121	454	2637	607	282	2963	155	871	1758	2756	714	1112	2232	2043	2931	2972	2907	1522	330	3041	600	1547	1374
Nashville, TN									539	906	703	747	686	1031	818	1715	569	1234	2405	1244	532	1269	2198	626	307	1675	954	2056	2360	2463	701	764	2597	679	748	1337
New Orleans, LA										1332	731	1121	653	1570	1245	1548	1108	1660	2663	1783	871	1643	2431	1002	690	1932	560	1846	2298	2731	668	1302	2865	1106	890	1755
New York, NY											1469	1258	1094	439	91	2481	367	313	2920	515	499	1716	2713	342	956	2189	1861	2839	2929	2864	1150	507	2998	228	1391	1665
Oklahoma City, OK												463	1388	1563	1408	1012	1124	1792	1934	1776	1237	871	1727	1331	505	1204	466	1370	1657	2002	1403	1295	2136	1350	161	1158
Omaha, NE													1433	1238	1228	1440	928	1561	1662	1451	1265	525	1455	1263	440	932	927	1630	1672	1719	1448	971	1853	1162	307	638
Orlando, FL														1427	1006	2169	963	1422	3091	1598	601	1955	2884	750	993	2360	1180	2467	2918	3149	82	1327	3283	860	1434	2025
Ottawa, ON															451	2575	545	382	2901	257	831	1696	2694	675	1050	2170	1981	2869	2910	2845	1483	268	2978	562	1485	1280
Philadelphia, PA																2420	306	419	2890	586	411	1686	2683	254	895	2160	1774	2779	2900	2835	1062	522	2968	140	1330	1633
Phoenix, AZ																	2136	2804	1335	2788	2249	1308	883	2343	1517	651	987	358	750	1513	2184	2307	1655	2362	1173	2075
Pittsburgh, PA																		690	2590	758	497	1386	2383	341	611	1859	1519	2494	2599	2534	1019	321	2668	240	1046	1332
Portland, ME																			3223	264	827	2019	3016	670	1279	2493	2189	3162	3233	3168	1478	668	3301	556	1714	1966
Portland, OR																				3114	2923	1268	578	2925	2057	771	2322	1093	638	170	3106	2633	313	2824	1775	1463
Québec, QC																					1003	1908	2905	846	1261	2381	2193	3080	3122	3057	1654	479	3190	732	1696	1523
Raleigh, NC																						1777	2716	157	825	2193	1398	2563	2894	2926	656	820	3060	265	1266	1724
Rapid City, SD																							1151	1720	963	628	1335	1372	1368	1195	1970	1429	1328	1620	712	792
Reno, NV																								2718	1850	524	1870	642	217	755	2899	2426	898	2617	1568	1867
Richmond, VA																									834	2194	1530	2684	2934	2869	805	660	3003	108	1274	1667
St. Louis, MO																										1326	968	1875	2066	2125	1008	782	2259	837	441	1075
Salt Lake City, UT																											1419	754	740	839	2375	1902	973	2094	1044	1455
San Antonio, TX																												1285	1737	2275	1195	1714	2410	1635	624	1621
San Diego, CA																													508	1271	2481	2601	1414	2720	1531	2209
San Francisco, CA																														816	2933	2643	958	2834	1784	2193
Seattle, WA																															3164	2577	140	2769	1843	1390
Tampa, FL																																1383	3297	916	1448	2039
Toronto, ON																																	2711	563	1217	1375
Vancouver, BC																																		2902	1977	1375
Washington, DC																																			1272	1566
Wichita, KS																																				956

Kilomètres

	Memphis, TN	México, MX	Miami, FL	Milwaukee, WI	Minneapolis, MN	Mobile, AL	Montréal, QC	Nashville, TN	New Orleans, LA	New York, NY	Oklahoma City, OK	Omaha, NE	Orlando, FL	Ottawa, ON	Philadelphia, PA	Phoenix, AZ	Pittsburgh, PA	Portland, ME	Portland, OR	Québec, QC	Raleigh, NC	Rapid City, SD	Reno, NV	Richmond, VA	St. Louis, MO	Salt Lake City, UT	San Antonio, TX	San Diego, CA	San Francisco, CA	Seattle, WA	Tampa, FL	Toronto, ON	Vancouver, BC	Washington, DC	Wichita, KS
México, MX	2566																																		
Miami, FL	1691	3466																																	
Milwaukee, WI	1004	3540	2378																																
Minneapolis, MN	1512	3400	2887	542																															
Mobile, AL	636	2294	1170	1640	2148																														
Montréal, QC	2101	4666	2689	1511	2019	2534																													
Nashville, TN	346	2912	1459	916	1426	724	1760																												
New Orleans, LA	637	2113	1406	1641	2151	235	2626	867																											
New York, NY	1807	4214	2090	1438	1948	1936	616	1458	2143																										
Oklahoma City, OK	784	2129	2589	1416	1276	1286	2615	1131	1176	2364																									
Omaha, NE	1165	2869	2661	827	616	1800	2092	1202	1804	2024	745																								
Orlando, FL	1335	3110	373	2023	2531	814	2359	1104	1051	1760	2233	2306																							
Ottawa, ON	2000	4566	2624	1408	1918	2383	194	1659	2526	706	2515	1992	2296																						
Philadelphia, PA	1665	4063	1948	1392	1900	1794	730	1316	2003	146	2265	1976	1619	726																					
Phoenix, AZ	2414	2388	3846	3044	2904	2674	4243	2759	2491	3992	1628	2317	3490	4143	3894																				
Pittsburgh, PA	1255	3821	1878	907	1418	1640	977	916	1783	591	1809	1493	1549	877	492	3437																			
Portland, ME	2335	4732	2618	1928	2438	2463	454	1986	2671	504	2883	2512	2288	615	674	4512	1110																		
Portland, OR	3833	4536	5329	3319	2779	4394	4767	3870	4285	4698	3112	2674	4973	4668	4650	2148	4167	5186																	
Québec, QC	2343	4909	2901	1751	2261	2747	249	2002	2869	829	2858	2335	2571	414	943	4486	1220	425	5010																
Raleigh, NC	1205	3461	1295	1538	2048	1175	1401	856	1401	803	1990	2035	967	1337	661	3619	800	1331	4703	1614															
Rapid City, SD	2006	3805	3501	1355	975	2640	2829	2042	2644	2761	1401	845	3146	2729	2713	2105	2230	3249	2040	3070	2859														
Reno, NV	3500	3809	4996	3170	2959	4095	4434	3537	3911	4365	2779	2341	4640	4335	4317	1421	3834	4853	930	4674	4370	1852													
Richmond, VA	1356	3673	1535	1446	1957	1385	1149	1007	1612	550	2142	2032	1207	1086	409	3770	549	1078	4706	1361	253	2767	4373												
St. Louis, MO	473	2936	1953	591	999	1107	1789	494	1110	1538	813	708	1598	1689	1440	2441	983	2058	3310	2029	1327	1549	2977	1342											
Salt Lake City, UT	2658	3435	4153	2327	2116	3218	3591	2695	3109	3522	1937	1500	3797	3492	3475	1047	2991	4011	1241	3831	3529	1010	843	3530	2134										
San Antonio, TX	1189	1372	2254	2161	2023	1083	3287	1535	901	2994	750	1492	1899	3187	2854	1588	2444	3522	3736	3529	2249	2148	3009	2462	1558	2283									
San Diego, CA	2962	2708	4325	3451	3241	3154	4716	3308	2970	4568	2204	2623	3969	4616	4471	576	4013	5088	1759	4956	4124	2208	1033	4319	3017	1213	2068								
San Francisco, CA	3450	3593	5052	3517	3306	3879	4782	3797	3697	4713	2666	2690	4695	4682	4666	1207	4182	5202	1027	5023	4656	2201	349	4721	3324	1191	2795	817							
Seattle, WA	3926	4821	5422	3204	2661	4504	4677	3963	4394	4608	3221	2766	5067	4578	4562	2434	4077	5097	274	4919	4708	1923	1215	4616	3419	1350	3660	2045	1313						
Tampa, FL	1360	3134	441	2047	2555	838	2449	1128	1075	1850	2257	2330	132	2386	1709	3514	1640	2378	4998	2661	1056	3170	4664	1295	1622	3821	1923	3992	4719	5091					
Toronto, ON	1569	4135	2465	977	1487	1953	531	1229	2095	816	2084	1562	2135	431	840	3712	516	1075	4236	771	1319	2299	3903	1062	1258	3060	2758	4185	4253	4146	2225				
Vancouver, BC	4142	5051	5638	3418	2877	4719	4893	4179	4610	4824	3437	2981	5282	4792	4776	2663	4293	5311	504	5133	4924	2137	1445	4832	3635	1566	3878	2275	1541	225	5305	4362			
Washington, DC	1442	3839	1714	1286	1794	1561	965	1093	1780	367	2172	1870	1384	904	225	3800	386	895	4544	1178	426	2607	4211	174	1347	3369	2631	4376	4560	4455	1474	906	4669		
Wichita, KS	961	2383	2663	1237	1025	1541	2489	1204	1432	2238	259	494	2307	2389	2140	1887	1683	2758	2856	2729	2037	1146	2523	2050	710	1680	1004	2463	2870	2965	2330	1958	3181	2047	
Winnipeg, MB	2187	3985	3614	1270	727	2875	2211	2151	2824	2679	1863	1027	3258	2060	2627	3339	2143	3163	2354	2451	2774	1274	3004	2682	1730	2341	2608	3554	3529	2237	3281	2212	2212	2520	1538

TEMPERATURE CONVERSIONS

°F	°C	°C	°F
110	43.3	40	104
100	37.8	35	95
90	32.2	30	86
80	26.7	25	77
70	21.1	20	68
60	15.6	15	59
50	10.0	10	50
40	4.4	5	41
32	0	0	32
30	-1.1	-5	23
20	-6.7	-10	14
10	-12.2	-15	5
0	-17.8	-20	-4
-10	-23.3	-25	-13
-20	-28.9	-30	-22
-30	-34.4	-35	-31
-40	-40.0	-40	-40
-50	-45.6	-45	-49

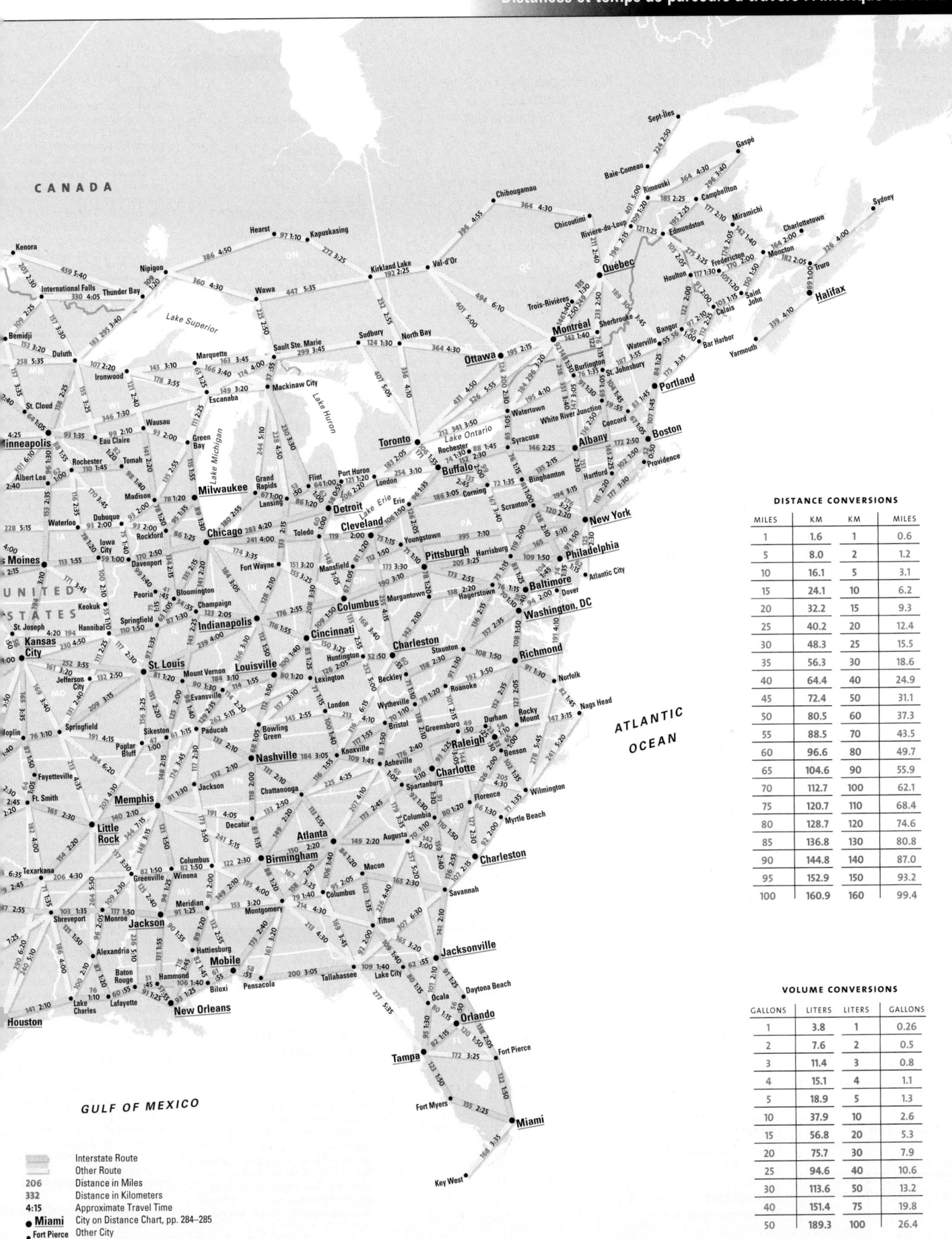

DISTANCE CONVERSIONS

MILES	KM	KM	MILES
1	1.6	1	0.6
5	8.0	2	1.2
10	16.1	5	3.1
15	24.1	10	6.2
20	32.2	15	9.3
25	40.2	20	12.4
30	48.3	25	15.5
35	56.3	30	18.6
40	64.4	40	24.9
45	72.4	50	31.1
50	80.5	60	37.3
55	88.5	70	43.5
60	96.6	80	49.7
65	104.6	90	55.9
70	112.7	100	62.1
75	120.7	110	68.4
80	128.7	120	74.6
85	136.8	130	80.8
90	144.8	140	87.0
95	152.9	150	93.2
100	160.9	160	99.4

VOLUME CONVERSIONS

GALLONS	LITERS	LITERS	GALLONS
1	3.8	1	0.26
2	7.6	2	0.5
3	11.4	3	0.8
4	15.1	4	1.1
5	18.9	5	1.3
10	37.9	10	2.6
15	56.8	20	5.3
20	75.7	30	7.9
25	94.6	40	10.6
30	113.6	50	13.2
40	151.4	75	19.8
50	189.3	100	26.4

Interstate Route
Other Route
206 Distance in Miles
332 Distance in Kilometers
4:15 Approximate Travel Time
● **Miami** City on Distance Chart, pp. 284–285
● Fort Pierce Other City

Distances and driving times may vary depending on actual
route traveled and driving conditions.

TOURISM INFORMATION

UNITED STATES

Alabama
334.242.4169
www.alabama.travel

Alaska
www.travelalaska.com

Arizona
866.275.5816
www.visitarizona.com

Arkansas
800.628.8725
www.arkansas.com

California
877.225.4367, 916.444.4429
www.visitcalifornia.com

Colorado
800.265.6723
www.colorado.com

Connecticut
888.288.4748, 860.256.2800
www.ctvisit.com

Delaware
866.284.7483
www.visitdelaware.com

District of Columbia
800.422.8644, 202.789.7000
www.washington.org

Florida
888.735.2872
www.visitflorida.com

Georgia
800.847.4842
www.exploregeorgia.org

Hawai'i
800.464.2924
www.gohawaii.com

Idaho
800.847.4843, 208.334.2470
www.visitidaho.org

Illinois
800.226.6632
www.enjoyillinois.com

Indiana
800.677.9800
www.visitindiana.com

Iowa
800.345.4692, 515.725.3084
www.traveliowa.com

Kansas
785.296.2009
www.travelks.com

Kentucky
800.225.8747, 502.564.4930
www.kentuckytourism.com

Louisiana
800.994.8626
www.louisianatravel.com

Maine
888.624.6345
www.visitmaine.com

Maryland
866.639.3526
www.visitmaryland.org

Massachusetts
800.227.6277, 617.973.8500
www.massvacation.com

Michigan
888.784.7328
www.michigan.org

Minnesota
888.847.4866
www.exploreminnesota.com

Mississippi
866.733.6477, 601.359.3297
www.visitmississippi.org

Missouri
800.519.2100, 573.751.4133
www.visitmo.com

Montana
800.847.4868
www.visitmt.com

Nebraska
402.471.3796
www.visitnebraska.com

Nevada
800.638.2328
www.travelnevada.com

New Hampshire
800.386.4664, 603.271.2665
www.visitnh.gov

New Jersey
800.847.4865, 609.599.6540
www.visitnj.org

New Mexico
505.827.7336
www.newmexico.org

New York
800.225.5697
www.iloveny.com

North Carolina
800.847.4862
www.visitnc.com

North Dakota
800.435.5663, 701.328.2525
www.ndtourism.com

Ohio
800.282.5393
www.discoverohio.com

Oklahoma
800.652.6552
www.travelok.com

Oregon
800.547.7842
www.traveloregon.com

Pennsylvania
800.847.4872
www.visitpa.com

Rhode Island
800.556.2484
www.visitrhodeisland.com

South Carolina
803.734.1700
www.discoversouthcarolina.com

South Dakota
800.732.5682, 605.773.3301
www.travelsd.com

Tennessee
800.462.8366, 615.741.2159
www.tnvacation.com

Texas
www.traveltex.com

Utah
800.200.1160, 801.538.1900
www.visitutah.com

Vermont
800.837.6668, 802.828.3237
www.vermontvacation.com

Virginia
800.847.4882
www.virginia.org

Washington
800.544.1800
www.experiencewa.com

West Virginia
800.225.5982, 304.558.2200
www.wvtourism.com

Wisconsin
800.432.8747, 608.266.2161
www.travelwisconsin.com

Wyoming
800.225.5996, 307.777.7777
www.wyomingtourism.org

Puerto Rico
800.866.7827
www.seepuertorico.com

CANADA

Alberta
800.252.3782
www.travelalberta.us

British Columbia
www.hellobc.com

Manitoba
800.665.0040, 204.927.7838
www.travelmanitoba.com

New Brunswick
800.561.0123
www.tourismnewbrunswick.ca

Newfoundland & Labrador
800.563.6353, 709.729.2830
www.newfoundlandlabrador.com

Northwest Territories
800.661.0788, 867.873.7200
www.spectacularnwt.com

Nova Scotia
800.565.0000, 902.425.5781
www.novascotia.com

Nunavut
866.686.2888, 800.491.7910
www.nunavuttourism.com

Ontario
800.668.2746
www.ontariotravel.net

Prince Edward Island
800.463.4734
www.tourismpei.com

Québec
877.266.5687
www.bonjourquebec.com

Saskatchewan
877.237.2273, 306.787.9600
www.tourismsaskatchewan.com

Yukon
800.661.0494
www.travelyukon.com

MEXICO

52.55.5278.4200
www.visitmexico.com

BORDER CROSSING INFORMATION

TRAVEL ADVISORY

All U.S. citizens are now required to present a passport, passport card, or WHTI (Western Hemisphere Travel Initiative)-compliant document when entering the United States by air, sea or land. U.S. citizens traveling directly to or from Puerto Rico and the U.S. Virgin Islands are not required to have a passport. For more detailed information and updated schedules, please see http://travel.state.gov.

CANADA

All persons entering Canada must carry both proof of citizenship and proof of identity. A valid U.S. passport, passport card other WHTI-compliant document satisfie these requirements for U.S. citizens. U.S. citizens entering Canada from a third country must have a valid U.S. passport. visa is not required for U.S. citizens to vis Canada for up to 180 days.

U.S. driver's licenses are valid in Canada; individual provinces and territories specify the length of time. Drivers should be prepared to present proof of their vehicle's registration, ownership, and insurance. International visitors to Canada who are not U.S. citizens must present a valid passport and visa (if required). Citizens of Mexico require a visa to enter Canada.

UNITED STATES (FROM CANADA)

Canadian driver's licenses are valid in the U.S.; lengths of time vary depending on state. Drivers should be prepared to present proof of their vehicle's registration, ownership, and insurance.

MEXICO

All persons entering Mexico must carry proof of citizenship, either a valid passport or their original birth certificate (U.S. citizens should bear in mind the requirements set by the U.S. government for re-entry to the U.S.). Visas are not required for stays of up to 180 days. Naturalized citizens and alien permanent residents should carry the appropriate official documentation. Individuals under the age of 18 traveling alone, with one parent, or with other adults must carry notarized parental/legal guardian authorization. All U.S. citizens visiting for up to 180 days must also procure a tourist permit, obtainable from Mexican consulates, tourism offices border crossing points, and airlines serving Mexico. However, tourist cards are not needed for visits shorter than 72 hours to areas within the Border Zone (extending approximately 25 km into Mexico).

U.S. driver's licenses are valid in Mexico. Visitors who wish to drive beyond the Baja California Peninsula or the Border Zone must obtain a temporary import permit for their vehicles. To acquire a permit, one must submit evidence of citizenship and of the vehicle's title and registration, as well as a valid driver's license. A processing fee must be paid. Permits are available at border crossings or selected Mexican consulates. Mexican law also requires the posting of a refundable bond to guarantee the departure of the vehicle.

All visitors driving in Mexico should be aware that U.S. auto insurance policies are not valid and that full-coverage insurance from a Mexican insurance company is mandatory. Many U.S. insurance companies sell short-term tourist auto insurance for travel in Mexico.

IMPORTANT WEB SITES

U.S. State Department,
www.travel.state.gov
U.S. Customs and Border Protection,
www.cbp.gov
Canada Border Services Agency,
www.cbsa-asfc.gc.ca
Citizenship and Immigration Canada,
www.cic.gc.ca
Mexican Ministry of Foreign Affairs,
www.sre.gob.mx
Mexican National Institute of Migration,
www.inm.gob.mx

OMMON ABBREVIATIONS

rch.	Archaeological	N.H.S.	National Historic Site
lld.	Battlefield	N.H.P.	National Historical Park
ons.	Conservation	N.M.P.	National Military Park
nt.	Entrance	N.R.A.	National Recreation Area
st.	Historic(al)	Pk. Hqtrs.	Park Headquarters
lem.	Memorial	Pres.	Preserve
lon.	Monument	Prov.	Provincial
ltn.	Mountain	Rec.	Recreation(al)
lts.	Mountains	Res.	Reservation–Reserve
lus.	Museum	S.H.S.	State Historic Site
atl.	National	S.P.	State Park
at.	Natural	Sta.	Station
		Vis. Ctr.	Visitor Center

ALABAMA	PAGE	GRID	LATITUDE LONGITUDE
ational Park & Rec. Areas			
orseshoe Bend N.M.P.-Main Road	128	B1	32.977130 -85.739600
orseshoe Bend N.M.P.-Vis. Ctr.	128	B1	32.977130 -85.739600
ussell Cave Natl. Mon.-Main Road	120	A2	34.980220 -85.809650
ussell Cave Natl. Mon.-Vis. Ctr.	120	A2	34.980400 -85.809800
uskegee Airmen N.H.S.	128	B2	32.424942 -85.691052
uskegee Airmen N.H.S.-Pk. Hqtrs.	128	B2	32.428600 -85.708500
uskegee Institute N.H.S.	128	B2	32.428751 -85.704120
uskegee Institute N.H.S.-Pk. Hqtrs.	128	B2	32.428600 -85.708500
tate Park & Rec. Areas			
ladon Springs S.P.	127	E4	31.730920 -88.195580
lue Springs S.P.	128	B4	31.661990 -85.508150
ucks Pocket S.P.	120	A3	34.469560 -86.049080
athedral Caverns S.P.	120	A2	34.572299 -86.221499
heaha S.P.	120	A4	33.474490 -85.807260
hewacla S.P.	128	B2	32.554520 -85.481920
esoto S.P.	120	A3	34.495460 -85.618860
lorala S.P.	136	B1	30.998590 -86.329980
rank Jackson S.P.	128	A4	31.291400 -86.255900
ulf S.P.	135	F2	30.270490 -87.582130
oe Wheeler S.P.	119	E2	34.793020 -87.379950
ake Guntersville S.P.	120	A3	34.367530 -86.222850
ake Lurleen S.P.	127	E1	33.295880 -87.676870
akepoint Resort S.P.	128	C3	31.990320 -85.114970
Meaher S.P.	135	E1	30.669720 -87.936030
Monte Sano S.P.	119	F2	34.745220 -86.511650
ak Mtn. S.P.	127	F1	33.324710 -86.758740
aul M. Grist S.P.	127	F2	32.595380 -86.996080
ickwood Caverns S.P.	119	F4	33.876870 -86.867230
oland Cooper S.P.	127	F3	32.055350 -87.245330
Wind Creek S.P.	128	A1	32.856820 -85.946540

ALASKA	PAGE	GRID	LATITUDE LONGITUDE
National Park & Rec. Areas			
Admiralty Island Natl. Mon.	155	E4	57.618060 -134.161110
Aleutian WWII Natl. Hist. Area	154	A4	53.888889 -166.527222
Aniakchak Natl. Mon. & Pres.	154	B4	56.833333 -158.250556
Bering Land Bridge Natl. Pres.	154	B2	65.595320 -164.301800
Cape Krusenstern Natl. Mon.	154	B1	67.471630 -163.312300
Denali Natl. Park & Pres.-Denali Vis. Ctr.	154	C2	63.737000 -148.895000
Denali Natl. Park & Pres.-Eielson Vis. Ctr.	154	C2	63.440900 -150.239000
Gates of the Arctic Natl. Park & Pres.-Anaktuvuk Pass Ranger Sta.	154	C1	68.139900 -151.735400
Gates of the Arctic Natl. Park & Pres.-Arctic Interagency Vis. Ctr.	154	C1	67.253700 -150.187000
Gates of the Arctic Natl. Park & Pres.-Bettles Ranger Sta.	154	C1	66.912500 -151.667100
Gates of the Arctic Natl. Park & Pres.-Coldfoot Ranger Sta.	154	C1	67.253700 -150.187000
Glacier Bay Natl. Park & Pres.-Glacier Bay Lodge & Vis. Ctr.	155	D3	58.454900 -135.882600
Katmai Natl. Park & Pres.	154	C3	58.667030 -156.524600
Kenai Fjords Natl. Park-Vis. Ctr.	154	C3	60.105300 -149.435000
Klondike Gold Rush N.H.P.	155	D3	60.113550 -149.441342
Kobuk Valley Natl. Park	154	B1	67.073230 -159.839500
Lake Clark Natl. Park & Pres.	154	C3	60.471450 -154.576390
Misty Fiords Natl. Mon.	155	E4	55.472600 -130.429700
Noatak Natl. Pres.	154	C1	67.320740 -162.646370
White Mts. N.R.A.	154	C2	65.524300 -147.156400
Wrangell-Saint Elias Natl. Park & Pres.-Kennecott Vis. Ctr.	155	D3	61.485600 -142.881100
Wrangell-Saint Elias Natl. Park & Pres.-Wrangell-Saint Elias Vis. Ctr.	155	D3	61.964300 -145.317900
Yukon-Charley Rivers Natl. Pres.	155	D2	65.341680 -143.120650
State Park & Rec. Areas			
Afognak Island S.P.	154	C4	58.227100 -152.067300
Chilkat S.P.	155	D3	59.211111 -135.398056
Chugach S.P.	154	C3	61.037440 -149.780830
Denali S.P.	154	C3	62.734600 -150.199600
Point Bridget S.P.	155	E3	58.671225 -134.958801
Shuyak Island S.P.	154	C4	58.533100 -152.486100
Wood-Tikchik S.P.	154	B3	59.909600 -158.672000

ARIZONA	PAGE	GRID	LATITUDE LONGITUDE
National Park & Rec. Areas			
Agua Fria Natl. Mon.	47	D4	34.276490 -112.114350
Canyon de Chelly Natl. Mon.-Vis. Ctr.	48	A2	36.153200 -109.539000
Casa Grande Ruins Natl. Mon.-Ent. Sta.	54	C2	32.994700 -111.537000
Chiricahua Natl. Mon.-Main Road	55	E3	32.009250 -109.382230
Chiricahua Natl. Mon.-Ent. Sta.	55	E3	32.007500 -109.388900
Coronado Natl. Mem.-Vis. Ctr.	55	E4	31.346300 -110.254000
Fort Bowie N.H.S.-Vis. Ctr.	55	E3	32.146600 -109.435000
Glen Canyon N.R.A.-Ent. Sta.	47	E1	36.943300 -111.493600
Grand Canyon Natl. Park-East Ent.	47	D2	36.038800 -111.828000
Grand Canyon Natl. Park-North Ent.	47	D2	36.334900 -112.116000
Grand Canyon Natl. Park-South Ent.	47	D2	36.000100 -112.121600
Grand Canyon-Parashant Natl. Mon.	46	C2	36.452170 -113.724367
Ironwood Forest Natl. Mon.	54	C3	32.478380 -111.530220
Lake Mead N.R.A.-Boulder City Ent.	46	C2	36.020800 -114.796000
Lake Mead N.R.A.-Henderson Ent.	46	C2	36.105400 -114.901200
Lake Mead N.R.A.-Las Vegas–Rt 147 Ent.	46	C2	36.161000 -114.905100
Lake Mead N.R.A.-South Ent.	46	C2	35.225600 -114.551000
Montezuma Castle Natl. Mon.-Vis. Ctr.	47	D4	34.611600 -111.839000
Navajo Natl. Mon.-Betatakin Ruin	47	E1	36.683500 -110.541470
Navajo Natl. Mon.-Inscription House Ruin-Closed To Public	47	E1	36.661250 -110.775940
Navajo Natl. Mon.-Keet Seel Ruin	47	E1	36.683500 -110.541470
Navajo Natl. Mon.-Vis. Ctr.	47	E1	36.678200 -110.541000
Organ Pipe Cactus Natl. Mon.-Vis. Ctr.	54	B3	31.954800 -112.801000
Petrified Forest Natl. Park-North Ent.	47	F3	35.069600 -109.778000
Petrified Forest Natl. Park-South Ent.	47	F3	34.799600 -109.885000
Pipe Spring Natl. Mon.-Vis. Ctr.	47	D1	36.862500 -112.737000
Saguaro Natl. Park-East	55	D3	32.178430 -110.737990
Saguaro Natl. Park-Vis. Ctr.	55	D3	32.180200 -110.736000
Saguaro Natl. Park-West	55	D3	32.251660 -111.191660
Sonoran Desert Natl. Mon.	54	C2	33.001730 -112.421220
Sunset Crater Volcano Natl. Mon.-Vis. Ctr.	47	E3	35.368800 -111.543000
Tonto Natl. Mon.-Vis. Ctr.	55	D1	33.645200 -111.113000
Tumacácori N.H.P.-Vis. Ctr.	55	D4	31.567800 -111.051000
Tuzigoot Natl. Mon.-Pk. Hqtrs.	47	D4	34.561000 -111.853000
Vermilion Cliffs Natl. Mon.	47	D1	36.806389 -111.741111
Walnut Canyon Natl. Mon.-Walnut Canyon Vis. Ctr.	47	E3	35.171700 -111.509000
Wupatki Natl. Mon.-Vis. Ctr.	47	E3	35.520300 -111.372000
State Park & Rec. Areas			
Alamo Lake S.P.	46	C4	34.234270 -113.553220
Boyce Thompson Arbrtum S.P.	55	D2	33.311150 -111.055790
Buckskin Mtn. S.P.	46	B4	34.255000 -114.134070
Catalina S.P.	55	D3	32.416760 -110.937500
Cattail Cove S.P.	46	B4	34.355075 -114.165877
Dead Horse Ranch S.P.	47	D4	34.748490 -112.022930
Homolovi Ruins S.P.	47	E3	35.023940 -110.630120
Kartchner Caverns S.P.	55	D3	31.840770 -110.342710
Lake Havasu S.P.	46	B4	34.473970 -114.345850
Lost Dutchman S.P.	54	C1	33.464920 -111.481350
Lyman Lake S.P.	48	A4	34.362870 -109.375370
Oracle S.P.	55	D2	32.610239 -110.740619
Patagonia Lake S.P.	55	D4	31.488970 -110.853790
Picacho Peak S.P.	54	C2	32.646340 -111.398090
Red Rock S.P.	47	D4	34.818920 -111.836700
Roper Lake S.P.	55	E2	32.758710 -109.709520
Slide Rock S.P.	47	D3	34.944340 -111.752810
Tonto Nat. Bridge S.P.	47	E4	34.323400 -111.449460

ARKANSAS	PAGE	GRID	LATITUDE LONGITUDE
National Park & Rec. Areas			
Fort Smith N.H.S.-Main Road	116	B1	35.387480 -94.429660
Fort Smith N.H.S.-Vis. Ctr.	116	B1	35.385800 -94.429800
Hot Springs Natl. Park-Main Road	117	D2	34.511660 -93.053980
Hot Springs Natl. Park-Vis. Ctr.	117	D2	34.513800 -93.053400
Pea Ridge N.M.P.-Main Road	106	C3	36.442600 -94.025980
Pea Ridge N.M.P.-Vis. Ctr.	106	C3	36.443800 -94.025900
State Park & Rec. Areas			
Bull Shoals-White River S.P.	107	E3	36.365590 -92.557490
Conway Cemetery S.P.	124	C1	33.101909 -93.683161
Crater of Diamonds S.P.	116	C3	34.038610 -93.667630
Crowley's Ridge S.P.	108	A4	36.044840 -90.666770
Degray Lake Resort S.P.-North Ent.	117	D3	34.248870 -93.116880
Degray Lake Resort S.P.-South Ent.	117	D3	34.217390 -93.085820
Hampson Arch. Mus. S.P.	118	B1	35.568990 -90.041060
Historic Washington S.P.	116	C4	33.774005 -93.683235
Hobbs S.P.-Cons. Area	106	C3	36.244880 -93.972640
Jacksonport S.P.	107	F4	35.641440 -91.305350
Jenkins' Ferry S.P.	117	E3	34.212070 -92.547490
Lake Charles S.P.	107	F4	36.066870 -91.132700
Lake Chicot S.P.	126	A1	33.373070 -91.194940
Lake Dardanelle S.P.	117	D1	35.251690 -93.213380
Lake Fort Smith S.P.	106	C4	35.654040 -94.150140
Lake Frierson S.P.	108	A4	35.988570 -90.717540
Lake Ouachita S.P.	117	D2	34.610990 -93.165520
Lake Poinsett S.P.	118	A1	35.535510 -90.688700
Louisiana Purchase S.P.	118	A2	35.150340 -90.734990
Lower White River Mus. S.P.	117	F2	34.977035 -91.495131
Mammoth Spring S.P.	107	F3	36.496010 -91.535960
Marks' Mills S.P.	117	E4	33.781085 -92.256427
Moro Bay S.P.	125	E1	33.298890 -92.348940
Mount Magazine S.P.	116	C1	35.149900 -93.563600
Mount Nebo S.P.	117	D1	35.224870 -93.229930
Ozark Folk Center S.P.	107	E4	35.883480 -92.116340
Parkin Arch. S.P.	118	A1	35.268607 -90.554809
Petit Jean S.P.	117	D1	35.128320 -92.898530
Poison Springs Battleground S.P.	117	D4	33.638340 -93.005250
Powhatan Hist. S.P.	107	F4	36.083234 -91.117858
Prairie Grove Bfld. S.P.	106	C4	35.983120 -94.305590
Toltec Mounds Arch. S.P.	117	E2	34.647370 -92.058510
Village Creek S.P.	118	A1	35.199650 -90.724540
White Oak Lake S.P.	117	D4	33.687490 -93.117240
Withrow Springs S.P.	106	C4	36.203800 -93.578200
Woolly Hollow S.P.	117	E1	35.286402 -92.285646

CALIFORNIA	PAGE	GRID	LATITUDE LONGITUDE
National Park & Rec. Areas			
Amboy Crater Natl. Nat. Landmark	53	E2	34.542196 -115.790920
Berryessa Snow Mountain Natl. Mon.	36	B2	38.902521 -123.411455
Carrizo Plain Natl. Mon.	52	B1	35.191000 -119.792000
Channel Islands Natl. Park	52	B2	34.248500 -119.267000
Death Valley Natl. Park-Furnace Creek Vis. Ctr.	45	F3	36.461800 -116.867000
Devils Postpile Natl. Mon.	37	E4	37.630330 -119.084300
Giant Sequoia Natl. Mon.-North Unit	45	D2	36.705501 -118.824821
Giant Sequoia Natl. Mon.-South Unit	45	E3	36.062389 -118.317784
Golden Gate N.R.A.-Marin Headlands	36	B4	37.830900 -122.525000
Golden Gate N.R.A.-Mott Vis. Ctr.	36	B4	37.799800 -122.460000
Joshua Tree Natl. Park-Indian Cove	53	E3	34.120000 -116.156000
Joshua Tree Natl. Park-North Ent.	53	E3	34.078300 -116.037000
Joshua Tree Natl. Park-West Ent.	53	E3	34.093600 -116.266000
Kings Canyon Natl. Park-East Ent.	45	D2	36.715870 -118.940420
Kings Canyon Natl. Park-West Ent.	45	D2	36.723720 -118.956490
Lassen Volcanic Natl. Park-Ent.	29	D4	40.537900 -121.571000
Lava Beds Natl. Mon.-Vis. Ctr.	29	D2	41.713900 -121.509000
Manzanar N.H.S.	45	E3	36.732260 -118.148500
Pinnacles Natl. Park-East Ent.	44	B3	36.483200 -121.162000
Pinnacles Natl. Park-West Ent.	44	B3	36.473300 -121.224400
Point Reyes Natl. Seashore-Bear Valley Vis. Ctr.	36	A3	38.043100 -122.799000
Point Reyes Natl. Seashore-Kenneth C. Patrick Vis. Ctr.	36	A3	38.027800 -122.961000
Point Reyes Natl. Seashore-Vis. Ctr.	36	A3	37.996500 -123.021000
Redwood Natl. Park-Kuchel Vis. Ctr.	28	A3	41.286800 -124.090900
Redwood Natl. Park-Prairie Creek Vis. Ctr.	28	A3	41.365300 -124.022000
San Gabriel Mountains Natl. Mon.	52	C2	34.286213 -117.884488
Santa Monica Mts. N.R.A.-Vis. Ctr.	52	B2	34.188600 -118.887000
Santa Rosa & San Jacinto Mts. Natl. Mon.	53	E3	33.755173 -116.729736
Sequoia Natl. Park-North Ent.	45	D3	36.647900 -118.826370
Sequoia Natl. Park-South Ent.	45	D3	36.487130 -118.836810
Shasta-Trinity N.R.A.	28	C4	40.633243 -122.601127
Trona Pinnacles Natl. Nature Landmark	45	F4	35.611944 -117.369444
Whiskeytown-N.R.A.	28	C4	40.751500 -122.320580
Yosemite Natl. Park-Arch Rock Ent.	37	D3	37.687500 -119.730000
Yosemite Natl. Park-Big Oak Flat Ent.	37	D3	37.800800 -119.874000
Yosemite Natl. Park-Hetch Hetchy Ent.	37	D3	37.893500 -119.842000
Yosemite Natl. Park-South Ent.	37	D3	37.507000 -119.632000
Yosemite Natl. Park-Tioga Pass Ent.	37	D3	37.910700 -119.258000
State Park & Rec. Areas			
Ahjumawi Lava Springs S.P.	29	D3	41.107140 -121.468600
Anza-Borrego Desert S.P.	53	E4	33.256550 -116.399340
Big Basin Redwoods S.P.	44	A2	37.168380 -122.221530
Bothe-Napa Valley S.P.	36	B3	38.553410 -122.525640
Butano S.P.	44	A2	37.200660 -122.344140
Carlsbad State Beach	53	D3	33.147530 -117.345280
Castle Crags S.P.	28	C3	41.149280 -122.317480
China Camp S.P.	36	B3	38.003990 -122.466480
Clear Lake S.P.	36	B2	39.009780 -122.805400
Cuyamaca Rancho S.P.	53	D4	32.933790 -116.562560
Del Norte Coast Redwoods S.P.	28	A3	41.603280 -124.100130
Doheny State Beach	52	C3	33.463820 -117.688830
Donner Mem. S.P.	37	D2	39.323880 -120.228370
Ed Z'Berg-Sugar Pine Point S.P.	37	D2	39.056290 -120.119200
Emerald Bay S.P.	37	D2	38.956710 -120.108850
Fremont Peak S.P.	44	B3	36.760340 -121.502670
Garrapata S.P.	44	B3	36.475310 -121.936280
Gaviota S.P.	52	A2	34.475250 -120.228590
Grizzly Creek Redwoods S.P.	28	B4	40.486630 -123.903520
Grover Hot Springs S.P.	37	D3	38.695230 -119.836760
Henry Cowell Redwoods S.P.	44	A2	37.044020 -122.070990
Henry W. Coe S.P.	44	B2	37.085600 -121.467340
Humboldt Lagoons S.P.	28	A3	41.284330 -124.089720
Humboldt Redwoods S.P.	28	A4	40.284740 -124.056950
Jedediah Smith Redwoods S.P.	28	A2	41.798190 -124.084030
Julia Pfeiffer Burns S.P.	44	B3	36.160700 -121.668210
Limekiln S.P.	44	B3	36.013380 -121.526870
Little River State Beach	28	A3	41.013580 -124.109680
Los Osos Oaks State Rec.	52	A1	35.310200 -120.835300
Manchester S.P.	36	A2	38.980450 -123.703020
Marina State Beach	44	B3	36.683030 -121.809440
McGrath State Beach	52	B2	34.227270 -119.256460
Mendocino Headlands S.P.	36	A2	39.307570 -123.798910
Morro Bay S.P.	44	B4	35.354020 -120.843800
Morro Strand State Beach	44	B4	35.435390 -120.888060
Mount Diablo S.P.	36	B4	37.844210 -121.950200
Mount Tamalpais S.P.	36	B3	37.904290 -122.604040
Navarro River Redwoods S.P.	36	A2	39.175000 -123.676390

290 Parks Index with GPS Coordinates
California–Georgia

Park	Page	Grid	Latitude Longitude
Pacheco S.P.	44	B2	37.055650 -121.016250
Palomar Mtn. S.P.	53	D3	33.325340 -116.893330
Patrick's Point S.P.	28	A3	41.135690 -124.150500
Pfeiffer Big Sur S.P.	44	B3	36.250930 -121.786550
Placerita Canyon S.P.	52	C2	34.377530 -118.470290
Plumas-Eureka S.P.	36	C1	39.758360 -120.695360
Point Dume State Beach	52	B2	34.003110 -118.807250
Point Sal State Beach	52	A1	34.897760 -120.642760
Prairie Creek Redwoods S.P.	28	A3	41.355490 -124.073670
Red Rock Canyon S.P.	52	C1	35.359734 -117.978351
Russian Gulch S.P.	36	A2	39.330990 -123.805050
Saddleback Butte S.P.	52	C2	34.689820 -117.824340
Samuel P. Taylor S.P.	36	B3	38.004660 -122.708400
San Gregorio State Beach	36	B4	37.321490 -122.401640
San Onofre State Beach	53	D3	33.383380 -117.580790
Sonoma Coast State Beach	36	A3	38.441060 -123.122970
Sunset State Beach	44	B2	36.897780 -121.835450
The Forest of Nisene Marks S.P.	44	B2	37.042024 -121.856231
Tolowa Dunes S.P.	28	A2	41.825800 -124.187500
Trinidad State Beach	28	A3	41.061090 -124.142290
Van Damme S.P.	36	A2	39.273990 -123.790490
Westport-Union Landing State Beach	36	A1	39.658350 -123.784930
Wilder Ranch S.P.	44	A2	36.962160 -122.080850
Zmudowski State Beach	44	B2	36.845580 -121.804300

COLORADO	PAGE	GRID	LATITUDE LONGITUDE
National Park & Rec. Areas			
Arapaho N.R.A.	41	D1	40.197870 -105.869440
Bent's Old Fort N.H.S.	41	F3	38.045980 -103.431440
Black Canyon-Gunnison Natl. Park-North Ent.	40	C3	38.586890 -107.695940
Black Canyon-Gunnison Natl. Park-South Ent.	40	C3	38.553980 -107.686390
Browns Canyon Natl. Mon.	41	D2	38.753093 -105.973528
Canyons of the Ancients Natl. Mon.	40	A4	37.587880 -108.916890
Colorado Natl. Mon.-Northwest Ent.	40	B2	39.117620 -108.730910
Colorado Natl. Mon.-Southeast Ent.	40	B2	39.032860 -108.631460
Colorado Natl. Mon.-South Ent.	40	B2	39.021100 -108.659540
Colorado Natl. Mon.-Southwest Ent.	40	B2	39.055070 -108.742500
Curecanti N.R.A.-East Ent.	40	C3	38.515010 -107.020560
Curecanti N.R.A.-North Ent.	40	C3	38.463380 -107.419580
Curecanti N.R.A.-South Ent.	40	C3	38.473160 -107.076450
Curecanti N.R.A.-West Ent.	40	C3	38.444680 -107.341980
Dinosaur Natl. Mon.-East Ent.	32	B4	40.443120 -108.517790
Dinosaur Natl. Mon.-South Ent.	32	B4	40.243920 -108.973750
Florissant Fossil Beds Natl. Mon.	41	E2	38.937440 -105.283400
Great Sand Dunes Natl. Park-Ent. Sta.	41	D4	37.725000 -105.519000
Hovenweep Natl. Mon.-Cutthroat	40	A4	37.413000 -108.720240
Hovenweep Natl. Mon.-Hackberry	40	A4	37.398890 -109.036680
Hovenweep Natl. Mon.-Holly	40	A4	37.398890 -109.036680
Hovenweep Natl. Mon.-Horseshoe	40	A4	37.464610 -108.974680
Mesa Verde Natl. Park-Ent. Sta.	40	B4	37.331100 -108.416000
Rocky Mtn. Natl. Park-Beaver Meadows Ent.	33	E4	40.367300 -105.578000
Rocky Mtn. Natl. Park-Fall River Ent.	33	E4	40.404000 -105.590000
Rocky Mtn. Natl. Park-Grand Lake Ent.	33	E4	40.267300 -105.833000
Rocky Mtn. Natl. Park-Wild Basin Ent.	33	E4	40.219000 -105.534000
Sand Creek Massacre N.H.S.	42	A3	38.541250 -102.505910
Yucca House Natl. Mon.	40	B4	37.251678 -108.684911
State Park & Rec. Areas			
Barr Lake S.P.	41	E1	39.938160 -104.733470
Boyd Lake S.P.	33	E4	40.428990 -105.045400
Castlewood Canyon S.P.	41	E2	39.325860 -104.737640
Crawford S.P.	40	C3	38.708000 -107.617550
Eleven Mile S.P.	41	D2	38.948570 -105.526450
Golden Gate Canyon S.P.	41	D1	39.875560 -105.453650
Harvey Gap S.P.	40	C1	39.606210 -107.659010
Highline Lake S.P.	40	B2	39.270910 -108.835930
Jackson Lake S.P.	33	F4	40.409110 -104.070130
James M. Robb-Colorado River S.P.-Corn Lake	40	B2	39.062709 -108.455110
James M. Robb-Colorado River S.P.-Island Acres	40	B2	39.165709 -108.300610
John Martin Reservoir S.P.	42	A3	38.065390 -102.927110
Lake Pueblo S.P.	41	E3	38.258130 -104.719160
Lathrop S.P.	41	E4	37.602830 -104.833740
Lone Mesa S.P.	40	B4	37.699890 -108.466750
Lory S.P.	33	E4	40.593143 -105.185413
Mancos S.P.	40	B4	37.399890 -108.266750
Mueller S.P.	41	E2	38.884940 -105.157710
Navajo S.P.	48	B1	37.067800 -107.407599
North Sterling S.P.	34	A4	40.787740 -103.264990
Paonia S.P.	40	C2	38.980440 -107.342900
Pearl Lake S.P.	33	D4	40.790160 -106.894610
Ridgway S.P.	40	B3	38.229710 -107.729410
Rifle Falls S.P.	40	B1	39.695290 -107.701090
Rifle Gap S.P.	40	B1	39.627460 -107.762520
Roxborough S.P.	41	E2	39.451300 -105.070200
San Luis S.P.	41	D4	37.663130 -105.734480
Spinney Mtn. S.P.	41	D2	39.014760 -105.625880
Stagecoach S.P.	33	D4	40.286100 -106.866920
Steamboat Lake S.P.	32	C4	40.805240 -106.943600
Sweitzer Lake S.P.	40	B2	38.712050 -108.042640
Sylvan Lake S.P.	40	C1	39.516710 -106.753170
Trinidad Lake S.P.	49	E1	37.149700 -104.563650
Vega S.P.	40	B2	39.226890 -107.810250
Yampa River S.P.	32	C4	40.533190 -107.444483

CONNECTICUT	PAGE	GRID	LATITUDE LONGITUDE
National Park & Rec. Areas			
Weir Farm N.H.S.	148	C2	41.255890 -73.455980
State Park & Rec. Areas			
Bigelow Hollow S.P.	150	B2	41.991600 -72.134840
Bluff Point S.P.	149	F2	41.335800 -72.033520
Chatfield Hollow S.P.	150	A4	41.361400 -72.580190
Day Pond S.P.	150	A4	41.553432 -72.418419
Devil's Hopyard S.P.	150	A4	41.486529 -72.342462
Gay City S.P.	150	A3	41.716100 -72.434470
Gillette Castle S.P.	150	A4	41.430670 -72.427990
Hammonasset Beach S.P.	149	E2	41.273640 -72.562350
Haystack Mtn. S.P.	94	C2	42.002010 -73.209960
Horse Guard S.P.	94	C3	41.807100 -72.848300
Hurd S.P.	150	A4	41.530650 -72.537650
John A. Minetto S.P.	94	C2	41.884020 -73.170280
Lake Waramaug S.P.	148	C1	41.706290 -73.382460
Mashamoquet Brook S.P.	150	B3	41.860320 -71.987230
Mount Riga S.P.	94	B2	42.028830 -73.428620
Putnam Mem. S.P.	148	C2	41.344200 -73.381500
Rocky Neck S.P.	149	F2	41.316920 -72.242690
Selden Neck S.P.	150	A4	41.287500 -72.331100
Silver Sands S.P.	149	D2	41.198410 -73.076180
Southford Falls S.P.	149	D1	41.455700 -73.166150
Squantz Pond S.P.	148	C1	41.508580 -73.471040
Stoddard Hill S.P.	150	B4	41.461900 -72.065500
Wadsworth Falls S.P.	150	A4	41.536080 -72.687380
West Rock Ridge S.P.	149	D2	41.347810 -72.968260

DELAWARE	PAGE	GRID	LATITUDE LONGITUDE
State Park & Rec. Areas			
Cape Henlopen S.P.	145	F3	38.782360 -75.103010
Delaware Seashore S.P.	145	F4	38.614420 -75.071540
Fenwick Island S.P.	145	F4	38.469740 -75.051550
Fort Delaware S.P.	145	E1	39.578700 -75.588320
Fort Dupont S.P.	145	E1	39.568930 -75.588590
Holts Landing S.P.	145	F4	38.584080 -75.128380
Killens Pond S.P.	145	E3	38.990320 -75.544920
Lums Pond S.P.	145	E1	39.570520 -75.733490
Trap Pond S.P.	145	E4	38.525860 -75.483170
White Clay Creek S.P.	146	B4	39.709810 -75.776560

FLORIDA	PAGE	GRID	LATITUDE LONGITUDE
National Park & Rec. Areas			
Biscayne Natl. Park-Dante Fascell Vis. Ctr.	143	F3	25.464400 -80.334900
Canaveral Natl. Seashore	141	E1	28.611410 -80.808390
Castillo de San Marcos Natl. Mon.	139	D3	29.897747 -81.311461
Dry Tortugas Natl. Park-Vis. Ctr.	142	B4	24.628500 -82.873400
Everglades Natl. Park-Ent.	143	E3	25.394400 -80.589300
Fort Matanzas Natl. Mon.	139	E3	29.715660 -81.234190
Gulf Islands Natl. Seashore	135	F2	30.362880 -87.139630
State Park & Rec. Areas			
Alafia River S.P.	140	C3	27.789920 -82.120830
Amelia Island S.P.	139	D2	30.543900 -81.449700
Anastasia S.P.	139	E3	29.874740 -81.285030
Anclote Key Pres. S.P.	140	B2	28.193070 -82.850660
Avalon S.P.	141	E3	27.542840 -80.318060
Bahia Honda S.P.	143	D4	24.659540 -81.277810
Bald Point S.P.	138	A3	29.902700 -84.408600
Big Lagoon S.P.	135	F2	30.322290 -87.401170
Big Shoals S.P.	138	C2	30.339915 -82.683182
Big Talbot Island S.P.	139	D2	30.460500 -81.421950
Blue Spring S.P.	141	D1	28.952270 -81.331300
Bulow Creek S.P.	139	E4	29.388000 -81.132399
Bulow Plantation Ruins Hist. S.P.	139	E4	29.433590 -81.144590
Caladesi Island S.P.	140	B2	28.059890 -82.813780
Cedar Key Mus. S.P.	138	B4	29.151172 -83.048299
Charlotte Harbor Pres. S.P.	140	C4	26.850691 -82.022026
Collier-Seminole S.P.	143	D2	25.991630 -81.591700
Crystal River Pres. S.P. & Arch. S.P.	140	B1	28.909530 -82.628680
Curry Hammock S.P.	143	E4	24.742640 -80.984793
Dade Bfld. Hist. S.P.	140	C1	28.654430 -82.124970
Deleon Springs S.P.	139	D4	29.131920 -81.360400
Delnor-Wiggins Pass S.P.	142	C1	26.272500 -81.826900
Dudley Farm Hist. S.P.	138	C3	29.649617 -82.630738
Eden Gardens S.P.	136	B2	30.361530 -86.125010
Egmont Key S.P.	140	B3	27.723490 -82.679390
Fakahatchee Strand Pres. S.P.	143	D2	25.961900 -81.364600
Faver-Dykes S.P.	139	E3	29.668050 -81.268030
Florida Caverns S.P.	137	D1	30.809160 -85.212270
Fort Clinch S.P.	139	D1	30.668010 -81.434300
Fort Cooper S.P.	140	C1	28.801300 -82.309200
Fort Pierce Inlet S.P.-East Ent.	141	E3	27.485160 -80.299430
Fort Pierce Inlet S.P.-West Ent.	141	E3	27.475930 -80.316980
Gasparilla Island S.P.	140	C4	26.718200 -82.261400
Grayton Beach S.P.	136	B2	30.328930 -86.155790
Henderson Beach S.P.	136	B2	30.387000 -86.447499
Highlands Hammock S.P.	141	D3	27.476554 -81.557148
Hontoon Island S.P.	141	D1	28.976680 -81.35769
Hugh Taylor Birch S.P.	143	F1	26.138220 -80.10445
Indian Key Hist. S.P.	143	E4	24.888056 -80.67805
John Gorrie Mus. S.P.	137	D3	29.725768 -84.98324
John Pennekamp Coral Reef S.P.	143	E3	25.127620 -80.40965
Jonathan Dickinson S.P.	141	F4	27.002920 -80.09998
Kissimmee Prairie Pres. S.P.	141	D3	27.538826 -81.02294
Lafayette Blue Springs S.P.	138	B2	30.115136 -83.22941
Lake Griffin S.P.	140	C1	28.857450 -81.90224
Lake Kissimmee S.P.	141	D2	27.971930 -81.38022
Lake Louisa S.P.	140	C1	28.460070 -81.75162
Lake Manatee S.P.	140	C3	27.475140 -82.33680
Little Talbot Island S.P.	139	D2	30.460500 -81.42195
Long Key S.P.	143	E4	24.821580 -80.81951
Lovers Key S.P.	142	C1	26.391000 -81.87780
Manatee Springs S.P.	138	B4	29.496230 -82.95863
Myakka River S.P.	140	C4	27.242670 -82.33224
Natural Bridge Bfld. Hist. S.P.	138	A2	30.284730 -84.15226
O'Leno S.P.	138	C3	29.809100 -82.55070
Olustee Bfld. Hist. S.P.	138	C2	30.214650 -82.42896
Oscar Scherer S.P.	140	B4	27.168840 -82.47736
Paynes Prairie Pres. S.P.	138	C3	29.520720 -82.30040
Perdido Key S.P.	135	F2	30.291480 -87.46536
Ponce De Leon Springs S.P.	136	C1	30.713260 -85.92249
Rainbow Springs S.P.	138	C4	29.103818 -82.43878
Ravine Gardens S.P.	139	D3	29.637490 -81.64683
River Rise Pres. S.P.	138	C3	29.859961 -82.60539
Saint Sebastian River Pres. S.P.	141	E3	27.815241 -80.51382
San Marcos de Apalache Hist. S.P.	138	A2	30.152890 -84.21003
Savannas Pres. S.P.	141	E3	27.245960 -80.25027
Sebastian Inlet S.P.	141	E2	27.870200 -80.45359
Silver River S.P.	139	D4	29.202550 -82.05361
Suwannee River S.P.	138	B2	30.389610 -83.15785
Three Rivers S.P.	137	D1	30.736800 -84.936500
Tomoka S.P.	139	E4	29.342210 -81.086200
Torreya S.P.	137	D2	30.553530 -84.946740
Troy Spring S.P.	138	B3	29.918000 -82.893300
Waccasassa Bay Pres. S.P.	138	B4	29.188100 -82.92550
Washington Oaks Gardens S.P.	139	E3	29.634670 -81.205500
Wekiwa Springs S.P.	141	D1	28.710490 -81.462810
Windley Key Fossil Reef Geological S.P.	143	E4	24.914100 -80.64280
Yulee Sugar Mill Ruins Hist. S.P.	140	B1	28.784730 -82.60737

GEORGIA	PAGE	GRID	LATITUDE LONGITUDE
National Park & Rec. Areas			
Chattahoochee River N.R.A.	120	C3	34.002910 -84.349180
Chickamauga & Chattanooga N.M.P.	120	B2	34.941430 -85.258790
Cumberland Island Natl. Seashore	139	D1	30.720300 -81.548760
Ed Jenkins N.R.A.	120	C2	34.682900 -84.198200
Fort Frederica Natl. Mon.	130	B4	31.219790 -81.386570
Fort Pulaski Natl. Mon.	130	C3	32.016520 -80.891680
Jimmy Carter N.H.S.	128	C3	32.034090 -84.401600
Kennesaw Mtn. Natl. Battlefied Park-Vis. Ctr.	120	C3	33.983000 -84.577900
Ocmulgee Natl. Mon.	129	D2	32.848560 -83.602140
State Park & Rec. Areas			
Amicalola Falls S.P.	120	C2	34.558940 -84.248890
Black Rock Mtn. S.P.	121	D2	34.918150 -83.400310
Bobby Brown State Outdoor Rec. Area	121	E3	33.979030 -82.588960
Cloudland Canyon S.P.	120	B2	34.830430 -85.482040
Crooked River S.P.	139	D1	30.844840 -81.559350
Elijah Clark S.P.	121	E4	33.854210 -82.391913
Florence Marina S.P.	128	C3	32.090988 -85.043263
Fort Mtn. S.P.	120	C2	34.763090 -84.689330
Fort Yargo S.P.	121	D4	33.984940 -83.733580
Franklin D. Roosevelt S.P.	128	C2	32.848670 -84.793230
General Coffee S.P.	129	E4	31.511490 -82.745360
George L. Smith S.P.	130	A2	32.570310 -82.103760
George T. Bagby S.P.	128	C4	31.739940 -85.074820
Georgia Veterans S.P.	129	D3	31.957951 -83.903787
Gordonia-Alatamaha S.P.	130	A3	32.081900 -82.123550
Hamburg S.P.	129	E1	33.208800 -82.774870
Hard Labor Creek S.P.	121	D4	33.677820 -83.593840
Hart State Outdoor Rec. Area	121	E3	34.376040 -82.910260
High Falls S.P.	129	D1	33.176590 -84.020280
Indian Springs S.P.	129	D1	33.247480 -83.921190
James H. "Sloppy" Floyd S.P.	120	B3	34.440260 -85.347580
John Tanner S.P.	120	B4	33.602750 -85.167070
Laura S. Walker S.P.	138	C1	31.143130 -82.212920
Little Ocmulgee S.P.	129	E3	32.100590 -82.886360
Magnolia Springs S.P.	130	A1	32.875760 -81.962560
Mistletoe S.P.	121	E4	33.638770 -82.390540
Moccasin Creek S.P.	121	D2	34.845160 -83.589140
Panola Mtn. S.P.	120	C4	33.622042 -84.173078
Providence Canyon State Outdoor Rec. Area	128	C3	32.068270 -84.929150
Red Top Mtn. S.P.	120	C3	34.145950 -84.720190
Reed Bingham S.P.	137	F1	31.161310 -83.538880
Richard B. Russell S.P.	121	E3	34.166778 -82.745691
Seminole S.P.	137	D1	30.811420 -84.873570
Skidaway Island S.P.	130	C3	31.947720 -81.052550
Sprewell Bluff State Outdoor Rec. Area	128	C2	32.857269 -84.482657
Stephen C. Foster S.P.	138	C1	30.827020 -82.361310

llulah Gorge S.P.	121	D2	34.736350 -83.391950
galoo S.P.	121	E3	34.501940 -83.082320
nicoi S.P.	121	D2	34.724620 -83.728170
ctoria Bryant S.P.	121	E3	34.299380 -83.158770
ogel S.P.	121	D2	34.766190 -83.922000
atson Mill Bridge S.P.	121	E3	34.041140 -83.126990

HAWAII	PAGE	GRID	LATITUDE LONGITUDE
ational Park & Rec. Areas			
aleakala Natl. Park-Main Road	153	D1	20.769130 -156.242850
aleakala Natl. Park-Kipahulu Ent.	153	D1	20.662000 -156.045600
aleakala Natl. Park-North Ent.	153	D1	20.769000 -156.243000
awaii Volcanoes Natl. Park-Ent.	153	F4	19.428700 -155.254500
onouliuli Natl. Mon.	152	A3	21.354145 -158.090528
alaupapa N.H.P.	152	C3	21.174110 -157.002830
tate Park & Rec. Areas			
hupuaa O Kahana S.P.	152	A2	21.555210 -157.873260
aena S.P.	152	B1	22.220930 -159.579600
aena Point S.P.	152	A2	21.551270 -158.244180
aumahina State Wayside Park	153	D1	20.871610 -156.170310
okee S.P.	152	B1	22.112580 -159.671050
akena S.P.	153	D1	20.634030 -156.444180
alaau S.P.	152	C3	21.174110 -157.002830
olihale S.P.	152	B1	22.084480 -159.756700
uaa Kaa State Wayside	153	D1	20.817560 -156.125800
aianapanapa S.P.	153	E1	20.786230 -156.003010
ailua River S.P.	152	B1	22.044180 -159.337250
ailua Valley State Wayside	153	D1	20.840110 -156.139980
ailuku River S.P.	153	F3	19.713340 -155.130490
aimea Canyon S.P.	152	B1	22.031990 -159.671100

IDAHO	PAGE	GRID	LATITUDE LONGITUDE
ational Park & Rec. Areas			
ity of Rocks Natl. Res.	31	D2	42.078950 -113.677650
raters of the Moon Natl. Mon. & Pres.	23	D4	43.462030 -113.559930
agerman Fossil Beds Natl. Mon.	30	C1	42.760980 -114.928220
inidoka Natl. Hist. Site	31	D1	42.636944 -114.232222
ez Perce N.H.P.-Clearwater Bfld.	22	B1	46.072600 -115.975400
ez Perce N.H.P.-East Kamiah Site	22	B1	46.216600 -115.992400
ez Perce N.H.P.-Vis. Ctr.	22	B1	46.446500 -116.817000
ez Perce N.H.P.-White Bird Bfld.	22	B1	45.794400 -116.282000
awtooth N.R.A.	22	C3	44.211000 -114.946000
tate Park & Rec. Areas			
ear Lake S.P.	31	F2	42.026180 -111.257690
runeau Dunes S.P.	30	B1	42.910940 -115.713890
astle Rocks S.P.	31	D2	42.135400 -113.670000
worshak S.P.	14	B4	46.577610 -116.327310
agle Island S.P.	22	B4	43.684510 -116.400300
arragut S.P.	14	B2	47.952790 -116.602170
arriman S.P.	23	F3	44.321000 -111.471200
ells Gate S.P.	14	B4	46.380500 -117.044780
enrys Lake S.P.	23	F3	44.620000 -111.373060
eyburn S.P.	14	B3	47.353840 -116.748770
ake Cascade S.P.	22	B3	44.520686 -116.046685
ake Walcott S.P.	31	D1	42.674850 -113.482570
and of the Yankee Fork S.P.	22	C3	44.475190 -114.208860
ucky Peak S.P.	22	B4	43.530880 -116.055160
assacre Rocks S.P.	31	D1	42.672200 -112.990800
cCroskey S.P.	14	B4	47.721080 -116.826310
ld Mission S.P.	14	B3	47.549420 -116.356940
onderosa S.P.	22	B2	44.926810 -116.083860
riest Lake S.P.	14	B1	48.622082 -116.827798
ound Lake S.P.	14	B2	48.166110 -116.634230
housand Springs S.P.-Box Canyon	30	C1	42.709800 -114.791900
housand Springs S.P.-Malad Gorge	30	C1	42.864400 -114.854600
housand Springs S.P.-Niagara Springs	30	C1	42.662800 -114.672400
hree Island Crossing S.P.	30	C1	42.945280 -115.314850
inchester Lake S.P.	22	B1	46.232280 -116.635570

ILLINOIS	PAGE	GRID	LATITUDE LONGITUDE
National Park & Rec. Areas			
incoln Home N.H.S.	98	B1	39.798120 -89.645150
onald Reagan Boyhood Home N.H.S.	88	B1	41.836700 -89.481100
State Park & Rec. Areas			
Apple River Canyon S.P.	74	A4	42.443990 -90.053280
Argyle Lake S.P.	87	F4	40.450680 -90.805080
Banner Marsh State Fish & Wildlife Area	88	B4	40.539600 -89.864500
Beall Woods S.P.	99	D4	38.351540 -87.836380
Beaver Dam S.P.	98	B2	39.214390 -89.959390
Big Bend State Fish & Wildlife Area	88	A2	41.634900 -90.044600
Buffalo Rock S.P.	88	C2	41.329720 -88.913090
Carlyle Lake State Fish & Wildlife Area	98	C3	38.768500 -89.193900
Castle Rock S.P.	88	B1	41.978230 -89.357040
Cave-In-Rock S.P.	109	D1	37.468010 -88.159950
Chain O'Lakes S.P.	74	C4	42.458390 -88.211950
Channahon S.P.	88	C2	41.415826 -88.223133
Coffeen Lake State Fish & Wildlife Area	98	B2	39.057000 -89.412400
Crawford County State Fish & Wildlife Area	99	D2	39.099800 -87.713100
Delabar S.P.	87	F3	40.957830 -90.939460
Des Plaines State Fish & Wildlife Area	88	C2	41.376600 -88.207400
Dixon Springs S.P.	108	C1	37.383600 -88.672830
Donnelley–Depue State Fish & Wildlife Area	88	B2	41.324000 -89.314100
Edward R. Madigan State Fish & Wildlife Area	88	B4	40.115280 -89.402240
Eldon Hazlet State Rec. Area	98	B3	38.667610 -89.327200
Ferne Clyffe S.P.	108	C1	37.532550 -88.966430
Fort Massac S.P.	108	C2	37.161720 -88.693850
Fox Ridge S.P.	99	D2	39.406020 -88.134810
Gebhard Woods S.P.	88	C2	41.357350 -88.440210
Giant City S.P.	108	C1	37.612250 -89.181790
Green River State Wildlife Area	88	B2	41.631600 -89.516500
Hamilton County State Fish & Wildlife Area	98	C4	38.065100 -88.404700
Hazel & Bill Rutherford Wildlife Prairie S.P.	88	B3	40.734180 -89.747270
Henderson County Cons. Area	87	F3	40.857505 -90.975005
Horseshoe Lake State Fish & Wildlife Area	108	C2	37.130465 -89.338505
Illini S.P.	88	C2	41.318770 -88.711070
Illinois Beach S.P.	75	D4	42.429920 -87.820150
Iroquois County State Wildlife Area	89	D3	40.994300 -87.598700
Jim Edgar Panther Creek State Fish & Wildlife Area	98	B1	40.011700 -90.177005
Johnson-Sauk Trail S.P.	88	A2	41.327510 -89.904850
Jubilee College S.P.	88	B3	40.844580 -89.827260
Kankakee River S.P.	89	D2	41.203400 -88.001880
Kaskaskia River State Fish & Wildlife Area	98	B4	38.229700 -89.879500
Kickapoo State Rec. Area	89	D4	40.138290 -87.737770
Lake Le Aqua-Na State Rec. Area	74	A4	42.422800 -89.823900
Lake Murphysboro S.P.	108	C1	37.771800 -89.382670
Lasalle Lake State Fish & Wildlife Area	88	C2	41.238400 -88.655500
Lincoln Trail S.P.	99	D2	39.346480 -87.696460
Lowden S.P.	88	B1	42.034860 -89.324950
Mackinaw River State Fish & Wildlife Area	88	B4	40.545801 -89.294301
Marshall State Fish & Wildlife Area	88	B3	41.007900 -89.410100
Matthiessen S.P.	88	C2	41.285010 -89.010050
Mautino State Fish & Wildlife Area	88	B2	41.323100 -89.718900
Middle Fork State Fish & Wildlife Area	89	D4	40.258300 -87.795900
Mississippi Palisades S.P.	88	A1	42.135820 -90.163300
Mississippi River State Fish & Wildlife Area	98	A2	38.991900 -90.542100
Morrison-Rockwood S.P.	88	A1	41.856350 -89.950120
Nauvoo S.P.	87	F4	40.543590 -91.386650
Newton Lake State Fish & Wildlife Area	99	D2	38.922400 -88.306700
Pere Marquette S.P.	98	A2	38.968110 -90.497430
Prophetstown S.P.	88	B2	41.672090 -89.920310
Pyramid S.P.	98	B4	38.003110 -89.425680
Ray Norbut State Fish & Wildlife Area	98	A1	39.685000 -90.648500
Red Hills S.P.	99	D3	38.728850 -87.838660
Rend Lake State Fish & Wildlife Area	98	C4	38.043800 -88.988900
Rice Lake State Fish & Wildlife Area	88	A4	40.476785 -89.949205
Saline County State Fish & Wildlife Area	109	D1	37.691300 -88.379100
Sam Dale Lake State Fish & Wildlife Area	98	C3	38.536005 -88.565605
Sam Parr State Fish & Wildlife Area	99	D2	39.011022 -88.126955
Sanganois State Fish & Wildlife Area	88	A4	40.091605 -90.283205
Sangchris Lake State Rec. Area	98	B1	39.656830 -89.487940
Shabbona Lake S.P.	88	C1	41.732250 -88.864930
Shelbyville State Fish & Wildlife Area	98	C2	39.566300 -88.566200
Siloam Springs S.P.	97	F1	39.899340 -90.955050
Silver Springs State Fish & Wildlife Area.	88	C2	41.627500 -88.518550
Snakeden Hollow State Fish & Wildlife Area	88	A3	41.030200 -90.080100
South Shore S.P.	98	B3	38.610250 -89.314570
Starved Rock S.P.	88	C2	41.321750 -89.010850
Stephen A. Forbes State Rec. Area	98	C3	38.718140 -88.743250
Ten Mile Creek State Fish & Wildlife Area	98	C4	38.081200 -88.594200
Turkey Bluffs State Fish & Wildlife Area	98	B4	37.877200 -89.771100
Walnut Point S.P.	99	D1	39.705150 -88.030390
Wayne Fitzgerrell S.P.	98	C4	38.089250 -88.937010
Weinberg-King S.P.	87	F4	40.226830 -90.899700
Weldon Springs S.P.	88	C4	40.125080 -88.921400
White Pines Forest S.P.	88	B1	41.988730 -89.461590
Wolf Creek S.P.	98	C2	39.488310 -88.680370
Woodford State Fish & Wildlife Area	88	B3	40.878900 -89.444800

INDIANA	PAGE	GRID	LATITUDE LONGITUDE
National Park & Rec. Areas			
George Rodgers Clark N.H.P.	99	D3	38.677880 -87.535350
Indiana Dunes Natl. Lakeshore	89	D1	41.653160 -87.062630
Lincoln Boyhood Natl. Mem.	99	E4	38.116800 -86.997860
State Park & Rec. Areas			
Bass Lake State Beach	89	E2	41.220100 -86.580200
Brown County S.P.	99	F2	39.197170 -86.215830
Chain O' Lakes S.P.	90	A2	41.336000 -85.422950
Charlestown S.P.	100	A3	38.448300 -85.644700
Clifty Falls S.P.	100	A3	38.761220 -85.420720
Fort Harrison S.P.	99	F1	39.871921 -86.018859
Harmonie S.P.	99	D4	38.089210 -87.934080
Indiana Dunes S.P.	89	E2	41.651470 -87.062620
Lincoln S.P.	99	E4	38.118370 -86.980080
McCormick's Creek S.P.	99	E2	39.283340 -86.726680
O'Bannon Woods S.P.	99	F4	38.200600 -86.254678
Ouabache S.P.	90	A3	40.728090 -85.111060
Pokagon S.P.	90	A1	41.707960 -85.029320
Potato Creek S.P.	89	E2	41.534950 -86.360290
Prophetstown S.P.	89	E4	40.500211 -86.829548
Shades S.P.	99	E1	39.941630 -87.057670
Shakamak S.P.	99	E2	39.181800 -87.232200
Spring Mill S.P.	99	F3	38.723330 -86.418460
Summit Lake S.P.	100	A1	40.018680 -85.302720
Tippecanoe River S.P.	89	E3	41.117330 -86.602750
Turkey Run S.P.	99	E1	39.882010 -87.200550
Versailles S.P.	100	A2	39.063900 -85.205330
Whitewater Mem. S.P.	100	B1	39.611300 -84.942300

IOWA	PAGE	GRID	LATITUDE LONGITUDE
National Park & Rec. Areas			
Effigy Mounds Natl. Mon.	73	F3	43.089310 -91.192350
Herbert Hoover N.H.S.	87	F1	41.671390 -91.346640
State Park & Rec. Areas			
Ambrose A. Call S.P.	72	B3	43.049650 -94.243430
Backbone S.P.	73	E4	42.600730 -91.532700
Beed's Lake S.P.	73	D4	42.767209 -93.241705
Bellevue S.P.	88	A1	42.247870 -90.416920
Black Hawk S.P.	72	B4	42.302700 -95.048680
Bobwhite S.P.	86	C3	40.710200 -93.393850
Cold Springs S.P.	86	B2	41.289540 -95.083810
Crystal Lake S.P.	72	C3	43.224895 -93.792925
Echo Valley S.P.	73	E3	42.944040 -91.776880
Elk Rock S.P.	87	D2	41.400470 -93.063050
Fort Defiance S.P.	72	B2	43.393260 -94.851290
George Wyth Mem. S.P.	73	E4	42.536980 -92.394210
Green Valley S.P.	86	B3	41.114490 -94.377270
Heery Woods S.P.	73	D4	42.766450 -92.675250
Honey Creek S.P.	87	D3	40.863940 -92.939050
Lake Ahquabi S.P.	86	C2	41.286710 -93.572690
Lake Anita S.P.	86	B2	41.434150 -94.762470
Lake Icaria S.P.	86	B3	41.053380 -94.756990
Lake Keomah S.P.	87	D2	41.286570 -92.541660
Lake Macbride S.P.	87	F1	41.803090 -91.570950
Lake Wapello S.P.	87	D3	40.824890 -92.570530
Ledges S.P.	86	C1	41.998970 -93.896110
Maquoketa Caves S.P.	87	F1	42.119890 -90.770950
McIntosh Woods S.P.	72	C3	43.132580 -93.457580
Mini-Wakan S.P.	72	B2	43.498460 -95.102320
Nine Eagles S.P.	86	C3	40.591250 -93.765130
Oakland Mills S.P.	87	E3	40.935400 -91.619370
Palisades-Kepler S.P.	87	F1	41.916880 -91.497050
Pammel S.P.	86	C2	41.295590 -94.073150
Pikes Point S.P.	72	A2	43.415320 -95.162860
Pilot Knob S.P.	72	C3	43.255470 -93.574840
Prairie Rose S.P.	86	A2	41.601590 -95.210660
Preparation Canyon S.P.	86	A1	41.901570 -95.911670
Rice Lake S.P.	72	C2	43.401350 -93.502490
Rock Creek S.P.	87	D1	41.760580 -92.835410
Spring Lake S.P.	86	B1	42.070600 -94.291500
Stone S.P.	35	F1	42.555460 -96.476050
Trappers Bay S.P.	72	A2	43.453630 -95.335510
Twin Lakes S.P.	72	B4	42.480180 -94.629860
Viking Lake S.P.	86	B3	40.973170 -95.053710
Wanata S.P.	72	A3	42.911340 -95.338080
Waubonsie S.P.	86	A3	40.677770 -95.683680
Wildcat Den S.P.	87	F2	41.467700 -90.869330

KANSAS	PAGE	GRID	LATITUDE LONGITUDE
National Park & Rec. Areas			
Fort Larned N.H.S.	43	D3	38.188740 -99.220620
Fort Scott N.H.S.	106	B1	37.843350 -94.704840
Monument Rocks Natl. Landmark	42	B2	38.790569 -100.762366
Nicodemus N.H.S.	42	C2	39.390833 -99.617500
State Park & Rec. Areas			
Atchison State Fishing Lake	96	B1	39.639010 -95.171830
Black Kettle State Fishing Lake	43	E3	38.229240 -97.509390
Bourbon State Fishing Lake	106	B1	37.793450 -95.069690
Brown State Fishing Lake	96	A1	39.847030 -95.373860
Cedar Bluff S.P.	42	C2	38.798230 -99.715060
Chase State Fishing Lake	43	F3	38.368480 -96.588000
Cheney S.P.	43	E4	37.732700 -97.844350
Clark State Fishing Lake	42	C4	37.391670 -99.784720
Clinton S.P.	96	A3	38.941970 -95.353960
Cowley State Fishing Lake	51	F1	37.104040 -96.795000
Crawford S.P.	106	B1	37.634320 -94.809820
Cross Timbers S.P.	106	A1	37.774514 -95.943431
Douglas State Fishing Lake	96	B3	38.796030 -95.165150
Eisenhower S.P.	96	A3	38.535720 -95.744270
El Dorado S.P.	43	F4	37.861420 -96.749460
Elk City S.P.	106	A2	37.251130 -95.774090
Fallriver S.P.	43	F4	37.653550 -96.043600
Glen Elder S.P.	43	D1	39.512160 -98.339140
Hain State Fishing Lake	42	C4	37.854250 -99.858020
Hamilton State Fishing Lake	42	B3	38.039090 -101.816940
Hillsdale S.P.	96	B3	38.660700 -94.894000
Kanopolis S.P.	43	E3	38.600340 -97.979500
Kingman State Fishing Lake	43	E4	37.651390 -98.306940
Kiowa State Fishing Lake	43	D4	37.612570 -99.299000
Leavenworth State Fishing Lake	96	B2	39.126970 -95.141700
Logan State Fishing Lake	42	B2	38.940280 -101.236940
Lovewell S.P.	43	E1	39.903310 -98.043090
Lyon State Fishing Lake	43	F3	38.546520 -96.058050
McPherson State Fishing Lake	43	E3	38.478667 -97.468267
Meade S.P.	42	C4	37.172220 -100.450000

Miami State Fishing Lake	96	B3	38.422220 -94.785280
Milford S.P.	43	F2	39.104290 -96.895520
Mushroom Rock S.P.	43	E2	38.722222 -98.032222
Nebo State Fishing Lake	96	A2	39.447220 -95.595830
Neosho State Fishing Lake	106	B1	37.430570 -95.202550
Ottawa State Fishing Lake	43	E2	39.103040 -97.573060
Perry S.P.	96	A2	39.140210 -95.492480
Pomona S.P.	96	A3	38.652400 -95.600800
Pottawatomie State Fishing Lake No. 1	43	F1	39.470370 -96.407510
Pottawatomie State Fishing Lake No. 2	43	F2	39.228100 -96.533660
Prairie Dog S.P.	42	C1	39.811810 -99.963920
Prairie Spirit Trail S.P.	96	A4	38.280278 -95.242222
Rooks State Fishing Lake	43	D2	39.398290 -99.315020
Saline State Fishing Lake	43	E2	38.903159 -97.657510
Sand Hills S.P.	43	E3	38.116667 -97.833333
Scott S.P.	42	B2	38.684867 -100.922500
Shawnee State Fishing Lake	96	A2	39.206940 -95.804170
Tuttle Creek S.P.	43	F2	39.255560 -96.583330
Washington State Fishing Lake	43	E1	39.929780 -97.118830
Webster S.P.	43	D2	39.407840 -99.454550
Wilson State Fishing Lake	106	A1	38.910450 -98.497950
Wilson S.P.	43	D2	38.915000 -98.500000

KENTUCKY	PAGE	GRID	LATITUDE LONGITUDE
National Park & Rec. Areas			
Abraham Lincoln Birthplace N.H.P.	110	A1	37.532280 -85.733570
Land Between the Lakes N.R.A.	109	D2	36.776912 -88.059988
Mammoth Cave Natl. Park-Vis. Ctr.	109	F2	37.186800 -86.101300
State Park & Rec. Areas			
Barren River Lake State Resort Park	110	A2	36.853220 -86.053850
Ben Hawes S.P.	109	E1	37.797034 -87.188186
Blue Licks Btfld. State Resort Park	100	C3	38.434960 -83.991340
Buckhorn Lake State Resort Park	111	D1	37.312890 -83.423040
Carter Caves State Resort Park	101	D4	38.371470 -83.108510
Columbus-Belmont S.P.	108	C2	36.761990 -89.107000
Cumberland Falls State Resort Park	110	C2	36.834390 -84.350170
Fishtrap Lake S.P.	111	E1	37.432048 -82.417926
Fort Boonesborough S.P.	110	C1	37.899345 -84.270040
General Butler State Resort Park	100	A3	38.669950 -85.146050
Grayson Lake S.P.	101	D4	38.208630 -83.014910
Greenbo Lake State Resort Park	101	D3	38.479130 -82.867630
Green River Lake S.P.	110	A2	37.277440 -85.338730
Jenny Wiley State Resort Park-East Ent.	111	E1	37.730120 -82.740990
Jenny Wiley State Resort Park-South Ent.	111	E1	37.687680 -82.725690
Jenny Wiley State Resort Park-West Ent.	111	E1	37.727250 -82.745880
John James Audubon S.P.	99	D4	37.889250 -87.556510
Kentucky Dam Village State Resort Park	109	D2	36.996880 -88.285716
Kingdom Come S.P.	111	D2	36.981850 -82.982210
Lake Barkley State Resort Park	109	D2	36.809190 -87.928310
Lake Cumberland State Resort Park	110	B2	36.930320 -85.040960
Levi Jackson S.P.	110	C2	37.085250 -84.059250
Lincoln Homestead S.P.	110	B1	37.760080 -85.215930
My Old Kentucky Home S.P.	110	A1	37.808140 -85.458840
Natural Bridge State Resort Park	110	C1	37.777470 -83.676310
Nolin Lake S.P.	109	F1	37.297641 -86.212624
Old Fort Harrod S.P.	110	B1	37.762130 -84.845670
Pennyrile Forest State Resort Park	109	E2	37.057410 -87.649390
Pine Mtn. State Resort Park	110	C3	36.735270 -83.700790
Rough River State Resort Park	109	F1	37.615410 -86.504410
Taylorsville Lake S.P.	100	A4	37.993990 -85.227813
Yatesville Lake S.P.	101	D4	38.093300 -82.617800

LOUISIANA	PAGE	GRID	LATITUDE LONGITUDE
National Park & Rec. Areas			
Cane River Creole N.H.P.	125	D4	31.739690 -93.083080
Jean Lafitte N.H.P. & Pres.-Chalmette Vis. Ctr.	134	A3	29.942100 -89.994400
Jean Lafitte N.H.P. & Pres.-French Quarter Vis. Ctr.	134	A3	29.954600 -90.065100
Jean Lafitte N.H.P.-Wetlands Acadian Cultural Center	134	A3	29.795969 -90.824480
Poverty Point Natl. Mon. & S.H.S.	125	F2	32.633370 -91.403880
State Park & Rec. Areas			
Bayou Segnette S.P.	134	B3	29.902720 -90.153800
Chemin-A-Haut S.P.	125	F1	32.913460 -91.847550
Chicot S.P.	133	E1	30.829870 -92.276180
Cypremort Point S.P.	133	F3	29.731960 -91.840740
Fairview-Riverside S.P.	134	B2	30.408730 -90.140360
Fontainebleau S.P.	134	B2	30.345470 -90.022850
Grand Isle S.P.-Temp. Closed	134	B4	29.256640 -89.958480
Hodges Gardens S.P.	125	D4	31.369280 -93.424860
Jimmie Davis S.P.	125	E3	32.265000 -92.540300
Lake Bistineau S.P.	125	D2	32.440250 -93.395910
Lake Bruin S.P.	126	A3	31.955370 -91.198080
Lake Claiborne S.P.	125	D2	32.713000 -92.923360
Lake D'Arbonne S.P.	125	E2	32.784850 -92.490310
Lake Fausse Pointe S.P.	133	F3	30.067820 -91.615790
North Toledo Bend S.P.	124	C4	31.558910 -93.732060
Palmetto Island S.P.	133	F3	29.862877 -92.144165
Poverty Point Reservoir S.P.	125	F2	32.540446 -91.421356
Saint Bernard S.P.	134	C3	29.864460 -89.899190
South Toledo Bend S.P.	125	D4	31.213889 -93.575000
Tickfaw S.P.	134	B2	30.382180 -90.631150

MAINE	PAGE	GRID	LATITUDE LONGITUDE
National Park & Rec. Areas			
Acadia Natl. Park-Cadillac Mtn. Ent.	83	D2	44.384400 -68.229800
Acadia Natl. Park-Park Loop Road	83	D2	44.338700 -68.183200
Acadia Natl. Park-Sieur de Monts Ent.	83	D2	44.360000 -68.205200
Acadia Natl. Park-Stanley Brook Ent.	83	D2	44.296300 -68.242000
State Park & Rec. Areas			
Aroostook S.P.	85	E2	46.612720 -68.005840
Baxter S.P.	84	C3	45.950290 -69.049080
Camden Hills S.P.	82	C2	44.232050 -69.046530
Cobscook Bay S.P.	83	E1	44.855290 -67.171680
Damariscotta Lake S.P.	82	C2	44.200070 -69.452900
Ferry Beach S.P.	82	B4	43.482410 -70.391520
Lake Saint George S.P.	82	C2	44.398950 -69.345710
Lamoine S.P.	83	D2	44.456000 -68.298520
Mount Blue S.P.	82	B1	44.721780 -70.417080
Peaks-Kenny S.P.	84	C4	45.256680 -69.254600
Popham Beach S.P.	82	C3	43.738740 -69.795830
Rangeley Lake S.P.	82	B1	44.919550 -70.696950
Range Ponds S.P.	82	B3	44.033540 -70.345080
Roque Bluffs S.P.	83	E2	44.614680 -67.479300
Saint Croix Island International Hist. Site	83	E1	45.128333 -67.133333
Sebago Lake S.P.	82	B3	43.916590 -70.570190
Shackford Head S.P.	83	F1	44.906191 -66.989979
Swan Lake S.P.	82	C2	44.568860 -68.981070
Vaughan Woods S.P.	82	A4	43.212680 -70.809320
Warren Island S.P.	82	C2	44.260445 -68.952255
Wolfe's Neck Woods S.P.	82	B3	43.827190 -70.084460

MARYLAND	PAGE	GRID	LATITUDE LONGITUDE
National Park & Rec. Areas			
Assateague Island Natl. Seashore	114	C2	38.239580 -75.140410
Harriet Tubman Underground RR Natl. Mon.	103	F3	38.322307 -76.176243
Thomas Stone N.H.S.	144	B4	38.529700 -77.032370
State Park & Rec. Areas			
Assateague S.P.	114	C2	38.250170 -75.156270
Big Run S.P.	102	B1	39.545090 -79.137254
Catoctin Mtn. Park-Vis. Ctr.	144	A1	39.633100 -77.449700
Cunningham Falls S.P.	144	A1	39.625040 -77.458130
Deep Creek Lake S.P.	102	B1	39.512110 -79.300150
Elk Neck S.P.	145	D1	39.482890 -75.983630
Fort Frederick S.P.	103	D1	39.616050 -78.007060
Gambrill S.P.	144	A1	39.468330 -77.495730
Greenwell S.P.	103	E4	38.364930 -76.525260
Gunpowder Falls S.P.	144	C1	39.536710 -76.502800
Hart-Miller Island S.P.	144	C2	39.251219 -76.376903
Janes Island S.P.	103	F4	38.009810 -75.846380
Martinak S.P.	145	E3	38.862920 -75.837790
North Point S.P.	144	C2	39.221910 -76.431600
Patapsco Valley S.P.	144	B2	39.296580 -76.781500
Patuxent River S.P.	144	B2	39.280790 -77.129620
Pocomoke River S.P.	114	C2	38.135410 -75.494870
Point Lookout S.P.	103	F4	38.066190 -76.336550
Rocks S.P.	144	C1	39.630140 -76.418120
Rocky Gap S.P.	102	C1	39.698430 -78.651150
Rosaryville S.P.	144	C3	38.778450 -76.799260
Saint Clement's Island S.P.	103	E4	38.225200 -76.749690
Saint Mary's River S.P.	103	E4	38.262940 -76.525640
Sandy Point S.P.	144	C3	39.021750 -76.420280
Seneca Creek S.P.	144	A2	39.152200 -77.247710
Smallwood S.P.	144	B4	38.556509 -77.185257
South Mtn. S.P.	144	A1	39.540058 -77.607422
Susquehanna S.P.	145	D1	39.599840 -76.154590
Swallow Falls S.P.	102	B1	39.506550 -79.448750
Tuckahoe S.P.	145	D3	38.967120 -75.943410
Washington Mon. S.P.	144	A1	39.499810 -77.631890
Wye Oak S.P.	145	D3	38.939150 -76.080230

MASSACHUSETTS	PAGE	GRID	LATITUDE LONGITUDE
National Park & Rec. Areas			
Adams N.H.P.-Vis. Ctr.	151	D1	42.257000 -71.011200
Boston Harbor Island N.R.A.	151	D1	42.319705 -70.928555
Cape Cod Natl. Seashore	151	F2	41.835890 -69.973730
Lowell N.H.P.-Market Mills Vis. Ctr.	95	E1	42.644400 -71.312800
Minute Man N.H.P.-Minute Man Vis. Ctr.	151	D1	42.449000 -71.268700
Minute Man N.H.P.-North Bridge Vis. Ctr.	151	D1	42.470800 -71.352600
New Bedford Whaling N.H.P.	151	D4	41.635570 -70.924250
Salem Maritime N.H.S.	151	D1	42.521490 -70.886980
Saugus Iron Works N.H.S.	151	D1	42.468230 -71.009110
Waquoit Bay Natl. Estuarine Research Res.	151	E4	41.581300 -70.524800
State Park & Rec. Areas			
Ames-Nowell S.P.	151	D2	42.113140 -70.975230
Ashland S.P.	150	C2	42.246380 -71.475560
Blackstone River & Canal Heritage S.P.	150	C2	42.099500 -71.618780
Borderland S.P.	151	D2	42.058560 -71.166330
Bradley Palmer S.P.	151	F1	42.652180 -70.911000
Callahan S.P.	150	C1	42.315140 -71.367710
Demarest Lloyd S.P.	151	D4	41.525790 -70.990530
Dighton Rock S.P.	151	D3	41.811230 -71.098440
Halibut Point S.P.	151	F1	42.686100 -70.631070
Hampton Ponds S.P.	150	A2	42.178350 -72.690030
Holyoke Range S.P.	150	A1	42.297270 -72.530890
Joseph Sylvia State Beach	151	E4	41.424140 -70.553870
Lake Wyola S.P.-Carroll Holmes Rec. Area	150	A1	42.500366 -72.430642
Moore S.P.	150	B1	42.312354 -71.954269
Nickerson S.P.	151	F3	41.775550 -70.028290
Pilgrim Mem. (Plymouth Rock) S.P.	151	E2	41.958850 -70.662870
Red Bridge S.P.	150	A2	42.175500 -72.406600
Robinson S.P.	150	A2	42.081680 -72.658650
Rutland S.P.	150	B1	42.371470 -71.997680
Savoy Mtn. State Forest	94	C1	42.626540 -73.015580
Skinner S.P.	150	A1	42.304220 -72.598790
South Cape Beach S.P.	151	E4	41.554582 -70.508194
Wahconah Falls S.P.	94	C1	42.491430 -73.120790
Watson Pond S.P.	151	D2	41.956260 -71.116090
Wells S.P.	150	B2	42.142290 -72.042400
Whitehall S.P.	150	C2	42.227210 -71.584330
Wompatuck S.P.	151	D2	42.218770 -70.866600

MICHIGAN	PAGE	GRID	LATITUDE LONGITUDE
National Park & Rec. Areas			
Father Marquette Natl. Mem.	70	C2	45.853912 -84.728874
Grand Island N.R.A.	70	A1	46.500405 -86.657605
Isle Royale Natl. Park-Rock Harbor Vis. Ctr.	65	F2	48.145530 -88.482220
Isle Royale Natl. Park-Windigo Vis. Ctr.	65	F2	47.912700 -89.156990
Keweenaw N.H.P.	65	F3	47.242160 -88.448020
Pictured Rocks Natl. Lakeshore-East Ent.	70	A1	46.657450 -86.021160
Pictured Rocks Natl. Lakeshore-West Ent.	70	A1	46.474000 -86.553000
Sleeping Bear Dunes Natl. Lakeshore	70	A4	44.785210 -86.049690
State Park & Rec. Areas			
Albert E. Sleeper S.P.	76	C2	43.972880 -83.205530
Algonac S.P.	76	C4	42.654760 -82.514510
Aloha S.P.	70	C3	45.525850 -84.464390
Baraga S.P.	65	F4	46.762070 -88.499320
Bewabic S.P.	68	C2	46.094260 -88.422290
Brimley S.P.	70	C1	46.412970 -84.555040
Burt Lake S.P.	70	C3	45.401305 -84.619505
Cambridge Junction Hist. S.P.	90	B1	42.066990 -84.225550
Charles Mears S.P.	75	E2	43.781980 -86.439670
Cheboygan S.P.	70	C2	45.644860 -84.420440
Clear Lake S.P.	70	C3	45.127390 -84.173910
Coldwater Lake S.P.	90	A1	43.665975 -84.948703
Craig Lake S.P.	68	C1	46.538810 -88.127700
Duck Lake S.P.	75	E3	43.354880 -86.397560
F.J. Mclain S.P.	65	F3	47.239400 -88.587190
Fayette Hist. S.P.	70	A2	45.717200 -86.664600
Fisherman's Island S.P.	70	B3	45.307550 -85.301540
Fort Wilkins Hist. S.P.	65	F3	47.466780 -87.878240
Grand Haven S.P.	75	E3	43.056100 -86.245990
Grand Mere S.P.	89	E1	41.995190 -86.538790
Harrisville S.P.	71	D4	44.649800 -83.293920
Hart-Montague Trail S.P.	75	E2	43.688800 -86.371900
Hartwick Pines S.P.	70	C4	44.744180 -84.648340
Holland S.P.	75	E4	42.780310 -86.201410
Indian Lake S.P.	70	A2	45.960420 -86.364400
Interlochen S.P.	70	B4	44.631370 -85.766630
J.W. Wells S.P.	69	D3	45.389070 -87.371360
Kal-Haven Trail S.P.	75	E4	42.324698 -85.667739
Lake Gogebic S.P.	68	B1	46.459950 -89.573110
Lakelands Trail S.P.	76	B4	42.408249 -83.964043
Lakeport S.P.	76	C3	43.129120 -82.501820
Leelanau S.P.	70	B3	45.209320 -85.546220
Ludington S.P.	75	E1	44.031100 -86.505460
Mackinac Island S.P.	70	C2	45.849880 -84.617650
Muskallonge Lake S.P.	70	B1	46.677100 -85.625210
Muskegon S.P.	75	E3	43.247900 -86.341480
Negwegon S.P.	71	D4	44.855020 -83.329240
Newaygo S.P.	75	F2	43.500600 -85.582260
North Higgins Lake S.P.	70	C4	44.515030 -84.753980
Onaway S.P.	70	C3	45.430530 -84.229020
Orchard Beach S.P.	75	E1	44.278860 -86.314480
Otsego Lake S.P.	70	C4	44.927770 -84.688980
P.H. Hoeft S.P.	70	C3	45.463700 -83.883560
P.J. Hoffmaster S.P.	75	E3	43.132870 -86.265460
Palms Book S.P.	70	A2	46.003280 -86.385130
Petoskey S.P.	70	B3	45.407950 -84.902160
Porcupine Mts. Wilderness S.P.	65	E4	46.816070 -89.621850
Port Crescent S.P.	76	C1	44.007570 -83.051290
Sanilac Petroglyphs Hist. S.P.	76	C2	43.649367 -83.018016
Saugatuck Dunes S.P.	75	E4	42.695990 -86.186840
Seven Lakes S.P.	76	B3	42.816750 -83.648120
Silver Lake S.P.	75	E2	43.663650 -86.492660
Sleepy Hollow S.P.	76	A3	42.925020 -84.408620
South Higgins Lake S.P.	76	A1	44.432818 -84.670299
Sterling S.P.	90	C1	41.921490 -83.342680
Straits S.P.	70	C2	45.858090 -84.720200
Tahquamenon Falls S.P.-East Ent.	70	B1	46.598030 -85.147890
Tahquamenon Falls S.P.-West Ent.	70	B1	46.564190 -85.292530
Tawas Point S.P.	76	B1	44.255820 -83.443050
Thompson's Harbor S.P.	71	D3	45.346705 -83.567431
Traverse City S.P.	70	B4	44.748050 -85.553800
Twin Lakes S.P.	65	E4	46.892210 -88.856560
Van Buren S.P.	75	E4	42.333830 -86.304830

Van Buren Trail S.P.	89	F1	42.211405 -86.171105
Van Riper S.P.	68	C1	46.525260 -87.991150
Walter J. Hayes S.P.	90	B1	42.072830 -84.137820
Warren Dunes S.P.	89	E1	41.900980 -86.595260
Warren Woods S.P.	89	E1	41.840680 -86.631290
Wetzel Rec. Area	76	C4	42.596720 -82.825140
White Pine Trail S.P.	75	F2	44.222900 -85.426700
Wilderness S.P.-East Ent.	70	B2	45.748160 -84.853500
Wilderness S.P.-West Ent.	70	B2	45.679360 -84.964170
William Mitchell S.P.	75	F1	44.236880 -85.453990
Wilson S.P.	76	A1	44.029620 -84.806070
Young S.P.	70	B3	45.235240 -85.041450

MINNESOTA	PAGE	GRID	LATITUDE LONGITUDE
National Park & Rec. Areas			
Grand Portage Natl. Mon.	65	E2	47.996274 -89.734256
Pipestone Natl. Mon.	27	F3	44.013150 -96.325360
Voyageurs Natl. Park-Ash River Vis. Ctr.	64	C2	48.435600 -92.850300
Voyageurs Natl. Park-Kabetogama Lake Vis. Ctr.	64	C2	48.446100 -93.030100
Voyageurs Natl. Park-Rainy Lake Vis. Ctr.	64	C2	48.584400 -93.161500
State Park & Rec. Areas			
Afton S.P.	67	D4	44.847930 -92.791020
Banning S.P.	67	D2	46.179730 -92.855170
Bear Head Lake S.P.	64	C3	47.792720 -92.083720
Beaver Creek Valley S.P.	73	E2	43.636790 -91.573190
Blue Mounds S.P.	27	F4	43.714340 -96.183100
Buffalo River S.P.	19	F4	46.866260 -96.469980
Camden S.P.	27	F3	44.362880 -95.917480
Caribou Falls State Wayside	65	D3	47.463890 -91.030660
Carley S.P.	73	E1	44.116790 -92.169320
Cascade River S.P.	65	D3	47.712950 -90.497930
Charles A. Lindbergh S.P.	66	C2	45.959410 -94.387640
Cross River State Wayside	65	D3	47.543420 -90.897770
Crow Wing S.P.	66	C1	46.272630 -94.316400
Father Hennepin S.P.	66	C1	46.144520 -93.484260
Flandrau S.P.	72	B1	44.294360 -94.482020
Flood Bay State Wayside	64	C4	47.038500 -91.642540
Forestville Mystery Cave S.P.	73	E2	43.637520 -92.220270
Fort Ridgely S.P.	72	B1	44.454810 -94.718310
Franz Jevne S.P.	64	B2	48.641140 -94.058260
Frontenac S.P.	67	E4	44.525200 -92.338730
George H. Crosby Manitou S.P.	65	D3	47.478990 -91.123070
Glacial Lakes S.P.	66	A3	45.540550 -95.529600
Glendalough S.P.	19	F4	46.313314 -95.679290
Gooseberry Falls S.P.	65	D3	47.145430 -91.462380
Grand Portage S.P.	65	E2	47.999150 -89.598690
Great River Bluffs S.P.	73	E1	43.939100 -91.430050
Hayes Lake S.P.	19	F1	48.641070 -95.570600
Hill Annex Mine S.P.	64	B3	47.327490 -93.277520
Inspiration Peak State Wayside	66	A1	46.136880 -95.578650
Itasca S.P.	64	A3	47.194490 -95.166740
Jay Cooke S.P.	64	C4	46.658790 -92.349200
John A. Latsch S.P.	73	E1	44.164720 -91.823860
Joseph R. Brown State Wayside	66	B4	44.750328 -95.324425
Judge C.R. Magney S.P.	65	E3	47.818090 -90.051230
Kilen Woods S.P.	72	B2	43.732140 -95.072220
Kodonce River State Wayside	65	E3	47.793930 -90.154140
Lac Qui Parle S.P.	27	F2	45.024680 -95.896580
Lake Bemidji S.P.	64	A3	47.536890 -94.832320
Lake Bronson S.P.	19	F1	48.730940 -96.630720
Lake Carlos S.P.	66	B2	46.000540 -95.334430
Lake Louise S.P.	73	D2	43.532620 -92.509250
Lake Maria S.P.	66	C3	45.304810 -93.935570
Lake Shetek S.P.	72	A1	44.105740 -95.699730
Maplewood S.P.	19	F4	46.549910 -95.966720
McCarthy Beach S.P.	64	B3	47.674110 -93.027350
Mille Lacs Kathio S.P.	66	C2	46.160740 -93.758020
Minneopa S.P.	72	C1	44.162190 -94.110310
Monson Lake S.P.	66	B3	45.321300 -95.270470
Moose Lake S.P.	64	C4	46.436360 -92.743090
Myre-Big Island S.P.	73	D2	43.623847 -93.289096
Nerstrand Big Woods S.P.	73	D1	44.327040 -93.111210
Old Mill S.P.	19	F2	48.369790 -96.569420
Ray Berglund State Wayside	65	D3	47.608200 -90.771930
Rice Lake S.P.	73	D1	44.095380 -93.063940
Rush River State Wayside	66	C4	44.507240 -93.931409
Saint Croix S.P.	67	D2	45.960615 -92.611630
Sakatah Lake S.P.	72	C1	44.218000 -93.509970
Sam Brown Mem. State Wayside	27	F1	45.596160 -96.841410
Savanna Portage S.P.	64	B4	46.819130 -93.176040
Scenic S.P.	64	B3	47.702450 -93.564710
Schoolcraft S.P.	64	B3	47.223040 -93.805320
Sibley S.P.	66	B3	45.318990 -95.011930
Soudan Underground Mine S.P.	64	C2	47.818130 -92.246090
Split Rock Creek S.P.	27	F4	43.907240 -96.367970
Split Rock Lighthouse S.P.	65	D3	47.189800 -91.395010
Temperance River S.P.	65	D3	47.558780 -90.867930
Tettegouche S.P.	65	D3	47.337210 -91.200670
Upper Sioux Agency S.P.	66	B4	44.734540 -95.456460
Whitewater S.P.	73	E1	44.068880 -92.040100
Wild River S.P.	67	D3	45.524100 -92.754500
William O'Brien S.P.	67	D3	45.223900 -92.763500
Zippel Bay S.P.	64	A1	48.840630 -94.849950

MISSISSIPPI	PAGE	GRID	LATITUDE LONGITUDE
National Park & Rec. Areas			
Gulf Islands Natl. Seashore	135	D2	30.407200 -88.749220
Natchez N.H.P.-Vis. Reception Ctr.	125	F4	31.553900 -91.412400
State Park & Rec. Areas			
Bogue Homa State Fishing Lake	127	D4	31.703200 -89.026400
Calling Panther State Fishing Lake	126	B3	32.197100 -90.265100
Clarkco S.P.	127	D3	32.108500 -88.693970
Columbia State Fishing Lake	134	C1	31.183500 -89.738400
Florewood S.P.	118	B4	33.525120 -90.250362
George Payne Cossar S.P.	118	B3	34.122710 -89.882100
Golden Mem. S.P.	126	C2	32.568560 -89.407640
Great River Road S.P.	118	A4	33.851733 -91.027574
Hugh White S.P.	118	B4	33.796080 -89.743010
J.P. Coleman S.P.	119	D2	34.924254 -88.171706
Jeff Davis State Fishing Lake	126	B4	31.567700 -89.839800
Kemper County State Fishing Lake	127	D2	32.804167 -88.730556
Lake Lincoln S.P.	126	B4	31.684354 -90.337142
Legion S.P.	127	D1	33.148690 -89.042460
Leroy Percy S.P.	126	A1	33.160500 -90.938250
Mary Crawford State Fishing Lake	126	B4	31.574900 -90.154000
Monroe State Fishing Lake	119	D4	33.941500 -88.568700
Natchez S.P.	126	A4	31.589580 -91.220350
Neshoba County State Fishing Lake	126	C2	32.706200 -89.010500
Oktibbeha County State Fishing Lake	118	C4	33.505700 -88.933400
Paul B. Johnson S.P.	134	C1	31.133800 -89.233910
Percy Quin S.P.	134	B1	31.189020 -90.510660
Perry State Fishing Lake	135	D1	31.132400 -88.899800
Prentiss Walker State Fishing Lake	126	C3	31.833200 -89.589500
Roosevelt S.P.	126	C2	32.321920 -89.664980
Simpson County State Fishing Lake	126	C3	31.913500 -89.794500
Tippah County State Fishing Lake	118	C2	34.794290 -88.950660
Tishomingo S.P.	119	D2	34.615670 -88.183390
Tom Bailey State Fishing Lake	127	D2	32.425030 -88.523069
Tombigbee S.P.	119	D3	34.231870 -88.628870
Trace S.P.	118	C3	34.260020 -88.886560
Wall Doxey S.P.	118	C2	34.660270 -89.459290
Walthall State Fishing Lake	134	B1	31.059184 -90.133939

MISSOURI	PAGE	GRID	LATITUDE LONGITUDE
National Park & Rec. Areas			
George Washington Carver Natl. Mon.	106	C2	36.986160 -94.351890
Ozark Natl. Scenic Riverways	107	F2	37.281400 -91.408000
State Park & Rec. Areas			
Bennett Spring S.P.	107	D1	37.725440 -92.856390
Big Lake S.P.	86	A4	40.092090 -95.347300
Big Oak Tree S.P.	108	C3	36.641990 -89.290180
Big Sugar Creek S.P.	106	C3	36.584106 -93.819122
Crowder S.P.	86	C4	40.082140 -93.669310
Cuivre River S.P.	97	F2	39.062380 -90.938640
Elephant Rocks S.P.	108	A1	37.652150 -90.690810
Finger Lakes S.P.	97	E2	39.075400 -92.314750
Graham Cave S.P.	97	F3	38.908850 -91.576090
Grand Gulf S.P.	107	F3	36.544100 -91.636370
Ha Ha Tonka S.P.	97	D4	37.975410 -92.762230
Harry S. Truman S.P.	97	D4	38.274650 -93.442390
Hawn S.P.	108	B1	37.833660 -90.241610
Johnson's Shut-Ins S.P.	108	A1	37.547920 -90.853020
Katy Trail S.P.	97	E3	38.975190 -92.750160
Knob Noster S.P.	96	C3	38.753020 -93.577440
Lake of the Ozarks S.P.	97	E4	38.133990 -92.564260
Lake Wappapello S.P.	108	A2	36.942210 -90.344400
Lewis & Clark S.P.	96	B1	39.538900 -95.052900
Long Branch S.P.	97	E1	39.767610 -92.526480
Mark Twain S.P.	97	E2	39.485270 -91.795340
Meramec S.P.	97	F4	38.215350 -91.123070
Montauk S.P.	107	F1	37.454710 -91.690970
Morris S.P.	108	B3	36.554166 -90.043220
Onondaga Cave S.P.	97	F4	38.064310 -91.230140
Pershing S.P.	97	D1	39.776270 -93.211130
Pomme de Terre S.P.	107	D1	37.874380 -93.318700
Prairie S.P.	106	B1	37.518510 -94.571280
Roaring River S.P.	106	C3	36.590110 -93.834420
Robertsville S.P.	98	A3	38.429120 -90.818110
Rock Bridge Mem. S.P.	97	E3	38.883350 -92.331890
Saint Francois S.P.	98	A4	37.972900 -90.536210
Saint Joe S.P.	108	A1	37.824990 -90.537480
Sam A. Baker S.P.	108	A2	37.254530 -90.505080
Stockton S.P.	106	C1	37.622470 -93.753070
Table Rock S.P.	107	D3	36.583440 -93.309150
Taum Sauk Mtn. S.P.	108	A1	37.669500 -90.673400
Thousand Hills S.P.	87	D4	40.185160 -92.643070
Trail of Tears S.P.	108	B1	37.452880 -89.490760
Van Meter S.P.	97	D2	39.262590 -93.267210
Wakonda S.P.	97	F1	40.004250 -91.526060
Wallace S.P.	96	C1	39.660760 -94.213290
Washington S.P.	98	A4	38.085600 -90.685650
Watkins Mill S.P.	96	C2	39.383920 -94.265130
Weston Bend S.P.	96	B2	39.392960 -94.863430

MONTANA	PAGE	GRID	LATITUDE LONGITUDE
National Park & Rec. Areas			
Bighorn Canyon N.R.A.	24	C2	45.330090 -107.871650
Fort Benton Natl. Hist. Landmark	16	A2	47.823210 -110.661910
Glacier Natl. Park-Many Glacier Ent.	15	D1	48.827150 -113.551540
Glacier Natl. Park-St Mary Ent.	15	D1	48.747120 -113.439650
Glacier Natl. Park-Two Medicine Ent.	15	D1	48.494210 -113.262250
Glacier Natl. Park-West Ent.	15	D1	48.499890 -113.987190
Grant-Kohrs Ranch N.H.S.	15	E4	46.398900 -112.736680
Little Bighorn Bfld. Natl. Mon.	24	C1	45.570080 -107.434710
Natl. Bison Range	15	D3	47.371674 -114.262066
Rattlesnake N.R.A.	15	D4	47.040775 -113.933333
State Park & Rec. Areas			
Ackley Lake S.P.	16	B4	46.947220 -109.936110
Anaconda Smoke Stack S.P.	23	D1	46.111037 -112.969599
Bannack S.P.	23	D2	45.159170 -112.997780
Beaverhead Rock S.P.	23	E2	45.383330 -112.458330
Beavertail Hill S.P.	15	D4	46.721660 -113.576420
Big Arm S.P.	15	D3	47.815360 -114.307930
Black Sandy S.P.	15	E4	46.756940 -111.888890
Brush Lake S.P.	17	F1	48.603000 -104.113000
Chief Plenty Coups S.P.	24	B2	45.429700 -108.532500
Clark's Lookout S.P.	23	E2	45.236110 -112.630560
Cooney S.P.	24	B2	45.435050 -109.225330
Council Grove S.P.	15	D4	46.912500 -114.150000
Finley Point S.P.	15	D3	47.763830 -114.078723
First Peoples Buffalo Jump S.P.	16	A3	47.494887 -111.525201
Fort Owen S.P.	15	D4	46.519440 -114.095830
Frenchtown Pond S.P.	15	D3	47.039530 -114.259220
Granite Ghost Town S.P.	23	D1	46.319000 -113.257000
Greycliff Prairie Dog Town S.P.	24	B1	45.767600 -109.794180
Hell Creek S.P.	17	D3	47.620290 -106.884510
Lake Elmo S.P.	24	C1	45.845280 -108.481310
Lake Mary Ronan S.P.	15	D2	48.204020 -114.330340
Lewis & Clark Caverns S.P.	23	E1	45.821840 -111.848510
Logan S.P.	14	C2	48.204020 -114.330340
Lone Pine S.P.	15	D2	48.175580 -114.339560
Lost Creek S.P.	23	D1	46.203020 -112.993810
Madison Buffalo Jump S.P.	23	F1	45.665140 -111.062770
Makoshika S.P.	17	F4	47.090240 -104.709970
Medicine Rocks S.P.	25	F1	46.046460 -104.456740
Missouri Headwaters S.P.	23	F1	45.909129 -111.497411
Painted Rocks S.P.	22	C1	45.706650 -114.282530
Pictograph Cave S.P.	24	C1	45.737500 -108.430830
Pirogue Island S.P.	17	E4	46.440560 -105.816670
Placid Lake S.P.	15	D3	47.138040 -113.524960
Rosebud Bfld. S.P.	25	D2	45.208270 -106.944460
Salmon Lake S.P.	15	D4	47.042270 -113.390390
Sluice Boxes S.P.	16	A3	47.211400 -110.939660
Smith River S.P.	16	A4	46.721219 -111.173819
Spring Meadow Lake S.P.	15	E4	46.612220 -112.075000
Thompson Falls S.P.	14	C3	47.618060 -115.387500
Tongue River Reservoir S.P.	25	D2	45.093520 -106.804670
Tower Rock S.P.	15	E3	47.181000 -111.816000
Travelers' Rest S.P.	15	D4	46.751000 -114.089000
Wayfarers S.P.	15	D2	48.057400 -114.079550
West Shore S.P.	15	D2	47.948780 -114.189160
Whitefish Lake S.P.	15	D2	48.204020 -114.330340
Wild Horse Island S.P.	15	D3	47.844640 -114.279970
Yellow Bay S.P.	15	D2	47.874500 -114.027080

NEBRASKA	PAGE	GRID	LATITUDE LONGITUDE
National Park & Rec. Areas			
Agate Fossil Beds Natl. Mon.	33	F2	42.423860 -103.791120
Chimney Rock N.H.S.	33	F3	41.719650 -103.336070
Pine Ridge N.R.A.	33	F1	42.625880 -103.205570
Scotts Bluff Natl. Mon.	33	F2	41.832380 -103.717550
State Park & Rec. Areas			
Chadron S.P.	34	A1	42.711540 -103.008500
Eugene T. Mahoney S.P.	35	F3	41.026387 -96.314180
Fort Robinson S.P.	33	F1	42.654050 -103.492100
Indian Cave S.P.	86	A4	40.263280 -95.586630
Niobrara S.P.	35	E1	42.747450 -98.051850
Platte River S.P.	35	F3	40.986840 -96.219290
Ponca S.P.	35	F1	42.600360 -96.714940
Smith Falls S.P.	34	C1	42.891670 -100.316670

NEVADA	PAGE	GRID	LATITUDE LONGITUDE
National Park & Rec. Areas			
Basin & Range Natl. Mon.	38	B3	37.931620 -115.350935
Devils Hole (Death Valley Natl. Park)	45	F3	36.423889 -116.305833
Great Basin Natl. Park-Vis. Ctr.	38	C2	39.005600 -114.220000
Lake Mead N.R.A.-North Ent.	46	B2	36.161180 -114.905200
Lake Mead N.R.A.-South Ent.	46	B2	36.021230 -114.796340
Lake Mead N.R.A.-West Ent.	46	B2	36.105980 -114.900940
Spring Mts. N.R.A.	46	A1	36.245200 -115.233910
Tule Springs Fossil Beds Natl. Mon.	46	A1	36.324457 -115.293643
State Park & Rec. Areas			
Berlin-Ichthyosaur S.P.	37	F2	38.880300 -117.607930
Big Bend of the Colorado State Rec. Area	53	F1	35.116730 -114.640820
Cathedral Gorge S.P.	38	C4	37.820280 -114.407890

	PAGE	GRID	LATITUDE LONGITUDE
embina S.P.	19	E1	48.964720 -97.240500
urtle River S.P.	19	E2	47.931660 -97.505390
hitestone Bfld. S.P.	27	D1	46.169190 -98.857330

OHIO	PAGE	GRID	LATITUDE LONGITUDE
ational Park & Rec. Areas			
harles Young Buffalo Soldiers Natl. Mon.	100	C1	39.689722,-83.891111
uyahoga Valley Natl. Park-Canal Vis. Ctr.	91	E2	41.372600 -81.613700
uyahoga Valley Natl. Park-Hunt Farm Vis. Info. Ctr.	91	E2	41.200900 -81.573100
opewell Culture N.H.P.	101	D2	39.298360 -82.917810
ames A. Garfield N.H.S.	91	E2	41.663600 -81.351260
tate Park & Rec. Areas			
.W. Marion S.P.	101	D1	39.633730 -82.885720
dams Lake S.P.	100	C3	38.812900 -83.519400
lum Creek S.P.	90	C4	40.226870 -82.981320
arkcamp S.P.	101	F1	40.047030 -81.031710
eaver Creek S.P.	91	F3	40.726220 -80.613590
lue Rock S.P.	101	E1	39.832780 -81.858370
uck Creek S.P.	100	C1	39.946410 -83.729550
uckeye Lake S.P.	101	D1	39.906540 -82.526270
urr Oak S.P.	101	E1	39.527740 -82.023260
aesar Creek S.P.	100	C1	39.515730 -84.041070
atawba Island S.P.	91	D2	41.573530 -82.855780
owan Lake S.P.	100	C2	39.387600 -83.882970
rane Creek S.P.	90	C2	41.603770 -83.192910
eer Creek S.P.	101	D1	39.649260 -83.246340
elaware S.P.	90	C4	40.377690 -83.071590
illon S.P.	101	E1	40.023600 -82.111910
ast Fork S.P.	100	C2	39.002050 -84.151210
ast Harbor S.P.	91	D2	41.540930 -82.820830
indley S.P.	91	D3	41.122990 -82.219390
orked Run S.P.	101	E2	39.085000 -81.770460
eneva S.P.	91	F1	41.852760 -80.963280
rand Lake Saint Marys S.P.	90	B4	40.549240 -84.436500
uilford Lake S.P.	91	F3	40.796100 -80.893760
arrison Lake S.P.	90	B2	41.637190 -84.361760
eadlands Beach S.P.	91	E1	41.752140 -81.294480
ocking Hills S.P.	101	D2	39.494180 -82.611910
ueston Woods S.P.	100	B1	39.573820 -84.715380
ndependence Dam S.P.	90	B2	41.282470 -84.313500
ndian Lake S.P.	90	B4	40.510360 -83.842980
ackson Lake S.P.	101	D3	38.902850 -82.596780
efferson Lake S.P.	91	F4	40.472050 -80.808930
ohn Bryan S.P.	100	C1	39.791020 -83.867790
elleys Island S.P.	91	D2	41.614080 -82.712110
iser Lake S.P.	90	B4	40.197650 -83.981740
ake Alma S.P.	101	D2	39.153450 -82.516810
ake Hope S.P.	101	E2	39.318500 -82.354920
ake Logan S.P.	101	D1	39.536400 -82.460590
ake Loramie S.P.	90	B4	40.359750 -84.359730
ake White S.P.	101	D2	39.109160 -83.040330
Madison Lake S.P.	100	C1	39.866250 -83.374930
Malabar Farm S.P.	91	D3	40.649590 -82.398390
Mary Jane Thurston S.P.	90	B2	41.409630 -83.881320
Maumee Bay S.P.	90	C2	41.678020 -83.353360
Mohican S.P.	91	D4	40.609510 -82.257600
Mosquito Lake S.P.	91	F2	41.301940 -80.767990
Mount Gilead S.P.	91	D4	40.547820 -82.816770
Muskingum River S.P.	101	E1	40.044140 -81.978260
Nelson-Kennedy Ledges S.P.	91	F2	41.330090 -81.040190
Paint Creek S.P.	100	C2	39.228360 -83.374450
Pike Lake S.P.	101	D2	39.158270 -83.220950
Portage Lakes S.P.	91	E3	40.966260 -81.565190
Punderson S.P.	91	E2	41.461540 -81.219590
Pymatuning S.P.	91	F2	41.580110 -80.541530
Quail Hollow S.P.	91	E3	40.970200 -81.325100
Rocky Fork S.P.	100	C2	39.188310 -83.529730
Salt Fork S.P.	91	E4	40.081830 -81.460400
Scioto Trail S.P.	101	D2	39.223620 -82.931210
Shawnee S.P.	101	D3	38.747670 -83.211220
South Bass Island S.P.	91	D2	41.644690 -82.835950
Stonelick S.P.	100	C2	39.226160 -84.057210
Strouds Run S.P.	101	E2	39.334320 -82.017690
Sycamore S.P.	100	B1	39.803410 -84.373470
Tar Hollow S.P.	101	D2	39.353790 -82.780200
Tinker's Creek S.P.	91	E2	41.276180 -81.368910
Van Buren S.P.	90	C3	41.138290 -83.644940
West Branch S.P.	91	E3	41.133310 -81.189660
Wolf Run S.P.	101	F1	39.789770 -81.540180

OKLAHOMA	PAGE	GRID	LATITUDE LONGITUDE
National Park & Rec. Areas			
Chickasaw N.R.A.	51	F4	34.497390 -96.970110
Winding Stair Mtn. N.R.A.	116	B2	34.749705 -94.793055
State Park & Rec. Areas			
Adair S.P.	106	B4	35.832230 -94.624100
Alabaster Caverns S.P.	51	D1	36.697490 -99.149430
Arrowhead S.P.	116	A1	35.168240 -95.639970
Beaver Dunes S.P.	50	B1	36.841129 -100.514988
Bernice S.P.	106	B3	36.626670 -94.901670
Black Mesa S.P.	49	F1	36.855620 -102.885680
Boggy Depot S.P.	51	F4	34.321747 -96.311302
Boiling Springs S.P.	51	D1	36.452950 -99.298900
Brushy Lake S.P.	116	B1	35.543680 -94.817676
Cherokee Landing S.P.	106	B4	35.758890 -94.908610
Cherokee S.P.	106	B3	36.480280 -95.050560
Clayton Lake S.P.	116	A2	34.549420 -95.308330
Dripping Springs S.P.	51	F3	35.611437 -96.068911
Fort Cobb S.P.	51	D3	35.203720 -98.464990
Foss S.P.	51	D3	35.578510 -99.186830
Gloss Mtn. S.P.	51	D2	36.367190 -98.576460
Great Plains S.P.	51	D4	34.730340 -98.985690
Great Salt Plains S.P.	51	E1	36.753170 -98.149930
Greenleaf S.P.	106	A4	35.623260 -95.180950
Hochatown S.P.	116	B3	34.197390 -94.766300
Honey Creek S.P.	106	B3	36.574060 -94.784370
Hugo Lake S.P.	116	A3	34.016384 -95.375061
Keystone S.P.	51	F2	36.137440 -96.264340
Lake Eucha S.P.	106	B3	36.353930 -94.824000
Lake Eufaula S.P.	116	A1	35.427900 -95.546100
Lake Murray S.P.	51	F4	34.154880 -97.120950
Lake Texoma S.P.	59	F1	33.997590 -96.651310
Lake Thunderbird S.P.	51	E3	35.232320 -97.247550
Lake Wister S.P.	116	B2	34.948700 -94.710400
Little Blue-Disney S.P.	106	B3	36.480260 -95.009130
Little Sahara S.P.	51	D1	36.532900 -98.890870
McGee Creek S.P.	116	A3	34.302927 -95.875467
Natural Falls S.P.	106	B4	36.151900 -94.673300
Okmulgee S.P.	51	F2	35.621900 -96.067700
Osage Hills S.P.	51	F1	36.757360 -96.176220
Raymond Gary S.P.	116	A3	33.997580 -95.253860
Red Rock Canyon S.P.	51	D3	35.456350 -98.358310
Sequoyah Bay S.P.	106	A4	35.886000 -95.276000
Sequoyah S.P.	106	A4	35.932960 -95.230650
Snowdale S.P.	106	A3	36.307710 -95.199040
Spavinaw S.P.	106	B3	36.385890 -95.053290
Talimena S.P.	116	B2	34.788290 -94.950690
Tenkiller S.P.	116	B1	35.598000 -95.031100
Twin Bridges S.P.	106	B2	36.804320 -94.757920
Wah-Sha-She S.P.	51	F1	36.926000 -96.091000
Walnut Creek S.P.	51	F2	36.251210 -96.280130

OREGON	PAGE	GRID	LATITUDE LONGITUDE
National Park & Rec. Areas			
Cascade-Siskiyou Natl. Mon.	28	C2	42.068300 -122.399940
Crater Lake Natl. Park-Annie Spring Ent. Sta.	28	C1	42.868700 -122.169000
Crater Lake Natl. Park-North Ent. Sta.	28	C1	43.086900 -122.116000
Hells Canyon N.R.A.-East Ent.	22	B1	45.500680 -116.806560
Hells Canyon N.R.A.-South Ent.	22	B1	44.903300 -116.957080
Hells Canyon N.R.A.-West Ent.	22	B1	45.176360 -117.040740
John Day Fossil Beds Natl. Mon.-Clarno Unit	21	D2	44.911250 -120.431780
John Day Fossil Beds Natl. Mon.-Painted Hills Unit	21	D3	44.661170 -120.254750
John Day Fossil Beds Natl. Mon.-Sheep Rock Unit	21	E3	44.555480 -119.645010
Lewis & Clark N.H.P.-Fort Clatsop	20	B1	46.138260 -123.876670
Lewis & Clark N.H.P.-Salt Works	20	B1	46.134551 -123.880420
Lewis & Clark N.H.P.-Sunset Beach	20	B1	46.099430 -123.936390
Newberry Natl. Volcanic Mon.	21	D4	43.716800 -121.376960
Oregon Caves Natl. Mon. & Pres.	28	B2	42.103910 -123.414300
Oregon Dunes N.R.A.-North Ent.	20	A4	43.885610 -124.120860
Oregon Dunes N.R.A.-South Ent.	20	A4	43.579470 -124.186490
State Park & Rec. Areas			
Ainsworth S.P.	20	C2	45.595720 -122.052980
Alfred A. Loeb S.P.	28	A2	42.113180 -124.188520
Beverly Beach S.P.	20	B3	44.726250 -124.057290
Bullards Beach S.P.	28	A1	43.150990 -124.395480
Cape Arago S.P.	20	A4	43.326140 -124.381770
Cape Blanco S.P.	28	A1	42.826660 -124.524640
Cape Lookout S.P.	20	B2	45.367667 -123.961127
Carl G. Washburne Mem. S.P.	20	A3	44.141990 -124.117490
Cascadia S.P.	20	C3	44.397100 -122.477480
Catherine Creek S.P.	22	A2	45.148890 -117.733990
Collier Mem. S.P.	28	C1	42.641810 -121.880630
Ecola S.P.	20	B1	45.916550 -123.967430
Elijah Bristow S.P.	20	C4	43.935470 -122.844270
Fort Columbia S.P.	20	B1	46.252580 -123.921500
Fort Stevens S.P.	20	B1	46.183200 -123.959940
Harris Beach S.P.	28	A2	42.067930 -124.305860
Hat Rock S.P.	21	E1	45.908260 -119.164510
Hilgard Junction S.P.	21	F2	45.342060 -118.236470
Humbug Mtn. S.P.	28	A1	42.686870 -124.445970
Illinois River Forks S.P.	28	B2	42.154870 -123.649870
Jessie M. Honeyman Mem. S.P.	20	A4	43.933440 -124.106440
Lake Owyhee S.P.	22	A4	43.638380 -117.229090
Lapine S.P.	21	D4	43.768452 -121.513399
Maryhill S.P.	21	D1	45.683060 -120.825830
Mayer S.P.	21	D1	45.682780 -121.301080
Milo Mciver S.P.	20	C2	45.306110 -122.372220
Molalla River S.P.	20	C2	45.294840 -122.696400
Nehalem Bay S.P.	20	B1	45.710000 -123.931470
Ona Beach S.P.	20	B3	44.518060 -124.075960
Oswald West S.P.	20	B1	45.770000 -123.958610
Port Orford Heads S.P.	28	A1	42.739470 -124.509730
Prineville Reservoir S.P.	21	D3	44.144660 -120.737770
Robert Straub S.P.	20	B2	45.183160 -123.965116
Rooster Rock S.P.	20	C2	45.546320 -122.236500
Shore Acres S.P.	20	A4	43.329940 -124.376510
Silver Falls S.P.	20	C2	44.853752 -122.662258
Smith Rock S.P.	21	D3	44.360540 -121.138400
South Beach S.P.	20	B3	44.598450 -124.059350
Starvation Creek S.P.	20	C1	45.688550 -121.690180
Stub Stewart S.P.	20	B1	45.739050 -123.199461
Sunset Bay S.P.	20	A4	43.339010 -124.353990
The Cove Palisades S.P.	21	D3	44.557460 -121.262110
Tumalo S.P.	21	D3	44.086760 -121.308730
Umpqua Lighthouse S.P.	20	A4	43.669610 -124.182830
Valley of the Rogue S.P.	28	B1	42.410770 -123.129310
Viento S.P.	20	C1	45.697240 -121.668310
Wallowa Lake S.P.	22	A2	45.280690 -117.208230
White River Falls S.P.	21	D2	45.166870 -121.087420
Willamette Mission S.P.	20	B2	45.080740 -123.031510
William M. Tugman S.P.	20	A4	43.623640 -124.181910

PENNSYLVANIA	PAGE	GRID	LATITUDE LONGITUDE
National Park & Rec. Areas			
Allegheny N.R.A	92	B1	41.943055 -78.867025
Allegheny Portage Railroad N.H.S.	92	B4	40.377020 -78.835870
Eisenhower N.H.S.	103	E1	39.818000 -77.232610
Flight 93 Natl. Mem.	92	B4	40.055200 -78.900900
Fort Necessity Natl. Bfld.	102	B1	39.816340 -79.584310
Friendship Hill N.H.S.	102	B1	39.777778 -79.929167
Gettysburg N.M.P.	103	E1	39.811600 -77.226100
Grey Towers N.H.S.	94	A3	41.325224 -74.871113
Hopewell Furnace N.H.S.	146	B2	40.206760 -75.773570
Johnstown Flood Natl. Mem.	92	B4	40.350710 -78.772480
Valley Forge N.H.P.	146	C2	40.102240 -75.422960
State Park & Rec. Areas			
Bald Eagle S.P.	92	C3	41.041960 -77.642780
Big Spring S.P.	92	C4	40.266850 -77.654410
Black Moshannon S.P.	92	C3	40.915190 -78.058570
Blue Knob S.P.	92	B4	40.265800 -78.584480
Buchanan's Birthplace S.P.	103	D1	39.872660 -77.953190
Caledonia S.P.	103	D1	39.905610 -77.478880
Chapman S.P.	92	B1	41.757850 -79.170350
Cherry Springs S.P.	92	C2	41.662778 -77.823056
Codorus S.P.	103	E1	39.783180 -76.908920
Colonel Denning S.P.	93	D4	40.281820 -77.416630
Colton Point S.P.	93	D2	41.711180 -77.465430
Cook Forest S.P.	92	B2	41.333790 -79.210440
Cowans Gap S.P.	103	D1	39.997980 -77.921530
Delaware Canal S.P.	146	C1	40.545565 -75.087831
Elk S.P.	92	B2	41.606100 -78.564780
Erie Bluffs S.P.	91	F1	42.008333 -80.410833
Evansburg S.P.	146	C2	40.197510 -75.407080
Frances Slocum S.P.	93	E2	41.347380 -75.893760
French Creek S.P.	146	B2	40.236580 -75.795660
Gouldsboro S.P.	93	F2	41.232250 -75.495730
Greenwood Furnace S.P.	92	C3	40.649610 -77.756090
Hickory Run S.P.	93	F3	41.035170 -75.736220
Hills Creek S.P.	93	D1	41.805190 -77.187600
Hyner Run S.P.	92	C2	41.359150 -77.623850
Kettle Creek S.P.	92	C2	41.377120 -77.930130
Keystone S.P.	92	A4	40.374250 -79.377830
Lackawanna S.P.	93	F2	41.575030 -75.711520
Laurel Hill S.P.	102	B1	39.984470 -79.234840
Laurel Mtn. S.P.	92	B4	40.179670 -79.131530
Laurel Ridge S.P.	92	B4	39.958400 -79.360160
Lehigh Gorge S.P.	93	F3	40.971900 -75.761840
Leonard Harrison S.P.	93	D2	41.698420 -77.450810
Little Buffalo S.P.	93	D4	40.454420 -77.169170
Little Pine S.P.	93	D2	41.371240 -77.360310
Lyman Run S.P.	92	C1	41.723650 -77.768470
Marsh Creek S.P.	146	B3	40.069360 -75.717320
Maurice K. Goddard S.P.	92	A2	41.428380 -80.145140
McConnells Mill S.P.	92	A3	40.963530 -80.168810
Memorial Lake S.P.	93	E4	40.424760 -76.590540
Mont Alto S.P.	103	D1	39.839130 -77.540630
Moraine S.P.	92	A3	40.940280 -80.098520
Nescopeck S.P.	93	E3	41.067100 -75.925300
Nockamixon S.P.	146	C1	40.463630 -75.242010
Ohiopyle S.P.	102	B1	39.865030 -79.504310
Oil Creek S.P.-East Ent.	92	A2	41.512130 -79.661810
Ole Bull S.P.	92	C2	41.543590 -77.709430
Parker Dam S.P.	92	C2	41.205140 -78.504310
Penn-Roosevelt S.P.	92	C3	40.726389 -77.702500
Pine Grove Furnace S.P.	103	D1	40.032910 -77.305070
Poe Paddy S.P.	93	D3	40.834150 -77.417380
Presque Isle S.P.	92	A1	42.114200 -80.153590
Prince Gallitzin S.P.	92	B3	40.669760 -78.575650
Promised Land S.P.	93	F2	41.313560 -75.210370
Pymatuning S.P.	91	F2	41.605440 -80.387840
Raccoon Creek S.P.	91	F4	40.503160 -80.424460
Ralph Stover S.P.	146	C1	40.440420 -75.106050

Park	Page	Grid	Latitude Longitude
Raymond B. Winter S.P.	93	D3	40.992340 -77.200450
Ricketts Glen S.P.	93	E2	41.336190 -76.300420
Ryerson Station S.P.	102	A1	39.892310 -80.450030
S.B. Elliott S.P.	92	C3	41.112740 -78.526100
Salt Springs S.P.	93	E1	41.911090 -75.868720
Samuel S. Lewis S.P.	103	E1	39.996580 -76.550410
Shawnee S.P.	102	C1	40.038060 -78.645850
Shikellamy S.P.	93	D3	40.879390 -76.802950
Sinnemahoning S.P.	92	C2	41.450650 -78.055090
Susquehannock S.P.	146	A3	39.805770 -76.283410
Swatara S.P.	93	E4	40.481480 -76.551350
Tobyhanna S.P.	93	F2	41.214130 -75.384030
Trough Creek S.P.	92	C4	40.311620 -78.131820
Tyler S.P.	146	C2	40.233330 -74.951170
Upper Pine Bottom S.P.	93	D2	41.325071 -77.394699
Warriors Path S.P.	92	C4	40.193330 -78.249880
Whipple Dam S.P.	92	C3	40.682250 -77.868410
Worlds End S.P.	93	E2	41.471880 -76.587060
Yellow Creek S.P.	92	B4	40.575830 -79.004420
RHODE ISLAND	**PAGE**	**GRID**	**LATITUDE LONGITUDE**
State Park & Rec. Areas			
Beavertail S.P.	150	C4	41.457030 -71.396950
Block Island State Beach	95	D4	41.180850 -71.566460
Brenton Point S.P.	150	C4	41.450430 -71.355870
Burlingame S.P.	150	C4	41.361610 -71.701370
Casimir Pulaski Mem. S.P.	150	C3	41.950000 -71.766670
Colt S.P.	151	D3	41.684590 -71.288860
Diamond Hill S.P.	150	C2	42.009620 -71.431630
East Matunuck State Beach	150	C4	41.378350 -71.525630
Fishermen's Mem. S.P.	150	C4	41.380630 -71.488000
Fort Adams S.P.	150	C4	41.469150 -71.339990
Goddard Mem. S.P.	150	C3	41.651030 -71.442040
Haines Mem. S.P.	150	C3	41.752960 -71.348600
Misquamicut State Beach	95	D4	41.324510 -71.800670
R.W. Wheeler State Beach	150	C4	41.372620 -71.495530
Scarborough State Beach	150	C4	41.389770 -71.474260
SOUTH CAROLINA	**PAGE**	**GRID**	**LATITUDE LONGITUDE**
National Park & Rec. Areas			
Charles Pinckney N.H.S.	131	D2	32.847150 -79.824090
Congaree Natl. Park	122	A4	33.836100 -80.827660
Kings Mtn. N.M.P.	122	A1	35.140120 -81.386890
Ninety Six N.H.S.	121	F3	34.162740 -82.010980
State Park & Rec. Areas			
Andrew Jackson S.P.	122	B2	34.839560 -80.810110
Barnwell S.P.	130	B1	33.329250 -81.300400
Calhoun Falls S.P.	121	E3	34.106792 -82.604200
Cheraw S.P.	122	C2	34.642370 -79.927640
Colleton S.P.	130	C1	33.063520 -80.613440
Devils Fork S.P.	121	E2	34.952527 -82.946085
Edisto Beach S.P.	130	C2	32.505410 -80.310310
Givhans Ferry S.P.	130	C1	33.031640 -80.382150
Hickory Knob State Resort Park	121	E4	33.884250 -82.416010
Huntington Beach S.P.	123	D4	33.502650 -79.081200
Jones Gap S.P.	121	E1	35.126360 -82.558350
Kings Mtn. S.P.	122	A1	35.113030 -81.394040
Lake Warren S.P.	130	B2	32.844830 -81.165070
Little Pee Dee S.P.	122	C3	34.331020 -79.282170
Myrtle Beach S.P.	123	D4	33.649210 -78.938600
N.R. Goodale S.P.	122	B3	34.281580 -80.525150
Oconee S.P.	121	E2	34.867297 -83.106098
Paris Mtn. S.P.	121	E2	34.924970 -82.365540
Poinsett S.P.	122	B4	33.804360 -80.544920
Santee S.P.	122	B4	33.500200 -80.489820
Table Rock S.P.	121	E2	35.022050 -82.710700
SOUTH DAKOTA	**PAGE**	**GRID**	**LATITUDE LONGITUDE**
National Park & Rec. Areas			
Badlands Natl. Park-Interior Ent.	26	B4	43.741900 -101.957000
Badlands Natl. Park-Northeast Ent.	26	B4	43.792400 -101.906000
Badlands Natl. Park-Pinnacles Ent.	26	B4	43.885500 -102.238000
Jewel Cave Natl. Mon.	25	F4	43.736500 -103.819940
Minuteman Missile N.H.S.	26	B4	43.833931 -101.899685
Mount Rushmore Natl. Mem.	26	A4	43.886730 -103.440610
Wind Cave Natl. Park-Vis. Ctr.	26	A4	43.556100 -103.478000
State Park & Rec. Areas			
Bear Butte S.P.	26	A3	44.460580 -103.433750
Custer S.P.	26	A4	43.770310 -103.440130
Fisher Grove S.P.	27	E2	44.883340 -98.356640
Hartford Beach S.P.	27	F2	45.398870 -96.665260
Lake Herman S.P.	27	F4	43.993120 -97.159790
Newton Hills S.P.	35	F1	43.218860 -96.569700
Oakwood Lakes S.P.	27	F3	44.454310 -96.989490
Palisades S.P.	27	F4	43.687970 -96.511470
Roy Lake S.P.	27	E1	45.703360 -97.419650
Sica Hollow S.P.	27	E1	45.740690 -97.229150
Union Grove S.P.	35	F1	42.922630 -96.785530
TENNESSEE	**PAGE**	**GRID**	**LATITUDE LONGITUDE**
National Park & Rec. Areas			
Andrew Johnson N.H.S.	111	D4	36.157710 -82.836880
Big South Fork Natl. River & Rec. Area	110	B3	36.475400 -84.752100
State Park & Rec. Areas			
Big Hill Pond S.P.	119	D1	35.078890 -88.718860
Big Ridge S.P.	110	C3	36.241600 -83.929280
Bledsoe Creek S.P.	109	F3	36.378050 -86.356660
Cedars of Lebanon S.P. & Forest	109	F4	36.093930 -86.335620
Chickasaw S.P.	119	D1	35.393241 -88.772298
Cove Lake S.P.	110	C3	36.305830 -84.210750
Cumberland Mtn. S.P.	110	B4	35.898460 -84.995130
David Crockett S.P.	119	E1	35.242690 -87.354850
Davy Crockett Birthplace S.P.	111	E3	36.221980 -82.662770
Edgar Evins S.P.	110	A4	36.086050 -85.812460
Fall Creek Falls S.P.	120	B1	35.622200 -85.208000
Frozen Head S.P. & Nat. Area-North Ent.	110	B4	36.122550 -84.433320
Frozen Head S.P. & Nat. Area-South Ent.	110	B4	36.102180 -84.446970
Harpeth River S.P.	109	E4	36.079240 -86.956920
Harrison Bay S.P.	120	B1	35.175850 -85.115350
Henry Horton S.P.	119	F1	35.596510 -86.698690
Hiwassee–Ocoee Scenic Rivers S.P.	120	C1	35.224557 -84.504269
Indian Mtn. S.P.	110	C3	36.583050 -84.139900
Long Hunter S.P.	109	F4	36.094340 -86.557330
Meeman-Shelby Forest S.P.	118	B1	35.336800 -90.029010
Montgomery Bell S.P.	109	E4	36.106750 -87.268690
Mousetail Landing S.P.	109	D4	35.581900 -87.859100
Natchez Trace S.P.	109	D4	35.839580 -88.252820
Nathan Bedford Forrest S.P.	109	D4	36.087900 -87.979750
Norris Dam S.P.	110	C3	36.234560 -84.127020
Old Stone Fort State Arch. Park	120	A1	35.487270 -86.101330
Panther Creek S.P.	111	D3	36.212760 -83.412420
Paris Landing State Resort Park	109	D3	36.441760 -88.090180
Pickett S.P.	110	B3	36.537374 -84.802126
Pickwick Landing S.P.	119	D2	35.051790 -88.242650
Pinson Mounds State Arch. Park	119	D1	35.504130 -88.683020
Reelfoot Lake S.P.	108	B3	36.414410 -89.426880
Roan Mtn. S.P.	111	E4	36.161110 -82.097000
Rock Island S.P.	110	A4	35.810000 -85.641550
Standing Stone S.P.	110	A3	36.458910 -85.437690
T.O. Fuller S.P.	118	B2	35.057810 -90.113650
Tims Ford S.P.	120	A1	35.220999 -86.255889
Warriors Path S.P.	111	E5	36.504610 -82.481090
TEXAS	**PAGE**	**GRID**	**LATITUDE LONGITUDE**
National Park & Rec. Areas			
Alibates Flint Quarries Natl. Mon.	50	A3	35.571900 -101.633880
Amistad N.R.A.	60	B2	29.449920 -101.053170
Big Bend Natl. Park-North Ent.	62	C4	29.680900 -103.167000
Big Bend Natl. Park-West Ent.	62	C4	29.306600 -103.523000
Fort Davis N.H.S.	62	B2	30.604120 -103.886010
Guadalupe Mts. Natl. Park-Vis. Ctr.	57	D3	31.894300 -104.822000
Lyndon B. Johnson N.H.P.	61	D2	30.276020 -98.411990
Padre Island Natl. Seashore	63	F3	27.553470 -97.248370
Palo Alto Btfd. N.H.P.	63	F4	26.011630 -97.481570
State Park & Rec. Areas			
Abilene S.P.	58	C3	32.241360 -99.879230
Atlanta S.P.	124	C1	33.229500 -94.249300
Balmorhea S.P.	62	B2	30.946270 -103.784890
Bastrop S.P.	61	E2	30.098960 -97.229090
Bentsen-Rio Grande Valley S.P.	63	E4	26.182530 -98.382360
Big Bend Ranch S.P.	62	B4	29.265070 -103.791910
Big Spring S.P.	58	A3	32.229650 -101.483090
Blanco S.P.	61	D2	30.093240 -98.423420
Bonham S.P.	59	F1	33.543100 -96.149640
Brazos Bend S.P.	132	A4	29.371480 -95.631890
Buescher S.P.	61	E2	30.073570 -97.176140
Caddo Lake S.P.	124	C2	32.684230 -94.177070
Caprock Canyons S.P. & Trailway	50	B4	34.406440 -101.048830
Choke Canyon S.P.-Calliham Unit	61	D4	28.460970 -98.356380
Choke Canyon S.P.-South Shore Unit	61	D4	28.467610 -98.239550
Cleburne S.P.	59	E3	32.265180 -97.560680
Colorado Bend S.P.	61	D1	31.062510 -98.504250
Cooper Lake S.P.	124	A1	33.305282 -95.648346
Copper Breaks S.P.	50	C4	34.113660 -99.747800
Daingerfield S.P.	124	B1	33.028720 -94.714510
Davis Mts. S.P.	62	B2	30.599520 -103.929220
Dinosaur Valley S.P.	59	E3	32.250020 -97.814620
Eisenhower S.P.	59	F1	33.822670 -96.616120
Fairfield Lake S.P.	59	F3	31.765910 -96.076220
Falcon S.P.	63	D3	26.583500 -99.144790
Fort Boggy S.P.	124	A4	31.189627 -95.986069
Fort Griffin S.H.S.	58	C2	32.924690 -99.219370
Fort Parker S.P.	59	F4	31.592650 -96.524370
Fort Richardson S.P. & Hist. Site	59	D2	33.206060 -98.164810
Franklin Mts. S.P.	56	C3	31.912060 -106.517140
Galveston Island S.P.	132	B4	29.196240 -94.956210
Garner S.P.	60	C2	29.600900 -99.744220
Goliad S.P.	61	E4	28.655190 -97.383580
Goose Island S.P.	61	F4	28.134060 -96.984350
Guadalupe River S.P.	61	D2	29.849890 -98.509590
Huntsville S.P.	132	A2	30.638130 -95.511370
Inks Lake S.P.	61	D1	30.738290 -98.366450
Kerrville-Schreiner S.P.	60	C2	30.007930 -99.117640
Lake Arrowhead S.P.	59	D1	33.759300 -98.396610
Lake Bob Sandlin S.P.	124	B1	33.054090 -95.10125
Lake Brownwood S.P.	59	D3	31.857370 -99.02128
Lake Casa Blanca International S.P.	63	D2	27.536739 -99.43244
Lake Colorado City S.P.	58	B3	32.313460 -100.9248
Lake Corpus Christi S.P.	61	E4	28.060360 -97.86769
Lake Livingston S.P.	132	B1	30.671300 -95.00820
Lake Mineral Wells S.P.	59	E2	32.814570 -98.04227
Lake Somerville S.P. & Trailway	61	F1	30.315760 -96.62508
Lake Tawakoni S.P.	59	F2	32.841610 -95.99071
Lake Texana S.P.	61	F3	28.953610 -96.56719
Lake Whitney S.P.	59	E3	31.924780 -97.35628
Lockhart S.P.	61	E2	29.857610 -97.69740
Longhorn Cavern S.P.	61	D1	30.686610 -98.35138
Lyndon B. Johnson S.P. & Hist. Site-Ranch Unit	61	D2	30.235180 -98.62910
Martin Creek Lake S.P.	124	B3	32.283090 -94.58347
Martin Dies Junior S.P.	132	C1	30.848980 -94.16472
Meridian S.P.	59	E3	31.892440 -97.69567
Mission Tejas S.P.	124	A4	31.546110 -95.23472
Monahans Sandhills S.P.	57	F4	31.634940 -102.81485
Mother Neff S.P.	59	E4	31.319150 -97.47421
Mustang Island S.P.	63	F2	27.677020 -97.17373
Palmetto S.P.	61	E2	29.597280 -97.58464
Palo Duro Canyon S.P.	50	B3	34.985710 -101.70319
Pedernales Falls S.P.	61	D1	30.273110 -98.25683
Possum Kingdom S.P.	59	D2	32.878970 -98.56174
Purtis Creek S.P.	124	A2	32.373340 -95.97453
Ray Roberts Lake S.P.	59	F1	33.444050 -96.92586
Rusk–Palestine S.P.-East	124	B3	31.803560 -95.19488
Rusk–Palestine S.P.-West	124	A4	31.739260 -95.57045
Sabine Pass Battleground S.H.S.	132	C3	29.726520 -93.87828
San Angelo S.P.	58	B4	31.491919 -100.54714
Sea Rim S.P.	132	C3	29.677900 -94.03990
Seminole Canyon S.P. & Hist. Site	60	A2	29.709000 -101.29848
South Llano River S.P.	60	C1	30.445430 -99.80461
Stephen F. Austin S.P.	61	F2	29.812030 -96.10820
Tyler S.P.	124	A2	32.481750 -95.28176
UTAH	**PAGE**	**GRID**	**LATITUDE LONGITUDE**
National Park & Rec. Areas			
Arches Natl. Park	40	A2	38.615570 -109.61692
Bryce Canyon Natl. Park	39	E4	37.641700 -112.16800
Canyonlands Natl. Park-East Ent.	40	A3	38.168510 -109.75098
Canyonlands Natl. Park-Horseshoe Canyon Unit	39	F3	38.497740 -110.20596
Canyonlands Natl. Park-North Ent.	40	A3	38.490150 -109.80793
Canyonlands Natl. Park-West Ent.	40	A3	38.255440 -110.18005
Capitol Reef Natl. Park	39	E3	38.291020 -111.26141
Cedar Breaks Natl. Mon.-East Ent.	39	D4	37.655230 -112.81135
Cedar Breaks Natl. Mon.-North Ent.	39	D4	37.665730 -112.83813
Cedar Breaks Natl. Mon.-South Ent.	39	D4	37.598730 -112.85008
Glen Canyon N.R.A.	39	F4	38.255440 -110.18005
Golden Spike N.H.S.	31	E3	41.620482 -112.54747
Grand Staircase-Escalante Natl. Mon.	39	E4	37.420000 -111.55000
Natural Bridges Natl. Mon.	39	F4	37.608120 -109.96628
Rainbow Bridge Natl. Mon.	47	E1	37.110810 -110.40605
Zion Natl. Park-East Ent.	39	D4	37.235370 -112.86447
Zion Natl. Park-Main Ent.	39	D4	37.201970 -112.98838
State Park & Rec. Areas			
Anasazi S.P. Mus.	39	E3	37.922399 -111.42574
Antelope Island S.P.	31	E4	41.089290 -112.11649
Bear Lake (Rendezvous Beach) S.P.	31	F2	41.962200 -111.40032
Bear Lake S.P.	31	F2	41.965360 -111.39948
Camp Floyd– Stagecoach Inn S.P.	31	E4	40.258360 -112.09727
Coral Pink Sand Dunes S.P.-North Ent.	47	D1	37.065540 -112.70553
Coral Pink Sand Dunes S.P.-West Ent.	47	D1	37.034580 -112.74126
Dead Horse Point S.P.	40	A3	38.510220 -109.72946
Deer Creek S.P.	31	F4	40.452620 -111.47782
Edge of the Cedars S.P.	40	A4	37.629760 -109.49173
Escalante Petrified Forest S.P.	39	E4	37.783820 -111.63022
Fremont Indian S.P.	39	D3	38.579537 -112.31477
Goblin Valley S.P.	39	F3	38.580620 -110.71258
Goosenecks S.P.	40	A4	37.174730 -109.92695
Green River S.P.	39	F2	38.995500 -110.15691
Gunlock S.P.-North Ent.	38	C4	37.275970 -113.76878
Gunlock S.P.-South Ent.	38	C4	37.251490 -113.77282
Huntington S.P.	39	F2	39.315200 -110.97710
Hyrum S.P.	31	E3	41.626220 -111.87217
Iron Mission S.P.	39	D4	37.688349 -113.06189
Kodachrome Basin S.P.	39	E4	37.501670 -111.99361
Millsite S.P.	39	E2	39.099020 -111.18424
Otter Creek S.P.	39	E3	38.167430 -112.02157
Palisade S.P.	39	E2	39.195800 -111.69160
Piute S.P.	39	E3	38.322530 -112.20420
Quail Creek S.P.	39	D4	37.105000 -113.57660
Red Fleet S.P.	32	B4	40.553300 -109.51847
Rockport S.P.	31	F4	40.751890 -111.36741
Sand Hollow S.P.	46	C1	37.144830 -113.38213
Scofield S.P.	39	E1	39.708600 -110.92100
Snow Canyon S.P.-East Ent.	38	C4	37.212120 -113.63087
Snow Canyon S.P.-North Ent.	38	C4	37.256790 -113.63299
Snow Canyon S.P.-South Ent.	38	C4	37.183380 -113.64501
Starvation S.P.	32	A4	40.104100 -110.33090

teinaker S.P.-North Ent.	32	A4	40.534870 -109.522440
teinaker S.P.-South Ent.	32	A4	40.504850 -109.528870
rritorial Statehouse S.P.	39	D2	38.965880 -112.353530
asatch Mtn. S.P.	31	F4	40.477770 -111.519990
illard Bay S.P.-North Ent.	31	E3	41.418810 -112.052390
illard Bay S.P.-South Ent.	31	E3	41.350610 -112.069060
uba S.P.	39	E2	39.381240 -112.028360

VERMONT	PAGE	GRID	LATITUDE LONGITUDE
ational Park & Rec. Areas			
arsh-Billings-Rockefeller N.H.P.	81	E3	43.635833 -72.538333
oosalamoo Natl. Rec. Area	81	D3	43.879457 -73.098532
tate Park & Rec. Areas			
llis S.P.	81	E3	44.051150 -72.626440
ranbury S.P.	81	D3	43.904250 -73.065370
urton Island S.P.	81	D1	44.779660 -73.180050
amp Plymouth S.P.	81	E4	43.475810 -72.694987
.A.R. S.P.	81	D3	44.058850 -73.409210
merald Lake S.P.	81	D4	43.283790 -73.002250
alf Moon S.P.	81	D3	43.699720 -73.223220
ingsland Bay S.P.	81	D2	44.226230 -73.277660
ake Saint Catherine S.P.	81	D4	43.483000 -73.202580
ittle River S.P.	81	D2	44.388940 -72.768360
olly Stark S.P.	94	C1	42.854920 -72.813790
orth Hero S.P.	81	D1	44.908210 -73.235110
icker Pond S.P.	81	E2	44.251467 -72.247550
tillwater S.P.	81	E2	44.280200 -72.275060
ownshend S.P.	81	E4	43.041920 -72.691600
nderhill S.P.	81	D2	44.528880 -72.843920
oodford S.P.	94	C1	42.894450 -73.037790
oods Island S.P.	81	D1	44.802500 -73.209283

VIRGINIA	PAGE	GRID	LATITUDE LONGITUDE
ational Park & Rec. Areas			
ppomattox Court House N.H.P.	112	C1	37.377367 -78.795290
ooker T. Washington Natl. Mon.	112	B2	37.120500 -79.733340
edar Creek & Belle Grove N.H.P.	102	C2	39.023500 -78.289000
olonial N.H.P.	114	A4	37.211390 -76.776730
umberland Gap N.H.P.-Vis. Ctr.	111	D3	36.602600 -83.695400
redericksburg & Spotsylvania Co. Bflds. Mem. N.M.P.	103	D4	38.254300 -77.451890
eorge Washington Birthplace Natl. Mon.	114	A2	38.192353 -76.927192
anassas Natl. Bfld. Park	144	A3	38.806030 -77.572810
ount Rogers N.R.A.	111	F2	36.811360 -81.420130
henandoah Natl. Park-Front Royal North Ent.	102	C3	38.903300 -78.192400
henandoah Natl. Park-Rockfish Gap South Ent.	102	C3	38.033900 -78.858900
henandoah Natl. Park-Swift Run Gap Ent.	102	C3	38.359100 -78.546700
henandoah Natl. Park-Thornton Gap Ent.	102	C3	38.662300 -78.320600
tate Park & Rec. Areas			
ear Creek Lake S.P.	113	D1	37.532970 -78.274890
elle Isle S.P.	114	B2	37.774526 -76.599222
hippokes Plantation S.P.	114	A4	37.140400 -76.748590
laytor Lake S.P.	112	A2	37.057620 -80.622140
outhat S.P.	102	B2	37.914520 -79.796740
airy Stone S.P.	112	B2	36.791790 -80.117890
alse Cape S.P.	115	F1	36.691370 -75.924410
irst Landing S.P.	114	B4	36.915601 -76.057000
rayson Highlands S.P.	111	F3	36.611920 -81.489900
olliday Lake S.P.	113	D1	37.404610 -78.644920
ungry Mother S.P.	111	F2	36.880860 -81.525750
ames River S.P.	112	C1	37.540400 -78.839300
iptopeke S.P.	114	B4	37.169292 -75.982919
ake Anna S.P.	103	D4	38.125850 -77.821690
eesylvania S.P.	103	E3	38.591200 -77.248400
ason Neck S.P.	103	E3	38.640740 -77.194400
atural Tunnel S.P.	111	E3	36.707520 -82.744090
ew River Trail S.P.	112	A2	36.870180 -80.868550
cconeechee S.P.	113	D3	36.633330 -78.525420
ocahontas S.P.	113	F2	37.366240 -77.573870
ailor's Creek Bfld. Hist. S.P.	113	D1	37.298470 -78.229470
ky Meadows S.P.	103	D2	38.988703 -77.968913
mith Mtn. Lake S.P.	112	B2	37.091110 -79.592110
win Lakes S.P.	113	D2	37.336900 -77.934100
estmoreland S.P.	103	E4	38.158690 -76.870120
ilderness Road S.P.	111	D3	36.621300 -83.512900
ork River S.P.	113	F1	37.414190 -76.713650

WASHINGTON	PAGE	GRID	LATITUDE LONGITUDE
ational Park & Rec. Areas			
olumbia River Gorge Natl. Scenic Area	21	D1	45.715322 -121.818667
ort Vancouver N.H.S.	20	C1	45.626940 -122.656310
anford Reach Natl. Mon.	13	E4	46.483333 -119.533333
ake Chelan N.R.A.	13	D2	48.309080 -120.657730
ake Roosevelt N.R.A.	13	F2	47.972680 -118.970580
ewis & Clark N.H.P.-Discovery Trail	12	B4	46.370033 -124.053503
ewis & Clark N.H.P.-Dismal Nitch	20	B1	46.249033 -123.862903
ewis & Clark N.H.P.-Sta. Camp	20	B1	46.263111 -123.932571
ount Baker N.R.A.	12	C1	48.714167 -121.805900
ount Rainier Natl. Park-Carbon River Ent.	12	C6	46.994810 -121.918090
ount Rainier Natl. Park-Nisqually Ent.	12	C5	46.741400 -121.919040
ount Rainier Natl. Park-Stevens Can. Ent.	12	C7	46.754730 -121.557010
Mount Rainier Natl. Park-White River Ent.	12	C8	46.902040 -121.554340
Mount Saint Helens Natl. Mon.	12	C4	46.277590 -122.218820
North Cascades Natl. Park-Golden West	13	D1	48.308200 -120.655000
North Cascades Natl. Park-Northern Cascades Vis. Ctr.	13	D1	48.666100 -121.264000
Olympic Natl. Park-Vis. Ctr.	12	B2	48.096700 -123.428000
Olympic Natl. Park-Vis. Ctr.-Hoh Rain Forest	12	B2	47.860700 -123.935000
Olympic Natl. Park-Vis. Ctr.-Hurricane Ridge	12	B2	47.969200 -123.498000
Ross Lake N.R.A.	13	D1	48.674250 -121.244730
San Juan Island N.H.P.	12	B2	48.534580 -123.016250
San Juan Islands Natl. Mon.	12	C2	48.531944,-123.029167
Whitman Mission N.H.S.	21	F1	46.040910 -118.468110
State Park & Rec. Areas			
Alta Lake S.P.	13	E2	48.031990 -119.934710
Anderson Lake S.P.	12	C2	48.014590 -122.810680
Belfair S.P.	12	C3	47.430630 -122.881400
Birch Bay S.P.	12	C1	48.903210 -122.757880
Bogachiel S.P.	12	A2	47.894790 -124.362820
Brooks Mem. S.P.	21	D1	45.950590 -120.664200
Camano Island S.P.	12	C2	48.131680 -122.503240
Cape Disappointment S.P.	20	B1	46.294210 -124.053610
Columbia Hills S.P.	21	D1	45.643030 -121.106410
Crawford S.P.	14	A1	48.992070 -117.370370
Curlew Lake S.P.	13	F1	48.719280 -118.661740
Damon Point S.P.	12	B4	46.945300 -124.132100
Deception Pass S.P.	12	C2	48.390970 -122.646880
Dosewallips S.P.	12	C3	47.687570 -122.899860
Fields Spring S.P.	22	A1	46.087520 -117.173650
Flaming Geyser S.P.	12	C3	47.280230 -122.041870
Fort Casey S.P.	12	C2	48.159760 -122.672410
Fort Okanogan S.P.	13	E2	48.102370 -119.678720
Fort Simcoe S.P.	13	D4	46.345340 -120.823460
Fort Townsend S.P.	12	C2	48.078260 -122.805690
Ginkgo Petrified Forest S.P.	13	E4	46.949010 -119.997490
Goldendale Observatory S.P.	21	D1	45.837090 -120.815890
Ike Kinswa S.P.	12	C4	46.555780 -122.536570
Jarrell Cove S.P.	12	B3	47.285940 -122.881080
Joseph Whidbey S.P.	12	C2	48.308370 -122.713170
Kitsap Mem. S.P.	12	C3	47.816580 -122.646840
Lake Chelan S.P.	13	D2	47.869430 -120.191110
Lake Easton S.P.	13	D3	47.249380 -121.190920
Lake Wenatchee S.P.	13	D3	47.816340 -120.729780
Larrabee S.P.	12	C2	48.650620 -122.489810
Lewis & Clark S.P.	12	C4	46.525850 -122.817910
Lewis & Clark Trail S.P.	13	F4	46.287600 -118.073340
Lincoln Rock S.P.	13	D3	47.535490 -120.282280
Millersylvania S.P.	12	B4	46.909610 -122.905950
Moran S.P.	12	C1	48.657700 -122.859630
Mount Spokane S.P.	14	B2	47.899290 -117.124350
Nolte S.P.	12	C3	47.267320 -121.943420
Ocean City S.P.	12	B4	47.038520 -124.158130
Osoyoos S.P.	13	E1	48.950060 -119.434350
Pacific Beach S.P.	12	A3	47.205980 -124.202220
Pacific Pines S.P.	12	B4	46.507610 -124.049150
Palouse Falls S.P.	13	F4	46.664030 -118.228660
Peace Arch S.P.	12	C1	49.000980 -122.751580
Pearrygin Lake S.P.	13	E2	48.496720 -120.146950
Peshastin Pinnacles S.P.	13	D3	47.578810 -120.613860
Potholes S.P.	13	E4	46.970780 -119.351180
Potlatch S.P.	12	B3	47.363000 -123.158140
Rainbow Falls S.P.	12	B4	46.631010 -123.237350
Rockport S.P.	12	C2	48.487920 -121.601870
Sacajawea S.P.	21	F1	46.210140 -119.046050
Scenic Beach S.P.	12	C3	47.649250 -122.845470
Seaquest S.P.	12	C4	46.295880 -122.820860
Sequim Bay S.P.	12	B2	48.040750 -123.030920
Shine Tidelands S.P.	12	C2	47.867990 -122.638700
Steamboat Rock S.P.	13	E2	47.828650 -119.134340
Sun Lakes S.P.	13	E3	47.596540 -119.387760
Triton Cove S.P.	12	B3	47.609112 -122.986526
Twenty-Five Mile Creek S.P.	13	D2	47.992520 -120.263610
Twin Harbors S.P.	12	B4	46.858850 -124.104210
Wallace Falls S.P.	12	C2	47.865610 -121.680050
Wanapum S.P.	13	E4	46.924760 -119.991690
Westport Light S.P.	12	B4	46.891700 -124.111630

WEST VIRGINIA	PAGE	GRID	LATITUDE LONGITUDE
National Park & Rec. Areas			
Bluestone Natl. Scenic River	112	A1	37.584300 -80.957900
Gauley River N.R.A.	101	F4	38.191800 -81.001920
Harpers Ferry N.H.P.	103	D2	39.318820 -77.759060
New River Gorge Natl. River	101	F4	37.875670 -81.077598
Spruce Knob Seneca Rocks N.R.A.	102	B3	38.681180 -79.544480
State Park & Rec. Areas			
Audra S.P.	102	A2	39.041110 -80.067500
Beartown S.P.	102	A4	38.051750 -80.275420
Blennerhassett Island Hist. S.P.	101	E2	39.273300 -81.644800
Bluestone S.P.	112	A1	37.623050 -80.934710
Cacapon Resort S.P.	102	C1	39.502980 -78.291330
Camp Creek S.P.	111	F1	37.508173 -81.132873
Carnifex Ferry Bfld. S.P.	101	F4	38.211290 -80.941850
Cass Scenic Railroad S.P.	102	A3	38.396520 -79.914280
Cedar Creek S.P.	101	F3	38.880780 -80.849420
Droop Mtn. Bfld. S.P.	102	A4	38.113200 -80.271670
Holly River S.P.	102	A3	38.653140 -80.382620
Little Beaver S.P.	112	A1	37.756570 -81.079780
Moncove Lake S.P.	112	B1	37.616950 -80.354730
Pinnacle Rock S.P.	111	F1	37.308190 -81.291430
Prickett's Fort S.P.	102	A1	39.514090 -80.099960
Tomlinson Run S.P.	91	F4	40.550660 -80.595950
Tygart Lake S.P.	102	A2	39.248160 -80.021060
Valley Falls S.P.	102	A2	39.392900 -80.070480
Watoga S.P.	102	A4	38.122510 -80.155660
Watters Smith Mem. S.P.	102	A2	39.174520 -80.414260

WISCONSIN	PAGE	GRID	LATITUDE LONGITUDE
National Park & Rec. Areas			
Apostle Islands Natl. Lakeshore	65	D4	46.812210 -90.820780
Saint Croix Natl. Scenic Riverway	67	E2	45.415700 -92.646270
State Park & Rec. Areas			
Amnicon Falls S.P.	64	C4	46.608210 -91.887850
Aztalan S.P.	74	B3	43.068310 -88.863750
Belmont Mound S.P.	74	A4	42.768611 -90.349444
Big Bay S.P.	65	D4	46.811030 -90.696960
Big Foot Beach S.P.	74	C4	42.567330 -88.436790
Blue Mound S.P.	74	A3	43.026990 -89.840740
Brunet Island S.P.	67	F3	45.176220 -91.161610
Buckhorn S.P.	74	A1	43.948280 -90.002130
Copper Culture S.P.	68	C4	44.887440 -87.897940
Copper Falls S.P.	65	D4	46.351710 -90.643670
Council Grounds S.P.	68	A3	45.184840 -89.734290
Devil's Lake S.P.	74	A2	43.429010 -89.734900
Governor Dodge S.P.	74	A3	43.019560 -90.141950
Governor Thompson S.P.	68	C3	45.326309 -88.219205
Harrington Beach S.P.	75	D2	43.499430 -87.811890
Hartman Creek S.P.	74	B1	44.318070 -89.194320
High Cliff S.P.	74	C1	44.166680 -88.291760
Interstate S.P.	67	D3	45.396410 -92.636580
Kinnickinnic S.P.	67	D4	44.837280 -92.733190
Kohler-Andrae S.P.	75	D2	43.672740 -87.719320
Lake Kegonsa S.P.	74	B3	42.978005 -89.230300
Lake Wissota S.P.	67	F4	44.980950 -91.313740
Merrick S.P.	73	E1	44.152740 -91.744120
Mill Bluff S.P.	74	A1	43.961610 -90.317980
Mirror Lake S.P.	74	A2	43.568770 -89.834930
Natural Bridge S.P.	74	A2	43.344930 -89.928290
Nelson Dewey S.P.	73	F4	42.743740 -91.037860
New Glarus Woods S.P.	74	B4	42.786830 -89.631980
Newport S.P.	69	D3	45.241470 -86.998830
Pattison S.P.	64	C4	46.535290 -92.121410
Peninsula S.P.	69	D3	45.133080 -87.213280
Perrot S.P.	73	F1	44.016350 -91.479670
Potawatomi S.P.	69	D4	44.849990 -87.407640
Rib Mtn. S.P.	68	B4	44.915800 -89.669360
Roche-A-Cri S.P.	74	A1	43.996120 -89.812370
Rock Island S.P.	69	E3	45.398990 -86.855970
Rocky Arbor S.P.	74	A2	43.647890 -89.808240
Straight Lake S.P.	67	E2	45.597399 -92.406609
Tower Hill S.P.	74	A3	43.147090 -90.043750
Whitefish Dunes S.P.	69	D4	44.928910 -87.182150
Wildcat Mtn. S.P.	74	A2	43.688870 -90.566800
Willow River S.P.	67	D3	45.017610 -92.672610
Wyalusing S.P.	73	F3	42.978770 -91.118560
Yellowstone Lake S.P.	74	A4	42.777360 -89.993540

WYOMING	PAGE	GRID	LATITUDE LONGITUDE
National Park & Rec. Areas			
Devils Tower Natl. Mon.	25	E3	44.586870 -104.706710
Flaming Gorge N.R.A.	32	A3	41.254860 -109.611400
Fort Laramie N.H.S.	33	E2	42.202530 -104.558590
Fossil Butte Natl. Mon.	31	F2	41.855370 -110.782340
Grand Teton Natl. Park-Granite Canyon Ent.	23	F4	43.597990 -110.801640
Grand Teton Natl. Park-Moose Ent.	23	F4	43.655860 -110.718350
Grand Teton Natl. Park-Moran Ent.	23	F4	43.843640 -110.511950
John D. Rockefeller Jr. Mem. Parkway	24	A3	44.108800 -110.685508
Medicine Wheel Natl. Hist. Landmark	24	C2	44.826200 -107.921717
Yellowstone Natl. Park-East Ent.	23	F3	44.489540 -110.001560
Yellowstone Natl. Park-North East Ent.	23	F3	45.006120 -109.991550
Yellowstone Natl. Park-North Ent.	23	F3	45.030110 -110.705460
Yellowstone Natl. Park-South Ent.	23	F3	44.134730 -110.666170
Yellowstone Natl. Park-West Ent.	23	F3	44.658720 -111.098970
State Park & Rec. Areas			
Bear River S.P.	31	F3	41.267257 -110.938030
Boysen S.P.	32	C1	43.270160 -108.115260
Buffalo Bill S.P.	24	B3	44.505020 -109.249540
Curt Gowdy S.P.	33	E3	41.175380 -105.243640
Edness K. Wilkins S.P.	33	D1	42.857220 -106.177370
Glendo S.P.	33	E1	42.476060 -104.998910
Guernsey S.P.	33	E2	42.287400 -104.763460
Hot Springs S.P.	24	C4	43.653980 -108.201790
Keyhole S.P.	25	E3	44.356490 -104.825810
Seminoe S.P.	33	D2	42.150350 -106.905870
Sinks Canyon S.P.	32	B1	42.752600 -108.804770

CANADA

ALBERTA	PAGE	GRID	LATITUDE LONGITUDE
National Park & Rec. Areas			
Banff Natl. Park-Banff Vis. Ctr.	164	B2	51.177400 -115.570900
Banff Natl. Park-Lake Louise Vis. Ctr.	164	B2	51.425200 -116.178400
Banff Park Mus. N.H.S.	164	B3	51.174300 -115.571100
Bar U Ranch N.H.S.	164	C3	50.420300 -114.244400
Cave and Basin N.H.S.	164	B3	51.168300 -115.591400
Elk Island Natl. Park	159	D4	53.572500 -112.841900
Jasper Natl. Park-Icefield Center	164	A1	52.233500 -117.234800
Jasper Natl. Park-Jasper Information Center	164	A1	52.877300 -118.080900
Rocky Mtn. House N.H.S.	164	C2	52.377590 -114.931237
Waterton Lakes Natl. Park-Waterton Vis. Ctr.	164	C4	49.051400 -113.906300
Wood Buffalo Natl. Park-Fort Chipewyan Vis. Ctr.	155	F2	48.714100 -111.154300
Provincial Park & Rec. Areas			
Aspen Beach Prov. Park	164	C2	52.454530 -113.975750
Beauvais Lake Prov. Park	164	C4	49.409500 -114.117000
Big Hill Springs Prov. Park	164	C3	51.251670 -114.386940
Big Knife Prov. Park	165	D2	52.489720 -112.210560
Birch Mts. Wildland Prov. Park	159	D1	57.509400 -112.957000
Bluerock Wildland Prov. Park	164	C3	50.642300 -114.654000
Bob Creek Wildland Prov. Park	164	C4	49.973700 -114.286000
Bow Valley Prov. Park	164	C3	51.040400 -115.077000
Bow Valley Wildland Prov. Park	164	B3	51.032600 -115.259000
Bragg Creek Prov. Park	164	C3	50.939170 -114.583330
Brown-Lowery Prov. Park	164	C3	50.813900 -114.430600
Calling Lake Prov. Park	159	D3	55.179720 -113.272500
Caribou Mts. Wildland Prov. Park	155	F3	59.205600 -114.897000
Carson-Pegasus Prov. Park	158	C3	54.295800 -115.645000
Chain Lakes Prov. Park	164	C3	50.200000 -114.183330
Chinchaga Wildland Prov. Park	158	B1	57.163400 -119.582000
Cold Lake Prov. Park	159	E3	54.602400 -110.072000
Cold Lake Prov. Park-North Shore	159	E3	54.644800 -110.103600
Crimson Lake Prov. Park	164	C2	52.466900 -115.048000
Cross Lake Prov. Park	159	D3	54.649300 -113.791000
Crow Lake Prov. Park	159	E2	55.800456 -112.152014
Dillberry Lake Prov. Park	165	E1	52.570200 -110.030000
Dinosaur Prov. Park	165	D3	50.770100 -111.480000
Don Getty Wildland Prov. Park	164	B2	50.893000 -114.993000
Dry Island Buffalo Jump Prov. Park	164	C2	51.929500 -112.975000
Dunvegan Prov. Park	158	B2	55.923600 -118.594400
Dunvegan West Wildland Prov. Park	158	B2	56.088900 -119.297000
Elbow Sheep Wildland Prov. Park	164	C3	50.703500 -114.939000
Fort Assiniboine Sandhills Wildland Prov. Park	158	C3	54.387100 -114.608000
Garner Lake Prov. Park	159	D3	54.183420 -111.741000
Gipsy Lake Wildland Prov. Park	159	E2	56.493500 -110.386000
Gooseberry Lake Prov. Park	165	D2	52.116940 -110.759170
Grand Rapids Wildland Prov. Park	159	D1	56.484200 -112.343000
Greene Valley Prov. Park	158	B2	56.140900 -117.242000
Gregoire Lake Prov. Park	159	E1	56.485000 -111.182780
Grizzly Ridge Wildland Prov. Park	158	C3	55.137700 -115.049000
Hay-Zama Lakes Wildland Prov. Park	155	F3	58.774100 -119.016000
Hilliard's Bay Prov. Park	158	C2	55.502900 -116.001000
Hubert Lake Wildland Prov. Park	158	C3	54.554100 -114.244000
Kakwa Wildland Prov. Park	158	A3	54.034600 -119.810000
Kinbrook Island Prov. Park	165	D3	50.437189 -111.910595
La Biche River Wildland Prov. Park	159	D3	54.987000 -112.626000
Lakeland Prov. Park	159	E3	54.759300 -111.557000
Lakeland Prov. Rec. Area	159	E3	54.721800 -111.398000
Lesser Slave Lake Prov. Park	158	C2	55.448000 -114.817000
Lesser Slave Lake Wildland Prov. Park	158	C2	55.497700 -115.567000
Little Bow Prov. Park	164	C3	50.227930 -112.926590
Little Fish Lake Prov. Park	165	D2	51.374246 -112.200944
Long Lake Prov. Park	159	D3	54.439986 -112.763465
Marguerite River Wildland Prov. Park	159	E1	57.638400 -110.266000
Midland Prov. Park	165	D2	51.478295 -112.771085
Miquelon Lake Prov. Park	159	D4	53.246900 -112.874000
Moonshine Lake Prov. Park	158	B2	55.883800 -119.216000
Moose Lake Prov. Park	159	E3	54.272986 -110.931143
Notikewin Prov. Park	158	C1	57.218300 -117.148000
Obed Lake Prov. Park	158	B4	53.558200 -117.101000
O'Brien Prov. Park	158	B3	55.065242 -118.822285
Otter-Orloff Lakes Wildland Prov. Park	159	D2	55.364200 -113.551000
Park Lake Prov. Park	164	C4	49.806621 -112.924681
Peace River Wildland Prov. Park	158	B2	55.983200 -117.765000
Pembina River Prov. Park	158	C4	53.611859 -114.985313
Peter Lougheed Prov. Park	164	B3	50.684100 -115.184000
Pigeon Lake Prov. Park	164	C1	53.029547 -114.150507
Police Outpost Prov. Park	164	C4	49.004503 -113.464980
Queen Elizabeth Prov. Park	158	B2	56.219128 -117.693540
Red Lodge Prov. Park	164	C2	51.947917 -114.243862
Rochon Sands Prov. Park	165	D2	52.461755 -112.892373
Rock Lake Solomon Creek Wildland Prov. Park	158	B4	53.413700 -118.118000
Saskatoon Island Prov. Park	158	B2	55.205201 -119.085401
Sheep River Prov. Park	164	C3	50.647300 -114.660000
Sir Winston Churchill Prov. Park	159	D3	54.832050 -111.976109
Spray Valley Prov. Park	164	B3	50.888700 -115.293000
Stony Mtn. Wildland Prov. Park	159	E2	56.211500 -111.244000
Sundance Prov. Park	158	B4	53.668700 -116.926000
Sylvan Lake Prov. Park	164	C2	52.315760 -114.092272
Thunder Lake Prov. Park	158	C3	54.131941 -114.725882
Tillebrook Prov. Park	165	D3	50.538593 -111.812268
Vermilion Prov. Park	159	E4	53.367679 -110.909771
Wabamun Lake Prov. Park	158	C4	53.565029 -114.441575
Whitehorse Wildland Prov. Park	164	B1	52.957900 -117.395000
Whitemud Falls Wildland Prov. Park	159	E1	56.703400 -110.084000
Whitney Lakes Prov. Park	159	E4	53.847100 -110.537000
William A. Switzer Prov. Park	158	B4	53.492000 -117.804000
Williamson Prov. Park	158	B3	55.081821 -117.560174
Willow Creek Prov. Park	164	C3	50.118067 -113.776021
Winagami Lake Prov. Park	158	C2	55.627500 -116.738000
Winagami Wildland Prov. Park	158	C2	55.611900 -116.635000
Woolford Prov. Park	164	C4	49.178498 -113.190438
Writing-On-Stone Prov. Park	165	D4	49.061400 -111.639000
Wyndham-Carseland Prov. Park	164	C3	50.827750 -113.436542
Young's Point Prov. Park	158	B3	55.148000 -117.572000

BRITISH COLUMBIA	PAGE	GRID	LATITUDE LONGITUDE
National Park & Rec. Areas			
Chilkoot Trail N.H.S.	155	D3	59.756667 -134.960833
Fort Langley N.H.S.	163	D3	49.168056 -122.569167
Fort McLeod N.H.S.	157	E1	54.992384 -123.039629
Fort Saint James N.H.S.	157	D2	54.440278 -124.255556
Gitwangak Battle Hill N.H.S.	156	C1	55.119444 -128.018056
Glacier Natl. Park-Eastern Welcome Sta.	164	A2	51.511700 -117.442000
Glacier Natl. Park-Rogers Pass Discovery Center	164	A2	51.300600 -117.521500
Gulf Islands Natl. Park Res.	163	D4	48.769400 -123.210000
Gulf of Georgia Cannery N.H.S.	163	D3	49.124722 -123.199722
Gwaii Haanas Natl. Park Res. & Haida Heritage Site	156	A3	52.349722 -131.433056
Kootenay Natl. Park-Radium Hot Springs Vis. Ctr.	164	B3	50.619500 -116.069800
Kootenay Natl. Park-Vermilion Crossing Vis. Ctr.	164	B3	51.000000 -115.966000
Mount Revelstoke Natl. Park-Western Welcome Sta.	164	A2	51.042000 -117.983900
Pacific Rim Natl. Park Res.-Broken Group Islands	162	B3	48.891100 -125.300800
Pacific Rim Natl. Park Res.-Pacific Rim Vis. Ctr.	162	B3	48.992000 -125.587200
Pacific Rim Natl. Park Res.-West Coast Trail	162	C4	48.704800 -124.866100
Pacific Rim Natl. Park Res.-Wickaninnish Interpretive Center	162	B3	49.012700 -125.674200
Yoho Natl. Park-Field Vis. Ctr.	164	B2	51.397800 -116.492000
Provincial Park & Rec. Areas			
Akamina-Kishinena Prov. Park	164	C4	49.032700 -114.178000
Alexandra Bridge Prov. Park	163	E2	49.700000 -121.399722
Alice Lake Prov. Park	163	D2	49.783056 -123.116667
Allison Lake Prov. Park	163	F2	49.683056 -120.599722
Anstey Hunakwa Prov. Park	164	A2	51.140600 -118.924300
Arctic Pacific Lakes Prov. Park	157	E2	54.384400 -121.553000
Arrow Lakes Prov. Park	164	A3	49.883056 -118.065667
Arrowstone Prov. Park	163	E1	50.879900 -121.273000
Atlin Prov. Park	155	E3	59.165400 -133.914000
Babine Lake-Pendleton Bay Marine Prov. Park	157	D2	54.533000 -125.724800
Babine Lake-Smithers Landing Marine Prov. Park	156	C1	55.098400 -126.600000
Babine Mountains Prov. Park	156	C1	54.913100 -126.928000
Babine River Corridor Prov. Park	156	C1	55.577400 -127.032000
Barkerville Prov. Park	157	E3	53.088889 -121.510833
Bear Creek Prov. Park	163	F2	49.930556 -119.520556
Bearhole Lake Prov. Park	158	A3	55.043400 -120.568000
Beatton Prov. Park	158	A1	56.333056 -120.933056
Beaumont Prov. Park	157	D2	54.050000 -124.616667
Beaver Creek Prov. Park	164	A4	49.066667 -117.600000
Big Bar Lake Prov. Park	157	E4	51.316667 -121.816667
Big Bunsby Marine Prov. Park	162	A2	50.120800 -127.504200
Big Creek Prov. Park	157	E4	51.301500 -123.158000
Bijoux Falls Prov. Park	157	E1	55.300000 -122.666667
Birkenhead Lake Prov. Park	163	D1	50.577900 -122.737000
Bishop River Prov. Park	162	C1	50.912500 -124.038000
Blanket Creek Prov. Park	164	A3	50.833056 -118.083056
Bligh Island Marine Prov. Park	162	A2	49.633300 -126.553000
Bowron Lake Prov. Park	157	F3	53.174100 -121.012000
Boya Lake Prov. Park	155	E3	59.380500 -129.090000
Brandywine Falls Prov. Park	163	D2	50.033056 -123.116667
Bridal Veil Falls Prov. Park	163	E3	49.183056 -121.733056
Bridge Lake Prov. Park	157	F4	51.483056 -120.700000
Bromley Rock Prov. Park	163	F3	49.416667 -120.258056
Brooks Peninsula Prov. Park	162	A2	50.180300 -127.657000
Broughton Archipelago Marine Prov. Park	162	A1	50.687100 -126.663000
Bugaboo Prov. Park	164	B3	50.794700 -116.808000
Callaghan Lake Prov. Park	163	D2	50.206900 -123.189000
Bull Canyon Prov. Park	157	E4	52.091667 -123.374722
Canal Flats Prov. Park	164	B3	50.183056 -115.816667
Canim Beach Prov. Park	157	F4	51.816667 -120.872667
Cape Scott Prov. Park	162	A1	50.765900 -128.246000
Cariboo Mts. Prov. Park	157	F3	52.852600 -120.538000

Name	Page	Grid	Latitude Longitude
Cariboo River Prov. Park	157	F3	52.873600 -121.2220
Carmanah Walbran Prov. Park	162	C4	48.654500 -124.6280
Carp Lake Prov. Park	157	E2	54.769400 -123.3870
Catala Island Marine Prov. Park	162	A2	49.835833 -127.0541
Cathedral Prov. Park	163	F3	49.069800 -120.1740
Champion Lakes Prov. Park	164	A4	49.184100 -117.6240
Charlie Lake Prov. Park	158	A1	56.316667 -120.9997
Chasm Prov. Park	157	F4	51.178900 -121.4380
Chilliwack Lake Prov. Park	163	E3	49.072200 -121.4360
Clayoquot Arm Prov. Park	162	B3	49.172800 -125.5600
Clayoquot Plateau Prov. Park	162	B3	49.225100 -125.4280
Clendinning Prov. Park	162	C1	50.429700 -123.7330
Codville Lagoon Marine Prov. Park	156	C4	52.060833 -127.8555
Conkle Lake Prov. Park	164	A4	49.166667 -119.1000
Coquihalla Canyon Prov. Park	163	E3	49.371944 -121.3666
Cormorant Channel Marine Prov. Park	162	A1	50.593500 -126.8509
Cowichan River Prov. Park	162	C4	48.780800 -123.9200
Crooked River Prov. Park	157	E2	54.466667 -122.6666
Crowsnest Prov. Park	164	C4	49.649722 -114.6997
Cummins Lakes Prov. Park	164	A2	52.104100 -118.0660
Cypress Prov. Park	163	D3	49.425800 -123.2090
Dahl Lake Prov. Park	157	E2	53.769900 -123.2930
Desolation Sound Marine Prov. Park	162	C2	50.101100 -124.7100
Diana Lake Prov. Park	156	B2	54.216667 -130.1666
Downing Prov. Park	163	E1	51.000000 -121.7830
Dry Gulch Prov. Park	164	B3	50.583056 -116.0330
Duffey Lake Prov. Park	163	D1	50.407500 -122.3370
Dune Za Keyih Prov. Park	155	E3	58.323000 -126.3550
Echo Lake Prov. Park	164	A3	50.199722 -118.7000
Edge Hills Prov. Park	163	E1	51.035900 -121.8710
Elk Falls Prov. Park	162	B2	50.041000 -125.3240
Elk Lakes Prov. Park	164	C3	50.480800 -115.0880
Ellison Prov. Park	164	A3	50.173333 -119.4330
Emory Creek Prov. Park	163	E3	49.516667 -121.4166
Eneas Lakes Prov. Park	163	F2	49.752400 -119.9360
Entiako Prov. Park	157	D3	53.221500 -125.4430
Epper Passage Prov. Park	162	B3	49.219167 -125.9497
Eskers Prov. Park	157	E2	54.081300 -123.2050
Ethel F. Wilson Mem. Prov. Park	157	D2	54.416667 -125.6830
Fillongley Prov. Park	162	C3	49.534100 -124.7552
Finger-Tatuk Prov. Park	157	D2	53.515600 -124.2260
Flat Lake Prov. Park	157	F4	51.499400 -121.5210
Flores Island Prov. Park	162	B3	49.291000 -126.1730
Francois Lake Prov. Park	157	D2	53.966667 -125.1666
French Beach Prov. Park	162	C4	48.383056 -123.9330
Garibaldi Prov. Park	163	D2	49.943200 -122.7510
Gibson Marine Prov. Park	162	B3	49.266667 -126.0666
Gitnadoiks River Prov. Park	156	B2	54.161700 -129.1620
Gladstone Prov. Park	164	A4	49.268900 -118.2690
God's Pocket Marine Prov. Park	162	A1	50.837200 -127.5620
Goldpan Prov. Park	163	E2	50.350000 -121.3830
Gordon Bay Prov. Park	162	C4	48.833056 -124.1997
Graham-Laurier Prov. Park	155	F4	56.594900 -123.4660
Graystokes Prov. Park	164	A3	49.986200 -118.8500
Green Inlet Marine Prov. Park	156	C3	52.918167 -128.4859
Green Lake Prov. Park	157	F4	51.400000 -121.1997
Hamber Prov. Park	164	A2	52.380300 -117.8820
Harmony Islands Marine Prov. Park	162	C2	49.862222 -124.0122
Ha'thayim Marine Prov. Park	162	C2	50.169400 -124.9550
Heather-Dina Lakes Prov. Park	157	E1	55.508300 -123.2850
Height of the Rockies Prov. Park	164	B3	50.488900 -115.2280
Herald Prov. Park	164	A3	50.788056 -119.2010
Hesquiat Lake Prov. Park	162	B3	49.500000 -126.3858
Hitchie Creek Prov. Park	162	C4	48.795556 -124.7375
Horne Lake Caves Prov. Park	162	C3	49.344167 -124.7555
Horsefly Lake Prov. Park	157	F3	52.383056 -121.3000
Inkaneep Prov. Park	163	F3	49.233056 -119.5330
Inland Lake Prov. Park	162	C2	49.953800 -124.4810
Itcha Ilgachuz Prov. Park	157	D3	52.711500 -124.9740
Jackman Flats Prov. Park	164	A1	52.950000 -119.4166
Jedediah Island Marine Prov. Park	162	C3	49.500000 -124.1997
Jewel Lake Prov. Park	164	A4	49.183056 -118.5997
Jimsmith Lake Prov. Park	164	B4	49.483056 -115.8330
Joffre Lakes Prov. Park	163	D2	50.344100 -122.4770
Johnstone Creek Prov. Park	164	A4	49.050000 -119.0497
Juan De Fuca Prov. Park	162	C4	48.489800 -124.2900
Junction Sheep Range Prov. Park	157	E4	51.801000 -122.4350
Juniper Beach Prov. Park	163	E1	50.785833 -121.0830
Kakwa Prov. Park & Protected Area	158	A3	54.057200 -120.2960
Kekuli Bay Prov. Park	164	A3	50.183056 -119.3402
Kentucky-Alleyne Prov. Park	163	F2	49.916667 -120.5666
Kianuko Prov. Park	164	B4	49.421600 -116.4560
Kikomun Creek Prov. Park	164	B4	49.233056 -115.2500
Kilby Prov. Park	163	E3	49.237500 -121.9608
Kinaskan Lake Prov. Park	155	E4	57.496100 -130.2340
Kiskatinaw Prov. Park	158	A2	55.950000 -120.5666
Kleanza Creek Prov. Park	156	C2	54.599722 -128.3997
Klewnuggit Inlet Marine Prov. Park	156	B2	53.688500 -129.6970
Kluskoil Lake Prov. Park	157	D3	53.202900 -123.8920
Kokanee Creek Prov. Park	164	B4	49.605722 -117.1330
Kokanee Glacier Prov. Park	164	B4	49.781800 -117.1360
Kootenay Lake Prov. Park	164	B3	50.085000 -116.9311

Kwadacha Wilderness Prov. Park	155	E3	57.820400 -125.058000
Lac Le Jeune Prov. Park	163	F1	50.483056 -120.483056
Lakelse Lake Prov. Park	156	C2	54.398900 -128.533000
Lawn Point Prov. Park	162	A1	50.333056 -127.966667
Lockhart Beach Prov. Park	164	B4	49.516667 -116.783056
Lockhart Creek Prov. Park	164	B4	49.497300 -116.705000
Loveland Bay Prov. Park	162	B2	50.049722 -125.450000
Lowe Inlet Marine Prov. Park	156	B2	53.555556 -129.580278
MacMillan Prov. Park	162	C3	49.283056 -124.666667
Main Lake Prov. Park	162	B2	50.210000 -125.215000
Mansons Landing Prov. Park	162	C2	50.121500 -124.928300
Maquinna Marine Prov. Park	162	B3	49.390500 -126.342000
Marble River Prov. Park	162	A1	50.544300 -127.526000
Martha Creek Prov. Park	164	A3	51.141667 -118.198122
McConnell Lake Prov. Park	163	F1	50.521944 -120.456667
McDonald Creek Prov. Park	164	A3	50.131056 -117.813667
Mehatl Creek Prov. Park	163	E2	50.036100 -122.054000
Moberly Lake Prov. Park	158	A2	55.800000 -121.700000
Momich Lakes Prov. Park	164	A2	51.327200 -119.353000
Monck Prov. Park	163	F2	50.178667 -120.533056
Moose Valley Prov. Park	157	E4	51.649800 -121.648000
Morton Lake Prov. Park	162	B2	50.116667 -125.483056
Mount Assiniboine Prov. Park	164	B3	50.937400 -115.761000
Mount Blanchet Prov. Park	157	D1	55.275500 -125.863000
Mount Fernie Prov. Park	164	C4	49.483056 -115.099722
Mount Pope Prov. Park	157	D2	54.490700 -124.331000
Mount Robson Prov. Park	164	A1	52.927000 -118.831000
Mount Seymour Prov. Park	163	D3	49.392400 -122.926000
Mount Terry Fox Prov. Park	164	A1	52.940800 -119.254000
Moyie Lake Prov. Park	164	B4	49.373333 -115.837222
Myra-Bellevue Prov. Park	164	A4	49.752100 -119.374000
Nahatlatch Prov. Park	163	E2	49.980200 -121.780000
Naikoon Prov. Park	156	A2	53.863400 -131.889000
Nairn Falls Prov. Park	163	D2	50.283056 -122.833056
Nancy Greene Prov. Park	164	A4	49.250000 -117.933056
Nickel Plate Prov. Park	163	F3	49.399722 -119.949722
Nicolum River Prov. Park	163	E3	49.366667 -121.341667
Nimpkish Lake Prov. Park	162	A2	50.337700 -127.005000
Niskonlith Lake Prov. Park	163	F1	50.795556 -119.777778
Norbury Lake Prov. Park	164	B4	49.533056 -115.483056
Nuchatlitz Prov. Park	162	A2	49.815700 -126.981000
Octopus Island Marine Prov. Park	162	B2	50.278400 -125.242100
Okanagan Lake Prov. Park	163	F2	49.683056 -119.719867
Okanagan Mtn. Prov. Park	163	F2	49.724600 -119.629000
Okeover Arm Prov. Park	162	C2	49.999722 -124.726667
One Island Lake Prov. Park	158	A2	55.300000 -120.266667
Paarens Beach Prov. Park	157	D2	54.416667 -124.399722
Paul Lake Prov. Park	163	F1	50.741667 -120.120556
Pinecone Burke Prov. Park	163	D3	49.526200 -122.721000
Porpoise Bay Prov. Park	162	C3	49.516667 -123.749722
Porteau Cove Prov. Park	163	D3	49.549722 -123.233056
Premier Lake Prov. Park	164	B4	49.900000 -115.650000
Princess Louisa Marine Prov. Park	162	C2	50.203722 -123.766667
Ptarmigan Creek Prov. Park	157	F2	53.487600 -120.880000
Puntchesakut Lake Prov. Park	157	E3	52.983056 -122.933056
Purden Lake Prov. Park	157	E2	53.928000 -121.912000
Quatsino Prov. Park	162	A1	50.491667 -127.816667
Rearguard Falls Prov. Park	157	F3	52.973333 -119.366667
Redfern-Keily Prov. Park	155	F3	57.405600 -123.878000
Roberts Creek Prov. Park	162	C3	49.433056 -123.666667
Rolley Lake Prov. Park	163	D3	49.250000 -122.400000
Rosebery Prov. Park	164	B3	50.033056 -117.400000
Rubyrock Lake Prov. Park	157	D2	54.677100 -125.348000
Ruckle Prov. Park	163	D4	48.766667 -123.383056
Rugged Point Marine Prov. Park	162	A2	49.963889 -127.238889
Saint Mary's Alpine Prov. Park	164	B4	49.877000 -116.348000
Sandy Island Marine Prov. Park	162	C3	49.616667 -124.849722
Schoen Lake Prov. Park	162	B2	50.176500 -126.245000
Schoolhouse Lake Prov. Park	157	F4	51.883600 -120.993000
Seeley Lake Prov. Park	156	C1	55.199722 -127.683056
Seven Sisters Prov. Park	156	C1	54.946900 -128.150000
Silver Beach Prov. Park	164	A2	51.240278 -118.955556
Silver Lake Prov. Park	163	E3	49.316667 -121.399722
Silver Star Prov. Park	164	A3	50.376900 -119.082000
Simson Prov. Park	162	C3	49.479700 -123.962900
Skihist Prov. Park	163	E2	50.249722 -121.500000
Skookumchuck Narrows Prov. Park	162	C2	49.744700 -123.915500
Smelt Bay Prov. Park	162	C2	50.033056 -124.983056
Sowchea Bay Prov. Park	157	D2	54.419167 -124.448333
Sproat Lake Prov. Park	162	C3	49.300000 -124.916667
Squitty Bay Prov. Park	162	C3	49.454167 -124.166667
Stagleap Prov. Park	164	B4	49.058700 -117.048000
Steelhead Prov. Park	163	E1	50.752778 -120.868056
Stemwinder Prov. Park	163	F3	49.366667 -120.133056
Stone Mtn. Prov. Park	155	E3	58.588600 -124.757000
Strathcona Prov. Park	162	B2	49.629300 -125.710000
Stuart Lake Marine Prov. Park	157	D2	54.650000 -125.000000
Sugarbowl Prov. Park	157	E2	53.801200 -121.589000
Sukunka Falls Prov. Park	157	E1	55.316667 -121.700000
Sulphur Passage Prov. Park	162	B3	49.412000 -126.094000
Summit Lake Prov. Park	164	A3	50.150000 -117.666667
Surge Narrows Prov. Park	162	B2	50.233056 -125.149722
Sutherland River Prov. Park	157	D2	54.338300 -124.818000
Sydney Inlet Prov. Park	162	B3	49.480000 -126.283000
Syringa Prov. Park	164	A4	49.378000 -117.906000
Tahsish-Kwois Prov. Park	162	A2	50.189100 -127.161000
Tatlatui Prov. Park	155	E4	56.996200 -127.386000
Tatshenshini-Alsek Prov. Park	155	D3	59.595900 -137.443000
Taylor Arm Prov. Park	162	B3	49.283056 -125.049722
Ten Mile Lake Prov. Park	157	E3	53.066667 -122.450000
Thurston Bay Marine Prov. Park	162	B2	50.383056 -125.316667
Ts'il-os Prov. Park	157	D4	51.191700 -123.971000
Tudyah Lake Prov. Park	157	E1	55.066667 -123.033056
Tunkwa Prov. Park	163	E1	50.615200 -120.887000
Tyhee Lake Prov. Park	156	C2	54.700000 -127.033056
Union Passage Marine Prov. Park	156	B3	53.410900 -129.436000
Upper Adams River Prov. Park	164	A2	51.682700 -119.228000
Valhalla Prov. Park	164	A4	49.873700 -117.567000
Vargas Island Prov. Park	162	B3	49.174000 -126.031000
Vaseux Lake Prov. Park	164	A4	49.268200 -119.474000
Walsh Cove Prov. Park	162	C2	50.268056 -124.800000
Wasa Lake Prov. Park	164	B4	49.793056 -115.738056
West Arm Prov. Park	164	B4	49.507000 -117.118000
West Lake Prov. Park	157	E2	53.733056 -122.866667
Whiskers Point Prov. Park	157	E1	54.900000 -122.933056
White Pelican Prov. Park	157	E3	52.284000 -123.031000
Whiteswan Lake Prov. Park	164	B3	50.145300 -115.487000
Woss Lake Prov. Park	162	A2	50.060400 -126.626000
Yahk Provincial Park	164	B4	49.083056 -116.083056
Yard Creek Prov. Park	164	A3	50.899722 -118.799722

MANITOBA	PAGE	GRID	LATITUDE LONGITUDE
National Park & Rec. Areas			
Lower Fort Garry N.H.S.	167	E3	50.136850 -96.940569
Riding Mtn. Natl. Park- Deep Lake Ranger Sta.	167	D3	50.860300 -100.836600
Riding Mtn. Natl. Park- Lake Audy Ranger Sta.	167	D3	50.712900 -100.230600
Riding Mtn. Natl. Park- McKinnon Creek Ranger Sta.	167	D3	50.787100 -99.579500
Riding Mtn. Natl. Park- Moon Lake Ranger Sta.	167	D3	50.995900 -100.067200
Riding Mtn. Natl. Park- South Lake Ranger Sta.	167	D3	50.655200 -100.061600
Riding Mtn. Natl. Park- Sugarloaf Ranger Sta.	167	D3	50.985300 -100.742100
Riding Mtn. Natl. Park- Whirlpool Ranger Sta.	167	D3	50.683300 -99.553500
Provincial Park & Rec. Areas			
Asessippi Prov. Park	166	C3	50.966400 -101.379700
Atikaki Prov. Wilderness Park	167	F2	51.532200 -95.547000
Bakers Narrows Prov. Park	161	D3	54.671100 -101.675000
Beaudry Prov. Park	167	E4	49.853900 -97.473300
Bell Lake Prov. Park	166	C1	52.541700 -101.241400
Birds Hill Prov. Park	167	E3	50.028800 -96.893200
Camp Morton Prov. Park	167	E3	50.710000 -96.990300
Clearwater Lake Prov. Park	161	D3	54.096200 -101.162000
Criddle–Vane Homestead Prov. Park	167	D4	49.707600 -99.596600
Duck Mtn. Prov. Park	167	D2	51.715600 -101.112000
Elk Island Prov. Park	167	E3	50.758300 -96.536500
Grand Beach Prov. Park	167	E3	50.567900 -96.554900
Grass River Prov. Park	161	D3	54.655500 -101.092000
Hecla–Grindstone Prov. Park	167	E2	51.198300 -96.660200
Hnausa Beach Prov. Park	167	E3	50.900300 -96.992200
Kettle Stones Prov. Park	167	D2	52.359200 -100.595300
Lake Saint George Prov. Park	167	E2	51.719703 -97.406772
Lundar Beach Prov. Park	167	E3	50.724000 -98.273000
Manipogo Prov. Park	167	D2	51.517000 -99.550000
Nopiming Prov. Park	167	F3	50.665200 -95.305600
North Steeprock Lake Prov. Park	166	C1	52.611800 -101.380000
Paint Lake Prov. Park	161	E2	55.492100 -98.018000
Patricia Beach Prov. Park	167	E3	50.467300 -96.575300
Pembina Valley Prov. Park	167	E4	49.038500 -98.296400
Pinawa Dam Prov. Park	167	F3	50.145200 -95.945700
Rainbow Beach Prov. Park	167	D3	51.099400 -99.718400
Saint Ambroise Beach Prov. Park	167	E3	50.275500 -98.074300
Saint Malo Prov. Park	167	E4	49.321400 -96.930490
South Atikaki Prov. Park	167	F3	51.041400 -95.417600
Spruce Woods Prov. Park	167	D4	49.703100 -99.141900
Stephenfield Prov. Park	167	E4	49.523400 -98.300500
Turtle Mtn. Prov. Park	167	D4	49.041500 -100.216000
Watchorn Prov. Park	167	E2	51.293100 -98.598500
Whitefish Lake Prov. Park	166	C2	52.333900 -101.587100
Whiteshell Prov. Park	167	F3	50.140900 -95.584400
William Lake Prov. Park	167	D4	49.055000 -100.038800
Winnipeg Beach Prov. Park	167	E3	50.512300 -96.967000

NEW BRUNSWICK	PAGE	GRID	LATITUDE LONGITUDE
National Park & Rec. Areas			
Beaubears Island N.H.S.	179	D3	46.972778 -65.569444
Fort Beauséjour N.H.S.	180	C1	45.865278 -64.290278
Fort Gaspareaux N.H.S.	180	C1	46.040833 -64.072778
Fundy Natl. Park-Vis. Ctr.	180	C1	45.659500 -65.132600
Kouchibouguac Natl. Park-Vis. Ctr.	179	D3	46.773200 -65.004900
Monument Lefebvre N.H.S.	180	C1	45.979167 -64.567222
Roosevelt Campobello International Park	180	A2	44.849722 -66.949722
Saint Andrews Blockhouse N.H.S.	180	A2	45.076389 -67.063889
Saint Croix Island International Hist. Site	180	A2	45.127778 -67.133333
Provincial Park & Rec. Areas			
De la République Prov. Park	178	B3	47.442778 -68.395556
Herring Cove Prov. Park	180	A2	44.866667 -66.933056
Mactaquac Prov. Park	180	A1	45.959025 -66.892556
Mount Carleton Prov. Park	178	C3	47.392300 -66.835500
Murray Beach Prov. Park	180	C1	46.016667 -63.983056
New River Beach Prov. Park	180	A2	45.133056 -66.533056
Parlee Beach Prov. Park	180	C1	46.233056 -64.499722
Sugarloaf Prov. Park	178	C2	47.974000 -66.671900
The Anchorage Prov. Park	180	A3	44.649722 -66.800000

NEWFOUNDLAND & LABRADOR	PAGE	GRID	LATITUDE LONGITUDE
National Park & Rec. Areas			
Castle Hill N.H.S.	183	E4	47.251389 -53.971111
Gros Morne Natl. Park-Vis. Ctr.	182	C2	49.571500 -57.877900
Hawthorne Cottage N.H.S.	183	E4	47.543333 -53.210833
L'Anse aux Meadows N.H.S.	183	F1	51.595000 -55.532778
Port au Choix N.H.S.	182	C1	50.712222 -57.375278
Red Bay N.H.S.	183	F1	51.733056 -56.415556
Ryan Premises N.H.S.	183	E3	48.648056 -53.112500
Terra Nova Natl. Park-Information Center	183	E3	48.394900 -54.204000
Terra Nova Natl. Park-Saltons Vis. Ctr.	183	E3	48.580600 -53.958900
Provincial Park & Rec. Areas			
Barachois Pond Prov. Park	182	C3	48.477100 -58.256600
Blow Me Down Prov. Park	182	C2	49.090833 -58.364444
Butter Pot Prov. Park	183	F4	47.390900 -53.071300
Chance Cove Prov. Park	183	F4	46.776900 -53.045400
Codroy Valley Prov. Park	182	C4	47.833333 -59.337778
Deadman's Bay Prov. Park	183	E2	49.331389 -53.692500
Dildo Run Prov. Park	183	E2	49.535556 -54.721667
Dungeon Prov. Park	183	E3	48.666667 -53.083611
Frenchman's Cove Prov. Park	183	D4	47.209444 -55.401667
Gooseberry Cove Prov. Park	183	E4	47.068056 -54.087778
J.T. Cheeseman Prov. Park	182	C4	47.631111 -59.249444
La Manche Prov. Park	183	F4	47.175200 -52.901200
Lockston Path Prov. Park	183	E3	48.437778 -53.379722
Notre Dame Prov. Park	183	E2	49.115833 -55.086389
Pinware River Prov. Park	183	F1	51.631667 -56.704167
Sandbanks Prov. Park	182	C4	47.607222 -57.646944
Sir Richard Squires Mem. Prov. Park	183	D2	49.354000 -57.213400
The Arches Prov. Park	182	C2	50.113333 -57.663056

NORTHWEST TERRITORIES	PAGE	GRID	LATITUDE LONGITUDE
National Park & Rec. Areas			
Nahanni Natl. Park Res.	155	E2	61.083333 -123.600000
Tuktut Nogait Natl. Park	155	E1	69.283333 -123.016667

NOVA SCOTIA	PAGE	GRID	LATITUDE LONGITUDE
National Park & Rec. Areas			
Alexander Graham Bell N.H.S.	181	F1	46.102778 -60.745556
Cape Breton Highlands Natl. Park-East Ent.	182	B4	46.642800 -60.404200
Cape Breton Highlands Natl. Park-West Ent.	182	B4	46.647300 -60.950200
Fort Anne N.H.S.	180	B3	44.741667 -65.519167
Fort Edward N.H.S.	180	C2	44.995556 -64.135278
Fortress of Louisbourg N.H.S.	181	F1	45.900300 -59.995100
Grand-Pré N.H.S.	180	C2	45.108889 -64.311944
Grassy Island N.H.S.	181	F2	45.336667 -60.973611
Kejimkujik Natl. Park (Seaside Adjunct)	180	C4	43.865800 -64.836900
Kejimkujik Natl. Park and N.H.S.	180	B3	44.336700 -65.268200
Marconi N.H.S.	181	F4	46.211111 -59.952778
Port-Royal N.H.S.	180	B3	44.712500 -65.610556
Saint Peters Canal N.H.S.	181	F1	45.655556 -60.870556
York Redoubt N.H.S.	181	D3	44.596583 -63.552439
Provincial Park & Rec. Areas			
Amherst Shore Prov. Park	180	C1	45.961181 -63.879025
Battery Prov. Park	181	F1	45.657022 -60.866764
Beaver Mtn. Prov. Park	181	E2	45.567556 -62.153583
Blomidon Prov. Park	180	C2	45.255869 -64.352056
Boylston Prov. Park	181	E2	45.426839 -61.510603
Cape Chignecto Prov. Park	180	C2	45.375800 -64.891300
Caribou–Munroes Island Prov. Park	181	D1	45.721800 -62.656914
Clam Harbour Beach Prov. Park	181	D3	44.731390 -62.891110
Ellenwood Lake Prov. Park	180	B4	43.929481 -66.005700
Five Islands Prov. Park	180	C2	45.407781 -64.021500
Graves Island Prov. Park	180	C3	44.565550 -64.218642
Laurie Prov. Park	181	D2	44.878175 -63.602194
Martinique Beach Prov. Park	181	D3	44.689911 -63.147567
Mira River Prov. Park	181	F1	46.026006 -60.037433
Porters Prov. Park	181	D3	44.691106 -63.308892
Rissers Beach Prov. Park	180	C3	44.232397 -64.423919
Salsman Prov. Park	181	E2	45.236856 -61.767150
Salt Springs Prov. Park	181	D2	45.545280 -62.878890
Shubenacadie Prov. Wildlife Park	181	D2	45.087222 -63.387500
Smileys Prov. Park	180	C2	45.013925 -63.961247
The Islands Prov. Park	180	B4	43.765503 -65.340347
Thomas Raddall Prov. Park	180	C4	43.844783 -64.919694
Valleyview Prov. Park	180	B2	44.875200 -65.316064
Wentworth Prov. Park	181	D2	45.627222 -63.567222
Whycocomagh Prov. Park	181	F1	45.968094 -61.109908

Parks Index with GPS Coordinates

Ontario–Yukon

ONTARIO	PAGE	GRID	LATITUDE LONGITUDE
National Park & Rec. Areas			
Battle of the Windmill N.H.S.	174	B4	44.722778 -75.486944
Bell Homestead N.H.P.	172	C3	43.107946 -80.273060
Bellevue House N.H.S.	173	F1	44.220556 -76.506667
Bruce Peninsula Natl. Park	170	C4	45.189100 -81.485500
Fathom Five Natl. Marine Park	170	C4	45.304800 -81.727600
Fort George N.H.S.	173	D3	43.252778 -79.051111
Fort Henry N.H.S.	173	F1	44.230833 -76.459444
Fort Malden N.H.S.	172	A4	42.108056 -83.113889
Fort Mississauga N.H.S.	173	D3	43.260833 -79.076667
Fort Saint Joseph N.H.S.	170	B3	46.063889 -83.944167
Fort Wellington N.H.S.	174	B4	44.713889 -75.510833
Georgian Bay Islands Natl. Park-Welcome Center	171	D4	44.803900 -79.720400
Glengarry Cairn N.H.S.	174	C3	45.121667 -74.490278
Merrickville Blockhouse N.H.S.	174	B4	44.916667 -75.837500
Peterborough Lift Lock N.H.S.	173	E1	44.308056 -78.300556
Point Clark Lighthouse N.H.S.	172	B2	44.073056 -81.756667
Point Pelee Natl. Park-Park Ent. Kiosk	172	A4	41.987700 -82.549900
Point Pelee Natl. Park-Vis. Ctr.	172	A4	41.931700 -82.513500
Pukaskwa Natl. Park-Information Center	170	A2	48.700400 -86.197200
Queenston Heights N.H.S.	173	D3	43.158056 -79.052778
Sault Ste. Marie Canal N.H.S.	170	B3	46.511667 -84.355556
Sir John Johnson House N.H.S.	174	C4	45.144444 -74.580000
Southwold Earthworks N.H.S.	172	B3	42.677778 -81.351389
Thousand Islands Natl. Park-Vis. Ctr.	174	A4	44.452300 -75.860300
Trent-Severn Waterway N.H.S.	173	E1	44.137500 -77.590100
Woodside N.H.S.	172	C2	43.466667 -80.499722
Provincial Park & Rec. Areas			
Abitibi-De-Troyes Prov. Park	171	D1	48.786500 -80.066300
Albany River Prov. Park	169	E1	51.358200 -88.134000
Algonquin Prov. Park	171	E4	45.605300 -78.323900
Arrowhead Prov. Park	171	D4	45.391700 -79.197200
Awenda Prov. Park	172	C1	44.854400 -79.989800
Balsam Lake Prov. Park	173	D1	44.642000 -78.864000
Bass Lake Prov. Park	173	D1	44.602000 -79.475000
Batchawana Prov. Park	170	B3	46.941900 -84.587010
Blue Lake Prov. Park	168	B3	49.904200 -93.525600
Bon Echo Prov. Park	171	E4	44.905600 -77.246600
Bonnechere Prov. Park	171	E4	45.658400 -77.570800
Bonnechere River Prov. Park	171	E4	45.674400 -77.661500
Brightsand River Prov. Park	169	D3	49.936700 -90.265400
Bronte Creek Prov. Park	173	D2	43.410490 -79.767830
Caliper Lake Prov. Park	168	B3	49.061670 -93.912780
Carson Lake Prov. Park	171	E4	45.502780 -77.746390
Chapleau-Nemegosenda River Prov. Park	170	B2	48.262300 -83.035300
Charleston Lake Prov. Park	174	A4	44.515400 -76.013600
Chutes Prov. Park	170	C3	46.219510 -82.071480
Craigleith Prov. Park	172	C1	44.535000 -80.367000
Darlington Prov. Park	173	D2	43.875480 -78.778300
Devil's Glen Prov. Park	172	C1	44.361000 -80.207800
Driftwood Prov. Park	171	E3	46.179000 -77.843000
Earl Rowe Prov. Park	172	C1	44.150000 -79.898000
Emily Prov. Park	173	D1	44.340530 -78.532860
Esker Lakes Prov. Park	171	D2	48.290100 -79.906100
Fairbank Prov. Park	170	C3	46.468070 -81.440410
Ferris Prov. Park	173	E1	44.293000 -77.788000
Finlayson Point Prov. Park	171	D3	47.055000 -79.797000
Fitzroy Prov. Park	174	A3	45.482680 -76.209400
French River Prov. Park	171	D3	46.008600 -80.620900
Frontenac Prov. Park	174	A4	44.540500 -76.512700
Fushimi Lake Prov. Park	169	F3	49.824800 -83.913800
Greenwater Prov. Park	170	C1	49.215900 -81.291000
Grundy Lake Prov. Park	171	D4	45.939800 -80.530400
Halfway Lake Prov. Park	170	C3	46.905700 -81.650500
Inverhuron Prov. Park	172	B1	44.298000 -81.580000
Ivanhoe Lake Prov. Park	170	C2	47.957600 -82.742600
John E. Pearce Prov. Park	172	B4	42.617000 -81.444000
Kakabeka Falls Prov. Park	169	D4	48.403290 -89.624130
Kap-Kig-Iwan Prov. Park	171	D2	47.789960 -79.884990
Kettle Lakes Prov. Park	170	C1	48.569400 -80.865400
Killarney Prov. Park	170	C3	46.099400 -81.386900
Killbear Prov. Park	171	D4	45.346200 -80.191200
Kopka River Prov. Park	169	D2	50.006300 -89.493000
Lady Evelyn-Smoothwater Prov. Park	171	D2	47.368500 -80.489300
Lake of the Woods Prov. Park	168	B3	49.221200 -94.606000
Lake on the Mtn. Prov. Park	173	F1	44.039940 -77.056080
Lake Saint Peter Prov. Park	171	E4	45.322000 -78.024000
Lake Superior Prov. Park	170	A2	47.595200 -84.756500
Larder River Prov. Park	171	D2	47.936300 -79.642800
La Verendrye Prov. Park	169	D4	48.138300 -90.431300
Little Abitibi Prov. Park	170	C1	49.637900 -80.922900
Little Current River Prov. Park	169	E2	50.724100 -86.211000
Long Point Prov. Park	172	C4	42.565000 -80.306000
Lower Madawaska River Prov. Park	171	E4	45.236200 -77.289300
MacGregor Point Prov. Park	172	B1	44.403700 -81.465600
Macleod Prov. Park	169	E3	49.676190 -86.931000
Makobe-Grays River Prov. Park	171	D2	47.617200 -80.376300
Mara Prov. Park	173	D1	44.589000 -79.349000
Mark S. Burnham Prov. Park	173	E1	44.299900 -78.257000
Marten River Prov. Park	171	D3	46.729000 -79.807000
Mattawa River Prov. Park	171	D3	46.315000 -79.108400
McRae Point Prov. Park	173	D1	44.569000 -79.320000
Mikisew Prov. Park	171	D4	45.820000 -79.512000
Missinaibi River Prov. Park	170	B1	49.101400 -83.234700
Mississagi Prov. Park	170	C3	46.596500 -82.682500
Mississagi River Prov. Park	170	C3	47.012600 -82.632700
Murphys Point Prov. Park	174	A4	44.774300 -76.240700
Nagagamisis Prov. Park	169	F3	49.475700 -84.771000
Neys Prov. Park	169	E4	48.750500 -86.591900
North Beach Prov. Park	173	E2	43.951050 -77.522660
Oastler Lake Prov. Park	171	D4	45.309000 -79.964800
Obabika River Prov. Park	171	D3	47.221200 -80.262600
Obatanga Prov. Park	170	A2	48.323000 -85.093700
Ojibway Prov. Park	168	C3	49.990900 -92.144400
Opeongo River Prov. Park	171	E4	45.576256 -77.887363
Otoskwin-Attawapiskat River Prov. Park	169	D1	52.235700 -87.491300
Ottawa River Prov. Park	174	A3	45.741700 -76.779800
Ouimet Canyon Prov. Park	169	D4	48.773350 -88.667400
Oxtongue River-Ragged Falls Prov. Park	171	D4	45.366900 -78.914100
Pakwash Prov. Park	168	B2	50.749800 -93.551400
Pancake Bay Prov. Park	170	B3	46.967200 -84.661100
Petroglyphs Prov. Park	173	E1	44.618300 -78.041700
Pigeon River Prov. Park	169	D4	48.025041 -89.572294
Pinery Prov. Park	172	B3	43.257200 -81.834000
Pipestone River Prov. Park	169	D1	52.244300 -90.313500
Point Farms Prov. Park	172	B2	43.804000 -81.700000
Port Bruce Prov. Park	172	B3	42.664000 -81.027000
Port Burwell Prov. Park	172	C3	42.646000 -80.816000
Potholes Prov. Park	170	B2	47.958700 -84.294020
Presqu'Ile Prov. Park	173	E2	44.007000 -77.735000
Quetico Prov. Park	168	C4	48.404500 -91.498700
Rainbow Falls Prov. Park	169	E4	48.830090 -87.389580
Renè Brunelle Prov. Park	170	C1	49.453700 -82.147900
Restoule Prov. Park	171	D3	46.080400 -79.839800
Rideau River Prov. Park	174	B4	45.060000 -75.672000
Rock Point Prov. Park	173	D3	42.854000 -79.552000
Rondeau Prov. Park	172	B4	42.278200 -81.865100
Rushing River Prov. Park	168	B3	49.681850 -94.234890
Samuel de Champlain Prov. Park	171	D3	46.301900 -78.864100
Sandbanks Prov. Park	173	F2	43.910200 -77.267200
Sandbar Lake Prov. Park	168	C3	49.491000 -91.555700
Sauble Falls Prov. Park	172	B1	44.673170 -81.257350
Selkirk Prov. Park	172	C3	42.824000 -79.961000
Sharbot Lake Prov. Park	174	A4	44.775500 -76.724600
Sibbald Point Prov. Park	173	D1	44.322160 -79.325570
Silent Lake Prov. Park	171	E4	44.907500 -78.047200
Silver Lake Prov. Park	174	A4	44.829770 -76.574680
Sioux Narrows Prov. Park	168	B3	49.429570 -94.037260
Six Mile Lake Prov. Park	171	D4	44.819500 -79.733500
Sleeping Giant Prov. Park	169	D4	48.419300 -88.795500
Solace Prov. Park	170	C3	47.189200 -80.683500
Springwater Prov. Park	173	D1	44.443500 -79.748500
Steel River Prov. Park	169	E3	49.161900 -86.812600
Sturgeon Bay Prov. Park	171	D4	45.623400 -80.414100
Sturgeon River Prov. Park	170	C3	46.949800 -80.523900
The Massasauga Prov. Park	171	D4	45.203400 -80.044300
The Shoals Prov. Park	170	B2	47.884800 -83.808000
Turkey Point Prov. Park	172	C3	42.694000 -80.333150
Turtle River-White Otter Lake Prov. Park	168	C3	49.129700 -92.042300
Upper Madawaska River Prov. Park	171	E4	45.513700 -78.078700
Wabakimi Prov. Park	169	D2	50.719100 -89.448500
Wakami Lake Prov. Park	170	C2	47.489700 -82.842000
Wasaga Beach Prov. Park	172	C1	44.494000 -80.027100
Wheatley Prov. Park	172	A4	42.098000 -82.448800
White Lake Prov. Park	170	A1	48.603500 -85.880900
Windy Lake Prov. Park	170	C3	46.619820 -81.455980
Woodland Caribou Prov. Park	168	B2	51.096900 -94.744900

PRINCE EDWARD ISLAND	PAGE	GRID	LATITUDE LONGITUDE
National Park & Rec. Areas			
Port-la-Joye–Fort Amherst N.H.S.	179	E4	46.195278 -63.133611
Prince Edward Island Natl. Park-Brackley Vis. Ctr.	179	E4	46.406200 -63.196600
Prince Edward Island Natl. Park-Cavendish Vis. Ctr.	179	E4	46.492300 -63.379700
Provincial Park & Rec. Areas			
Brudenell River Prov. Park	179	F4	46.209583 -62.588556
Buffaloland Prov. Park	179	F4	46.092500 -62.617778
Cabot Beach Prov. Park	179	E4	46.557250 -63.704250
Cedar Dunes Prov. Park	177	E4	46.622222 -64.381944
Chelton Beach Prov. Park	179	E4	46.303944 -63.747167
Green Park Prov. Park	177	F4	46.590972 -63.890333
Jacques Cartier Prov. Park	177	F4	46.851222 -64.013000
Kings Castle Prov. Park	179	F4	46.019167 -62.567389
Linkletter Prov. Park	179	E4	46.402694 -63.850361
Lord Selkirk Prov. Park	179	F4	46.091889 -62.906000
Mill River Prov. Park	177	F4	46.749722 -64.166667
Northumberland Prov. Park	179	F4	45.966667 -62.716667
Panmure Island Prov. Park	179	F4	46.133056 -62.466667
Red Point Prov. Park	179	F4	46.366667 -62.133056
Wood Islands Prov. Park	181	D1	45.949722 -62.749722

QUÉBEC	PAGE	GRID	LATITUDE LONGITUDE
National Park & Rec. Areas			
Lieu Historique Natl. du Fort-Lennox	175	D4	45.120556 -73.268056
Lieu Historique Natl. du Fort-Témiscamingue	171	D2	47.295000 -79.456667
Parc Natl. de Forillon-North Ent.	179	D1	48.960100 -64.339000
Parc Natl. de Forillon-South Ent.	179	D1	48.854300 -64.396300
Parc Natl. de la Mauricie-East Ent.	175	D1	46.752600 -72.792600
Parc Natl. de la Mauricie-South Ent.	175	D1	46.650000 -72.969200
Réserve de Parc Natl. de l'Archipel-de-Mingan	177	F1	50.237100 -63.606900
Provincial Park & Rec. Areas			
Parc d'Aiguebelle	171	D1	48.510300 -78.745800
Parc d'Anticosti	182	A2	49.463200 -62.819000
Parc de Frontenac	175	E3	45.848600 -71.184600
Parc de la Gaspésie	178	C1	48.941500 -66.214400
Parc de la Gatineau	174	A3	45.566667 -75.949722
Parc de la Jacques-Cartier	175	E1	47.317300 -71.347000
Parc de la Pointe-Taillon	176	C3	48.717300 -71.993600
Parc de la Yamaska	175	D3	45.429400 -72.601800
Parc de l'Île-Bonaventure-et-du-Rocher-Percé	179	E1	48.496389 -64.161944
Parc de Miguasha	178	C2	48.110556 -66.369444
Parc de Plaisance	174	B3	45.597900 -75.123600
Parc de Récréation du Mont-Orford	175	D3	45.344700 -72.212900
Parc des Grands-Jardins	176	C4	47.681300 -70.836900
Parc des Hautes-Gorges-de-la-Rivière-Malbaie	176	C3	47.918700 -70.498700
Parc des Monts-Valin	176	C3	48.598600 -70.825300
Parc du Bic	178	A1	48.355300 -68.797600
Parc du Mont-Mégantic	175	E3	45.450700 -71.167300
Parc du Mont-Saint-Bruno	175	D3	45.555278 -73.309722
Parc du Mont-Tremblant	174	C2	46.443000 -74.344600
Parc du Saguenay	176	C3	48.289900 -70.243400
Parc Marin du Saguenay-Saint-Laurent	178	A2	48.133056 -69.733056
Parc Régional du Massif du Sud	175	F2	46.581389 -70.467778

SASKATCHEWAN	PAGE	GRID	LATITUDE LONGITUDE
National Park & Rec. Areas			
Batoche N.H.S.	165	F1	52.752800 -106.116700
Battle of Fish Creek N.H.S.	165	F1	52.550000 -106.180300
Fort Battleford N.H.S.	165	E1	52.713800 -108.259600
Fort Espèrance N.H.S.	166	C3	50.451400 -101.712800
Fort Livingstone N.H.S.	166	C2	51.903880 -101.960620
Fort Pelly N.H.S.	166	C2	51.795900 -101.951800
Fort Walsh N.H.S.	165	E4	49.559100 -109.901700
Grasslands Natl. Park-East Block Vis. Ctr.	166	A4	49.370800 -106.384800
Grasslands Natl. Park-West Block Vis. Reception Ctr.	166	A4	49.203800 -107.732700
Prince Albert Natl. Park-Waskesiu Vis. Ctr.	160	B3	53.922500 -106.081800
Provincial Park & Rec. Areas			
Blackstrap Prov. Park	166	A2	51.755600 -106.458300
Buffalo Pound Prov. Park	166	B3	50.576200 -105.361000
Candle Lake Prov. Park	160	B4	53.845000 -105.252000
Cannington Manor Prov. Hist. Park	166	C4	49.712900 -102.027300
Clearwater River Prov. Park	159	E1	56.929300 -109.043000
Crooked Lake Prov. Park	166	C3	50.592200 -102.741400
Cumberland House Prov. Hist. Park	160	C4	53.948000 -102.421400
Cypress Hills Interprovincial Park	165	E4	49.632400 -109.809000
Danielson Prov. Park	166	A2	51.252200 -106.866000
Douglas Prov. Park	166	A3	51.025300 -106.480000
Echo Valley Prov. Park	166	B3	50.808500 -103.891900
Fort Carlton Prov. Park	166	A1	52.867100 -106.542700
Fort Pitt Prov. Park	165	E1	53.577000 -109.806300
Good Spirit Lake Prov. Park	166	C2	51.543500 -102.707000
Greenwater Lake Prov. Park	166	C1	52.532000 -103.448000
Katepwa Point Prov. Park	166	B3	50.693165 -103.626025
Lac La Ronge Prov. Park	160	C3	55.249200 -104.769000
Last Mtn. House Prov. Park	166	B3	50.722800 -104.823300
Makwa Lake Prov. Park	159	E3	54.016800 -109.234000
Meadow Lake Prov. Park	159	E3	54.501400 -109.076000
Moose Mtn. Prov. Park	166	C4	49.821300 -102.424000
Narrow Hills Prov. Park	160	C3	54.091300 -104.643000
Pike Lake Prov. Park	166	A2	51.893200 -106.819000
Rowan's Ravine Prov. Park	166	B3	50.995600 -105.179700
Saint Victor Prov. Park	166	A4	49.395300 -105.873200
Saskatchewan Landing Prov. Park	165	F3	50.664600 -107.997000
Steele Narrows Prov. Park	159	E3	54.025900 -109.318400
The Battlefords Prov. Park	165	E1	53.132500 -108.381300
Touchwood Hills Prov. Park	166	B2	51.306400 -104.014100
Wildcat Hill Prov. Park	166	C1	53.273946 -102.492828
Wood Mtn. Post Prov. Hist. Park	166	A4	49.320833 -106.379167

YUKON	PAGE	GRID	LATITUDE LONGITUDE
National Park & Rec. Areas			
Dawson Hist. Complex N.H.S.	155	D2	64.050000 -139.433330
Ivvavik Natl. Park	155	D1	69.519722 -139.525000
Kluane Natl. Park and Res.-North Vis. Ctr.	155	D3	60.991800 -138.520800
Kluane Natl. Park and Res.-South Vis. Ctr.	155	D3	60.752900 -137.510100
Vuntut Natl. Park	155	D1	68.306944 -140.047500
Provincial Park & Rec. Areas			
Herschel Island-Qikiqtaruk Territorial Park	155	D1	69.592100 -139.092400

DISCOVERING USA EAST NATIONAL PARKS

Everglades National Park, Florida

Continued from page 11.

 ## ARKANSAS
Hot Springs National Park★★

58mi southwest of Little Rock (take I-30 South to US-270 West to Rte. 7/Central Ave.). Visitor center located in the Fordyce Bathhouse on Central Ave. in Hot Springs, AR. ⚠ ⚙ *P*501-620-6701. www. nps.gov/hosp.

Hot Springs' therapeutic waters have been attracting visitors for hundreds—perhaps thousands—of years, beginning with the early Indians who bathed here. Extraordinarily pure water from the springs is heated thousands of feet below the earth's surface and bubbles up through faults in the underlying sandstone at a constant 143°F. The warm water flows from 47 springs at the average total rate of 850,000 gallons per day.

Begin your tour at the visitor center on magnolia-lined Central Avenue, also known as **Bathhouse Row★**. The 1915 **Fordyce★** is the grandest of the eight remaining early-20C bathhouse structures, most of which went out of business when public bathing declined in the 1970s. It has been completely restored and offers visitors a vivid look at what "taking the waters" once meant.

Today visitors can still enjoy a traditional bathing experience at two of the original bathhouses currently open to the public. Most of the springs have been capped, but the spring at the corner of Central Avenue and Fountain Street is easily accessible. It tumbles down the hillside like most of the springs originally did.

A short drive from town, the 216ft **Hot Springs Mountain Tower** (take Central Ave. to Fountain St. to Hot Springs Mountain Dr.; *P*501-623-6035; www. hotsprings.org) offers fine **views★** of the town and surrounding countryside.

FLORIDA
Everglades National Park★★★

40001 State Rd. 9336, 11mi southwest of Homestead, FL. *P*305-242-7700. www.nps.gov/ever.

Renowned throughout the world, the vast "river of grass" known as the Everglades covers the southern end of the Florida peninsula. Everglades National Park is one of only a few American parks that enjoy status as a UNESCO World Heritage Site and as an International Biosphere Reserve. This immense subtropical wetland nurtures such diverse ecosystems as hardwood hammocks and mangrove swamps that harbor mammals, reptiles and many bird species. The Everglades is actually a slow-moving river—formed during the last Ice Age—which starts at Lake Okeechobee in south-central Florida and slopes south, where it drains into the Gulf of Mexico.

The Southern Everglades includes the **Pahayokee Overlook★★**, an elevated platform that provides a sweeping view of a seemingly endless prairie of sawgrass, the Everglades' most dominant flora. The Northern Everglades encompasses the **Big Cypress National Preserve** (52mi west of Miami; accessible from US-41 & I-75), habitat of the endangered Florida panther, and **Fakahatchee Strand State Preserve★** (north of Everglades City; accessible from US-41 and Rte. 29).

KENTUCKY
Mammoth Cave National Park★★★

8mi west of Cave City via Rte. 70 (or 9mi northwest of I-65 from Exit 48 at Park City). *P*301-722-1257. ⚠✕♿🅿 Park information; *P*270-758-2180. www.nps. gov/maca.

The world's longest cave (more than 350mi of the five-level labyrinth have been mapped), Mammoth underlies three Kentucky counties. Known to Woodland Indians over 4,000 years ago and rediscovered by frontiersmen in the late 18C, Mammoth Cave was established as a national park in 1941.

A variety of guided tours are offered into Mammoth's depths, taking visitors as far as 360ft below ground. Among the sights are the ruins of a c.1810 saltpeter mining operation; a decorative stone formation called **Frozen Niagara;** and the underground **River Styx,** home of eyeless fish. Designated a UNESCO World Heritage Site and an International Biosphere Reserve, the cave is home to the world's most diverse cave ecosystem, including some life forms that cannot survive outside its walls. (🚶Tours last 1-6 hours, with varying degrees of difficulty. Reservations recommended. Cave temperatures average 54°F year-round; bring a sweater or light jacket. Wear sturdy, comfortable shoes and be prepared to climb.)

MAINE
Acadia National Park★★★

170mi north of Portland via US-1 North & Rte. 3 South. ⚠✕ *P*207-288-3338. www.nps.gov/acad.

Located primarily on **Mount Desert Island★★★**, with smaller sections on **Isle au Haut** (off Deer Isle; access by boat from Stonington) and **Schoodic Peninsula** (across Frenchman Bay; access via US-1 North to Rte. 186 South), Acadia National Park welcomes some 4 million visitors each year. More than one-third of the park's 40,000 acres (33,000 of which fall on Mount Desert Island) were donated by John D. Rockefeller, Jr., who created the 45-mi of carriage paths that web the eastern side of the island. Bordering the temperate and subarctic climate zones, Acadia harbors 1,100 plant species and almost 300 types of birds.

The park's main attraction, **Loop Road★★★** (20mi) parallels a spectacular section of open coast with myriad scenic overlooks affording vistas from sweeping seascapes of island-studded waters. Many observation areas have benches from which to enjoy the breathtaking views of the Atlantic.

DISCOVERING USA EAST NATIONAL PARKS

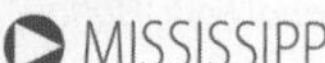

▶ MISSISSIPPI

Melrose Plantation/Natchez National Historical Park★★★

1 Melrose-Montebello Pkwy. ☎601-446-5790. www.nps.gov/natc.

Now owned by the National Park Service, Melrose is an authentic antebellum town estate (c.1845) complete with slave quarters and other "dependencies," including a kitchen, stables and privies.

A guided tour of the house and grounds informs visitors about the lives of slave owners and the enslaved alike, including the slaves' individualized bell-summoning system and the tragedies linked to a then-innovative lead-lined cistern system.

In 1910 an heir of the former owners moved to Melrose with his bride, who restored the house and opened it for the first pilgrimage tour in 1932. Original furnishings include a set of carved Rococo Revival chairs in the drawing room, from whose rose pattern the Gorham sterling silver flatware pattern "Melrose" was derived.

▶ NORTH CAROLINA–TENNESSEE

Great Smoky Mountains National Park★★★

107 Park Headquarters Rd., Gatlinburg, TN. ⚠️&🅿️ ☎865-436-1200. www.nps.gov/grsm.

Straddling the North Carolina–Tennessee border, the lofty mountains that form the nation's most visited park are named for the ever-present shroud of blue-gray mist that inspired Cherokee Indians to call them Shaconage, or "place of blue smoke." Today, Great Smoky is a UNESCO World Heritage Site and an International Biosphere Reserve; it preserves the best examples of eastern deciduous forest and is the habitat for more than 60 mammals, including black bears (more than 1,500 live in the park), white-tailed deer, elk and more than 200 species of birds. Near the park's northern entrance lie the regional commercial centers of **Gatlinburg** and **Pigeon Forge,** Tennessee. From Newfound Gap, pick up the winding 7mi spur to **Clingmans Dome,** the park's tallest mountain (6,643ft). Take the steep, paved .5mi trail from the parking lot to the **observation tower** for a dizzying panorama that extends across the Carolinas, Georgia and Tennessee. This lookout is also the perfect place to watch the sunset on a clear evening.

Nestled in a stunning secluded valley surrounded by the forested peaks of the Great Smoky Mountains, **Cades Cove** was settled in the 19C by pioneers from Virginia, North Carolina and east Tennessee who came in search of farmland.

▶ PENNSYLVANIA

Valley Forge National Historical Park★★

20mi northwest of Center City via I-76 West. Take Exit 26B and continue 1.5mi in King of Prussia, PA. &🅿️ ☎610-783-1000. www.nps.gov/vafo.

Initiated into the national park system for the 1976 US Bicentennial, the 3,500-acre park preserves the fields and ridges where George Washington's exhausted and poorly provisioned 12,000-man Continental Army camped from December 19, 1777 to June 19, 1778. Begin at the visitor center to view the 18min film dramatizing the travails of Washington's men, and to see artifacts used by the encamped army. Take a 10mi self-guided **driving tour★** past earthworks and historic stone buildings, including Washington's Headquarters, where George and his wife, Martha, spent that stark winter; a free cell phone tour (☎484-396-1018); or a self-guided tour on the park's 18mi of trails.

▶ VIRGINIA

Colonial National Historic Park at Jamestown★★

West end of Colonial Pkwy. &🅿️ ☎757-898-2410. www.nps.gov/colo.

In 1607 this 1,500-acre James River Island became the site of the first permanent English-speaking colony in America. Now administered by the National Park Service, most of the island has been returned to its natural state and 3- and 5mi loop drives weave across its bogs and woodlands.

On the northwest corner of the island, the Jamestown Visitor Center (🅿️ ☎757-856-1250) exhibits recovered artifacts. Behind the visitor center an excavated street grid outlines the foundations of the buildings from the former colonial capital. The brick tower from a church begun in 1639 is the only early structure remaining. East of the tower, the brick replica Memorial Church was built in 1907 on the cobblestone foundations of the 1617 church.

A 10min walk from the visitor center, the **Jamestown Archaerium** tells the story of the early English settlers through some 2,000 objects unearthed at the Jamestown Fort site. A causeway connects the island to the mainland, where the park maintains its popular **Glasshouse★** (take the first right after park entrance), site of the ruins of the original 1608 glass house and the replica where costumed artisans demonstrate colonial glass-making.

▶ WISCONSIN

Apostle Islands National Lakeshore★★

Visitor center is located in the 19C Bayfield County Courthouse, Washington Ave. between 4th & 5th Sts. in Bayfield, WI. ⚠️🅿️ ☎715-779-3397. www.nps.gov/apis.

Though trapped, hunted, logged, fished, farmed, quarried and visited for 400 years, this cluster of islands off Wisconsin's Bayfield Peninsula remains unspoiled. Today accessible by private boat and a regular schedule of cruises run by the **Apostle Islands Cruise Service** (☎715-779-3925, www.apostleisland.com) out of Bayfield, these 21 islands were exposed by retreating glaciers during the last Ice Age.

Characterized by pink-sand beaches, dense forests, sandstone cliffs and sea caves, the Apostles offer sailing, hiking and kayaking in summer and a variety of winter pastimes for those adventurous enough to cross the ice. Six historic light stations built between 1857 and 1891 still mark the treacherous outer islands, and park staff conduct interpretive programs at several of them. The park also includes 12 mainland miles along the northwest coast of the peninsula at **Little Sand Bay** (off Rte. 13 between Meyers Rd. and Little Sand Bay Rd.).

Reenacting history, Valley Forge National Historical Park, Pennsylvania

© NPS Photo

Notes

MICHELIN NORTH AMERICA, INC.

Michelin Travel & Lifestyle North America
One Parkway South
Greenville, SC 29615 U.S.A.

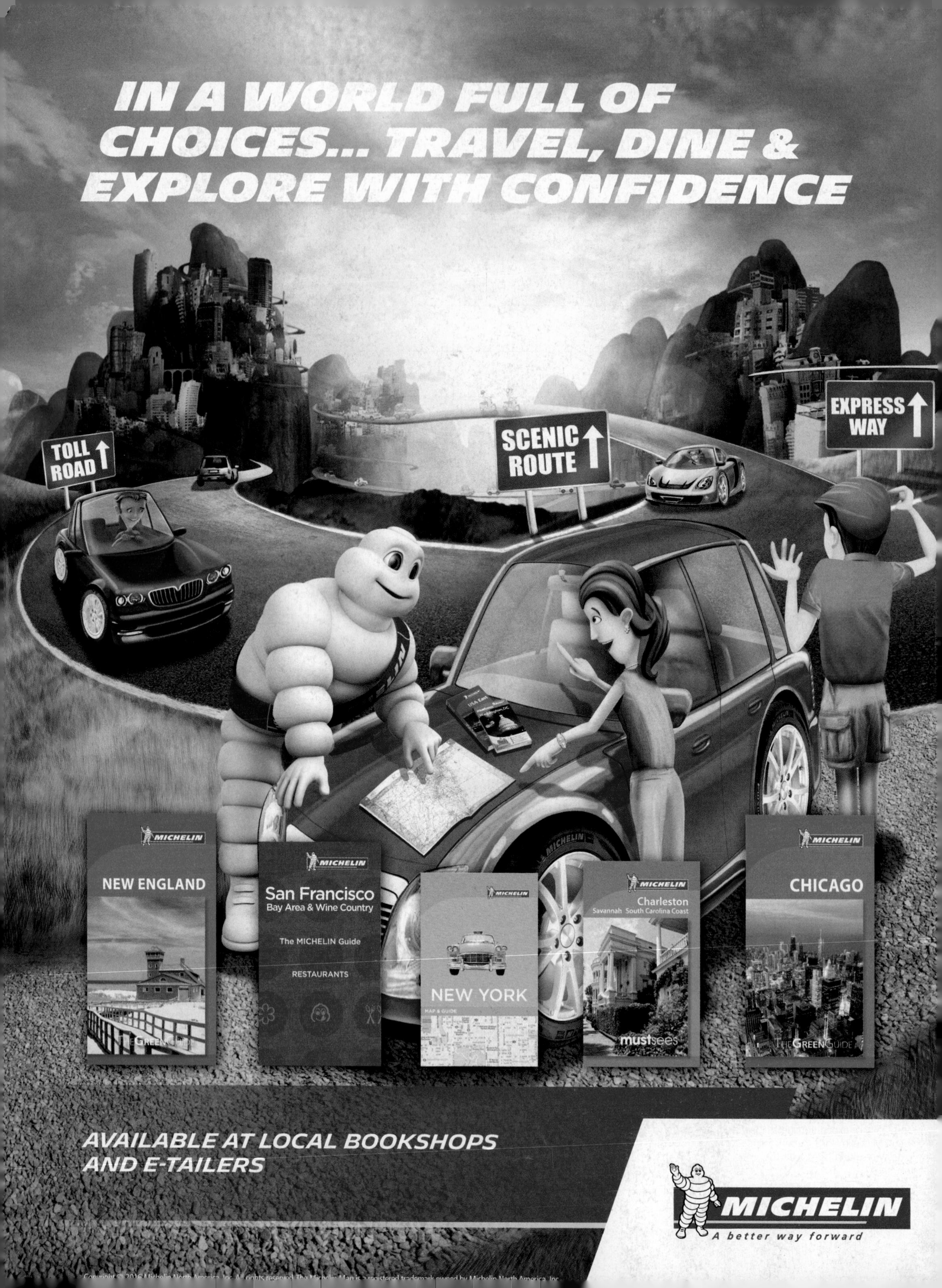